I0120821

Ukraine vs. Russia: Revolution, Democracy, and War

REVOLUTION, DEMOCRACY, AND WAR

UKRAINE VS. RUSSIA

SELECTED ARTICLES AND BLOGS, 2010-2016

ALEXANDER J. MOTYL

Westphalia Press
An Imprint of the Policy Studies Organization
Washington, DC
2017

Ukraine vs. Russia: Revolution, Democracy and War
All Rights Reserved © 2017 by Policy Studies Organization

Westphalia Press
An imprint of Policy Studies Organization
1527 New Hampshire Ave., NW
Washington, D.C. 20036
info@ipsonet.org

ISBN-10: 1-63391-513-1
ISBN-13: 978-1-63391-513-8

Cover and interior design by Jeffrey Barnes
jbarnesbook.design

Daniel Gutierrez-Sandoval, Executive Director
PSO and Westphalia Press

Updated material and comments on this edition
can be found at the Westphalia Press website:
www.westphaliapress.org

PREFACE

vii

PART ONE:

THE RISE AND FALL OF VIKTOR YANUKOVYCH

1

PART TWO:

DEMOCRATIC UKRAINE AFTER YANUKOVYCH

111

PART THREE:

RUSSIA'S WAR AGAINST UKRAINE

225

PART FOUR:

THE DECLINE OF PUTIN RUSSIA

383

PART FIVE:

HISTORY, LANGUAGE, AND NATIONAL IDENTITY

477

PREFACE

I wrote close to 400 blogs and articles on Ukraine and Russia in 2010–2016, most for the *World Affairs Journal* website (www.worldaffairsjournal.org) and the others for the websites of Foreign Affairs, Foreign Policy, The Atlantic Council, CNN, Al Jazeera, The Huffington Post, The Kyiv Post, The Wall Street Journal, Open Democracy, The Monkey Cage, and the European Leadership Network. Many thanks to James Denton, editor of the *World Affairs Journal*, for suggesting in 2010 that I do a weekly blog, "Ukraine's Orange Blues."

This collection contains many of these pieces, organized thematically into five self-contained parts, each of which has some semblance of a narrative structure. I did not include articles that were outdated, too specific, flippant, or uninteresting. I did include most of the articles that were written during the especially dramatic, tragic, violent, and nerve-wracking times of revolution, repression, and war, even if later events disproved my direst expectations.

I was right in predicting Viktor Yanukovych's end. I did not expect Putin to invade Ukraine, thinking it would be a strategic mistake. He did invade, but I still believe that his annexation of Crimea and the war in the eastern Donbas have brought Russia no benefits and will cost it dearly. I am firmly persuaded that the post-Yanukovych government has, despite its many faults, introduced enormous changes, which largely go unrecognized by an impatient population (and an impatient West) that, in their impatience, may yet negate modern Ukraine's best chance of becoming a full-fledged member of the world. And I remain certain that Putin and his regime will eventually join Hitler, Mussolini, and other fascist dictators on the dust bin of history.

The articles are all analytical, sometimes even theoretical, but they are firmly rooted in certain normative beliefs. I openly and proudly detest Putin's fascist dictatorship and Yanukovych's corrupt sultanistic regime. I unabashedly support democracy, human rights, liberalism, and market reform. I firmly believe that an independent, democratic, and prosperous Ukraine—as well as an independent, democratic, and prosperous Russia—would be good for Ukraine, good for Russia, good for Europe, good for America, and good for the world. And I fear—greatly—that Putin's brutality, European fecklessness, and American indifference could do irreparable harm to the world order.

A.J.M.
New York, December 2016

PART ONE

THE RISE AND FALL OF VIKTOR YANUKOVYCH

The Ukrainian 'W', *Moscow Times*, March 1, 2010

Ukrainian President Viktor Yanukovych bears a striking resemblance to former President George W. Bush.

Although Bush was born rich and Yanukovych poor, both were rowdy as youths, with the former drinking and carousing and the latter serving two jail terms for hooliganism.

Eventually both became serious, went into politics and became governors of large and economically important states—Texas and Donetsk—that served as springboards for their presidential ambitions. Both are—or claim to be—deeply religious: Bush is a born-again Christian, Yanukovych is an Orthodox Christian, and both love to hunt.

Like Bush, Yanukovych has an embarrassing proclivity to get his facts wrong. He has confused poet Anna Akhmatova with his billionaire backer Rinat Akhmetov, the Jewish writer Isaac Babel with the German socialist August Bebel, Slovenia with Slovakia and genocide with genetics. He has called playwright Anton Chekhov a Ukrainian poet and the Helsinki Treaty the Stockholm Treaty.

Yanukovych's best-known gaffe was to have misspelled "proFFessor" back in 2004—a mistake that is doubly embarrassing inasmuch as he claims to have two degrees, a master's of international law and a doctorate of economic sciences. Bush only has an MBA from Harvard University, but his academic record was respectable and the degree is real. Yanukovych, in contrast, somehow managed to acquire both degrees and write a dissertation while serving as full-time deputy governor and then governor of Donetsk.

Both rose to power with the support of a regionally concentrated and ideologically focused base. Bush's was in the red states in the middle of the United States and among Christian fundamentalists. Yanukovych's was in the east and south of Ukraine and among pro-Soviet and anti-Western fundamentalists. Both also had the support of powerful billionaires who helped propel them to power.

Unsurprisingly, educated elites looked down on both men as crude, simplistic, dull-witted and undiplomatic. Although the two claimed to be unconcerned with such criticism, they quickly made adjustments in their image, polished their language and brushed up on their knowledge of the world. They also both relied heavily on U.S. public-relations and campaign consultants.

Like Bush's victory over candidate Al Gore in the 2000 presidential vote, Yanukovych's narrow victory over Yulia Tymoshenko on February 7 produced several weeks of legal contestation and political maneuvering that was resolved only after the intervention of higher courts.

There is one final point of similarity. Both men promised to unify a deeply divided country. Bush failed to do so in his first term because he adopted a polarizing rhetoric and pursued partisan politics that alienated half the country. His attempts to rectify the situation in his second term came too late to save his reputation.

Yanukovych now faces a choice. He can pander to his base in Donetsk, divide Ukraine and be first-term Bush. Or he can appeal to the whole country, alienate some of his base and be second-term Bush.

If Yanukovych does the latter, he'll succeed as president, and Ukraine will in all likelihood emerge from its current economic and political crisis. If he does the former, the Ukrainian "Dubya" will go down in history as an ignominious failure.

*

Ukraine's 'Prorizna Street Rebellion' Shows Democracy Internalized, *Open Democracy*, March 25, 2010

Ukrainians are keeping a wary eye on the new government of Viktor Yanukovych following his victory in the two-round presidential election of January–February 2010. Some of them are also setting him an example of what collective action in the public interest can mean—and in central Kyiv, just one block away from the site of the "orange revolution" of November 2004–January 2005. There, on Prorizna Street, just above Khreshchatyk (the main artery of Ukraine's capital city) a citizens' initiative is demanding that unlawful construction of a "polyfunctional establishment"—including a restaurant, sauna, and underground garage—be halted and the existing "green zone" be preserved.

This "Prorizna Street rebellion" could very well define the new, socially active, and civically mobilised Ukraine that Viktor Yushchenko's successor will have to confront in the years to come.

Yushchenko and his ally-turned-adversary, former prime minister Yulia Tymoshenko, failed to live up to the promise of the orange revolution—that great outpouring of defiance and hunger for change on the streets of Kyiv in 2004. But Ukraine still managed to change fundamentally in the five years that followed. Today's Ukraine is a democracy capable of holding fair elections. It is free, and its media, parties, and people revel—sometimes with excessive enthusiasm—in that freedom.

Ukraine's population has also become deeply disillusioned with politics and politicians, and cynical about their ability to deliver the goods. Whether they like or not, people have been forced to rely on themselves to get things done. To put it in a more positive way: they have in effect been obliged to internalise the values of the orange revolution. As one of the Prorizna Street activists puts it: "Our initiative would have been impossible before the orange revolution."

There is no going back to the days of Leonid Kuchma, the pre-revolution president who could manipulate the people with a clever mix of harsh measures and occasional concessions before the epic popular demonstrations of 2004 swept him away.

A City's Cause

The Prorizna Street rebellion embodies that new attitude of self-initiative. It began in late January 2010, when workers started constructing a fence around the square. Some residents spontaneously began picketing the site and demanding an explanation. Activists tore down the fence. Up it went again; and again down.

The protest centred on two issues. First, the developer—Parus—had failed to undertake a study of its project's impact on surrounding buildings and the ecology of the square, and may have even forged a work-permit. Second, residents suspected that a "polyfunctional establishment" could ultimately be transformed into a casino, strip-club, or anything else that would enrich Kyiv's criminal establishment.

Within days, the rebellion became a political cause célèbre. Vitaly Klitschko, the Ukrainian boxer who heads the Vitaly Klitschko Bloc and hopes to become Kyiv's next mayor, joined the rebel side; so did the Save Old Kyiv and Our Country citizens' movements, the Kyiv Landscape Initiative fund, the Civic Position group, and the Coalition of Orange Revolution Participants. Meanwhile, the media picked up the story, writing extensively and sympathetically about the rebellion. The little square on Prorizna Street had clearly captured Kyivites' attention and become a symbol of official indifference that resonated with their growing frustration at the political deadlock and corruption in the country.

The Prorizna rebels ultimately place the blame on Kyiv's loopy and allegedly corrupt millionaire banker-turned-mayor, Leonid Chernovetsky. Since he was elected (with 32 percent of the votes) in 2006, Chernovetsky has allegedly used his office to enrich himself and his cronies from the capital city's real-estate boom—especially in the downtown area, where most of Kyiv's historic buildings and monuments are located. Luxury high-rises, hotels, and office buildings have gone up in every possible space, while traffic has increased to unmanageable levels; at the same time, preparations for Kyiv's participation in the European football championship of 2012 (which Ukraine is co-hosting with Poland) have been neglected.

Chernovetsky survived an effort to unseat him in 2008 by distributing favours to his primarily elderly electorate, but public opinion has again turned against him in recent months. In the tough winter of 2009–2010, city authorities neglected to remove a large accumulation of snow, with the result that Kyiv's streets soon became covered with several inches of treacherous ice. As Kyivites were slipping and breaking limbs, Chernovetsky was vacationing in sunnier climes. To add insult to injury, he eventually expanded budgetary outlays—not for the clean-up, but for plaster casts. Even more insulting to many Kyivites was the claim by his daughter, Khrystyna, that on a trip to Paris on 15 February 2010 she had been robbed of jewellery worth €4.5 million ($6m).

Chernovetsky's political future is therefore uncertain. The population of Kyiv as a whole detest him, and local elections in Ukraine are likely to take place in 2010. The tussle between Yanukovych and Tymoshenko gives him some breathing-room, but time is short: he and his cronies may have only a few more months to enrich themselves by appropriating more real-estate. But the Prorizna rebels know that too and are not about to give up. Whatever the ultimate outcome of the standoff between the builders and the citizens, the lesson of the initiative is that individuals who had never met or greeted one another in the past have developed a sense of solidarity, mission, and community. In effect, they have demonstrated just how and why civil society, the kind that can make a difference, emerges.

A President's Warning

The Prorizna Street rebellion, like many other similar such projects across Ukraine, demonstrates that the country now has genuine citizens able and willing to defend themselves against the predations of corrupt political and business elites. Ukrainian citizens are angry with their rulers and exploiters, and they are again refusing to accept it.

Yanukovych, Tymoshenko, and their colleagues must now live with the empowering consequences of the orange revolution and the five years of endless politicking—and the resulting popular revulsion—that followed. To find a modus vivendi with an empowered population will be especially difficult for Viktor Yanukovych, who is used to exerting strict control of his hometown of Donetsk. Two-thirds of Kyivites voted against him in the presidential elections. Yanukovych will have to learn to talk to a sophisticated city that distrusts all politicians. If he tries to rule Kyiv and Ukraine as a whole as if they were extensions of Donetsk, the Prorizna Street rebellion may turn out to be a foretaste. For Ukrainians have indeed—despite their politicians—become citizens.

*

Ukraine's Democracy in Danger, *Wall Street Journal*, April 5, 2010

As Ukraine's recently elected President Viktor Yanukovych prepares to visit Washington in April, he will aim to project an image of stability, confidence, and control. In reality, Mr. Yanukovych has committed a series of mistakes that could doom his presidency, scare off oreign investors, and thwart the country's modernization.

Mr. Yanukovych's first mistake was to violate the Constitution by changing the rules according to which ruling parliamentary coalitions are formed, making it possible for his party to take the lead in partnership with several others, including the Communists. That move immediately galvanized the demoralized opposition that clustered around his challenger in the presidential elections, former Prime Minister Yulia Tymoshenko.

His second mistake was to appoint as prime minister his crony Mykola Azarov, a tough bureaucrat whose name is synonymous with government corruption, ruinous taxation rates, and hostility to small business. The appointment dispelled any hopes Ukrainians had that Mr. Yanukovych would promote serious economic reform.

His third mistake was to agree to a cabinet consisting of 29 ministers as opposed to 25 before—an impossibly large number that will only compound its inability to engage in serious decision making. That the cabinet contained not one woman—Mr. Azarov claimed that reform was not women's work—only reinforced the image of the cabinet as a dysfunctional boys' club.

His fourth mistake was to appoint two nonentities—a former state farm manager, and an economics graduate from a Soviet agricultural institute—to head the ministries of economy and finance. Meanwhile, he created a Committee on Economic Reform, consisting of 24 members, to develop a strategy of economic change. The size of the committee guarantees that it will be a talk shop, while the incompetence of the two ministers means that whatever genuinely positive ideas the Committee develops will remain on paper.

His fifth mistake was to appoint the controversial Dmitri Tabachnik as minister of education. Mr. Tabachnik has expressed chauvinist views that democratically inclined Ukrainians regard as deeply offensive to their national dignity, such as the belief that west Ukrainians are not real Ukrainians; endorsing the sanitized view of Soviet history propagated by the Kremlin; and claiming that Ukrainian language and culture flourished in Soviet times. Unsurprisingly, many Ukrainians have reacted in the same way that African Americans would react to KKK head David Duke's appointment to such a position—with countrywide student strikes, petitions, and demonstrations directed as much at Mr. Yanukovych as at Mr. Tabachnik.

These five mistakes have effectively undermined Mr. Yanukovych's legitimacy within a few weeks of his inauguration. The 45.5 percent of the electorate that voted against him now feels vindicated; the 10–20 percent that voted for him as the lesser of two evils now suspect that their fears of Mrs. Tymoshenko's authoritarian tendencies were grossly exaggerated. And everyone worries that Mr. Yanukovych and his band of Donbas-based "dons" are ruthlessly pursuing the same anti-democratic agenda that sparked the Orange Revolution of 2004.

Several other key dismissals and appointments have only reinforced this view. The director of the Security Service archives—a conscientious scholar who permitted unrestricted public access to documentation revealing Soviet crimes—has been fired. The National Television and Radio Company has been placed in the hands of a lightweight entertainer expected to toe the line. Most disturbing perhaps, several of Mr. Yanukovych's anti-democratically inclined party allies have been placed in charge of provincial ministries of internal affairs—positions that give them broad scope to clamp down on the liberties of ordinary citizens.

Democratically inclined Ukrainians are increasingly persuaded that Mr. Yanukovych wants to become Ukraine's version of Belarus's dictator, Aleksandr Lukashenka. But Mr. Yanukovych's vision of strong-man rule rests on a strategic, and possibly fatal, misunderstanding of Ukraine.

First, the Orange Revolution and five years of Viktor Yushchenko's presidency empowered the Ukrainian population, endowing it with a self-confidence that it lacked before 2004 and consolidating a vigorous civil society consisting of professionals, intellectuals, students, and businesspeople with no fear of the powers that be. Mr. Yanukovych's efforts to establish strong-man rule already are, and will continue to be, resisted and ridiculed by the general population.

Second, Ukraine's shambolic government apparatus cannot serve as the basis of an effective authoritarian government. Tough talk alone will fail to whip a bloated bureaucracy into shape. Worse, Ukraine's security service and army are a far cry from those in Belarus. Mr. Yanukovych may try to emulate Mr. Lukashenka, but without a strong bureaucracy and coercive apparatus, he will fail.

Third, with an ineffective cabinet, all decision making will be concentrated in Mr. Yanukovych's hands. Even if one ignores his deficient education and poor grasp of facts, Mr. Yanukovych's appointment of Mr. Tabachnik demonstrates that Ukraine's president is either completely out of touch with his own country, or arrogantly indifferent to public opinion.

Fourth, Ukraine is still in the throes of a deep economic crisis. If Mr. Yanukovych does nothing to fix the economy, Ukraine may soon face default, and mass discontent among his working-class constituency in the southeast is likely. If Mr. Yanukovych does embark on serious reforms, that same constituency will suffer and strikes are certain. So negotiating the crisis will require popular legitimacy—which Mr. Yanukovych is rapidly squandering; a strong government—which he does not have; and excellent judgment—which is also missing from the equation.

Indeed, if Mr. Yanukovych keeps on making anti-democratic mistakes, he could very well provoke a second Orange Revolution. But this time the demonstrators would consist of democrats, students, and workers. The prospect of growing instability will do little to attract foreign investors, while declining legitimacy, growing incompetence, and tub thumping will fail to modernize Ukraine's industry, agriculture, and education. Mr. Yanukovych could very well be an even greater failure as president than Mr. Yushchenko.

Although the outlook is grim, it is not yet hopeless for Ukraine's new president. He could still grasp a modest victory from the jaws of an embarrassing defeat by ruling as the president, not of Donetsk, but of all Ukraine. All he has to do is restrain his appetite for power and learn to rule with the opposition and with the population. It's not so complicated—it's democracy.

*

End of Ukraine and Future of Eurasia, *Atlantic Council*, May 10, 2010

For the first time in 20 years, Ukraine's disappearance as a state is imaginable. Since Ukraine is a pivotal state of great geopolitical significance to the stability of both Europe and Asia, its collapse could have considerable geopolitical consequences.

If Ukraine fails as a state, future historians will place the blame on four factors:

- NATO enlargement up to Ukraine's western border. Expanding the North Atlantic Treaty Organization to include East Central Europe and the Baltic states effectively placed Ukraine in a strategically untenable no-man's land between a united West and an increasingly hostile Russia.

- President Viktor Yushchenko's catastrophic mismanagement of the country in 2005–2009. Yushchenko neglected the economy, permitted corruption to flourish, demoralized the population, polarized the country, and destroyed the unity of pro-Western Ukrainian elites.

- Europe's criminal indifference to Ukraine's strategic dilemmas and experiment in democracy after the Orange Revolution of 2004. Europe—and especially Germany—courted authoritarian Russia and turned its back on Ukraine's pleas for assistance, at precisely the time that even a vague promise of eventual membership in the European Union would have united Ukraine's pro-Western elites around a democratic reform agenda.

- President Viktor Yanukovych's rush to dismantle democracy and destroy Ukraine's Ukrainian identity. In the two months that Yanukovych has been in office, he and his comrades in the Party of Regions have launched a full-scale rollback of Ukraine's democratic institutions, a full-scale attack on Ukrainian language and culture, and a full-scale shift oward Russia.

Yanukovych's actions could result in three possible scenarios, arranged below according to long-, medium-, and short-term probability:

1. Least likely in the short term is Ukraine's transformation into a vassal state of Russia. Although critics of Yanukovych's agreement to extend the Black Sea Fleet's base in Sevastopol for 30 years accuse him of selling out to Russian President Dmitry Medvedev, the short-term reality is that the fleet would have stayed in Crimea until 2017 anyway. The long-term prospects, however, are different. The continued presence of the fleet until 2047—in conjunction with Yanukovych's apparent desire to forge the closest possible economic, cultural, political, and military ties with Russia—will draw Ukraine into Russia's sphere of influence and could then, in a process of creeping re-imperialization, transform Ukraine into a Russian protectorate.

2. The real importance, in the short to medium term, of the Black Sea Feet deal is that it demonstrates that Yanukovych is not an economic reformer committed to introducing

genuine market relations in Ukraine. The deal rests on an anti-market approach to economics and shows that Yanukovych is less interested in making Ukraine modern and productive than in acquiring easy money to sustain his hyper-centralized rule and make painful reforms unnecessary. Yanukovych, in sum, is rapidly transforming Ukraine into a backward sultanistic regime, in which authoritarianism and corruption flourish and the economy stagnates. Such regimes are inherently unstable and, as they lose the support of even their die-hard supporters in the medium term, become vulnerable to people power, radical movements, and terrorism.

3. The most immediate—and most likely—short-term consequence of Yanukovych's anti-Ukrainian and anti-democratic measures is the mobilization of Ukrainian democrats and the radicalization of Ukrainian nationalists. The harder Yanukovych pushes, the harder will they push back. A second Orange Revolution would be the best-case outcome, but rather more likely is the abandonment of moderation by Ukrainians fed up with being treated as second-class citizens by a chauvinistic regime determined to push Ukrainian identity into Bantustans. As social tensions rise, both violence and an attempt by Western Ukraine to secede become increasingly conceivable. Yanukovych will try to crack down, but how the resulting conflict will be resolved is anybody's guess. One thing is sure: Ukraine will be destabilized.

What would be the consequences for Eurasia of the end of Ukraine?

First, the European project will collapse. If the European Union is unwilling or unable to defend democracy in its back yard and to prevent Ukraine's transformation into a second Yugoslavia, then the EU is as meaningless as its commitment to supposedly humane European values is hollow.

Second, Russian democracy will be set back for generations, as Ukraine's collapse will be said to demonstrate that Eastern Slavs are congenitally incapable of democratic self-rule. In turn, the case for autocracy will be made with increased vigor, and the authoritarian character of the Putin-Medvedev regime will be strengthened.

Third, Putin Russia's neo-imperial agenda will have been vindicated. The end of Ukraine will seemingly prove that Russia can, should, and must reestablish imperial sway over the formerly Soviet states. If a Russian empire is reestablished, a second cold war with the United States is inevitable, an arms race in Central Europe is probable, and a hot war with imperial Russia's non-Russian neighbors, including China, becomes possible. If the imperial project fails—as a result, perhaps, of misguided imperialist adventures that lead to disaster and discredit the Russian regime—Russia will be destabilized and Eurasia will suffer the contagion. At the very least, Central Asia, the Caucasus, and the Middle East will remain unstable for many decades to come.

Are such trends inevitable? Europe could easily correct Ukraine's trajectory by promoting Ukraine's integration into Euro-Atlantic structures—but will not as long as it frames the issue as Ukrainian democracy vs Russian gas. The United States could impress Yanukovych with the need to keep his sultanistic ambitions in check—but won't as long as it deems Russia indispensable to its geopolitical designs.

That means that Ukrainians alone will have to stop the destruction of their state. The chances of such an outcome are greater than Yanukovych may think. He's already alienated one third to one half of the country and transformed most of its truculent intellectual and cultural elites into his enemies. As the country continues to stagnate economically under his sultanistic rule, disenchantment will spread to those Ukrainians who are still willing to give Yanukovych a chance. As the gap between his increasingly brittle sultanistic regime and the increasingly angry population grows, elite defections will multiply and a second Orange Revolution could very well take place.

Whatever the scenario—vassalage, popular upheaval, or civil conflict—Ukraine will be unstable. And Yanukovych will go down in history as even more ineffective than the hapless Yushchenko.

*

Ukraine: Containing the Con, *Atlantic Council,* May 12, 2010

For five years Viktor Yanukovych claimed to be a democratic, moderate, and unifier—everything that the Orange elites presumably were not. In the two months that he has occupied the president's seat, Yanukovych has shown that he is an authoritarian, radical, and disunifier—everything that the Orange revolutionaries had accused him of being in 2004.

The con, as it turned out, was a conman and his supposed makeover by U.S. political consultant Paul Manafort was nothing but an elaborate con.

Having succeeded in "coordinating" government within two months—the term the Nazis used for Hitler's identical feat in 1933 was *Gleichschaltung*—Yanukovych and his band of dons are on a roll. Having openly embraced dictatorship, they cannot retreat. They must now consolidate their power, eliminate all opposition, and transform Ukraine into the Donbas, both because their legitimacy depends on it and because anything less than complete success for a dictator spells defeat.

Ukrainians should therefore expect the assault on democracy and Ukrainian identity to continue. Indeed, because Ukrainian language, culture, and identity have become so closely bound with democracy and the West, and because the Russian language, culture, and identity have—unfortunately—become so closely bound with authoritarianism and the Soviet past, Yanukovych must attack both democracy and Ukrainian identity with equal vigor. Yanukovych's Führerist ambitions are merely the flip side of Education Minister Dmitri Tabachnik's anti-Ukrainian hysteria.

If undeterred, the continued assault on democracy and Ukrainian identity is likely to take the following forms:

- The progress transformation of the Rada into a rubber-stamp institution along the lines of the Russian Duma.

- The dispersal of demonstrations by means of force and, if need be, violence.

- The harassment, persecution, and possible "disappearance" of opposition leaders in general and of outspoken national-democratic and nationalist leaders, in particular.

- The curtailment of university autonomy.

- The progressive reintroduction of censorship in and the gradual imposition of financial, bureaucratic, and legal constraints on the independent media. The harassment, persecution, and possible "disappearance" of outspoken journalists, scholars, and writers.

Fortunately, Ukraine is not, as the perceptive President Leonid Kuchma once wrote, Russia. Ukraine still has a vigorous civil society and political opposition. It also has a vibrant diaspora that may be expected to monitor Yanukovych's dictatorial plans.

Who will win—the Yanukovych authoritarians or the national democrats?

Yanukovych must destroy the opposition to win. A dictator cannot be a dictator as long as there is an opposition. The opposition must only contain Yanukovych to win. It has only to demonstrate that he can be stopped.

Yanukovych faces by far the more daunting task, if only because his coercive resources are fewer than his sultanistic ambitions require and because civil society and the opposition are too strong and too large to be cowed, killed, or deported as in the good ol' days of Comrade Stalin. Besides, mass arrests or mass disappearances might even lead Berlin and Paris to raise an eyebrow.

In sum, Yanukovych will fail—ineluctably and inevitably—but he will cause enormous damage to Ukraine in the process of failing. The east-west split in Ukraine will be amplified, radicals will mobilize and be tempted to engage in violence, the regime will turn a blind eye to the growth of anti-Semitism within its energized pro-Russian constituency, and foreign direct investment will dry up.

For several reasons, 2012 may be the year of Yanukovych's downfall.

First, his dictatorial ambitions will be absolutely clear by then, even to those Ukrainians who are still willing to give him the benefit of the doubt. The Stalinists will of course be delighted by full-scale *Gleichschaltung*, but those Ukrainians with some sense of alternatives, human dignity, and decency—which is to say the majority—will not.

Second, his inability or unwillingness to reform the economy and improve living standards will also be equally manifest. Contrary to their populist rhetoric, dictators are primarily interested in their own and their cronies' enrichment and generally do little more for the people than make the trains run on time.

Third, civil society, the independent media, and the political opposition will, even in the face of open repression, still be alive, if not quite well. After a few years of persecution and harassment, they will be angry, focused, and more united, while the Orange-era incompetence of opposition politicians will be a distant memory.

Fourth, parliamentary elections slated for 2012 will, as in late 2004, serve as an excellent occasion for mobilizing the people against the regime. Even fascistoid Russia continues to hold national elections, and Yanukovych will have no choice but to follow in Vladimir Putin's footsteps.

Fifth, fissures will open in Yanukovych's regime, as former supporters concerned with political survival become defectors and join the opposition camp. Authoritarian regimes are always and everywhere brittle; they are especially susceptible to elite splits as popular opposition grows and the possibility of defeat, and punishment, grows real. Expect Serhii Tihipko to bolt by no later than early 2012 or late 2011.

Sixth, Ukraine will be co-hosting the UEFA-2012 soccer championship and will, as a result, be subject to intense international scrutiny, tourism, and media coverage. The soccer championship will force the regime to adopt the veneer of democracy and lessen its harassment and persecution of the opposition, thereby providing regime opponents with both a window of opportunity and a cover.

These six factors could easily create a "perfect storm." Disillusioned and angry at a time of electoral mobilization, average Ukrainians could join forces with existing and defecting elites and, with political repression relaxed due to the UEFA championship, make demands that the regime will not be able to repress or resist.

With any luck, Yanukovych will then buy a one-way ticket on the Kyiv-Vladivostok express.

*

Ukrainian Blues, *Foreign Affairs*, July/August 2010

In February 2010, Viktor Yanukovych made a remarkable political comeback. In the 2004 Ukrainian presidential election, Yanukovych, who was then Ukraine's prime minister and the handpicked successor to President Leonid Kuchma, was accused of fraud and ousted by the Orange Revolution, which was led by Viktor Yushchenko and Yulia Tymoshenko. Just over five years later, surrounded by his party's blue-and-white banners, Yanukovych became president.

When it first came to power, Ukraine's Orange government seemed like it would fulfill popular demands for radical political reform and rapid integration into Europe. But those expectations were quickly dashed. Yushchenko, as president, and Tymoshenko, as prime minister, proved incapable of working together, continually clashing and publicly criticizing each other. Soon, Ukraine's dysfunctional political system became known to Ukrainians as a *durdom*, or "madhouse."

Then, the global economic crisis sent Ukraine's economy into a tailspin. In 2009, the country's GDP fell by about 15 percent, exports by 25 percent, and imports by just under 40 percent. The consumer price index rose by more than 12 percent. Popular anger and frustration set in. Yearning for stability, Ukrainians were willing to support anyone in this year's election who could fix the mess. Tymoshenko, Yanukovych's main challenger, was seen to share fault for Ukraine's problems and could not easily claim to be that person.

Wisely, Yanukovych presented himself as a moderate, democratic professional who could unify a country increasingly divided over whether it should align with Russia or the West. He claimed that he would be able to strike the right balance between the two and could transform Ukraine into an economic tiger, making it one of the world's 20 richest nations. Yanukovych's campaign slogan—"Ukraine is for people"—captured the right tone to counter his previously negative image. It suggested that he was a man of the people who would place the interests of citizens above his own, in contrast to the supposedly power-hungry Tymoshenko. Yanukovych also claimed to have learned from his mistakes in 2004. In December 2009, he wrote in *Dzerkalo Tyzhnya*, one of Ukraine's most widely read newspapers, that although he still believed that the real goal of the Orange Revolution had been "to weaken Russia," he accepted that it represented a popular call for democracy. He further noted that a government "cannot promote serious socioeconomic plans without the active participation of the entire society."

Whatever the reasons for Yanukovych's victory, it was a surprisingly narrow one. In the first round, Yanukovych received just over 35 percent of the vote and made it into the runoff round with Tymoshenko. He received just under 49 percent of the vote in that round, compared with Tymoshenko's 45 percent. But really he had won over only about one-third of Ukraine's electorate since turnout was around 69 percent. Moreover, had Yushchenko not encouraged his supporters to select the "against all" option on the ballot, Tymoshenko would probably have won.

With such a slim mandate, most expected Yanukovych to pursue a moderate course after the election, reaching out to the opposition and working toward economic stability and political reform. Instead, he immediately took actions that undermined democracy, neglected the country's badly broken economy, and aligned Ukraine too closely with Russia for the comfort of much of the electorate.

Democratic Roadkill

After the Yushchenko government was dismissed, on March 3, Yanukovych had 30 days to form his own. Because his Party of Regions lacked a clear majority of seats in the Verkhovna Rada, Ukraine's parliament, it needed a coalition partner and so began negotiations with the Our Ukraine-People's Self-Defense (NU-NS) Bloc, led by Yushchenko.

The NU-NS knew that no majority coalition could be formed without it, and so it demanded control over a range of portfolios, including the prime ministership.

The Party of Regions responded by changing the Rada's rules so that it could form a coalition without the NU-NS by joining with willing individual deputies. In mid-March, Yanukovych's party formed a governing coalition called Stability and Reform with the Communists, the Lytvyn Bloc (the bloc allied with the Rada's Speaker, Volodymyr Lytvyn), and 16 individuals who crossed party lines to join the coalition. Those who crossed over have come to be known as *tushki*, a pejorative Russian term roughly meaning "roadkill." Although the *tushki* gave Stability and Reform just enough votes to form a government, Yanukovych's willingness to use unconstitutional measures to do so—in 2008, Ukraine's Constitutional Court explicitly outlawed the use of individual deputies to form coalitions, although it has now refused to challenge Yanukovych—set a disturbingly anti-democratic precedent. As the German political scientist Andreas Umland noted in late March in the *Kyiv Post*, "Ukraine is now less democratic than it was ... With their change of allegiance the *tushki* have grossly misrepresented the preferences of the Ukrainian voters."

After the coalition was formed, Ukrainians expected Yanukovych to live up to his campaign promises and appoint professionals, reformers, and moderates to government posts, but he did the opposite. Most of Yanukovych's political appointees hail from his home region, Ukraine's highly Sovietized rust belt, the Donbas, and have little experience with democratic politics or the technical know-how required to run a clean government and a functioning market economy. Like the old Donbas Communist Party bosses did, with whom many of these appointees cut their political teeth, Yanukovych acts as a patron. He doles out favors, provides access to power, and makes most decisions.

The position of prime minister, for example, went to Yanukovych's longtime ally Mykola Azarov. As head of the Rada's budgetary committee and the State Tax Administration in the 1990s, Azarov turned a blind eye to government graft and imposed ruinously high tax rates on small businesses. His relationship with Yanukovych was cemented when he served as the first deputy prime minister and finance minister to notoriously unscrupulous cabinets headed by Yanukovych in 2004 and 2006–2007. Together, Yanukovych and Azarov have doled out 29 cabinet seats to their cronies. Such a large cabinet, with two more members than even the ineffective Council of the European Union, is almost certain to become a talking shop that, like the Council of the European Union, is incapable of reaching consensus or making tough decisions. Meanwhile, the positions of economic minister and finance minister have gone to politicians who lack experience in either field but are dependent on Yanukovych for power and are thus unlikely to cross him. Contrary to his campaign slogans, reform and democracy are clearly not Yanukovych's priority.

To be sure, Yanukovych and his chief of staff, the economist Iryna Akimova, have created—and will be heading up—the new Committee on Economic Reform. Although there are some economists among the committee's 26 members, there are also many political appointees beholden to Yanukovych. The inclusion of political appointees and the committee's impractically large size suggest that it will be as ineffective as Yanukovych's cabinet. And even if it does develop some real economic reforms, they are likely to fall victim to turf battles between the Economy and Finance Ministries and the committee itself. Parallel organizations with overlapping jurisdictions are doomed to tussle over control, even with wise, professional management—something Yanukovych is unlikely to provide.

Yanukovych's hub-and-spokes political system—with Yanukovych at the center and key political roles filled by yes men—has put the president "on top of [the] Ukrainian power pyramid," as analysts at Kyiv's Penta Center, a political think tank, have put it. Yanukovych even went so far as to redefine democracy as "order" in a press conference in Strasbourg on April 27. But political order is not democracy. Such hypercentralized political systems are rarely efficient and almost always corrupt. There is no reason to think that the Donbas-based dons who man the Yanukovych system will be able or willing to pursue the economic reform Ukraine so badly needs.

Eastward Bound

Just as Yanukovych has failed to live up to his democratic and economic promises, he has acted against his campaign promise to unify the country. As president, Yushchenko actively favored his ethnic Ukrainian base by promoting the Ukrainian language, culture, and identity in schools, government, and the media. In the process, he alienated many of the ethnic Russians and Russian-speaking Ukrainians in the country's east and south. Most observers expected Yanukovych to calm the tense situation by neither advocating nor disparaging Ukrainian heritage. Instead, he surprised everyone by attacking it.

Dmitri Tabachnik, Yanukovych's appointment for minister of education and science, has spearheaded this assault. Tabachnik is an odious choice because, besides having a weak academic pedigree, he openly espouses anti-Ukrainian views. He claims that the ethnic Ukrainians in the west of the country are too westernized to be true Ukrainians. He believes that Ukrainian culture flourished in Soviet times, when it was in fact suppressed in favor of the colonial power's culture. He also insists that today the Russian language is discriminated against, even as Russian-language publications and broadcasts make up the overwhelming majority of media available in Ukraine. Since assuming his new position, Tabachnik has reduced the role of Ukrainian in schools, urged the cessation of Ukrainian-language dubbing of foreign films, and expressed indifference to the construction of a statue of Stalin in the southern city of Zaporizhzhya. Unsurprisingly, his assault on Ukrainian identity has provoked demonstrations, student protests, and petitions—directed as much at Yanukovych as at Tabachnik.

Yanukovych's overly centralized, anti-Ukrainian regime has been unable to forge a genuine national consensus on the country's political and economic direction, either. A case in point is the April 2010 Russian-Ukrainian pact, in which Yanukovych agreed to extend until 2047 the basing rights of Russia's Black Sea Fleet in Sevastopol, a port city on the southern part of the Crimean Peninsula, which juts off Ukraine and into the Black Sea, and Russian President Dmitri Medvedev agreed in return to lower the price Ukraine pays for Russian natural gas by 30 percent through 2019.

The agreement's critics charge that Yanukovych has sold out to Russia. This may be true, but the more damning criticism is that the agreement was pushed through the Rada without regard for transparency or democratic procedure. As one senior Ukrainian diplomat told me, "The haste with which the agreement was signed is daunting. There was no expert evaluation of the draft and no proper consideration of the issue in parliamentary committees ... The decision was taken by a small group of individuals, if not by one person."

There are four separate issues concerning the Sevastopol deal that the Rada should have had the opportunity to debate: the geopolitical implications for Ukraine of basing the Black Sea Fleet in Sevastopol, the fair rate that Russia should pay in rent for using the base, the price Ukraine should pay for Russian gas, and the cost to Russia of transporting gas through Ukraine's pipelines. But instead of airing these issues individually in the Rada, Yanukovych bundled them and thus bartered away Ukraine's security by ceding informal control of Crimea, its potentially vital sea-lanes, and the natural gas deposits that surround it to Russia for the foreseeable future. In return, Yanukovych secured gas prices that will likely save Ukraine some $1–$3 billion annually for only the next nine years. Worse, Russia merely agreed to cut its gas prices to current average world rates, pay below-market gas transit fees, and pay a long-term rent on the base that, at $100 million per annum, is about one-fifth of what experts calculate it should be, based on rents for comparable bases around the world. With open consideration of the agreement's terms in the Rada and a team of professional negotiators, Ukraine could have gotten much more out of the deal: it should at least have demanded European-level transit fees and a higher basing rent.

The deal's passage unleashed a riot in the Rada, complete with egg throwing and smoke bombs. Yanukovych's subsequent negotiations with Russia over closer cooperation on aviation, nuclear energy, transportation, and gas transit have led to protests across Ukraine. Intellectuals and opposition leaders have accused Yanukovych of treason, declared unconditional opposition to his regime, and predicted that civil war was in the offing. Even if this response is exaggerated, it shows that a significant portion of the population—at least the one-third or more who are opposed to closer ties with Russia—now detests Yanukovych.

Can't Hold Us Down

The rise of such discontent matters. Ukraine is home to a politically conscious civil society that, thanks to the Orange Revolution, is more vigorous than at any time in Ukraine's almost 20-year independent existence. Professionals, intellectuals, students, and businesspeople will increasingly resist Yanukovych's efforts to establish strongman rule and will continue to protest if he kowtows to Russia or the economy grows worse. They have already started to organize: in mid-March, over 300 representatives of the so-called New Citizen movement met in Kyiv to begin monitoring the activities of the Yanukovych government; in May, branches of the similar Save Ukraine Committee were operating across the country. Local elections in 2011 and parliamentary elections in 2012 could also mobilize the population against Yanukovych and his regime. If he continues on his current course, radical nationalists may be the big winners.

Faced with growing popular resistance, Yanukovych may contemplate cracking down on dissent. But such a move would likely provoke violence and destabilize Ukraine. Moreover, authoritarianism along the lines of Belarus in the mid–1990s or Russia at the start of this century is almost certainly not a viable option for Yanukovych. When Aleksandr Lukashenko became president of Belarus in 1994, he inherited an intact Soviet security apparatus. And former Russian President Vladimir Putin could rely on thousands of *siloviki*, political operatives in the secret police and the army, for support. Ukraine's security service and army are a far cry from those in Belarus or Russia. Without a strong coercive apparatus, Yanukovych cannot succeed even as an authoritarian.

Ukraine's first president, in office from 1991 to 1994, the generally cautious Leonid Kravchuk, has joined the chorus of Yanukovych critics. In an open letter published in March, he wrote, "Your team has many people who want to continue along the path of lawlessness, permissiveness and corruption. They're developing a taste for solving complex problems by force. This has nothing in common with democracy." Kravchuk's comments should worry Yanukovych. They demonstrate that even neutrally inclined Ukrainian elites (Kravchuk did not support the Orange Revolution) are turning against him.

Sleight-of-Hand Reform

If Yanukovych keeps on his current course, he could very well provoke a second Orange Revolution. Lacking the ability, capacity, and will to change the system, Yanukovych will probably try to enhance his regime's legitimacy by continuing to rally the more radical of his constituents at the expense of the Ukrainian language, culture, and identity; do everything possible to appease the gas-hungry oligarchs of eastern Ukraine; and use the Union of European Football Associations (UEFA) championship, which Ukraine will host in partnership with Poland in 2012, to promote his image as a pro-European modernizer.

Viewed through this lens, Yanukovych's choice of the incendiary Tabachnik as education and science minister makes some sense. As Tabachnik antagonizes nationally conscious Ukrainians, he enhances Yanukovych's appeal among his pro-Russian constituents in the country's south and east. That said, this course risks encouraging ethnic violence between radical ethnic Russians and ethnic Ukrainians. Additionally, Yanukovych cannot provoke moderate ethnic Ukrainians without limit. They are the ones who took to the streets in 2004 to prevent him from coming to office and could do so again to kick him out.

The lower natural gas price that Yanukovych negotiated with Russia will bring immediate benefits to the oligarchs who run Ukraine's heavily industrialized southeast. Lower gas prices will allow them to keep the costs of their products low and globally competitive without forcing them to modernize or become more efficient. This will certainly endear them to Yanukovych in the short term. In the medium term, however, Ukraine's overarching economic stagnation will eat into their profits. And even if the population welcomes lower gas prices at first, the Yanukovych regime is likely to become more corrupt as it draws closer to Russia's notoriously unscrupulous energy business. Sooner or later, as their living standards stagnate or deteriorate, Yanukovych's working-class constituents may begin to realize that they got the short end of the deal.

Yanukovych's best chance to rally public support (and address some economic problems) might be the 2012 UEFA championship. Ukraine's roads are in terrible shape; its railroads, although efficient, require modernization; and its airports and hotels are in need of significant improvement. A state-led campaign to fix these problems before the influx of tourists in 2012 could generate economic activity, create jobs, and attract more capital. Unsurprisingly, readying Ukraine for the championship has become a priority for Yanukovych, who in April created a special committee to oversee the preparations.

The UEFA preparations will buy Yanukovych time but cannot fix Ukraine's underlying economic and political problems. To do that, Yanukovych would have to democratize his regime, control corruption, cease his anti-Ukrainian campaign, and persuade his compatriots to accept the economic pain that goes with serious reform. He may eventually come to realize that democracy is preferable to ignominy. Or oligarchs worried about their long-term economic interests may persuade him that hypercentralization will destabilize Ukraine. Rather than waiting for these eventualities to happen, however, Russia and the West should help Yanukovych change his course now, before it is too late.

Helping Yanukovych Help Himself

At the start of his presidency, Yanukovych laid out his foreign policy priorities: restoring Ukraine's close ties with Russia, European integration, and building relationships with strategic partners such as the United States. By playing to these priorities and, at the same time, pursuing their own interests in the region, Russia, the European Union, and the United States can help stabilize the Yanukovych presidency and Ukraine.

Russia considers Ukraine part of its sphere of influence and would prefer it to be a weak state rather than an independent, strong democracy. But although a weak Ukraine may be to authoritarian Russia's benefit, a deeply dysfunctional Ukraine on the verge of popular revolution is not. For his part, Yanukovych has said that he wants Ukraine to serve as a bridge between Russia and the West. But a bridge must be sturdy. With the gas and fleet deal, Yanukovych has amply demonstrated his fealty to Russia and solidified his pro-Russian credentials with his base. The Kremlin should return the favor by encouraging Yanukovych to fire the controversial Tabachnik to appease some of his critics in the rest of the country.

The West has an even greater role to play in nudging Yanukovych in the right direction. The International Monetary Fund—which gave Kyiv an emergency loan at the start of the global economic crisis and will likely need to do so again—should insist on strict conditionality. It should not only demand that Yanukovych balance his budget but also pressure him to undertake significant structural economic reforms, including reducing taxation, simplifying business registration procedures, raising the retirement age, and raising the cost of utilities.

Europe should hold to the European Parliament's February 2010 resolution, which reaffirmed Ukraine's strategic importance to the EU and stated that the country could apply for membership if it "adheres to the principles of liberty, democracy, respect for human rights and fundamental freedoms, and the rule of law." As the European Parliament recommended, Europe should assist Ukraine in meeting these standards and should deepen ties between the two by working toward visa-free travel, better energy cooperation, and a free-trade zone. Yanukovych has affirmed that he is interested in further integration with the EU. Europe should take him at his word and offer Yanukovych the prospect of associate member status for Ukraine if he tackles some of the country's political and economic problems.

Washington must remind Yanukovych that Ukraine—especially a democratic Ukraine—remains important to the United States, even as the Obama administration works to improve U.S. relations with Russia. Historically, the U.S.-Ukrainian relationship has atrophied when the United States has pursued closer ties with Russia and has grown stronger when U.S.-Russian relations were strained. But President Barack Obama should resist this pattern. Just as a stable Ukraine is in Russia's interests, so, too, is a stable and democratic Ukraine in the United States' interests. If Yanukovych precipitates a government collapse or state failure, Russia may be tempted to step in, disrupting the balance of power in eastern Europe.

If no popular revolution intervenes, Russia and the West will have to deal with Yanukovych and his "blue counterrevolution" for the next five years. Unfortunately, during that time, Yanukovych will probably grow increasingly ineffective and embattled, destabilizing Ukraine. Yet it remains conceivable that Yanukovych could reverse course, democratize Ukraine, and enact genuine economic reform. But this is likely only if Russia and the West act soon to save Yanukovych from himself.

*

Yanukovych's Democratic Steamroller, *Wall Street Journal*, September 16, 2010

Ukraine's already weak democracy has just received three body blows from the government of President Viktor Yanukovych.

On September 7, Ukraine's parliament passed a law effectively depriving the inhabitants of Ukraine's capital city, Kyiv, of self-rule. According to the law, the executive functions of the city now belong to the so-called Kyiv City State Administration. Who appoints the head of that body? The president. The parliamentary measure now gives Mr. Yanukovych control over the one city in Ukraine that has consistently voted against him, his party, and his cronies; that was the site of the Orange Revolution that disgraced him in 2004; and that has the country's highest concentration of foreign diplomats, journalists, and business people. Mr. Yanukovych knows that he cannot control Ukraine without controlling Kyiv. Now he does.

Controlling Ukrainians' intellects is also key. On September 8, the young historian Ruslan Zabily was interrogated by the Security Service for 14 hours. The alleged reason was Mr. Zabily's supposed dissemination of state secrets. His real crime? Mr. Zabily studies the Holodomor (the deliberately engineered famine that took the lives of millions of Ukrainians in 1932–1933) as well as the Ukrainian nationalist resistance to Soviet rule in the post-World War II period. Both topics have been declared taboo by the Yanukovych government. In classic KGB style, the Security Service confiscated Mr. Zabiliy's computer, suggested he think about the fate of his family, asked him about his foreign academic contacts, and initiated a criminal case against him.

Back in May, the rector of the Ukrainian Catholic University, Father Borys Gudziak, also received a cautionary visit from the Security Service. This Harvard-educated Ukrainian-American's students don't take kindly to strong-arm tactics, having helped defeat Mr. Yanukovych in the Orange Revolution in 2004 and having protested his moves since his inauguration in February. At the time Father Gudziak's visit seemed like it could have been an isolated incident. Now, Mr. Zabily's case suggests the crackdown on dissident academics has only just begun.

Let's not forget the judiciary. On September 9, three members of Ukraine's Constitutional Court resigned. They just happened to be critics of Mr. Yanukovych's electoral machinations in the run-up to the Orange Revolution. Unsurprisingly, Mr. Yanukovych's allies have tarred the three as corrupt. Their departure transforms an already spineless institution into a rubber-stamp body, and opens the way for Mr. Yanukovych and his allies to introduce further anti-democratic measures. This bodes well for Mr. Yanukovych's goals of increasing presidential powers and lengthening his legal term in office, in the mold of Kazakhstan, Russia, and other post-Soviet authoritarian states.

These latest developments come as Ukraine's democrats deal with the Yanukovych era's first "disappeared" dissident, editor Vasyl Klimentyev, who left his house in Kharkiv in early August and never returned. Kharkiv's mayor, a Yanukovych crony, pooh-poohed Mr. Klimentyev's disappearance and implied that he may have fled for personal reasons. But the timing of his disappearance is striking: Mr. Klimentyev was investigating local government corruption by allies of Mr. Yanukovych. By now, the consensus is that Mr. Klimentyev is dead and that he is "Gongadze II"—a reference to Georgi Gongadze, the journalist who disappeared and was beheaded in 2000 for opposing the regime of then-President Leonid Kuchma.

Mr. Yanukovych's message to Ukraine—and the world—is clear: The courts and the capital city are now in his pocket, and free thinkers have been put on alert. Democracy can now be steamrollered at an accelerated pace. R.I.P., Ukrainian liberty. We hardly knew ye.

*

Yanukovych in Wonderland, *Atlantic Council*, September 27, 2010

The policy and business elites who attended the Atlantic Council's September 24th luncheon in New York with Ukraine's President Viktor Yanukovych may be wondering just what he meant by what he said—and, more important, by what he did not say.

The good news is that his "address" was probably written by his minions—possibly in Ukrainian, possibly in Russian—and then translated into barely adequate English (with a noticeable absence of definite and indefinite articles). The speech may therefore be assumed to reflect Yanukovych's views, and not those of his American handler, the political consultant Paul Manafort.

It's important to remember that, despite Yanukovych's claim to be a straight shooter, he is above all a product of Soviet politics and ideology and their current incarnation in his bailiwick—Ukraine's reactionary rustbelt, the Donbas. That means he knows that words, and their manipulation, matter.

So, as Americans try to maneuver through Yanukovych's linguistic Wonderland, they may be advised to keep the following translation manual in mind. Let's go through some of the main claims made by Yanukovych and determine what they really mean or what really lies behind them.

Claim: "for the first time in the modern history of Ukraine—the President, the Government and the Parliament (to be exact the coalition majority that has been formed) are moving in the same strategic direction, not in the three different ones as was the case earlier."

Reality: Yanukovych fails to mention that this unprecedented unanimity is the product of crude constitutional shenanigans that enabled his Party of Regions to form a majority in the Parliament and thus a government.

Claim: "I put forward tough, but accomplishable requirements to reduce licensing procedures by 90 percent, to cut the number and scope of activities of the controlling bodies to the fullest extent possible in order to substantially decrease the tax pressure."

Reality: Revenue collection by the government is woefully below target, with the result that tax collectors have been set loose on the small and medium-sized businesses Yanukovych claims to support. More important, Yanukovych fails to explain just how the liberalizing measures he ostensibly supports can be reconciled with an authoritarian bureaucracy dominated by one party—his own—and intent on never giving up power to an opposition that Yanukovych's people have publicly vowed to destroy.

Claim: "This and other measures have already brought in first considerable results—we have not only stopped an unprecedented economic downslide in a time of peace, but set forward a steady economic development—more than 6 percent GDP growth in the first six months of this year."

Reality: As everybody knows, no government policies can affect GDP immediately.

PART ONE: THE RISE AND FALL OF VIKTOR YANUKOVYCH

There's always a time lag of several months, maybe more. Ukraine's economic growth in the first half of 2010 is thus due either to the policies of the Tymoshenko government or, more likely, to the general upswing in the global economy. We'll see what impact Yanukovych's policies will have only in 2011.

Claim: "I think you will be interested to know how I understand democracy. Of all its various definitions, the following is the closest to me: Democracy means stable state institutions, broad civic freedoms and justice. A state in which these principles are being violated is doomed to have a corruption, chaos, lawlessness or authoritarianism."

Reality: No self-respecting political theorist anywhere would define democracy as stability plus broad civic freedoms plus justice. Democracy, Yanukovych may be interested in knowing, is about "rule of the people"—and that means, above all, fair and free elections in which competing and viable parties take part. That Yanukovych says nothing about elections is his way of saying that his party plans to stay in power for the indefinite future, despite the inconvenience of local elections in October 2010 and parliamentary elections in 2012. Note also that Yanukovych fails to mention specific freedoms, such as freedom of assembly and speech, as those have been violated systematically since he came to power. Last, Yanukovych pointedly avoids the term "rule of law," which is about impartial institutions and procedures, and prefers to speak of "justice," which all authoritarian leaders, from Russia's Putin to Belarus's Lukashenka, claim to be best qualified to dispense.

Claim: "National public discussion of the public television concept that I initiated has been completed. In the nearest future a bill paving the way for the principally different mass media—the ones which policy will be determined by the civil society - will be submitted to the Parliament for consideration."

Reality: Note that Yanukovych states that the policy of public television will be determined by "civil society"—implying, among other things, that the current media, and especially his critics, are not reflective of civil society. You can therefore be certain that his notion of civil society excludes the opposition. More important, you can be equally certain that "civil society" will be represented by some Yanukovych-appointed "civic" body, whose members will all be Yanukovych allies and/or creatures. And you can be absolutely certain that they will transform public television into a mouthpiece of the president.

Claim: "I categorically disagree with statements that claim freedom of speech is on decline in Ukraine. As for separate turf wars in media sphere that have recently been widely discussed, I have to responsibly stress that the government has nothing to do with them. They are clashing of business interests or disputes between the media management and its staff."

Reality: Yanukovych fails to mention that these turf wars involve Ukraine's largest media mogul, Valery Khoroshkovsky—who just happens to be the head of Ukraine's intelligence service, which just happens to have begun a process of selective intimidation of academics, journalists, and foreigners. Khoroshkovsky, by the way, was appointed by Yanukovych.

23

Claim: "Will correction of our Euro-Atlantic integration course and defining our non-aligned status as the main guidance point in the security sphere leave a mark on our relations? ... By the way, the term "non-aligned" or "non-alignment" is not the most adequate one since the era of military blocks has long ended together with the Cold war. But at least, it is concise and understandable. I think the principle of non-participation of our country in any military-political alliance most adequately fits the current geopolitical realities."

Reality: Note that Yanukovych eschews the word neutrality. That's no accident. As he knows, neutrality would imply removing the Russian military presence from Crimea. Non-alignment, in contrast, can be fudged, and, as we know from history, non-aligned countries could be non-aligned with the West (like Yugoslavia) or with the East (like India). Even so, Yanukovych should know that even non-aligned countries do not permit foreign militaries to have bases on their territories. When they do—and Yanukovych extended the Russian Black Sea Fleet's basing rights by 25 years—they effectively abandon non-alignment.

Claim: "Taking this decision was conducive to defusing tensions that existed both in Ukraine and on the entire European continent in connection with the possibility that Ukraine would join NATO."

Reality: Yanukovych forgets to mention that Ukraine's joining NATO was on President Kuchma's and his own agenda before the 2004 Orange Revolution disgraced both of them. The "tensions" about NATO that enveloped Ukraine after 2004 were entirely the handiwork of Yanukovych and his minions in the Party of Regions.

In the end, just what did Yanukovych really say to the Atlantic Council? That he's right, that his critics are wrong, and that he has no intention of leaving office.

That may be stability—but only in Wonderland.

*

Counterrevolution in Ukraine, *World Affairs Journal*, October 12, 2010

Almost six years after it began, the Orange Revolution formally ended on October 1, 2010, when Ukraine's Constitutional Court **reversed** the "political reform" imposed on the presidency as part of the popular democracy movement's uprising.

In the wake of widely criticized presidential elections in November 2004, several weeks of "people power" that came to be known as the Orange Revolution propelled Viktor Yushchenko ahead of his establishment opponent, Viktor Yanukovych—then the prime minister (not to mention the man for whom the people in the streets believed the elections had been rigged). As part of the regime's negotiated exit, however, the Yanukovych camp imposed power-sharing reforms on the presidency before Yushchenko took office—reforms that transferred power from the president to the legislature in an effort to weaken the new leader. The move worked, eventually producing an inherently conflict-ridden relationship between Yushchenko and his prime minister, Yulia Tymoshenko. The turmoil helped Yanukovych topple Yushchenko when he ran again last year, this time as a champion of stability. However, the October 1 Constitutional Court ruling now shows what Yanukovych really thinks of "people power"—not to mention "power-sharing."

After assuming office in late February, Yanukovych amassed a great deal of power. Still, he chafed at the constitutional restrictions on his office—the same restrictions he once favored during Yushchenko's administration—so now, he has angled to reverse them. Well aware that only Ukraine's parliament, the Rada, can change the Constitution— and equally aware of how hard it would be to mobilize enough votes there in favor of such a reversal—Yanukovych turned to the pliant Constitutional Court (which some Ukrainians call the *Konstytutka*, a play on *prostytutka*). The new president had leaned on the court at least once before since taking office, pressuring it to approve an anti-constitutional change in the rules governing the formation of parliamentary coalitions. And prior to this recent reversal he had packed the court with friendly jurists. It's no surprise, then, that this ruling weaseled its way through the back door of a technicality—that the 2004 political reform was a law, and not a constitutional change—to declare the reform unconstitutional.

Now, as a result, Ukraine has officially entered an era of counterrevolution—with Yanukovych as the undisputed master of the nation, able to appoint and dismiss prime ministers at will. In other words, the court's recent decision turned back the clock to the Constitution of 1996, effectively propelling Ukraine into a state of constitutional ambiguity.

Did the Constitutional Court act legally and, if not, who's to challenge it, and where? In a court? In the Rada? Or in the streets? If the 1996 Constitution were in effect again, would all the laws passed since 2004 be unconstitutional? Were the elections that brought Yanukovych to power legal? Should parliamentary elections be held in 2012, as the reforms dictate, or in 2011, as the 1996 Constitution mandates? Are any of Ukraine's political institutions legitimate? No one knows.

As Ukraine descends into a constitutional "time of troubles," Yanukovych will insist that he has no choice but to rule with an iron fist: after all, won't he be the last hope standing between Ukraine and utter chaos? (And surely only irresponsible democrats and meddlesome Americans want that!) This logic will please his Stalinist base in the Donbas, but his democratic critics in the rest of the country—who may be more than half the electorate by now—will see this tyranny for what it is.

There is, however, some underlying good news here:

First, counterrevolution always makes the ideals of the revolution it superseded attractive: the Orange Revolution stood for democracy, human rights, tolerance, and dignity. Expect those values—tarnished by five years of Orange squabbling and ineffectiveness—to creep back into Ukrainian debates. Second, having become "Sultan of Yanukstan," Yanukovych will be responsible for everything that transpires on his watch—the good, of which there has been none thus far, as well as the bad, which is increasing on a daily basis. Only his sycophants expect him to morph into a philosopher king and rule brilliantly. Last, the 1996 Constitution and the systemic presidential abuses it engendered arguably caused the Orange Revolution. Another popular upheaval is perfectly possible—and will become more likely with every presidential abuse.

Pity poor Yanukovych: he's set himself up for a major fall.

*

Ukrainian FEMENists against Putin, *World Affairs Journal*, November 8, 2010

Ukraine's wars of symbols took an especially interesting turn on October 27.

Vladimir Putin, Russia's prime minister, came to Kyiv that day to pursue negotiations with his Ukrainian counterpart, Mykola Azarov, over energy. While policymakers and pundits debated the pros and cons of closer Russo-Ukrainian energy cooperation, FEMEN—a Ukrainian feminist group—staged a symbolically fascinating anti-Putin demonstration in downtown Kyiv (see the video clip **here**).

Six young women, bare-chested, clad in stylish, tight-fitting jeans, and wearing beribboned wreaths typical of traditional Ukrainian folk costumes, held placards and shouted slogans in front of the capital city's most famous statue of Lenin, at the foot of Shevchenko Boulevard. The site is witness to periodic tussles between anti-Communists, who detest Lenin and want to deface his image, and Communists, who worship the Father of Communism and want to preserve it.

This time, the Communists were nowhere to be seen. After all, why worry about a few half-naked girls? Little did Ukraine's Stalinists suspect that FEMEN's topless protest could be far more destructive than anything the anti-Communists could do. One can always fix or clean a statue. Nudity, on the other hand, is freedom from social constraints par excellence; as such, it stands in diametrical opposition to the dictatorship of the prudish proletariat and Lenin's baleful totalitarian legacy.

FEMEN's demonstration made two more politically important points. First, the antics were an obvious dig at Putin's painfully embarrassing **attempts to project a bare-chested macho image**. And second, FEMEN's attire struck a symbolic blow against the Yanukovych regime's determination to marginalize Ukrainian identity and reduce Ukrainian culture to a museum curio. The combination of svelte bodies, trendy jeans, and Ukrainian folk costumes loudly declared that being Ukrainian is both hip and modern.

What the FEMENists had to say was also quite striking. Several of their placards read

"Ukraine is not Alina"—a sexually charged reference to Alina Kabaeva, the 27-year-old Olympic-medal-winning Russian gymnast rumored to be Putin's girlfriend. Another read: "We won't give ourselves to the dwarves"—another sexually charged reference to Prime Minister Putin and President Medvedev, Russia's diminutive leaders. The FEMENists also chanted "Putin go home" and "You can't force us down so easily." A spokeswoman stated, in Russian no less, that the group wants Putin "to know … that Ukraine doesn't want to see him here. Ukraine knows why he came. He wants to break off parts of Ukraine. We won't give him that. All of Ukraine won't permit that. We simply reflect the views of all of Ukraine."

Whether FEMEN reflects the views of all of Ukraine is debatable. Public opinion surveys show that significant parts of the population in the southeast of the country might be quite happy with giving Putin "parts of Ukraine." And FEMEN itself, established in 2008 by a group of Kyiv university students, has hardly become a mass movement. On the other hand, FEMEN probably does reflect the views of significant portions of Ukrainian students and its ability to attract media attention with well-publicized happenings has transformed it into an important part of Ukraine's ongoing symbolic wars.

Significantly, FEMEN has managed to combine several seemingly disparate ideological trends. The group is unquestionably feminist and hopes to shock Ukraine's straight-laced society and sexist establishment. But it is also openly modern and nationalist, aspiring to a contemporary, independent, and liberal homeland. It has also adopted a progressively broader and more overtly political agenda—beginning in 2009 with actions against sexual harassment at universities, the Miss Universe competition, and sex tourism, then moving to protests against electoral fraud, the absence of women in the Yanukovych-appointed cabinet, and, now, Vladimir Putin.

Committed to "the principles of social awareness and activism, intellectual and cultural development" and "the European values of freedom, equality and comprehensive development of a person irrespective of the gender," the FEMENists are clearly the intellectual and cultural offspring of the Orange Revolution.

Yanukovych's Stalinist supporters will consider FEMEN to be one more reason to damn everything Orange. Ukraine's young people, on the other hand, may take heart. The "Sixties" could finally be coming to Ukraine.

*

Remembering the Orange Revolution, Somberly—yet Hopefully, *World Affairs Journal*, November 23, 2010

Yesterday marked six years since the start of **Ukraine's Orange Revolution**—the mass upheaval that reversed a fraudulent election, catapulted Viktor Yushchenko to the presidency and Yulia Tymoshenko to the premiership, and promised to transform the country into a modern, democratic European state. Despite expectations at the time, the Orange coalition only held for a few months. Embroiled in seemingly endless bickering, Yushchenko and Tymoshenko neglected reform and enabled the man who had been humiliated by the uprising, Viktor Yanukovych, to stage a comeback in 2010 and win the presidency.

Since then, Yanukovych, who campaigned as a moderate promising to unify the nation and fix the country, has embarked on a systematic rollback of the revolution's ideals. He's substituted Russia for the West, authoritarianism for democracy, and Russian supremacism for Ukrainian patriotism, thereby establishing himself as a radical willing to do anything—even deepen regional, national, ethnic, and class divides—to get and keep power. The many Ukrainian democrats who thought of Yanukovych as the lesser of two evils have now descended into despair—German reporter Konrad Schuller **has called it** "the return of fear"—and increasingly view Yanukovych's administration as an "occupation" regime and his Party of Regions as a throwback to the Communist Party of the Soviet Union (CPSU).

And they have a point. Established in 2001 by the former Soviet functionaries who had run Ukraine's industrial heartland, the Donbas, for decades, the Party of Regions stole the proletarian constituency of the neo-Stalinist Communist Party of Ukraine—and, backed by tycoons with enormous holdings in the steel, coal, chemicals, and media businesses, quickly became hegemonic in southeastern Ukraine.

The Regionnaires (as party members are known) share other similarities with the Communist Party of the Soviet Union. Like the CPSU, the Party of Regions is a formidable vote-manufacturing machine, possessing dedicated cadres, vast resources, and unscrupulous leaders. Like the CPSU, the Party of Regions is an efficient moneymaking machine, serving as a get-rich-quick scheme for its activists, promoting the interests of Ukraine's elites, and maintaining warm relations with organized crime. Like the CPSU, the Party of Regions is also a powerful mythmaking machine, idolizing all things Soviet, exalting Russian language, culture, history, and identity, and conferring "separate and unequal" status on their Ukrainian equivalents. And finally, the Party of Regions is inherently incompatible with democracy, the market, and rule of law, as was the CPSU. Even if Yanukovych is the bold reformer his defenders say he is, he will—like Mikhail Gorbachev—soon discover that the main obstacle to perestroika is his own party.

Although the Regionnaires may make the trains run on time, their rule—called "thugist" by the Russian democratic analyst Yulia Latynina—cannot make Ukraine truly modern. Small wonder that they still can't accept the Orange Revolution as a genuine manifestation of popular will. It's not just that the upheaval repudiated and exposed them as fraudsters. Far worse, it demonstrated that Ukrainians could and, given the chance, *would* resist the rule of reactionaries and authoritarians. The revolution proved that Ukrainians were mature enough politically to understand that they had rights—and that the Yanukovych people were the interlopers incapable of withstanding people power.

Few Ukrainians today regard the Orange Revolution with more than a smirk. That's not surprising, as the pain and disillusionment produced by Yushchenko and Tymoshenko's incompetence are still too palpable. That said, the uprising represents one of the most important junctures in Ukraine's modern history. The revolution brought down an authoritarian regime in an inspiring example of popular engagement; it did so peacefully; and it did so while invoking and practicing progressive political and humanitarian ideals. Future historians will doubtless depict the Orange Revolution as a major step along Ukraine's democratic trajectory.

Those same historians will treat the Yanukovych interlude as a typical example of counterrevolution that, like all counterrevolutions, cannot succeed in fully turning back the clock. Indeed, the longer Yanukovych and the Regionnaires practice "thug-ism," the more Ukrainians will regard the revolution's values as those befitting a modern Ukrainian state. The residents of both the tiny village of Plesetske, outside Kyiv, and the large industrial city of Kharkiv have already invoked those ideals in their ongoing protests against the Regionnaires' manipulation of the October 31 local elections. And the tens of thousands of small business people currently demonstrating against the regressive new tax code have just issued a formal ultimatum to Yanukovych, vowing to "defend our right to life, our right to entrepreneurial activity, and other civic rights and liberties with continuing strikes and actions of civil disobedience" unless he vetoes the code.

A desire for truth, integrity, and, above all, human dignity motivated the millions of mostly young Ukrainians who took part in and supported the Orange Revolution. Not surprisingly, those values may have been best expressed by the unofficial anthem of the Revolution—a rap song by the group GreenJolly. The first stanza declares just what the young Orange revolutionaries expected from their government: "Falsifications—No! Machinations—No! Connivance—No! No to lies!" They were, of course, to be grossly disappointed.

But the second stanza gets to the heart of the matter:

> We're not chattel, we're not fools.
> We're the sons and daughters of Ukraine.
> Now or never, no more waiting:
> Together we are many, we cannot be defeated.

These sentiments, so similar to the slogans of the civil rights movement in the United States, underscore the fact that the Regionnaires have no future in Ukraine's future. Sooner or later, the next generation of Orange revolutionaries—and there always is a next generation—will realize that they too deserve to be treated as human beings.

*

Who Needs Education? *World Affairs Journal*, December 20, 2010

Ukraine's Ministry of Education and Science is now the Ministry of Education, Science, Youth, and—no kidding, honest—Sports. This bizarre transformation took place on December 10, when President Viktor Yanukovych announced an administrative reform abolishing a bunch of ministries and reorganized a few others. Youth and sports were attached to education and science in a move that testifies either to the president's improbable belief in *mens sana in corpore sano* or to the sorry state of Ukraine's educational system.

Soviet education was always faulted—correctly—for failing to inculcate critical thinking in students, but it excelled in the natural sciences, which could be pursued without pressure from the Communist Party's ideological machine. Ukraine traditionally produced outstanding physicists and mathematicians and, in the 1960s, was even a leader in the emerging field of cybernetics. Translating the theoretical achievements of scientists into workable technology was another failing of the Soviet Union, but the scientists themselves were world-class, and those who emigrated to the West often found top jobs in the IT sector.

Everything changed after the USSR's collapse. Independent Ukraine's economy went into steep decline, state financing dried up, state institutions—and all universities were state-run—withered, corruption became rampant, and education in general and higher education in particular fell into disrepair. At present, university administrators and professors are overworked and underpaid, bribe-taking is rampant, standards have crashed, and plagiarism is commonplace. Reform, while imperative, has been resisted. Too many state bureaucrats and too many university administrators have a stake in the system as it currently exists.

Unsurprisingly, alternatives to Soviet institutions have multiplied, but their quality is usually substandard. One notable exception is the Ukrainian Catholic University in Lviv, whose rector is a Harvard-educated, Ukrainian-American priest, Borys Gudziak. Another is the Kyiv-Mohyla Academy, established in 1632 by the Kyiv Metropolitan Petro Mohyla, shut down in 1817 by Tsar Alexander I, and reestablished in 1991 as a formally state-run institution with an exceptional degree of autonomy. That autonomy—and the academy's commitment to Western standards, openness to visiting professors from throughout the world, refusal to engage in bribe-taking, insistence on English-language instruction, and support of the Orange Revolution's democratic values—has made Mohyla (as it's known) one of Ukraine's leading universities and its students the equals of the very best the United States has to offer.

Autonomy, openness, and critical thinking are, of course, anathema to the Yanukovych administration and, in particular, to Minister of Education, Science, Youth, and Sports Dmitri Tabachnik, said to be Moscow's point man in Kyiv (where, by the way, he's reputed to be a real estate wheeler-dealer with sizable holdings). Ukrainian democrats generally append the modifier "odious" to Tabachnik, viewing him—and his unabashed endorsement of discriminatory policies toward Ukrainian language, culture, history, and identity—as Ukraine's equivalent of an anti-Semitic education minister in Israel.

Tabachnik's appointment back in March 2010 led to countrywide protests by students (many of whom were subsequently expelled) and to public criticism by Mohyla's outspoken rector, Serhii Kvit. Tabachnik shrugged off the attacks, but he must have secretly begun sharpening his knives. He has now prepared a draft law on higher education that envisions curtailments of university autonomy and contains language forbidding universities—read: Mohyla—from making knowledge of English a requirement of admission. If the law is adopted in its current form, Mohyla's special status—and excellence—would end.

Kvit recently issued an open letter to Yanukovych urging him to junk Tabachnik's proposal. Democratic intellectuals have sided with Kvit, as they understand that Mohyla could become their Thermopylae (here is a petition in defense of Mohyla), while Mohyla graduates have issued an appeal in which they decry the law as "leading to Ukraine's self-isolation and the further degradation of science and education in our state."

Yanukovych has also signaled his views of the matter. His administrative reform not only expanded Tabachnik's powers, but it also increased his opportunities for self-enrichment by including sports within his portfolio. The Union of European Football Associations' soccer championship will be held in four Ukrainian cities in 2012: that means billions will be poured into hotels, infrastructure, and tourism in the next two years. Surely a bit of that filthy lucre will end up in Tabachnik's ministry. No one's betting that the money will go to critical thinking.

When asked by the press to explain Tabachnik's hostility to Mohyla, Kvit stated: "Obviously, he doesn't care for an effective university without corruption. Obviously, he doesn't care for an autonomous university. In reality, there is no autonomy in Ukraine. The state exerts authoritarian control over universities in all their activities. We are in spirit a free university."
Still.

*

Regionnaires' Disease in Ukraine, *World Affairs Journal*, December 28, 2010

Last winter's health scare in Ukraine was swine flu. This year's is far worse: Regionnaires' Disease, an illness that eats away at political organisms and turns them into ethical zombies.

The carriers of this terrible illness are the cadres of the Party of Regions, the hierarchically organized, anti-democratic, and Russian supremacist political force that brought President Viktor Yanukovych to power and serves as his political base. The Regionnaires control the Parliament, the cabinet, and most regional and local governments.

Many Ukrainians refer to the Regionnaires as *bandyty*, a word best translated as "thugs." The term fits them well. All too many of them resemble Hollywood versions of gun-toting mugs. They generally lack anything resembling a political program—and the "vision thing," to quote George H. W. Bush, is completely absent from their mindset. Instead, like the gangster Johnny Rocco in John Huston's 1948 film *Key Largo*, their goal is simply "more." More power and more wealth, to be precise. More insight, more knowledge, and more sensitivity are not exactly on their agenda.

Neither are more manners. On December 16, a band of Regionnaire thugs broke into the Ukrainian Parliament and viciously attacked opposition politicians protesting government harassment of Yulia Tymoshenko. This wasn't just an instance of the run-of-the-mill fisticuffs for which the Parliament has become known. It was, as one democratic website put it, nothing less than a "pogrom." Take a look at the YouTube video of the attack. The big guys throwing punches and swinging chairs are Regionnaires. The little guys hiding for cover are the opposition politicians. Oh, and by the way, the Regionnaires have officially declared that the violence was "provoked" by the opposition.

Just a few days earlier, another Regionnaire deputy, the 34-year-old pretty boy, Vitalii Khomutynnik, exhibited his party's classy side. When asked by a female journalist to name the date of the Treaty of Pereiaslav—the Russo-Ukrainian accord was signed in 1654, and it's about as elementary a part of Ukrainian, Russian, and Soviet history textbooks as 1776 is in American texts—the married head of the Regionnaire youth wing refused to answer the "provocation," as he put it, and quipped that, after all, he wasn't asking her about her bust size. Sounds like unacceptably crude sexism, right? Sure, but who cares? Back in March, 63-year-old Prime Minister Mykola Azarov stated that the reason there were no women in his cabinet was that, well, politics wasn't women's work. Like fathers, like sons, I guess.

With lugs like these running the country, just what chance does Ukraine have of implementing anything resembling serious reform? Zilch might be an optimistic answer, and most Ukrainians expect the Regionnaires to grab "more" in the few years they stay in power. And maybe then, after Ukraine becomes a kind of Zimbabwe lite, things will change.

Yanukovych, who knows that thuggishness is not the best way to people's hearts, is now caught between a rock and a hard place. Without the Regionnaires, he's nothing—and both he and they know it. Small wonder that he failed to condemn the pogromchiks explicitly, stating instead that he's "categorically against using physical force in the Parliament." Indeed, Yanukovych's hyper-centralization of power in no small measure made the pogrom possible. What else are Mickey Mouse parliamentarians with no responsibilities—and lots of testosterone—to do?

But with Regionnaires' Disease, Yanukovych is doomed to become a reviled tin-pot dictator. He could even give Robert Mugabe a run for the money—unless vanity or common sense intervenes and the Ukrainian president decides to accept a democratic cure.

In the meantime, the West may want to consider the advice of my fellow *World Affairs* blogger Vladimir Kara-Murza that we issue travel bans for evildoers—and impose a quarantine on pogromchiks with Regionnaires' Disease.

*

Cracking Down and Cracking Up, *World Affairs Journal*, January 10, 2011

The dialectic was alive and well in Ukraine in 2010. On the one hand, the regime of President Viktor Yanukovych appeared strong, moving decisively toward authoritarianism. On the other hand, it appeared weak, manifesting a breathtaking serial incompetence.

The transition from democracy consisted of three steps.

First, Yanukovych concentrated vast power in his hands, effectively creating a "sultanistic" regime in which all subordinates are accountable to him alone.

Second, the Party of Regions seized control of the parliament, the central government, almost all provincial and district governments, and the "strategic heights" of the economy.

Third, the regime assaulted institutional sites of potential opposition, curtailing university autonomy, limiting press freedom, encroaching on NGOs, and persecuting the opposition.

Weakness, ineptness, and bungling are direct consequences of these authoritarian trends.

Sultanism promotes administrative irresponsibility, bureaucratic infighting, and risk avoidance, as subordinates become sycophants who know that their livelihoods depend on the sultan and his whims. Sultanism is also incompatible with policy effectiveness, since contemporary societies and economies are too complex for any one leader to guide.

One party's domination of government promotes corruption even in the best of circumstances. When that party resembles the mafia, absolute power, to misquote Lord Acton, corrupts more than absolutely, and government loses even its residual ability to facilitate entrepreneurship, creativity, and innovation.

Cracking down on civil society is a surefire way of reducing information flows to rulers and, thus, of enhancing their incompetence. Repression also corrodes regime legitimacy, thereby making it increasingly dependent on coercion. As Talleyrand pointed out many years ago, however, one cannot sit on bayonets—at least not without tearing one's pants.

The Yanukovych regime's serial incompetence manifested itself most strikingly—and embarrassingly—in three easily avoidable policy disasters.

The first was the April Kharkiv accords with Russia, in which Ukraine's rulers couldn't tell the difference between business (the price of gas) and strategy (the basing of the Black

Sea Fleet). Only a tyro would confuse or couple the two. And only an incompetent tyro would agree to an excessively high gas price and an excessively low base rent in exchange for Sevastopol and possibly Crimea.

The second was the Entrepreneurs' Rebellion over the Tax Code. The draft code had been the target of sustained criticism and entrepreneur-led demonstrations throughout Ukraine since the middle of the year. When the business people announced they would assemble in Kyiv's Independence Square, the site of the Orange Revolution, on November 22, the sixth anniversary of the uprising, only an obtuse regime could not have foreseen trouble. (Incredibly, Yanukovych's advisers said he hadn't read the code, thereby demonstrating both the sultan's limitations and his sycophants' inability to lie imaginatively.) The thousands of entrepreneurs who assembled peacefully for almost two weeks forced Yanukovych to revise the code and decisively demonstrated that the people still had the power to stop the bulldozer regime.

The third mistake was the persecution in late December of former Prime Minister Yulia Tymoshenko and former Interior Minister Yuri Lutsenko. Before the harassment began, most Ukrainians would have agreed that both politicians were washed up. Now Tymoshenko and Lutsenko look like political martyrs, and their popularity can only grow. Yanukovych, in contrast, will look punitive at best and maladroit at worst.

The coming months will likely see both continued crackdowns and crack-ups. With its legitimacy in tatters and economic prosperity nowhere on the horizon, the regime will have no choice but to use coercion to elicit what social scientists call "societal compliance." After all, when your soft power is nil and the Putin option of neo-imperial, macho-man chest-beating is unavailable, you have to use, and sit on, hard bayonets. But, as the Entrepreneurs' Rebellion showed, society is in no mood to comply: people know there is strength in numbers, and they know the numbers are on their side. Once the pensioners, housewives, and coal miners join the students and the entrepreneurs, even club-swinging and tear gas won't help.

As the regime weakens, expect intra-elite tensions and defections to increase. The *tushki* (the defectors to the ruling coalition) will go first; as parliamentary elections and the 2012 soccer championship approach, fair-weather friends like Speaker of Parliament Volodymyr Lytvyn and reform-oriented oligarchs like Serhii Tihipko and Rinat Akhmetov will be the next to jump ship. Yanukovych will then go the way of all weak authoritarian rulers: he'll wrap himself in the flag of patriotism. With 2011 marking 20 years of Ukraine's independence, he'll have ample opportunities to play the great statesman and nation builder. It's even possible that the anti-Ukrainian Minister of Education Dmitri Tabachnik will be fed to the wolves. If that doesn't work, Yanukovych will have to make direct overtures to the democrats. If those in jail can get their act together with those outside (a big if, to be sure), Yanukovych's future—and Ukraine's—will be in their hands. Let's just hope that, this time, Viktor Yushchenko stays on his bee farm.

*

PART ONE: THE RISE AND FALL OF VIKTOR YANUKOVYCH

A Ukrainian Martin Luther King? *World Affairs Journal*, January 20, 2011

Now that Americans have finished celebrating Dr. Martin Luther King Jr. Day, it may be worth asking whether Ukraine could ever get such an inspired, and inspirational, leader.

It certainly deserves to. The current crop of democratic leaders is mediocre at best and shabby at worst. They can issue statements and bang their fists, but they are unlikely to move people to self-sacrifice and solidarity.

The Orange Revolution showed that Ukrainians can be mobilized into a nationwide movement professing humanitarian goals, community, and nonviolence. Yulia Tymoshenko and Viktor Yushchenko had their chance to be world-historical figures, but they blew it, preferring the political low ground to the moral high ground.

The failure of the Orange leaders has many reasons, but surely one of the most important was their personal inability to view politics from an irreproachable ethical vantage point. What distinguishes Martin Luther King, Mohandas Gandhi, the Dalai Lama, Desmond Tutu, Vaclav Havel, and Nelson Mandela from run-of-the-mill politicos is their ethics—their strong sense of right and wrong and their willingness to place the good of the community ahead of personal gain.

Ukraine deserves to have a Martin Luther King, if only because Ukrainians so strongly resemble African Americans. Both peoples were held in humiliating captivity until the 1860s; both suffered savage discrimination and systematic violence in the last 150 years; both still experience the very similar consequences of their national traumas—from broken homes and broken cultures to dysfunctional males and overburdened females to excessive pride and excessive humility.

Back in the 1960s, during the heady days of the civil rights movement, some black Americans sought solutions in violence. The system seemed unalterably racist and ripe for smashing. Some Ukrainians may be tempted to respond the same way. The Yanukovych regime appears determined to transform Ukraine into a Slavic version of the Jim Crow American South, in which the knout rules, thugs go unpunished, and Ukrainian lan-guage, culture, and identity are confined to "Colored Only" waiting rooms. The tempta-tion to strike back may be strong, but it should be resisted. Ukrainians must understand that violence is not only wrong but also ineffective, leading tyrants to crack down and reinforce their own ugly rule.

Dictators don't fear bullets; they fear numbers. Dr. King, the Mahatma, the Dalai Lama, Bishop Tutu, Mandela, and Havel have shown that nonviolence and people power work. And most Ukrainians, at least those that spent weeks freezing on Kyiv's Independence Square during the Orange Revolution and the Entrepreneurs' Rebellion, know that too.

Charismatic, inspirational leaders cannot be predicted. Somehow, almost magically, they just emerge. Who would have expected an obscure Baptist minister in Atlanta to change America? Who would have imagined that a lawyer in South Africa would end British rule in India? Or that a writer of absurdist plays would bring down communism in Czechoslovakia? Such unpredictability is good news, however, as it means that, no matter how hard the Yanukovych regime cracks down on the current crop of leaders, it will never be able to find the future visionary.

The other bit of good news is this: Inspirational leaders emerge when the times are tough, when times *demand* inspirational leaders. The uglier the Yanukovych regime becomes, the likelier the appearance of a Ukrainian Martin Luther King. Ukrainian democrats may take heart. Sooner or later, they too shall overcome.

*

Viktor Yanukovych, Splittist, *World Affairs Journal*, February 7, 2011

Few things were worse in the Communist catalog of sins than "splittism"—or the promotion of splits within the "united front" of the proletariat. Splittists were "deviationists" who preached unity while abandoning the Party "line" and going off in their own, invariably destructive directions.

Thanks no doubt to the mysterious workings of the Marxist dialectic, the ranks of the splittists have recently acquired a new member: Ukraine's President Viktor Yanukovych who, in typically splittist fashion, preaches unity while promoting discord.

Here's an excerpt from his January 21st speech commemorating Ukraine's Unity Day:

> I strongly condemn any attempts to jeopardize the unity of Ukraine and the unity of our nation, as well as any efforts to set a part of our citizens against another. I advocate us searching for something that is common for people, regardless of whether they live in the west or the east of Ukraine.

Nice words, but how can one reconcile them with Yanukovych's actions?

A genuine unifier would never have appointed a Russian supremacist as minister of education. Dmitri Tabachnik makes about as much sense in that position as Oleh Tyahnybok, a Ukrainian extremist. After all, you don't promote racial unity in the United States by placing a Ku Klux Klansman or a Black Panther in charge of the Department of Education.

Nor would a genuine unifier promote the hegemony of one of Ukraine's three Orthodox churches—the one affiliated with the Moscow Patriarchate—and thereby encourage in the other two legitimate fears of persecution and liquidation. Indeed, a genuine unifier would, like every one of Ukraine's past presidents, be tolerant and ecumenical, maintaining a dialogue with all of Ukraine's many faiths, and not just the one that gets him Brownie points with the Kremlin. (By the way, that service has not gone unappreciated by the Russian Orthodox Church: on January 21, Yanukovych received the $50,000 Patriarch Aleksei II Prize for "strengthening the unity of Orthodox peoples.")

Nor, finally, would a genuine unifier promote only his Donetsk cronies to positions of authority and let them feed at the trough, while charging his centrist political opponents with corruption and looking the other way as his supporters fund Tyahnybok in the hope of creating a regionally strong, though nationally unelectable, bogeyman.

Why is Yanukovych pursuing splittism? He may have a hidden unificationist agenda—of attaching Ukraine or, at least its eastern provinces, to Russia. Or he may be trying to turn eastern Ukrainians against western Ukrainians on the *divide et impera* rationale. Or, just as plausibly, he may, as a deeply provincial politico, not understand that a complex and diverse country cannot be run like his Donbas fiefdom.

Whatever the reason, Yanukovych had better keep his eyes open, as his splittism could lead to civil conflict and possibly even destroy Ukraine. Some of his Regionnaire pals wouldn't mind that outcome, but Yanukovych should—especially if he wants to keep having photo-ops in Brussels, Paris, and Washington. At the very least, Yanukovych should realize that his splittism could lead to a split between him and the rest of the country. His base in the east still tolerates him (though just barely) as their native son, but much of the rest of the country regards him with distrust at best and disdain at worst. And now that he's insulted Ukrainian women in Davos, where he encouraged investors to come to Kyiv in the spring and watch them disrobe, Yanukovych may be widening the gender gap as well.

More immediately worrisome for Ukraine's president is that his splittism is already generating splits in his outwardly solid, though inwardly decrepit, regime. The latest indication of growing cracks is an article by Lieutenant-General Oleksandr Skipalsky, the former deputy head of the Security Service of Ukraine (SBU). Here's what Skipalsky had to say about the Yanukovych regime:

> The people who have now come to power in our State are those for whom Ukraine is a foreign concept. These people believe that Ukraine should become their private property. Their goal is to privatize Ukraine completely. And persistently, step by step, they are heading toward that goal. The people are mired in poverty, but they are swimming in luxury. While pensioners are counting their pennies, they are buying up yachts, planes, villas, and banks. They regard the Ukrainian force structures, the Ukrainian courts, and the Prosecutor's Office of Ukraine as their private property. They look upon the Security Service of Ukraine as a security service for their clans. They are not only destroying our language and our history, they are destroying public morale. They are destroying the future of our children, grandchildren, and great-grandchildren. They represent not so much a diffe ent ideology as a diffe ent civilization.

Pretty strong stuff, but the important thing is that Skipalsky (and former SBU head Valentyn Nalyvaychenko, who is also a determined opponent of Yanukovych) must have many high-ranking supporters within the secret police. As Skipalsky says, "We do not want our age-old hopes betrayed. We desire the achievement of our goals. That is why my comrades in arms and I—those members of the force structures who have not lost sight of honesty and honor—will not be changing our profession for a long time to come."

As Egypt's President Hosni Mubarak could tell Ukraine's president, no illegitimate regime can survive for long without the support of the army and secret police. Ukraine's army is decrepit, so Yanukovych can't count on it. The SBU has retained some of its élan, but if Skipalsky's views are commonplace in its ranks, then Yanukovych can't count on it either.

So who's left? Tabachnik and his band of Regionnaire supremacists? Unfortunately for Ukraine's splittist president, when the going gets rough, as it surely will in 2011–2012, Tabachnik and the thugs will be the first to split.

*

Viktor Yanukovych, Revolutionary, *World Affairs Journal*, February 18, 2011

President Viktor Yanukovych's rhetoric has recently taken a scary turn. At a February 2nd Polish-Ukrainian economic meeting in Warsaw, he spoke like a bona fide revolutionary committed to forcible change from above. To be sure, given his decidedly casual relationship to language, words, and meaning, the Ukrainian president may not have understood just what he was saying. On the other hand, he just may have. And if he did, Ukraine—and the rest of the world—should be prepared for a significant increase in coercion, instability, and conflict.

All revolutionaries share several characteristics. First, they insist on the need for total change. Second, they claim to be empowered by some higher force—the class, the nation, the race, or God. Third, they insist that the opposition must be destroyed—for the good of the revolution and the higher force that inspires it. And last, they blame their own failures on traitors. Look at the writings of Robespierre, Lenin, Stalin, Hitler, Mao, and the Ayatollah and you'll find all these features. Why? Because they go together. If you believe you have the right to transform a society completely, then you must appeal to some abstract force for legitimacy, as real people would never opt for total change. If you believe you know exactly what must be done to improve society, then all who oppose you must be enemies of the revolution and of the higher force you represent. If, despite your superior wisdom, things go wrong, then the fault cannot be yours. It must be the work of devious wreckers.

Consider Yanukovych's comments in light of the above:

1. The need for total change: "The country must be changed, it must be changed; its face must be changed. We must change our approaches by, as they say, 180 degrees. And we'll do it."

2. Empowerment by an abstract higher force: "The Ukrainian people is wise—it knows what to do ... We get our stimulus from the Ukrainian people."

3. Opposition must be destroyed: "When such a strong, crushing blow is

delivered to the bureaucratic system, it obviously reacts with like force."

4. Failures are caused by traitors: "They lie without conscience, twisting facts; with the money they stole they hire hirelings in Europe, the USA, and within the country ... and confuse the whole world and Ukrainian society."

If we take Yanukovych's comments seriously (and since he's president, we should, shouldn't we?), then they amount to nothing less than a call for "revolution from above"—that is, total change initiated and carried out by the state in the manner of a "great leap forward." Such a goal should worry Ukrainians and the rest of the world, not just because revolutions from above are always coercive and always violent (after all, people always resist and their resistance must be crushed)—but, no less important, because they do not work. The three prime examples of revolutions from above are Stalin's, Hitler's, and Mao's. Each of them changed his country completely—and almost destroyed it, and its neighbors, in the process. If this is what Yanukovych has in mind for Ukraine, then heaven help it.

Now, I'm sure that Yanukovych's people will say that I'm overreacting—that the president was just talking tough. Could be. On the other hand, his alarmingly total appropriation of super-presidential power was anything but rhetorical. And, if Yanukovych just wants to talk tough, why talk tough like a fanatical revolutionary? Why not talk the tough talk of reform, democracy, and liberalism? Why not state that 180-degree shifts are necessary in a few areas—such as government corruption, rent-seeking by highly placed state functionaries, and outright theft, graft, and shakedowns by the president's buddies—and that society, culture, education, business, democracy, and other policy areas need adjustments? Maybe by 10 degrees, maybe by 20 or 30, maybe even by 90—but surely not by 180. Why not eschew the language of "crushing blows," and instead speak calmly of providing incentives to change behavior? Why not admit that even the president can make mistakes? Why not, finally, fess up that mendacity is not exactly foreign currency to his cronies? (Are you listening, Hanna Herman?)

What's behind this outburst of revolutionary talk (especially as Yanukovych's foreign minister has just published an article castigating Yulia Tymoshenko for being—you guessed it!—a revolutionary)? It's possible that Yanukovych is desperate, having come to realize that his presidency is a complete failure and that, unless he does something big quickly, he will soon follow in former Egyptian President Hosni Mubarak's footsteps. It's also possible that sultanism has gone to Yanukovych's head. Now that he's concentrated all the powers of the state in his own hands, he may believe that, like Robespierre, he's been anointed by destiny to bring happiness and virtue to humanity, even if cooler heads in his own cabinet are against it. Finally, it's possible that Yanukovych has decided that his presidency is beyond salvaging, but that tough-guy talk just might salvage his image.

Take your pick. Alas, whatever the interpretation, it is Ukrainians who will pay the price for Yanukovych's gross mishandling of their country.

Ya-nuking Democracy in Ukraine, *World Affairs Journal*, March 4, 2011

What's the condition of democracy in Ukraine after one year of Viktor Yanukovych's presidency? He and his supporters say democracy is alive and well. His critics say it's dead or decaying. Who's right?

Obviously, the answer depends on what you mean by democracy.

Here's a very short and, I submit, non-controversial list of modern democracy's minimal features:

1. A balance of power among the executive, the legislature, and the judiciary.

2. Rule of law rooted in independent courts and a functioning constitution.

3. Fair and free elections involving genuine parties.

4. Freedom of assembly and speech.

Here's why these features matter.

A balance of power precludes the over-concentration of power in the hands of any one individual or institution—as in a monarchy or dictatorship—and guarantees the independence of courts. Neutral laws determine how those branches of power interact with one another and with society; laws can be neutral only if they are interpreted by an independent judiciary and grounded in a consensual document known as a constitution. The individuals who run the executive and the legislature are not appointed by some power-holder, but, acting as representatives of social and political interests called parties, are elected by the people. Elections and rule of law cannot be meaningful unless citizens and policymakers can meet and speak openly and freely.

Where does Yanukovych's Ukraine stand on this scale? For the sake of convenience, let's assign scores of 3, 2, 1, or 0 for each of these categories (with 3 representing fully democratic and 0 fully non-democratic) for both Yanukovych and his predecessor, former President Viktor Yushchenko.

1. Yanukovych has concentrated all power in his hands, thereby making the Parliament a rubber-stamp institution and the courts, anything but independent under Yushchenko, completely subordinate to the all-powerful president's whims. Yushchenko: 2, Yanukovych: 0.

2. Under Yanukovych, as under Yushchenko, some laws are honored, some are not. The Constitution and judicial independence are adhered to when it's convenient for the president and violated when it's not. Yushchenko: 1, Yanukovych: 1.

3. The elections that brought Yanukovych to power were fair and free, but the October 2010 local elections that produced Party of Regions' hegemony were not. The regime is doing its best to destroy the Yulia Tymoshenko Bloc, to

support the extremist Svoboda Party, and to entrench the Party of Regions as the only game in town. Yushchenko: 3, Yanukovych: 1.

4. As many independent international observers have noted, freedom of assembly and speech has taken a big hit under Yanukovych. Yushchenko: 3, Yanukovych: 1.

Add up the scores and you get 9 for Yushchenko (out of a possible 12) and 3 for Yanukovych. That's quite a difference, and Ukrainians feel it. Even if you bump up Yanukovych's scores by 1 or 2 points—on the grounds that I was just too darned harsh—the trend is still downward. Translated into letter grades, Yushchenko gets a B and Yanukovych gets a D, or possibly a C-minus. He hasn't yet failed, but he's failing and might want to consider remedial work in democracy summer school.

Whimsy aside, the important question is this: Is Yanukovych's Ukraine, with a score of 3, still a democracy or has he ya-nuked it? If you figure that a 6 would be the minimum for a really crummy democracy, then the answer is: he's ya-nuked it. If you're inexplicably generous and bump up Yanukovych's scores by 1 or 2 points, then his Ukraine doesn't even qualify as a really crummy democracy.

Now, four more questions:

Is this the best way to promote Ukraine's integration with Europe? Take a wild guess.

Is this the best way to promote Ukraine's transformation into Belarus? Take an even wilder guess.

Is this the best way to transform Ukraine into a backward province of Russia? Go ahead and hit the ball outta the park.

Finally, the question that's dearest to Yanukovych: Is this the best way to promote stability and order? The Ukrainian president thinks so, but any political science undergraduate could tell you why he's dead wrong. For one thing, every rapid institutional shift is destabilizing. For another, every rapid institutional shift away from democracy is especially destabilizing if citizens are not compensated for their loss of freedom with economic goodies or a feel-good ideology. As Ukrainians know all too well, their living standards are in free fall and their identity is under assault. Ironically, by ya-nuking democracy Yanukovych is also ya-nuking his presidency and, ultimately, Ukraine.

Back in the days of the Cold War, that kind of irrational behavior was known as Mutually Assured Destruction—and the solution to MADness was nuclear disarmament.

So how about dismantling those ya-nukes, Mister President, before you destroy yourself and your country?

*

Viktor Yanukovych, Terminator, *World Affairs Journal*, March 18, 2011

President Viktor Yanukovych's main claim to fame is political stability. Say what you will about the rollback of democracy and the absence of economic reforms, his supporters say, but you gotta admit that Ukraine has become more stable in the year since he's been president. After all, Yanukovych is the undisputed boss, he gives all the orders, his minions follow them, and things get done. That's stability, and stability is good, right?

The argument couldn't be more wrong.

All authoritarian leaders—and Yanukovych is no exception—believe that the more power they have, the better, the more stable, the more predictable things must be. But the historical experience of dictatorships conclusively shows that the hyper-concentration of power is actually a guarantee of political, social, and economic *instability*. The Soviets took the case for centralization to its logical conclusion, constructing a totalitarian polity and a centrally planned economy—and you know how that ended. The fact is that democracy is not just nice. It's also more stable and more effective than dictatorship.

Unsurprisingly, Yanukovych the would-be authoritarian stabilizer will succeed only in becoming a Terminator and destabilizing Ukraine—and here's why.

First, although Yanukovych is the undisputed master, he is woefully inadequate in his understanding of modern societies, economies, and polities. Absolute rulers can be successful if and only if they are philosopher kings, and Yanukovych, a tough kid from a tough neighborhood with two suspect degrees from fly-by-night educational institutions, is not. Knowledge underload and information overload will wear him down very quickly.

Second, and far more important, Yanukovych has, by grabbing all the power, effectively destroyed Ukraine's political institutions. The Parliament is a joke; the courts are a joke; and the cabinet—along with all the ministries of government—is merely a tool of the president. But here's the rub. Modern states and societies cannot be run without effective institutions, even if leaders are philosopher kings. Modern states and societies are too complex for any one person to do the job. Sultanistic rule á la Yanukovych might have worked in Ukraine back in the fifteenth century, but not in the twenty-first.

Third, and even more important, by declaring himself sultan and destroying institutions, Yanukovych has provided government administrators with irresistible incentives to engage in buck-passing, evasiveness, obstructionism, toadyism, and corruption. Place yourself in the position of some cog in Ukraine's vast bureaucratic machine. You know that your job depends *entirely* on being in good graces with your boss, whose job depends on being in good graces with his boss. And so on, all the way up the food chain. Will you assume responsibility for anything? Of course, not: you'll pass the buck. Will you take a stand? No, you'll be evasive. Will you help your colleague get the job done? Hardly: far better to trip her up, as that makes you look better. Will you speak your mind to your boss? Never: you'll always suck up. Will you be honest? Not a chance: you know that, since you could be fired at any minute, you need to steal as much as you can when you can. Add to the mix the fact that Yanukovych's Regionnaire thugs have seized control of the government apparatus, and its incompetence and venality are sure-fire bets.

Fourth, and most important, a hyper-centralized system consisting of a misguided leader, absent institutions, and thuggish party hacks cannot be reformist, effective, or legitimate. Genuine reform is impossible, because it serves no one's interests. Ineffectiveness is inevitable, because running a complex society in so primitive a fashion is certain to result in terrible mistakes. Nor will you learn from your mistakes, as the mechanisms for providing the leader with good information—functioning institutions and responsible administrators—are missing.

Legitimacy is also out of the question. Big bosses may be feared, but they are never loved. And, when their mistakes become endemic, they always come to be despised and ridiculed. (It took Yanukovych only a few months in office to become a laughing stock.) The result is that he is doomed, at best, to become a second Leonid Brezhnev—the Soviet leader who presided over the inglorious "era of stagnation" and probably made the USSR's collapse inevitable. The Ukrainian president should ask himself just why Yanukovych jokes are now as popular as Brezhnev jokes used to be in the 1970s and 1980s.

Such a system is not stable. It *looks* stable, but only because the boss is the only one speaking and all his underlings *pretend* to be listening. And the Yanukovych system is especially prone to instability, because the Ukrainian president is not content, as Brezhnev was, with doing nothing. Yanukovych wants to consolidate one-man rule as quickly as possible by *proactively* destroying institutions. But the unintended outcome of institutional evisceration is a vicious circle: his rule will only get weaker, which in turn will lead him to strike out at and further weaken institutions. As his regime becomes increasingly ineffective and he becomes increasingly illegitimate, people will increasingly lead their lives outside the state. Some will emigrate; others will "drop out" into the shadow economy and parallel social institutions. Still others will resist: some actively, most passively, in the time-honored manner of the weak and powerless—by slacking, lying, stealing, and pretending.

At the rate it's decaying, the Yanukovych system will be on the verge of collapse in a few years. Like some recently deposed Arab potentate, Yanukovych will smile, wave his hand, and look powerful. His acolytes will smile, wave their hands, and look adoring. In reality, he will be presiding over a house of cards. At some point, a spark—some crisis, some serial stupidity, some act of self-immolation—will bring it all down and his adoring acolytes will be the first to terminate the Terminator.

*

Mistrusting Yanukonomics, *World Affairs Journal*, March 24, 2011

You gotta see things in perspective, President Viktor Yanukovych's apologists say. Sure, democracy may not be doing too well, but just look at the economy. Bold reforms are being adopted. Just give Yanukovych a few years, and Ukraine will become an Eastern European tiger. Growl.

Were that the trade-off—less democracy, more growth—one might rationalize Yanukovych's authoritarianism as the price an underdeveloped country must pay for economic modernization. After all, it's true that Ukraine needs a systemic overhaul and that the process of reforming the tax code, the legal system, the pension system, the educational system, and a myriad of other socio-economic spheres will be painful. And it's true that the country must be reformed sooner rather than later, lest it continue on the path to oblivion. And it's also true that the Orange leadership's bungling only intensified Ukraine's troubles and left Yanukovych with a big mess.

For better or for worse, however, authoritarianism is not an option for Ukraine or for Yanukovych. As I've been arguing in this blog, authoritarianism á la Yanukovych is in-trinsically unstable. Hence, to think that one can *force* Ukraine to modernize is absurd. It won't work, and the likely consequence of such an effort is a social upheaval leading to government collapse.

That leaves Yanukovych with one option: *coaxing* Ukraine toward reform. But that can work only if Ukrainians trust their president and are willing to assume economic hardships for the good of the country. Poles, for instance, accepted shock therapy back in the early 1990s because they were happy to make sacrifices for a government they believed in.

Public opinion surveys show that trust in Yanukovych has plunged, and it's not hard to see why. He could have reached out to the national democrats who had voted for Yulia Tymoshenko, but chose instead to bulldoze his way to super-presidential status, roll back Ukrainian language, culture, and identity, and attack the democratic opposition. He could have tried to produce a fair tax code, but chose instead to ignore the centerpiece of any serious economic reform, thereby generating mass protests that culminated in the Entrepreneurs' Rebellion of late November 2010.

Yanukovych's assault on the national democrats lost him the support of nationally conscious Ukrainians, and his indifference to the needs of small and medium-sized enterprises lost him the support of the nascent middle class in both eastern and western Ukraine. Yanukovych then lost everybody's support by failing to understand the obvious: that a reformer asking the people to make sacrifices must be perceived as honest, frugal, and incorruptible. People—and especially people living on the margins of subsistence, like most of his proletarian constituency in eastern Ukraine—will endure pain only if they believe their leader will endure pain.

Yanukovych has done the exact opposite. He's been living high on the hog in a huge villa on a questionably appropriated estate; he dresses like a hotshot Wall Street investment banker; he's driven to work in a limo, thereby causing massive traffic jams in downtown Kyiv; he's surrounded himself with corpulent ministers who appear to have their fingers in every conceivable pot. And his rule rests on the Party of Regions, a political machine consisting of beefy pogromchiks, shifty crooks, and unabashed corruptioneers. Ukrainians would sacrifice for a Martin Luther King; they'd be crazy to sacrifice for a Nero.

Yanukovych has also failed to acquire the trust of foreign investors, without whom modernization is impossible. In 2010, his first year in office, foreign direct investment grew by only 12 percent. In the first year of Orange rule, 2005, FDI almost *doubled*—growing by 96 percent. And, in the intervening Orange years, FDI grew by 12 percent in 2009 (when Ukraine was virtually ungovernable during Viktor Yushchenko's disastrous last year in office), 21 percent in 2008, 39 percent in 2007, and 29 percent in 2006.

Why are investors skittish? Cause they ain't stupid. They want s tability, b ut they u nderstand that invocations of stability are no substitute for the foundation of any stable economic environment—rule of law—and that rule of law is impossible in a dictatorship. Unfortunately, Yanukovych doesn't get this elementary point. As he noted on February 17th, "Ukraine is a state that is attractive to investors. But it is imperative to create mo-tivations for investors, the most important of which are the stability of the country, the transparency of its economy, and an effective policy of deregulation." No word, not even a peep, about rule of law. But as German Foreign Minister Guido Westerwelle recently put it, "There a re i n Germany entrepreneurs who would gladly invest i n U kraine. But they fear legal instability and corruption."

As long as Yanukovych continues to be viewed as an anti-Ukrainian and anti-entrepreneurial Godfather who prefers bling to bowling and one-man rule to rule of law, Ukrainians will continue to make ends meet in the shadow economy, and investors will continue finding more attractive opportunities elsewhere.

Is the situation hopeless? Winning back the trust one unwisely squandered is extraordinarily difficult, as the public response to the recently initiated investigation of former President Leonid Kuchma's involvement in the 2000 murder of journalist Heorhii Gongadze demonstrates. Although a welcome development, the investigation will do little to help Yanukovych. Since no one trusts him anymore, everyone's working assumption is that justice was the last thing motivating his decision to bite the hand that once fed him.

That said, Yanukovych might be able to regain some credibility by reversing course in several dramatic ways. Firing his Russian-supremacist minister of education, Dmitri Tabachnik, would be a good start. Ending Tymoshenko's harassment would help. Crafting a tax code that promotes small and medium-sized business would be nice. Moving to a modest apartment in Kyiv and walking to work would do wonders for his image—and his tennis game. And letting the courts be independent might persuade investors that rule of law is not yet quite dead.

That's a tall order, but is it possible? Sure. The only catch is that Yanukovych would have to stop being Yanukovych.

*

The Yanukovych Bulldozer Breaks Down, *World Affairs Journal*, April 26, 2011

Viktor Yanukovych made an astonishing admission recently. In his annual address to the Parliament on April 7th, Ukraine's faltering president stated that "Of the intentions and plans we had for 2010, we succeeded in accomplishing at most a third." In a word, Yanukovych's presidency has been a bust—and he knows it. And if you consider that he, like any politician, exaggerates, then that third probably amounts to a sixth.

Remember the swagger that Yanukovych and his Regionnaires displayed just one year ago, after they squeaked into power and proceeded to twist every possible rule to consolidate it? Well, that bravado and braggadocio are all gone. The Yanukovych bulldozer has broken down, and it sits, dripping oil and emitting gusts of brown steam, in a deep ditch on the side of the road.

A one-sixth success rate is about as impressive as former President Viktor Yushchenko's, and you know what happened to him. And don't forget that the things Yanukovych accomplished—such as dismantling democracy, concentrating all power in his own hands, and creating a sultanistic regime—would have been better not accomplished.

What went wrong?

According to Yanukovych, the reasons are three, and—surprise!—none of them has anything to do with his administration's faults. First, the "bureaucratized state machine" is unwilling to abandon its corrupt ways. Second, "national business, both large and small, has adopted a wait-and-see attitude." And third, "millions of our people have after 20 years of independence genuinely tired of waiting for qualitative changes."

Yanukovych is right, of course, except that he doesn't address the causes of these problems. After all, how can you expect a state apparatus that is dominated by one of the world's most corrupt money-making machines, the Party of Regions, to warm up to reform? Why should business trust a president who's done absolutely nothing to earn trust and keep the fat cats from the trough? And why shouldn't people be tired now that months of presidential tub-thumping have resulted only in higher prices for everything?

But readers of this blog know that the Yanukovych regime and real reform are pretty much antithetical notions. What's much more significant than the breakdown of the bulldozer is Yanukovych's public recognition of that breakdown. He clearly understands that he's losing, that his regime is tottering on the edge of disaster, and that the result could be a social explosion on the order of the Orange Revolution. According to recent polls, the "alienation index" of Ukrainians has reached 83 percent; 40 percent would be willing to defend their rights and interests by means of protests; only 16.7 percent would vote for Yanukovych; and 15.7 percent would support the Regionnaires. The president has good reason to be desperate.

Desperate people often do desperate things. One analyst suggests Yanukovych has embarked on a "thaw." True, there have been some personnel changes, but there has still been no change of course—a genuine *cultural* thaw would have to start with the firing of the Russian-supremacist education minister—and there certainly hasn't been anything resembling "deyanukization." But some bold move will become increasingly necessary if Yanukovych hopes to avoid a second humiliation that would earn him a place in the Guinness Book of World Records among other stupendously failed leaders.

Investigating former President Leonid Kuchma's role in the disappearance, murder, and cover-up of journalist Heorhii Gongadze could be one such bold move. Alas, like so much that Yanukovych does, it smacks of populist seat-of-the-pantism. Only a truly desperate leader who knows that his back is against the wall would try to save himself by taking on the establishment that made him possible. Kuchma, after all, doesn't just represent himself. He's got the backing of heavyweight state administrators and oligarchs, all of whom will fight Yanukovych to the finish.

Yanukovych's apparent seriousness about moving toward the European Union and resisting Vladimir Putin's blandishments about joining the Russia-led Customs Union could be another such bold move. Domestically weak presidents often look for salvation in foreign-policy victories. Alienating Russia would certainly alienate much of Yanukovych's constituency, but many of them hate him anyway. On the other hand, effectively courting Europe has cross-national appeal throughout Ukraine and would enable Yanukovych to argue that he is the people's president.

Ironically, if unsurprisingly for an entity that preaches soft power but responds mostly to its hard variant, Europe may be more serious about courting Yanukovych than it was about courting Viktor Yushchenko. A democratic Ukraine with pro-Western leanings could easily be taken for granted, found fault with, and subordinated to Europe's geopolitical interest in Russian gas. An authoritarian Ukraine with pro-Russian leanings could threaten the stability and security of Europe and might therefore need accommodating. Yushchenko's pro-European policy foundered on Europe's hypocritical commitment to promoting democracy. Yanukovych's pro-Yanukovych policy may resonate with Europe's genuine commitment to promoting its self-interest.

You'll know that Ukraine is really moving closer to Europe when former German Chancellor Gerhard Schröder calls Yanukovych what he called Vladimir Putin during the Orange Revolution—a "true democrat."

*

Regime Incoherence in Yanukovych's Ukraine, *World Affairs Journal*, June 2, 2011

How can you explain the jaw-dropping incoherence of the Yanukovych regime? They blithely give away the store to the Russians in the April 2010 Kharkiv Accords, but they're skittish about joining the Russian-led Customs Union. They pursue integration with the European Union, but crudely violate European legal standards by persecuting their political opponents. They declare an anti-corruption drive, but retain fantastic villas and shamelessly fix tenders. They pass a law on freedom of information, but constrict freedom of the press. With this kind of record, can anyone be certain that the Parliament's recently passed endorsement of a free-trade zone with the EU represents an irreversible turn toward Europe?

There are three possible explanations of this incoherence. Let's look at them, in order of increasing likeliness.

It could be that these aren't examples of incoherence, but of profound cleverness. Accordingly, President Yanukovych and his buddies know exactly what they're doing: They're trying to strike a balance between competing interests and priorities, while following a centrist policy devoted to Ukraine's interests only. Sound plausible? Maybe for relations with Russia, with the Kharkiv Accords representing Yanukovych's attempt to make nice with the Kremlin and the skittishness about the Customs Union representing a justifiable fear of the Kremlin's embrace. But this rationale just doesn't work for the other examples of incoherence. If you're serious about the EU, you don't arrest your former minister of the interior, Yuri Lutsenko, keep him in jail for close to half a year, and respond indifferently to his brush with death during his just-discontinued hunger strike. That's callous or stupid or both. Nor do you go about harassing former Prime Minister Yulia Tymoshenko on trumped-up charges. A clever regime would have dealt with the political threat posed by these individuals by appointing Lutsenko and Tymoshenko as ambassadors to Lichtenstein and Andorra.

Let's consider a second explanation. Incoherence could be symptomatic of a cognitive inability to recognize contradictions as contradictions. This would bespeak an inability to think logically and to understand that A and minus-A are incompatible. Sound plausible? You betcha. Neither Yanukovych nor any of his ministers is a genius. More important, they are all members of the Donetsk political elite, whose roots extend to Soviet times and whose mentality is still Soviet. Despite incessant Soviet invocations of the Marxian dialectic, the USSR's planners and policymakers had little sense of contradiction. After all, everything they did was, by definition, correct and every revision of the Communist Party line was, by definition, also correct. That arrogance and ignorance are equally characteristic of the Yanukovych folks. They're right even when—or especially if—they are wrong. So why worry about contradictions that cannot, by definition, be contradictions?

The third explanation is simplest and probably most persuasive. Accordingly, "the regime" isn't contradictory, because "the regime" isn't adopting decisions as a unitary actor. Instead, different factions or power holders within the regime are going in different directions, with the result that "the regime" looks like it's going in different directions. Thus, the pro-Russian faction goes for the Kharkiv Accords and gives away basing rights in Sevastopol for a song, while the pro-Ukrainian faction tries to move Ukraine away from the Customs Union and toward the EU. The hard-line authoritarians crack down on Lutsenko and Tymoshenko, while the quasi-democrats court the EU and push for anti-corruption measures and freedom of information. Sound plausible? Absolutely, but this explanation is also least flattering and most worrisome for Yanukovych. It suggests that, despite having amassed enormous powers, Ukraine's president is unwilling or unable to keep his subordinates in line. And if Yanukovych really has lost control of a divided regime, its incoherence—and instability—can only grow.

Incoherent regimes are doomed to ineffectiveness and prone to breakdown. Unfortunately for Yanukovych, he cannot afford to sit back and have a beer, while watching the boys duke it out. Ukraine's economy is a mess, his popularity is almost nil, and the people are no longer afraid to say no to the thugs running the country. Bold choices and radical reform really are necessary. And Yanukovych's choices are essentially two. He can opt for the status of a corrupt, non-democratic, and permanently backward hinterland of Russia or he can try to join Europe and the world economy as a struggling democracy and modernizing economy. The former choice means becoming another Belarus. The latter choice means becoming another Poland. You can't be both. Nor can you flip flop back and forth between Russia, authoritarianism, and corruption on the one hand and the world, democracy, and decency on the other. You gotta choose once and for all—not just for the sake of logic, but because the longer you wait, the longer the contradictions fester, the angrier society will get, and the more likely will your regime collapse.

*

Yanukovych Losing Support in the Texas of Ukraine, *World Affairs Journal*, June 17, 2011

Just how deep is the hole President Viktor Yanukovych is in? Take a look at Luhansk Province, Ukraine's easternmost. With a mostly Russian-speaking population of about 2.5 million (54 percent Ukrainian, 42 percent Russian) and an economy highly dependent on a decaying coal-mining industry, the province has been a bastion of pro-Soviet, pro-Russian, and pro-Regionnaire sentiment since 1991, consistently producing huge majorities for parties and candidates opposed to national-democratic ideals. Luhansk, like its neighbor, Donetsk Province, is to Yanukovych and the Regionnaires as Texas was to George W. Bush and the Republicans.

According to two recent public opinion surveys, electoral support for the Regionnaires in Luhansk has crashed. One university study has shown that, while 53.8 percent of the region's inhabitants would have voted for Yanukovych's party in November 2009, only 30.7 percent would do so today. A poll conducted by the SocioLab Group puts the number even lower, at 26 percent. In other words, the Regionnaires, while still the strongest party in the province, have lost about 50 percent of their support in two years. At this rate, they'll be down to 20-25 percent by the time of next year's parliamentary elections and to 5–10 percent by the 2015 presidential elections.

It's not hard to see why the Regionnaires' core is turning against Yanukovych and his pals. Life under their rule has turned out to be a disaster. Another university survey shows that 75.9 percent of the province's inhabitants identify high prices as their main economic concern; 67.2 percent point to low wages. In addition, 49.2 percent say their living standards deteriorated in 2010, while 42.9 percent say their health got worse. According to a second SocioLab study, 83 percent accuse the authorities of dealing poorly with inflation,

77 percent blame them for not doing enough to fight corruption, and 75 percent believe that the economy will remain bad or very bad six months from now.

The local Regionnaire authorities are as clueless about getting Luhansk's economy going as are their counterparts in Yanukovych's administration and the Parliament. And for obvious reasons. Economic reform means both abandoning the economic model the Regionnaires prefer—a corruptocratic alliance of Regionnaire elites, organized crime, and oligarchs that enables all three to expropriate the country's wealth—and encouraging local entrepreneurship and small business to flourish within the context of a genuine market economy. A people's capitalism, however, requires democracy and at least some rule of law, both of which are anathema to the Regionnaires.

Unsurprisingly, the Luhansk authorities are, like their comrades in Kyiv, responding to popular immiseration with cheap symbolism. In late May, they gave Russian the status of a "regional language" in the province, thereby bringing coal to Newcastle by enthusiastically endorsing the hegemonic status quo. After all, Russian is ubiquitous in Luhansk. It's hard to see just how such an absurdly irrelevant motion could possibly help a destitute population with little hope in the future, but no matter. The Regionnaires know they own the province and that, in the absence of bread, innovative ideas, or democracy, circuses will have to do.

It's not clear that Luhanskites are taking such abuse lying down. On June 7th, an anonymous caller claimed to have placed a bomb in the building occupied by the Provincial State Administration. The odd thing is that this was only the latest of a series of bomb threats in Luhansk city this year—the first apparently coming on February 15th and the ninth coming on April 18th—for a total of ten in under four months. There's no way that the authorities can blame these incidents on their favorite bogeyman, radical nationalists from Western Ukraine. So what gives? Is Luhansk going crazy or do the threats reflect both popular dissatisfaction with Regionnaire misrule and the absence of institutional forms of protest? Whatever the answer, it's a fair bet that the Luhansk bosses aren't draw-ing the obvious conclusion: that more democracy is the answer, not less.

In any case, if Luhansk is a bellwether of Ukraine, then Yanukovych, whose ratings have plummeted in the last year, must be as desperate as his Luhansk comrades. If he can't hold on to his Texas, then the only thing between his party and inevitable electoral humiliation is massive voter fraud. Unfortunately, they tried that already, in 2004, and you know what that led to.

*

Integrating an Authoritarian Ukraine into Democratic Europe? *World Affairs Journal,* June 24, 2011

A distinguished group of Ukrainian and Western analysts has recently argued that

Europe should make Ukraine's integration into European institutions conditional on the Yanukovych regime's adherence to democratic standards.

Thus, they argue: "The EU should advance free trade and political agreements only if the Yanukovych administration demonstrates its clear commitment to European values." In other words, no democracy in Ukraine, no integration with Europe.

Alas, "no democracy, no Europe" is the worst possible advice—for Ukraine, for Europe, and, by the way, also for Russia. This is not to say that Europe shouldn't be tough with Ukraine. Nor is it to say that an authoritarian Ukraine should become a member of the European Union. It is to say, however, that strategic goals should guide strategic choices and that even an authoritarian Ukraine should be integrated into European institutions. Let me explain.

What's the best imaginable outcome for Ukraine? I suspect most more or less reasonable people would agree that it should be democratic, market-oriented, modern, and Western. You can interpret those words any way you like, but it's clear that their polar opposites are authoritarian, oligarchic, backward, and anti-Western.

Remember: Ukraine is not a small country comfortably surrounded by prosperous and peaceful democracies. Ever since NATO and the European Union expanded to its borders, Ukraine's been trapped in a geopolitically untenable no-man's-land between Europe and Russia. Moreover, Ukraine currently stands at a crossroads. If it signs a free-trade agreement with the EU and moves toward associate membership, its chances of becoming democratic, market-oriented, modern, and Western will grow. If it does not move toward Europe, Ukraine will either remain isolated in that no-man's-land or, far more likely, move toward the Russia-led Customs Union, membership in which guarantees that Ukraine will become authoritarian, oligarchic, backward, and anti-Western.

Why is that?

Whether or not Ukraine becomes democratic and market-oriented—and modern—pretty much depends on Ukraine, its government, and its people. That said, international institutions can and do nudge countries in specific directions. Democratic and market-oriented institutions promote democracy and markets, while authoritarian and oligarchic institutions do not. Institutions have this effect because they compel governments and people to play by their rules, and repeated rule-following, even if rules are frequently violated, tends, over time, to lead to an internalization of rules. Ask yourself this. What's better for Ukraine? That Ukrainian oligarchs should hobnob with the rich and mighty in Davos or in Minsk? That Regionnaire elites should negotiate with Brussels or with Moscow? Where are they more likely to learn, or be forced to adapt to, democracy and markets?

Here are two more equally rhetorical questions. Is it better for an authoritarian and oligarchic Ukraine to be in a free-trade zone with democratic and market-oriented Europe or in a customs union with authoritarian and oligarchic Russia, Belarus, and Kazakhstan? And is it better for Europe for an authoritarian and oligarchic Ukraine to be in a free-trade zone with democratic and market-oriented Europe or in a custom union with authoritarian and oligarchic Russia, Belarus, and Kazakhstan?

As I argued above, an authoritarian and oligarchic Ukraine will be nudged toward democracy and the market by Europe's institutions. Obviously, Ukraine won't become fully democratic and market-oriented overnight. But it will *creep* in that direction, as Ukrainians travel to Europe, as European economic ties with Ukraine are strengthened, as Ukrainian elites are forced to walk and talk like Europeans, as Ukraine slowly enters the European vocabulary and consciousness, and as European values slowly enter the Ukrainian vocabulary and consciousness. In contrast, an authoritarian and oligarchic Ukraine will only become more authoritarian and more oligarchic as part of any economic and political association led by today's authoritarian and oligarchic Russia. Indeed, such an outcome would condemn Ukraine to economic backwardness for decades to come, as Ukraine would be transformed into Russia's hinterland. And since Russia is the hinterland of the West, that would make Ukraine the hinterland of a hinterland. Some prospect, right? So take your pick—creeping Europeanization or rapid hinterlandization.

The analysts I cited above appear to believe that keeping an authoritarian and oligarchic Ukraine out of Europe would be good for Europe. But the exact opposite is true. Such a Ukraine would be prone to instability—after all, authoritarian states with weak economies are unstable—and likely become a neo-colonial appendage of a neo-imperial Russia. For a pivotal state the size of Ukraine to be unstable cannot be good for Europe, and for a pivotal state the size of Ukraine to become subservient to Russia cannot possibly be good for European, and more generally Western, hopes of a normal relationship with a "normal" Russia.

One last rhetorical question. Is it better for a *democratic and market-oriented Russia* (a country that does not yet exist) for an authoritarian and oligarchic Ukraine to be in a free-trade zone with democratic and market-oriented Europe or in a customs union with authoritarian and oligarchic Russia, Belarus, and Kazakhstan? Naturally, Russian imperialists and authoritarians prefer an ingathering of Soviet lands, but just because they want that doesn't make it right for Russia. If democracy, the market, modernity, and the West are good for Ukraine, then they must also be good for Russia. And there's no way that such a Russia will be more likely to emerge if an authoritarian and oligarchic Ukraine joins up with an authoritarian and oligarchic Russia.

Ukraine's moving toward Europe is good for Ukraine, good for Europe, and good for Russia. It's also good for the Ukrainian opposition: where would you prefer to be a harassed democrat—in Europe or in Russia? And, yes, if Viktor Yanukovych manages to push Ukraine toward Europe, it'll also be good for him. But so be it. The interests of the Ukrainian people must surely trump those of Yanukovych. To insist that today's Ukraine shouldn't join Europe until Yanukovych becomes a democrat is not to cut off one's nose to spite one's face. It's to cut off ne's face to spite one's nose.

*

PART ONE: THE RISE AND FALL OF VIKTOR YANUKOVYCH

The Serial Stupidity of Trying Tymoshenko, *World Affairs Journal*, June 30, 2011

Forgive the blunt question, but are the Regionnaires really that dumb? Evidently, yes. The latest bit of evidence for their serial stupidity is the trial of Yulia Tymoshenko. If you haven't heard, the former Orange prime minister has been charged with "abuse of office," something that supposedly transpired when she negotiated a gas deal with Russia a few years ago. That deal was apparently bad for Ukraine and, since it was bad, Tymoshenko must be guilty. Of something—well, of anything, actually. And abuse of office will do: it has the ring of substance, while at the same time being so broad as to be meaningless.

Forget the hypocrisy. Abuse of office is about the only thing Ukrainian elites have been doing consistently, and well, since 1991. President Viktor Yanukovych abuses his office every time he takes a breath in his questionably appropriated estate outside of Kyiv. His pals abuse their offices every time they rig tenders, rake in millions, and pass legislation that favors their buddies. And if Yulia's gas deal was criminal, what is one to say of Viktor's Kharkiv Accords?

And forget the impossibility of making any sense of Ukraine's opaque gas relationship with Russia. Who makes the decisions in Kyiv? No one knows. Are the deals good for Ukraine? Mebbe yes, mebbe no. Are they bad for Ukraine? Mebbe yes, mebbe no. About the only thing anybody does know is that the deals never fail to benefit Russia's Gazprom on the one hand and the oligarchs, industries, and Regionnaires of eastern Ukraine on the other. Is that accident, design, or divine providence? Take a wild guess.

And, obviously, forget justice. Everyone knows that there's as little substance to the charges as there is a high collective IQ in the Ukrainian cabinet. Everyone knows that the only reason the regime is hounding Tymoshenko is to neutralize her in advance of the 2012 parliamentary and 2015 presidential elections. And everyone knows that the courts are the tools of the Yanukovych regime. I mean, for chrissakes, this is Ukraine, and not Canada, and any claim of judicial independence is about as persuasive as the claim of Regionnaire honesty.

So forget all that. The only important question is this: why are the Regionnaires so utterly incapable of understanding that they're committing another mega-blunder, one that will redound to Tymoshenko's favor, provide the Ukrainian opposition with a shot in the arm, mobilize society against them, raise European and American eyebrows, and produce a public relations disaster—at precisely the time that the regime has manifestly failed to deliver on anything and is desperately hoping for a miracle to save it from ignominy?

If you really want to get rid of Tymoshenko, then appoint her ambassador to, say, Brussels or Paris or London or, even, Moscow—any important place that'll flatter her, but also keep her busy and out of the way. Or make her your minister of foreign affairs, along the lines of Barack Obama's appointment of Hillary Rodham Clinton as secretary of state, or, if you really want to give her a migraine, your minister of culture. Or send her on a five-year fact-finding mission among all the Ukrainian diaspora communities in the world. Or give her a television talk show during prime time.

The very last thing you do with a prominent, influential, charismatic, smart, articulate, rich, and photogenic political opponent is put her on trial—for anything. Unless, of course, you really do have a smoking gun and your evidence is incontrovertible. A bad case against a tough defendant is guaranteed to transform Tymoshenko into an international cause célèbre and bring down fire and brimstone on the regime—especially in Europe, which Yanukovych says he wants to join. Worse, the trial is likely to drag on and dominate headlines for months. Ukraine's image will be mud, as witness after witness—the prosecution alone intends to call some 30 people, including former President Viktor Yushchenko—reveals just how rotten Ukraine's political and economic elites are. If the Regionnaires think that stink won't rub off n them, they've got a big surprise coming.

My guess is that this time, as so many times in the past, this mess traces back to the shocking incompetence and arrogance of the Yanukovych camp. I can just see the meeting in the president's office. The vodka's flowing, the boys are slurping up the caviar, they're comparing the size of their bank accounts in the Caymans, they're trying to figure out how to fool all the people all of the time, and some crackerjack has the bright idea of putting Yulia behind bars. Wotta concept, says Prime Minister Azarov. And a piece of cake, too, says Education Minister Tabachnik. Well, now the boys are likely to choke on that cake.

Small wonder that Yanukovych insists he has nothing to do with the trial. Blame it on our super-duper independent courts, he says. Naturally, that's what he's got to say. At the same time, I'm guessing Viktor may have realized that he better put some daylight between himself and the proceedings—like, uh, ASAP. When the stuff hits the fan, Yanukovych wants to be sure that his pals are left holding the bag and that he has some plausible deniability.

That's the extraordinary thing about the Regionnaires. They're rank amateurs who are too arrogant to know just how little they know. And amateurs who don't even know what's good for themselves can't possibly know what's good for the country they claim to be running.

*

Yanukovych Shows off His Estate to Select Journalists, *World Affairs Journal*, July 7, 2011

After months of ignoring journalists asking to see his estate outside Kyiv, President Viktor Yanukovych finally broke down in late June and took six select representatives on a tour of his house and gardens. Afterward, the seven sipped tea on a veranda and chatted about Ukraine.

It was all very casual and laid back—although Yanukovych did look a bit stiff in his pin-stripe, button-down shirt and dress slacks—and hardly newsworthy, except for the little details. For starters, the journalists included only men. You'd think that the president's advisers would have thought to include at least one woman—if only to give the topless activists of FEMEN one less thing to protest about—but no, Yanukovych and his advisers remained true to form. Also interesting: five of the six journalists were bona fide professionals, while one, Mikhail Podolyak, was until recently working as a consultant to Yuri Ivanyushchenko, the president's boyhood pal, a key behind-the-scenes player in the administration, and an alleged underworld kingpin. Podolyak, by the way, was the only journalist without a jacket and in jeans. And his shirt wasn't even tucked in.

The front of Yanukovych's house is adorned with four gigantic columns, which he added to the modest original structure. If it weren't for the sleek exterior and the excessively elaborate ironwork, you'd think for a moment that you're viewing an antebellum planta-tion house in the American South. The inside, on the other hand, is a post-Soviet *nouveau riche* dream come true. You expect shiny marble to be everywhere, and it is. Naturally, the furniture is all heavy, without a hint of modernism or even IKEA-style lightness. The candelabra, the candle holders (yes, there are candle holders on the mantle above the marble fireplace!), the chairs, and tables all have the Baroque quality beloved by Soviet and post-Soviet hotel designers—and readily available to Americans in mall home-fur-nishing outlets with a flair for the excessive. Unsurprisingly, there are curlicues galore. But, to Yanukovych's credit, there are also paintings galore—in the hallways, along the staircase, and in all the rooms—with heavy gilded frames and spotlights. It's hard to tell just what their subject matter is, but they don't seem to be socialist realist master-pieces. Many appear to be landscapes in brown and green tones. One appears to depict the Grand Canal in Venice. The long thin painting above his bed looks like an Italian or Roman cityscape.

And then there's the president's office—a small room with a tiny, neatly ordered desk, photographs of the family (sons, grandkids, and daughters in law, but no wife), and a chaise longue that, to tell the truth, looks a bit small for the big Yanukovych. There don't seem to be any bookcases, at least not in the office. Outside, there's a three-tiered foun-tain, old-style street lamps, an artificial waterfall and pond, a swimming pool, and a nicely groomed garden, where the president works out. As he also told the journalists, he plays tennis three to four times a week, for one and a half to two hours, and swims every day. *How much?* one journalist asked. "Up to five kilometers," said Yanukovych. As one uninvited reporter, Mustafa Naim, observed, that would mean swimming about 400 lengths. Well, if Mao Zedong could swim the Yangtze, why not? By the way, I don't want to sound catty, but with so much exercise, Yanukovych really should look slimmer. (Don't forget your caloric intake, Mister President!)

Why did the president choose to open his digs to public scrutiny just now? That's easy. He's in trouble with the public, and the visit was an obvious public relations ploy intend-ed to humanize him—to show that he's just a regular guy. Of course, since the place is a mansion, Ukrainians may also come away wondering just how a working-class kid from the Donbas, who's never been a businessman, was able to cough up the dough for a palace on a measly government salary.

The visit was also a ploy—or an attempt, if you prefer—to reach out to the media. Most journalists are, or have become, extremely critical of him and his administration, and it's at least possible that some of the six will now have a slightly different view of the president. Or not. Like the Ukrainian public, they'll want to know who paid for the house. (It's been valued at a cool $10 million.) They're also likely to wonder why they didn't get to see the many acres of public property appended to the mansion, where Yanukovych has built a fabulous club house for himself and his friends.

Oh, two more things. Yanukovych likes to give very long and plodding answers to pointed questions and he keeps bees. Guess which other Ukrainian president also talked too much and kept bees. Viktor Yushchenko.

Uh-oh.

*

Ukraine's Intellectuals against Yanukovych, *World Affairs Journal*, August 12, 2011

Some of Ukraine's most prominent intellectuals have recently weighed in on the scandalous Tymoshenko show trial. In an open letter addressed to Ukrainian society, they condemn the trial and call on Ukrainians not to be indifferent to the injustice being perpetrated by the Yanukovych regime: "We still have the chance to stop all this! We dare not be silent!"

The signatories read like a Who's Who and include a diverse group of 28 writers, scholars, and commentators, ranging from former Soviet dissidents Ivan Dzyuba, Bohdan Horyn, and Levko Lukyanenko to former Soviet Ukrainian writers Roman Ivanychuk, Dmytro Pavlychko, and Yuri Mushketyk to the liberal philosopher Myroslav Popovych to the hottest current writers Yuri Andrukhovych, Larysa Denysenko, Serhii Zhadan, Vasyl Shklyar, and Iren Rozdobudko to the excellent political commentators Mykola Ryabchuk and Serhii Hrabovsky.

According to the authors, the Tymoshenko trial will open the door to similar acts of repression "against all those who are politically inconvenient for the regime, against pensioners and small business, against activist young people, against all who oppose the country's descent to a condition of feudal-criminal oligarchic control and the destruction of Ukrainian national identity."

Here's the punch line:

> The roll-back of democracy, which we are currently witnessing, will close Ukraine's road to Europe, while at the same time opening more widely the eastern gates to our Soviet past. The Yulia Tymoshenko case concerns each one of us. Here and now we face a Rubicon. If the authorities cross it, they will try many of us tomorrow. But then there will be no one to write appeals and call meetings.

They will crush us quietly and singly. It's already clear today just how the authorities want to frighten us and sow loss of faith and terror among those who have not yet lost the capacity to struggle for their national, economic, social, and political rights.

Correctly, the signatories of the appeal view the trial as a watershed for Ukraine. If Tymoshenko is found guilty, then the Yanukovych regime will have publicly, openly, and proudly proclaimed to the world that it has consciously chosen the path of authoritarianism. The claim that it is only building a strong state, consolidating authority, and establishing stability will no longer persuade anyone but Aleksandr Lukashenka of Belarus and Viktor Yanukovych's dwindling band of apologists. Moreover, the signatories are quite right to state that the trial will transform Ukraine's government into a pariah of no interest to an already indifferent Europe. If that happens, Moscow will have a field day with Kyiv, while Viktor Yanukovych and his merry band of Regionnaire pranksters will have no place to camp out but the political equivalent of Siberia's barren tundras. Why any sensible elite would opt for a political, economic, and cultural dead end that promises only opprobrium, poverty, and disgrace beats me, but then again the Regionnaires have never been known for their smarts. And if Siberia is what they want, Siberia is what they'll get.

Where the signatories are probably wrong is in claiming that the trial will lead to further repressive measures. True, the Regionnaires will surely give repression their best shot. What else do you expect from thugs? But they will fail. Ukrainians almost to a person hate them, and a decrepit army and a few thousand elite police troops just aren't enough to keep a country of more than 40 million on its knees. Look at Belarus's beleaguered dictator, Lukashenka. With far stronger repressive forces than Yanukovych and a much weaker society than Ukraine, he's managed to terrorize his country for some 15 years. That's an impressive run, except that he may now be on the verge of collapse. Yanukovych would be lucky to pull off a Lukashenka for a few lousy months. And that, in turn, means that, while the Tymoshenko show trial will lead Europe to ostracize the Yanukovych regime, Ukraine's "road to Europe" will be blocked only temporarily—until the regime follows in Hosni Mubarak's footsteps and collapses.

In the meantime, the most interesting things about the appeal may be its very appearance and the Yanukovych regime's response. Readers with a familiarity with Soviet dissent will recognize just how eerily reminiscent the appeal is of Soviet-era open letters by brave dissidents protesting Communist Party injustice. The authors suggest that Soviet times may be returning to Ukraine. Possibly. More likely than not, Ukraine is on the verge of the kinds of upheavals that rocked the country in *late-Soviet* times—the period of perestroika under Mikhail Gorbachev, when Ukrainians, Russians, Balts, and many others toppled a totalitarian empire.

Equally Soviet was a second letter by another group of intellectuals that appeared a few days after the above appeal. This one, addressed to Yanukovych personally, stated that "You are right that democracy is not chaos and disorder. The government administration is the civilian army that serves the people; there must be order in it. And you are right to introduce it severely. Go along the road you chose bravely: reform Ukraine, do not permit the rollback of reforms, crush corruption, and lead the state to democratic rule. With you are the people."

No less shocking than the Soviet language of leader adulation were the signatories, who included Serhii Kvit, the president of the elite Kyiv Mohyla University, who has been relentless in his criticism of the Yanukovych regime's anti-Ukrainian cultural and educational policies. What happened? Did Kvit lose his marbles? It turns out that he, like most of the signatories, signed on to the letter after they had been read bits of it over the telephone. Another supposed signatory, the ex-dissident Les Taniuk, says that "he had been called and asked whether he'd like to take part in signing a group letter in defense of Serhii Kvit"!

Unsurprisingly, and most typically Soviet, no one wants to fess up to authorship. The author may be one of the signatories or it may be someone within the Yanukovych administration or, possibly, within the Security Service. Who knows? In any case, the president's minions immediately seized on the letter as proof of "the intelligentsia's" support of Yanukovych. Obviously, nothing could be further from the truth. All the second letter demonstrates is that the regime is getting so desperate as to resort to transparently stupid measures that will persuade only octogenarian Stalinists with fond memories of Leonid Brezhnev.

*

Ukraine Turns 20, *World Affairs Journal*, August 19, 2011

Independent Ukraine turns 20 on August 24th. Some Ukrainians are celebrating, some are demonstrating. Most are too busy making ends meet, going on vacation, tending to their private plots, or worrying about the price of buckwheat to care too much.

Polls show that only about half the population would vote for independence today. About a third wouldn't. And the rest don't know. That looks worse than it is. Compared to such highly nationalistic populations as the Poles and French, Ukrainians look confused. Compared to everybody else, Ukrainians are probably par for the course. Actually, more worrisome than the large number of opponents of independence is that their percentage has remained stable over the last 20 years and that they are concentrated in the Russian-speaking south and east of the country.

Of course, most of these Ukrainians have also gotten used to living in Ukraine. They take it as a given. They don't like it, but what the heck. Some say they'd prefer living in the Soviet Union, but, in case they missed it, the glorious Land of the Soviets collapsed a while back, so that option is, well, off the table. Others say they'd prefer living in some Russian-led entity, but, since that dream could easily be fulfilled with a cheap one-way train ticket, one can't but wonder how seriously they mean it.

The bottom line is that most people in most places and in most times adapt to their circumstances. True, it'd be nicer if most Ukrainians felt a deep love for their prosperous, democratic country, but since their country isn't prosperous or very democratic, their lack of enthusiasm may be forgiven.

In contrast, Ukraine's current ruling class loves Ukraine. And why shouldn't they? They live well—and they own the place. Unfortunately, their love is the love of the mafia. They love Ukraine because it's an easy mark. For them, Ukrainians are just plain suckers, and you know what W.C. Fields said about suckers: Never give 'em an even break.

In an ideal world, the benighted masses would drive the thieves out of town. That almost happened during the Orange Revolution and could easily happen again. Then, supporters of Ukrainian independence wanted to clean the stables. Those who opposed or were indifferent to independence were on the other side of the Orange barricade. Now, mafia misrule has led even the opponents and "indifferents" to want to throw the bums out.

The mafia has resisted by playing the independents against the opponents. It's also trying to pick off challengers. And it has, like any group of scoundrels, wrapped itself in the flag. But that isn't fooling anyone. The independents can't be persuaded by their faux patriotism, and the opponents and "indifferents" don't care.

Might the mafia change its ways? Not if it's left to its own devices. After all, why should thugs get religion? Might someone force them to see the light? Western democrats and do-gooders haven't a chance. After all, they're suckers. The only one who could out-mafia the mafia is a stronger mafia. And, unfortunately for Ukraine's current mafia, their thuggish godfather to the north is stronger than they are.

Like Johnny Rocco, the gangster in John Huston's *Key Largo* who always wants "more," Vladimir Putin's Russia knows no bounds on its appetites toward Ukraine. The vigorish keeps going up, the cuts keep getting larger, and the demands keep getting more outlandish. If you give them an inch, they'll take a mile. If you give them a mile, they'll take ten. Jeeze, what's a poor Ukrainian capo to do?

The answer is obvious: go straight. Get rid of those black shirts and wide lapels, stop smoking cigars and packing heat, cut your fingernails, brush your hair, buy yourself a nice house and mow the lawn, start a respectable business, and join a country club, preferably in Brussels.

Oh, and one more thing. Declare Putin and his sidekick Dmitri Medvedev Heroes of Ukraine. They deserve it. Their thuggishness might just make Ukraine fully independent.

*

Regionnaire Plagiarism Rears Its Head, *World Affairs Journal*, September 16, 2011

Who hasn't heard by now of the charges of plagiarism made against President Viktor Yanukovych's recently published English-language book, *Opportunity Ukraine*? The evidence is persuasive. Many sections were clearly **lifted without attribution from other texts**. And that's plagiarism, period.

The president's many critics have seized on the texts as evidence—if any were still necessary—of the regime's dishonesty. The president's official defenders dismiss the charges as absurd. They have to, of course. What else can they say in the face of incontrovertible proof? In the final analysis, however, both sides aren't quite getting the real point.

It goes without saying that plagiarism is dastardly, dishonest, and demeaning and it must be condemned wherever and whenever it rears its ugly little head. But it's also stupid—profoundly, deeply, screamingly, and unforgivably stupid—especially when committed by people with money, advice, knowhow, and clout who know, or should know, that every single word uttered by Yanukovych is always subjected to minute scrutiny by armies of critics in Ukraine and abroad.

I mean, how dumb must the Regionnaires be to engage in open-faced plagiarism in an English-language book intended to be read—not in party headquarters in Donetsk—but in the West? For chrissakes, man—don't these guys get it *at all*? Don't they understand that the West abjures plagiarism and that most Western scholars, journalists, and policymakers would never engage in it? It's a matter of professional honor. And besides, they know they'd get caught. And getting caught in the age of fancy Internet programs that compare millions of texts is a piece of cake.

So how could the Regionnaires have done it?

One possible explanation is that the Yanukovych people truly didn't know that what they were doing was plagiarism. Possible? Sure, but in that case these punks shouldn't be running a country. They should be shining shoes in Grand Central Station. You can forgive a regular guy's ignorance of quantum mechanics, but for the policy honchos of a big country not to know the elementary rules of citation is unpardonable.

Another explanation is that they knew what they were doing, but thought they'd get away with it. That is to say, the Regionnaires figured that the rest of the world is just one big Donbas and that their provincialism and arrogance wouldn't raise eyebrows in Paree and the Big Apple. Possible? Sure, but then these guys shouldn't even be shining shoes in Grand Central. They'd better stick to the Donetsk train station until they learn the ways of the world.

A final explanation is that the book was a collective enterprise and that too many cooks spoiled the broth. Pyotr didn't know what Pavlo was doing, both assumed Ivan would check for mistakes, while Ivan figured they would—and none of them could read English anyway. Accordingly, the Yanukovych folks could plead sloppiness. Possible? Absolutely, but then they'd be well advised not to shine shoes even in Donetsk. I mean, if these guys can't get their act together—which, of course, means that they had no leadership from the gentleman who put his name to the book—then no one should trust their shoes to them anywhere.

Whichever explanation you favor, the upshot is the same: the Regionnaires are clods. When they made jaw-dropping mistakes right after Yanukovych became president in early 2010, one could argue that, with time, they'd eventually learn. But if they still can't get something as simple as proper citation right, it's clear that they're incapable of learning.

That's not because they're ignoramuses. If they were merely ignorant, there'd be hope. No, the Regionnaires are know-it-alls—but not, alas, your run-of-the-mill breed. What makes their case hopeless is that these guys are *aggressively ignorant* know-it-alls. Fortunately, like all garrulous drunks with half-baked opinions about everything, they'll eventually fall under the table.

*

The Underdevelopment of the Donbas, *World Affairs Journal*, October 7, 2011

A just-released study by the International Center for Future Research has some bad news for southeastern Ukraine. According to the center's calculations, the quality of life is lowest in a coherent swath of territory running from south to east. Of Ukraine's 27 provinces, Zaporizhzhya is 22nd, Mykolaiv is 23rd, Kherson is 24th, Luhansk is 25th, Donetsk is 26th, and Dnipropetrovsk is dead last. The two outliers are Kharkiv in the northeast, which is 2nd, and Chernihiv in the north, which is 21st.

As you'd expect, Kyiv City is at the top, while the Autonomous Republic of Crimea, with its tourism, comes in 3rd. Visitors to western Ukraine won't be surprised to learn that it does quite well in the rankings: Ternopil Province is 4th, Lviv is 5th, Chernivtsi is 6th, Ivano-Frankivsk is 8th, Volyn is 10th, Zakarpattya is 11th, and Rivne is 13th.

Since the rankings were based on five criteria—material well-being, education, health, security, and environment—there are some interesting variations. Kyiv City, Crimea, and Kharkiv, Dnipropetrovsk, Zaporizhzhya, and Donetsk provinces score well on both well-being and education. In contrast, the western Ukrainian provinces, and just above everyone else in the country, do far better than the southeastern provinces in terms of health, security, and environment. To put it somewhat crudely, the Donbas is an ecological disaster and dangerous slum populated by smart and prosperous folks.

Note that the most unlivable part of Ukraine—the southeast in general and the Donbas in particular—is the heart of Viktor Yanukovych country and has the highest concentration of oligarchs and Regionnaires. Coincidence?

The Donbas was once the jewel in the Stalinist crown of Soviet socioeconomic development—the showcase of Soviet central planning. Twenty years ago, when Ukraine became independent, the industrial southeast was past its prime, but neither had it yet become a slum. That transformation took place in the last two decades—partly as a result of the collapse of central planning, partly as a result of the collapse of the Ukrainian economy in the 1990s, and, last but not least, partly as a result of the region's political mismanagement and economic exploitation by post-Communist functionaries, corrupt Regionnaires, organized criminals, and rapacious oligarchs.

Those nefarious groups have effectively conspired to promote the Ukrainian industrial heartland's progressive development into an economic wasteland, ecological nightmare, and social disaster. They've done that by appropriating worthwhile assets for themselves, neglecting everything else, and distracting the people with red flags, bogus claims of language discrimination, culture wars, and the like.

The puzzle is not that venal Regionnaires and oligarchs managed to suck the southeast dry, but that the people let them. After all, they're relatively affluent and well-educated, and relatively affluent and well-educated people are supposed to be capable of recognizing a crook when they see one. So what happened?

First, the population of the southeast is and remains highly Sovietized, with cultural values and political aspirations that are fundamentally at odds with modernity—and that means, among other things, effective market relations, rule of law, and democracy. Second, the population is isolated and has difficulty imagining itself in the context of a globalized world, a changing Europe, or, for that matter, even a stagnant Ukraine. And third, the population still regards the Donbas as the apex of civilization and takes umbrage at suggestions that their self-perceptions may be a tad off the mark. In these respects, the Ukrainian southeast is not unlike the American Jim Crow South: wedded to beliefs, practices, and institutions that are outmoded and downright deleterious—to everybody.

But there is also good news, potentially. It's hard to imagine that smart people won't eventually decide they can do better than live in a slum run by thugs. Public opinion polls show that southeastern Ukrainians are rapidly losing faith in Yanukovych and the Regionnaires. With any luck, that trend will continue. It should, if only because the long-term well-being of the southeast will be unsustainable if the region does not become livable again—soon.

In a word, time is running out for southeastern Ukrainians. If the Regionnaires and oligarchs transform the southeast into Ukraine's outpost in the third world, locals will face an unenviable choice: accept grinding poverty or get the hell out. Unless, of course, they realize that there's a third way: kick the Regionnaires out.

*

The Serial Stupidity of Sentencing Tymoshenko, *World Affairs Journal*, October 19, 2011

The obtuseness of the Yanukovych regime appears to know no bounds. After a puppet court sentenced former Prime Minister Yulia Tymoshenko to seven years in jail on October 11th, after that verdict provoked howls of protest from everybody—from Washington to Brussels to Moscow—the Yanukovych folks have just lodged new criminal charges against Tymoshenko, this time for her business activities back in the 1990s. In doing so, they have effectively thumbed their noses at Europe.

That leaves one option only on Ukraine's international front—subservience to Russia and devolution into a third-world colonial hinterland doomed to underdevelopment and poverty. Integration into the Russian-led Customs Union will enable the Regionnaires to retain their wealth and power for a while, but when Vladimir Putin becomes president for life, the party will be over. He knows the Regionnaires are clowns and will treat them accordingly. They deserve Siberia. Unfortunately, Ukraine doesn't deserve being consigned to the Stone Age.

How can Yanukovych and the Regionnaires not understand what's good for them, if not what's good for Ukraine? The irrationality of the Tymoshenko ruling has mystified everybody and provoked a range of hypotheses. One of the most popular is that Yanukovych has been persuaded to act against his own interests by some nefarious group. Some speculate that it's headed by the billionaire Dmytro Firtash, but that just begs the question: even if it's true that Firtash managed to outmaneuver the supposedly pro-Western oligarchs supporting the president, why would Yanukovych buy his arguments? After all, doesn't he get it?

Apparently not. And that brings me to my own favorite explanation: that the Regionnaires and their president really are ignorant hicks who haven't a clue about how the world out-side the Donbas works. Consider Yanukovych's statement, made a few days after the verdict: "If such a situation happened in any other country in the world, even in the most democratic country, no one would have said a word ... We are currently being examined with a microscope. Is that pleasant for us? No, it's not pleasant."

Now, consider what's so shockingly wrong with this short statement. First, political show trials *would* elicit condemnation if they took place in other countries. Second, the reason they wouldn't elicit condemnation if they occurred in the most democratic country is, *ahem*, because they would *never occur* in the most democratic country. And third, yes, all countries that aspire to integrate with Europe are placed under a microscope. That's what Euro-integration is all about. If Yanukovych really doesn't get these three elementary points of modern politics, then he really doesn't get much of anything at all and may want to consider beekeeping as a full-time profession.

*

Finding Ukrainian President Yanukovych's Book, *World Affairs Journal*, November 10, 2011

I have some really swell news.

I finally managed to get my hands on Viktor Yanukovych's bestselling book, *Opportunity Ukraine*. No one I know in Ukraine has ever laid his or her eyes on the volume, but I have it—my very own copy.

I'll discuss the actual volume in subsequent blogs, but for the time being let me tell you how I found it.

It wasn't easy. I scoured the bookstores of Kyiv and Lviv a few weeks ago, but to no avail. Silly me: why would an English-language book by its president be sold in Ukraine?

But, surely, it'd be available in Vienna, right? I mean, the publisher, Mandelbaum Verlag, is based in Vienna, and, surely, they'd have an interest in selling it there? Right?

Wrong.

I scoured the bookstores of Vienna, but with no luck. The city's answer to Barnes and Noble, Morawa, didn't even have the book in its computer system—which was a bad sign, of course, and led me to think I should just go straight to the source.

It turns out that Mandelbaum Verlag is located on the ground floor of an old building at Wipplingerstrasse 23, in the First District. I walked in and encountered two men sitting amid shelves and piles of books. The older one asks me, in German, if he could help me. I say that I'm looking for President Yanukovych's book—that I've looked in all the bookstores of Vienna but wasn't able to find it.

"*Es ist vergriffen*," he says, "but I may still have a copy or two."

"Sold out?" I respond. "You mean here in Austria?"

"*Nein*," he says, "the books have been shipped to Ukraine."

"Aha," I say and ask him how much the book costs.

"Nineteen euros and ninety cents."

I give him a twenty and he rummages in a box, where he finds five copies wrapped in plastic. He hands me one and returns ten cents. I thank him profusely and rush out, a broad smile on my face.

After all, I may be the only person outside the presidential administration to own a copy of the volume.

So, what's the book like?

Mandelbaum did their job well: the book at least *looks* professional. Too bad Yanukovych's ghost writers didn't bother with such niceties as citation, preferring plagiarism instead, but there's at least one good thing to be said about the tome—that someone, perhaps Yanukovych himself, had the good sense to understand that an English-language volume by a Ukrainian president could be an effective way of telling the world about Ukraine. None of Ukraine's three other presidents understood that, so Yanukovych deserves some credit for seeing the importance of reaching out.

Naturally, since his book is a Regionnaire operation, it's not surprising they did a lousy job. Forget the plagiarism. The truly bizarre thing about the volume is that it's intended for Western investors. Yanukovych and his minions really appear to have believed that your typical investor would make a far-reaching business decision involving millions or billions of dollars by reading a book. And one by a president no less.

Anyone with even a grade-school understanding of how investment decisions are made could have told the Regionnaires that investors mistrust broad smiles and vague assurances by smooth-talking honchos promising to take care of everything personally. What any investor wants and needs to know is simple: Can I make money? And is my investment safe from political and criminal predators? A president can turn blue in the face with claims that all will be well, but the bottom line for any investor is a country's economic numbers and the quality of its legal system. After all, there are close to two hundred countries in the world. Why invest in some place whose president promises you'll make money when you can invest in another place where other businesspeople are already making money? You'd have to be dumb—or a Regionnaire with criminal connections—to fall for that.

And it doesn't help when the Regionnaire in question doesn't have his facts straight. Yanukovych claims that "registering a business" takes 27 days in Ukraine, as compared to four in Singapore, 23 in Japan, and 15 in Germany (p. 247). According to the authorita-tive Doing Business ratings calculated by the World Bank and the International Finance Corporation, the only number Yanukovych got right was four for Singapore. In reality, "starting a business" takes five days in Hong Kong, 107 in Japan, 98 in Germany—and 112 in Ukraine.

Yanukovych's book might have attracted some investor attention if it had been a hard-hitting, honest, and self-critical memoir—a Horatio Alger story of one Donbas hooligan's rise to the presidency of a big country. That kind of book might even have found a big publisher in New York, and it's not inconceivable that readers—and there *would* have been readers for that kind of book—would have come away thinking that this Yanukovych fella must be a straight-shootin' kind of guy.

Naturally, such a book could work only if it were honest, and that pretty much rules it out for a Party of Regions author. Alas, if Yanukovych weren't so vain and pompous—signs, perhaps, of a deep-seated inferiority complex?—he might actually look like a nice guy. Small wonder that, like the American comedian Rodney Dangerfield, he "don't get no respect."

Yanukovych: The Man Who Would Be King, *World Affairs Journal,* November 22, 2011

Viktor Yanukovych owes African Americans an apology.

Not for permitting his Regionnaire pals to devastate Ukraine. For that he should apologize to his own people, who elected him to improve the country and not destroy it.

No, Yanukovych owes African Americans an apology for comparing himself to Martin Luther King Jr. He does that in the concluding chapter of his recently published English-language book, *Opportunity Ukraine.* The chapter, titled "I Have a Dream," consists of numerous paragraphs that begin with those very words to express the Ukrainian president's vision of Ukraine.

The choice is not accidental. As Yanukovych writes on page 288:

"I Have a Dream" was the name of a famous speech by Martin Luther King, the great American advocate of civil rights and a Nobel Peace Prize winner. I too have a dream: a strong and prosperous Ukraine. And I am going to talk about this dream of mine below. I will tell you about the dream that will, without a hint of doubt, certainly come true.

In other words, Yanukovych thinks of himself as the Ukrainian Martin Luther King.

That takes chutzpah, gall, cynicism, and ignorance.

After all, Martin Luther King and Viktor Yanukovych couldn't be more different. King was a deeply devout man who was unconditionally committed to justice and human rights for all human beings—for blacks and for whites. King confronted prejudice and was willing to sacrifice his life for the good of humanity. King abjured power and wealth because he knew that they interfered in his quest for the good. King stood for love, not for hate.

King would never have rolled back democracy, violated human and civil rights, amassed virtually limitless power, privileged the secret police, consorted with criminal elements, appropriated an enormous estate, surrounded himself with luxury, ignored the misery of the population, promoted ethnic chauvinism, and divided the people.

King would never have abused religion. He would never have falsified elections. He would never have twisted the courts. He would never have regarded the people as chattel. He would never have discriminated against any language or culture. He would never have jailed his political opponents. He would never have aspired to be president for life.

Shame on you, Mister President, for suggesting that you and Martin Luther King have *anything* in common.

What's next? A Sermon on the Mount—delivered from your helicopter?

It's time, Mister President, to examine your conscience and take a deep look at yourself and your friends.

If you truly want to follow in Martin Luther King's footsteps, start by apologizing to African Americans for insulting his memory. Then beg your own people to forgive you. I doubt that they will. Having been systematically pillaged and exploited by your friends, they may be rather more inclined to curse the day you seized power. Finally, tell the thugs who serve you to don sackcloth and ashes.

If Canossa isn't where you want to go, then permit me, respectfully, to propose another destination: Port-au-Prince—and a more appropriate role model: Papa Doc Duvalier. He ruled Haiti with an iron fist, let the Tontons Macoutes run roughshod over his critics, presided over Haiti's decay, and left he Haitians with a corrupt heir—Baby Doc.

With two Baby Docs in tow, you and your sons can aspire to misrule Ukraine even longer than the Duvaliers. But at least be honest about it.

Let Ukrainians know that your dream is their nightmare.

*

Will Yanukovych Start Cracking Heads? *World Affairs Journal*, December 9, 2011

Many Ukrainians think so, and they may have a point.

Here's the way their argument goes. Start with the fact that President Viktor Yanukovych is so widely detested as to be bereft of the least shred of legitimacy. Continue with the fact that his regime is screamingly incompetent, corrupt, and hostile to reform. Add an internal economic crisis that is compounded by a global economic crisis. And stir in mounting popular discontent that will only get more brazen as the threefold crisis—of leader, regime, and economy—deepens.

What's left or the regime? What is its only remaining power resource?

The answer is: force and violence.

All governments, after all, maintain popular support, elicit compliance, and thereby stay in power with some combination of five resources.

If leaders are charismatic, people will support them because they believe in their wisdom. Yanukovych, needless to say, does not fit the bill.

If regimes have ideological appeal, people will support them because they believe in their visions for the future. The Yanukovych regime, as all Ukrainians know, has only one vision: plunder.

If regimes have economic resources, people will support them because of the material advantages that accrue to them. As even the Yanukovych people admit, they have no goodies to distribute and can stay afloat only by increasing taxes and cutting social programs.

If regimes have generous outside benefactors who provide them with the resources they lack, people will support them because of their ability to get free rides. Yanukovych has nowhere to go for such support: the Europeans insist on democracy in return, while the Russians insist on vassalage.

Which leaves violence. If regimes have powerful coercive apparatuses, people will acquiesce in them because they fear for their lives. Does the otherwise bankrupt Yanukovych regime have the coercive wherewithal to force Ukrainians to love it?

The thousands of militiamen and special-forces agents that invariably appear, clad like Star Wars extras, at demonstrations would appear to suggest that the answer is yes. If so, then violence is not only possible but likely, especially as the regime's illegitimacy, incompetence, and isolation grow.

But the picture is much more complicated than that. Bona fide authoritarian regimes always need the support of the army and the secret police in order to stay in power. Ukraine's armed forces are underfed, undersupplied, underpaid, and undertrained. They can't be relied on to tie their shoe laces, much less to crack down.

Ukraine's Security Service is a fair-weather friend. It may have connived to undermine President Leonid Kuchma; it appears to have played some role in preventing a crackdown during the Orange Revolution. And it knows too much—both about the rottenness of the Yanukovych regime and the hatred of the public—to blithely throw in its lot with a lost cause.

The militia, which may number about 350,000, is also unreliable. Look at their fuzz-covered faces at a demonstration. They're always looking away, as if they were ashamed of what they're doing. And rightly so. Many of them are new recruits. Few of them believe in the regime. Most have joined because of the money and especially the bribes they extort from citizens. In sum, they're mercenaries, and mercenaries, as we know from world experience, often flinch when push comes to shove and they have to crack the heads of friends and relatives and realize they have no place to hide when the regime comes crashing down.

That leaves the special forces. These guys are tough, and they're probably ruthless. But even thugs can't be counted on in crises. After all, what made Iran's Revolutionary Guard, the USSR's KGB, or Germany's SS so formidable is that they were true believers in the regime and its leader. What exactly do Ukraine's elite forces believe in?

The Yanukovych regime is now in the unenviable, but richly deserved, position of having nothing but coercion and violence to keep it in power. But resorting to violence is a very risky bet. The forces of coercion may carry out your orders—or they may not, especially if the protestors are senior citizens and coal miners in the Donbas. And even if they do carry them out, they're likely to provoke a mass outburst of people power that will only hasten the regime's collapse. Knowing that a large-scale use of coercion will probably fail, the Regionnaire thugs are likely to use violence selectively. But that strategy, too, is a dead end, as it won't eliminate the opposition while continuing to enrage the population.

Worse, Yanukovych's role model—Vladimir Putin's repressive regime—is showing some big cracks. The United Russia party can hang on to power only by falsifying the recent Duma elections, while regular Russians, who are supposed to be quiescent, happy, or apathetic, have taken to the streets in protests. And, unlike Yanukovych, Putin is charismatic—and has ideological appeal, economic resources, and effective forces of coercion.

So what's a powerless autocrat to do? Pray? Take to the bottle? Consult a fortune teller?

Now that he's backed himself into a corner, you can be sure of one thing: if Yanukovych does decide to spill the blood of his citizens, that won't be a sign of strength, but of weakness, decrepitude, and despair.

Yanukovych would be sweating bullets—if he had any.

*

Who's Afraid of Yulia Tymoshenko? *World Affairs Journal,* January 27, 2012

Which two Ukrainians most detest Yulia Tymoshenko, most fear her, and most obsess about her?

It's the two Viktors, of course: Yushchenko and Yanukovych.

Most Ukrainians have very strong opinions about the former prime minister turned political prisoner, but it's only the two Viktors who've let their feelings about her become borderline psychotic.

In the last three years of his presidency, 2006 to 2009, Yushchenko abandoned whatever reform aspirations that may have guided him during the Orange Revolution and concentrated almost exclusively on squabbling with and attacking Tymoshenko, never passing up an opportunity to denounce her, regardless of whether his audience was listening or cared. I personally witnessed him bore two roomfuls in New York with hour-long attacks on Tymoshenko: the first group consisting of some 50 potential American investors who wanted to hear about Ukraine's economy; the second, of some 100 Ukrainian-Americans who wanted to hear about Ukraine's culture.

Just as Yushchenko let his obsession with Tymoshenko define, and ultimately destroy, his presidency, so too has Yanukovych. After she lost the presidential election of 2010, Tymoshenko was washed up as a national politician. All Yanukovych had to do to keep her that way was to ignore her. Instead, by persecuting Tymoshenko, by jailing her at precisely the time that he's ostensibly courting Europe and hoping to negotiate a gas deal with Russia, he's given her the ethical stature she never had, undermined his standing at home and abroad, sabotaged Ukraine's attempts to integrate more closely with the European Union, and provided the Kremlin with additional reasons for stonewalling Kyiv. Like that other Viktor, this one has let his obsession with Tymoshenko define, and ultimately destroy, his presidency.

So what gives? Although Yanukovych has moved toward many of Yushchenko's positions in the last year, the fact is that the two are profoundly different presidents. Yushchenko was, despite his multitudinous faults, significantly more pro-democratic, pro-Ukrainian, and pro-market than the unabashedly anti-democratic, anti-Ukrainian, and anti-market Yanukovych. They are also very different politicians, with Yushchenko preferring the safety of a podium and Yanukovych preferring the safety of a designer suit.

Why would two such different policymakers share the same fear and loathing of Tymoshenko?

I suspect it's because they're the same kind of guys. It's not Tymoshenko the politician they hate, but Tymoshenko the too-strong woman who knows they're both pushovers and treats them as such. After all, Yushchenko knows how to deal with male enemies. He bores them to death or, as in the case of Yanukovych, cuts a deal with them.

Yanukovych's approach is even simpler, and usually involves a sock to the jaw. Neither approach works with Tymoshenko. She can run rhetorical circles around Yushchenko and knock Yanukovych off is leaden feet.

Tymoshenko, as the strong woman of Ukrainian politics, has exposed both fellas for the vain weaklings they really are. When Yushchenko lost his charms after being poisoned and disfigured in the summer of 2004, Tymoshenko not only threatened his authority and standing as president. She also threatened his manhood and his sense of self as a ladies' man. Moreover, she didn't fall for his act precisely because she wanted what he only half-wanted: power. And she never failed to pursue it, for better or for worse, while Yushchenko never failed to let it slip out of his fingers.

Yanukovych is an even more transparently self-doubting male who is also burdened with the sense of inadequacy that comes from being a hoodlum-turned-honcho. Hence the big mouth and big talk and big fists. Hence the absence of women in his prime minister's cabinet. When wife Ludmilla went off the deep end during the Orange Revolution, Yanukovych could respond only by banishing her to Donetsk. When political opponent Yulia claimed that he was a thug and a crook during the 2010 presidential campaign, he could respond only by banishing her to a jail. Small wonder that his leading female cheerleader, Hanna Herman, gets big bucks for her efforts.

Self-confident politicians and self-confident men would have treated Tymoshenko as just what she was—a strong-willed, tough, and ruthless politician—regardless of her sex. But neither Yushchenko nor Yanukovych can, evidently, see past that. And that obviously drives both fellas crazy, to the point of preferring political suicide to rational policymaking.

Tymoshenko's inevitable comeback will be a traumatic defeat for both Viktors. When the queen bee returns, expect both of them to take up bee-keeping full-time.

Ukraine's Future Amidst an Unstable Russia, EU, *World Affairs Journal*, February 17, 2012

I wrote in a recent posting for this blog that Europe's troubles and Russia's turbulence herald an "unhappy new year" for Viktor Yanukovych and the Regionnaires. Let's up the ante and ask what the European Union's meltdown and Russia's breakdown might mean for Ukraine. Both possibilities may still strike us as unlikely, but, in contrast to the conventional wisdom that ruled over the last decade, they're no longer unimaginable. Indeed, one can easily imagine the EU's transformation into a loose economic association without political aspirations or a tight political-economic entity under German leadership. And one can just as easily imagine Russia's experiencing popular uprisings, coups d'état, and regional secessionist movements that would make it a weak, brittle, and possibly even failed state.

Recall why both the EU and Russia are important for Ukraine. Economically, they're Ukraine's largest trading partners, the most significant sources of foreign direct investment, and the most important destinations for Ukrainian migrant labor. Russia is also Ukraine's prime supplier of energy. Geopolitically, Russia—with its military, atomic weapons, natural resources, and population—is a superpower compared to Ukraine, while the EU, with its incestuous relationship with a confused NATO, represents only a minor balancing opportunity for Ukraine. Normatively, Russia's authoritarianism is a source of emulation for Ukrainian authoritarians, while EU democracy is a source of inspiration for Ukrainian democrats. Culturally, Russia exerts a far greater pull on Ukraine—via proximity, open borders, population, and media hegemony—than the more distant and more aloof EU.

A simultaneous economic decline in both the EU and Russia will knock the wind out of Ukraine's economy. Trade, investment, and migrant remittances will fall, while Ukraine's unemployment rate will rise and GDP will crash. Worse, energy flows could be disrupted, while natural gas is likely to become even more expensive. In sum, Ukraine's economy could experience another 1990s-style depression, and social tensions, possibly even mass revolts, are certain. With their backs to the wall, Ukraine's elites may finally have to choose between packing their bags or reforming the country. They won't be able to count on Russia or the EU to save them and they won't have Russia or the EU to blame for their own incompetence and venality. When forced to sink or swim, Ukraine might finally begin swimming. Or not.

In contrast to an economic breakdown, a geopolitical breakdown could on balance enhance Ukraine's security. Europe isn't much of a geopolitical player anyway, and a decline of its military capacities won't make much of a difference. Russia's transformation into a weak, weaker, or even failed state, on the other hand, will be a significant boon to Ukraine's geopolitical status. Indeed, all of Russia's non-Russian neighbors will breathe more easily with the decline of a superpower with a predilection for neo-imperial rhetoric. The potential downside is that a Russian breakdown could result in civil war, secessionist struggles, mass refugees, loose nukes, and hyper-nationalist rhetoric that will, willy-nilly, affect Ukraine's, as well as Eurasia's, security. Facing direct threats to their sovereignty, Russia's non-Russian neighbors will beef up their militaries and police apparatuses, strengthen border controls, and emphasize their identities as separate states and nations. Under conditions such as these, Ukraine's army may finally be transformed into a genuine military. Ukraine's integrity as a state will also be boosted: no one will want to secede, as there will be no place to secede to.

State building under conditions of outside threats is rarely good for democracy, but, in Ukraine's case, the outcome isn't so clear. After all, the main source of authoritarian legitimation in Ukraine is Russian authoritarianism. If the latter fails, then the prospects for the former correspondingly grow weaker. Of course, if the EU fails, then that source of democratic legitimacy will also grow weaker. On balance, therefore, the condition of Ukraine's (as it is) barely sentient democracy may not be greatly affected by these scenarios.

Finally, Russia's breakdown will greatly weaken its immense cultural pull on Ukraine, while Europe's breakdown will have far less impact on Europe's far weaker cultural attractiveness. For better or for worse, that means Ukraine will likely begin to develop an identity and culture that will be its own—not Russian, but, quite possibly, also not European.

In sum, if both Europe and Russia break down, Ukraine will confront an economic catastrophe, a geopolitical boon, a series of massive security challenges, a normative boost, and a cultural shot in the arm. One of Ukraine's most intelligent analysts, Borys Kushniruk, has argued that, "in expecting Russia's destabilization, we should be aware that it will bring nothing good to Ukraine or the world." In point of fact, Russia's, and the EU's, destabilization will bring a mixed bag of goods to Ukraine and the world.

Ukraine's challenge will be to take advantage of enormous economic and security threats as well as of significant geopolitical, normative, and cultural opportunities to move its economy into high gear, enhance the effectiveness of the state and the identity of its nation, and retain at least its current parlous commitment to democratic procedure. In principle, Ukraine's notoriously fractious and incompetent elites should understand that it's better to hang together than to hang separately, but, then again, who knows? If they get their act together, Ukraine could finally prosper and, as a stable prosperous state, could even exert a positive influence on a destabilized Russia. If they don't get their act together—well, then all bets are off, and Ukraine will likely join Russia as a failed or failing state.

*

The Mega-Stupidity of Imprisoning Yuri Lutsenko, *World Affairs Journal*, March 9, 2012

Throwing opposition leader Yulia Tymoshenko in jail was profoundly dumb, but sentencing her minister of the interior, Yuri Lutsenko, to four years was jaw-achingly, eye-poppingly dumber. After all, Tymoshenko actually posed a threat to President Viktor

Yanukovych. She almost beat him in the last presidential election, and she would almost certainly have crushed him in the next one. Worse, as a self-confident woman, she undermined his desperately fragile male ego. To be sure, jailing her also subverted Ukraine's chances of moving toward Europe and exposed it to Russia's predations—strategic considerations that most leaders would have acknowledged as trumping the frailty of their personalities—but at least her imprisonment served some of Yanukovych's immediate interests.

Nothing of the sort can be said about Lutsenko's imprisonment. First, his trial was even more of a farce than Tymoshenko's. Second, the charges were so manifestly petty and stupid—helping his driver financially—as to make even the most fierce of his critics cringe. The anti-Ukrainian Regionnaire apologist Oles Buzyna, for instance, observed Lutsenko's behavior at the trial and concluded that "The clown became a martyr and a victim. As well as a hero."

Third, Lutsenko posed absolutely no threat to anybody. He was never going to challenge Yanukovych, and he was highly unlikely ever again to become a minister after his dismal performance in Tymoshenko's cabinet. At most, he would have become a fringe politician, able to appeal to and mobilize a few thousand followers. There are scores of wannabe leaders like that in Ukraine and one more would have made no difference to Regionnaire rule.

Fourth, only a dolt could believe that his sentencing will scare Ukrainians. Regionnaire legitimacy is nil, Yanukovych's popularity is approaching nil, popular anger is enormous, approaching the explosive range, and societal mobilization—whether of students, miners, veterans, entrepreneurs, writers, or human rights activists—continues unabated. Quite the contrary, sentencing Lutsenko will only make people angrier.

Fifth, freeing Lutsenko would have cost nothing and brought possibly significant dividends. Lutsenko became a martyr, victim, and hero—in a word, a symbol—*after* he was sentenced. Releasing him on some technicality would have led to some gloating by the democrats, but only briefly, since Lutsenko was washed up and not yet a symbol. Indeed, had the Regionnaires been smart enough to free him, they could have claimed to be magnanimous, fair, and just. Most Ukrainians would have seen their self-righteous stance for what it is—bunk—but some might not have, and when you're down to single digits in popular support, every person counts.

Sixth, and most important, not sentencing Lutsenko would have enabled the Yanukovych regime to suggest to the Europeans that it was changing its way, that it was going straight, and that the Tymoshenko verdict was an unfortunate aberration. Like Ukrainians, Europeans aren't as dumb as the Regionnaires think they are, but the signal would have been loud and clear, and it could not have been ignored in Brussels. Had the Regionnaires really been smart, they could even have hinted that the Lutsenko case was a foretaste of things to come with respect to Tymoshenko. At the very least, such a gesture would have won the Yanukovych regime a bit more time and breathing space.

Instead, the Yanukovych people decided to act against their own interests. Having shot themselves in one foot with Tymoshenko, they proceeded to shoot themselves in the other foot with Lutsenko. Not accidentally—but purposefully, after carefully taking aim and pulling the trigger.

Such suicidal behavior bespeaks either a complete breakdown of coordination within the regime, or complete incompetence, or complete stupidity. As I've suggested on several occasions, all three outcomes are intrinsic features of Sultanistic regimes that centralize too much power in a poor leader.

Tymoshenko commented on Lutsenko's sentencing with the following words:

> Their end will come and it will come soon. Their infamous end will not come from abroad, but from within Ukraine: from Lviv and Donetsk, from Odessa and Poltava, from Chernihiv and Kharkiv. Today we are behind bars. But if that is the price we must pay to free the country, then we are willing to pay it. Yuri, I know, will agree with me ... Till we meet again in freedom!

This is the language of martyrs, victims, and heroes. If the Regionnaires weren't so narrow-minded and so dumb, they'd know that, in today's day and age, you can't beat Martin Luther King, Nelson Mandela, or Vaclav Havel. You can imprison them and you kill them, but you can't beat them.

*

Ukraine: The Yanukovych Family Business, *World Affairs Journal*, March 23, 2012

Just when did people start referring to the inner circle around President Viktor Yanukovych as "The Family"? The term is now commonplace, but my impression is that it started entering the political vocabulary of Ukraine about six to twelve months ago, when son Oleksandr joined Viktor Senior and Viktor Junior to form a triumvirate of power holders and all three began promoting their buddies to positions of authority in the government or to positions of unbounded rapaciousness in the economy.

Little Viktor has long been active in the youth branch of the Party of Regions—call them the "Regionnairettes"—and has served as a dutiful member of Parliament, where he's been filmed acting uprightly by voting on behalf of absent comrades (a constitutional infraction, by the way, but what the hell). His big brother, Oleksandr, is the dentist extraordinaire whose mastery of gums and teeth somehow propelled him to the ranks of Ukraine's one hundred richest individuals at precisely the time that Big Viktor was president.

The head of the central bank, the 36-year-old Serhii Arbuzov, is a friend of "The Family," as is the recently appointed minister of finance, the 38-year-old Yuri Kolobov. See the pattern? Where money's at stake, the Yanukovych brothers make sure their pals are in charge, and Dad says, "Da."

Who knows just how much the Yanukovych boys are worth? After all, every dollar of visible wealth is probably matched with another hundred stashed away in hidden assets or foreign bank accounts. And there's lots of very visible wealth, from Junior's fast cars to the Dentist's real estate holdings.

But corruption isn't my point. All authoritarian leaders and their cliques raid state coffers and grow very rich, very quickly. Rather more important is that only very few authoritar-ian leaders rule by means of bona fide family members. Most prefer to surround them-selves with loyal cops, soldiers, and other lugs.

Good ol' Leonid Brezhnev, the man who brought the "era of stagnation" to the Soviet Union, had a "Family" of his own, centered on his corrupt daughter, Galina. Every North Korean leader in the last few decades has relied on his sons. Romania's notorious Nicolae Ceausescu made wife Elena a member of the Politburo and permitted his dissolute son Nicu to harass half the country's women. Saddam Hussein had a stable of powerful, and thuggish, sons. Syria's Hafez al-Assad made sure son Bashar succeeded him. Hosni Mubarak hoped son Gamal would take his place. And where would Cuba's Fidel Castro be without his brother Raúl?

In all these instances, authoritarian rulers employ family members to misrule their countries. The inevitable result is, of course, vast corruption, as evident in Yanukovych's Ukraine as in Ceausescu's Romania or Brezhnev's USSR. But the inevitable cause of rule by family is the ruler's lack of trust in his own supporters and his isolation from both the ruling elites and society. Why would you want your untested offspring to run a country if you had smart elites whom you trusted? You wouldn't. What distinguishes the incompetent son or daughter from the competent policymaker or technocrat is that you, as the supreme leader, can count on the former to follow your every wish and command. You can trust them—or, at least, you think you can trust them. In contrast, smart policymakers, even if they're your supporters, can never be fully trusted. They may decide to jump ship, or worse, to stab you in the back.

The rise of the Yanukovych Family is thus a sign of Yanukovych's growing helplessness. When a president of a big country must rely on Junior and the Dentist to run the place, you know he's in trouble. And the trouble will only increase. After all, what do Junior and the Dentist know about running a state? Nothing. And would either of them tell Dad the bad news or would they be more inclined to sugarcoat it? The latter, obviously. Which means that the more Yanukovych relies on the boys for information and advice, the more misinformed and ill-advised he will be, and the more incompetent and unprofessional his policies will become.

The amassing of Yanukovych Family power heralds nothing less than the fall of Papa Yanukovych. I wouldn't be surprised if Junior and the Dentist were licking their chops and preparing political eulogies.

Truth and Hopelessness in Luhansk, *World Affairs Journal*, March 30, 2012

I recently came across the saddest commentary on Ukraine's eastern provinces that I have ever encountered. It's a video blog by one Stanislav Tsikalovsky from the city of Luhansk. The 34-year-old Tsikalovsky goes by the name of Proctologist. His slogan is: "Believe me, because madmen always speak the truth."

The truth that recently caught the attention of some 30,000 Ukrainians came in a video Tsikalovsky made after a trip to Lviv, in western Ukraine. Here's what he had to say:

> I would like to dedicate this video blog to the city of Lviv, which I visited, and to those people who hosted us, showed us their city, and told us about its beauty and prospects for the future. I wasn't sure what to say until I sat down in the Lviv-Luhansk train and arrived in my native Luhansk. I disembarked and understood that, besides crying in front of a camera, I wouldn't succeed in describing the beautiful city of Lviv. And not because there's nothing to say. You understand that quite well, if you've seen my photographs. There are, I'm ashamed to admit, many, many, many interesting things there. But when I stepped onto my native Donbas-Luhansk land and looked around, I saw and understood that we don't even have a future. We have no city authorities and no provincial authorities. And it's not even a question of having no prospects of large-scale change. We have no prospects of any kind of change whatsoever. All that's left for us, for you, is at a minimum for us, the Donbas, to be enclosed with barbed wire and not be let out, so as not to interfere with normal people's efforts to develop themselves and build a good country. And at a maximum, I guess, simply to drink ourselves silly. Bye.

The bit about hopelessness and lack of prospects is depressing enough. But for a native of Luhansk to recommend enclosing the Donbas with barbed wire is enough to drive one to drink. If Tsikalovsky were a punk with a dog collar and a mohawk, one could dismiss his comments as the rant of an adolescent. But the Proctologist has a university degree in management and has been working for the Luhansk-based Web portal TOP since 2004. And, with a balding pate and intelligent face, he looks as respectable as he sounds.

It's easy to understand Tsikalovsky's despair. Lviv is an architectural, historical, and cultural gem. Its infrastructure is a mess and too many of its streets and buildings require capital repairs, but it feels like a place that will, one day, be a fabulously prosperous town. Small wonder that the *Financial Times* recently included it on its list of top 10 European "cities of the future."

In contrast, Luhansk is your quintessential Soviet, and Sovietized, city. Obviously, dreadful architecture need not doom a city. As every New Yorker knows, with a little bit of imagination, even ugliness can be made interesting and drabness can be made more livable. But, as Tsikalovsky understands, his city's real problem is that it's still misruled by people who don't see beyond the Stalinist past: "We have no city authorities and no provincial authorities." And note Tsikalovsky's triple emphasis: "We have no prospects of any kind of change whatsoever."

If you want to get a sense of the reality that Tsikalovsky finds so depressing, look at a Russian-language film *Coal Mine No. 8*, by Marianna Kaat of Estonia. It's a documentary about a bunch of kids making ends meet in the depressed coal-mining town of Snizhne, almost equidistant from Donetsk and Luhansk. If you don't understand Russian, don't worry. Just look at the houses, the devastated countryside, and the young boy who goes down into abandoned mine shafts to scrabble for coal, which he then sells or uses to heat his makeshift home. Or look at the "fecal geyser" that gushed forth from a break in Luhansk sewage pipes on March 20th. Or consider the wave of suicides that has swept Luhansk Province.

When you're done watching Kaat's film, you may want to draw barbed wire around the Regionnaires who banned it in Kyiv and the Donbas authorities who remain utterly indifferent to the people they claim to serve.

*

Extremism in Ukraine, *World Affairs Journal*, April 13, 2012

Which Ukrainian political parties are extremist? Most people would point to the right-wing Svoboda party under the leadership of the charismatic demagogue, Oleh Tyahnybok. And they'd be right. Svoboda (or, ironically, "Freedom") is xenophobic, radical, and anti-democratic: the three defining features of extremism.

But they'd be only partly right. No less xenophobic, no less radical, and no less anti-democratic are two other political groups—the Communist Party of Ukraine and the Party of Regions. Suffice to say that Ukraine's Communists are still Stalinist and proud of it. As for the Regionnaires, two years of their rule have relegated Ukrainian language, culture, and identity to Bantustans, exacerbated tensions between Ukrainian speakers and Russian speakers, intentionally promoted Russian chauvinism and Svoboda extremism, efficiently dismantled democracy, bequeathed the economy to rapacious corruptioneers, squeezed civil society, and eroded freedom of the press, speech, and assembly. If that isn't extremism, I don't know what is. Contrary to President Viktor Yanukovych's assertions that he is a moderate, the fact is that he is an extremist par excellence.

But to put the matter in these terms misses the whole picture. After all, Svoboda captured a mere 0.76 percent of the vote in the 2007 parliamentary elections. It does have influence in Ternopil Province and the city of Lviv, but it is also, despite Tyahnybok's assurances to the contrary, never likely to increase its share of the total vote in Ukraine over five percent. Five percent is five percentage points too many, but it's also a tiny amount. Not so with the Communists, who polled 5.39 percent in the parliamentary elections of 2007 and 38 percent in the presidential elections of 1999. Not so, as well, with the Party of Regions, which got 34 percent of the vote in the 2007 parliamentary elections and whose candidate, Yanukovych, won 49 percent in the presidential elections of 2010. Since Yanukovych's party effectively stole the Communist vote, the Regionnaires may be viewed as a non-ideological version of the former Communist machine. The Communists were extremists because that was the best way to build Stalinism; the Regionnaires are extremists because that's the best way to steal. Choose your poison.

As odious as Svoboda is, therefore, the main extremist threat to Ukraine comes not from it, but from the Regionnaires and Communists. Indeed, unless you believe in miracles, Svoboda will never become a major political force, whereas the Regionnaires are and will long remain one. Moreover, Regionnaire extremism is primarily responsible for galvanizing Svoboda extremism. The moral for Ukrainian democrats should therefore be clear: avoid collaborating with extremists of all stripes, whether Svobodites, Regionnaires, or Communists.

Unfortunately, reality is more complicated. The Regionnaires are in power and will do everything it takes to stay in power. Should democrats shun and oppose them, and thereby lose every chance of influencing the course of events, or should they collaborate—or is the better word *cooperate*?—with them and hope to moderate their extremism? Power is a heady brew, and Yanukovych knows full well that he can co-opt democrats by offering them symbolically important positions in his regime. On the other hand, there is a case to be made for infiltrating the regime and attempting to change it from within.

Who's right? What's clear is that both stances are bets. Principled opposition to Regionnaire rule could turn out to be right or it could consign the democrats to impotence. Pragmatic cooperation could turn out to be effective or it could consign the cooperators to collaborationist infamy. Petro Poroshenko, the millionaire chocolate-maker and former good guy, has just joined the Yanukovych government as minister of economic development and trade. He obviously thinks that working with extremists might make a difference for the collapsing Ukrainian economy. If you agree, buy Roshen chocolates. If you don't, switch to Hershey's.

Naturally, if these qualms are valid with respect to the Regionnaire extremists, they must also be valid with respect to the Communist and Svoboda extremists. Back in the days of the USSR, some well-meaning Ukrainians chose to become principled dissidents while others joined the Party. The USSR's collapse made the former look right, but for most of Leonid Brezhnev's rule many viewed them as hopelessly unrealistic idealists. By the same token, some Ukrainian democrats are willing to include Svoboda in an anti-regime electoral coalition, while others are not. Their dilemma is identical to that faced by Russian democrats, who have to decide whether an anti-Putin coalition should or should not have room for nationalists and communists. If you think collaborating with Regionnaire extremism is permissible, you have no choice but to permit collaboration with Communist or Svoboda extremism. If you think all extremists are equally odious, you have no choice but to view cooperation with the Regionnaires as as wrong as cooperation with the Communists or Svoboda. Unless, of course, you believe that extremists with power are less odious than extremists without power, in which case you won't collaborate with Svoboda until they make it into office.

Fortunately, democrats may be able to sidestep these moral dilemmas—but only at this time—precisely because the Regionnaire regime is crumbling, while the Stalinists and

Svoboda are likely to remain minority parties (or so I hope). The democrats don't need any of them to regain power. If they want to win the trust of the people, they should position themselves as *anti*-extremists and don the mantle of tolerance, moderation, and inclusion—the opposites of xenophobia, radicalism, and anti-democracy—and make the case for an anti-extremist Ukraine in which people, and not thieves, thugs, chauvinists, and anti-Semites, will be served. After all, Ukrainians want to live *normalno*, and normality is anything but extremist.

*

Yanukovych's Shady Royalties, *World Affairs Journal*, April 23, 2012

President Viktor Yanukovych has stepped into another scandal, this one over his assets. He declared his total income for 2011 as being 17,362,024 hryvnia, which, at 8.03 hryvnia to the dollar (the exchange rate on April 15th), comes out to $2,163,257.

Not bad enough for a populist president who claims to be one of the regular folk, but the real scandal concerns the source of Yanukovych's money. A mere 757,615 hryvnia ($94,396) constitute his presidential salary, while 155,409 hryvnia come from dividends and interest. (He's got 14,521,454 hryvnia stashed away in banks.) So what's the source of the remaining 16,449,000 hryvnia ($2,049,497)?

Turns out those are his "author's royalties" and other income due to "intellectual property." How so? you ask. Well, according to the UNIAN Information Agency, the Donetsk-based *Novyy svit* (New World) publishing house paid Yanukovych the money for the rights to four books Yanukovych penned from 2005 to 2010, as well as for "literary works that the author will create in the future." The prolific Prez's books are primarily collections of his speeches and articles, which, as one democratic website points out, "are usually distributed for free by his party." As to the literary works, let's not even go there.

So is all this stuff really worth two million bucks? Seems like a stretch to me. Yanukovych ally Volodymyr Semynozhenko, the head of the State Agency for Science, Innovations, and Informatization, disagrees: "I didn't speak with the president about this issue, but, as far as I understand, we're talking about an advance for the future memoirs of the head of state. I think Viktor Yanukovych has agreed to give a long interview after 2020 and to relate his dramatic life's destiny, his work as prime minister, how he experienced the Orange Revolution, stayed in opposition in 2005 and 2008–2009, and finally succeeded in winning the presidential elections and introducing reforms." What's the big deal? asks Semynozhenko. After all, Ronald Reagan, George W. Bush, Barack Obama, and Bill Clinton also got big advances.

You gotta wonder what's scarier: the thought of Yanukovych writing fiction or the preposterousness of Semynozhenko's comments. Say what you will about those American presidents, but they were world-historical personalities whose memoirs were guaranteed important and large readerships. Are there more than 100 Ukraine experts (sorry—99 not counting myself) who'll care to buy Yanukovych's memoirs? A nice Ukrainian folk saying is quite appropriate here: "As the smith is placing a horseshoe on the horse, the frog extends its leg."

By the way, note that Semynozhenko assumes that Yanukovych will be around after 2020 to give long interviews. Given the Prez's current ratings, his winning the 2015 election fair and square is virtually impossible. And if Yanukovych just grabs power and has himself declared president again in opposition to the popular will, he may be too busy running from Interpol in 2020 to have time to sit down for a chat.

Now, the Regionnaires may be dumb, but they know money, and no self-respecting Regionnaire can possibly believe that Yanukovych deserves so large an advance for books that nobody will read. So what's going on? According to the opposition *Ukrainska Pravda* website, the New World publishing house is behind Yanukovych's scandalous book, *Opportunity Ukraine*, which wasn't only a snooze, but, after it was revealed that parts had been lifted from other published sources, was quickly withdrawn from the market—at some loss, I assume, to the state budget.

The director of the press is one Hennadii Ustymenko, who, as it turns out, is also the "head of the transportation-technical administration of the Administration of the State Special Service of Transportation of the Ministry of Infrastructure." What the hell is that? you wonder. Turns out that the "State Special Service of Transportation is a specialized state organ of transportation in the Ministry of Transportation and Communications of Ukraine, which is intended to ensure the reliable functioning of transportation in times of peace and under conditions of war and emergencies."

Got that? Well, if you ever wondered just how impenetrable and absurd Ukraine's bureaucracy is, the good news is that now you know. By the way, it's even funnier. On January 12, 2012, Ustymenko was appointed a member of the Ministry of Economic Development and Trade's "Offset Commission." What's that? As with Yanukovych's lit-erary works, let's not even go there. Oh, and Ustymenko is apparently affiliated with Biznesrazvedka.RF, a marketing firm that gathers "business intelligence." If you want to visit the multitasking Ustymenko and get your own memoirs published, New World is on Batyshcheva Street 2-a in Donetsk.

Anyway, the bottom line is clear. The shady Ustymenko is part of the state bureaucracy, and New World appears to be at the beck and call of the president. I figure that a good chunk of the state budget—lemme take a wild guess and say it's about 16 million hryvnia—somehow made its way to Ustymenko's publishing outfit, which in turn … Well, let's not even go there.

The other thing that's clear is that Yanukovych has been stung by criticism of his authorial lucre. On April 15th, Orthodox Easter, he told journalists: "This year the money I received from the publication of some of my books will be directed only at helping the poor, the ill, and of course above all children."

The ease with which Yanukovych donated the $2 million suggests that he regards it as chump change, the price of a cup of coffee. Only a man who's worth billions could think that way.

*

Ukraine's Opposition Declares War, *World Affairs Journal*, May 25, 2012

Ukraine's united democratic opposition recently adopted an Action Program that defines its goals in stark opposition to the Regionnaire regime of President Viktor Yanukovych. Since the democrats can lose the October parliamentary elections only if the Regionnaires engage in massive fraud and get away with it, the Action Program may be a harbinger of things to come.

The preamble says it all:

> Today Ukraine needs change as never before. All power in the country belongs to the criminal-oligarchic regime headed by president [sic] Yanukovych, who is leading Ukraine toward an abyss.

> Ukraine is ever more becoming a country without laws, rights, freedom, and justice. It is no longer a rule-of-law, democratic, social state.

> The national wealth created by the labor of the whole society is being divided to the benefit of a few scores of families.

> The resources that belong to current and future generations of Ukrainians—land, minerals, forests, rivers, invaluable landmarks of history and culture—are being privatized, sold, and stolen.

> Individuals get billions, foreign accounts, and real estate. The majority gets miserable wages, growing prices and fees, and ruinous taxes. The rich are getting richer, while the poor are getting poorer. This is the essence of Yanukovych's policies. Constitutionally granted human and civil rights have become a fiction. Courts have become puppets in the hands of the ruling regime. The militia, instead of protecting citizens from criminals, protects the power of criminals from citizens. The opponents of the regime are subject to political repression.

> Today's power holders treat citizens as a herd supposed to labor quietly for their enrichment. They believe that power can be bought with money and that the more money they have, the stronger will be their rule.

> They think they will remain in power forever and that Ukraine will always be as it is today.

They are wrong.

The criminal occupation of Ukraine will be put to an end. We will remove the Yanukovych regime from power by means of honest and democratic elections.

For the first time in the history of Ukraine the opposition political parties have joined together in a large and powerful team whose primary goals are:

A JUST STATE, AN HONEST GOVERNMENT, A DIGNIFIED LIFE

I'd say the diagnosis is spot on and that the slogans, which so closely mirror those that motivated Ukrainians to join the Orange Revolution in 2004, are smart. Ukrainians want to live well, of course, but what they want above all is justice, honesty, and dignity. They want to be treated as human beings, and not as a herd of dumb Regionnaire cattle.

The document then goes on to list the opposition's seven immediate policy goals:

1. We will give people the opportunity to work and earn a dignified wage.

2. We will introduce dignified wages and just pensions.

3. Corruptioneers will be taken to task.

4. We will bring back justice.

5. Instead of expensive Russian gas, there will be cheap Ukrainian energy.

6. We will remove the criminal-oligarchic Yanukovych regime.

7. We will place the government under the control of society.

All these goals are worthwhile, but all but two will take time. Points one and two—dignified wages and pensions—can happen only if the Ukrainian economy gets going again. Point three will be difficult because corruption has become an integral part of Ukrainian life. Point five requires a massive transformation of Ukraine's corrupt and inefficient energy sector. Point seven presupposes the emergence of a post-Soviet citizenry that actually wants to take charge of its life.

In contrast, points four and six—bringing back justice and removing the regime—can be accomplished rather more quickly, and it is they that will define the opposition's policies should it be permitted to run the Parliament. Naturally, the Regionnaire faction in Parliament will resist tooth and nail legislation intended to place them all in jail. Scuffles, blockades, and other extralegal measures will become the order of the day and both the legislature and the government could become completely dysfunctional. Yanukovych will then have to rule by decree, thereby assuming complete responsibility for his incompetent regime. Under conditions such as these, Anybody But Yanukovych will be a shoo-in for president in the elections of 2015.

What chance is there that Yanukovych might decide to save his skin by working with the opposition and divesting his family of some of its ill-gotten gains? The record of the world's tyrants suggests that they would rather go down in flames, and drag their countries with them, than go straight. Just look at Anastasio Somoza, Mobutu Sese Seko, Robert Mugabe, Slobodan Milosevic, Vladimir Putin, and Benito Mussolini. Worse, Yanukovych's own inability to learn—consider his stubbornly self-destructive behavior regarding European demands that Yulia Tymoshenko be released—suggests that he, too, will prefer to crash and burn rather than admit to being wrong.

Well, crash and burn he will if he stays on course. Let's just hope that, this time, the democrats who eventually replace him don't repeat the mistakes of the Orange revolutionaries by dithering and squabbling and, instead, immediately take measures to free the economy from the stranglehold of corruptioneers and bureaucrats and, above all, incorporate the much-abused Ukrainian citizenry into the process of government and self-government.

*

Urban Politics and Regionnaire Corruption in Ukraine, *World Affairs Journal*, June 15, 2012

Two recent studies cast interesting light on urban life and Regionnaire policy in Ukraine. Unsurprisingly, most of the cities they misrule are sorely neglected slums, while the only two that matter to them politically—Donetsk and Luhansk—are recipients of government largesse. As it turns out, President Viktor Yanukovych's Party of Regions would be better termed the Party of Two Cities.

In *Kommentarii* magazine's livability rating of 45 Ukrainian cities, those in the bottom half, the 22nd through the 45th, are, with but three exceptions, in the southeastern provinces that support the Regionnaires. The top half, the 1st through the 21st, are all in the central and western provinces that support the national democrats, with the exception of six major Regionnaire-run cities—Sevastopol (3rd), Dnipropetrovsk (5th), Kryvyy Rih (10th), Simferopol (14th), Donetsk (16th), and Odessa (18th). Note the pattern. The Regionnaire-run cities that do relatively well are all large; the provincial cities they misrule are all in the dumps.

The Regionnaire record looks worse if we exclude Sevastopol and Simferopol from the list (the former, as the site of the Russian Black Sea Fleet, gets big bucks from Moscow, while the latter is relatively near Crimea's beaches) and look at the number of points the cities score. The highest possible point total is 1,125 (with 45 points per 25 criteria). Kyiv, which is 1st on the list, gets 896 points, or 80 percent of the total. The Regionnaire strongholds, Donetsk and Luhansk, get only 57 percent and 43 percent, respectively. And the cities that score under 50 percent are, with but two exceptions, Regionnaire bastions.

The Regionnaires know where their bread is best buttered and obviously feel free to condemn the rest of the provinces they run to stagnation. These findings are consistent with a study I cited last year that showed that the quality of life is lowest in a coherent swath of territory running from south to east. Of Ukraine's 27 provinces, Zaporizhzhya was 22nd, Mykolaiv was 23rd, Kherson was 24th, Luhansk was 25th, Donetsk was 26th, and Dnipropetrovsk was dead last.

Keep these ratings in mind as we look at some other data, on state budget transfers to provinces. As it turns out, Donetsk Province, which is Yanukovych's power base and contributes 12 percent of Ukraine's GDP, received 21 percent of budget transfers in 2010 and a whopping 27 percent in 2011. Luhansk Province, which is a Regionnaire power base and contributes a mere 4 percent to Ukraine's GDP, got 8 percent in 2010 and 11 percent in 2011. The capital city, Kyiv, contributes 18 percent of GDP and, justifiably, received 15 percent of outlays in 2010 and 18.3 percent in 2011.

Several conclusions follow from these data.

First, the claim made by Donbas residents that they "feed" the rest of Ukraine is clearly false. If anyone is being fed, it's them.

Second, in light of the fact that most southeastern cities are dumps, it's clear that the subsidies being received by Luhansk and Donetsk provinces are going to Luhansk and Donetsk cities, and not the towns and villages in the provinces. In other words, the Donbas provinces are feeding Donetsk and Luhansk.

Third, and most interesting, the money going to Luhansk and Donetsk is obviously not having the intended effect. Kyiv gets a lot of cash, but it contributes its share to the total pot and is highly livable. In contrast, despite being the targets of Regionnaire lucre, Luhansk and Donetsk rank relatively low on the livability scale.

Why?

Part of the answer may be that they suffered disproportionately from Ukraine's economic collapse in the 1990s and must therefore catch up more to reach Kyiv's level. The problem with this explanation, however, is that the Donbas has been highly subsidized by Kyiv since independence in 1991. Every Ukrainian president has known that he must win the region's loyalty, or at least neutrality, by buying it off ith goodies.

So the more convincing answer for Luhansk and Donetsk's continued underdevelopment must have to do with the nature of their rulers—the Regionnaires (and pre-Regionnaires) who pocket state expenditures with a wild abandon that would make Al Capone's head spin. Is it pure coincidence that Kyiv's subsidies to Donetsk exploded at precisely the same time that Yanukovych's dentist son, Oleksandr, became one of Ukraine's 100 richest individuals?

The lesson is obvious. Were the Party of Regions a city, it would be at the very top of the heap, with a 200 percent rating. Were the Yanukovych clan a city, it would score even higher.

PART ONE: THE RISE AND FALL OF VIKTOR YANUKOVYCH

Street Protests in Ukraine, *World Affairs Journal*, August 17, 2012

Talk to Ukrainians and the view you'll hear from almost everyone is that "they"—Ukrainians—are passive, apathetic, and inert. I've heard this line in Lviv, Kyiv, and Donetsk as well as in Western Europe and North America. I've even heard it at, of all places, demonstrations in Ukraine.

The question that invariably follows is: "Why don't they rise up and finally do something?"

The fact is that Ukrainians are doing something almost every day. Walk down most main streets in most cities and towns and you'll usually encounter some protesters handing out leaflets or some groups raising a ruckus. Maybe not every day, but often enough to persuade you that at least some Ukrainians aren't passive.

Naturally, most Ukrainians aren't impressed by that kind of protest action. It's too run-of-the-mill, too easy, too small, too quiet, too unimpressive. In a word, it's no Orange Revolution, when millions rose up throughout the country to demand their rights in the face of the Kuchma-Yanukovych camarilla that had falsified the presidential elections of 2004.

The problem with revolutions, uprisings, and other displays of people power is that they are, by definition, infrequent. It takes an unusual concatenation of forces to induce millions to disregard their everyday concerns—such as survival—go into the streets, and, most important, stay there for weeks or even months. And when the result of a mass mobilization is failure, don't be surprised if people become skeptical and wait.

On the other hand, that skepticism can also vanish overnight. Remember Poland's Solidarity movement? It emerged seemingly out of nowhere in 1980 and survived as a mass movement for about a year, until General Jaruzelski cracked down. But its activists continued to promote their cause until, finally and almost miraculously, the regime toppled like a house of cards in mid–1989, and they, the dissidents who had languished in jail just a few weeks before, suddenly emerged victorious.

I mention Poland because the similarities between Yanukovych's Ukraine and Jaruzelski's Poland are too striking to ignore. Both regimes came to power after democratic mass movements failed to reach their agendas. Both regimes represented a restoration of the status quo ante and, as such, had absolutely nothing to offer their populations. Both regimes represent momentary pauses in inevitable social and political processes. Both leaders were singularly unimaginative and both ruling parties were hopelessly corrupt. Both democratic movements remained alive and well, in that significant parts of the population had internalized their values and rejected the loutish regimes in power. And both countries generated impressive civil societies that kept making demands during the dark years of repression and stasis. The next few years will see the final similarity: the Yanukovych regime, like the Jaruzelski regime some 30 years ago, will collapse under the weight of its own rot.

Meanwhile, Ukrainians *are* protesting like there's no tomorrow. According to a study by the Center for the Study of Society, Ukraine has experienced 100 to 300 protest actions every single month of 2010 and 2011. The numbers are usually highest, between 200 and 300, when you'd expect them to be highest—during the spring months of March, April, May, and June and during the fall months of October and November.

Now that's a helluva lot of protests, especially in a country that's supposedly disinclined to protest. In the social sciences, you'd say that the evidence disproves the "passivity hypothesis." In any case, it certainly doesn't support it.

The numbers for this year are especially impressive. There have been about 100 to 150 more protest actions per month in March, April, May, and June than for corresponding months in 2010 and 2011. A more recent study (by the same center) of protests in July shows that, at 404, they exceeded the previous month's 330 by 74. That's a record, sparked largely by the Regionnaire-controlled Parliament's adoption in late June of a law on lan-guages that is as stupid as it is supremacist. Significantly, July also saw another record: the number of repressive responses went up from 70 in May and June to 101—a 44 percent increase.

Clearly, the Yanukovych regime has seen the writing on the wall and is terrified. And rightly so. If the upward protest trend keeps up, a second Orange Revolution becomes perfectly possible. And since the Regionnaires have to cheat in the forthcoming October parliamentary elections (cheating, you see, is as much a political imperative as a genetic predisposition), a fraudulent ballot could again serve as the spark that drives the masses into the streets.

The regime is currently working overtime, trying to rig the electoral rules, gerrymander districts, split the opposition, manipulate the press, buy votes, and so on. Some of that will work, if only because the oligarch-funded Regionnaires have billions of dollars to throw around. But you can't fool all the people all of the time and, as Jaruzelski discovered in 1989, you can't even fool some of the people some of the time—especially if you're a deadbeat leader who is perceived by everyone as a deadbeat leader. Note that, in just the last two months, support for the Regionnaires has fallen five percentage points—from 28 percent to 23.

The protests in Ukraine will continue, of course. Unlike Jaruzelski, who dared to crack down in 1981 because the Soviet Union had amassed its soldiers on the Polish border, Yanukovych knows that the thousands of new militiamen he's recently hired are just regular guys trying to make ends meet. When push comes to shove, they'll join their friends and neighbors and give the Regionnaires a mighty heave-ho.

*

Delinquents vs. Democrats in Ukraine, *World Affairs Journal*, September 14, 2012

Word's out in Ukraine that there is "no difference" between the Regionnaires and the opposition. The implication is obvious: it doesn't matter whom you vote for in the October 28th parliamentary elections and it doesn't even matter whether you vote. After all, whoever wins, whether Regionnaires or the opposition, there's "no difference."

This is nonsense.

Let's consider a few dimensions along which one might measure difference.

- Moral qualities: There are, as everyone knows, far too many crooks and corruptioneers among the democrats, but the crucial difference between them and the Regionnaires is that, while the former tolerate thugs within their ranks, the latter *are* thugs. It's like the difference between Fortune 500 CEOs and the mafia. Are there criminals among the former? Of course. Do most of them probably do things we'd consider a tad shady? Sure. But they ain't the mafia. Even that notorious thief, Bernie Madoff, was no Al Capone. Or to put it a different way: Whom would you prefer to encounter in a dark alley—a typical democrat or a typical Regionnaire? Arsenii Yatseniuk or Viktor Yanukovych Junior?

- Democratic proclivities: There's no question that the Orange democrats screwed things up royally while in power from 2005 to 2010. Reform was zilch, and the government seemed to be in permanent crisis. But, by any measure, Ukraine was democratic and Ukrainians were free. And that's because the Orange and post-Orange democrats genuinely value things like democracy and freedom. Now, compare their record to that of the Regionnaires. In the last two years, since Viktor Yanukovych's election as president in 2010, Ukraine's democracy has been dismantled: the president has become all-powerful, the parliament is a joke, and the courts are puppets of the executive. Moreover, freedoms of speech, of assembly, and of the press have been and are being constricted. Does anyone have any doubts that in three more years the condition of democracy and freedom in Ukraine will be even worse?

- Competence and dedication to reform: Yup, the Orange democrats proved to be dreadful managers and terrible governors, so much so that they made Yanukovych look like an attractive alternative in the presidential elections of 2010. But what he and his Regionnaire cronies have managed to accomplish in the last two years is even more astounding: their level of incompetence and their complete indifference to anything resembling systemic reform have been so screamingly obvious that they've succeeded in making ex-president Viktor Yushchenko look like a model of competence. And small wonder. While thugs may be able to keep order in a small province, where kicking butts usually suffices to get things done, they cannot, by definition, run anything resembling a modern state and a modern economy. Street smarts, which Yanukovych acquired while running with gangs in the Donbas, just aren't enough in government.

- Statecraft: This one is easy. After five years, the Orange democrats managed to have lousy relations with Putin's Russia and decent, though uninspired, relations with the United States, the European Union, the International Monetary Fund, and other major international actors. After just two years, the Yanukovych regime has managed even to alienate Russia, its putative pal, and is barely on speaking terms with the Americans, Europeans, and IMF. Only the Chinese have deigned to acknowledge the Regionnaires, although it's not yet clear that their offer to lend Ukraine billions won't be undermined by some Regionnaire blundering.

- Personal wealth: Yes, the democrats have tons of cash, much of it illicitly or semi-illicitly acquired. But no, their level of wealth doesn't even come close to that of the Regionnaires. And do you really think that any democratic president would have built a Spanish galleon as his, or her, playground? Oh, and last I looked, the mega-gazillionaire ex–card sharp Rinat Akhmetov was a Regionnaire.

I could go on, but the point should be clear: there's a ton of difference between the Regionnaires and the democrats.

So why the widespread perception that there isn't any?

Well, partly that's just the line that pro-Regionnaire publicists and politicians (like the former Orange president, Yushchenko) are pushing on all the media outlets the Regionnaires control, and if you push something long and loud enough, some people will begin believing it.

But mostly the perception is due to the fact that the democratic opposition has failed to inspire the population. The democrats are regular guys, but they lack charisma and they're not, as one lady in Kyiv complained to me, George Washingtons. Fair enough, but what's so bad about uninspiringly regular guys? And shouldn't you prefer them to the mafia?

And if that doesn't persuade you, consider this. Can Ukraine survive several more years of Regionnaire rapine? Wouldn't Ukraine be just a jot better off if the Regionnaires got a punch in the nose in the forthcoming elections and were told to back off?

The sad fact is that, if Ukrainians keep on insisting that they'll vote only for angels, they may just ensure rule by the devils.

*

PART ONE: THE RISE AND FALL OF VIKTOR YANUKOVYCH

Yanukovych after the Fall, *World Affairs Journal*, October 26, 2012

What will Viktor Yanukovych do after he falls from power?

That's a question that should concern Ukraine's current president, especially as Ukrainians are preparing to go to the polls on October 28th. After all, just about everyone in Ukraine hates him: from the regular folk to the intellectuals to the elites to his supposed supporters. It didn't have to be that way. Even a half-hearted commitment to reform and good government would have won him accolades. Since it's too late to save his ruined presidency, there's nothing left o do but wait for it to end.

And sooner or later end it will. It could happen in 2015, if the oligarchs who back him decide he's a loser and send him to the showers. It could happen in 2020, after his second term is up and Ukraine has been devastated so thoroughly that no one in the country—not even well-fed Regionnaires—will want him around. It could happen between now and 2020, if some Regionnaire cabal decides that his incompetence has gotten to the point of undermining their privileged status or if the people realize that the prospect of endless Regionnaire rapine is no way to live one's life and chase poor Viktor out of the presidential palace. Or it could happen anytime Yanukovych's health begins to crumble under the pressure of too many late nights.

After all, although Yanukovych the man may not believe it now, he's just human and humans have been known to suffer from creeping mortality. And although Yanukovych the president certainly can't envision the end of his presidency—what aspiring tin-pot dictator doesn't dream of misruling forever?—that presidency will end. Presidencies always do, even good ones, and Viktor, like his role models Vladimir Putin of Russia and Aleksandr Lukashenka of Belarus, will someday just be a bad memory

Were Viktor a bit more inclined to pick up an occasional book, he'd do well to read up on Poland. He might notice that independent Ukraine, which is supposed to resemble post-Communist Poland, actually resembles Communist Poland. Ukraine's independence in 1991 was pretty much a repeat of Poland's abandonment of Stalinism in 1956. Ukraine's first two presidents, Leonid Kravchuk and Leonid Kuchma, are strikingly similar to Poland's Communist leaders, Stanislaw Gomulka and Edward Gierek. The Orange Revolution of 2004 was virtually identical to Solidarity's revolution of 1980–1981.

Which means that the man who crushed Solidarity, General Wojciech Jaruzelski, is none other than Viktor Fedorovych Yanukovych himself.

Jaruzelski was incapable of doing anything but cracking down on the democratic opposition. Poland stagnated, regime legitimacy declined, and the ruling Communist Party decayed. Similarly, Yanukovych is incapable of doing anything but cracking down on the democratic opposition. Ukraine is stagnating, regime legitimacy is declining, and the ruling Party of Regions is decaying.

When 1989 came along, the Jaruzelski regime was exposed as a house of cards, and the collective efforts of the opposition and population brought it down in a matter of days. Ukraine's 1989 will also come and, when it does, the Regionnaires will head for the hills and Yanukovych will become a pariah.

Where will the Regionnaires go? Their wealth is in Western Europe and the United States, but it's unlikely that any Western democracy will open its doors to thousands of crooks. Russia and Belarus might welcome some of them, but will they want a mass influx of embittered and impoverished Regionnaire schemers? Probably not. That leaves such offshore havens as the Cayman Islands. Keep that in mind when you're planning your vacation a few years from now.

And how about ex-president Yanukovych?

If Putin's still in charge, Russia won't be an option, since Vlad famously detests Vik. Minsk might work, but who wants to live in what Lukashenka proudly called Europe's last dictatorship? Either way, Yanukovych would have to say good-bye to all the goodies his family has squirreled away in the West. And besides, the West is likely to put him and his sons on some black list anyway, so forget the Riviera or Palm Beach.

Which leaves three options: the first is some pariah state, such as North Korea (too cold), Zimbabwe (too hot), or Somalia (too dangerous). The second is to try to make it to the South Pacific on his Spanish-style Galleon (too leaky). The third is to stay in Ukraine and face the music. He'll have to do it on his own, of course, as all his erstwhile yes-men will publicly denounce him and claim that they had secretly supported democracy all along.

At a minimum, some future democratic Ukrainian court will strip him and his sons of all their assets. Will the former president then get a job as a security guard at some Donetsk coal mine? At a maximum, the court will put him in jail, and, if the judges have a sense of humor, they'll also do so on the same grounds as Yanukovych's imprisonment of opposition leader Yulia Tymoshenko.

Viktor Fedorovych may then take some consolation from the poetry of it all. His political career will have ended in the same place it began.

*

Is 2013 the End for Ukraine's Regionnaires? *World Affairs Journal*, January 3, 2013

Last year ended with a series of portentous developments for the Yanukovych regime. And, more and more, it looks like the regime's ready to break down or crack up. Consider the signs.

- The almighty Regionnaires couldn't even cheat their way to a majority in the new Parliament and, instead, had to settle for what effectively amounts to a power-sharing arrangement with the opposition. Worse, they will now have to deal with a raucous collection of right-wing deputies, the "Svobodites," who will harass and jeer them at every step of the way.

- The much-vaunted professionalism of the Regionnaires received two fatal blows, when, first, the government was snookered into signing a billion-dollar deal with an imposter claiming to represent a Spanish energy firm and, second, all the expensive Hyundai trains procured by former Infrastructure Minister Boris Kolesnikov just before the Euro 2012 soccer championships last summer broke down in the harsh Ukrainian winter.

- In moves that could impress only Leonid Brezhnev in the final years of his inglorious reign as Communist Party leader, the newly appointed speaker of the Parliament became Viktor Yanukovych's crony from Donetsk, the aging, dull, and thoroughly uninspiring Volodymyr Rybak, while the prime minister's job went to the equally dull and uninspiring incumbent, Mykola Azarov.

- The notoriously Ukrainophobic Dmitri Tabachnik remained minister of education, science, youth, and sport, thereby demonstrating the president's mindboggling inability to understand that replacing him with anyone would have won him easy brownie points with the electorate.

- That two of the brightest, if morally compromised, members of the old Cabinet, Serhii Tihipko and Valery Khoroshkovsky, have left—the former for Parliament, the latter for his business empire—demonstrates, first, that Yanukovych's primary criterion in choosing ministers was not talent or brains, but loyalty and, second, that the pro-regime elites are jumping ship.

- Since the new Cabinet consists mostly of Yanukovych loyalists who are beholden to his "Family," the clan run by the president and his two sons, the newly appointed ministers will focus their energies on fulfilling the sultan's wishes, thereby aggravating the regime's hypercentralization, indecisiveness, incompetence, ineffectiveness, and instability.

- Because Yanukovych yes-men also control all the most important financial and economic ministries, the Ukrainian economy will continue to decay, while the Family's plundering of the economy will accelerate, perhaps in anticipation of the rapidly approaching end and, hence, the limited amount of time left or untrammeled theft.

- All the other seats on the Cabinet went to Donetsk hyper-billionaire Rinat Akhmetov's flunkies, a sign that Yanukovych has formalized his alliance with Ukraine's richest man, accepted that his power base has been reduced to a sliver of the country, the Donbas, and effectively acknowledged that he has no legitimacy among the people or even—no less important—the other oligarchs and elites.

- The last-minute cancelation of the Ukrainian president's planned trip to Moscow, the European Union's continued dissatisfaction with his regime, Secretary of State Hilary Clinton's harsh criticism of Ukraine's democratic backsliding, and China's deafening indifference demonstrate that Yanukovych has managed to achieve the near-impossible in international relations: complete isolation.

I could go on, and on, but this brief list should suffice to show that the regime may very well be on its last legs. As shockingly incapable as it was of getting anything right between 2010 and 2013, its incompetence, thievery, and resistance to common sense will probably only grow in the months ahead. As more and more power is concentrated in the Family and its *pater familias*, the regime will eventually be reduced to an inglorious royal court whose only concerns are self-enrichment and self-preservation. Since Yanukovych loyalists also control the power ministries, the temptation to crack down in order to avert a crack-up will be overwhelming. Cracking down won't work, however, because most of the population no longer fears the dullards running the country into the ground.

The new year therefore begins on a hopeful note for Ukraine and its democratic aspirations. The writing is on the wall for the regime. If they'd only read more and steal less, they might even see it.

*

The Yanukovych Ruin and Its Aftermath, Part 1, *World Affairs Journal*, January 10, 2013

Although Ukraine may have to endure another three to eight years of Viktor Yanukovych's misrule—until the presidential elections of 2015 or 2020—the end, fortunately, is in sight, and the challenges of post-Yanukovych reconstruction may be envisioned, at least in broad outlines. Following the extensive institutional destruction wrought by Yanukovych and the Party of Regions, Ukraine will have to be reconstructed from top to bottom. Mere reform will no longer be enough. Even "radical reform" may not quite accurately capture the magnitude of change that Ukraine will have to endure to emerge from the "Yanukovych Ruin" politically energized and rejuvenated, rather than enervated and ossified.

Whether or not Yanukovych remains in office through 2015 or 2020 almost does not matter. The institutional destruction he initiated in 2010 is more or less complete, a brittle sultanistic regime has emerged, and neither three nor eight years of additional misrule will significantly deepen or extend the *political* damage. Naturally, Ukraine's economy and society will experience far more destruction from eight years of ruin than from three. By the same token, the likelihood of an oligarch-led putsch or a popular rebellion involving violence will grow the longer Yanukovych and his Regionnaires remain in power. But the political regime he created—sultanism—will not change qualitatively anymore, except to break down.

After his election as president in early 2010, Yanukovych quickly accumulated vast powers, thereby transforming the presidency into a near-dictatorial office, while subordinating the other two branches of government—the Parliament and the courts—to himself and his party. Despite claiming to be a moderate, Yanukovych proved to be a quintessential revolutionary committed to destroying the existing political order as rapidly and as thoroughly as possible. Yanukovych's power base, the Party of Regions, quickly became the functional equivalent of the Communist Party of the Soviet Union under Leonid Brezhnev: a vehicle for acquiring power, accumulating wealth, and dispensing patronage. Whatever ideological visions the Regionnaires claimed to have were abandoned, and they became little more than the greedy clerks who once mismanaged the Soviet empire.

Given the evisceration of the non-presidential branches of government and the emergence of the Regionnaires as the party of both power and theft, it was inevitable that Yanukovych would become the focus of increasingly personalized rule, while his closest confidantes would join him in plundering the country. The logical end point of this institutional development was reached in 2012: the triumph of Yanukovych and his "Family," the reduction of the Rada and the courts to meaninglessness and buffoonery, and the transformation of the Party of Regions into nothing more than an instrument of rapine.

Having attained the "highest stage" of sultanism, such a regime can experience little institutional development in the next three to eight years. Yanukovych and his family cannot acquire more power, the other institutions of government cannot become more meaningless, and the Regionnaires cannot become more rapacious. Because sultanistic regimes are invariably corrupt and conservative, there is no reason to think that the avaricious mediocrities who man the Yanukovych system will be able or willing to sacrifice their well-being to vague notions of reform, especially if reform undermines their power and privilege.

On the other hand, such a deeply dysfunctional regime is a leading candidate for stagnation and decay. And, sooner or later, the sultanistic Yanukovych system will collapse under its own dead weight. Most probably, that collapse will come in 2015, during the next presidential elections, or in 2020, after Yanukovych finishes his second term. The only question facing Ukraine is whether or not collapse will occur peacefully.

It is perfectly possible for the tycoons whose assets are being stripped by the Yanukovych Family to join the forces of coercion and, in the manner of many third-world countries, stage a coup. It is also possible for mass-based violence to occur. It generally does when societies are humiliated and exploited, when oppressors look vulnerable and weak, and when individuals or groups with violent agendas exist. The first two conditions are already present in Ukraine and both will only intensify as the economy continues to stagnate and Regionnaire abuse of the population continues. The third could easily emerge, especially if a brittle sultanistic regime resorts to violence itself. Weak regimes often employ violence in the hope of quashing internal opposition. More likely than not, their violence only induces radically inclined individuals and groups within society to respond with violence.

The collapse of sultanism will mean the collapse of a meaningless Parliament, meaningless courts, and an all-powerful presidency. The Party of Regions will also collapse. Were the Regionnaires an ideological party, some of them might stay and fight. But inasmuch as their primary concern is self-enrichment, they will head for the hills as soon as the writing appears on the wall.

The task facing Ukrainians after the Yanukovych Ruin will be enormous. Inasmuch as Yanukovych and the Regionnaires have effectively destroyed post-Soviet Ukraine's political institutions, Ukrainians will have to construct a political regime *de novo*.

*

The Yanukovych Ruin and Its Aftermath, Part 2, *World Affairs Journal*, January 18, 2013

While the Yanukovych regime's likely disintegration (discussed last week in Part 1) is not tantamount to an institutional void, the destruction wrought by sultanism will place post-Yanukovych Ukraine in the extraordinary position of being a country without effective political institutions. Indeed, Ukraine will approximate a failed state. Under conditions such as these, the most important political actors will be the oligarchs, forces of coercion, civil society and opposition movements, and charismatic individuals.

The oligarchs, the military, the militia, and the security service will survive collapse intact, even if the regime's downfall is accompanied by social upheaval and mass violence:

- Ukraine's tycoons will remain fabulously wealthy and influential, regardless of whether they hide on their estates or in their villas in the West. Their primary interests will, as always, be the protection of their assets and privilege, which means stability and security. Although sultanism offered some measure of both, the collapse of sultanism and Ukraine's subsequent time of troubles will likely incline the oligarchs to seek to align Ukraine with the global economy in general and the West in particular as the only reliable guarantors of both.

- The forces of coercion will remain relatively strong, although, in all likelihood, despised by, and illegitimate in the eyes of, most of the population.

- A variety of civic and political groups, movements, and organizations will survive, and perhaps even thrive, in a stagnant sultanistic regime, and all of them will make claims on the right to guide Ukraine in the aftermath of Yanukovych's fall. Their claims will be persuasive, legitimate, and popular, but they will be effective only if civil society resists the temptation to squabble and self-destruct.

- In transitional circumstances such as these, charismatic leaders will thrive. Articulate individuals with forceful agendas and moral authority will be best positioned to play such roles, and it is they who could provide civic and political organizations with a unifying agenda and a common purpose. It is also they who could conduct negotiations with strong, but weakened forces of coercion and win them over to the side of the people. If she survives until then, whether in jail or in exile, Yulia Tymoshenko could easily emerge as Ukraine's Nelson Mandela.

With institutional destruction, regime collapse, and Regionnaire flight on the one hand, and oligarch influence, coercive uncertainty, social mobilization, and charismatic leaders on the other, Ukraine could be in the position to do away with more than 24 years of regime ineffectiveness and achieve an institutional breakthrough along the lines of East Central Europe in 1989–1991. Then, too, the existing Communist regimes had eviscerated political institutions, promoted state decay, and tolerated powerful civic institutions such as Solidarity, dissident movements such as Charter 77, and charismatic individuals such as Lech Walesa and Vaclav Havel.

When the Communist regimes collapsed and the forces of coercion remained indecisive and were unwilling to crack down, civic/political organizations were able to join forces with charismatic individuals to promote breakthroughs that enabled their countries to abandon communism and embark on democratic and free-market reform. The forces of the *ancien régime* were too weak, too confused, or too preoccupied with saving their own skins to stop them, and success was assured.

The choice before Ukraine's future democratic elites will mirror that before Poland and Czechoslovakia more than twenty years ago. Post-Yanukovych Ukraine will remain unified, like Poland, if its civic-political institutions, oligarchs, and leaders can agree on some degree of federalization or decentralization that enables Ukrainian-language speakers and Russian-language speakers to use Ukrainian as a lingua franca and to enjoy linguistic choice at other levels of social interaction. Post-Yanukovych Ukraine will go the way of Czechoslovakia if some such consensus is not found.

Chances are that the Polish scenario will get the upper hand. The Yanukovych regime's endorsement of Russian supremacism may appeal to diehard Russian-language speakers, but it will, several years from now, likely be as discredited as the regime that spawned it. Unless the post-Yanukovych democrats engage in linguistic maximalism, it's a good bet that Ukraine will survive intact and that a "social contract" between East and West will emerge, especially if the oligarchs endorse it, as they are likely to do. That said, we should remember that, if Ukraine follows in Czechoslovakia's footsteps, both the Czech Republic and Slovakia prospered in the aftermath. A central-western Ukrainian Ukraine will move unhindered toward the West and do well economically. A southeastern Russian Ukraine will probably join the Russian Federation and, while certain to stagnate economically, will be able to enjoy the Russian language and Soviet traditions.

A more substantive danger to post-Yanukovych Ukraine will be Vladimir Putin's Russia. The chances that a declining quasi-fascist petro-state such as Russia will become strong and stable are few. A beleaguered Putin will almost certainly not choose democracy as the means to save himself and his regime. Instead, Putin will tighten the reins and increase his neo-imperialist rhetoric, perhaps hoping for a "quick little war" that could provide his tottering regime with a shot in the arm.

Will Ukraine survive a possible military intervention? It could go the route of Yugoslavia, and the resulting instability could also spell Russia's doom. Or post-Yanukovych democrats and oligarchs may succeed in drawing on burgeoning popular patriotism and organizing a mass mobilization in defense of the "homeland." Given the parlous nature of the Putin state, the outcome could easily be a stalemate, which would be tantamount to a victory for Ukraine. Naturally, a defeat would mean Ukraine's loss of Crimea and some southeastern territories to Russia. That would be painful, but it could also consolidate a post-Yanukovych consensus around a breakthrough agenda in independent Ukraine.

Future historians are likely to credit the Yanukovych Ruin with having cleaned Ukraine's slate institutionally and thereby prepared the way for a consolidated democracy and a free-market economy. It took Poland a little more than three decades to become independent after the uprising of 1956. With the acceleration of time in the present age, Ukraine's 1989 may even come in 2015. And then, with a little luck, the country may finally be in the position to join the world.

*

Citizens Derail Oligarch's Mining Development Plans in Ukraine, *World Affairs Journal*, March 1, 2013

Here's more evidence busting the myth of Ukrainian passivity and indifference.

The residents of Kremenchuk, a city of 230,000 southeast of Kyiv on the Dnipro River, and its environs are up in arms over oligarch Kostyantyn Zhevago's plans to build the Bilaniv Mining and Enrichment Combine (HZK) on the Psol River in Kremenchuk District. According to Zhevago's plans, about 12 villages comprising one fifth of the district's territory would have to go to make room for the combine.

Besides opposing the displacement of thousands of villagers, the inhabitants of the region, together with community activists and scientists, fear an environmental catastrophe—ranging from the destruction of the Psol to massive air and water pollution to permanent changes in the area's ecological balance. The specific bone of contention is the "Draft Plan of the Territory of Kremenchuk District" developed by the Urban Construction Division of the local government, the Kremenchuk District Administration. The activists insist that it fails to safeguard the region's environment and must be revised. The bureaucrats and Zhevago people say it's fine.

The 39-year-old Zhevago is worth a few billion and has a growing mining and minerals empire in Ukraine. He controls the "Finances and Credit" group and has been a parliamentary deputy since 1998, usually as a member of the Yulia Tymoshenko Bloc. Most recently, in the October 2012 parliamentary elections, he ran as an independent candidate in the town of Komsomolsk and won 60 percent of the vote. Komsomolsk happens to be the site of one of his plants, the Poltava Mining and Enrichment Combine (HZK).

As Lyudmyla Kucherenko, an environmental activist, president of the Poltava Province Media Club, and critic of Zhevago's plans, says bitterly: "It's unlikely that the oligarch, who lives mostly abroad and views Kremenchuk District as a colony for acquiring large profits from the extraction of resources, will listen to the people or heed the laws that he, as a legislator, approves! It's small wonder that Karl Marx wrote in *Capital* that there is no crime a capitalist wouldn't commit for the sake of 300 percent profits."

Construction of the Bilaniv plant is part of an ambitious plan for Kremenchuk District developed by Ferrexpo, a Swiss-based iron-ore-producing company controlled by Zhevago. Ferrexpo built the Poltava HZK and is currently completing construction of the Yerystiv HZK. Also in the works is the mega-plant, Vorskla-Stal. According to its website, "the management company Vorskla Steel AG is currently managing metallurgical assets in Ukraine, Hungary, and Denmark. Currently our largest asset that is being built is an electric steel plant of direct reduced iron with the use of natural gas in Komsomolsk, Poltava region, Ukraine. ... The capacity of Vorskla Steel plant is 3 million tons annually that is 8–10 percent of production volume of metallurgical branch of Ukraine."

Read the following, also from Vorskla's website, and you'll understand just why local inhabitants are worried (and English-language purists should be aghast):

> As of today 410 000 m^3 of soil has already being taken out, 350 km of drainage trenches have being laid out and filled with 400 000 m^3 of macadam and 2 mln m^3 of sand. In a peak period up to 360 people and 180 pieces of equipment have been working on the site. ... Now project has full support of local authorities and community. Vorskla Steel is a socially responsible company that is why it has started plenty of philanthropic projects, like supporting local school and kindergarten, patronage of local veterans organization. The company cares of cultural and educational development of region, therefore constantly supports organization of ethnic festivals, competitions, and various celebrations. Vorskla Steel is aware that this project is an extraordinary one. There are no analogues in Ukraine, therefore obviously, certain problems and obstacles can occur, but having the team of professionals it successfully overcomes them. The factory will be built on time. And along with development of this project the whole region will be developing.

Extraordinary, perhaps—but the "full support of local authorities and community"? The local authorities for sure, but that's because Zhevago runs Komsomolsk. As to the community, it's pushing back, while the self-satisfied tone of the above paragraph more than lends credence to villager complaints that the developers are running roughshod over the countryside and ignoring their interests.

The push-back has been going on for about two years, and its latest expression was a public demonstration on February 13th before the Kremenchuk District Council and District Administration. (Significantly, right-wing Svoboda activists were there, winning brownie points with the local population.) Holding posters with the following demands—"Hands off our God-given land!" "Shame on the enemies of the environment!" "Poltava Province is the heart of Ukraine: Don't rip out its heart!"—the activists insisted that the draft plan be taken off the council's agenda. Amazingly, the council caved, at least for now.

What's next? Kucherenko isn't optimistic: "There are no guarantees that the oligarchs and venal bureaucrats will abandon their intention to transform the district into a gigantic quarry, while making billions by neglecting the rights of their poor countrymen and women and by mercilessly exploiting natural resources."

Still, Zhevago and the other oligarchs now know that their greed has to be curbed—if only a bit. More important, the people are fired up. They care.

The Ukrainian rock star Skriabin sings an awfully sad song with the following refrain: "My country is a total ruin / How can they detest it so much?" He may be right about much of Ukraine—but definitely not about Kremenchuk District.

*

An Isolated Yanukovych, *World Affairs Journal*, March 15, 2013

A behind-the-scenes powerbroker most people have never heard of has some interesting things to say about the Yanukovych regime and the Regionnaires in a recent interview. The 63-year-old Hennadii Moskal has occupied a variety of highly placed positions in the Ministry of Internal Affairs and the Security Service and has also served as governor of Luhansk and Zakarpattya provinces and as President Yushchenko's permanent representative to Crimea. In a word, Moskal knows both the "power ministries" and the country. He also happens to have been a parliamentary deputy for a few years, most recently having been elected in October 2012 on the democratic-opposition ticket.

Yevgenii Kuzmenko, of the Social Communication website Obkom, interviewed Moskal on January 29th. What, Kuzmenko asks, does Moskal think of the fact that President Yanukovych is appointing "his exclusive little soldiers" to positions of authority?

> I believe that today the president's greatest mistake is to form his team on the basis of their common regional roots. That's the road to nowhere. ... Ceausescu also picked his team on that basis. And as soon as there appeared a revolutionary situation—when Ceausescu was met with shouts of "Down with Ceausescu!" at a meeting—within ten minutes the minister of defense, the minister of internal affairs, and the head of the Securitate ran away. ... The same will happen in Ukraine! Someone will take a pot shot and you'll see how quickly Yanukovych's team will disperse.

But, says Kuzmenko, isn't Yanukovych giving all the important positions to his son's friends so as to avoid the Ceausescu scenario?

> The people he appoints should be moral authorities. Just because they're going to

say something doesn't mean anyone will follow orders! ... You can't appoint only people from Donetsk to the 300,000-strong militia. That's impossible. So they replace the leaders. But are these leaders moral authorities for the rank and file? Of course they're not! Do they provoke annoyance? Of course, they do! ... I speak to these people every day. There's no love for the party and no love for the leaders! The situation in the country is now such that we have people to give orders—the hierarchy has been formed—but there's no one to follow them. And once the situation in Ukraine becomes more complicated, no one will follow orders!

Unfortunately, the interviewer says, the opposition looks weak and powerless.

So do you want the opposition to call for an armed uprising? Are Tyahnybok, Yatseniuk, or Klitschko supposed to climb atop a tank?

So, wonders Kuzmenko, just how is the regime to be removed? By another colored revolution, via elections, or, "heaven forbid," by means of violence?

There are several components here. First, the opposition in today's Parliament is much stronger and much better than in 2007. Second, the economic situation in the country undermines the position of the authorities. And third, the government and presidential administration are sitting on a branch that they themselves are cutting with their incorrect internal and external policies. At some point these three factors will combine to form a powerful mixture. And I can state unequivocally that it's inevitable. ... I understand that people's expectations today are more radical and that society is radicalizing, and that's what they expect from the opposition. I understand that perfectly, but the fruit must ripen. It shouldn't be eaten when it's still green.

Then Kuzmenko shifts the conversation to the power ministries and the Regionnaires. So what's going on in the Security Service?

Believe me, there are no pro-presidential attitudes there. Quite the contrary, there is hidden sabotage and lack of acceptance. But these are people who speak little. They'll share their views only with people they know. ... The country's leaders also overstate the role of the Ministry of Internal Affairs.

Well, asks Kuzmenko, doesn't Moskal think that the recently formed Ministry of Income and Taxes will become the key instrument of repression of the "late Yanukovych epoch"?

But how can you repress someone who has nothing? What will they take from me? My jeans, my jacket, my tie? ... People like me comprise 99 percent of the country. Only 1 percent has something that can be taken. And they are the authorities and the Party of Regions.

So, says Kuzmenko, will they start expropriating their own people?

Who else? They'll do what the Bolsheviks did: steal what was stolen. Who else can you steal from?

The Regionnaires, suggests Kuzmenko, can't be too happy with the current state of affairs in the country.

> Indeed, discontent is very large. They've understood that brute force no longer works. ... Their attitude is defeatist, like that within the Soviet Army in 1941. I know many in the Party of Regions: there are enough smart, literate, and educated people there (it's not true that the Party of Regions consists only of criminals, although it's true that there have never been as many in the party as today). These people look around them and say: "Where is this all leading?" This is no longer the monolithic Party of Regions that came into Parliament in 2007.

Yanukovych must sense that his own cadres are grumbling and could at some point even be tempted to go against him. Why else would the Higher Administrative Court, which consists of Yanukovych flunkies, strip Yulia Tymoshenko's defender, Serhii Vlasenko, and Regionnaire small-fry Andrii Verevsky of their status as parliamentary deputies on the grounds that the law forbids having outside jobs? Yanukovych is signaling to all disgruntled deputies that one false step could lead to their forfeiture of the goodies that come with deputy status. The opposition already knew that, just as they knew that opposition could land them in jail. Now the Regionnaires know it as well. Worse, Yanukovych's Ministry of Income and Taxes can now swoop down on them and seize their assets.

Yanukovych's moves are acts of desperation, and the Regionnaires, who are well versed in the art of treachery, know full well that the new ministry and the court's decision are just signs of the regime's isolation, illegitimacy, and weakness. Now is the time to start looking for ways to jump ship. Of course, Yanukovych knows they know, so expect him to react in the only way he knows how: by accumulating still more power, waving his fists, and retreating into even more complete isolation.

Moskal's final two sentences nicely summarize the condition of the Yanukovych regime:

> Well, since they've gotten into this dead end, it's necessary to find a way out. Instead, they're only making things worse ...

*

Ukraine's Regionnaire Party Panics, *World Affairs Journal*, April 22, 2013

The Regionnaires are panicking. They know they're in trouble and they don't know what to do about it.

On February 28th, the Donetsk provincial leadership met with local leaders. One of them, the mayor of Kramatorsk, Hennadii Kostyukov, informed the assembled big shots of the following:

> Young people use the Internet today. I am more than certain that in no other country, aside from Russia and us, do they write such filth about the first persons of the state.

... They sow mistrust in young people and thereby raise an entire generation of nihilists. ... This is very serious. The year 2015 is before us, and we're losing time.

Kostyukov doesn't get it: the Regionnaires haven't just lost time in the run-up to the 2015 presidential elections. They've lost the hearts and minds of everyone under the age of 50. In particular, Internet-savvy young people—and Donetsk, with its many universities, is full of them—know that the people running the Party of Regions (and, not incidentally, running the Donbas into the ground) just don't measure up. The Regionnaires have lost that constituency and, thus, the battle for the future. Small wonder that, when Kostyukov finished his talk, someone from the audience drew the logical conclusion and cried out: "Kill them all!"

On March 30th, the Donetsk mayor, Oleksandr Lukyanchenko, gave the Donetsk provincial conference of the Party of Regions more bad news:

> Mistakes and difficulties in the economy and the slow pace of reform have disappointed the population and sown popular mistrust of the authorities. The number of our supporters is declining. Some of the center's decisions directly harm urban and rural territorial communities. Thanks to the center's mistakes, the people in our region are suffering.

Ignore Lukyanchenko's wooden bureaucratese, which is typical for old Communist apparatchiks. Consider only that he is accusing the Yanukovych regime of failing its own voters. To be sure, he puts the blame on vague mistakes and difficulties and on "some" of the center's decisions. But Regionnaire ex-Communists know full well that those seemingly anodyne references conceal a blistering criticism of Kyiv's incompetence. And the kicker is, of course, this sentence: "The number of our supporters is declining." When a Regionnaire is forced to admit that his party's hegemony may be impermanent, you can be sure that the situation is dire.

Then, on April 4th, a meeting of the Donetsk provincial council heard one of its deputies, a certain Ordash Dadashov, engage in this complaint:

> After the provincial council voted on drilling for nontraditional gas in the region there was unleashed a campaign of discrediting the members of the Party of Regions who, as provincial deputies, voted for this decision. The Artemovsk city website contained a large portrait of our president and provincial deputies with the caption "Traitors of the Donbas." I ask that you task the appropriate agencies to find out who's behind this. As we approach important electoral events, the Party of Regions and the party's members in the provincial council do not need this.

Dadashov is quite right: the last thing the Regionnaires need is free speech.

That Dadashov's party agrees with him was made evident on April 3rd, when the Press Service of the Party of Regions interpreted an incident in which some of its members were pelted with snowballs in Kyiv as heralding the rise of fascism.

101

The Party of Regions will not ignore this occurrence and demands that the organs of order find these brutes and give an appropriate legal response to their crimes ... Sowing enmity and hatred among Ukrainian citizens, the opposition leaders Tyahnybok, Yatseniuk, and Klitschko are pushing the country toward chaos, thereby satisfying their political ambitions. Promoting fascistically inclined fighters is nothing less than the demonstratively public manifestation of political terrorism and a resurgent neo-Nazism.

Meanwhile, one Regionnaire has decided to jump ship. Valery Konovaliuk, appointed President Yanukovych's adviser in 2010, provided this spot-on analysis of the failures of the regime on his Facebook page in late April:

So there it is! I'm no longer an adviser to the president of Ukraine ... And nothing connects me to the Party of Regions for the last year ... I have nothing to say to Viktor Yanukovych ... All my many statements and comments about the situation in the country, about the disastrous and ineffective economic policy, about the absence of real reforms, about the extent of corruption and abuse, about the low level of executive authority and discipline and much, much more ... What is currently taking place (and I have issued many warnings to this effect) is the direct route to crisis and the country's bankruptcy. It's a complete rejection of the promises and commitments made three years ago, and a betrayal of those who for many years gave their support and believed in the development and blossoming of Ukraine!!!

*

Yanukovych Could Divide and Destroy Ukraine, *World Affairs Journal*, May 24, 2013

Start with the president's overriding strategic interest: survival by reelection. Back in 2010, when he was elected, it was power and wealth. Now, after imprisoning opposition leaders, closing down the free press, and otherwise delegitimizing himself, Viktor Yanukovych wants only one thing: to be reelected in 2015. Not because he has plans for the country. But because he has plans for himself: he knows that the alternative to power is exile or, more likely, jail.

Continue with the fact that the only way Yanukovych can induce anybody to vote for him is by polarizing society. Conclude with the fact that, even if Ukrainian society is transformed into two hostile camps on the brink of civil war, there is still no way that a leader as bad as Yanukovych could ever get elected in a free and fair election. Fraud is therefore inevitable, and a violent crackdown in the aftermath of defeat or mass protest becomes the inevitable Plan B.

So there you have it. In order to stay in power, Yanukovych will almost certainly do the following: first, transform Ukraine into a country consisting of two irreconcilable parts, thereby guaranteeing that it is unstable and ungovernable. And, second, he'll support one side against the other with coercion and, in effect, attempt to rule with martial law.

If that happens, Ukraine's conversion into an authoritarian sultanate will be complete. Worse, since the country's survival and integrity as a state will then depend entirely on Yanukovych and his dubious ruling abilities, it's quite possible that the sultanate will collapse and that either Ukraine will descend into civil conflict or its eastern provinces will be annexed by a Russia fearful of spill-over and mass refugees.

After all, having polarized Ukraine in order to rule it by force, a president of Yanukovych's questionable caliber will never be able to "un-polarize" it, at least not in the short run.

Ukraine's tragedy consists in being misruled by an inept leader and thuggish party that will not relinquish power voluntarily. Western and Ukrainian analysts frequently concoct scenarios of how the opposition might win the elections and return to power. Those scenarios are well and good—and I've spun many of them myself—but their ultimate plausibility rests on one overriding factor: the willingness of Yanukovych and the Regionnaires to abdicate if they lose. Democracy can work only if power-holders who lose elections step down. If they don't, or announce they won't, elections become meaningless rituals, and democracy, along with all hope of democratic change, becomes a pipe dream.

At that point, when systems become clogged and refuse to countenance normal change, "extra-democratic" action becomes virtually inevitable. When regimes become thuggish, they generate thuggish responses: to put it another way, violence begets violence. Perhaps not immediately. If Yanukovych assumes dictatorial control over a divided society, the losers are likely to respond with confusion, apathy, and despair. Very quickly, however, some losers will decide they want to be winners. They'll survey the regime and its forces of coercion and conclude that it's led by an illegitimate leader with only tenuous support among a demoralized army and militia. Other losers will conclude that, having lost it all, they have nothing left to lose. Anomic violence will lead to organized violence and organized violence will destabilize the regime and, in all likelihood, the country itself.

I have no doubt that Yanukovych and the Regionnaires don't care about Ukraine's continued existence as a country several years from now. By then, they will have accumulated enough lucre to be able to live comfortably in Europe. Once le déluge begins, they'll just board their private jets and abandon the country to its fate.

So how is such a dreadful outcome to be avoided? If one can no longer rely on Yanukovych and the Regionnaires to act in the country's interests, then everything will depend on the population, the opposition, and the West. Ukrainians will have to resist Regionnaire calls to split into two warring factions and, instead, recognize that, if they don't hang together, they'll hang separately. The opposition will be able to promote consolidation if it presents itself as a serious democratic alternative with concrete proposals for improving people's everyday lives. Europe can reduce the likelihood of violence by holding its nose and signing an Association Agreement with Yanukovych. Finally, both Europe and America can make sure Yanukovych leaves before the deluge by giving him a place to hang his hat. The West has provided refuge for dictators in the past. Why not for a sullied sultan in the future?

Mugging FEMENist Protesters in Ukraine, *World Affairs Journal*, August 5, 2013

The first attack took place in downtown Kyiv on Wednesday, July 24th, sometime between 10 and 11 at night. Several goons beat to a pulp Viktor Svyatsky, a political sci-entist who serves as adviser to the FEMEN group of Ukrainian women activists, whose bare-chested demonstrations have been a constant thorn in the sides of both the Putin and Yanukovych regimes.

The next attack took place in Kyiv in the evening of Saturday, July 27th. This time, a single goon pummeled FEMEN leader Hanna Hutsol and stole her notebook computer.

One beating might be a random mugging. Two, especially in so short a time span, suggest a pattern that warrants asking two related questions: Who did the beatings? And why?

Given other detentions and beatings taking place during the same period, it seems nearly certain that this is part of a strategy orchestrated by the Yanukovych regime. The same Saturday as the second attack, at around 4 p.m., the Kyiv militia detained three FEMEN activists, charged them with public nudity, and subsequently beat them up. They were fined on Sunday for "petty hooliganism." The FEMENists insist they were clothed when arrested, though they were apparently on the way to a demonstration that would have presumably involved public nudity. So, who's telling the truth? The militia's version is unpersuasive, as the arrest took place far from where the demonstration was scheduled to occur, raising the question—why would the FEMENists have bared their breasts *before* the demonstration?

It's worth mentioning that it would surprise no one if a Putin hack or henchman was involved as well. After all, the Russian president flew down to Kyiv for the celebration of the 1,025th anniversary of the adoption, in 988, of Christianity by the Kyivan prince, Volodymyr (Vladimir in Russian; later canonized). There was a big to-do on July 27th involving the Orthodox Churches, President Putin, and President Yanukovych. And it was that to-do, which FEMEN called "a holy meeting of post-Soviet dictators headed by KGB agents in frocks" (a reference to the disreputable secret-service pasts of the heads of the major Orthodox leaders), that the FEMENists were hoping to disrupt.

Neither Yanukovych nor Putin (nor, for that matter, the Putin-friendly Patriarch Kirill of the Russian Orthodox Church) would have wanted their carefully orchestrated Slavic love-fest to be upstaged by the FEMENists. Both regimes have employed freelance thugs to attack democratic demonstrators in the past, and there is ample reason to think they would do so again. But the attackers could just as easily have been employees of the mi-litia, special forces, or security services of either country. After all, it's an open secret that Russia's spies freely trawl Ukraine and have numerous agents, as well as agents of influence, in the country. The detained FEMENists say the militia told them their per-secutors were members of the Security Service of Ukraine (a charge the service's official spokeswoman denies).

Svyatsky's attackers openly told him that his beating was just a warning to FEMEN to lay off the festivities. When the FEMENists refused to be cowed, it was Hutsol's turn to be beaten, and her colleagues' turn to be detained.

Hutsol believes that both Putin and the patriarch were behind the beatings. As she later told the German broadcaster Deutsche Welle: "This is a continuation of their attempts to intimidate FEMEN ... As fighters for freedom and democracy, we've conducted many ac-tions in Russia and Ukraine against the dictator, Putin, and the growing influence of the Moscow Patriarchate ... The brutality of these latest attacks on us is the personal revenge of Putin and Gundyayev." (Gundyayev is Patriarch Kirill's last name.)

Meanwhile, a few hours before Hutsol was beaten, at a meeting with the heads of the Orthodox Churches, Yanukovych had the temerity to say the following. Try not to gag as you read the full official press release:

> "Ukraine requires restoring Christian values in conditions of modern challeng-es," the President noted. "Challenges and controversies of the modern world are without exaggeration extremely difficult. That's why Ukraine and other coun-tries need restoring of Christian values—foundation of public morality and spirituality," Viktor Yanukovych said at the meeting with representatives of Orthodox churches and heads of church delegations that arrived to Kyiv in order to celebrate the 1025th anniversary of Christianization of Kyivan Rus. The Head of State expressed gratitude to the heads of churches for their efforts aimed at strengthening the unity in the Orthodox world.

That same day, both Yanukovych and Putin also joined the Orthodox church leaders in a "prayer" near Kyiv's St. Volodymyr monument. "After the solemn measures," according to Yanukovych's press office, "the presidents venerated the relics and icon of St. Vladimir."

My heavenly sources tell me that the good prince regrets his choice in 988 and is consid-ering conversion to Catholicism, Judaism, or Islam.

*

Yanukovych Faces EU Integration and History, *World Affairs Journal*, September 23, 2013

It's not every day that a president gets to look history in the eye. It's not every day that a leader must make a choice that will determine both his country's trajectory and his own legacy for decades, perhaps even for centuries. Most leaders at most times just muddle through their years of rule and end up as footnotes or failures in subsequent historical accounts. Many make the wrong fateful choice and thereby doom themselves to infa-my and their countries to disaster. Only few—usually the exceptional leaders—make the right fateful choices.

Given the profoundly unexceptional nature of Viktor Yanukovych's presidency, he has no right to stand face to face with history. He's no George Washington. He's no Charles de Gaulle. He's no Margaret Thatcher. Heck, he's not even Jimmy Carter. And yet, history, like the Lord, moves in mysterious ways, and, lo and behold, it's Yanukovych who, of all people, is in the unique, and uniquely unlikely, position of being able to propel Ukraine into the world.

Nothing in Yanukovych's past suggests that he should be even remotely interested in Ukraine's integration into Europe and eventual membership in the European Union. Ukraine's current president is the product of one of the most Soviet, most Communist, least Western, least European, and least Ukrainian regions in the entire Soviet Union. He should be looking east. Instead—*mirabile dictu*—he's looking west.

Two years ago, when Yanukovych first intimated that he'd pursue EU integration, it seemed like a bad joke or a sly ruse. Now, just a few short weeks before a November summit in Vilnius is supposed to decide whether Ukraine gets to sign an Association Agreement with the European Union, Yanukovych's continued commitment to integration seems to be genuine. Indeed, it's now conceivable that Yanukovych could pull off a Nixon. Just as it took a lifelong anti-Communist to pursue rapprochement with China and end the war in Vietnam, so too it may take a lifelong pro-Russian politician to move Ukraine out of Russia's sphere of influence and into Europe's.

It's highly unlikely that Yanukovych and his entourage care greatly about the Ukrainian population's global integration or about European values. But they understand full well that moving toward Russia and joining the Moscow-led Customs Union means subordinating themselves to Vladimir Putin's fascistoid regime, and subordinating their wealth, as well as that of Ukraine's oligarchs, to the far larger capital resources of Russia's super-rich. Simply put, integrating with Russia means being transformed into the impotent vassals of an underdeveloped thuggish state. In contrast, EU integration means subordinating themselves to the EU's light political touch and inconsistently implemented values, a legal system that won't encroach upon their ill-gotten wealth, and a civilized form of capitalism that is structured according to rules that Ukrainian oligarchs have long since mastered.

Notwithstanding Yanukovych's motives for pursuing westward integration, it's actually a great thing for everybody concerned—for Ukrainians, for Europeans, and for Russians.

Ukrainians will benefit from finally becoming part of a decent, liberal, democratic, stable, and prosperous community, whose decency, liberalism, democracy, stability, and prosperity will progressively rub off on Ukraine. Europeans will benefit from finally having an increasingly decent, liberal, democratic, stable, and prosperous country—which also happens to be one of the continent's largest and geopolitically most important—in their front yard. Russians will benefit from finally having an increasingly decent, liberal, democratic, stable, and prosperous country—which also happens to like Russian language and culture and be unwaveringly supportive of good relations with Russia and Russians—in their back yard.

Unsurprisingly, the only one to kick and shout against Ukraine's EU integration is Russia's President Vladimir Putin, and that's because he's the only loser. Putin's legitimacy as a charismatic fascistoid leader rests on his ability to claim that he, and only he, can reestablish the lost empire, reclaim the Soviet golden age, and restore imperial Russia's place in the sun. None of these promises makes any sense without Ukraine. Seen in this light, the panic, demagoguery, and alarm with which the Putin regime has greeted Ukraine's moves toward Europe smack of desperation—not so much at the prospect of Ukraine's becoming increasingly decent, liberal, democratic, and prosperous (after all, what normal leader wouldn't want all his country's neighboring states to be like that?) as at the prospect of the Russian regime's own looming illegitimacy and instability.

As the Vilnius summit approaches, Yanukovych should remember that the choice he makes will determine how history views him. If he stays the course, addresses the Tymoshenko issue, and opts for Europe, history will probably overlook most of his incompetence and underscore his bold Nixonian move, perhaps even calling it a stroke of genius. If he blinks and opts for integration with Russia, history will remember him as a Putin clone and consign both of them to the ash heap of failed dictators.

*

The EU Faces Ukrainian Integration and History, *World Affairs Journal*, September 27, 2013

After writing last week's blog, "Yanukovych Faces EU Integration and History," I was sorely tempted to write this week's first draft by simply taking last week's text and substituting "European Union" wherever "Yanukovych" occurred. Now, now, you might say, that's no way to treat Europe, which, as everyone knows, is the most "decent, liberal, democratic, stable, and prosperous community" (my words from the blog) in world his-tory. After all, these modifiers don't exactly spring to mind when one thinks of Ukraine's president. Indeed, you might say their opposites do.

Personally, I like Europe: I travel there all the time, study the place, read its literature, and admire its cultures and languages. But—and there is always a "but" after such a grand opening statement—I have no illusions about the European Union. Although it's definitely a "decent, liberal, democratic, stable, and prosperous community," I'm not at all sure it represents, as Lenin might have put it, the "highest stage" in human development. The EU, as anyone who's been to the place knows, is profoundly flawed.

The ongoing crisis in Greece and a few other countries is only the tip of the iceberg. The EU has shown a remarkable capacity to avoid making important decisions—in no small measure due to its cumbersome decision-making rules—and an equally remarkable tendency to rush headlong into world-changing decisions (the fateful introduction of the Euro in 2002 and the 10-country expansion of the EU in 2004 being just two examples). The EU suffers from a "democratic deficit" that has turned many of its own citizens against it. It meddles in everyday life, while lacking anything resembling a strategic vision. And, finally, it and its member states routinely sacrifice the "European values" that supposedly lie at the core of the entire European project on the altar of crude self-interest. A case in point is Europe's relations with Vladimir Putin's fascistoid Russia. Were Europeans—and especially Germans—motivated solely by the lofty ideals of their founding documents, they would have broken off relations with the Kremlin years ago. Instead, those relations thrive.

As hypocritical as that is, it's also perfectly understandable. Despite the rhetoric, all states, all international organizations, and all do-gooding NGOs are motivated by both ideals and self-interest. As well they should be. If human rights and other moral absolutes determined all foreign policy, no one would be on speaking terms with anyone, and the world would not be a better place.

Which brings me to Ukraine, of course, and the question of whether the European Union should sign an Association Agreement with President Yanukovych. The answer is yes, precisely because the EU has been, is, and should be motivated by both human rights *and* self-interest.

Ask yourself this question: Will the human and civil rights of Ukraine's 40 million–plus citizens be better off with or without the agreement, inside or outside the EU's front yard? The answer should be obvious. The agreement will provide Ukrainians with a certain cover, a shield against the predations of the Yanukovych regime. No agreement, in contrast, will mean both the absence of such a shield and, far worse, Ukraine's likely drift into the Putin-dominated Customs Union, where human and civil rights are violated as a matter of course.

Is Yanukovych Ukraine's association with Europe the best possible outcome for human rights? Of course, not. That would be a democratic Ukraine's association with a democratic Europe. But not only is the best the enemy of the good, but the second best is good enough. A few weeks ago, Ukraine's LGBT organizations wrote to Brussels, asking that Europe's visa regime with Ukraine not be liberalized until Ukrainian law guarantees all rights to the LGBT community, on the grounds that opposition to sexual discrimination is an "absolute imperative" of EU laws.

Beware of blithe invocations of absolute imperatives that privilege human rights over humans. According to the absolutist logic of this appeal, no one—including Ukraine's gays—should have the right to travel more easily to Europe until everyone—including Ukraine's gays—enjoy full protection against discrimination. Extend that logic to the Association Agreement and you must conclude that it's better for Ukraine to be consigned to Yanukovych's authoritarianism and Putin's despotic bloc than to be associated with Europe, because Ukraine is not yet fully democratic. If that makes sense to you, please consider cutting off our nose to spite your face ...

Or consider Yulia Tymoshenko, Ukraine's most prominent political prisoner. Should she be freed as a condition of the agreement's being signed? According to the "absolute imperative," yes. Will she be freer if the agreement is not signed? Hell, no. Unsurprisingly,

Tymoshenko supports the agreement. Among other things, she knows quite well that her fate, like Ukraine's, is likely to be far rosier if Brussels has some leverage with Kyiv than if Moscow calls all the shots.

How about self-interest? It's obvious that Ukraine would benefit from an Association Agreement, but would Europe? Once again, the answer is yes.

First, thanks to Vladimir Putin's aggressive neo-imperialism, it's become perfectly clear that failure to sign the agreement will mean that Ukraine will be swallowed up by Russia or the Customs Union, or both. By upping the ante and revealing his intentions, Putin has done everyone, and especially Europe, a great service. One can't pretend any longer that Ukraine will somehow muddle through without the agreement. It won't. Europe's self-interest in all this is obvious. If it feeds Ukraine to Putin, it will encourage an aggressive Kremlin foreign policy that will have immediate destabilizing consequences for the security of the EU's easternmost members—Estonia, Latvia, Lithuania, Poland, Slovakia, Romania, and Bulgaria. So if you want to destabilize the EU, keep Ukraine out. It's that simple.

Second, irrespective of Putin's designs, having a big, geostrategically pivotal state with enormous economic potential on the EU's side is obviously good for the EU's security and, in time, prosperity. There is no scenario in which Ukraine's progressive transformation into Europe's Zimbabwe could be good for Europe. In contrast, an increasingly "decent, liberal, democratic, stable, and prosperous" Ukraine can only enhance Europe's own security, stability, prosperity, as well as decency, liberality, and democracy.

In sum, Europe is facing history as much as Yanukovych is. So let me put the case for human rights and self-interest in a way that Europeans—and especially Germans—may immediately understand. If they want to continue sipping their cappuccinos in peace and quiet, they'll take a moment to look up from their smartphones, stare history in the face, and permit imperfect Ukrainians inside their cafes.

PART TWO
DEMOCRATIC UKRAINE AFTER YANUKOVYCH

The Resilience of Ukrainians, Despite Yanukovych, *World Affairs Journal*, August 30, 2013

Nothing quite lifts my spirits about Ukraine's liberal-democratic prospects like an extended trip to the country. Reading the websites and blogs leaves me feeling pessimistic and bilious. The news is usually bad—Ukraine's journalists know how to dig up the Yanukovych regime's seemingly endless supplies of dirt—and the popular response often seems too anemic: a demonstration here, a flag-waving collection of irate citizens there, and little else. As persuaded as I am that the regime is incompetent, weak, brittle, and doomed, it's sometimes hard to escape the conclusion that, just maybe, it's my hopes and expectations and theoretical schemes that are incompetent, weak, brittle, and doomed.

And then I visit the country and interact with its people and come away feeling that so boorish and cloddish a regime can't possibly survive long when facing so smart and resilient a population.

The most amazing thing about the country is that, after close to 25 years of economic mismanagement and political misrule and despite every effort made by the Regionnaires to thwart the people and sabotage their well-being, many Ukrainians not only manage to scrape by, they're actually doing relatively well. Forget the statistics and take a walk in any Ukrainian city or town. The number of cafes and restaurants, especially in such larger places as Kyiv and Lviv and Odessa, is up to Western standards. And the joints are full, while the prices are anything but dirt cheap. Look at the cars. There are too many to be the sole property of Regionnaire fat cats and oligarchs. Or take a ride on the Hyundai fast train from Kyiv to Kharkiv: the prices are outrageous by Ukrainian standards, but the trains are packed with regular people, and not just shady *biznessmeny*.

Imagine how well the country would be doing if the Regionnaires took a long hike and the mega-intrusive, mega-incompetent, and mega-bloated Ukrainian state bureaucracy were to go on a crash diet. I wager that Helmut Kohl's vision of East Germany's transformation into a "blossoming landscape" might just come true in Ukraine's vast steppes.

Resilience is the key word here. In that sense Ukrainians are exactly like their neighbors, Poles and Jews. You can knock them down, you can beat them up—but they keep getting on their feet and starting all over again. It's small wonder that the oppressors eventually lose. Poles have shown what they can do when given a chance in post-Communist Poland. Jews have done the same in Israel. Give Ukrainians a chance in their own country, and I have no doubt the brain drain out of the country will reverse itself.

I've also concluded that the brain drain from Ukraine is no big deal. So Ukraine has lost a whole bunch of educated people. So what? It's not as if those who've stayed are all dolts and flakes. No less important, ambitious people emigrate all over the world and somehow the world keeps chugging along. Most important, to fixate on the "best and the brightest" is to forget what makes countries thrive. Americans have an obsession with super stars, the super rich, and even superheroes—as if it were they who made countries rich. Not so. In reality, it's the regular folk—the hardworking regular folk—who make countries prosperous, if the institutional conditions are right and if they are allowed to place their shoulders to the grindstones and reap the benefits of their labor. If the conditions are lousy, as they are in Ukraine, no one prospers, neither the superheroes nor the regular folk.

That's why I'm bullish on the country. The supposedly best and the brightest have left and are leaving, the Regionnaires are stealing as if there were no tomorrow, and yet, and yet, the regular folk are managing to live, and some of them are managing to live well. With that kind of resilience, the people can't lose and, with a little luck, this past August 24th may have been one of Viktor Yanukovych's last official celebrations of Ukraine's independence.

*

Yanukovych's Choice, *Foreign Affairs*, November 7, 2013

Ukrainian President Viktor Yanukovych has a decision to make. On November 28–29, Ukraine could sign an Association Agreement with the EU that will expand their political and trade ties, security cooperation, and cultural connections. Success or failure to sign the agreement will not only reshape Ukraine's domestic political landscape; it could force Yanukovych, ever the authoritarian in democrat's clothing, to change too. If Ukraine doesn't sign it, Yanukovych may have to fashion himself as an anti-Western autocrat with a political future bound to Russia. If it does, he just might reinvent himself as a pro-Western national democrat who saved his country by bringing it closer to the EU. Each strategy carries risks, but only the second one promises stability.

The Association Agreement is, according to the EU, "a pioneering document" and "the first agreement based on political association between the EU and any of the Eastern Partnership countries." It focuses on core economic and political reforms while promoting "democracy and the rule of law, respect for human rights and fundamental freedoms, good governance, a market economy and sustainable development," as well as "enhanced cooperation in foreign and security policy and energy." It would create a Deep and Comprehensive Free Trade Area to open up markets and bring trade competition up to EU standards. If Yanukovych signs the agreement at the Vilnius summit in late November, it then will have to be ratified by Ukraine's rubber-stamp parliament and all EU-member state parliaments. But ratification will hinge on Germany, which is uneasy about integrating Ukraine at the cost of antagonizing Russia given its own dependence on Russian gas.

If the agreement is signed and ratified, Ukraine has much to look forward to as part of the most successful and most democratic economic and political association in the world. Over half of the electorate—the pro-Western, pro-Ukrainian, and anti-Soviet electorate in the center, north, and west that regularly votes against Yanukovych—will rejoice at the agreement's passage. But over a third, located in the uncompromisingly pro-Russian, pro-Soviet, and anti-Western regions of Ukraine's south and east that have served as the die-hard base for both Yanukovych and his Party of Regions, will be outraged. Ukraine could suffer some short-term economic distress as European goods flood its markets, domestic production adjusts to the new economy, and unemployment likely increases. Punitive Russian trade restrictions imposed in October 2012 to keep Ukraine from signing the agreement will remain in place. Any chance of lifting them will disappear due to Russian President Vladimir Putin's anger at having lost Ukraine.

But if Ukraine does not sign the agreement, it will be thrown into a geopolitical no-man's land between an indifferent EU (and NATO) and a Russia eager for Ukraine's inclusion in the Moscow-led Customs Union, which consists of Belarus, Kazakhstan, and Russia. By joining the Customs Union, Ukraine could become a permanently underdeveloped supplier of raw materials and low-tech goods to Russia. That might go over well in Ukraine's pro-Russian and anti-Western southeast. But it would incense the rest of the country, which is proudly nationalist, pro-Western, and deeply anti-Soviet and knows that Ukraine's rejection of the West and the promises of greater economic integration would be catastrophic.

Either scenario will put a wrench in Yanukovych's attempt to win the presidency in 2015. In the elections of 2004 and 2010, his strategy was clear: draw on his base, attract disillusioned democrats, and appeal to certain narrow constituencies and special interests such as the country's wealthy oligarchs. And, if that didn't work, falsify the results. In 2004, that strategy only half succeeded, which led to a degree of vote-rigging that sparked popular fury and the Orange Revolution. In 2010, as public disenchantment with the Orange governments of President Viktor Yushchenko and Prime Minister Yulia Tymoshenko deepened, Yanukovych didn't look so bad after all. He applied that strategy and won what international observers called a free and fair election.

But that strategy won't work in 2015. If the agreement is not signed, the pro-Western electorate will have more reason than ever to detest Yanukovych for failing to bring Ukraine closer to the EU. His anti-Western base, meanwhile, will have second thoughts about supporting a man who pushed for integration with Europe, rather than Russia. And rightly so. His supporters in Ukraine's depressed southeast know that they have nothing to lose from integration with Russia. In contrast, Yanukovych and his closest allies, including most of Ukraine's oligarchs, know that a closer association with Putin's Russia would transform them into vassals of the Kremlin. They also know that their power and status would be safe within the EU and its rule of law. Many anti-Western Ukrainians could then drift toward the high-living Stalinist leader of Ukraine's Communist Party, Petro Symonenko, who managed to garner 38 percent of the vote in the presidential elections of 1999.

Without the agreement, the only way for Yanukovych to keep the presidency is to court his own electorate by appealing to its authoritarian values, rig the elections, fully appropriate the autocratic powers that his base admires, and rule with an iron fist. It probably wouldn't be enough to win, however, since his regime lacks the coercive, ideological, charismatic, and material resources that make authoritarianism effective. The army is weak, the police forces are untested, and his regime has no ideological appeal. Yanukovych himself is generally perceived as comical or inept, a mirror of Ukraine's economy, which is perpetually on the verge of default. Meanwhile, Yanukovych's aggression would likely provoke massive civil disobedience from the country's robust civil society organizations and violence from right-wing radicals.

Ukraine would be a very different—and far more stable—place if it signs the EU agreement. The people in Yanukovych's base will abandon him: after all, the agreement contravenes everything they stand for. They'll rush to the Communist Party, and the Party of Regions will be left to struggle as it tries to reconcile its anti-Western sympathies and authoritarian tendencies with Ukraine's turn toward the rest of Europe. If Yanukovych hews too closely to his authoritarian past, however, he'll be doomed politically. EU monitoring will guarantee that he'll lose fair and free elections.

Yanukovych's only path to re-election in this scenario is his own reinvention: abandon his anti-Western values, jettison the intransigent elements within his southeastern base, and reach out to the Orange electorate. Civic and political mobilization is much lower in Ukraine's southeast than in the rest of the country, which should keep the anger of the anti-Western base, and their ability to do anything about it, in check. Russia might threaten intervention in support of its Russian-speaking brethren in Ukraine, but that would probably just be rhetoric; it is unlikely to want to disrupt relations with the EU and the United States, especially in the aftermath of the Sochi Olympics.

Transforming himself into a democrat would be easier for Yanukovych with the charismatic Tymoshenko, currently in jail on political charges, out of the picture. Yanukovych could outflank his democratic opponents, including Arsenii Yatseniuk and Vitaly Klitschko, who do not inspire much faith among voters, given what many consider their lack of principles and their penchant for corruption. Surveys show that Yatseniuk and Klitschko would beat Yanukovych in presidential elections, but mostly because Yanukovych is so unattractive. He could address that problem by trying to change popular perceptions of his rule.

Yanukovych could court Orange voters by embracing the pro-European "civilizational choice" that the Association Agreement represents. Claiming to be more European than his democratic opponents alone won't do the trick. Yanukovych would have to make a few striking personnel changes, take some symbolic steps, and adopt several policy shifts in order to persuade voters that his Europeanism is real.

For starters, he would have to replace the universally detested pro-Russian and pro-Soviet minister of education and science, Dmitri Tabachnik, with someone who has a less jaundiced view of Ukrainian language, history, culture, and identity. Vyacheslav Bryukhovetsky, the former president of Ukraine's most Western-oriented university, the elite Kyiv-Mohyla Academy, comes to mind. Yanukovych would also have to sack the current, ineffective prime minister, Mykola Azarov, and replace him with a moderate technocrat with relatively clean hands, perhaps the multimillionaire confectionary magnate Petro Poroshenko, known as the chocolate king. Or, if Yanukovych really wanted to push the envelope, he could turn to Yatseniuk or Klitschko. The head of the Security

116

Service of Ukraine, Oleksandr Yakymenko, who spent most of his career in the Russian armed forces and is too closely associated with Yanukovych, would have to go, as a sign of changing times.

To show Ukrainians that he's turning a new leaf, Yanukovych should vacate his palatial (and dubiously acquired) residence outside of Kyiv and donate it to the people as a conference center, think tank, foundation, or museum. He could consider moving into an apartment downtown in walking distance of his office, abandoning the traffic-inducing motorcades that rile city residents. Reining in his older son Oleksandr's excesses in the banking world and even encouraging him to go back to dentistry would also impress voters.

Yanukovych would also have to adopt new policies. To cut back on red tape and corruption, he could fire a good portion of the do-nothing state bureaucracy and raise the salaries of the remaining officials. To encourage healthy economic competition and wealth distribution, he could introduce a raft of policies that promote small and medium business and ensure that tenders are competitive. Promoting Ukrainian language and culture on the one hand while guaranteeing the linguistic and cultural rights of Ukraine's ethnic minorities on the other would also underscore his serious commitment to supporting cultural diversity.

None of these measures is too difficult to pursue for an autocrat-president who currently has all the powers he needs to twist arms, distribute incentives, and implement his policy preferences—especially with European support. Still, for Yanukovych, it comes down to a choice. He could transform himself from the president of a minority of Ukraine to the president of most of Ukraine, from an authoritarian detested by most Ukrainians to a democratic leader of all the people, from a source of European embarrassment to a showcase of EU effectiveness. With his political survival on the line, Yanukovych just might make the leap and change. After all, the ultimate survivor in Ukraine's untamed political world already overcame his criminal convictions as a teenager and the disgrace of the Orange Revolution to become president.

*

Ukraine's President Yanukovych Dithers on EU, *World Affairs Journal*, November 14, 2013

It was sometime this week, as I was reading yet another news item about President Viktor Yanukovych's continuing unwillingness to make up his mind about the pending Association Agreement with the European Union, that it struck me. I'm awfully tired—and I mean honest-to-goodness, god-awfully tired—of the guy. It's not that I wish he'd go away (although I do: very much), but that I wish he'd finally make a decision.

No, it's not even that anymore. I've been waiting over two years for him to make up his mind about Ukraine's integration into Europe. And now, just two weeks before the Vilnius summit that will decide Ukraine's future, I can no longer listen, watch, or read about the guy. You see, I suffer from Yanukovych Fatigue.

It's not Ukraine Fatigue: the country and its people remain as interesting as they've always been, and I wish them well. Nor is it Regionnaire Fatigue: my feelings toward Yanukovych's party are better summed up by the term Regionnaire Catarrh. When I see those distinguished gentlemen, I feel the need to clear my throat.

No, it's good, ol' fashioned fatigue. Here's a man who claims to be a Big Decision-Maker, yet he can't make a decision, even one so obviously in his and his country's interests. Associating with the EU is a no-brainer. Associating with the Russia-led Customs Union is an equal and opposite no-brainer. But whatever one's view of either institution, and whatever one's view of the costs and benefits for Ukraine of associating with the European Union or Russia, a real decision-maker, a real leader, someone with a backbone and a strong will, would have made up his or her own mind long ago. Ya wanna go west? Fine. Go west. Ya wanna go east? Fine. Go east. But don't abuse people's patience.

After all, Yanukovych has taken everyone for a long and expensive ride. The Europeans, who have better things to do than to waste their time on tiresome Ukrainian quasi-leaders, must be sick of him. The Russians, who respect strength and will, must wish he'd retire to the Donbas. Ukraine's oligarchs, who need clarity and stability to run their businesses, must be wondering what made them crazy enough to support his run for the presidency. Yanukovych's erstwhile south and east Ukrainian supporters know he's betrayed them by flirting with the EU; Yanukovych's west and central Ukrainian opponents know he's betrayed them by dancing around the Association Agreement. Few Ukrainians could have escaped disappointment by now.

In a way, it no longer matters—for Yanukovych, that is—whether Ukraine and Europe sign an Association Agreement or not. His reputation is shot, along with his credibility, and his continual hemming and hawing have disqualified Ukraine's anti-presidential president from membership in any possible political elite.

Ironically, this is all the more reason for him to go west. A faux-president will always be able to find someone to listen to his stories in Monte Carlo's famed casinos. Perhaps some faded aristocrat, asthmatic princeling, or pretender to a non-existent throne. In Europe, after all, they have a long tradition of tolerating unserious policymakers who still dream of what might have been. Not so in Russia. There, losers have a tendency to wind up in real or imagined Siberias.

But none of that matters to Yanukovych, whose immaturity, indecisiveness, and lack of professionalism have sabotaged the Association Agreement and driven Ukraine into the wilderness of the developing world. He is isolated from reality, isolated from rationality, and now, thanks to his treatment of Yulia Tymoshenko, he is even isolated from his own country and the world. The irony is inescapable. The man who began his political career in jail as a teenage hoodlum is ending it in a golden cage of his own making.

Yanukovych Chooses Russia over EU for Ukraine, *World Affairs Journal*, November 25, 2013

So how are we to interpret the decision by Ukrainian President Viktor Yanukovych, to turn his back on an Association Agreement with the European Union?

The underdevelopment of Ukraine's economy will now be accelerated, as the country becomes even more isolated from that of the world; its population will become significantly poorer. The opposition will become more implacable, more radical, and more intransigent, and its popular support will grow. The polarization within Ukraine between Europhiles and Russophiles will intensify and major civil disturbances are now quite possible, especially in the run-up to the 2015 presidential elections, which Yanukovych cannot possibly win fairly, freely, or even quasi-fairly and freely.

As Ukraine descends into poverty, ungovernability, and instability, what could Yanukovych have possibly been thinking?

Remember that Yanukovych acts on the basis of two simple principles:

- *The absolute imperative of power.* Schooled in the Leninist understandings of politics as a battle between dominants and subordinates ("*Kto kogo,*" or "Who whom," as Lenin put it), Yanukovych believes that loss of power spells capitulation. But, having mismanaged Ukraine for three years, he must also fear that, if he loses power, his successor will imprison him, just as his regime did to the head of the previous government. Finally, a product of Donetsk economics, Yanukovych believes that wealth can be acquired only be means of power.

- *A deep mistrust of liberalism and a concomitant preference for authoritarianism.* Both features flow from his Leninist-Donetsk-style understanding of power and are exacerbated by his inexperience in international relations and apparent distrust of more worldly political figures, especially when they're women (witness his treatment of political opponent and former Prime Minister Yulia Tymoshenko).

Seen in this light, Yanukovych's decision to abort the EU agreement makes perfect sense—for him, that is.

Integrating with Europe would mean that he would have to try to meet Western electoral standards and get reelected cleanly in 2015—which would never work—or make himself attractive enough to Europhile voters to get their votes—which would mean talking and acting like a liberal. Rejecting the Association Agreement makes Yanukovych unelectable on any legitimate basis, but leaves the door open to fraud and coercion, which appeals to his authoritarian impulse. Integrating with Europe would also mean living up to Western judicial standards and releasing Tymoshenko from prison. That was a deal-breaker both because rule of law is anathema to him and because it would have meant losing face by caving in to a woman.

And what of Ukraine's seemingly inevitable decay? Given the principles that underlie Yanukovych's behavior, the country's immiseration, underdevelopment, and instability are good things for him. After all, the weaker and more isolated the country is from the Western world's inconvenient standards, the easier it is to control politically and exploit economically. Now that Yanukovych has donned Leonid Brezhnev's mantle and transformed Ukraine into a stagnant version of the late USSR, expect Ukraine's downward slide, if undeterred, to be purposefully promoted by the regime.

The only silver lining in this cloud is that these same principles will also militate against Yanukovych's joining Vladimir Putin's neo-imperialist pet project, the Customs Union made up of such, er, thriving market economies as Russia, Kazakhstan, and Belarus. Joining the CU would bring Yanukovych and his corrupt operations within the Kremlin's sphere of influence and undermine his power and wealth.

Fortunately, all is not lost. Like all tin-pot authoritarians, Yanukovych thought he could pull a fast one on the people. He was wrong. On Sunday, November 24th, hundreds of thousands of Ukrainians took to the streets in protest against the regime's anti-European moves. The opposition called for the government's resignation and Yanukovych's impeachment. They may or may not succeed this time, but one thing is clear, and Yanukovych must know it. Sooner or later, his regime will come crashing down. The only question is: will the collapse be peaceful or not?

*

What the Mass Demonstrations in Ukraine Mean, *World Affairs Journal*, November 27, 2013

Whatever the outcome of the mass demonstrations that rocked capital city Kyiv on Sunday, November 24th, their meaning is clear. The spirit of the 2004 Orange Revolution is alive and well in Ukraine, and the Yanukovych regime had better watch out.

Some 100,000 to 150,000 Ukrainians assembled in downtown Kyiv to protest the regime's rejection of an Association Agreement with the European Union. (Another 20,000 to 30,000 marched in Lviv on November 25th, and hundreds of Crimean Tatars set out for Kyiv on November 26th.) For them, and for countless others, the agreement represents much more than a trade pact and access to European goods. It was, first and foremost, a "civilizational choice"—an irreversible move by their country toward European democracy and away from Russian despotism. In snubbing the agreement, the regime effectively told Ukrainians that they would never be free and independent.

In mobilizing in Kyiv and other cities, however, the people effectively told Yanukovych and his Regionnaire cronies that they would not accept tyranny. As one journalist put it: "The Sunday events once again demonstrated something that is the object of envy of many residents of Moscow: people in Kyiv are freer. ... They conduct themselves as the citizens of a republic, and not the subjects of an all-powerful tsar."

For several years now, Ukrainian and foreign analysts have been insisting that Ukrainians had become apathetic, passive, and indifferent, and that mass protests would never again take place. There was massive evidence to the contrary: continual demonstrations throughout all of Ukraine, by Ukrainian- and Russian-speaking students, businesspeople, pensioners, veterans, feminists, environmentalists, urban preservationists, and many others. Contrary to the claims of many dispirited analysts, civil society was vibrant, if only one looked closely. Discontent was ubiquitous. Meanwhile, regime predations continued unabated: unjustified political arrests, rampant corruption and outright theft of state property, the falsification of history and the denial of memory, attempts to curb freedom of speech, assembly, and press. The emergence of the Yanukovych "Family," a money-grubbing camarilla centered on the president and his two sons, illustrated just how closely his regime had come to resemble the "socialism in one family" once practiced by Romanian dictator Nicolae Ceausescu, his wife Elena, and their playboy son Nicu.

Seen in this light, the government's rejection of the Association Agreement was the last straw: the spark that mobilized the people and revealed the depths of their hatred of the Yanukovych regime. Some scholars, and many revolutionaries, might call the ensuing condition a "revolutionary situation." And they'd be right to do so. For the first time since Yanukovych's unfortunate election as president in early 2010, his corrupt regime could be toppled (especially if demonstrations acquired renewed force after the EU's Vilnius Summit takes place on November 28th and 29th and Yanukovych fails to backtrack and sign after all). Should Ukraine's president eventually fall, he would have the richly deserved distinction of possibly being the world's only leader to have been humiliated twice by people power.

Of course, it's possible that the demonstrators will be dispersed or that Yanukovych will satisfy their demands by dismissing the Azarov government and signing the agreement at Vilnius. At the moment, the situation is too fluid for the ultimate denouement to be even remotely predictable. But one fact remains indisputable: mass protests on the scale of the Orange Revolution are taking place. The regime now knows that the Ukrainian people's democratic aspirations have not withered and died. It knows that it's lost the hearts and minds of the young (the students of Kyiv's top two universities joined the demonstrators en masse on November 26th) and has no future. It knows that the people want to be free. And the regime knows that they detest it.

Worse for the regime, it has stupidly provided the opposition with the ideal slogan and the perfect brand. Ukraine's democrats are now all Europhiles. Their goals boil down to one word—Europe. Their fears boil down to two—Putin's Russia. Their allies are all people who support Ukraine's European choice. Their opponents are all authoritarians who insist that Ukraine remained mired in its Soviet past and aspire to be a colony of a despotic, neo-imperial, and chauvinist petro-state.

If Yanukovych had welcomed the Association Agreement, he could have positioned himself as Europe's champion. Now, he's defined himself as Europe's enemy. Had he freed Yulia Tymoshenko, as the EU requested, he could have claimed to be magnanimous.

Now that she's declared an open-ended hunger strike on November 25th, he can look, at best, vindictive or weak.

Whichever way you look at it, the regime is rapidly maneuvering itself into a dead-end.

The Ukrainian anthem begins with the words, "Ukraine still lives." Despite the regime's best efforts to transform the population into a mindless rabble, Ukraine's pro-European demonstrators have shown that it's alive and kicking. It's just a matter of time before one of their kicks lands squarely on Yanukovych.

*

Dear President Yanukovych, Resign! *World Affairs Journal*, December 3, 2013

Viktor Yanukovych!

You were elected president of Ukraine in 2010. After several years of ineffective rule by your predecessor, you had a golden opportunity. You could have become president of all the people. You could have committed yourself to promoting the well-being and dignity of the people who elected you. You could have dedicated yourself to setting Ukraine on the path of political and economic reform and European and global integration. You could have promoted democracy, freedom, tolerance, and human rights. You could have served the people selflessly.

Instead, you chose to use your office for your own ends.

Instead of becoming president of all the people, you turned Eastern Ukraine against Western Ukraine and promoted linguistic divisions.

Instead of promoting the well-being and dignity of the people who elected you, you chose to impoverish them, deny their identity, and treat them as chattel.

Instead of dedicating yourself to setting Ukraine on the path of political and economic reform and European and global integration, you created a backward gangster state that fears Europe and the world and everything they stand for.

Instead of promoting democracy, freedom, tolerance, and human rights, you centralized power in your hands, transformed the Parliament into a rubber-stamp institution, jailed your critics, squeezed media and civil society freedoms, inflamed inter-ethnic, inter-confessional, and inter-cultural tensions, promoted extremism, chauvinism, and supremacism, and tried to transform Ukrainians from citizens to subjects dependent on your power and whim.

Instead of serving the people selflessly, you and your family amassed fabulous wealth and, as people's living standards dropped precipitously, flaunted it shamelessly.

You betrayed the people's trust. You violated their confidence. You dashed their hopes and expectations. You transformed yourself from a defender of the people to a predator on the people. You once had legitimacy. Now you have none.

In losing all legitimacy, you transformed yourself from a president who promotes the people's interests with the authority vested in his office by the Constitution to a power-holder who serves his own interests with the knout.

Rule by the knout is ineffective, inefficient, and unstable. It never lasts—especially when the citizens you degrade refuse to be treated as chattel.

You should not be surprised that they have risen up against you, the system you built, and everything you represent.

All Ukrainians, regardless of their linguistic preferences, want dignity, freedom, democracy, and human rights. They desire to live normal lives in a normal country free from the predations of venal power-holders who know only how to swing the knout.

In marching in the streets of Kyiv, Lviv, and other cities, Ukrainians have demonstrated that, after three years of your predations, they have not lost their spirit, dignity, and desire for freedom. They have shown that you have lost and that your attempt to build a gangster state has failed.

Permit me to inform you that they have demoted you from president of Ukraine to the provisional occupant of the presidency of Ukraine.

You should act accordingly and resign.

The fact of the matter is that you have maneuvered yourself into a hopeless position. You have no allies in the world. You have minimal support in Ukraine. The economy is on the verge of collapse. The government is ineffective. Your regime is cracking. Your rule is evaporating.

You know better than anyone that violence is not an option. The army and militia are unreliable, the internal troops are untested, and the special forces are too few. Do you really want to risk provoking a civil war that could destroy the country and that you will not be able to win?

Reform is still an option, and it just could restore some of your legitimacy, but your personal stubbornness and unwillingness to countenance concessions close off hat route.

Even if, by some miracle, you succeed in dispersing the demonstrators demanding your resignation, Ukraine will become ungovernable, you will be reviled, and your rule will be doomed.

The choice before you is simple: resign now with dignity and guarantees of security or resign later without dignity and without guarantees of security.

Ukrainians have made their choice: they want you to go.

Now make yours.

*

Ukraine's Multiple Crises, *World Affairs Journal*, December 6, 2013

If current conditions in Ukraine look revolutionary to you, that's because the Yanukovych regime has maneuvered the country and itself into a series of reinforcing crises. If the regime holds on to power, the crises will only deepen. If the opposition comes to power, with or without Regionnaire participation, it will face monumental tasks requiring almost superhuman wisdom and skill. In a word, whatever the denouement of the ongoing standoff between opposition and regime in Kyiv, Ukraine will be a mess for some time to come.

Crisis is a sexy word that means all things to all people, but, if used rigorously, it usually means a life-threatening condition, one in which, to pursue the medical analogy, the patient faces a 50–50 chance of recovery. It's impossible to apply the word with equal precision to social reality, but the point is that we should use crisis only with reference to extremely serious conditions that appear to be unsustainable for more than the short term.

Seen in this light, the Yanukovych regime has created three crises: a crisis of the regime, a crisis of the economy, and a crisis of presidential legitimacy. Significantly, all three are the result of the system of centralized rule Yanukovych introduced, or what I have called sultanism.

As I have repeatedly argued in this blog, sultanism is intrinsically unstable:

> Yanukovych quickly accumulated vast powers, thereby transforming the presidency into a near-dictatorial office, while subordinating the other two branches of government—the Parliament and the courts—to himself and his party. ... Given the evisceration of the non-presidential branches of government and the emergence of the Regionnaires as the party of both power and theft, it was inevitable that Yanukovych would become the focus of increasingly personalized rule, while his closest confidantes would join him in plundering the country. The logical end point of this institutional development was reached in 2012: the triumph of Yanukovych and his "Family," the reduction of the Rada and the courts to meaninglessness and buffoonery, and the transformation of the Party of Regions into nothing more than an instrument of rapine. Because sultanistic regimes are invariably corrupt and conservative, there is no reason to think that the avaricious mediocrities who man the Yanukovych system will be able or willing to sacrifice their well-being to vague notions of reform, especially if reform undermines their power and privilege. ... [S]uch a deeply dysfunctional regime is a leading candidate for stagnation and decay.

Sultanism is also responsible for the economic crisis, which is best described by Anders Aslund:

> Rather than following its commitments to the IMF, the Ukrainian government has imposed strict currency regulations to make it exceedingly difficult to take money out of the country. It has also pursued very high interest rates. ... The high interest rates have kept inflation at zero, but they have also killed investment and thus liquidated economic growth. Output has fallen for the last five quarters. The expected contraction for 2013 is now 1 percent, but it might become 1.5 percent.

> It is difficult to imagine a worse economic policy. ... Why would any government pursue such a harmful and mindless economic policy? The simple answer is that it benefits the ruling "family" and its closest friends. Previously unknown individuals, who are presumed to be connected with people at the top, have taken over a large number of private companies at low prices. The worse the economic situation is, the cheaper Ukrainian companies become for these selected buyers ...

> Yanukovych is walking on eggshells. Ukraine's economic situation is precarious. The risk for a run by ordinary Ukrainians both on banks and the Ukrainian currency is evident, though Ukraine has been on the brink for so long that no panic is apparent. The rating agencies mercilessly downgrade Ukraine ever lower, and corporate defaults are all too common. Ukraine is in desperate need of an IMF agreement, but Yanukovych has recently firmly rejected any (necessary) increase in domestic gas prices, and it should depreciate the hryvnia in any case.

Finally, sultanism is responsible for the evisceration of Yanukovych's legitimacy. Having arrogated to himself all the state's powers, Yanukovych, unsurprisingly, proved incapable of meeting popular expectations. No one can be a sultan in today's complex world. And least of all is a provincial politician with no understanding of politics and economics able to play that role.

In sum, the Yanukovych regime, the Ukrainian economy, and Yanukovych himself are in crisis. The only things in Ukraine that are not in crisis are civil society and the political opposition, which have been getting progressively stronger in the three years since their partial demobilization in the aftermath of Viktor Yushchenko's disastrous administration.

Small wonder that this "Euro Revolution" has broken out. On the one hand, there's a crisis-ridden president, regime, and economy. On the other hand, a vigorous civil society and opposition. Look at any historical revolution and you'll find these same ingredients present.

Given the severity of this contradiction, do not discount the possibility of a regime collapse. There are ample precedents for just such an outcome. Also possible is a "managed transition," involving regime and opposition, or a protracted standoff that intensifies the political and economic crises and makes Ukraine ungovernable and ripe for another mass uprising. Least likely is a Pinochet-like crackdown: crisis-ridden regimes lack the resources to pull off uch feats.

Which outcome will produce a government most capable of dealing with Ukraine's multiple crises?

Obviously, both a protracted standoff and a crackdown would only push Ukraine to the brink of systemic collapse.

Since Yanukovych and the Regionnaires caused the crises, their absence is probably the necessary condition of any sustained attempt at resolution. The sufficient condition is, of course, the ability of the democratic opposition to eschew cheap populism and promote wise policies. In principle, that's possible. Riding on a wave of popular support, they could have the legitimacy to introduce painful measures that the people would be willing to accept. After the disaster of Orange rule, the opposition may have also learned a thing or two about effective policymaking. The problem with this scenario is that, rightly or wrongly, most Ukrainians have little regard for their opposition leaders—which might incline them to engage in the very populism they need desperately to avoid.

Since Yanukovych and the Regionnaires will be unwilling to leave the scene voluntarily, a managed transition and the formation of a coalition government will be more palatable to them. On the other hand, Regionnaire involvement in policymaking could easily doom new plans to ineffectiveness. After all, how likely are they to agree to the dismantling of the sultanistic system that feeds them (even though it created the crises)? That in turn means that such a government could work if and only if the Regionnaires were to be assigned a distinctly secondary role in policymaking. And that could happen only if the West, the opposition, and the people left hem no choice.

There is, then, no easy way out of the Yanukovych-induced mess. But, for the first time in many years, there is hope in Ukraine. And for Ukrainians, who have had to live with the prospect of continued regime predations, that may be the most important thing.

*

Lenin's Final Fall in Kyiv, *World Affairs Journal*, December 10, 2013

Whatever the outcome of the ongoing "Euro Revolution" in Ukraine, future historians will view the destruction of the Lenin statue in downtown Kyiv as a milestone in the country's move away from its Soviet past and Regionnaire present.

Vladimir Illich Lenin was a brilliant polemicist and strategist who arguably made the Bolshevik Revolution. But he was also a tyrant who countenanced, encouraged, and committed what we would today call massive crimes against humanity. Regardless of whether or not Leninism directly led to Stalinism, Lenin and Leninism made Stalin and Stalinism possible and, indeed, likely. No country claiming to be civilized would honor mass murderers in one of the most visible and central parts of its capital city. Until the evening of December 9th, Ukraine did.

The young Ukrainians who tore down Lenin were acting in the spirit of anti-regime protesters the world over. Hungarians felled a huge Stalin statue during the Revolution of 1956. Russians toppled a monument to Feliks Dzerzhinsky, the bloodthirsty founder of the Bolshevik secret police, in 1991. And Iraqis destroyed a statue of Saddam Hussein in 2003. Like the Iconoclasts in the Byzantine Empire, rebels and revolutionaries understand that symbols can sustain oppressive regimes as much as violence.

Lenin's felling may mark a caesura in Ukrainians' self-understanding. Having been victimized by two world wars, a genocidal famine, and decades of totalitarianism and imperialism, many Ukrainians developed a range of survival mechanisms that rested on self-abasement and self-denial. The marble Lenin guarding the intersection of Shevchenko Boulevard and Kyiv's Broadway, the Khreshchatyk, was a permanent reminder of their servile status. With Lenin smashed to pieces, all Ukrainians are now free to reinvent themselves as empowered human beings capable of deciding their own fates.

The contrast between how many Ukrainians already view themselves and how the regime still views them was best captured by the mayor of Viktor Yanukovych's home town, who assured a small group of regime supporters that "Big Daddy [Yanukovych] will never betray his children." As the "father of the revolution," Lenin was of course the ultimate Big Daddy. His departure paves the way for the current Big Daddy's departure.

The Ukrainians taking part in the Euro Revolution already consider themselves to be rational adults with no need of any Big Daddy's solicitude. In marching, protesting, and demanding their rights as human beings, they are explicitly demonstrating that they have broken with the subaltern psychology that helped keep Communist and post-Communist tyrants in power.

It is especially fitting that Lenin's fall should have taken place just two weeks after Ukrainians commemorated the 80th anniversary of the Holodomor, the famine-genocide that took the lives of millions in 1932–1933. If anything broke the people's spirit and reduced Ukrainians to serfs, it was the Holodomor. A mass murder is bad enough. But no less debilitating for the survivors was that they were not only compelled to deny that the famine had ever taken place. For several generations, they were also forced to glorify its perpetrators. It's as if Jews had to deny the Holocaust and praise Hitler, Himmler, and Goebbels. Whatever the psychological consequences of living in such a twisted world, they cannot have been good.

Although it was Stalin, and not Lenin, who engineered the Holodomor, Lenin's felling on December 9th opens the door to a full-scale national psychological convalescence. Most Ukrainians now recognize the Holodomor as genocide; in so doing they are finally coming to grips with the trauma it produced. Now that Lenin is gone from downtown Kyiv, Ukrainians are in the position to state that no Big Daddy, whether on the left or on the right, will ever again determine their fates.

Yanukovych Must Go, *Foreign Affairs*, December 11, 2013

For the second time in nine years, anti-regime protesters have filled the streets of Ukraine. But now, the stakes for the European Union and the United States have risen. Ukraine's latest political upheaval, which pro-European protesters have dubbed the Euro-Revolution, began in late November when President Viktor Yanukovych rejected a long-awaited agreement to boost political and trade ties with the EU. Demonstrations exploded after riot police brutally attacked protesters camped out in Independence Square, the site of the 2004 Orange Revolution, on November 30. Within a week, mass protests demanding Yanukovych's resignation spread across the country. Several hundred thousand marched in Kyiv, while mostly young activists set up barricades around government buildings and knocked down a statue of Lenin.

Mykola Azarov, Ukraine's prime minister, called the peaceful demonstrators in Kyiv "Nazis" and compared the statue's toppling to the Taliban's destruction of the giant Buddhas of Bamiyan in Afghanistan in 2001. European Commission President José Manuel Barroso, meanwhile, praised the "young people in Ukraine's streets" for "writing a new history of Europe." The demonstrators' slogan ("Ukraine is Europe!") signifies much more than a desire to join the EU. For them, as for most Ukrainians, Europe is a symbol of democracy, national dignity, human rights, and freedom—everything they believe, correctly, the Yanukovych regime opposes.

Although much of the world has focused on the demonstrations in Kyiv, anti-regime discontent is hardly limited to the capital. Opposition channels, Web sites, and social media have broadcast continuously from Independence Square or the Euromaidan ("Eurosquare" in Ukrainian), providing accurate information and countering the slanted reporting of regime-controlled and Russian sources. Several journalists have even resigned from Ukraine's First National TV station in protest. Up to 50,000 Ukrainians have marched repeatedly in Lviv, where the elite Berkut police units pointedly refused to intervene. In the west, the Europe-leaning officials who run the Ivano-Frankivsk, Lviv, Ternopil, and Volyn provinces have effectively escaped the regime's control.

Demonstrations have even erupted in the country's south and east, long the home of Yanukovych's traditional support base. Sensing danger, his ruling Party of Regions has called emergency sessions in two formerly quiescent eastern cities, Kharkiv and Luhansk, in order to nip homegrown anti-regime sentiments in the bud. In Donetsk, Yanukovych's stronghold, the authorities had to cancel a pro-regime demonstration when it became clear that the turnout would be embarrassingly small. In Yenakievo, Yanukovych's hometown, the mayor assured nervous regime supporters that "Big Daddy"—Yanukovych— "will never betray his children."

Since it lost the battle for hearts and minds very early, a desperate regime bared its teeth. In the early hours of December 11, Berkut units assaulted the Euromaidan, but protestors held their positions and the police retreated after daybreak. As opposition leaders called on Ukrainians to march on Independence Square, Assistant Secretary of State Victoria Nuland handed out food to protesters, after Catherine Ashton, the European Union's foreign policy chief, visited the square. In a statement, Secretary of State John

Kerry expressed "disgust" with the Ukrainian authorities' use of "riot police, bulldozers, and batons" against peaceful protesters. "This response is neither acceptable nor does it befit a democracy." Yanukovych proved, yet again, that he only speaks the language of force and cannot be trusted.

Even if the regime eventually disperses the Euromaidan protesters, the crisis is far from over. Mass demonstrations will likely continue; protesters can encamp in another square in Kyiv. The Yanukovych regime will remain weak and popular opposition will remain strong. Lacking legitimacy and economic resources, the regime will rest on force and be viewed as an occupying power. And occupation always provokes resistance. The pro-European protesters know something that Yanukovych and his cronies still cannot comprehend: that Ukraine's only path to stability and prosperity is democracy.

The Message from the Maidan

Although Yanukovych's decision to spurn the Association Agreement with the EU sparked the Euro-Revolution, its underlying causes run much deeper. In his three years in office, Yanukovych has created a dysfunctional system of sultanistic rule, concentrating power in his less-than-able hands and turning the government and parliament into rubber-stamp institutions. He has eviscerated the courts, joined forces with Ukraine's richest oligarch, Rinat Akhmetov, and used his Party of Regions as a vehicle for self-enrichment. The result is an ineffective, incompetent, and corrupt government apparatus that systematically ignores popular needs and violates human and civil rights.

Beyond that, the protests have also exposed three truths about Ukraine. First, the emperor, Yanukovych, has no clothes and everybody inside and outside Ukraine now knows it. It is no longer possible to claim, as many observers have for years, that his regime is benign and that he has a democratic mandate. Quite the contrary, he has lost all legitimacy. Second, Ukrainians are not, as was frequently asserted in the last few years, apathetic and indifferent to their fate, to democracy, and to freedom. They want to run their lives without Yanukovych's paternalistic interference in a way that accords with what Europe represents. Third, Ukrainians will not submit to the predations of an authoritarian regime. They rebelled in the late 1980s against Soviet rule. They rebelled in 2000–2001 against the authoritarianism of President Leonid Kuchma. They rebelled in the 2004 Orange Revolution against Yanukovych's falsification of presidential elections. And they rebelled in the 2013 Euro-Revolution against Yanukovych's sultanism. They will continue to rebel as long as sultanism exists.

If the Yanukovych regime survives the current crisis intact but refuses to change its ways, Ukraine will be ungovernable: the regime will continue to stagnate, the already slumping economy will go into freefall, Ukrainian civil society and the democratic opposition will grow stronger, and pro- and anti-regime radicals will mobilize. Another rebellion will be all but inevitable. And that will bring violence, especially if a desperate regime miscalculates and cracks down on civilians, provoking a counter-response.

Yanukovych has no future in such a Ukraine, with nothing positive to offer a population that knows that its poverty and degradation are the direct result of his malfeasance. Nor does he have the coercive resources to reestablish stability in a country the size of France by force. The army is decrepit, the internal troops untested, and the elite riot police number only several thousand. Even Russia cannot save him. Billions of dollars of credits and lower gas prices may reduce the budget deficit and keep gas prices down, but they will do nothing to address the sources of the current crisis. Yanukovych's chances of winning the 2015 presidential elections fairly and freely are nil, and electoral falsification will produce another popular uprising. Yanukovych is in no less of a crisis than the system he built.

The only stable solution to Ukraine's state of permanent revolution is a democratic government. Only it would have the legitimacy and popular support to dismantle an authoritarian, crony system, take on corruption, embark on painful reforms, and turn Ukraine toward Europe and the world. Yanukovych still had a chance to become a reformer before he rejected the EU agreement; he may not get it again. At some point, it will be up to the democratic opposition to try its hand. When that time comes, it will have to avoid the post-revolutionary Orange government's mistakes—the failure to develop a clear reform agenda and lines of authority within the new government—and follow, instead, the path of post-Communist reformers in Estonia, Lithuania, and Poland who quickly adopted painful economic reforms, streamlined their government bureaucracies, and willingly borrowed ideas and personnel from the West. When Ukrainian democrats extend a hand to the West, the European Union and the United States would do well to reciprocate.

As Ukraine Goes

Ukraine's descent into instability might not matter if it were a tiny country tucked away in some corner of Eurasia. But today, as much as at independence in 1991, Ukraine matters precisely because it is a pivotal state, populated by 45 million people, that borders both Europe and Russia. Ukraine's independence is, as former National Security Adviser Zbigniew Brzezinski has repeatedly argued, a guarantee of Russia's non-imperial future and Europe's security. An unstable Ukraine could produce instability next door, in Hungary, Poland, Romania, Slovakia, and the Baltic states. In contrast, a stable, democratic, and prosperous Ukraine will reinforce stability in both Europe and Russia, two key U.S. interests.

None of this is new. Ukrainian and Western analysts have well understood Ukraine's potential role in the region since 1991, but few policymakers listened. After the Orange Revolution in 2004, President Viktor Yushchenko's government hoped for a quick rapprochement with the EU, but Brussels stayed silent. Germany, the EU's power holder, was loath to disturb relations with Russian President Vladimir Putin (Chancellor Gerhard Schröder even called Putin a "true democrat" at the height of the Orange Revolution). But with the Orange government's descent into perpetual squabbling, the EU finally appreciated its strategic interest in the countries of the former Soviet Union and developed the Eastern Partnership, which was supposed to culminate in the Association Agreement. This time Kyiv, responding to Putin's sticks and carrots, turned its back on Europe and ignited the Euro-Revolution.

Although a weak, unstable, stagnant, and authoritarian Ukraine cannot be in the interest of a democratic Russian state, it suits Putin just fine. Having amassed vast powers, Putin needs to bring former Soviet territories under Moscow's umbrella to bolster his legitimacy at home and project newfound Russian strength abroad. The strategy has been heavy-handed. Putin's adviser Sergei Glazyev warned that borders could be revised in case Moldova and Ukraine signed the Association Agreement, spurning Russia. Equally aggressive are Putin's pursuit of a Customs Union with Belarus and Kazakhstan (and, if it joins, Armenia) and his promotion of a plan to create a Eurasian Union to supersede the mostly defunct Commonwealth of Independent States. Neither scheme makes much economic or political sense in a globalized world. But, in transforming their non-Russian member states into Russian appendages, both would serve Putin's ideological interests. The very last thing Putin wants is a successful revolution in Ukraine that would energize and inspire Russia's democratic opposition.

Massive human rights violations and the collapse of Ukraine's democratic potential should trouble all Europeans and Americans. An economic basket case on the EU's eastern border will produce huge numbers of labor migrants and refugees. An ungovernable Ukraine will not be a reliable transit country for the large amounts of natural gas that flow from Russia to Europe. A stagnant authoritarian regime that generates periodic mass uprisings could at some point provoke a civil war or, not inconceivably, result in state failure. Permanent instability may even tempt Putin to consider military intervention along the lines of Georgia, unleashing a wider conflagration.

Asked how they think the West can support their democratic aspirations right now, most Ukrainians say that Europe and the United States should squarely tell Yanukovych that a violent crackdown and a refusal to negotiate would have two immediate consequences. First, the West will take advantage of the Magnitsky Act, the 2012 U.S. law that bars Russian officials from traveling to the United States and accessing their U.S. bank accounts, and impose travel bans on top Ukrainian officials and their families. At the same time, visa restrictions could be loosened on ordinary Ukrainians. Second, Europe and the United States will freeze the billions of dollars of illegally acquired assets held by Yanukovych's inner circle and their cronies in the West.

Ukrainians understand that these measures will not dismantle Yanukovych's broken system: that is their job. But such measures would send a powerful signal to Ukraine's democratic forces and provide the regime with incentives to lessen its exploitation of the population and its repression of the opposition, take round-table negotiations seriously, and perhaps even agree to new elections or a coalition government. Should the regime come to its senses, Ukrainians hope that Europe will leave the door open to an Association Agreement. Should the regime collapse, Ukrainians know that continued Western support of Ukrainian democracy will be critical to its survival. Above all, the United States and Europe will have to appreciate that their own interests require denying Putin his neo-imperial hopes for a weak Ukraine.

But even with their vital interests at stake in Ukraine, it remains to be seen whether Washington and Brussels understand that if they do too little to support Ukrainians in the streets now they will have to deal with far more instability later. U.S. and European officials have told Yanukovych to refrain from violence. Most Ukrainians would argue that, however positive, such vague admonitions without a clearly stated "or else" will have no impact on a brutal regime concerned only with power and self-enrichment.

*

Watching Yanukovych's Mafia Regime Squirm, *World Affairs Journal*, December 20, 2013

It's been fun watching the Yanukovych regime squirm these last few weeks. Ukraine has exploded with the Euro Revolution. The world is in awe of the tenacity, spirit, nonviolence, and democratic ideals of the demonstrators. The United States has openly threatened the regime with sanctions. The European Union has expressed its displeasure. The people hate President Yanukovych and openly treat him as a buffoon.

And if that weren't bad enough, the regime even failed to mobilize a mass demonstration in its own support on the weekend of December 14th and 15th. People were paid 300 hryvnia (about $37) and/or threatened with dismissal from their jobs. The regime had all the buses and trains it needed at its disposal. And instead of the 200,000 who were supposed to descend on Kyiv, something like 10,000 to 20,000 showed up. They stood around for a few hours and then rushed for the exits. Contrast that laughably small turnout with the hundreds of thousands who've voluntarily marched against the regime four weekends in a row.

If you've ever wondered what an emperor with no clothes looks like, look at Yanukovych.

The emperor hasn't just been exposed as a weak and desperate tyrant; worse: he's cornered. No one likes him; no one trusts him—neither inside nor outside Ukraine. So, what's a cornered emperor to do? There are two ways of reacting to such a predicament. The smart way is to evaluate how you got there, correct your mistakes, and seek a way out. The stupid way is to revert to all the instincts that got you cornered in the first place.

Guess which path the Yanukovych regime has chosen?

Might the regime consider offering the opposition a compromise, if only as a devious means of splitting it? Of course, not. The Yanukovych camarilla refuses to make any concessions whatsoever. The government must stay. Prime Minister Azarov must stay. And all talk of political alternatives is treason. Basta.

How about engaging the opposition in an honest dialogue? Are you kidding? Azarov called the peaceful demonstrators Nazis, while Yanukovych convened a round table, ostensibly with the opposition, but made sure to pack it with his acolytes. And the authorities have begun investigating individual democratic activists, including the winner of the 2004 Eurovision Song Contest, Ruslana Lyzhychko.

Might the regime tone down its mendacity? Well, you know the answer. The Regionnaire deputy party boss in Parliament has called US Senators John McCain and Chris Murphy, who visited Kyiv on December 14th and 15th, "extremists." Five local elections were also held that weekend and—surprise!—the regime unabashedly employed its usual shenanigans.

Might Yanukovych, who runs everything, at least take some responsibility for the brutal-ity of his own riot police? No way. Yanukovych had the chutzpah to suggest that police and demonstrators were equally responsible for the violence. (And you can appreciate his logic: after all, if the protesters' heads weren't in the way, police clubs would have swung harmlessly through the air.) Then he tried to foist all the blame on three subordinates. When one of them accused national security adviser Andrei Klyuyev, an oily man who's never refrained from employing the perks of office to pursue the just cause of self-enrich-ment, of having given the orders, the procurator's office stepped in and absolved Klyuyev of wrongdoing.

Many years ago, when I was still in grad school, one of my professors said, "All these elaborate political science models of Soviet politics miss the point. The best model is the mafia." He was right about the Soviet Communist Party then and he would have been equally right about the Yanukovych regime now. As Rajan Menon of New York's City College says about Yanukovych, he is "id-driven." Like any capo, he understands only force, greed, and fear.

How would a mafia boss respond to popular protests? Exactly in the manner of Yanukovych. He'd snarl and bang the table and fly into a rage and lie, lie, lie. Oh, and continue stealing—just to be on the safe side. Anders Aslund of the Peterson Institute for International Economics estimates that "embezzlement and corruption alone have probably generated $8 billion to $10 billion a year to the 'Yanukovych family' during the last three years."

And if snarling didn't work, the don would go to the *capo di tutti capi*—Russia's Vladimir Putin—with hat in hand. Don Vlad apparently promised Yanukovych $15 billion in cred-its and a 33 percent reduction in the price of gas. The billions should save Yanukovych from looming default; the price decrease will line the pockets of Regionnaires and their oligarch pals. Meanwhile, the deal will guarantee that the Ukrainian economy will con-tinue to spiral downward and be at the mercy of the regime's predations.

And don't be so certain that Putin will hand over the dough just like that. Russia's econ-omy is projected to be stagnant for the next 5 to 10 years, and easy money isn't that easy anymore. Besides, Putin's own fortune is, according to the New School's Nina Khrushcheva, $40 to 70 billion. The fella knows the value of a hard-earned buck and is unlikely to shower a lazybones like Yanukovych with limitless lucre. He'll attach so many strings that Yanukovych will be reduced to a puppet and Ukraine will be reduced to an underdeveloped colony with an exploited population determined to drive the camarilla from power.

Buoyed by his capitulation to Putin, Yanukovych has staved off humiliation for a while.

His back is still to the wall, and he still has no idea of how to extricate himself from the mess he created. So expect him to continue promising the world, accelerating his "family's" plundering of the economy, and trying to wear down the opposition by means of attrition and targeted repressions. Since most of the population detests him, do not expect the opposition to buckle under. Meanwhile, the risk for Yanukovych is obvious. The longer he stands in that corner with no clothes, the more likely will his increasingly desperate henchmen start squirming and looking for alternatives. Once pro-regime rats start jumping ship, you can say "*hasta la vista*, baby" to the emperor.

In the weeks ahead, Ukrainians, their friends in the world, and especially Don Vlad would do well to remember two things. (1) Never believe anything Yanukovych says or signs. (2) Always expect him to stab you in the back.

As the saying goes, you can't teach an old thug new tricks.

*

Rethinking the Euro Revolution and the Yanukovych Regime, *World Affairs Journal*, December 25, 2013

The Euro Revolution and the Yanukovych regime's shameful deal with Putin's Russia are as momentous conceptually as they are politically, requiring a new way of thinking about what has transpired in Ukraine and how Ukraine may be best understood. Now more than ever, as the regime attempts to redefine reality according to its twisted Orwellian categories, calling things by their rights names is imperative. Here's a brief primer. The key terms are: *declaration of independence, social contract, freedom, legitimacy, tyranny, occupation, colony, resistance movement*, and *national-liberation struggle*.

First, in taking part in mass anti-regime demonstrations for more than five weeks, Ukrainians declared that the Yanukovych regime was ruling without their consent and was therefore illegitimate. In effect, Ukrainians made a *declaration of independence* from the regime, using the same logic (and oftentimes the same language) employed by American revolutionaries in 1776. Because Yanukovych systematically abused the Ukrainian people, neglected their interests, and violated the *social contract* between democratically elected rulers and the people who elected them, he ceased to be their "sovereign." Once the sovereign turns against the people and acts tyrannically, he transforms himself into a usurper and the people are no longer obligated to obey him. Indeed, like the American revolutionaries, they have both the right and the obligation to defend themselves from his predations.

Second, in standing up for their rights, Ukrainians demonstrated to themselves, to the regime, and to the world that they are free and will fight for that *freedom*. The demonstrations began as protests against the government's decision to snub the European Union; but they quickly morphed into assertions of the dignity and autonomy of the self. Now that Ukrainians have freed themselves from the fear, impotence, and self-denigration that many decades of Communist and post-Communist despotism promoted, there is no going back. Free Ukrainians—and they are now a majority of the country—have also sent a clear signal to the regime: that the Euro Revolution is only the first stage in what is likely to be a protracted struggle to replace an illegitimate regime with popular sovereignty.

Third, in violating the people's trust, Yanukovych lost all the democratic *legitimacy* he had acquired in the 2010 presidential election. Some analysts continually invoke Yanukovych's democratic election as if it were an unconditional mandate. It is anything but. A democratic election is not a mandate to abuse the people who elected you. A democratic election is an obligation to protect the people and promote their welfare. By violating that obligation, by systematically exploiting the people and enriching himself in the process, by undermining their very security and safety, by breaking the social contract, and ignoring the people's legitimate demands that he step down, Yanukovych nullified the election and the legitimacy it bestowed on him and ceased to be president. He embraced *tyranny*—and thereby became a tyrant—and transformed his rapacious regime into an *occupation* force and his Party of Regions and their oligarch supporters into a collection of collaborators.

Fourth, in mortgaging Ukraine to Vladimir Putin in exchange for his temporary financial support, Yanukovych began the process of Ukraine's transformation into a *colony* of Russia. Having torn up his social contract with the Ukrainian people, Yanukovych signed a new one with Putin. Yanukovych accepted the status of a lowly satrap in exchange for the ability to continue exploiting Ukraine economically and brutalizing Ukrainians politically. Yanukovych's cultural policy is already determined in Moscow. Now his economic and foreign policy will also be determined in Moscow. Were he logically consistent with his own actions, he would shut down Ukraine's embassies and consulates, return the buildings to the Ukrainian diaspora that bought them, and disband the Ministry of Foreign Affairs or rename it the Ministry of Liaison with the Kremlin.

The Yanukovych regime's transformation into an occupation force and Ukraine's creeping transformation into a semi-colony mean that Ukrainians, who now know that they too are fully human beings fully capable of self-rule, are engaged in a pro-democracy movement that is also a *resistance movement* and a *national-liberation struggle*. The Euro Revolution, a.k.a. the Maidan people's movement, established in Kyiv on December 22nd, is just such a broad-based movement with the potential to become some combination of Poland's Solidarity, the American civil rights movement, the black struggle against apartheid in South Africa, and Gandhi's nonviolent movement in India. Brutality, violence, and repression are ultimately powerless against such a potent mix of invigorating ideas, uplifting morals, just causes—and millions of people.

Ukrainians have demonstrated their confidence, humanity, autonomy, and maturity during the Euro Revolution. As expected, Yanukovych has displayed his desperation, incompetence, and weakness; unexpectedly, Putin has revealed a proneness for strategic miscalculations. Yanukovych is certain to be as unreliable a satrap as he has been rapacious as a sultan. Worse, Putin apparently doesn't understand that Russia lacks the economic resources and state strength to dominate a country as large and unstable as

Ukraine. The costs of imperialism will prove too great for Putin's economically stagnant and crumbling petro-state to bear—especially as a popular movement that supports democracy, human dignity, resistance to occupation, and national liberation is too powerful a contender for an illegitimate satrap to contain. Ukraine's neo-colonial status will be short-lived and the collapse of Putin's neo-imperial project may mean the collapse of Putin. And without Putin, Yanukovych will have nowhere to turn and nothing to do but run for the hills. This time, Interpol is likely to be on his heels.

*

Taking Yanukovych to the International Criminal Court? *World Affairs Journal,* January 1, 2014

The savage beating on December 25th of investigative journalist Tetyana Chornovol has led Ukrainians to speculate about three possible explanations. The first is that the Yanukovych regime is directly responsible. The second is that rogue elements within the Ministry of Internal Affairs are responsible. The third is that it's the Russians.

The third is least persuasive. Accordingly, the Putin regime is trying to destabilize Ukraine and weaken Yanukovych, in the hope, presumably, that both will be more pliant and open to the Kremlin's machinations. But Ukraine is already unstable, Yanukovych is already in Putin's pocket, and the Kremlin already calls the shots thanks to the neo-colonial deal it signed with Kyiv. I suppose it's possible for Putin to be simultaneously stabilizing and destabilizing Yanukovych and Ukraine, but forgive me for suspecting this version is too clever by half.

The second is also unpersuasive, as it ignores the fact that Chornovol's beating is just the latest in a long string of attacks on opposition activists. If rogues are trying to undermine Yanukovych, then they're an odd lot, as their actions correspond exactly to the regime's brutal treatment of the opposition since 2010. It's the Yanukovych regime, after all, that's been beating and jailing its opponents for the last three years. There were 101 instances of physical violence against Ukrainian journalists in 2013, up from 65 in 2012. And, if you recall, I had commented on the savage beatings of several FEMEN members last summer. If the regime's previous violations of human and civil rights weren't the handi-work of rogues, why should the Chornovol incident be?

Moreover, consider the following, probably incomplete, list of assaults on opposition ac-tivists since the Euro Revolution began.

- November 22nd: Crimea, Serhii Mokreniuk is attacked.

- November 23rd: Zhytomyr, Vlad Puchych is beaten.

- November 25th: Dnipropetrovsk, demonstrators attacked.

- November 27th: Crimea, Mokreniuk's car is vandalized.

- November 27th: Kyiv, Oleksandr Danyliuk's car is set on fire.

- November 28th: Zhytomyr, Vlad Puchych is beaten again.

- November 29th: Ivano-Frankivsk, Maksym Kytsiuk is beaten.

- November 30th: Ternopil, Volodymyr Khanas is beaten.

- December 6th: Luhansk, Ihor Chudovsky's car is set on fire.

- December 13th: Kharkiv, demonstrators' microbus is set on fire.

- December 15th: Zhytomyr, Viktor Brokar is attacked.

- December 16th: Uzhhorod, Yaroslav Shafar's car is set on fire.

- December 20th: Kharkiv, demonstrators' headquarters are attacked.

- December 20th: Crimea, Serhii Kovalsky's car is shot at.

- December 21st: Odessa Province, Yevhen Burkut's care is set on fire.

- December 21st: Kharkiv, Ivan Varchenko is attacked.

- December 21st: Volodymyr Moralov is attacked; his car is set on fire.

- December 22st: Zhytomyr, Dmytro Tkachuk is attacked.

- December 23rd: Kharkiv, local activist's car is set on fire.

- December 24th: Kharkiv, Dmytro Pylypets is knifed.

- December 25th: Kyiv, Tetyana Chornovol is beaten.

- December 27th: Dnipropetrovsk, local activist's car is vandalized.

- December 27th: Kharkiv, local activist's car is set on fire.

- December 28th: Kharkiv, Ivan Varchenko's car is set on fire.

I suppose it's remotely possible that Yanukovych knows nothing about this violence, but it's having begun just as soon as the Euro Revolution took off can't be an accident. As the U.S. Embassy in Kyiv correctly observed, "We express our concern at a strikingly simi-lar series of events over the last few weeks, targeting individuals, property, and political activity, apparently aimed at intimidating or punishing those linked to the Euromaidan protests."

The first version—that Yanukovych's forces are directly responsible for the Chornovol beating—is the most persuasive, both because it fits the facts and because it's the simplest (and the social sciences always prefer the simplest explanations). The regime is thuggish and has been using violence and force since its inception. Yanukovych is thuggish and has been using violence and force throughout his entire career. Facing a mortal threat to their existence—the Euro Revolution—he and his regime are responding in the only way they know how. And, having no legitimacy and popular appeal, they are responding in the only way they can. If you can't charm the people, or fool them, or buy them off, you have no choice but to beat them into submission. Not surprisingly, most of the assaults have taken place in the south and east, where the democratic opposition is making inroads and the Regionnaires are panicking.

It may be that Yanukovych gave the order for all these acts of violence or it may be that he simply instructed his underlings to get the job done. Whatever the case, as the man who runs the show, he carries all the responsibility for any such violence his people carry out.

That violence may very well continue through 2014. The Euro Revolutionaries are not about to go away, and the regime knows that its back is to the wall. The 2015 presidential elections are approaching and, although Yanukovych has no chance of winning a fair and free ballot, now more than ever he must win. But everyone knows that the only way he can do so is by means of more violence and more intimidation and more beatings.

Imagine that this sad scenario comes true. Imagine that the violence becomes widespread and systematic. Yanukovych may then be open to prosecution for "crimes against humanity." According to Article 7 of the Rome Statute of the International Criminal Court of July 17, 1998:

> For the purpose of this Statute, "crime against humanity" means any of the following acts when committed as part of a widespread or systematic attack directed against any civilian population, with knowledge of the attack: (a) Murder; (b) Extermination; (c) Enslavement; (d) Deportation or forcible transfer of population; (e) Imprisonment or other severe deprivation of physical liberty in violation of fundamental rules of international law; (f) Torture; (g) Rape, sexual slavery, enforced prostitution, forced pregnancy, enforced sterilization, or any other form of sexual violence of comparable gravity; (h) Persecution against any identifiable group or collectivity on political, racial, national, ethnic, cultural, religious, gender as defined in paragraph 3, or other grounds that are universally recognized as impermissible under international law, in connection with any act referred to in this paragraph or any crime within the jurisdiction of the Court; (i) Enforced disappearance of persons; (j) The crime of apartheid; (k) Other inhumane acts of a similar character intentionally causing great suffering, or serious injury to body or to mental or physical health.

The Yanukovych regime may already be guilty of "imprisonment or other severe deprivation of physical liberty in violation of fundamental rules of international law" and "persecution against any identifiable group or collectivity on political, racial, national, ethnic, cultural, religious, gender ... or other grounds." It's not too hard to imagine an increasingly desperate regime's resorting to "murder" and the "enforced disappearance of persons" in 2014.

Given the complexity of the International Criminal Court's procedures, I'm not sure I'd bet on Yanukovych visiting The Hague in handcuffs. That said, miracles do happen, and concerned lawyers could increase the likelihood of their happening by preparing a case against Yanukovych ASAP.

In the meantime, as Ukrainians hope for Yanukovych's appearance before the ICC and demand that the United States and Europe impose sanctions on the regime's most thuggish thugs, the West may want to consider a policy measure it could easily and effortlessly adopt today. I wrote about it in a blog post of December 2, 2011.

Many Europeans probably don't know that Ukraine has a 1998 statute on the books that permits just about anybody to acquire a diplomatic passport granting its bearer visa-free travel. As you'd expect, the president, prime minister, minister of foreign affairs, and genuine diplomats get to have a diplomatic passport. But so, too, do all parliamentary deputies, all cabinet ministers, all heads of provincial councils, the head of the secret police, a ton of other officials, and, just in case someone's job description is not on the list, anybody with the "written approval of the Ministry of Foreign Affairs of Ukraine, on condition that the President of Ukraine approves it."

The EU could end the Regionnaires' monopoly on the real Europe in a flash. It wouldn't have to blacklist Regionnaires, as some opposition democrats suggest. All it needs to do is quietly change a few rules and insist that the only Ukrainians who get to travel to the EU with diplomatic passports are bona fide diplomats engaged in bona fide diplomatic activity. Basta.

Everyone else—all the parliamentary deputies, all the provincial council heads, all the cabinet ministers, and all the president's cronies—must get on line at the appropriate European consulate, wait in stuffy rooms, fill out endless forms, pay exorbitant fees, produce invitations and bank accounts, and experience the same exact humiliation and frustration that regular folk do when they hope to go abroad.

*

A Free Donetsk? *World Affairs Journal*, January 10, 2014

Want more proof of the fact that the Yanukovych regime is crumbling? Take a look at recent goings-on in his bastion, Donetsk.

Communists ruled the city with an iron fist for decades; then the equally thuggish and equally corrupt Regionnaires took over. The Yanukovych Family, their cronies, and Ukraine's richest man—indeed one of the world's richest men—Rinat Akhmetov control everything, making sure that most the population reads, hears, and sees only what they want them to read, hear, and see and snuffing out opposition by means of intimidation, coercion, and violence.

Think of poor Donetsk as a mafia town that is also a company town. Small wonder that, while privately expressed criticism is rampant—especially by the city's sizable educated elite—open opposition is minimal. To protest publicly could mean sacrificing your career, your family's life chances, and, possibly, your health. With the population cowed, why shouldn't the Regionnaires feel confident? Until now.

There have been rumblings of discontent in the past, but nothing—and I mean absolutely nothing—like what's been going on since the Euro Revolution was launched in Kyiv. The people have spoken, and Donetsk will never again be the Regionnaire stronghold it used to be.

At first, it was only a small group of about 20 to 30 demonstrators who repeatedly assembled at the Shevchenko monument in central Donetsk. Then, a few weeks ago, several hundred brave protesters—young and old, male and female, Russian speakers and Ukrainian speakers—carried pro-democracy, pro-Europe, and anti-Yanukovych banners in a march through downtown. Some intemperate babushkas denounced them in the manner of white supremacists reacting to 1950s civil rights marchers in the American South. Most people just watched. About 20 percent applauded, smiled, or flashed victory signs.

As if so much downright chutzpah weren't enough, the demonstrators went on to produce a New Year's video greeting to Yanukovych, in which they calmly, coolly, civilly, and bilingually restated their democratic, pro-European aspirations, thanked Yanukovych for "uniting the country around one idea," and encouraged him to make a "heroic decision and resign," a move that "all Ukraine and all its citizens" would greet "with applause."

For 500 marchers to assemble in Donetsk is the equivalent of 50,000 in Lviv or 500,000 in Kyiv. This is an earthshattering development, almost as important as the Euro Revolution itself. Think about it: Regionnaire hegemony in Donetsk has been broken. The place will never be the same again.

Watching the marchers, I couldn't help but think of the three 1965 marches led by Dr. Martin Luther King Jr. in Alabama, from Selma to Montgomery. The civil rights activists, both black and white, marched into the belly of the beast—and emerged triumphant.

Like the American racists who could respond to the marchers only with violence and intimidation, so too the Regionnaires and their hired thugs have been responding to the democratic activists throughout Ukraine with violence and intimidation. But violence and intimidation are the weapons of the terrified, of the desperate, of the weak. Strong, self-confident, and popular rulers know they have nothing to fear from dialogue, concessions, and negotiations.

As a matter of fact, the Donetsk power-holders appear to be panicking. And nothing demonstrates that better than Akhmetov's bizarre exchange on December 31st with picketers and journalists outside his estate. They had been reporting that he was absent, presumably in his luxury apartment in London. And then something remarkable happened. Ukraine's richest man drove up to them in his own car—without his guards and wearing a running tracksuit (which suggests that he made the move spontaneously)—and started haranguing them about "promoting lies." Which lies? That he was in London. (Uh, Rinat, that's usually called a mistake, not a lie.) "Come to me with the truth, and I'm with you." And on and on he went, in what can only be termed an intemperate rant, without permitting any comments from the people with whom he claimed to want a conversation.

The most striking thing about the performance was that Akhmetov had so visibly lost his cool. He was agitated and rambled on in an embarrassingly defensive manner. And if it's true, as I suggested above, that he interrupted whatever he was doing to confront the picketers and journalists, then he must have been agitated indeed. After all, it's not normally the case that a multibillionaire feels impelled to defend himself before a handful of the *hoi polloi*. Clearly, Akhmetov feels threatened by the Euro Revolution. Just as clearly, he knows that handful represents the coming Euro Revolution in Donetsk. Akhmetov, the ultimate survivor, knows the wind is blowing in a different direction.

He's right. Donetsk is changing. Donetsk is becoming free. And a free Donetsk, maybe even more than a free Ukraine, spells the end for the Yanukovych mafia regime.

*

Standoff in Ukraine: Mafia Regime vs. Mobilized Citizens, *World Affairs Journal*, January 21, 2014

At first glance, the world appears to be coming to an end in Ukraine: President Yanukovych is still in power, he's signed a neocolonial deal with Russia, and he approved a whole raft of repressive legislation on January 16th. But wait: Take a deep breath, examine all the evidence, and you may conclude that things aren't quite as bad.

Let's compile a ledger of the things that have gotten worse in the last few months, the things that haven't changed, and the things that have gotten better. And then let's see whether we can come up with a more or less reasonable assessment. It goes without saying, of course, that by better or worse I mean better or worse for Ukrainian democracy, for the Ukrainian people, for freedom. By extension, what's bad for Yanukovych is good for Ukraine.

Here are three things that belong on the bad side of the ledger:

1. The Yanukovych–Putin pact saved the Ukrainian tyrant's skin and pushed Ukraine along the road toward neocolonial status vis-à-vis Russia.

2. Regime violence has increased and is likely to continue increasing.

3. Anti-regime violence, provoked by years of regime violence, finally occurred on January 19th.

Here are a few that haven't changed and are unlikely to change:

1. The Yanukovych mafia regime's authoritarianism, corruption, and weakness.

2. Yanukovych's despotism, incompetence, and callousness.

3. Regime determination to manipulate the 2015 presidential elections.

4. The Yanukovych economy's inability to grow.

5. The fascistoid Putin regime's authoritarianism, corruption, and weakness.

6. Putin's charisma and macho bluster.

7. The Putin economy's inability to grow.

8. The end of Putin's energy monopoly.

9. The European Union's interest in Ukraine.

Here are several things that have changed for the better:

1. The illegitimacy of Yanukovych and his regime is fully evident.

2. Ukrainians have demonstrated that they are not apathetic, want to be free, and are capable of sustained and repeated mass mobilization.

3. Ukrainians formed a mass movement, the "Maidan People's Association," with the potential to become a stable mass-based opposition.

4. The United States has abandoned its "Ukraine fatigue" and is now concerned about the country.

5. The Ukrainian diaspora has mobilized around the Euro Revolution and will become a permanent thorn in the side of the Yanukovych regime.

Pessimists generally place many of the points in my second category—of things that haven't changed—into the bad column and thereby render a less rosy picture. But the fact of the matter is that the Yanukovych regime has remained quite consistent since 2010. It was a thuggish, brutal, nasty, and corrupt dictatorship before the Euro Revolution. And it's remained true to itself ever since. We shouldn't be surprised that such a regime would fail to listen to the demonstrators, and thereby further weaken itself.

The January 16th measures hurriedly passed by a rump parliament are illegal, but then again everything the regime has been doing since late 2010, when Yanukovych arrogated to himself the powers of a super-presidency and transformed himself into a sultan, has been anti-constitutional and, thus, illegal. The significance of the January 16th measures is not that they ushered in a repressive, violent, thuggish dictatorship, but that the Regionnaires openly and brazenly violated the Constitution in adopting them. Knowing full well that their legitimacy is nil, they adopted not laws, but threats. As opposition leader Vitaly Klitschko said, the "authorities declared war on the people of Ukraine."

And the regime did so consciously, knowing that it is an occupation force.

Not surprisingly, anti-regime hotheads responded in kind on Sunday, January 19th. Violence always begets violence, and it was probably inevitable that individuals unaffili-ated with the peaceful Maidan movement should have taken to attacking the police and firebombing their vehicles—on the order of disaffected minority rioters in the United Kingdom and France. I've put this in the bad column, because the regime could take advantage of it to attack and discredit the peaceful demonstrators. On the other hand, if it's true that the Yanukovych mafia regime understands only force, then the riots may put the fear of God into it.

The other thing that hasn't changed is the brittleness of the fascistoid Putin regime. I've written extensively about this elsewhere, but the reality is that a leader-centered corrupt authoritarian regime that rests on easy energy money is only strong if the leader remains charismatic and young, the corruption keeps getting fed easy money, and easy money keeps coming from oil and gas. But even Putin is getting old, the Russian economy is about to enter a decade of minimal growth, and Russia's famed energy card looks de-cidedly less impressive in light of shale gas and liquid natural gas developments in the United States and Europe. Putin can beat his chest and talk empire—after all, he must in order to maintain his image as the Big Man on Horseback—but his state and economy are too weak to sustain empire.

So, when you consider these features in relation to the neocolonial implications of the Yanukovych–Putin pact, you may want to relax a bit. Being a semi-colony will bring Ukraine no good, but Ukraine is highly unlikely to acquire genuine colonial status and it is highly likely to morph out of semi-colonial status as both the Yanukovych regime and the Putin regime experience their inevitable times of troubles.

Increasing Yanukovych regime violence is a definite bad, but it too must be viewed in relation to all the goods that have emerged in the last two months. A mafia regime can do—and already has done—untold harm to innocent human beings, but violence pure and simple is not a sustainable strategy in the medium term, especially in a country with a highly-developed civil society, mass-based opposition movement, and a demonstrated capacity to respond in kind. Does the Yanukovych regime want to provoke mass violence and a civil war that it may not win?

Moreover, forces of coercion are very expensive and they produce nothing of value eco-nomically. Any regime that relies on them only for its existence is doomed to economic contraction, which in turn means declining opportunities for elite theft, growing popular discontent, and the growing likelihood of anti-regime violence. (As the French diplomat Talleyrand once said, "The only thing you cannot do with a bayonet is sit on it.") Such a condition is inherently unstable—especially if rapacious regime elites begin to feel the heat, as they will if the United States, Canada, and the European Union impose sanctions on the most egregious crooks and the Ukrainian diaspora helps expose illegally financed Regionnaire assets in the West.

Even if you disagree with my threefold categorization, you may agree that a closer look at

Ukraine's current straights suggests that things aren't quite as bad as they look to a some-times-despondent popular movement that expected the camarilla exploiting the country to cease being a camarilla and cease exploiting the country after several weeks of mass protests. I'd say the situation resembles an unstable standoff between the mafia regime and the mobilized people. Regime violence and thuggishness will not let up, at least for the foreseeable future. But neither will popular resistance and outside pressure. As one American ex-pat wrote to me from Kyiv, "I think we're looking at years' worth of low-grade revolution over here. Seems like every time I go outside I walk into a demonstration in front of this official office or that one, and I see no indication that people are not in this for the long, long, long haul."

The possibilities for change, especially for the good, are immense, and that uncertainty is terrifying. Still, the "correlation of forces" (as the Soviets used to put it) favors the dem-ocratic opposition, particularly in the medium to long run, for the simple reason that, whatever the weaknesses of the Euro Revolutionaries, the Yanukovych regime is much weaker. I've been betting against Yanukovych and Putin for the last few years. I still am.

*

Yanukovych Invites Violence, *World Affairs Journal*, January 22, 2014

It was all quite predictable. How could the gangster regime of an avaricious sultan not pro-voke an uprising by a population tired of being systematically and relentlessly plundered and abused? You don't have to be an expert on revolutions and rebellions to know that, at some point, all decent people will say to their oppressors: enough is enough.

The only question now is: Is sporadic violence enough for the regime? Disappearances, beatings, and even killings have become more common. Will the regime now go into full occupation mode and employ mass violence against the protestors in Kyiv and elsewhere?

Hired thugs and riot police (in case you're wondering what the difference between the two is, the latter wear helmets) are being bused into Kyiv. The troops confronting the protesters appear to have developed increasingly itchy fingers, firing rubber bullets and explosive devices into the crowds. Push appears to be coming to shove.

The risks associated with a violent crackdown are extremely high, and the sultan knows that. After all, if there's one thing Viktor Yanukovych understands, it's violence. He grew up in a violent environment; he employed violence as a teenage gangster; he was both the object and subject of violence in prison; he uses well-placed punches to keep his minions in line. Indeed, considering his abysmal record as president of Ukraine—which essen-tially ended when he willfully, consciously, and voluntarily abandoned that position by betraying the people's trust and opting for occupation—violence may be the only thing the man understands.

If all goes according to plan, the riot police will clean out the Maidans in Kyiv and other cities quickly and efficiently. Heads will be cracked, lives will be lost, but let the stupid liberals in the West worry about that. Putin will shower the sultan with accolades for having resisted Western imperialism. The Regionnaire thugs will congratulate one another on a job well done. As the people return to servitude, the occupation regime will be able to get on with its *raison d'être*: plunder. All will be well again.

But what if things do not go according to plan? After all, Yanukovych must know that the only person who is perfectly predictable and reliable when it comes to violence is himself. What if the riot police don't act as quickly and efficiently as he would? What if they clean out some Maidans, but not others? What if all the heads that need to be cracked and all the lives that need to be lost aren't? And what if the people don't return to servitude? What if they continue to resist—some openly, some covertly, some peacefully, and some violently?

Yanukovych knows one thing from the gangster world that molded him as a young man: that violence works only when it works completely. He must therefore know that a violent crackdown has to be total and totally successful. Anything short of the complete elimination of a rival gang is unacceptable. Anything short of the complete elimination of the Euro Revolution is equally unacceptable.

Are the militia, internal troops, and riot police as dependable as Yanukovych himself? Will they blink when ordered to initiate a bloodbath? Will they shoot women? Will they stand fast in the face of determined opposition and Molotov cocktails? Will they be able to look their neighbors, their wives, their children, their friends in the eye? That's the problem with being the coercive handmaidens of a non-foreign occupation regime: you have to both kill people and continue to live among the people you're killing. There have been reports suggesting that some units have engaged the democrats in negotiations about immunity. If so, Yanukovych must be cursing the fact that there's only one of him.

No less worrisome is the possibility of continued resistance. Ukraine is a big country and at least two-thirds is populated by people who detest the occupation regime. Imagine that the crackdown in Kyiv succeeds. Is Yanukovych ready for the emergence of small-scale, hit-and-run actions in the provinces? If destroying the physically compact Maidan in Kyiv is a challenge, just imagine how much more difficult it will be to put an end to resistance in hundreds or thousands of cities, towns, and villages? The sultan does have an enormous security apparatus, but will local militia men be willing to kill their friends and neighbors? And what will local Regionnaires do when they and their property become the targets of local resistance movements?

Yanukovych has no good options. If he does nothing, the Euro Revolution continues. If he cracks down, the Euro Resistance continues. Either way, Ukraine becomes ungovernable and his occupation regime becomes even more unstable. A smart politician would negotiate in good faith. A violence-prone sultan will do what comes naturally to him. Yanukovych thinks he's tightening the noose around the opposition. In actuality, it's his head that's in the rope.

One more thing, just in case some European politicians are reading this blog. If you want to forestall a bloodbath or a civil war in a neighboring country, you easily can. The Yanukovych criminals all have their banking accounts and real-estate assets in your countries. Freeze them. Just say no to Regionnaire violence. Unless, of course, it's easier to say yes to Regionnaire money.

*

Ukraine's Three Revolutionary Breakthroughs, *World Affairs Journal*, January 28, 2014

The end of the criminal Yanukovych mafia regime may be nearer than we think. Three developments in the last week mark sea changes that favor the democratic opposition.

First, the regime's elite guards—the Berkut riot police—shot and killed several demonstrators. Another man was disappeared by a death squad, tortured, and killed. These actions were criminal, but they were also profoundly stupid. In killing at least five young men, the Yanukovych regime has provided the democratic revolutionaries with something every revolution needs: martyrs and symbols. The Ukrainian revolution of 2014 now has its Nathan Hale (hanged by the British in 1776), its Medgar Evers (killed by white racists in 1963), its Benno Ohnesorg (killed by the West German police in 1967), and its Steve Biko (killed by the apartheid South African regime in 1977).

As Yanukovych will soon learn, you can't fight martyrs, and you definitely can't fight symbols. They will remain permanently alive, inspiring the struggle and promoting implacability and irreconcilability. In martyring five men, the regime made them into invincible enemies who will hasten its end.

Second, the democratic opposition declared that it was forming an alternative parliament—the People's Rada. Thus far, the democratic Rada is a paper institution, but, unless the democrats suffer a sudden loss of political will, it will progressively grow into a real parliament that issues legislation, appoints governing bodies, and rewrites the Constitution. Local branches of the Rada have already banned the Regionnaires and Communists in Ternopil, Ivano-Frankivsk, Chernivtsi, and Khmelnytsky provinces. Unless nipped in the bud—and there is hardly any way the regime can do that without crushing the entire country—the People's Rada will quickly evolve into a contender for sovereignty. Since it will enjoy popular legitimacy, it will eventually reduce the Supreme Rada, the discredited faux parliament run by the Regionnaire thugs, to a sideshow of political has-beens. When that happens, the regime is pretty much dead.

Yanukovych, who may still remember some of the Soviet history he learned in grade school, will recognize this as a condition of "dual sovereignty" similar to what emerged in Russia after the February Revolution of 1917. Then the socialists established the Soviet of Workers' and Soldiers' Deputies, thereby spelling the beginning of the end of the provisional government. Yanukovych may also remember that the Soviet had armed self-defense detachments. The Maidans in Kyiv and elsewhere may soon have them as well. When they do, the Berkut thugs, whose courage extends only to beating defenseless and wounded protesters, will head for the hills.

Finally, the Euro Revolution in Kyiv has become the Ukrainian Revolution. Grassroots Ukrainians throughout the country have begun to seize the buildings housing Yanukovych's governors, thereby taking control of the Provincial State Administrations they ran. As of this writing, the state administrations in Lviv, Ternopil, Ivano-Frankivsk, Rivne, Lutsk, Zhytomyr, Khmelnytsky, Chernivtsi, Vinnytsya, Poltava, and Kyiv (city) are in the hands of revolutionaries; those of Kyiv, Chernihiv, and Kherson province are under assault; those of Dnipropetrovsk, Zaporizhzhya, Sumy, and Cherkasy have been recaptured by pro-state forces. Government forces are relying on hired goons known as "*titushky*" for help; they will prove to be unreliable as the standoffs continue and the weather refuses to get warmer. In the meantime, expect Ukrainians to continue seizing the levers of local power and claiming their bit of sovereignty at home.

This development has, in effect, "decentered" the Kyiv Maidan. At this point, if the Kyiv revolutionaries lose the territory of the Maidan to the riot police (and there are rumors that the long-awaited crackdown will soon come), nothing will change in terms of the overall correlation of forces. After all, only thousands of Ukrainians could travel to Kyiv from the provinces to participate in the Maidan. Millions can now pursue revolutionary goals by staying right at home—on their own turf, where the Berkut is far outnumbered by the people. They can either seize the state administrations or other offices or, like the soccer fan clubs of Kyiv, Odessa, Sevastopol, Kharkiv, Donetsk, Luhansk, and Dnipropetrovsk, join in protecting local Maidans from the predations of regime-hired goons. By the way, these clubs are not just groups of beer-guzzling fans: given the extreme weakness of self-organization in Ukraine's southeast, fan clubs may be said to represent local civil society.

Yanukovych's worst nightmare is coming true: the revolution has spread and will continue to spread. It is no longer focused on the capital. It is now completely beyond his control. Regionalization of the revolution also has important tactical consequences. Up to now, the regime could concentrate its police forces in Kyiv. It can't do that anymore—which is good for Kyiv. But neither does the regime have enough riot police and internal troops—at most 35,000—to control a huge country with 25 provinces. And some of them have already begun defecting from what is becoming an increasingly obvious lost cause.

The writing is on the wall.

After the Bastille fell on July 14, 1789, Louis XVI asked, "Is it a revolt?" The Duke de La Rochefoucauld answered: "No, Sire, it's a revolution." Louis, as you know, lost his head.

*

The Crisis in Ukraine and Its Possible Aftermaths, *Al Jazeera*, January 30, 2014

Anti-government protesters hold a rally on Independence Square in Kyiv on December 8, demanding association with the European Union. The protesters' grievances have since broadened to include corruption and misrule by Ukraine's ruling party.

Ukraine is in the throes of a revolutionary situation. On the one hand stands the regime—illegitimate, battered, weak, completely reliant on violence for its survival. Opposing the regime is a coalition of protesters, which enjoys vast popular support, is acquiring momentum in the provinces and hopes to transform the country into a genuine democracy.

Amid growing protests, President Viktor Yanukovych announced on Thursday that he is taking unspecified medical leave, citing severe respiratory disease and fever. The latest development leaves efforts to resolve the nearly three-month-old political crisis through negotiated settlement in limbo. Shortly after announcing the sick leave, the embattled president accused opposition leaders of escalating the situation simply to fulfill their own selfish "political ambitions."

The choice before the regime is no longer survival or defeat. It is between forms of defeat. Yanukovych and his regime, as well as Ukraine, would benefit most from his immediate and voluntary resignation. Yanukovych could probably negotiate an amnesty for himself, and the country would be spared a civil war.

A continuation of the current standoff, followed by regime collapse, is the next best alternative. Violence would be avoided, but an amnesty would be less likely and the economy would continue to deteriorate, to no one's benefit. A bloodbath followed by civil conflict and regime collapse would obviously be bad for everyone. Yanukovych might not in fact survive. Many Ukrainians are now referring to him as Yanuchescu, after Romanian dictator Nicolae Ceausescu, who met a bloody end in 1989. The country would experience enormous hardship, and a breakup of Ukraine then becomes possible.

Modest Demands

Two months ago, when mass demonstrations first rocked Ukraine's capital, Kyiv, protesters insisted on only two demands: that the government sign an association agreement with the European Union, which Yanukovych had scuttled, and that Prime Minister Mykola Azarov be fired for rejecting the agreement. The protesters' grievances have grown over time to include the complete overhaul of the Yanukovych system of government. Protesters want to replace dictatorship with democracy, crony capitalism with a genuine market economy, and massive state corruption with the rule of law.

The regime turned a deaf ear to the protesters' initially modest demands and instead responded with sustained violence involving daily beatings, fire bombings, disappearances and killings. These actions radicalized the opposition, which is now demanding a new constitution, the resignation of the president and early parliamentary and presidential elections. As the protesters' demands expanded, the regime intensified its use of force, introducing a raft of repressive legislation on January 16 and killing several demonstrators in the street fighting that followed.

The opposition then proceeded to establish a People's Council, as an alternative to the Supreme Rada, the corrupted regime-controlled legislature, while local democratic activists throughout the country began seizing the buildings occupied by Yanukovych's governors, the Provincial State Administrations, and establishing local People's Councils. Pro-regime riot police, with the assistance of hired hooligans called "*titushky*," launched counterattacks in various cities including Kyiv, Donetsk, and Zaporizhzhya, thereby adding to the sense of growing chaos.

The situation has clearly slipped out of the Yanukovych regime's control. The regime enjoys the support of no more than 25 percent of the population, overwhelmingly concentrated in three provinces in the southeast: Donetsk, Luhansk and Crimea—which have traditionally served as the largely Russian-speaking base of both the Communist Party and Yanukovych's Party of Regions. The rest of the population detests the regime and its leadership. Large numbers of leading intellectuals, artists and journalists have openly declared their opposition to the regime.

Ukraine's top oligarch and key supporter of Yanukovych, the Donetsk-based multibillionaire Rinat Akhmetov, has twice stated his opposition to a violent resolution of the crisis. About 80 members of the Party of Regions appear to have broken ranks with their comrades, thereby potentially creating a split within the regime's institutional base of support. The economy is in free fall: the Ukrainian currency, the hryvnia, has lost 25 percent of its value, the deficit is growing and GDP is declining. For a regime that relies only on the forces of coercion, there are now some worrisome signs that members of the armed forces, riot police and militia are ready to defect or declare their neutrality.

Faced with such destabilizing prospects, on January 28 Prime Minister Azarov resigned, while the regime rescinded some of the repressive laws it had adopted earlier. Whether this was made in good faith is doubtful. More than half the draconian laws adopted in violation of the Constitution remain in force. The regime seems unwilling to consider the opposition's key demands—early presidential and parliamentary elections and a revision of the Constitution that would prevent a president's ability to amass dictatorial powers.

On January 29, the regime adopted a 15-day amnesty for jailed protesters contingent on the clearing of the protester-controlled Maidan, the area around Independence Square in downtown Kyiv. The amnesty was immediately rejected by the opposition as a ruse intended to extract maximum concessions from them in exchange for a partial reversion of the regime's illegal use of violence. The savage beatings, disappearances and killings—which continue unabated in the provinces—underscore the regime's bad faith.

Negotiations are currently taking place under the patronage of Ukraine's first president, Leonid Kravchuk, and they may result in some positive changes. Much will be clearer when Yanukovych appoints a new Cabinet. Although they have formally resigned, all former ministers except Azarov are still carrying out their official duties. If this condition persists, it will be clear that Yanukovych has no intention to compromise. If he replaces the current Cabinet with an even worse collection of anti-reformist individuals drawn exclusively from his political camp, his message to the opposition will be clear: No change is forthcoming, and violence is the only thing you may expect. A positive sign would be a technocratic Cabinet of reform-minded individuals acceptable to both ends of the political spectrum. Such a Cabinet could draw on the near-rebellious members of the Party of Regions who are aligned with Western-leaning oligarchs Serhii Tihipko and Rinat Akhmetov.

A Simple Choice

The reality is far less cheerful for Yanukovych than he may think. His regime has lost control of the country, and it is losing the loyalty of its own cadres. No regime can rely solely on the use of force for long, especially if most the population and the elite are against it, the economy is collapsing and the international community is poised to impose painful sanctions on key officials. The United States, Canada and the European Union have all said they would impose sanctions if a violent crackdown were to occur.

As a matter of fact, the Yanukovych regime is effectively doomed. If it fails to crush the opposition in a bloodbath, the regime will wither away as opposition increases. If it succeeds in crushing protest in the Maidan in Kyiv and elsewhere, it will only spark a massive national resistance movement that will, ultimately, wear down the regime and, possibly, lead to a breakup of the country, with Luhansk and Donetsk provinces splitting away and Crimea being swallowed by Russia.

The choice before Yanukovych is quite simple. He can save himself and the country, or he can destroy himself and Ukraine.

The only question is: Does he see it?

*

Ukraine's Day of Infamy, *World Affairs Journal*, February 19, 2014

Tuesday, February 18, 2014, will go down in European history as a day of infamy. It was then that Viktor Yanukovych declared war on his own people.

In retrospect, his decision to kill and maim Ukrainians looks inevitable. In 2010, he arrogated to himself the powers of a sultan. Thereafter, he progressively dismantled all of Ukraine's democratic institutions and undermined all its freedoms. Finally, he and his cronies systematically looted the country to the tune of more than $10 billion. Having consistently treated the Ukrainian people as second-class citizens whose sole function consisted in serving the needs of the ruling Regionnaires, Yanukovych finally took his disdain for the nation to its logical conclusion: he began to butcher them.

Yanukovych claims that he is Ukraine's legitimate president, that the protesters reject the constitutional solutions that he, the supposed moderate, supports, and that they are responsible for the violence. Don't believe him for a second.

Democratically elected leaders become illegitimate tyrants the moment they turn against the people who elected them. Yanukovych abandoned whatever minimal claims to legitimacy he may have had back in 2010. The amazing thing is that Ukrainians actually hoped against hope for three years before deciding that the man had to go.

For three years, the democratic opposition has been pleading with Yanukovych to adhere to Ukraine's Constitution. To no avail. He's violated it at whim. For three months now, ever since the protests in Kyiv began in late November, the protesters have pleaded with him to talk, to compromise, to acknowledge their existence and the legitimacy of their demands. To no avail. Yanukovych's only response has been violence: beatings, killings, fire-bombings, and disappearances. The massive violence of February 18th is just the logical conclusion of the daily violence he's engaged in since November.

In declaring war on Ukrainians, Yanukovych has sealed his own fate. He thinks he's re-establishing control. In reality, the violence is an act of desperation that will only hasten his own downfall.

Regionnaire parliamentarians have begun fleeing the country and taking their hard currency with them. One of the most thuggish Regionnaires, Oleg Tsaryov, has publicly distanced himself from "Yanukovych's decision" to engage in violence. More than half of Ukraine is already up in arms: government buildings have been seized, central authority has been rejected, and riot police have been disarmed. Even if Yanukovych succeeds in crushing the demonstrators on Kyiv's Independence Square, the Euromaidan epicenter, opposition will simply go underground or morph into other forms.

What Yanukovych doesn't understand—and has never understood—is that you can't stop millions of people from wanting to live freely and in dignity.

It's high time for the European Union to understand that as well. Do Europeans really believe in their vaunted European values? Do they care that Ukraine may be on the verge of becoming another Bosnia? Do they care that Yanukovych could be on his way to becoming another Slobodan Milosevic? If democracy and human rights mean anything to Europe, if they mean at least as much as access to Russian gas and ample supplies of beer and wine, then the European Union must move from declarations of support and threats of sanction to actual sanctions. Immediately.

As it is, the European Union lacks credibility with Yanukovych. Explicitly stating that sanctions might be imposed only if bloodshed occurs was an invitation to Yanukovych to continue with harsh crackdowns. Like the Regionnaires in general, Yanukovych doubts that the Europeans will ever act forcefully—even if Ukraine becomes another Bosnia and the cost of EU intervention skyrockets. As the democratic analyst Oleksii Haran rightly said last week, "If the EU does not take decisive steps, it will share responsibility for bloodshed in Ukraine and hundreds of thousands of refugees." Now blood has been shed—lots. Yanukovych bears all the responsibility for the crimes. But the Europeans, alas, have committed a serious sin of omission. They could have made a difference. But didn't. They looked the other way.

Sanctions will no longer stop the bloodshed. It's too late for that. But they would have two important consequences. They'd redeem Europe morally. And they'd hasten Yanukovych's end. And that end is inevitable. No tyrant can declare war against his own people and hope to survive for long. When Yanukovych finally decides to flee the country, Europe could at least have the decency to deny him entry.

*

Brutality Won't Save Ukraine's President, *CNN*, February 21, 2014

Viktor Yanukovych is probably doomed—even if he does not yet know it. He should just step down.

As the embattled Ukrainian President hides in the presidential administration in central Kyiv, medical authorities report from 70 to 100 demonstrators have been killed and hundreds wounded. His minister of internal affairs has authorized police units to employ live ammunition. There are also fears that army units are moving on Kyiv, the capital city.

These appear to be the desperate measures of a dying regime.

The turning point took place on Tuesday when Yanukovych ordered police units to storm the Maidan—the area centered on Independence Square that has been occupied by the democratic opposition since late November. Regime forces killed at least 25 demonstrators in pitched street battles, set buildings on fire and initiated a campaign of mass terror.

Yanukovych hoped the opposition in Kyiv would disperse. Instead, the violence only spurred demonstrators to greater resistance and underscored their determination to fight to the end. More important, the brutality has had several important consequences.

First, democratic forces began seizing government buildings, attacking and disarming police units, and rejecting central authority throughout much of the country. As of this writing, Yanukovych has effectively lost control of at least half of Ukraine—mostly in the west and center—and demonstrations and disturbances are constant in many parts of the southeast, his power base.

Second, in many of the cities and provinces captured by the revolutionaries, riot police and militia have thrown down their weapons and joined the resistance.

In Kyiv on Thursday, several scores of internal troops and their commander surrendered to the opposition. The coercive forces represent Yanukovych's last line of defense; such defections mean that his regime may soon be exposed to assault by an enraged and increasingly armed population.

Third, dozens of prominent members of Yanukovych's Party of Regions have left the party and repudiated his rule. Some are genuinely appalled by the brutality of the regime; all sense which way the wind is blowing and want to save their skins—such as up to 30 pro-regime parliamentary deputies who reputedly fled the country for Western Europe. Even Yanukovych's appointee, the de facto mayor of Kyiv, has turned against Yanukovych. The regime's own power base is crumbling.

Fourth, Ukraine's oligarchs, who have so far supported or refused to turn against Yanukovych, are now hedging their bets. Massive bloodshed and a potential civil war is not in their interest, and the more things escalate, the more likely will their dissatisfaction with Yanukovych turn into opposition.

Yanukovych faces a no-win situation.

If he backs down, the revolutionaries will sweep the country, seize the presidential administration and in all likelihood arrest him. Given the popular anger that his butchery has unleashed, it's not inconceivable that his fate could be that of Romania's Communist dictator, Nicolae Ceausescu, in 1989.

If he doesn't back down, he can no longer hope for a return to the stalemate that existed until February 18. The revolutionaries are no longer in the mood for compromise with a regime that is willing to kill its own citizens to stay in power.

Given these options, Yanukovych might decide that his only hope of salvation lies with an escalation of violence. If the criminal bands of the Berkut riot police—in cahoots perhaps with select units of the internal troops and army—begin shooting indiscriminately and employing heavy weaponry, they could certainly crush the Kyiv demonstrators, although probably at the cost of thousands of dead.

In light of Yanukovych's proven indifference to human life, this option is, alas, not impossible.

But even massive bloodletting won't change the balance of forces. Kyiv's demonstrators will just go underground and initiate a guerrilla struggle against the regime. More important, the rest of the country will remain in the hands of the democratic opposition.

Its determination to oust Yanukovych and his criminal regime will become implacable, while defections in the coercive forces and Party of Regions could continue. Meanwhile, the economy is on the verge of collapse, social unrest will likely break out in the southeastern rust belt, and the regime may soon have no money to pay its defenders.

It could be that Yanukovych's days are numbered, and even Russian President Vladimir Putin might not be able to help him. Putin could decide it is not worth his while to invade Ukraine to prop up a doomed regime. And an invasion of Ukraine could unleash a new cold war with the West and transform Russia into a pariah state.

Yanukovych's friend, the mayor of Kharkiv, has suggested that he evacuate to his city. That—or flight to Russia—may be Yanukovych's last real hope.

A House United: Why Analysts Touting Ukraine's East-West Division Are Just Plain Wrong, *Foreign Policy*, February 22, 2014

Throughout the crisis in Ukraine, experts real and imagined have persistently invoked the country's vaunted East-West "divide." According to this interpretation, Ukraine is neatly divided into two homogeneous, coherent, and irreconcilable blocs. The implicit message is that partition is inevitable and desirable. As Viktor Yanukovych fled Kyiv for the pro-Russian and "separatist" Kharkiv on February 22, analysts feared he would ignite a civil war between Ukraine's irreconcilable factions. But as is often the case with such binary oppositions, they conceal and obfuscate more than they reveal and clarify, creating a simplistic image of a complex condition.

As is obvious to any visitor, Ukraine's westernmost large city, Lviv, differs fundamentally from its easternmost counterparts, Luhansk and Donetsk. Lviv is pro-Western; it supports Ukrainian independence; it has consistently voted against Viktor Yanukovych and his Party of Regions; it speaks Ukrainian and promotes Ukrainian culture, while being multilingual, multicultural, and remarkably diverse; and it rejects the Soviet past. In contrast, Luhansk and Donetsk are more pro-Russian; they have doubts about Ukrainian independence; they support Yanukovych and the Party of Regions (and when they voice their discontent, they often vote for the Stalinist Communist Party); they speak Russian and favor Russian culture; they are monolingual, monocultural, and homogeneous; and they embrace the Soviet past.

But this neat picture becomes muddled in the environs of Luhansk and Donetsk. For example, the official website of the Bilokurakyn district of Luhansk Province (which borders Russia) is in Ukrainian, and the website's sentiments are distinctly anti-Yanukovych. The countryside and smaller towns of both provinces tend to speak Ukrainian and practice Ukrainian culture. And even in the cities themselves, the clear majority of the population—minus the pro-Russian chauvinists—will happily engage Ukrainian speakers in conversation. One Ukrainian history professor at Donetsk State University has been conducting all his lectures in Ukrainian for over a decade. At first some students grumbled—and he responded by pointing out that if they lack the intellectual ability to understand Ukrainian, they shouldn't be university students. Since then, there have been no complaints and no problems.

Go to Lviv in the West, and you encounter similar subtleties. The overwhelming majority of Lviv residents are at least proficient in Russian, gladly speak the language, read Russian newspapers and books, and watch Russian television. If a radio is playing in a restaurant or café, chances are as high that it'll be tuned to a Russian station rather than a Ukrainian one. Lviv is especially popular with Russian tourists, who like it for its Middle European feel, old architecture, and Ukrainian distinctiveness. A favorite Russian watering hole is the Kryyivka (Bunker) restaurant, modeled after the underground hideouts used by anti-Soviet Ukrainian nationalists after World War II.

And between the far East and far West, the supposed East-West divide gets ever fuzzier. Go from far West to far East and the percentage of individuals who speak Ukrainian in everyday circumstances progressively declines. By the same token, go in the opposite direction and the percentage of Russian-speakers declines. In much of the country, and especially in its middle, most people speak both languages. Most ethnic Russians, who comprise about one fifth of the population and primarily reside in Luhansk and Donetsk provinces and in Crimea, have a working knowledge of Ukrainian, and only some, primarily ultranationalists in Crimea, refuse to speak it. Meanwhile, most ethnic Ukrainians are effectively bilingual, regardless of where they live. The capital, Kyiv, illustrates this point very well. Most of the conversations one hears in public are in Russian—but address Russian speakers in Ukrainian and most will respond in Ukrainian.

Kyiv nicely illustrates another important nuance. It's often said that Kyiv speaks like the East and votes like the West: most Kyivites are fluent in Russian, and most also support the ongoing anti-government revolution, just as they supported the 2004 Orange Revolution. (In the photo above, anti-government protesters in Kyiv sing the Ukrainian national anthem.) This means that language preference does not as easily correlate with cultural preferences (Russia versus the West) or political choices (Yanukovych versus the democrats), as the East-West paradigm suggests. In that vast space between far East and far West, many Russian-speaking ethnic Ukrainians vote against the Party of Regions, support Ukrainian independence, and fear Putin's Russia. Voters in Dnipropetrovsk, Poltava, Chernihiv, and Kharkiv provinces are known to cast votes for other parties. Neither Yanukovych nor the Party of Regions received 100 percent of the vote in any province. Not surprisingly, about one-fifth of the demonstrators in Kyiv hail from Ukraine's "pro-Russian," south-eastern provinces.

Just as unsurprisingly, every major south-eastern city—Kharkiv, Donetsk, Dnipropetrovsk, Zaporizhzhya, Mykolaiv, Odessa, and, even Crimea—has held anti-Yanukovych demonstrations in the last three months. A few weeks ago, some 5,000 people marched in support of the anti-government demonstrators in Yanukovych's stronghold, Donetsk—a remarkable figure considering the violence they knew could await them from the local security forces. Equally indicative of the degree to which anti-Yanukovych sentiment has permeated the southeast is the fact that, from early November to early February, when pro-regime forces engaged in daily beatings, killings, and disappearances of anti-regime activists throughout the country, most of the victims were from the east.

Even the Crimean Autonomous Republic isn't quite as solidly pro-Russian and pro-Putin as it's often depicted. The northern part of the peninsula is populated by ethnic Ukrainians, most of whom are bilingual and are likely to have some loyalties to Ukraine. The central and southern parts are populated by Crimean Tatars, who currently comprise about 15–20 percent of the total population. Most of them speak Russian on a daily basis, yet most also oppose Crimea's annexation by Russia and strongly support the Kyiv revolution. Several hundred have even joined the revolutionaries in downtown Kyiv.

In sum, the image of two competing blocs is just dead wrong. Ukraine happens to be an extremely diverse place, with a range of languages, cultures, identities, and political preferences throughout the country. In that respect, Ukraine's diversity is pretty much on par with that found in just about any country of the world: the United States, Canada, Italy, Germany, Turkey, Brazil, India, and so on. Diversity can sometimes spell trouble (as in Great Britain with Scotland and in Spain with Catalonia) and it can sometimes mean vitality (as in the United States and Canada), but we rarely assume, a priori, that it must lead to ungovernability and partition—except, apparently, in Ukraine, where what is business as usual elsewhere is assumed to be a fatal flaw. There are many reasons for such a flawed perception, but the central one may be the inability of Russian elites and their sympathizers in the West to concede that Ukraine is a real country and that Ukrainians are a complex people.

The real divide in Ukraine is not between East and West, but between the democratic forces on the one hand and the Party of Regions on the other. The latter is strongest in the southeast, mostly because its cadres (who are mostly former Communists) have controlled the region's information networks and economic resources since Soviet times and continue to do so to this day. Their domination since Ukraine's independence rests on their having constructed alliances with organized crime and the country's oligarchs, in particular, with Ukraine's richest tycoon, Rinat Akhmetov. They have enormous financial resources at their disposal, control the local media, and quash—or have quashed—all challengers to their hegemony. Their rule has been compared, not inaccurately, to that of the mafia. Ukrainians in the southeast tend to vote for them, less because they're enamored of Yanukovych (they are not), and more because they have no alternatives and, due to the Region Party's control of the media, see no alternatives.

This real divide could very well end in the near future. Yanukovych's regime is on the verge of collapse. Most of the country has escaped his control; prominent members of the Party of Regions —including Yanukovych himself—are fleeing Kyiv; and the Ministry of Interior declared vowed to support the "people of Kyiv," not the government. The parliament—now under opposition control—has reasserted its control, reinstating the 2004 Constitution that truncates presidential powers and empowers the legislators to appoint a reform-oriented cabinet. When the regime does collapse, the Party of Regions is likely to collapse with it, and its hegemony over the southeast will end. At that point, Ukraine—still happily diverse—may finally become a normal country as well.

*

Ukraine's Opportunity for Genuine Democracy, *World Affairs Journal*, February 25, 2014

After 23 years of formal independence, Ukraine stands poised to take the final steps toward genuine independence by liberating itself from what has become the legacy of Soviet communism throughout its former empire—rule by criminal and thuggish regimes and oligarchs. Ukraine finally has the opportunity to join the civilized world where constitutions and rule of law, not party hacks and bullies, reign supreme.

The sudden, rapid, and comprehensive collapse of the criminal Yanukovych regime surprised many—especially after the butchery that just preceded it—but it was preprogrammed by the nature of the regime. Extreme centralization of authority in the hands of an incompetent sultan whose entire agenda consisted of self-enrichment guaranteed bureaucratic fragmentation, regime illegitimacy, and popular anger. Lacking an ideological *raison d'être* and resting only on the willingness of security forces to sustain it, the brittle regime crumbled once President Yanukovych ordered mass killings, democratic revolutionaries in Kyiv refused to be cowed, provincial uprisings swept the country, and Regionnaires realized their careers—and lives—were on the line. As soon as the Regionnaire thugs began fleeing *en masse*, the security forces became isolated, Yanukovych's cronies jumped ship, and he had to run. Graft, theft, and coercion proved to be insufficient to keep the mafia regime intact.

The Party of Regions has become eviscerated; it and the Communist Party are still represented in Parliament, but both must rethink the retrograde Soviet values that inspired them in order to survive. Propelling that rethinking is the fact that democratic Ukraine intends to try the top 25 regime representatives for crimes against humanity. If and when Yanukovych, who heads the list, is captured and put on trial, the full extent of the regime's criminality will come to light and discourage Regionnaire holdouts from attempting a comeback. The democratic authorities are also planning a "lustration" similar to investigations of criminal wrongdoing by regime collaborators in Central Europe and South Africa.

A key part of the repudiation of the Soviet past is the continued toppling of Ukraine's approximately 1,300 remaining Lenin statues and the renaming of streets, squares, and the like. Twenty-five Lenins met their end in just two days last week. In a foretaste of things to come, the eastern Ukrainian city of Dnipropetrovsk renamed Lenin Square "Heroes of the Maidan Square," in honor of the demonstrators shot and killed by Yanukovych's hirelings on Kyiv's Independence Square. The Soviet star adorning the Parliament has also been removed.

These and many other measures stand a good chance of moving Ukraine in the direction of post-Communist Poland, the Baltic states, and their Central European neighbors, which understood, when the USSR collapsed, that a radical break with the Soviet past was the precondition of a lasting shift toward sustainable democracy, rule of law, and a market economy. In effect, Ukraine is now at the same point they were in 1989–91.

Except that Ukraine is also far worse off. In addition to 70 years under Communist totalitarianism and Russian imperialism, Ukraine suffered incalculable damage due to four years of untrammeled Regionnaire exploitation. The treasury is empty. State institutions have been eviscerated. The economy is on the verge of collapse. Rule of law has disappeared. And, unlike in 1991, when Russia was weak and in retreat, Putin's Russia is much stronger and more aggressive.

Will the democratic revolution succeed?

Cautious optimism is the order of the day. Repudiation of the Soviet past and the institutional devastation caused by the "Yanukovych Ruin" give the democrats the opportunity to start from a clean slate. The Regionnaires and Communists are on the run and, quite possibly, on the verge of extinction. Three months of intense struggle and close to 100 dead have created an unprecedented *esprit de corps* among democrats. For the first time, they agree on strategic goals: Europe, democracy, rule of law, and the market; most of the population supports the goals of the revolution; and the United States and Europe support Ukraine. Once the EU Association Agreement is signed, it will provide Kyiv with a road map of change. The democrats also know that, if they fail, Ukraine will fail, and that the Maidan activists who fought the regime and sacrificed their lives will fight them if they dither and squabble.

Will Russia lead a charge to reinstall the *ancien régime* or break off bits of Ukraine? The former scenario is almost impossible, as the regime has melted away and there is no one left to reinstall. The latter is theoretically possible—at least in Crimea—although it would mean that President Putin has lost all his geopolitical marbles. If Putin does throw all caution to the wind and acts only on irrational impulse, he will only consolidate democratic rule in Ukraine (nothing rallies people around the flag as much as foreign intervention: even Yanukovych's financial backer, the multibillionaire Rinat Akhmetov, spoke out against partition on February 24th) and provoke Russian democrats and Crimean Tatars to take to the streets (or, possibly, to arms—in which case, you can kiss the peninsula's vaunted beaches good-bye). Such action would also be warning Belarus and Kazakhstan that they might be next. When the dust settles, democratic Ukraine will still be standing, Putin's Russia could be destabilized, and his Customs Union and Eurasian Union would essentially be kaput. An intervention or economic embargo would bring Putin's Russia nothing at best and enormous risks at worst.

The next few months will be heady, as the Parliament and government adopt a variety of important measures to pull back the country from bankruptcy, reintroduce democracy, and move Ukraine irreversibly toward Europe. There will be setbacks. Euphoria will alternate with despair. There may be pushback from desperate Regionnaires. In time, policy details will come into play and divisions will appear in the ranks of the democrats. Ideals will be sullied. Compromises will be reached. Charges of spinelessness will be leveled. Fortunately, these charges will probably be leveled after strategic shifts have taken place and Ukraine has seceded from its Soviet past. And then, with just a little luck, Ukraine could become a normal polity where democratic politics, both clean and dirty, becomes the norm.

*

'Experts' on Ukraine, *World Affairs Journal*, March 20, 2014

An astoundingly large amount of nonsense has been written about Ukraine ever since it came to occupy center stage in the public mind. That's not surprising: most people in most countries barely knew the place existed or assumed it was "really" Russia. The number of Ukraine specialists outside of Ukraine is probably no greater than a few hundred in the entire world. Their expertise was of little interest to people who had no interest in or use for the country.

Now that Ukraine is in the news, it's equally unsurprising that non-experts with an abysmal knowledge of Ukraine are claiming to be able to speak authoritatively about it. Media that feature such people are doing their consumers an enormous disservice. No one would ask a plumber to speak about nuclear weapons or a nuclear physicist about plumbing. And yet it doesn't seem to occur to news outlets that Professor Stephen F. Cohen, a life-long specialist on Russia who has never written anything academic about Ukraine, might be unqualified to opine about Ukraine. Worse, it doesn't trouble Cohen, who has spent a good part of his distinguished academic career insisting that evidence and expertise are indispensable to genuine knowledge. Nor does ignorance of Ukraine keep Henry Kissinger from producing a *Washington Post* op-ed that gets nearly every-thing wrong about the country.

Here's a rule of thumb for media, policymakers, and consumers of news. Before you listen to, read, or watch self-styled experts discussing this topic, first find out whether they read Ukrainian, or at least Russian, and whether they've written anything serious about Ukraine.

The latest two examples of such blather come from two professors, David Hendrickson and Robert English. Like Kissinger, they are specialists in international relations; their views on Ukraine's place in the world order might therefore be trustworthy. Naturally, neither evinces any deep knowledge of Ukraine's history, politics, or culture.

Both scholars set off a larm b ells d iscussing t he p resence i n U kraine's g overnment o f several members of right-wing political organizations, Svoboda and the Right Sector. English even thinks that their presence is more dangerous than Vladimir Putin's invasion of Ukraine's southernmost province, Crimea. Both say these organizations are fascist.

One cannot help but wonder if either scholar has read any of the official Uk rainian-language statements or programs of either organization. For myself, I am fairly certain that neither has availed himself of the extensive academic literature on Ukrainian nationalism. Hendrickson cites one scholar, Per Rudling, whose views on Ukrainian nationalism are as extreme as Noam Chomsky's on American foreign policy. There's nothing wrong with reading Rudling (one suspects Hendrickson didn't read too closely, though, as he misspells Rudling's name twice), but, as any serious scholar and journalist knows, one should always familiarize oneself with a variety of perspectives.

Are Svoboda and the Right Sector fascist? Let's compare them to a bona fide fascist regime. Vladimir Putin's Russia is an authoritarian dictatorship that has a charismatic strong man as its undisputed leader, glorifies him in an unabashed personality cult, and employs hyper-nationalism and neo-imperialism as a source of legitimacy. These features are found in equal measure in Hitler's Germany and Mussolini's Italy, and we justifiably call regimes with such defining characteristics fascist. Unsurprisingly, such regimes are usually violent and intolerant of various minorities.

Now let's look at Svoboda and the Right Sector. Neither group supports authoritarian dictatorship or neo-imperialism. Svoboda aspires to the kind of "ethnocracy" found in Israel—a system of government that, while neither ethnically neutral (Israel is a Jewish state) nor as liberal as the ACLU might desire, is not undemocratic. The Right Sector professes to be more liberal than Svoboda and expresses a moderate form of nationalism, while Svoboda's has significantly diminished during, and possibly as a result of, the Euro Revolution. Both groups, while on the Maidan in Kyiv, actively and easily cooperated with Russian speakers and ethnic minorities. (Ukraine's Jewish leaders have not expressed alarm at their presence in the revolution or government.)

Svoboda has a charismatic leader, Oleh Tyahnybok, but his chances of winning a presidential election and becoming a strongman are virtually nil. The Right Sector's leader, Dmytro Yarosh, lacks even Tyahnybok's charisma and has zero chances of becoming president. Neither movement envelops the leader in a personality cult.

Both Svoboda and Right Sector are on the right. They are decidedly not liberals—and some of them may be fascists—but they are far more like the Tea Party or right-wing Republicans than like fascists or neo-Nazis. I for one wouldn't want them to be setting the tone for Ukrainian policy. But neither would I want the Tea Party to be in charge of Washington. No less important, their role in the Kyiv government is at best tertiary (they would probably win no more than 5 percent of the vote in a national election), and policy is set not by them but by the broad coalition of unquestioned liberal democrats.

Should both groups be monitored? Of course. Might they evolve in a worrisome fashion? Possibly. But Hendrickson and English might be advised to direct most of their monitoring zeal at the activity of Putin and his fascist state. He invaded Ukraine. Neither Tyahnybok nor Yarosh has invaded Russia. Putin may start a land war with Ukraine. Both Tyahnybok and Yarosh will at most defend their country.

Who's the greater threat to Ukraine? Right-wing organizations such as Svoboda and Right Sector, who have a few hundred "fighters" at their disposal, or a full-fledged fascist such as Putin, who has 750,000 soldiers at his? You don't have to be an international relations expert to answer that question.

*

Putin's Warlords vs. Ukraine's Presidential Ballot, *World Affairs Journal*, April 29, 2014

Vladimir Putin appears determined to disrupt the May 25th presidential elections in Ukraine.

The dictator and his warlords have already gone on a rampage in eastern Ukraine's Putinstans: they control two cities, Sloviansk and Kramatorsk, and occupy administrative buildings in several others. Their efforts to destabilize Ukraine will continue, but Putin's warlords will likely share the fate of terrorists the world over and fail to stifle the people's voice.

In the absence of a full-scale war, the elections will take place, they will be fair and free, the international community will recognize them as such, and they will move Ukraine along the road to democracy. After all, Ukrainians want to vote and Kyiv wants them to vote. According to a recent poll conducted by the International Republican Institute, "Despite the fact that 64 percent of respondents believe Russia will try to disrupt or discredit the May 25 presidential election, an overwhelming 84 percent said they either will or are likely to vote. Although enthusiasm for the presidential election is highest in the west (91 percent) and center (92 percent), a majority in all regions say they either will or are likely to vote, 79 percent in the east and 62 percent in the south."

As Russia tries to stop a genuinely democratic, internationally recognized, fair and free ballot, it risks what little reputation it has left. No one, anywhere, will be able to hang on to the illusion that Putin's fascistoid regime is a constructive force—for peace, for democracy, or, indeed, for anything that normal, decent human beings could support. Even German business may have to agree that Putin's Russia is a nasty piece of work.

Putin and his warlords must resort to terrorism precisely because they have so little support among the people they claim to be liberating from the "fascists" in Kyiv. According to the IRI poll:

> Despite Russian propaganda and the claims of pro-Russia militants that Russian-speaking citizens need protection from Moscow, an overwhelming majority of respondents (85 percent) oppose Moscow sending troops to protect Russian-speaking citizens.

> This overwhelming majority opposed to Russian intervention extends to every region (97 percent, west; 94 percent, center; 69 percent, east; 75 percent, south), to all age groups (18–29 year olds, 85 percent; 30–49 year olds, 85 percent; 50 and older, 85 percent), and to men and women (men, 84 percent; women, 86 percent). In addition, 68 percent of Russian-speaking citizens oppose military intervention by Moscow ...

> When asked if it was necessary for the Russian military to come into eastern and/ or southern Ukraine to protect Russian speakers and ethnic Russians, an overwhelming majority (88 percent) said no. That majority was seen across all regions of the country, 98 percent in the west, 95 percent in the center, 73 percent in the east, and 86 percent in the south.

Lacking popular support in Ukraine, Putin's warlords will do what terrorists do: seize buildings, promote anti-Semitism, imprison and kill opposition leaders, attack Roma and other minorities, take neutral observers and journalists hostage, and abuse the population of whichever cities or towns they terrorize. One especially brutal terrorist, the warlord of the Sloviansk Putinstan, Vyacheslav Ponomaryov, recently told a female journalist the following: "We'll adopt all necessary measures to prevent elections in the southeast from taking place. We'll take someone prisoner and hang him by his balls. Got it?" It was Ponomaryov's terrorist pals who, under the leadership of the Russian intelligence officer Igor Strelkov, took hostage a group of OSCE military inspectors on April 25th.

Although Putin and his slippery foreign minister, Sergei Lavrov, will tell the world that the warlords have the support of the people, no one will believe them. Just as no one believes that al-Qaeda or the Taliban represent the people. Indeed, as Putin's terror bands operate in Ukraine ahead of the elections, expect policymakers, journalists, and, most important, residents of the terrorized regions to reach the obvious conclusion: that Putin and his warlords are depriving the people of their voice, their livelihoods, and their lives.

Once that connection is made, watch eastern Ukrainian sentiment turn decisively against Putin. Ukrainians will be determined to vote precisely because Putin and his warlords want them not to vote. Watch Putin's supporters in Russia scratch their heads and wonder why they voted for a loose cannon. Putin doesn't know it yet, but his criminal decision to set up Putinstans could herald his own demise.

Is it possible that Putin's terror will disrupt or shut down the elections? Why should it? Elections take place in extreme circumstances all the time. Look at Iraq and Afghanistan. Despite the best efforts of terrorists and warlords, Iraqis and Afghanis regularly go to the polls, thereby rebuffing warmongers and violence peddlers. Ukraine need only make sure its elections are fair and free—and with the good-faith effort of the democratic government in Kyiv and the technical assistance of the United States, the European Union, and the Organization for Security and Cooperation in Europe, the May 25th ballot will be fair and free and the people's choice will be legitimate.

Putin will insist that the poll was illegitimate. But he's been saying that all along, so why would anyone expect him to change his tune—especially after he's been exposed as a sponsor of terrorism? Besides, who cares what he says? How many people heed the pronouncements of Kim Jong-un and Bashar al-Assad on human rights and democracy?

So why listen to a fascistoid dictator who supports terrorism and warlordism? Why listen to the Kremlin's illegitimate ruler rant and rave about the illegitimacy of a democratic process?

Remember: It's not a democratic ballot in Ukraine that Putin fears most. It's a democratic ballot—period.

*

Ukraine's Election Exposes Putin's Lies, *World Affairs Journal*, May 28, 2014

Despite the best efforts of Vladimir Putin and his terrorist commandos in the eastern Donbas region, Ukraine's presidential elections did in fact take place on May 25th, under conditions that international observers concur were fair and free. As of this writing, Petro Poroshenko appears to have won in one round.

Herewith a few lessons:

First, Ukraine is hardly the unstable almost-failed state that Putin and his Western apologists say it is. The terrorist violence was confined to two provinces—Luhansk and Donetsk. In the rest of the country, the voting proceeded smoothly. On top of that, Ukraine's security forces maintained law and order in much of the country, a positive development that builds on the armed forces' creditable performance in their "anti-terrorist operations" in April and May.

Second, Ukraine is anything but the illegitimate state Putin and his western apologists say it is. Voting participation for the entire country was high: about 60 percent. Not including the two provinces that were terrorized by Putin's commandos, participation was even higher. Everyone knows that the only thing that kept Ukrainians in the Donbas from voting was Putin's terrorists.

Third, Putin's terrorist commandos have been outflanked by the elections. People want stability; they want a return to normality. And they know that elections can bring about both. The terrorists, like Putin, have nothing but violence to offer. That is not a winning electoral platform. Nor is it any way to win the hearts and minds of the eastern Ukrainian population the terrorists claim to be defending from wild-eyed Ukrainian "fascists." Small wonder that, after hemming and hawing for several months, even Ukraine's richest oligarch, Rinat Akhmetov, got off the fence and denounced the terrorists, while calling on Donbas residents to take to the streets and march in protest. (And, in an indication of just what is still so wrong with the Donbas, hundreds of thousands heeded his call. Were they not, one might well ask, capable of acting on their own—without being told to do so by some higher-up?)

Fourth, while Ukraine now has a legitimately elected president, Putin has egg on his face—lots of it. Russia's fascistoid dictator can continue questioning democratic Ukraine's legitimacy, and he is perfectly entitled to believe that fair and free elections are unfair and un-free, but at some point such truculence becomes nothing more than childishness, stupidity, and petulance. Come to think of it, haven't those three qualities defined Putin's behavior since the fall of 2013, when he coerced Ukraine's since-deposed sultan, Viktor Yanukovych, into backing out of the Association Agreement with the European Union? Ask yourself this: just what has Putin gotten out of this entire crisis? An arid peninsula with enormous economic and political problems, a spike in his popularity, and affirmations of love from his Western apologists. And just what has he lost? Good relations with the West, good relations with Ukraine, and the prospect of a rapid recovery of Russia's moribund economy. Isn't it time to recognize the obvious: that Putin's statecraft is about as refined as Yanukovych's?

Fifth, Ukraine's much touted, much decried, and much denounced "radical, right-wing extremists" attracted about 1–2 percent of the vote—which surprised no one who knows a bit about Ukrainian politics. (Contrast that with the 25 percent achieved by France's National Front in the May 25th elections to the European Parliament.) In a word, Ukraine's right-wingers are a fringe phenomenon that has played no serious role in Ukraine's national politics, is playing no serious role in Ukraine's national politics, and will continue to play no serious role in Ukraine's national politics. All those Western, Russian, and Ukrainian analysts who've been beating the drum about the nefarious influence of Ukraine's right in the last few years—while turning a blind eye to the extremism of Yanukovych's thuggish regime and the even worse extremism of the pro-Russian hyper-chauvinists who eventually became the core of Putin's terrorist commandos in eastern Ukraine—have some serious crow to eat. And some serious apologies to make: for diverting attention from the real danger in Ukraine to their own personal obsessions.

Sixth, it may be time to be guardedly optimistic about democratic Ukraine's prospects. True, the Donbas will remain a problem for a long time, but Putin's terrorists are unlikely to branch out to other parts of the country. As Turkey, Israel, Colombia, and many other countries have shown, life can go on, even when terrorists are ensconced in regional strongholds. More important, Putin and his terrorists appear to be in a dead end. The government of Prime Minister Arsenii Yatseniuk has a serious reform program that should bring about radical economic change and a whole-scale decentralization of authority. The newly elected president has good credentials and a huge popular mandate. The West—the United States, the European Union, the International Monetary Fund, and the North Atlantic Treaty Organization—supports Ukraine and will make sure that reforms are in fact implemented. Finally, the capital city, Kyiv, has a new mayor, the pro-Western reformer, Vitaly Klitschko.

Not bad for a country that, according to Putin's Russian propagandists and Western apologists, is supposedly on the verge of collapse.

*

Ukrainians Die, as Europe Coos, *World Affairs Journal*, July 3, 2014

Excuse the lurid title, but it's only a variant of a headline that appeared many years ago in a New York tabloid: "Mother Dies, as Baby Coos." I can't speak for the accuracy of that headline, but today's variant is, alas, all too valid. Because the fact is that Ukrainian soldiers are dying at the hands of Vladimir Putin's terrorist hirelings as European states—and the European Union—are engaging the Kremlin with baby talk and diplo-babble.

Twenty-seven Ukrainian soldiers were killed by the terrorists during the cease-fire declared by President Petro Poroshenko more than a week ago (and which he ended on June 30th). Putin and his foreign minister, Sergey Lavrov, liked the cease-fire and wanted it to continue. What's not to like from the Kremlin's twisted point of view? As the terrorists continued to shoot at Ukrainians, Ukrainian soldiers continued to be sacrificed at the altar of diplo-babble.

Putin's acquiescence in killing Ukrainians makes sense. After all, he's demonized them as fascist vermin, and fascist vermin must, as every good Russian knows, be exterminated. European complicity in the killings makes rather less sense. After all, Europe is supposed to be a community of values. Europe is supposed to be committed to the promotion of democracy and human rights. Europe is supposed to be opposed to wars and fighting and killing.

Do European values stop at Ukraine's borders? Evidently. But then why don't they stop at Russia's? Surely the Germans must see that Russia is not exactly a thriving democracy. Surely the French must see that Russia has engaged in an aggression against Ukraine. Or are they so self-absorbed or dependent on the Kremlin mob that they are blinded to the atrocities taking place in Europe's back yard?

If so, it's small wonder that the European Union is experiencing a crisis. Its financial problems can be fixed. The EU's real crisis is the mismatch between their words, their values, and their actions. If the EU really is a community of values, then it should act like one. If it's too pusillanimous to defend the values it claims are at its core, then it should abandon all pretense of defending democracy and human rights and reinvent itself as a values-free zone.

If you think Ukrainian lives aren't worth a café au lait in Paris or a stein of beer in Munich, then please say so. Have the courage to tell the Ukrainians: "You are not worth my comfort. Your lives are not worth the price of a steak frites. Your existence is of less importance to me than the existence of a juicy Schnitzel on my plate."

So, France, deliver the two Mistral amphibious assault ships to Russia as the Kremlin continues its assault on Ukraine. A few more Ukrainians will die, but the espressos will flow in Paris.

And, Germany, by all means remain committed to sweet-talking Putin, even though you of all countries should know the difference between perpetrators and victims, aggression and resistance, dictatorship and democracy. A few more Ukrainians will die, but the beer will flow in Berlin's *Kneipen*.

And, Austria, even though you should remember just what an Anschluss is, keep signing those pipeline deals. A few more Ukrainians will die, but the wine will continue flowing in Vienna's wine gardens.

What's not to like?

*

What's Next for Ukraine? *European Leadership Network*, September 2014

Unless Vladimir Putin launches a full-scale war against all of Ukraine—in which case all bets are off and prognostications are futile—Ukraine will remain a sovereign state that moves, slowly though inexorably, toward becoming a consolidated democracy, a market economy, a rule of law state, and a member of both the West and the wider community of nations. This optimistic outcome will transpire even if the current Russo-Ukrainian War in eastern Ukraine results in a "frozen conflict" as the result of a Russian occupation of the disputed territory.

The Maidan—or the Revolution of Dignity—that culminated in former President Viktor Yanukovych's flight from Kyiv in late February, 2014, reversed the radical course toward authoritarianism that he and his Party of Regions had pursued since his election in early 2010. As a result, Ukraine's elites and civil society now share an unprecedented consensus on the need for radical reform, while the primary opponents of reform—the Party of Regions, the Donbas elites, and the Communist Party—have been irreversibly weakened and no longer pose a challenge to the democratic, pro-Western forces. For the first time in its history as an independent state, Ukraine also enjoys the support of the West in general and of key Western institutions and states, in particular. Internally and externally, Ukraine resembles Poland in the early 1990s and, as such, is poised to make a reform breakthrough.

Western support is only partly due to the Maidan's endorsement of democratic values and human rights. Far more important in turning the West decisively toward Ukraine was Russia's aggression and its violation of the international order. That aggression went through four, increasingly more violent stages. The first was the occupation and annexation of Ukraine's Crimean Autonomous Republic. The second was the transformation of an armed pro-Russian separatist movement in the eastern provinces of Donetsk and Luhansk into a Russian-led proxy force supported with armaments, money, and personnel. The third was the Russian proxies' employment of terror, wanton destruction, and anti-civilian violence (which included the downing in July of Malaysian Airlines Flight MH17) in their struggle against the Ukrainian army's attempt to reassert control over those parts of the Donbas they controlled. The fourth was the open invasion of eastern Ukraine by Russian regular troops in late August.

The upshot of the Russian aggression in eastern Ukraine was the emergence in most of Ukraine of an unprecedented patriotism and sense of Ukrainian identity as well as the formation of a more effective Ukrainian state apparatus and army. Putin's imperialist policies succeeded in creating what Ukrainian elites had unsuccessfully pursued since 1991: state and nation building. The Russian invasion of eastern Ukraine also led to the progressive destruction of large parts of the Donbas, the very region Moscow claimed to be "liberating" from the "fascist junta" in Kyiv. In turn, the destruction of the Donbas produced a humanitarian catastrophe that Putin insisted had to be rectified with a further Russian intervention.

The destruction of the Donbas has several additional consequences for Ukraine and Russia. First, whatever its future status, the Donbas will never again have the same clout that once enabled it to obstruct reform and strong-arm Kyiv into tailoring its policies to its demands. Second, whoever eventually comes to control the disputed parts of the Donbas will have acquired an economic mess requiring enormous expenditure of resources. If Russia takes control, it will have to expend its own resources, under conditions of declining economic growth and painful international sanctions. If Ukraine seizes control, its already strained budget will be taxed, while the West is likely to assist with significant economic assistance. Third, if Russia manages to transform parts of the Donbas into a zone of frozen conflict, the political benefit to it and the political harm to Ukraine will be close to nil. Russia will be saddled with the very humanitarian catastrophe its imperialism produced, Western sanctions will increase, and its ongoing transformation into a rogue state will be complete.

In contrast, although Ukraine will have lost territory and suffered a blow to its pride, the emergence of a frozen conflict in the Donbas will only consolidate the nation around the state, enhance Ukrainian patriotism and identity, increase the international community's sympathy for Ukraine's victimhood, and in no way prevent Ukraine's progressive integration into the West and the world. After all, Moldova and Georgia, with their own frozen conflicts in, respectively, Transnistria and Abkhazia/South Ossetia, signed Association Agreements with the European Union in advance of Ukraine. Azerbaijan has enjoyed rapid economic growth despite its loss of Nagorno-Karabakh to Armenia. Frozen conflicts are inconveniences, but not impediments to modernization and Westernization.

In principle, the solution to the Russo-Ukrainian war is simple. Russia withdraws its troops and its proxies; Ukraine agrees to grant what remains of the destroyed Donbas far-reaching decentralization of authority and language rights. Both sides agree to rebuild the region in cooperation with the international community, to base their economic relations on free-market principles, and to respect each other's security, sovereignty, and stability. Ukraine could even sweeten the pot by agreeing not to seek NATO membership.

The problem is not with finding a thinkable solution that would benefit both Ukraine and Russia. The problem is with finding a solution that Putin would accept. The wild card in all these scenarios is Russia's unconstitutionally elected president, who has revived its imperial ambitions and constructed a hyper-dictatorial regime that shares the characteristics of interwar Italy and Germany. Thanks to his mendacity, ruthlessness, and unpredictability, he has engaged Ukraine in a (thus far) limited war and made a massive war in Europe imaginable for the first time since the end of the Cold War. Ukraine and the West must pursue every possible diplomatic solution to the conflict and be ready for every possible reasonable compromise, but they have no choice but to regard Putin and his aggressive regime with the utmost suspicion. The West, if it wants to survive, also has no choice but to view Ukraine as the front line of Europe's own defense against Russian imperialism. If the West fails to do so, Putin's destruction of the post-Cold War European order may be inevitable.

*

Ukraine's Real and Unreal Elections, *World Affairs Journal*, November 12, 2014

Ukraine recently witnessed one real election and one pseudo-election, but both may be turning points in the country's history.

The real election, to the Rada (Ukraine's Parliament in Kyiv), took place on October 26th; the pseudo-election, in the Donbas enclave occupied by Russia and its proxies, took place on November 2nd. The former was fair and free and, as a referendum on popular attitudes, produced a clear victory for pro-Western, pro-democratic, and pro-Ukrainian parties. The latter was a staged event overseen by thugs with guns that, unsurprisingly, produced a clear victory for the pro-Russian thugs with guns.

The online newspaper *Ukrainska Pravda* conveniently broke down electoral outcomes by province according to their pro-European and pro-Russian tendencies. Importantly, every single Ukrainian province—including all those in the southeast (Odessa, Mykolaiv, Kherson, Zaporizhzhya, Dnipropetrovsk, Kyiv-controlled Donetsk and Luhansk, and Kharkiv)—had more pro-European votes than pro-Russian votes. These were also the regions where the pro-Russian parties did best, but, no less importantly, their best was a far cry from what it had been in the parliamentary elections of 2012. In a word, a political sea change—toward the West, democracy, and Ukraine, and away from everything Russia stands for—appears to have taken place in Ukraine's southeast.

A closer look at the figures will bear out these conclusions. I calculated for each of the southeastern provinces the percentage increase of the pro-European vote and the percentage decrease of the pro-Russian vote. Here are the results: Odessa (+61 percent, –37 percent); Mykolaiv (+82 percent, –47 percent); Kherson (+68 percent, –53 percent); Zaporizhzhya (+74 percent, –37 percent); Dnipropetrovsk (+63 percent, –40 percent); Donetsk (+264 percent, –33 percent); Luhansk (+245 percent, –30 percent); Kharkiv (+47 percent, –29 percent). These are impressive trends. Just how impressive is clear from a comparison with the same percentages for three regions where the pro-Europeans did exceptionally well: Lviv Province (+7 percent, –71 percent), Kyiv city (+16 percent, –60 percent), and Poltava Province (+42 percent, –66 percent). Since these three are already very pro-European, they have less room for improvement than the southeast. But if current trends in the southeast continue, it should be making leaps and bounds and catch up within a decade or so. Not bad for a region that is still considered unremittingly pro-Russian and pro-Soviet by clueless Western "experts."

In contrast to these elections, the ballot in the Donbas enclave tells us nothing about popular preferences. Its importance lies elsewhere. Clearly, the Russian proxies who control the territory are determined to acquire as much independence as they can and to do so regardless of international agreements and norms. That's no surprise, of course, as they've flouted all civilized norms ever since they appeared in the spring of 2014. What's new is that no one, anywhere, can still harbor any illusions about their intentions. They will stay in the enclave until they are driven out. Indeed, they may even want to expand their sphere of influence by attacking Ukraine. Although they say they want to negotiate with Kyiv, their indifference to dialogue, their commitment to violence, and their predilection for creating *faits accomplis* demonstrate that there is nothing to talk about with them. Ironically, even Russia's illegitimately elected ruler, Vladimir Putin, may have come to a similar conclusion, having pointedly refrained from recognizing the elections or from holding talks with the terrorists.

Kyiv, correctly, revoked the autonomous status it granted the enclave as part of the Minsk agreement of September 5th. Prime Minister Arsenii Yatseniuk also announced that Ukraine would cease providing the enclave with subsidies amounting to some 34.2

billion hryvnia (about $2.3 billion). At the same time, Yatseniuk also noted that gas and electricity would continue to be provided to the enclave—gratis.

Kyiv faces a dilemma. The enclave has declared independence from Ukraine and is waging a bloody war against Ukrainian troops. It's quite possible that the Russian proxies may soon launch a large-scale offensive against Ukrainian positions in the Donbas and, possibly, elsewhere. At the same time, in providing billions of hryvnia to the enclave's (oftentimes anti-Ukrainian) government institutions (as well as non-functioning coal mines!), not to mention free gas and electricity, Ukraine is effectively subsidizing the very terrorists it claims to be opposing. Kyiv would say it has an obligation to keep its citizens in the enclave warm. True. But it also has an obligation to keep its citizens outside the enclave safe. So which is the greater priority: the security and survival of a huge country with some 40 million people or the warmth of a small Russian-controlled enclave with some 4 million? At the very least, Kyiv could insist that some dummy entity in the enclave pay Ukraine the exact same price for the gas that it's agreed to pay Russia—$385 per 1,000 cubic meters.

The terrorists may soon make that question moot. If, as seems likely to an increasingly large number of sober Ukrainian analysts, they attack Ukraine, and if, as also seems likely, Russian artillery and bombers rain destruction on Ukrainian soldiers and civilians, Kyiv's hand will be forced and the subsidies will likely cease. The result of Putin's continued aggression cannot be foretold, but you can be certain that the tens of thousands of dead Ukrainians and Russians (one Russian analyst **estimates** that 35,000 Russians would die in a war against Ukraine) will unfortunately give Russia's cruel dictator few sleepless nights.

*

Does Ukraine's Reform Plan Measure Up? *World Affairs Journal*, November 21, 2014

The reform plan of Ukraine's coalition government-in-the-making has received mixed reviews from a team of Ukraine experts affiliated with the policy discussion website VoxUkraine.

According to the analysis:

> We assign PASS to 3 sections out of 17, and CONDITIONAL PASS to 6 sections out of 17. We find that the draft does not have a coherent ideology and that many sections advocate Soviet style command economy approach to reforms, while only few sections address the structural causes of the problems in Ukraine.

The good news is that the team rates three of 17 sections as excellent, six as subject to improvement, five as "water" (or boilerplate), and only four as bad. That's nine of 17 that are at least good enough. And those nine include law enforcement, national security, and energy independence (pass) as well as anti-corruption, decentralization, regulation and competition policy, infrastructure and transportation, electoral reform, and ecology (conditional pass).

The bad news is that eight of 17 don't pass muster, and, worse, these include such key sectors as judicial and financial reform ("water") and agricultural, constitutional, and economic-growth reform (fail). If you believe that judicial reform underpins all the other reforms, then none of the reforms will take off without a fundamental restructuring of the courts. If, alternatively, you believe that economic growth is the *sine qua non* of many of the other reforms, then you're likely to view the bad news as really, really bad.

Unlike the VoxUkraine team, Anders Aslund of the Washington-based Peterson Institute for International Economics believes the entire document is a disaster:

> The draft coalition agreement even reminded me of reading Leonid Brezhnev's speech at the 26th Party Congress of the Communist Party of the Soviet Union in 1981. This is not a reform program but an old-style bureaucratic Soviet document for the preservation of the old system. Such a conservative document will never bring reform. There is no declaration of will or strategy. The document does not even start with a set of goals but with a bureaucratic laundry list.

Aslund and VoxUkraine can't both be right: the document cannot be both wholly conservative and partially reform-oriented. Their disagreement may be rooted in the fact that Aslund is assessing the document primarily from the economic point of view, while the VoxUkraine team looked at all its dimensions.

Be that as it may, political realists might interject by arguing that no (democratic) government ever adopts or promotes fully consistent reform programs or implements all its stated goals. Seen in this light, the fact that a coalition of five squabbling parties managed to produce a document that is more than half passable is quite an impressive achievement. And were Ukraine to introduce serious reforms in nine of 17 sectors, we should, once again, probably thank the gods.

My own sense is that, while many of the reforms do go together and need either to be passed simultaneously in order to work or depend on some one key sector to work, many are also discrete. I can agree that judicial and constitutional reform underpins anti-corruption and electoral reform, but I'm not sure that building an effective army (national security) and constructing infrastructure and transportation depend (as much or at all) on good courts. America, for instance, became a regional power and expanded its railroads westward in the second half of the nineteenth century, and yet its courts were highly deficient. Which is only to say that much progress can probably be made in the nine areas that get a pass or conditional pass even without equal progress in the eight areas that fail.

There are two more upsides to the coalition document.

First, it's an extensive list of all the reforms the coalition has in mind. As a result, it's open to evaluation by such groups as the VoxUkraine team. Whether or not the governing coalition actually listens to criticism is another thing. But, at the very least, Western states and Ukrainian civil society will be able easily to monitor the government's progress and make aid conditional on forward movement in neglected areas. As the VoxUkraine team says:

> Interestingly, the best sections are those on Energy Independence, National Security, and Law Enforcement, which are the key areas for the survival of the sovereignty of Ukraine. Some other good areas are based on the EU directives (see ecology, e.g.). The less pressing areas offer a more depressing picture. This gives support to the argument that the change for the better in Ukraine can come only because of the external pressure to the state. The sections that are supposed to respond to domestic challenges such as social sphere, public utility services, and healthcare are low quality.

Second, the document assigns deadlines to the accomplishment of individual reforms. That, too, will enable Western states, experts such as Aslund, and Ukrainian citizens to keep track of government progress.

All in all, the coalition document has probably earned a conditional pass. That's not great, compared to the ideal requirements of experts. Compared to what Ukraine's previous governments have accomplished in the past 25 years, however, it may be borderline amazing.

And that may be the final bit of good news: Ukrainians now demand more of their government. Barely good enough just isn't good enough anymore. You can thank the Orange Revolution and the Revolution of Dignity for that.

*

Ukraine's Pro-Reform Cabinet, *World Affairs Journal*, December 22, 2014

Ukraine may finally have a cabinet able to introduce radical reforms. For the first time in independent Ukraine's history, its ministers are young and Western. Youth matters, as it's a measure of the degree to which individuals are still captives of the Soviet past. Western attitudes and experience also matter, as they presumably reflect the willingness and ability of the ministers to embark on pro-Western reforms.

The composition of the new cabinet was announced on December 2nd. Most commentators focused on the fact that three of the ministers were foreigners—an American, a Lithuanian, and a Georgian. That was certainly indicative of Kyiv's willingness to think "out of the box," especially as two of the three received the crucial economic development and finance portfolios.

But the objective characteristics of the 20 cabinet members are no less important. Their mean age is 43.7; their median age is 44.5. (I was unable to find the date of birth of one minister: judging from his appearance, I calculated it at 45.) Here's the age breakdown: 59, 50, 49, 49, 49, 47, 47, 47, 46, 45, 44, 44, 43, 40, 38, 38, 38, 36, 35, 30. The majority have spent more time living in post-Soviet than in Soviet conditions. The 59-year-old was 36 when the USSR collapsed, and the 30-year-old was only 7, but all the others were somewhere between 12 and 26 in 1991. And if you consider that Mikhail Gorbachev's perestroika marked the end of Soviet totalitarianism, then the caesura gets moved back to 1986—which means that most of the ministers were between 7 and 21 when the Soviet world began to end.

No less important, the ministers are remarkably Western. Exactly one-half have studied abroad for some time; one-half have also had some form of extended experience with the West, whether in business, politics, or diplomacy. If you count all the individuals with either Western educations or Western experience (Western education and experience don't always go together), then the number of ministers with some acquaintance with the West rises to 12—or 60 percent. In other words, these people know the West. They understand Western institutions and Western rules of the game. According to economist Anders Aslund, "All but two of the 20 ministers speak English, while only two ministers spoke English in President Viktor Yanukovych's last government."

Do these characteristics automatically mean that the ministers will promote pro-Western reforms? Of course, not. On the other hand, these are just the features we would expect to see in a pro-Western, pro-reform cabinet. Naturally, one can criticize each individual minister for this or that—and the Ukrainian press has gleefully, and rightly, done just that. (Thus far, no exceptionally embarrassing skeletons have been found.) In the aggregate, however, this is an excellent group that has the knowledge and experience to introduce radical change. No less important, this is a group that probably understands that Ukraine's economy could collapse in the absence of reforms and that the West will help Ukraine only if it embarks on reform.

So, the news from Ukraine, at least with respect to the government, is quite good—finally. Given the positive nature of this development, it's all the more bizarre for liberal, level-headed Western commentators to repeat the Kremlin's line on the continuing threat of fascism in Ukraine. Here's the celebrated author Anatol Lieven, currently a professor at Georgetown University's School of Foreign Service in Qatar:

> Kyiv's dependence on ... oligarchs and on nationalist militias to fight the war in eastern Ukraine represents a serious and growing threat to Ukrainian democracy and to the spread of liberal values in Ukraine.

> A worrying sign in this regard was the appointment last month of Vadim Troyan as regional chief of police in Kyiv. His regiment, the Azov battalion, is known for links to the far right and his promotion seems largely in reward for his group's participation in the fighting in eastern Ukraine.

But wait: doesn't Kyiv's appointment of a democratic cabinet represent a serious and growing promotion of Ukrainian democracy and of the spread of liberal values? Isn't it at least worth mentioning, if only to provide some balance? Doesn't the appointment of 20 pro-reform ministers trump the appointment of one right-wing cop?

And just why was Troyan appointed? Lieven obviously doesn't know (hence his use of two conditionals "seems largely", but if he had done some research, he might have learned that Interior Minister Arsen Avakov "seems largely" to have wanted a tough individual with the guts to implement his planned radical reform of the militia in a key province.

Personally, I don't care for the Azov Battalion's ideological leanings, and I share Lieven's knee-jerk distaste for anyone sharing them. On the other hand, Troyan completed the Kharkiv University of Internal Affairs, proved himself in difficult fighting in eastern Ukraine, and was associated with Avakov's former business partner, Oleksandr Lypchansky. None of this excuses Troyan's politics—whatever they are—but it does sug-gest that Avakov wasn't rewarding Azov when he promoted Troyan. Instead, he was pro-moting his own reform agenda and drawing on someone with the requisite experience and the old-boy connections. Avakov was acting like a *Western* politician, but that banal-ity does not, alas, fit the sexier narrative of fascists lurking behind every tree.

*

Is Ukraine Fascist? *Huffington Post*, February 3, 2015

So which is it? Is Ukraine a hotbed of fascism, as the Kremlin and its supporters insist? Or is it a tolerant democracy, as Kyiv and its supporters insist?

The issue is important to sort out since members of the new Greek government, including Prime Minister Tsipsas, have suggested in the recent past that the new government in Kyiv has neo-fascist links that harken to memories of World War II. And that has been the view often promoted by the Kremlin from the outset of the conflict.

Although there are often two sides to a story, in this case, there really isn't. The Kremlin is dead wrong, and even though Ukraine isn't quite the consolidated democracy that its government says it is, the country is certainly far more democratic now than it was just over a year ago. And, despite some zigzags, it is becoming more democratic with every day.

Let's start with a brief discussion of what fascism is and then ask whether any of Ukraine's present or past government fits the bill.

What Is Fascism?

Fascism is often used as an epithet, especially by the left, but it is a perfectly respectable academic term that refers to a particular type of political system. Everyone can agree that fascist states are authoritarian—that is, they lack the fundamental attributes of democracy. Unlike democracies, fascist systems lack meaningful parliaments, judiciaries, parties, political contestation and elections. In fascist systems, as in all authoritarian systems, parliaments are rubber-stamp institutions, judiciaries do what the leader tells them, opposition parties are marginal and electoral outcomes are preordained.

Like all authoritarian states, fascist states are highly centralized and hierarchical, they give pride of place within the power structure to soldiers and policemen, usually secret policemen, and they always have a supreme leader. Indeed, there can be no fascist state without a supreme leader. Like authoritarian states, fascist states limit freedom of the press, freedom of speech and freedom of assembly; and espouse some form of ethnocentrism glorifying their nation and their state and their fabulous past, present and future.

But fascist states are not just run-of-the-mill authoritarian states. The latter typically connotes images of dour old men ruling a sullen population. Fascist states exude youth and vigor, and they always implicate the population in its own repression. Fascist leaders strut. They want to appear youthful, manly and active: they are machos, par excellence. They also appeal to those qualities in the population, usually co-opting the young into their movements or parties. No less important, fascist states are popular: they incorporate the population into the system of rule, promising it a grand and glorious future in exchange for its enthusiasm and support.

Not surprisingly, fascist states tend to sound and act aggressively. The soldiers and policemen that run fascist states have a natural proclivity to toughness and weaponry. The ethnocentrism appeals to national and state glory, and cult of vigor sees enemies everywhere. The machismo-based cult-like status of leaders encourages them to pound their chests with abandon. And the population's implication in its own repression leads it to balance its self-humiliation with attempts to humiliate others.

Seen in this light, Franco's Spain, Pinochet's Chile and the Greece of the colonels were just your average authoritarian states. So, too, is today's China. In contrast, Mussolini's Italy was clearly fascist, as was Hitler's Germany and Atatürk's Turkey. What of today's Ukraine?

I trust the question answers itself. Ukraine has a tri-partite government structure characterized by an independent presidency and parliament and a semi-independent (though corrupt) judiciary, a vigorous multi-party system, fair and free elections—most recently, of both president and the parliament—a free (if sometimes irresponsible) press and protection of human, civil and minority rights. Of special importance is the fact that Ukraine's government is run by civilians only and that its president—Petro Poroshenko—has none of the strongman features that a fascist supreme leader promotes via a machismo-based cult of personality. Last but not least, Ukraine has not pursued any of the repressive policies associated with fascism. Oppositions, minorities and marginal groups thrive, civil society is strong, and, if anything, Ukrainians accuse the government of being too weak—and certainly not too strong.

Ukraine is far from a consolidated democracy. Its democratic institutions are young and weak; its commitment to democratic practices has not yet stood the test of time. Police, judges and politicians are often corrupt, and bad policies are frequently adopted. These faults make Ukraine a flawed democracy, possibly a very flawed democracy, but they do not come anywhere near to making it a fascist state.

Is Ukraine Ruled by Fascists?

Supporters of the Ukraine-is-fascist argument might say that Ukraine is not fascist, but its rulers are fascists who want to establish a fascist system of rule. Alas, this claim is absurd.

Poroshenko and his predecessor, Acting President Oleksandr Turchynov, are obviously not fascists. None of the current cabinet members has anything resembling fascist credentials. The government that succeeded the corrupt Yanukovych dictatorship in late February 2014 consisted of 19 individuals: only two (Defense Minister Ihor Teniukh and Deputy Prime Minister Oleksandr Sych) were members of the right-wing Svoboda party and one, the Secretary of the National and Security Defense Council Andrii Parubii, had right-wing ties until 2004.

In early 2014, Svoboda had 38 seats in Ukraine's parliament—out of a total of 450. Svoboda's leader, Oleh Tyahnybok, had run for president in the 2010 elections that brought Yanukovych to power and received 1.43 percent of the vote. He ran again, in the presidential ballot of May 25, 2014, and received 1.16 percent. Dmytro Yarosh, head of the right-wing Right Sector, received a mere 0.70 percent in 2014. In the October 26, 2104, parliamentary elections, Svoboda and the Right Sector got, respectively, six seats and one seat.

Tyahnybok has made some anti-Semitic and anti-Russian statements in the past but his language and behavior changed significantly during, and as a result of, the Maidan Revolution that ousted Yanukovych. He has since attempted to position himself as a moderate nationalist.

Svoboda's approach to ethnic relations has been termed fascist but in fact it is strikingly similar to official policy in Estonia, Latvia and Israel. In effect, Svoboda aspires to create a "lite" version of what Israeli scholar Oren Yiftachel calls an "ethnocracy," a system of rule within which the titular nation holds a position of dominance over the other nations inhabiting the land, such as Estonians and Latvians vis-à-vis Russians or Jews vis-à-vis Palestinians. As the Baltic and Israeli examples show, ethnocracies can be democratic, but they're obviously not as democratic as liberal democracies and, with their penchant for hierarchy, can easily violate the civil rights of minorities.

Although Tyahnybok has gone on record praising Israel for the fact that all its parties are nationalist, Svoboda does not call for disenfranchising minorities in the manner of the Balts and Israelis. Instead, it supports a radical affirmative-action policy that would decisively promote Ukrainians and their language and culture within all spheres of the Ukrainian state and restrict citizenship to ethnic Ukrainians, everyone born in Ukraine and foreigners who speak Ukrainian. It goes without saying that Svoboda is anything but liberal (its representatives often deride Ukrainian liberals as "liberasts"—a combination of liberal and pederasts) and that its ranks also include genuine anti-Semites, xenophobes and racists (the openly neo-Nazi ideologue, Yuri Mykhalchyshyn, comes to mind). But their relative presence in the party is probably no greater than that of Russian supremacists and Ukrainophobes in Yanukovych's Party of Regions and the Communist Party of Ukraine.

Svoboda's socio-economic program, which is a mishmash of socially conservative, capitalist and socialist elements and often reads like a Tea Party document, is pretty much irrelevant to its supporters. It is not surprising that the party has done next to nothing in the provincial councils it controls in western Ukraine. Svoboda has neither implemented xenophobic policies nor bothered with economic issues. What they have done is engage in the shrill, anti-establishment, populist rhetoric that got them elected in the first place. Their inactivity is probably due to their ingrained preference for street politics, their absence of economic knowledge and their paucity of intellectual skills. In the first and second respects, the nationalists resemble Ukraine's Communists. In the second and third, they resemble the Party of Regions.

The Right Sector, meanwhile, only emerged during the Maidan Revolution. Its members have indeed been among the foremost anti-Russian and anti-Yanukovych militants who then manned the barricades. Since then, they have actively participated in volunteer battalions in the fighting in eastern Ukraine. There are probably no more than a few hundred or a few thousand members, and their support within the population at large is under one percent. Interestingly, Yarosh, their leader, has criticized Svoboda for being anti-Semitic, while one of Right Sector's leading activists is a practicing conservative Jew.

In sum, the right-wing presence in Ukraine's post-Yanukovych government has been so slight as to be virtually invisible.

Why Putin Calls Ukraine Fascist

So why, then, do Putin and his supporters see fascism ablaze in Kyiv? There are several reasons for this bizarre charge.

First, as the above characterization of fascism's key features should have suggested, the country that possesses all of them is not Ukraine—but Putin's Russia. Its democratic institutions are at best moribund, having been transformed into pliant tools of the Kremlin; civil society and the press have been severely circumscribed; representatives of the military and secret police dominate all ruling elites and suffuse them with their anti-democratic ethos; the Russian nation and state are unabashedly glorified; Putin is the undisputed leader, and his macho image exudes vigor, youth and manliness; a variety of rabidly pro-Putin youth groups act as the vanguard of the state; the population overwhelmingly supports Putin and has done so since he assumed the presidency; ethnocentrism, a mistrust of both internal and external foreigners and a corresponding glorification of Russia's past (including its criminal Stalinist period) and present are the official worldview; Russia has taken to asserting its "rightful" place in the sun by engaging in war against Georgia and Ukraine.

It makes a great deal of sense for Putin and his propaganda apparatus to accused Ukraine of the very crime that he has committed—to deflect world attention from his own transformation of Russia into a repressive state.

Second, the Kremlin needs to insist that Ukraine's democrats are fascists because it insists that Yanukovych was a democratic leader. Yanukovych was corrupt and dictatorial. He was rapidly closing down Ukrainian civil society and transforming the parliament into a rump institution, but he was too incompetent and too comical to be able to project the he-man image that Putin had perfected. Since the Kremlin refuses to acknowledge the right of people to oust tyrants, it must insist that Ukraine is ruled by a "junta"—which is just shorthand for fascism. According to this logic, Americans had no right to rebel against King George, and the government led by Washington, Jefferson and Hamilton was nothing but a junta!

Finally, the Kremlin's insistence that democratic Ukraine is fascist goes back to old Soviet—as well as tsarist Russian—stereotypes of Ukrainians who insisted on their democratic and/or national rights as traitors, agents of imperialism, capitalist stooges and, of course, fascists. Ironically, continued use by Putin and his supporters of such terminology demonstrates just how deeply they are still ensnared in Stalinist political culture.

The bottom line is this: Putin has transformed Russia into a fascist state. Ukraine ousted Yanukovych in order to avoid becoming fully authoritarian. The war Putin unleashed against Ukraine is his way of telling Ukraine that fascism and democracy are incompatible.

*

Why Russia Will Lose in Ukraine, *World Affairs Journal*, February 24, 2015

So, who's winning the war in eastern Ukraine—Russia or Ukraine? The answer is not as simple as it might seem, because victory means different things for each side.

A Russian victory could take one of two forms: territorial expansion into large parts of southeastern Ukraine or the imposition on Ukraine of disadvantageous peace terms. Or it could take both forms. But neither has happened, and neither is likely to happen.

Anything short of such a victory amounts to a defeat for Russia. Having destroyed the Russian economy, transformed Russia into a rogue state, and alienated Russia's allies in the "near abroad," Vladimir Putin loses if he doesn't win big.

In contrast, Ukraine wins as long as it does not lose big. If Ukraine can contain the aggression, it will demonstrate that it possesses the will and the military capacity to deter the Kremlin, stop Putin and his proxies, and survive as an independent democratic state.

The balance of forces could change. Russia could throw hundreds of thousands of regular troops against Ukraine in order to seize Kyiv or build a land corridor to Crimea. But this would dramatically increase Putin's risk factor. In that case, Ukrainians would fight to the finish, a partisan war would ensue, the United States would supply weapons to Ukraine, other Eastern European countries might get involved in the fighting, Western sanctions would be ratcheted up, and Russia would be excluded from the SWIFT international banking system. Russian losses—human, financial, and material—would likely be enormous, inviting a palace coup against Putin.

Although Putin is driven by a bizarre vision of reestablishing Holy Russia's greatness, he is enough of a realpolitik policymaker to understand that attempting to overrun Ukraine would have dire consequences for Russia and himself.

Putin is therefore likely to maintain the military pressure on Ukraine—having the separatists strike here, strike there, withdraw, regroup, make nice, and then repeat the cycle—in the hope of draining Ukraine's economic, military, and human resources.

But that, too, won't result in territorial expansion into large parts of southeastern Ukraine or the imposition on Ukraine of disadvantageous peace terms.

Thus far skittish about military aid, the Obama administration is coming under increasing pressure to provide Ukraine with lethal weapons and real-time intelligence. Provided that meaningful economic reforms move forward in Kyiv, chances are good that other Western states and institutions will give Ukraine significant economic assistance, especially now that the IMF has committed itself to a $40 billion aid package. And the more Western money is sunk into Ukraine, the greater the likelihood that Western states will follow with military aid, if only as a guarantee of their financial investment. Meanwhile, Ukrainian elites—prodded by the West and compelled by Putin's threat to annihilate Ukraine—will embark on (more or less) radical economic reforms.

The Ukrainian armed forces are getting stronger and more effective by the day, inflicting high casualties on the militants and Russians and maintaining their positions. Even the retreat from the Debaltsevo salient, mistakenly portrayed in the Western press as a "debacle," was anything but. (In order to know that, however, you need to be able to read Ukrainian- and Russian-language sources.) According to one of Ukraine's top military analysts, Yuri Biryukov, Ukraine's losses were 179 dead and 89 missing and presumed dead in the period from January 18th to February 18th, while Russian and proxy losses amounted to 868 dead—roughly three to four times as many. And small wonder. As Ukraine's other top military analyst, Yuri Butusov, has repeatedly argued on his Facebook page, there is simply no comparison between the Ukrainian army of today and the ragtag band of soldiers that was Ukraine's armed forces in March of 2014, when Putin seized Crimea. More important, Ukraine's less than competent military command appears to be on the verge of a major change in personnel.

The situation on the front is a military stalemate that is as deleterious to the Donbas enclave's economic viability as it is beneficial to Ukraine's ability to survive as an independent political entity. As this blog has argued ad nauseam, a frozen conflict—which may be in the process of emerging, even though everyone denies it—would be the best thing that could possibly happen to Ukraine.

Finally, although Ukrainians are one-fourth as many as Russians, Ukrainians are fighting for their homeland. In both eastern and western Ukraine, they know this is perhaps their last chance to break free of Moscow's imperial grip. The remarkable thing about Ukraine's dedicated volunteer battalions is the high number of eastern Ukrainians in them. Western Ukrainians dominated in both the 2004 Orange Revolution and the 2014 Maidan Revolution. Russian-speaking eastern Ukrainians have demonstrated that, when it comes to defending their own homes, they're more than willing to step up.

Russia can't win big. Ukraine can't lose big. And that means that Russia is losing and Ukraine is winning—and that Russia will lose and Ukraine will win.

The West should know that, in supporting Ukraine, it's not just doing the right thing. It's also betting on the winner.

*

Is There Economic Reform in Ukraine? *World Affairs Journal,* March 23, 2015

If you listen to Ukrainians tell it, there's been absolutely no reform within the last year. Their frustration is understandable—they want the positive effects of major change *now*—but their perception just doesn't correspond to the facts.

The much-awaited reform process is actually under way—though quietly and unobtrusively. The Education Ministry and the Ministry of Internal Affairs have led the way with restructuring universities and the police force, probably because they don't deal directly with high-stakes corruption and the power of the oligarchs. Some personnel cuts have been introduced in the presidential administration and the government bureaucracy; more are forecast. A law (albeit flawed) on lustration has been adopted and has already led to some high-level resignations and prosecutions. An Anti-Corruption Bureau has been approved, and a head is currently being sought.

Perhaps most important, economic reform is a reality. According to the invaluable VoxUkraine Index for Monitoring Reforms, compiled by Tymofiy Mylovanov, an economist at the University of Pittsburgh, and a team of economists with specialized knowledge of Ukraine, the level of Ukraine's economic reform efforts—when measured on a –5 to +5 scale, with the +2–3 range being "acceptable"—is moving in the right direction. (The index measures the quality of reform measures adopted in a two-week period, and not the overall progress of reform.) Here are Ukraine's scores for 2015:

- January 11th: 1.1

- January 25th: 1.3

- February 8th: 1.5

- February 22nd: 0.3

- March 8th: 2.2

If you discount the February 22nd score as an outlier, then the trend is clearly upward. More important than the overall score are the individual components for these five dates and the averages of the five scores (in parentheses):

- Governance and anti-corruption: 0.9, 1.8, 2.0, 1.0, 2.9 (1.72)

- Public finance: 1.0, 1.5, 2.0, 0.0, 2.0 (1.3)

- Monetary policy and financial markets: 0.8, 1.0, 2.5, 0.0, 3.0 (1.46)

- Energy independence: 2.0, 1.0, 0.8, 0.0, 3.0 (1.36)

- Foreign trade: 0.6, 1.0, 0.0, 0.5, 0.0 (0.42)

The foreign trade sector is obviously unreformed—with an average of 0.42—but all the others have decent, though not yet acceptable, average scores. If the February 22nd scores are excluded—for the simple reason that almost no legislation was adopted in that two-week period—then the overall trend for the individual category scores is very clearly upward and the four-score averages (in parentheses) look very different:

- Governance and anti-corruption: 0.9, 1.8, 2.0, 2.9 (1.9)

- Public finance: 1.0, 1.5, 2.0, 2.0 (1.63)

- Monetary policy and financial markets: 0.8, 1.0, 2.5, 3.0 (1.83)

- Energy independence: 2.0, 1.0, 0.8, 3.0 (1.7)

- Foreign trade: 0.6, 1.0, 0.0, 0.0 (0.4)

The averages for the first four categories are almost acceptable, being just beneath 2.0, but the last two individual scores for Governance and anti-corruption, public finance, and monetary policy and financial markets are already acceptable, being, respectively, 2.0/2.9, 2.0/2.0, and 2.5/3.0.

Naturally, Ukraine still has a long way to go. But reform *has* begun, and if Kyiv sustains its political will, the West continues to insist on change, and Vladimir Putin continues to remind Ukraine that the alternative to reform is subjugation to Russia—then 2015 may be the year of reform in Ukraine. Perhaps that's why the IMF's permanent representative in Ukraine, Jerome Vacher, stated on March 19th that the IMF expects economic growth to resume in late 2015 and to constitute 2 percent in 2016—nothing to write home about, but significantly better than the 5.5 percent drop expected in 2015.

Ukraine Doesn't Have a Warlord Problem, *Foreign Policy*, March 26, 2015

One analyst has claimed that "Eastern Ukraine is awash with weapons and armed militia groups on both sides." Another has spoken darkly of "independently operating warlords and armed groups." A third has written of "independent and semi-independent battalions, some of which descend from Ukrainian nationalist groups, extreme elements of the Maidan self-defense forces, and criminal groups." Even Vladimir Putin has chimed in, warning of a "foreign legion, in this particular case, a NATO foreign legion, which is not pursuing Ukraine's national interests of course."

One would think Ukraine is on the verge of collapse.

The target of these alarmist statements, and the perpetrators of the supposed chaos, are Ukraine's volunteer fighting units. Are these units really a threat to Ukraine's stability and democratic prospects? The answer is no, at least not now and not for the foreseeable future. Although the First Deputy Speaker of Ukraine's parliament, Andrii Parubii, may have gone too far in saying (at a New York briefing at Dentons LLP on February 27) that the units are "disciplined Ukrainian warriors about whom films will be made and books will be written," he was right to suggest that panic is unwarranted.

Who They Are

Some basic facts and numbers, mostly gleaned from Ukrainian- and Russian-language sources inaccessible to many Western journalists, tell a less alarming story. These volunteer units emerged in the immediate aftermath of Russia's annexation of Crimea in March 2014. Ukraine's armed struggle against pro-Russian separatists picked up in the spring and summer of 2014, and the regular army, neglected since Ukraine's independence in 1991 and starved of resources under the Viktor Yanukovych regime in 2010–2013, proved not quite up to the job. At the same time, significant parts of the militia in Ukraine's southeastern provinces had either defected to the separatists or refused to take sides. It was in March and April of 2014 that the government adopted a variety of constitutionally grounded measures legalizing the formation of volunteer units under the aegis of both the Ministry of Defense and the Ministry of Internal Affairs. Most were formed in April–May 2014.

According to a September 2014 report of the *Kyiv Post*, Ukraine had 44 volunteer Territorial Defense Battalions subordinate to the Ministry of Defense, 32 volunteer special purpose patrol battalions subordinate to the Ministry of Internal Affairs, 3 volunteer special purpose National Guard battalions, and several Ukrainian Volunteer Corps battalions. Another source lists 43 Territorial Defense Battalions and 26 Internal Affairs special police units; while Minister of Internal Affairs Arsen Avakov noted on September 30, 2014 that there were 34 volunteer battalions. Part of the problem in identifying the exact number of units in each category is that the units and their roles often overlap. Another part is that the units, being volunteer-based, appear to ebb and flow.

The newspaper compiled incomplete data about 37 units, drawn from each of the above three categories. Nine units hailed from Kyiv Province, 7 from Dnipropetrovsk, 2 from Luhansk, Poltava, Kharkiv, and Chernihiv, and one apiece from Donetsk, Lviv, Odessa, Ivano-Frankivsk, Kherson, Volyn, Kirovohrad, Mykolaiv, Vinnytsia, Khmelnytsky, and Ternopil provinces. That is, 19 came from eastern and southern Ukraine, 9 from the capital city and its environs, and only 7 from west of the Dnipro River. A more recent source places 10 Volunteer Defense Battalions in provinces west of the Dnipro, 7 from Kyiv and other central provinces, and 16 from Ukraine's east and south. The tilt toward the southeast in both accounts makes sense, as that is where the imperative to defend one's home from the invading Russian forces is strongest.

According to the *Kyiv Post*'s calculations, the smallest of the units, from Odessa, Mykolaiv, and Chernihiv provinces had, respectively, 50, 50, and 46 soldiers. The largest, from Dnipropetrovsk and Donetsk, had, respectively, 4,000 and 600 men. About half had 100–200 men, and about half had 400–500. The total number of soldiers was 10,919; the average size of a unit was 352 men. All the units have actively participated in the fighting in eastern Ukraine. As of January 15, 2015, they suffered 232 deaths. In comparison, Ukraine's armed forces incurred 1,232 deaths in 2014 and 2015. (If the number were to include soldiers who are missing in action, and probably dead, it would probably be 2,500–3,000.)

Unlike conscripts, the volunteers are far more motivated, idealistic, and willing to place their lives on the line. Many are close to or above middle age, have families and professions, and served in the Soviet army. The commander of the Donbas battalion, for instance, is an ethnic-Russian ex-businessman from Donetsk. Indeed, although all the volunteers would characterize themselves as Ukrainian patriots, many are ethnic Russians or Russian speakers. Jews also form a noticeable contingent within some of the battalions. That said, the volunteer units generally have the same problems as Ukraine's regular armed forces: lack of supplies, lack of training, lack of integration into an effective command and control structure.

Anything but Warlords

Contrary to the impression that the Western media often convey, the volunteer battalions are not "incipient warlords." For one thing, they have no territorial bases and independent sources of financing (such as drugs). For another, they have families and jobs and are only part-time soldiers. Finally, with the exception of the Ukrainian Volunteer Corps, they are all subordinated to the Ministry of Internal Affairs or the Ministry of Defense, which does anything but favor them over the regular troops. Quite the contrary, although the armed forces rely greatly on the volunteers, especially in close fighting with Russian troops, the battalions remain less well supplied with equipment, weapons, and ammunition than the regular forces.

Of the 79-plus volunteer units, only three—Aidar with 500 fighters, Azov with 500, and Right Sector with 250 (according to the *Kyiv Post*, which attributes 120 to one Right Sector Unit and has no data for the second one: so I multiplied 120 by two)—have attracted consistent media attention in both Ukraine and the West. This fact needs to be underlined. That is, only 4 percent of the units and 11 percent of the volunteers have been implicated in controversy. (The numbers of volunteer fighters has probably grown since the *Kyiv Post*'s calculations, but the proportions are probably the same.) Given that the volunteers are quickly mobilized irregulars with too much motivation and too little training, the most striking thing about them is not the presence of a few bad apples, but the absence of many more.

Consider in this light an October 20, 2014 Amnesty International report, "Summary Killings during the Conflict in Eastern Ukraine," which critics of the units always cite as evidence of their having gone rogue. A *Newsweek* article discussing the report was even entitled "Ukrainian Nationalist Volunteers Committing 'ISIS-Style' War Crimes." In fact, the Amnesty report is far more ambiguous: "Amnesty International was able to identify three grave sites, containing a total of nine bodies, five of which appear to have been [separatist] DNR fighters killed in the course of hostilities. There is strong evidence pointing to the conclusion that the four remaining bodies, found in two grave sites, were extra-judicially executed by Kyiv-controlled forces." But, as Amnesty then goes on to admit, the evidence is even weaker than the first statement had suggested: "Three of the bodies that were found need to be identified, and the circumstances of all four deaths need to be promptly, thoroughly and impartially investigated. It is clear, however, that at least one of the victims, Nikita Kolomeytsev, who was restrained at the time of his death, is a victim of extrajudicial execution; the available evidence implicates Kyiv-controlled forces in his killing." One-to-four victims are obviously one-to-four too many, but they hardly constitute evidence of "ISIS-style war crimes."

The Three Controversial Units

Aidar draws many of its fighters from Luhansk Province; Azov and the Right Sector also draw heavily on volunteers from eastern Ukraine. Contrary to prevalent stereotypes of Ukrainian nationalists as being hostile to all things Russian, the Russian language dominates in all three units. Their origins in Ukraine's easternmost provinces are significant. Like the pro-Russian separatists fighting on the other side of the barricades, these pro-Ukrainian volunteers are the products of Donbas political culture, which is illiberal, intolerant, and oftentimes racist. It would be shocking if the pro-Ukrainian volunteers were to have diametrically opposite attitudes from those of the pro-Russian separatists.

Only Aidar genuinely seems to be a rogue unit or, more accurately, a unit with many rogue elements. According to Luhansk Province Governor Hennadii Moskal, "Aidar is changing from a military unit that is supposed to defend the territorial integrity and sovereignty of Ukraine to an armed bandit formation." However, he has also said that "a significant part of the Aidar battalion is selflessly fighting on the front line ... but there's another part of that unit, which has long since deserted from Aidar, that has assumed an illegal position and engages in looting, thievery, racketeering, automobile thefts, and other crimes in population centers of Ukrainian-controlled territory." Minister of Internal Affairs Avakov has called these elements "pseudo-Aidar" and "Aidar-2." An Aidar fighter, meanwhile, says that the battalion consists of a subunit—the "black ones," rumored to be its commander's private army and consisting of "criminals, fighters, and fighter-criminals." There are reports of tensions and fighting between the two Aidars, though whether it's over power, booty, or principle isn't clear.

The modifier that is invariably appended to Azov is "neo-Nazi." The unit's leader, Andrii Biletskii, is in fact a member of an unabashedly extremist and racist organization, Patriot of Ukraine. That said, Biletskii comes across as a hardline Republican in his interviews with the press, saying such things as "our battalion stands on a right-wing, patriotic platform.... We're called Nazis, but we pay no attention to these names.... Our central ideological platform is: fight for what's yours and destroy everything that interferes in the life of your people and your state. Today our primary enemy is the Putin regime and the band of outcasts who call themselves his 'family'." To add to the complexity, Azov has received funds from Igor Kolomoisky, the no-nonsense governor of Dnipropetrovsk Province and a leading Jewish Ukrainian philanthropist.

A recent *USA Today* article interviewed one self-styled Azov Nazi, Alex, and described his views as follows: "He said he supports strong leadership for Ukraine, like Germany during World War II, but opposes the Nazis' genocide against Jews. Minorities should be tolerated as long as they are peaceful and don't demand special privileges, he said, and the property of wealthy oligarchs should be taken away and nationalized." These views may be populist and borderline illiberal, but they are anything but Nazi. Since Alex more accurately belongs in America's Tea Party, Hungary's Fidesz, or in Israel's Likud, his claim that "no more than half his comrades are fellow Nazis" cannot be accepted at face value. Josef Zissels, a Kyiv-based Ukrainian Jew who is chairman of the General Council of the Euro-Asian Jewish Congress, downplays the neo-Nazi label, saying that Azov may have 30–40 genuine Nazis: what matters most, he says, is that all the volunteers are united in defending their country against Russia. It was, as Zissels points out, Azov that, in early May of 2014, liberated the port city of Mariupol. Azov's uncertain Nazi credentials may be why journalistic reports of the unit never reveal any "typical" neo-Nazi activities such as organizing underground cells, distributing *Mein Kampf*, or staging anti-Jewish pogroms.

The Right Sector, which emerged on the political scene during the Maidan Revolution in 2014, is the driving force behind the Ukrainian Volunteer Corps. Unlike all the other volunteer units, which are subordinated to the Ministry of Defense or the Ministry of Internal Affairs, the Volunteer Corps has retained its autonomy. In early 2015, the Right Sector turned down an official offer to go "legal," as presidential advisor Yuri Biryukov put it, and have a contractual relationship with the Ministry of Defense. Notwithstanding their go-it-alone approach, the Right Sector's volunteer units coordinate their activities with Ukraine's military command, fought together with regular army units in defense of Donetsk Airport, and have not been implicated in any major public scandals.

The Right Sector is generally criticized, not for its rogue behavior on the battlefield, but for its political views. Russian propaganda has demonized the group, suggesting that it amounts to a Ukraine-wide movement that is sharpening its knives in preparation for a final assault on Russia. In reality, the Right Sector amounts to no more than a few thousand members. (One source says the group "boasts" of having 5,000 to 10,000, but that sounds like bravado.) Formed on November 28, 2013 as a coalition of far-right groupings,

184

the Right Sector eventually morphed into a political party on March 22, 2014. Although the group's ideology is unquestionably right-wing, its electoral program was a collection of largely anodyne proposals for better governance and less corruption. Only the opening line—"Ukraine is a neocolonial creation and exists in a condition of internal and external occupation"—sounds radical. Even that impression quickly fades as soon as the document identifies the external occupant as Russia, and the internal one, not as Jews (the group pointedly rejects anti-Semitism and one of its leading activists is an Orthodox Jew, Borislav Bereza), but as Ukraine's corrupt, and justifiably reviled, oligarchs. Although few Ukrainians—and few Westerners—would disagree with that assessment of Ukraine's ills, the Right Sector received only 1.8 percent of the popular vote in the October 26, 2014 parliamentary elections. Its candidate for president received only 0.7 percent in the May 25 presidential elections.

Ukraine's Volunteer Movement

Although the volunteer battalions are generally viewed as part of Ukraine's armed forces, it may be more appropriate to think of them as part of the burgeoning self-help movement that has swamped Ukraine since the days of the Maidan Revolution. The Maidan's "regulars"—who numbered about 10,000 permanent activists—were all volunteers. Many of them then went on to continue the struggle after Russia annexed Crimea and intervened in eastern Ukraine. Some of Ukraine's revolutionaries went into politics; others joined NGOs; and still others abandoned the barricades, took up arms, and went to war, in the manner of their predecessors in the American and French Revolutions.

Their efforts have been supplemented by an army of civilian volunteers, who have contributed to a veritable flowering of Ukraine's civil society. (And domestic volunteers have in turn been assisted by hundreds of thousands of diaspora Ukrainians, who contribute large sums of money for medical supplies and other necessities.) As of late 2014, the volunteer movement in Ukraine consisted of 750,000 individuals and about 100 groups with no fewer than 100 permanent members. They provide food supplies, medicine, and equipment to the military as well as a whole range of services for the 1.8 million refugees from the Donbas in Ukraine. That number amounts to about 2 percent of Ukraine's actual population (about 40 million). In addition, run-of-the-mill Ukrainians, most of whom exist on the verge of poverty, have provided hundreds of thousands of dollars for their cause. One volunteer activist estimates that people willing to give large donations on a regular basis amount to about 2-3 percent (0.8-1 million), while those who give one-time small donations are about 10–15 percent (4–6 million).

Although volunteerism is an intrinsically positive phenomenon reflective of the strength of civil society, it can also be a measure, as in today's Ukraine, of the weakness of the state. Many tasks—such as economic entrepreneurship, religion, culture, and self-help— are best left outside the purview of the state; some—such as defense and emergency response—are best performed by the state. As Denys Kobzyn, the director of the Kharkiv Institute for Social Research, has stated: "The good news is that Ukraine has developed an enormous potential for self-organization. ... The bad news is that the state's monopoly of the use of violence ... could be destroyed."

185

<u>Yuri Butusov</u>, probably Ukraine's best military analyst and a merciless critic of Ukraine's political and military establishment, disagrees, questioning the units' ability to "engage in a revolt." According to Butusov, "amidst chaos organized and patriotic volunteer units are the most disciplined foundation of the government." President Poroshenko's unwillingness to support the volunteer units, says Butusov, is "irrational. ... Yes, the battalions are politicized. ... But they're no army. So why regard them as if they were a regular army? Let's arm and train them, and then we'll give them regular army tasks. Let's replace their incompetent commanders with competent ones. And then let's raise our standards toward them."

Both Kobzyn and Butusov have a point. The emergence of a huge volunteer movement in Ukraine in 2014 was testimony to both the strength of Ukrainian civil society and the abysmal weakness of the post-Maidan, post-Yanukovych Ukrainian state. That movement—and the armed units within it—played a critical role in sustaining the state in 2014 and continues to play such a role today. It will be a measure of the success of Ukrainian state building that the volunteer movement—and the armed units—eventually wither away and assume "normal" proportions.

If current state-building, nation-building, and economic-reform efforts proceed apace and Ukraine manages to withstand Russian military pressure, the volunteer units will fade into obscurity. If those efforts fail and Russia overruns large parts of Ukraine, the volunteer units will be the least of Ukraine's—and the West's—problems. In the meantime, all talk of warlordism, fascism, and imminent chaos is just hyperventilation. The volunteer units are anything but warlords, only a tiny number is extremist, and the true source of chaos in Ukraine comes from Putin's armies in the east.

*

Putin's War Has Consolidated Ukraine, *Atlantic Council*, March 26, 2015

Viewed historically, the ongoing Russo-Ukrainian war is the product of four deeper causes and one trigger. First, the Soviet empire's collapse in 1991 propelled its successor state, Russia, to seek reimperialization for structural and ideological reasons. Second, the emergence of a "fascistoid" (or almost fully fascist) regime made imperial revival a central feature of Vladimir Putin's hyper-masculine strategy of self-legitimation. Third, European Union and NATO expansion placed Ukraine in an untenable security vacuum, between a Europe manifestly uninterested in Ukraine and an imperial Russia that was increasingly making claims on Ukrainian sovereignty. Fourth, the "colored revolutions" in Georgia, Ukraine, and Kyrgyzstan in 2003–05 directly threatened Putin's imperial regime and legitimacy—compelling him to wage war against Georgia and launch a variety of protective measures vis-à-vis Ukraine and Kyrgyzstan.

Finally, Ukraine's 2014 Maidan Revolution was the trigger that led Putin to exploit that country's post-revolutionary weakness by invading Crimea and eastern Ukraine in the hope of promoting Russia's empire and consolidating his regime.

1. The normal trajectory of imperial decline is the decay of ties between the empire's core and its peripheries or colonies, followed by progressive territorial attrition. Sometimes, empires collapse rather suddenly, usually the result of wars. In the Soviet case, that shock came from within. Once Mikhail Gorbachev embarked on perestroika in the mid–1980s and began dismantling totalitarianism, he subverted the empire, resulting in the end of core Russian rule over its non-Russian peripheries by 1991.

Several factors led to reimperialization in post-Soviet Russia. The non-Russian ex-periphery remained linked to the Russian ex-core with respect to energy, trade, culture, and language. Facilitating continued core dominance was Russia's relative state strength and the openness of borders. Soviet-style imperial discourse, culture, and ideology also survived in Russia, as they usually do in post-collapse successor states such as Weimar Germany. Opposition to and demonization of NATO expansion and Ukrainian nationalism were part of that mindset, which was evident in Russia even in the democratic 1990s.

2. Russia suffered all the typical consequences of imperial collapse: economic distress, humiliation, loss of faith. Blame fell on the democrats who ruled Russia following that collapse, and on non-Russians—specifically Ukrainians—who had supposedly betrayed Russia. Boris Yeltsin, who embodied the democratic '90s, left office in disgrace, while his successor, Putin, assumed control in 1999, promising to reestablish Russia's place in the sun. By the mid–2000s, Putin had eviscerated Russia's democratic institutions and succeeded in constructing a fascistoid regime with three institutional features. The first was standard authoritarianism (centralizing the power ministries; subordinating business to the state; restricting rights; forming mass pro-regime movements; controlling the media; and establishing a massive propaganda apparatus). The second was Putin's undisputed supreme leadership. The third was Putin's hyper-masculine personality cult and neo-imperialism, which he used to legitimize the regime. That cult drew on and reinforced the sexism within Russian political culture. The Putin regime eventually came to resemble those of interwar Italy and Germany, and Putin himself came to resemble Mussolini and Hitler.

3. EU-NATO expansion created a no-man's land between Russia and Europe, with Belarus, Ukraine, and Moldova finding themselves in an untenable security vacuum. By expanding European economic, political, and security institutions just short of them (and of course Georgia), Europe effectively signalled to Moscow that it had no interest in these countries—precisely as Russia's neo-imperial tendencies were taking off and the Putin regime's fascistoid features were consolidating. The timing couldn't have been worse. In effect, if not in intent, NATO enlargement enhanced the security of countries like the Czech Republic, Poland, Hungary, Slovakia, and Bulgaria that faced no conceivable security threat. It extended security guarantees to countries such as the Baltics that could not easily be defended by NATO. And it failed to extend security guarantees to countries like Belarus, Ukraine, and Moldova that suddenly faced existential threats thanks to NATO's enlargement, which annoyed the Russians. NATO—an institution in crisis—did not threaten Russia and the Kremlin, with its many spies in Brussels, knew it. What worried Moscow was the symbolism of the West's "strength" in the face of Russia's

post-collapse "weakness."

4. The colored revolutions posed the first concerted outside threat to Putin's regime, but his response was as spontaneous and unplanned as they were. Regime change in Georgia, Ukraine, and Kyrgyzstan suggested that people power could succeed. That mattered because Putin was well aware of the continued strength of the democratic movement in Russia's key cities, Moscow and St. Petersburg. Georgia's 2003 Rose Revolution empowered pro-Western forces led by President Mikhail Saakashvili. His determination to join NATO and other Western institutions eventually led Putin to provoke a "glorious little war" in 2008 that resulted in the partition of Georgia. The 2004 Orange Revolution caught Putin flatfooted, which was unsurprising, given his belief in an ideology that sees Ukraine as a weak, feminine Little Russia. Putin resolved to solidify Viktor Yanukovych's puppet rule in Ukraine, to such a degree that both of them helped bring about the next Ukrainian uprising in 2013. In Kyrgyzstan, Moscow opposed the 2005 Tulip Revolution, but then learned from its mistake and supported the 2010 uprising.

With these four factors in place, all that was necessary for full-scale war with Ukraine to break out was a trigger. That came in the form of the 2013–14 Maidan Revolution—a genuinely democratic movement that heralded Ukraine's abandonment of Russia's imperial domain and fundamentally challenged fascism and Putin himself. Putin's threat perception had little if anything to do with potential Ukrainian membership in NATO, since neither Ukraine nor NATO had traditionally shown much interest in each other. Putin's answer to the Maidan was to annex Crimea, promote separatism in Ukraine's southeast, and wage war—in the manner of Saddam Hussein's 1980 attack against revolutionary Iran.

The upshot of Putin's war has been the exact opposite of what he hoped to achieve. Ukraine has not collapsed. Instead, Putin has consolidated the Ukrainian state, nation, army, and security apparatus, pushing the country toward the EU, NATO, and reform. For the first time since independence in 1991, Ukraine's people and elites are united around a pro-Western, pro-reform, pro-democracy agenda. And for the first time, Ukraine has the West's support. Although Putin is straining that country's economy to the maximum, he has lost Ukraine, which should pull through and become stronger.

At the same time, the weakness of Putin's fascistoid regime is evident. Institutional decay and ineffectiveness are rampant; the elite appears to be divided; the cult of hyper-masculinity will diminish as Putin ages. In addition, Russia suffers from economic decay, declining energy revenues, the pain of Western sanctions, the costs of war, and growing non-Russian assertiveness. Regime collapse, a putsch, massive instability, or even civil war is no longer unimaginable, as the recent discussions of Putin's inexplicable absence showed. But there is nothing the West can do to prevent Russia's possible collapse as long as Putin is in power. All it can do is try to protect itself and Russia's neighbors from the consequences of collapse by supporting the front-line states: Ukraine, the Baltics, Belarus, Moldova, Georgia, and Kazakhstan. In short, the West must finally appreciate that Ukraine's continued existence as an independent democratic state is vital to its own security.

Ensuring Ukraine's independence means one of two things—and the haphazard dithering that has characterized Western policy toward Ukraine in 2014 is neither of them. The West must provide Ukraine with either massive military assistance or massive economic support far in excess of the few billions hitherto made available. Put another way, the West must choose whether to draw Ukraine into NATO or into the EU. If, as many Western analysts and policymakers argue, massive military assistance or NATO membership would only provoke Moscow to escalate its war, then the West has no choice but to transform Ukraine into its economic and political protectorate—and that means EU membership. *Tertium non datur.* There is no third alternative.

*

US-Ukraine Strategic Partnership Lacks Strategy, Partnership, *World Affairs Journal*, June 23, 2015

When three influential American Russia experts call for a substantive US-Ukrainian strategic partnership, it's time to listen.

Matthew Rojansky, director of Washington's prestigious Kennan Institute at the Woodrow Wilson International Center for Scholars, Thomas E. Graham, former senior director for Russia on the National Security Council staff and currently with Kissinger Associates, and Michael Kofman, a public policy scholar at Kennan, recently wrote an important op-ed in which they criticized the "U.S.-Ukraine strategic partnership" for "lack[ing] both strategy and partnership."

Please take note: the three experts take for granted that such a partnership exists and strongly imply that it should exist. They're calling, not for establishing such a relationship, but for filling it with appropriate substance.

Here are their recommendations:

> First, Washington should endorse Kyiv's leading political figures and their agenda with the same degree of caution and circumspection as the Ukrainian people support them. ... Instead, the U.S. objective should be to work on the overarching problems that create instability and threaten Ukraine's future: the disastrous state of the economy and the conflict with Russia. ... [Second], Washington should work with Kyiv to lay the framework for a bilateral strategic partnership. This should be based on a clear definition of mutual interests and values, and realistic expectations for the short, middle and long term. Instead of a few favored partners or signature projects in Ukraine, Washington should look for spheres of cooperation that serve the interests of both nations. It must forget the tired formula of persuading Ukrainians to pick a pro-Western path as a vehicle for foiling Russian-led integration projects. A new approach can build a foundation for sustained bilateral engagement with Ukraine as a whole—well beyond the

period after the fighting with Russia has ended. As it eventually will. [Third], Washington must demonstrate strategic patience. Ukraine will likely progress more slowly and more fitfully than Americans would prefer. A strategic partnership based on clearly defined values and interests will help both sides navigate the potential misunderstandings and significant challenges that lie ahead.

The first point is spot on. America's goals vis-à-vis Ukraine cannot be to promote any particular leader or leaders, but to advance good solutions to Ukraine's main problems. As a result, Ukrainian policymakers should earn Washington's support by bringing about the changes that regenerate the economy and end the war. That said, Washington must understand that reform cannot, and will not, ever come to pass if the former Regionnaires now grouped in the Opposition Bloc or the Communists return to power. America must be cautious and circumspect with respect to the national democrats, but it must reject outright the political groupings that embody corruption, thievery, thuggishness, lack of reform, Putinism, and Sovietism.

The second point is a bit too circumspect for my taste. In fact, the United States and Ukraine have a perfectly clear short- and middle-term interest: stopping Russian aggression and ending the war in eastern Ukraine. They also have an obvious long-term interest: promoting civilized international behavior by Russia. As to bilateral engagement with Ukraine "well beyond the period after the fighting with Russia has ended," that too is obvious. Ukraine has the human capital and economic potential to become a leading middle power that could, if its transition to a consolidated democracy and prosperous market economy succeeds, play a positive, stabilizing role in Eurasian politics. Whether inside or outside the European Union and NATO, Ukraine could be as important an American ally as South Korea or Israel.

The third point is on the mark again. Ukrainians and Americans who think reforms are proceeding too slowly must get a grip on themselves and their expectations. For starters, reforms *are* taking place. Substantial macroeconomic stabilization has been achieved—no small feat. Decentralization is about to be introduced, while the budgets of local governing bodies have already been increased. New police patrols are about to take to the streets in a few cities. No less important, painful measures have been implemented without undermining Ukraine's democratic procedures. Supporters of faster reform forget that democracy is generally incompatible with vastly unpopular change. That Ukraine has managed to promote reform while transitioning to a post-Yanukovych democracy (and fighting a ruinous war!) is almost miraculous. Promoters of "big bangs" should remember that the greater and faster the reforms, the greater the concentration of political power, and the greater the likelihood of authoritarian rule.

These are all quibbles about the op-ed. The important thing is to recognize and promote the US-Ukraine strategic partnership and to supplement it with an EU-Ukraine strategic partnership.

*

Ukraine's Bumpy Road to Normalcy, *World Affairs Journal*, June 29, 2015

The most striking thing about Lviv, Kyiv, and a number of small towns and villages I've recently visited is their normalcy. Walk down the streets or dirt roads and you'd never think Ukraine's economy is depressed and that the country is at war. A village church I visit is full of people dressed in their Sunday best. Lviv's cafes are packed. Kyiv's main drag, the Khreshchatyk, is as fashionable as before Russia's onslaught.

But that's just the outward appearance. Talk to people and their current or impending economic travails—inflation, stagnant wages, corruption, and the growing cost of gas and electricity—quickly come to the fore. Talk a little longer and the war in the east soon becomes a topic of conversation.

The appearance of normalcy is both a façade and a coping mechanism. People know full well that times are hard and that soldiers are dying—usually one or two a day, sometimes up to four or five a day. They know that Vladimir Putin and his proxies are threatening to unleash a devastating war against Ukraine and kill thousands more.

Ukrainians seek to live as normally as possible, as if all were well. In their memoirs, Soviet gulag inmates claimed to do the same, trying to recreate some semblance of everyday familiarity in their otherwise dreadful lives. A friend tells me he only reads the good news. Another focuses all her attention on her grandchildren. A villager worries about the tomatoes she's planted.

"The war has forced our ambivalent elite to consider genuine reform," says a political analyst in Kyiv. "If it hadn't been for Putin's invasion of Crimea and the Donbas, the Maidan would probably have ended with a return to the status quo ante."

"Putin as the promoter of Ukraine's reforms?" I say. "Putin as Ukraine's nation builder?"

"Exactly," my interlocutor smiles. "But we still have a long way to go. True, Russian speakers have now been integrated into the nation, but the language question remains. It's just been bracketed for the time being. The problem is that Russian speakers still don't get that Ukrainian speakers also have rights. They assume everyone should naturally prefer Russian."

I witnessed an example of this mind-set the day before. A friend and I went to a popular Kyiv coffee shop. She asked the young boy serving us to speak Ukrainian. When asked politely, wait staff invariably switch to Ukrainian. This one refused. "Why?" she asked. "Can't you speak Ukrainian?" "I can," he responded, "but I won't."

His behavior strikes me as incomprehensible. If addressed in English, he'd probably respond in broken English. Address him in an "inferior" tongue, however, and he'll refuse to use it, even though he knows how. I know the comparison is overdrawn, but I can't help think of what blacks must have experienced when they were refused service in the Jim Crow South.

What mystifies me, however, is why some kid should make such a big deal of language use. "In America," I explain to him afterwards, "waiters try to adapt to clients' cultural and linguistic preferences because they know that'll get them a bigger tip." "Sorry," he says—in Russian.

Almost everyone in Ukraine believes that absolutely nothing has changed in the last year. The "absence of reform" has become a mantra. The pervasiveness of the view is understandable. People's lives have gotten worse, and may get even worse before they start to improve. The press has become freer and reports constantly on official malfeasance, creating the impression that corruption is on the rise. The war in the Donbas looks like it's going to be permanent. And the government has poorly communicated its intentions—thereby underscoring Ukrainians' innate mistrust of the authorities.

A journalist points to Mikheil Saakashvili's "brilliant" image-building in Odessa Province, which, as its newly appointed governor, he's promised to clean up. Georgia's former president has even taken to using public transport to commute to work. Why doesn't Ukraine's president, Petro Poroshenko, occasionally visit some popular eatery and have a plate of potato pierogis with the common folk? I ask. "Good question," she says.

A businessman in Lviv tells me things *are* changing. "They're not demanding bribes as brazenly as before," he says. "The fear of getting caught or exposed in the media seems to be having some effect." Local budgets are also being increased, and the result is much-needed repairs to Ukraine's awful roads. A resident of a dreadfully depressed Western Ukrainian town notes that one of its pockmarked roads is finally being fixed.

People's patience is wearing thin, or so they say. Reforms have taken place—in education, in law enforcement, in the army, and in the economy—but their immediate effect on people's lives has been either insignificant or negative. A radical decentralization of authority and budgets is in the works, but it won't be fully complete for another two years.

A university administrator in Lviv tells me that "Poroshenko could be ousted by the end of the year, especially as winter approaches and people find they have no money to pay their bills." In contrast, the Kyiv-based analyst doesn't expect a third Maidan. "There'll be localized demonstrations, but there's none of the deep moral outrage that led to the Orange and Euro revolutions."

"For all its faults, the current government is nothing like the Yanukovych regime," an American journalist tells me, speaking of the previous government. "We could easily trace the lines of theft and corruption under [Viktor] Yanukovych. There's no evidence of anything like that at present."

An article in the Ukrainian-language weekly *Tyzhden* notes that, when it comes to the economy, people believe either that "all is lost" or that "we've won." In fact, the author argues, both claims are true. Macroeconomically, Ukraine is on the way to recovery. Microeconomically—which is where the average citizen lives—life has gotten harder.

That dialectic is evident in all aspects of Ukrainian life.

Ukraine *is* changing, rapidly and significantly—partly as a result of the Maidan revolution, partly as a result of Putin's mad war, partly as a result of pressure from Ukrainian civil society, partly as a result of pressure from the West, and partly as a result of the efforts of Ukraine's "ambivalent" elites.

But change is always disruptive, even, or especially, if its ultimate effect is positive. And change is always viewed as either insufficient or excessive.

The griping in Ukraine will continue. The elites will continue to move the country in the right direction—too slowly for some, too quickly for others. In about a year or two, I'm betting Ukraine won't just look normal. It'll be normal.

*

Ukrainians Impatient with Pace of Reforms, *World Affairs Journal*, September 15, 2015

Ukrainians are angry. The standard refrains are that there are no reforms and that Ukraine is worse off han it used to be.

Such deep-seated anger was at the root of the violent demonstration at the Parliament a few weeks ago. Most commentators focused on the violence and its implications for Ukraine's democracy. In fact, despite the Western media's bizarre infatuation with Ukraine's radical right, it is tiny and poses no threat to the system.

Far more worrisome is the widespread popular anger and growing popular radicalism.

Angry people who make radical demands—of the we-want-everything-immediately variety—and mistrust their leaders make for illegitimate and unstable rule. At some point, illegitimate and unstable rule can crumble. If Ukraine ever comes unglued, it'll be because popular anger produced a third Maidan that destroyed Ukraine's fledgling institutions and either created chaos or brought radicals to power. All Ukrainians would lose. Vladimir Putin would win.

Radicalism is appropriate in revolutionary situations such as the second Maidan in early 2014. Radical talk can also remind established elites of what they need to do. Consider Martin Luther King's "I have a dream" speech in Washington, DC: "This is no time to engage in the luxury of cooling off or to take the tranquilizing drug of gradualism. ... It would be fatal for the nation to overlook the urgency of the moment.... The whirlwinds of revolt will continue to shake the foundations of our nation until the bright day of justice emerges."

Radicalism makes for awful politics in normal or semi-normal conditions. People who want it all right away are making demands that no system, no matter how effective or legitimate, can meet. Normal politics is about compromise, about second or third best, about good enough. If everyone insists on everything right away, violence or dictatorship is often the result.

A just-released public opinion survey by the respected Democratic Initiatives organization suggests what ails Ukrainians. Thus, 48.4 percent believe there have been no reforms; 24.6 percent that only a tenth of possible reforms have taken place.

When asked to identify who was responsible for the absence of reform, Ukrainians targeted the oligarchs (51.5 percent), the government (51.5 percent), the majority coalition in Parliament (44.5 percent), the bureaucrats (44 percent), and the president (39.1 percent).

When asked who drives reform, 36.8 percent said it's the president, 32 percent the government, 22.1 percent the coalition majority, 6.9 percent the oligarchs, and 5.5 percent the bureaucrats.

Subtract the latter percentage from the former and you get each actor's reform-mindedness: –44.6 for the oligarchs, –38.5 for the bureaucrats, –22.5 for the coalition, –19.5 for the government, and –2.3 for the president.

The distribution of responsibility is about right. Ukraine's main political problem is the symbiosis between a bloated and corrupt state bureaucracy and the oligarchic class. Even if the president, Rada, and government did everything according to some reformist blueprint, weakening that monstrous apparatus would be difficult and take time.

But consider this: despite the fact that the state apparatus remains unreformed, comprehensive reform has taken place. Look at the assessments by VoxUkraine and the Carnegie Endowment for International Peace. There may be too little reform, and it may be too slow, but it is not unimpressive—especially compared to where Ukraine was a year ago. Dare I suggest that reform is possible even in a corrupt state? Look at Italy, a very nice country that is probably marginally less corrupt than Ukraine.

The survey also shows which reform areas Ukrainians consider most and least important. The former include corruption (65.2 percent), law and order (58 percent), pensions (39.9 percent), and health (35.9 percent). The latter include taxes (21.5 percent), decentralization (17.8 percent), deregulation and investments (14 percent), and land reform (8.1 percent).

In a word, Ukrainians want change in the areas that affect their lives immediately and closely. They regard as unimportant the very things experts consider most important—the components of a healthy economy.

The reasons for popular anger now become clearer.

First, Kyiv has focused on the macro-economy, while people want change where they can feel it.

Second, Kyiv has poorly communicated its successes, failures, and intentions to the people.

Third, the oligarchic state apparatus and its leading representatives are not just a brake on reform. They remain unpunished for their malfeasance, corruption, and past crimes—something people who lived through the Revolution of Dignity, have experienced steep drops in living standards, and are sacrificing their lives to defend Ukraine from Putin's aggression find intolerable, and rightly so.

The good news is that the macro-economy has been stabilized and some economic growth looks likely. The semi-good news is that communicating with folks isn't rocket science: all the more reason to wonder why the president and prime minister don't have an occasional borscht with the regular folk.

Fixing the state apparatus will be hardest. I know from my experience with university administrations that they are corrupt, nepotistic, bloated, and resistant to change. If changing them is hard, imagine how much harder changing the apparatus of a large country must be.

That said, sentencing a few high-level corruptioneers and criminals is no rocket science either. President Poroshenko would be well advised to consider this option in addition to slurping down some beet soup.

*

Promising Structural Change Begins to Show in Ukraine, *World Affairs Journal*, November 11, 2015

The seemingly unchanging nature of Ukraine's dysfunctional politics can easily mask the reality: Ukraine itself is changing. Three sets of data illustrate the point.

The *Ukrainian Week* recently published numbers on the changes in Ukraine's ethnic composition brought about by general demographic trends and, above all, Russia's annexation of Crimea and occupation of one third of the Donbas. According to the magazine's demographic extrapolations from the 2001 census, the number of ethnic Russians in Ukraine has fallen from 8.34 million to 4.58 million—a 45 percent decrease. Ethnic Russians used to constitute 21.1 percent of Ukraine's total population; now, they constitute 11.8 percent. In contrast, the ethnic Ukrainian share of the total population has grown from 72.7 percent in 1989 to 83.8 percent today.

In effect, if not in intent, Vladimir Putin's aggression has transformed Ukraine into an ethnically Ukrainian state. Russia's war against Ukraine has also imbued those Ukrainians with a sense of identity and patriotism that they failed to develop on their own. Both trends are likely to be mutually reinforcing in the years ahead—which bodes well for Ukraine's nation and state building efforts as well as for its ability to sustain painful reforms. As many social scientists argue, culturally solidary communities are more prone to agree and to sacrifice than culturally fragmented communities.

Less optimistic is Ukraine's overall demographic condition. As demographers Anatole Romaniuk and Oleksandr Gladun argue in *Population and Development Review* (June 2015):

> Ukraine experienced, during the first half of the twentieth century, a series of de-mographic catastrophes almost unparalleled in history. It withstood these largely thanks to high fertility. It now imposes a demographic crisis on itself. Even with fertility having recovered from its lowest point and emigration having slowed, it is difficult to foresee a future in which Ukraine's population does not continue to decline—age structure alone will see to that—albeit at a more moderate pace. … There are three possible responses to ameliorate the trend: reduce the hemor-rhage of young people leaving the country, increase fertility, or improve health, especially male health.

Note that all three responses identified by Romaniuk and Gladun presuppose a prosper-ous economy, one that will offer young people opportunities, enable couples to envision a future for their children, and improve health facilities. And a prosperous economy pre-supposes painful economic reforms.

Kyiv's reforms have been sluggish, but there may be more going on than meets the eye. That at least is what the indispensable website VoxUkraine suggests in a recent article measuring the degree of personnel change in Kyiv's state bureaucracy. The results are heartening:

- The Central Apparatus of the Central Executive Authorities has been down-sized, but the change is minor. Average reduction for the period from the beginning of 2014 till mid 2015 is 5 percent.

- At the ministry level, the picture is more nuanced and heterogeneous. Some authorities have cut the number of employees: Ministry of Economic Development and Trade—34 percent, Ministry of Social Policy—15 percent, State Property Fund—13 percent, Anti-Monopoly Committee, Ministry of Infrastructure, Ministry of Finance, Ministry of Agrarian Policy—11 per-cent, Ministry of Ecology—8 percent, Ministry of Regional Development and Trade—3 percent, Ministry of Culture—2 percent.

- Others have increased the number of employees of their central offices from the beginning of 2014 till mid 2015: e.g. NBU [National Bank of Ukraine] increased for 3 percent, Ministry of Justice for 12 percent, Prosecutor General Office for 11 percent, and Ministry of Youth and Sports for 15 percent.

- Some Authorities have substantively reduced their regional units. The lead-ers are law enforcement authorities and the central bank. The Ministry of Internal Affairs has cut 14 percent of local people, the Ministry of Justice and Prosecutor General Offices reduced their sizes for 22 percent, the central bank—21 percent.

- The renewal rate among the top levels of the government (ministers, deputies, heads of departments) is about 80 percent, benchmarked to the beginning of 2014. The management of the State Fiscal Service and the Prosecutor General Office are renewed at 91 percent.

- The renewal rate drops dramatically for lower levels of the hierarchy in the government.

In other words, the bureaucracy is getting streamlined, though not evenly, and outsiders are increasingly getting positions of authority. The current Poroshenko-Yatseniuk government may be indifferent to rooting out corruption and introducing radical reform, but the proverbial facts on the ground may be making systemic change inevitable.

*

Slowly but Surely Kyiv Comes Around, *Atlantic Council*, November 16, 2015

How has Ukraine changed since the Euromaidan Revolution?

In attempting to answer this question, I've used the governance-related categories in Freedom House's Nations in Transit study, which tracks the reform record of post-Com-munist countries in Europe and Eurasia, and supplemented them with a few of my own. (Full disclosure: I've been involved in the Nations in Transit project since its inception in the mid–1990s.)

Freedom House assigns scores between 1 and 7 (with 1 being the best and 7 the worst) to seven institutional categories: electoral process, civil society, independent media, national democratic governance, local democratic governance, judicial framework and independence, and corruption. As these categories focus primarily on politics, I've added seven more to round out the picture: international relations, security, armed forces and police, education, culture and identity, economic well-being, and economic stability and reform. (Unlike Freedom House, which assigns scores to Ukraine together with its Russian-occupied territories, I will assign scores only to "free" Ukraine.)

In the chart below, I've listed Freedom House's scores for its seven institutional categories for three years: 2009, the last year of "Orange" government; 2013, the last year of former President Viktor Yanukovych's government; and 2014, the year of post-revolution instability and war. I've added my estimates for the seven additional categories for those three years, as well as for all fourteen categories for 2015, the year of post-revolution consolidation, as Freedom House's scores for this year haven't yet been published. For the sake of clarity, Freedom House's scores are in blue.

Year	2009	2013	2014	2015
Electoral Process	3.50	4.00	3.50	3.25
Civil Society	2.75	2.50	2.25	2.00
Independent Media	3.50	4.25	4.00	3.75
National Democratic Governance	5.00	6.00	6.00	4.75
Local Democratic Governance	5.25	5.50	5.50	5.50
Judicial Framework and Independence	5.00	6.00	6.00	6.00
Corruption	5.75	6.25	6.00	6.00
International Relations	5.00	6.00	5.00	4.00
Security	5.00	5.50	6.50	5.50
Armed Forces and Police	6.00	6.50	5.00	4.00
Education	5.00	6.50	6.25	5.25
Culture and Identity	4.50	6.00	4.50	3.75
Economic Well-Being	5.00	6.00	6.50	6.75
Economic Stability and Reform	5.00	6.00	6.50	6.25

Across the board, Freedom House's scores deteriorate sharply between 2009 and 2013, then improve slightly in 2014, after Yanukovych's departure. That's not surprising: Yanukovych was a disaster for Ukrainian politics, and although his departure improved things, that improvement was marginal, given the conditions of post-revolution instability and war in the east.

My own scores for 2009, 2013, and 2014 both reflect and deviate from this trend. My seven categories show across-the-board declines between 2009 and 2013, as well as significant selective declines between 2013 and 2014. On the other hand, Ukraine's international relations improved significantly in 2014, as the country became a strategic concern of the West; so, too, did its armed forces, which developed into a genuine fighting force, and its culture and identity, with the former becoming freer and the latter becoming more consolidated. Education improved only slightly in 2014, mostly because Yanukovych's education minister, Dmitri Tabachnik, left office. However, security, economic well-being, and economic stability and reform all experienced large drops, mostly as a result of the war with Russia and turmoil in the east.

In contrast to revolutionary and war-torn 2014, 2015 was a year of post-revolution consolidation, demonstrating improvements in many categories. The score for electoral process improved in light of October 2015's largely free and fair local elections. Civil society became even more active, and the media became a tad more independent. National democratic governance improved significantly, as the government of President Petro Poroshenko and Prime Minister Arsenii Yatseniuk reestablished control over the country and began functioning as a genuine government.

Local governance remained unchanged (given the planned decentralization, it could change for the better in 2016), as did judicial framework and corruption. Ukraine's international relations, security, and armed forces and police improved, as the war became a stalemate and the West continued to value Ukraine; culture and identity, as well as education, also improved. The economy was a mixed bag: living conditions declined greatly, while macroeconomic stabilization and some tax reform merited a slight improvement from 2014.

In sum, even if my scores are too generous, it's clear that Ukraine experienced improvements of some kind in ten out of fourteen categories. Only four categories were characterized by a lack of positive change: local governance, judicial framework, corruption, and economic well-being. Significantly, the lack of any noticeable improvement in just these four categories explains why many Western policymakers and analysts remain dissatisfied with Ukraine's progress, and why most Ukrainians insist that "nothing has changed."

Western policymakers and analysts are unhappy with Ukraine's progress because they prioritize corruption, where no improvement whatsoever is visible. Although the West must continue to pressure Kyiv to adopt serious anti-corruption measures, Western governments and organizations may also want to reconsider their "fetishization" of corruption.

For starters, no country ever moves with lightning speed from a condition of deep corruption to no corruption. The struggle against corruption, in Ukraine and elsewhere, is a long-term and arguably never-ending process. Second, corrupt countries can and do change for the better. Ukraine is proof of that, as is virtually every country in the world, including the United States. Indeed, corrupt countries can experience rapid economic growth (China), enjoy democracy (India), and be pleasant places to live (Italy). Finally, a truly radical, full-scale attack on corruption would almost certain impair Ukraine's democratic institutions.

Obviously, profoundly corrupt countries that remain profoundly corrupt are probably dooming themselves to permanent underdevelopment, but that eventuality is likely only in authoritarian states like Zimbabwe and Russia, where dictators impose such a trajectory on the population. Ukraine's strength has been its civil society and independent media, which, even during the worst days of President Leonid Kuchma in the 1990s or Yanukovych in 2010–2013, made it difficult for dictators to ignore society's preferences.

Ukrainians want two things above all. First, after twenty-five years of penury, they want their lives to finally get better. Instead, GDP declined by over a fifth between 2014 and 2015. The reason may be war and not government inaction, but Ukrainians cannot be blamed for holding their President and Prime Minister accountable.

Second, after two impressive displays of "people power" in 2004 and 2013–2014, Ukrainians want justice. They want the corruptioneers, thugs, oligarchs, and authoritarians who limited their livelihoods for twenty-five years and opposed their revolutionary upheavals to pay. The Euromaidan Revolution in particular was about justice, and it raised popular expectations enormously. Instead, not a single Yanukovych crony, Party of Regions bigwig, oligarch, or shooter of demonstrators has been prosecuted.

In sum, while Ukrainians' well-being has deteriorated sharply since the Euromaidan, their enhanced desire for justice has remained unsatisfied. Ukraine may have become a better place according to the above 14 indices, but Ukrainians don't care—and they are right.

There are signs that things may be changing. The Ukrainian parliament displayed remarkable dynamism in the last few days, as it dismissed 227 judges, passed a law forbidding workplace discrimination on the basis of sexual orientation, created a State Bureau of Investigation, and adopted a measure replacing the corrupt Soviet-era militia with a national police. These steps could amount to little, as is often the case in Ukraine, or they just might herald a shift, however halting, toward genuine anti-corruption reform.

There are several things to watch for in particular. We'll know Kyiv is serious about justice if the already existing Anti-Corruption Bureau is paired with an independent procurator and independent judges and if Poroshenko replaces the current Procurator General, Viktor Shokin, a man virtually everyone believes is corrupt, with a genuine reformer. And we'll know Kyiv is serious about reforming the economy—and promoting popular welfare—if the 345 state-owned firms that are at the core of oligarchic schemes for robbing the state are privatized by early 2016.

Will Ukraine finally get serious? Next year, 2016, could show real movement toward addressing Ukrainians' demands for an improvement in living standards and justice for three reasons. The indispensable West appears to be losing its patience, and Ukrainian elites know it. Increasing numbers of Ukrainians are also losing their patience, with some even insisting that a third Maidan revolution is necessary. Finally, the high probability of continued Russian aggression in the east should serve as a constant reminder to Kyiv that it really has no choice but to change—however slowly and fitfully.

*

A Frenchman Comes to Ukraine, *World Affairs Journal*, November 20, 2015

Meet one of Ukraine's most determined pro-Western politicians and Ukrainian patriots. He's the mayor of Hlukhiv, a small city located northeast of Kyiv, in Sumy Province, just a few miles from the border with Russia.

His name is Michel Terestchenko.

Until March 2015, the 61-year-old Terestchenko was a French citizen, born and raised in Paris. That month he acquired a Ukrainian passport straight from the hands of President Petro Poroshenko. Why the hullabaloo? Because Terestchenko is a descendant of the Tereshchenko family, one of Ukraine's grandest, having produced a number of prominent entrepreneurs, philanthropists, art collectors, and diplomats in the 18th–20th centuries. The family fled to France during the bloody years of the Bolshevik Revolution. Their expropriated art collection then formed the core of what eventually became the Kyiv National Museum of Russian Art.

Michel—described by one source as an "art patron, entrepreneur and descendant of the legendary dynasty" and by another as a "cordial bon vivant clad in a brown bomber jacket"—returned to Ukraine about a decade ago. Apparently, "a sudden desire to see his ancestral home nearly a decade ago moved Tereshchenko to resettle from Paris and turn part of the old family mansion into the office of a profitable flax and hemp production plant."

Terestchenko's decision to get involved in politics was just as unexpected. He speaks Russian slowly, slightly ungrammatically, and with a charming French accent:

> I love Ukraine very much. It's the homeland of my ancestors. It's now my homeland. I was on the Maidan. I was no hero, just a simple man. I was still French then. ... I was there all the time. I saw how they brought down the Lenin monument on December 8 [2013]. ... I saw fourteen corpses. I will never forget this. Until then, I believed it was possible not to take part in politics. But then I saw what had happened. ... Things are difficult at the state level. There are reforms, but they're proceeding very slowly. ... Many people have died, over 7,000. Every family has experienced a trauma. And in Hlukhiv there are no reforms. ... The city is dying. ... There are no investments, no future. ... When the residents of Hlukhiv suggested I run for mayor, I said to myself: Michel, you can't say no.

In the October 25th local elections, Terestchenko trounced his opponent, winning two-thirds of the vote.

He has no illusions about the size of the task before him. But he remains optimistic:

> Tereshchenko told Agence France Presse that he hoped to establish a flourishing, corruption-free democratic government like the one his grandfather had hoped to establish in Tsarist Russia. "It failed in Russia. But it will succeed in Ukraine," he said.

Terestchenko's victory is important for several reasons. First, it demonstrates that anti-system candidates can win office in the post-Maidan Ukraine. Just these individuals will be able to parlay the greater authority and resources that Ukraine's soon-to-be-implemented decentralization grants them into more effective local government. Terestchenko could succeed in fixing Hlukhiv.

Second, Terestchenko's deeply rooted Ukrainian patriotism gives the lie (yet again) to Russian and Western pro-Russian propaganda that insists the Euromaidan Revolution was the handiwork of fascists and Nazis and that Kyiv is in the hands of a vicious junta. The Nation magazine might want to take note.

Third, Terestchenko's election and acceptance by the local population suggests that Ukrainians may not be the xenophobes that the Russian right and the Western left says they are. More important, the emergence of a Russian-speaking, French-born Ukrainian as a prominent local political figure suggests that a new post-Maidan Ukrainian identity is indeed in the process of formation.

Fourth, the Terestchenko phenomenon would have been impossible without the Euromaidan Revolution, showing once again that this overwhelmingly impressive demonstration of "people power" has already had and will continue to have enormous positive consequences for Ukrainian politics and culture.

Small wonder that Vladimir Putin hates and fears Ukraine. If, as Terestchenko hopes, free democratic government "will succeed in Ukraine," Russia could be next.

*

The Negativists Are Wrong on Ukraine, *World Affairs Journal*, January 15, 2016

It was at the California Republican state convention in San Diego on September 11, 1970 that Vice President Spiro Agnew immortalized his speech writer, William Safire, by saying the following memorable words: "In the United States today, we have more than our share of nattering nabobs of negativism. They have formed their own 4-H club —the hopeless, hysterical hypochondriacs of history."

Too bad the witty and erudite Safire, who eventually went on to become a *New York Times* columnist, isn't alive today. If he were, he might be tempted to direct his rhetoric at the nattering nabobs and hopeless, hysterical hypochondriacs who comment on Ukraine.

Some live in the West; many of whom never cared much about Ukraine and decided they were experts after surfing the Internet. Many more live in Ukraine; they're the populists, the right- and left-wing hotheads, the intellectuals who spin pristine theories and then cry foul when reality fails to meet their expectations, and the analysts who refuse to admit that a half-empty glass is better than an empty one.

I'd be rich if I had a hryvnia for every article that said Ukraine was on the "brink of disaster" or the "verge of collapse." And I'd be richer if I had half a hryvnia for every time people have said that "nothing has changed" in Ukraine since the Euromaidan Revolution.

Here are some of the most popular examples of hopeless hysteria:

- *The economy is on the verge of collapse.* No, it's not. The macro-economy has been stabilized. A reasonable budget has been adopted. The banking system is being fixed. Energy prices are beginning to make sense. And, thanks to Russia's Putin, all of Ukraine's trade will be with EBR (Everybody but Russia) as of 2016. Expect Ukraine's economy to become more competitive and globally oriented this year.

- *Ukraine is unstable.* Say that again? More Ukrainians are patriotic and committed to statehood than at any time in recent history. The far right is weak; the far left is even weaker. The former Regionnaires organized in the Opposition Bloc are mostly a nuisance. Few people like the president and prime minister, but virtually no one wants to replace them with radicals or bring back Yanukovych. True, many, perhaps most, elites are corrupt, but corruption isn't instability.

- *Neo-Nazis are poised to seize power.* This claim says more about the West's phobias than about Ukraine's problems and about the Western media's love affair with the country's few score genuine neo-Nazis. This ragtag group is to topple a government? C'mon!

- *Free Ukraine will split in two.* If the country controlled by Kyiv didn't fracture in 2014, when the government and army were weak, polarization was high, and Putin could have invaded with impunity, it won't in 2016. In any case, Ukraine's vaunted East-West "divide" is no more threatening to the country's unity than America's red state/blue state divide.

- *The volunteer militias in free Ukraine are powerful and destabilizing warlords.* They were always too few to be destabilizing, and they have long since stopped being powerful. And how can you be a warlord, if you control no territory?

- *Ukraine will never be normal as long as the Donbas is occupied.* Quite the contrary. Ukraine's chances of becoming normal are high as long as the Donbas cancer remains outside its body politic—which, thanks to Putin, is likely to be a long time

The fact is that, although it still has a very long way to go, Ukraine has changed enormously, and mostly for the better, in the last two years. For statistical evidence, look at an excellent joint study recently published by VoxUkraine and the *Ekonomichna Pravda* website.

You may even conclude that the nabobs and hypochondriacs are right about one thing. Ukraine *is* on the brink—of success.

*

Ukraine Expands Trade Routes, Bypasses Russia, *World Affairs Journal*, January 26, 2016

Ukraine is taking two important steps toward expanding its ties with the global economy.

The Beskyd-Skotarske train tunnel in the Carpathians is being widened from one track to two, thanks to funding provided by the European Bank for Reconstruction and Development and the European Investment Bank. The project will more than double the speeds at which trains can travel through the tunnel as well as double the number of trains undertaking the journey. Since 60 percent of Ukraine's current trade with countries to its west goes through the tunnel (originally built in 1886), the result will be a vastly enlarged capacity for imports and exports with the European Union, which already is Ukraine's largest trading partner and with which Ukraine now shares a free trade zone. The work is scheduled to be completed by the end of 2017; trains will start using it by mid-2018.

Even more impressive is Ukraine's participation in the Trans-Caspian international transport route that extends from Georgia, through Azerbaijan and Kazakhstan, to China, thereby bypassing Russian territory. The first trial run of a Ukrainian train consisting of 10 cars and 20 40-foot containers began in mid-January in the Ukrainian port city of Illichevsk. It was transported by ship to Batumi, Georgia. Thence by train to the Azerbaijani port city of Alyat, where it was loaded onto a ferry and crossed the Caspian Sea to Aktau in Kazakhstan. Some cargo will stay in Kazakhstan; some will go on to China, Kyrgyzstan, Uzbekistan, Tajikistan, and Turkmenistan. Naturally, Chinese and Central Asian goods will also flow westwards.

The journey to Aktau is supposed to take about nine days. The train will run three times a week starting in March. Ukraine has high hopes, planning to transport up to 10 million tons of cargo annually via this route.

Ukrainians can thank Russia's hapless president for their country's involvement in the Silk Road. Moscow imposed an embargo on the transit of Ukrainian goods in early 2016, as punishment for Ukraine's pursuit of closer economic ties with the European Union via the Deep and Comprehensive Free Trade Area agreement. That move, like Vladimir Putin's decision to destroy Western food products and reduce economic ties with Turkey, has only forced Russia's neighbors to search for alternatives to their traditional over-dependence on Russia. Since the alternatives are there, the big loser is Russia, which, thanks to Putin, will increasingly become isolated, economically and politically. Ukraine will be a big winner, since ending its economic dependence on Russia's backward energy-based economy is a *sine qua non* of the still-backward Ukrainian economy's finally becoming globally competitive. Over time, going global will help create commercial conditions that will allow Ukraine's trade to expand and its economy to advance and modernize, while Russia's remains unreformed and antediluvian.

Perhaps the most striking and encouraging aspect to Ukraine's linkage to the Trans-Caspian trade route is that the country's leadership could successfully navigate and negotiate a complex deal swiftly and efficiently through an intelligent and sustained diplomatic effort.

According to one source:

> To organize the running of trains, the Ministry of Infrastructure, Ukrainian Railways, and the Coordination Committee of the Trans-Caspian international transport route made significant and hard work in 2015. The inclusion of Ukraine in the Great Silk Road was first recorded in the Ukrainian-Chinese inter-agency protocol. The possibilities of the project of Trans-Caspian international transport route were presented on 16 November 2015 during a road show and on 3 December 2015 at the International forum "Connecting Europe and Asia: a new

look at the formation of the transcontinental route system" in Odessa.

The bottom line is this: Ukraine's policymakers wisely anticipated the Kremlin's embargo and even more wisely addressed the looming potential crisis well before it became one. That's impressive, suggesting that Ukraine can get the job done when it needs to.

*

At Last, Military Reform Makes Headway in Ukraine, *World Affairs Journal*, February 3, 2016

When a close observer and frequent critic of Ukraine's military establishment has something good to say about it, we may want to listen.

Yuri Butusov, military analyst and editor of the censor.net website, describes a January 21 roundtable on defense reform he attended at the Ministry of Defense. He lists a number of firsts:

- For the first time, a draft reform strategy was developed on the basis of the new National Security Strategy and the new Military Doctrine. It's impossible to begin structural reforms of the Ministry of Defense and the Armed Forces without such a plan.

- For the first time, outside experts were invited to provide criticism, and not praise.

- For the first time, discussion focused on a finished document, and not a concept.

- For the first time, "NATO standards" were defined as not something abstract, but as certain concrete obligations.

In a word, Ukraine's military establishment appeared to be serious and willing to listen. Moreover, the focus of the discussion—the Strategic Defense Bulletin—elicited, according to Butusov, a generally positive response from the civilian participants. There was also substantive criticism, especially of the document's suggestion that NATO standards be introduced only by 2018. Obviously, notes Butusov, changing military hardware and training takes time. But "to change the administrative system, to replace our absolutely ineffective administrative formula with NATO's decentralized system of decision-making and greater leadership responsibility does not require many resources or time. We have the cadres. We know how to do it."

Butusov notes that the document's main shortcoming is that it fails to specify military threats. Without that, it's impossible to establish reform priorities and the depth of desired changes. "We don't need standards for the sake of standards," says Butusov, "but results" in case of a "massive Russian aggression." After all, "we need to know the war and scenarios for which we're preparing."

Another military analyst, Dmytro Tymchuk, puts the matter this way:

> The main goal of any reform of any armed forces is to create a structure able to oppose effectively the most likely military threat. For us that's an open and massive aggression by the Russian Federation, regardless of how improbable it may be.

> Instead of focusing on the main threat, however, "we are currently situationally reforming the army in terms of the hybrid war with Russia" and the Anti-Terrorist Operation against the separatists in the eastern Donbas. That's too bad, because the needs of conducting hybrid war are different from those of conducting a massive land war.

Rather more bullish on the prospects of reforming the Ukrainian defense establishment is Andrii Zahorodniuk, the head of the Ministry of Defense's Reform Office. In addition to the Ministry's own staff, an "enormous number of people are taking part in developing reform," he says, and reforms are already taking place on several levels. Zahorodniuk has big hopes for 2016:

> Our main task in the new year is to unite all the reform initiatives. ... At present, we have about ten reform initiatives at the Ministry of Defense and the General Staff, with no coordination among them. ... The Strategic Defense Bulletin is a kind of roadmap for defense reform.

Butusov might be less sanguine about the Bulletin's serving as an effective road map, but he would agree with Zahorodniuk that the major obstacle to reform is the bloated, obstructionist bureaucracy. "90 percent of our work goes to fighting it," says Zahorodniuk. "Everyone whose signature is required can slow down or stop the process. One of our colleagues recently calculated that gathering the signatures for just one document required walking nine kilometers within the corridors of the Ministry."

All bureaucracies change slowly and unwillingly, as Zahorodniuk understands. "The things we'll be doing this year will affect many people," he says hopefully. The good news is that he expects "a great deal of resistance." This may mean that those nine kilometers could soon be reduced—but only if Ukraine's Butusovs, Tymchuks, and Zahorodniuks keep pushing.

*

Managing Kyiv's Government Crisis, *World Affairs Journal*, February 29, 2016

For those who are puzzled by current goings-on in Ukraine's government, here are a few tips.

First, let's not confuse "crisis of government" with "crisis of Ukraine." True, Prime Minister Arsenii Yatseniuk is unpopular and should probably resign. Also true, his cabinet needs reshuffling. But it's illogical to jump from the claim that the government is dysfunctional to the claim that Ukraine is experiencing a "grim slide." Governments are not countries, even when they're absolutist, as in Louis XIV's France, or fascist, as in Vladimir Putin's Russia. Ukraine is a poorly functioning democracy—which means that its poorly functioning democratic institutions do not determine the fate of the country as a whole.

Second, let's not assume that resignations by reformist ministers mean that "there have been no reforms" or that "reforms have stalled." When Minister of Economy and Trade Aivaras Abromavicius resigned a few weeks ago, most commentators bemoaned his leaving because he was a "reformer" while simultaneously claiming "nothing had changed." These declarations are incompatible. If he was a reformer, then something must have changed under his tutelage. If nothing had changed, then good riddance to him. In fact, as virtually all objective analysts in Ukraine and in the West say, Ukraine has changed much in the last two years. It needs to change much more—especially in rule of law, where reforms have been hesitant. But the country *has* indeed changed.

Third, let's not assume that Ukraine's current governmental crisis cannot be managed. Ministers resign all the time; prime ministers are detested all the time; cabinets are re-shuffled all the time. The current Ukrainian crisis is no different from scores of similar crises in other countries. Sometimes they end well; sometimes they end badly. One big difference about Ukraine's crisis is that Western institutions and leaders hold significant leverage now, and they are applying pressure and insisting that Kyiv find a solution. The jury is still out with respect to Kyiv's ability to manage the crisis.

Fourth, let's not assume that the language of gloom, doom, despair, and betrayal that Ukrainians so relish offers a way out of the crisis. If everything is hopeless, then why bother crafting effective policy? If they're all crooks and traitors, then why not just bring back Viktor Yanukovych and his thugs? This is not to suggest that we don rose-tinted glasses. However, it is to suggest that how Ukrainians "frame" the challenges ahead directly affects how, or whether, they address them.

Finally, one example of how not to think about Ukraine and one of how to think about it.

The first is a piece in *Time* magazine by Serhii Lyovochkin, identified as "a member of the Ukrainian parliament and one of the leaders of the Opposition Bloc political party." *Time* shamelessly omits to mention that Lyovochkin—Ukrainians usually append the modifier "odious" to his name—was also Yanukovych's right-hand man. For Lyovochkin to talk about "fixing my country's broken system" is, thus, the height of gall. He helped break the system that is now so difficult to repair. Lyovochkin had no qualms as the Yanukovych gang ravaged the place he now calls "my country." Truly fixing Ukraine means instituting rule of law, which in turn means making Lyovochkin's return to Ukrainian politics as unthinkable as Joseph Goebbels's to Germany's.

The second piece is a smart and balanced analysis of the ongoing crisis in the indispensable VoxUkraine. The authors judiciously analyze its causes, isolate several cons *and* pros of the crisis, and suggest a variety of possible outcomes. Their conclusion is worth quoting at length:

> The failed No Confidence Motion is neither a unique occurrence for Ukraine nor a catastrophe. Such a scenario has been played out in many other countries. In Ukraine, we observe not only the political struggle and negotiations between major political parties, but also an attempt of a minority coalition parties to strengthen their voice and increase the share and loyalty of electorate by speaking openly against the governing parties.

> Despite the bitter scent of renewed political bickering, the failed NCM has helped to avoid an even greater disaster (early elections would not only take a lot of precious time, but could give rise to populist politics and endanger the success of reforms). Still, the coalition parties have to avoid the political stalemate by quickly reaching agreement over changes in the government and accelerating the reforms. Hopefully, this will be done, given the pressure of domestic audience and international partners. The memories about the 2005 post-Maidan political fiasco and the second anniversary of Euromaidan sacrifices should also help.

> Such conflicts are likely to happen again if the underlying reasons for political instability are not addressed. The constitutional conflict between the PM and the President, low quality of "old" elites, absence of ideology based parties and imperfect election laws threaten the long-term success of reforms in Ukraine. One of the possible solutions could be constitutional changes developed by an impartial Constitutional Assembly with wide participation of experts and civil activists that would finally answer the question—is Ukraine a parliamentary or a presidential republic, i.e. who is the head of the executive branch—the president or the prime-minister? This would decrease the potential for political infighting and make politicians more accountable to the people by drawing clear responsibility lines within the government.

So, drop your unwarranted assumptions, dump Lyovochkin on the ash heap of history, and listen to the *vox* of reason.

*

Decentralizing Government Power Is Key to Reforming Ukraine, *World Affairs Journal*, March 4, 2016

It's not surprising that Kyiv's convoluted politics color what we think about Ukraine and its prospects. But don't let the turmoil in Kyiv obscure the hopeful developments taking place in Ukraine's provinces. Take agricultural reform. As Kyiv's policymakers squawk and squabble, real Ukrainians must live real lives. And they do, frequently developing innovative new schemes that qualify as no less important reforms than those contemplated and adopted in the capital.

Lviv Province, 39 percent of whose population lives in the countryside, has just adopted an ambitious five-year Complex Plan of Supporting and Developing Agro-industrial Production, developed by the Province State Administration's Agro-industrial Department, which is headed by the dynamic Natalia Khmyz, described by her coworkers as a "fount of ideas." The State Administration is allocating 11 million hryvnia (about $425,000 toward agriculture in 2016. According to Taras Verveha, the head of the Lviv Provincial Council's Agro-industrial Commission, 1.5 million will pay the interest farmers owe on existing loans; 1 million is earmarked for replenishing the soil; and 8.5 million will serve as low-interest loans for agricultural improvements. Verveha expects agricultural production to increase by 10 percent in five years.

In addition to the 11 million coming from the province in 2016, Khmyz and her colleagues expect Kyiv to provide 16 million, international donors to come up with 6 million, and co-financing partnerships (involving local budgetary allocations and farms to account for 42 million—for a total of 75 million hryvnia. Since the State Administration intends to spend 86 million hryvnia during the next five years (or about $3.3 million at the current exchange rate, the actual total will likely be seven times as much, or 602 million hryvnia ($23 million.

The Lviv Province Fund for Supporting Individual Housing Construction in Villages, which has been providing villagers with cheap loans for fixing their homesteads since 2000 on a transparent and competitive basis, will administer most of the monies involved (8.5 million in 2016 and 68 million in 2016–2020. The Fund expects to provide 1-to-3-year loans at 5 percent interest (compared to the 30-percent interest offered by banks to 104 small farmers, individual homesteads, and village cooperatives in 2016 and to a total of 605 in 2016–2020. The interest is earmarked for promoting the program, providing training and instruction, and covering direct administrative costs.

According to Zenoviy Drevnyak, the head of the Fund, the loans will be awarded on the same kind of transparent and competitive basis that has characterized the Fund's loan-making activity hitherto. Farmers will be obliged to submit detailed business plans to the State Administration's Agro-industrial Department, which will select those proposals that promise to contribute most to increasing production of milk, fruits, vegetables, and meat and to creating jobs. The Fund will sign contracts with the farmers, provide the financing, and monitor the projects. The Agro-industrial Department's outside experts will then evaluate the projects on an ongoing basis. The financing will pay for up to 50 percent of the proposed project's total budget ensuring that the individual farmers share the risks. When farmers eventually pay off their loans, the monies will be ploughed back into the program and go toward financing future agro-industrial projects.

The program's process, says Drevnyak, has been carefully designed to minimize opportunities for corruption by stipulating that each part of the process—competition, financing, and evaluation—be performed by different individuals or entities. Information about the entire process will be available on a special website; the Fund will also train farmers to develop their business plans. In time, the authorities hope to have a list of the "500 Most Successful Farms" that would serve as models for other farmers and cooperatives.

Perhaps the most promising aspect of the Plan is that it is a local initiative entailing negligible involvement of Kyiv's heavy-handed, inept, and corrupt bureaucracy. Small wonder that other provinces are expressing great interest in Lviv's initiative. On March 1, several hundred farmers and entrepreneurs from throughout Ukraine met in the Lviv Arena conference center for an extensive discussion about how to improve agriculture production. The name of the event reflected the hopeful enthusiasm of its participants: "A Million from Each Hectare."

The road to effective administration is long, and it remains to be seen whether Lviv's provincial government is up to the task. However, the Agro-industrial Department's effort to revitalize agriculture has exhibited a degree of professionalism that has eluded Kyiv. The Lviv experiment needs to be monitored, as well supported from within and without. And the clear lesson for Ukraine's reformers is obvious: cut the central bureaucracy and its intrusiveness—radically.

*

Ukraine as a Vital Security Interest for Europe, *World Affairs Journal*, March 31, 2015

An American official in Brussels recently informed me of a meeting he had with a highly placed European Union diplomat during which the latter "stressed that Ukraine is an 'almost existential' issue for Europe."

The phrase "almost existential" is worth looking at more closely. Existential issues concern the life or death of the subject concerned. A Russian attack on Germany would be an existential issue for Germany. A Russian attack on Tajikistan would be an existential issue for Tajikistan, but a non-existential issue for Germany. An almost existential issue for some country is thus something that almost concerns—or is almost equivalent to—the life and death of that country. Seen in this light, the claim that Ukraine is almost existential for Europe amounts to saying that Ukraine's life or death is almost equivalent to the life or death of Europe.

Another way of making this point is to say that Ukraine is a *vital strategic interest* of the West. That is, Ukraine isn't just an interest to Europe: lots of countries are. Nor is it just strategic: something on which the well-being, security, and survival of Europe depend. Ukraine is also vital: the well-being, security, and survival of Europe depend on it *directly*.

These are very strong words. They'll come as no surprise to Ukrainian policymakers and analysts, who've been making just this point for at least a year—if not since Ukraine's independence in 1991—to no avail. Although the United States and the United Kingdom supposedly guaranteed Ukraine's security in the 1994 Budapest Memorandum on Security Assurances, no Western country paid much attention to Ukraine or its security for more than two decades. Quite the contrary, the EU and NATO expanded all the way up to Ukraine's borders and few Western policymakers considered what that meant for Ukraine: its relegation to a security no-man's-land between a visibly indifferent West and a visibly aggressive Russia.

Had Europe recognized Ukraine's almost existential importance one or two decades earlier, Russia might not have invaded Crimea and the Donbas and the human tragedy of the ongoing Russo-Ukrainian war could have been avoided. Put this way, Europe's very belated understanding of its own vital strategic interests is a terrible indictment of its self-absorption, hypocrisy, and inefficiency. Clearly, Ukraine must reform itself radically. But so, too, does the EU.

One Western analyst has recognized Ukraine's strategic importance from the get-go: the former national security adviser Zbigniew Brzezinski, who's consistently argued that the only thing standing between Russia and empire is an independent Ukraine. Just recently, Brzezinski expanded on these sentiments in an interview with Poland's *Gazeta Prawna*:

> If the war in Ukraine turns into an easy military success for Russia, its victory, then we must reckon with something in the Baltic states. That would be the first step. Further flare-ups could take place in Moldova, Georgia, and Azerbaijan. That would be the logic of events. Next in line could be Poland.

When asked whether NATO would defend Poland, Brzezinski offered sobering advice. "Poland should arm itself," he said. The complexity of NATO procedures means that the alliance "could be paralyzed for some time" after a Russian attack on Poland, which "should count on itself so as to be able to defend itself for as long as possible." These are scary recommendations for a country that's been partitioned four times in modern history.

Sadly, Brzezinski is right about NATO's inability to rush to the rescue even of its own members—not to mention such non-members as Ukraine. But his comments also suggest that Europe's perception of Ukraine's "almost existential" importance still has some way to go before it becomes more than a rhetorical claim. As Russian analyst Vladimir Ryzhkov **says**:

> The West's reaction [to Putin's aggression] was not only weak, but is growing weaker by the day. It only reluctantly and belatedly imposed sanctions, without imposing an oil or gas embargo or disconnecting Russia from the SWIFT banking system—moves that would have threatened the survival of Putin's regime.

What's more, after less than a year of sanctions, a growing number of Western states are already clamoring to weaken or repeal them.

Europe will truly understand the meaning of "almost existential" when it appreciates that its commitment to Ukraine must be "almost" as great as its commitment to itself.

*

A Grand Strategy for Ukraine, *Foreign Affairs*, April 5, 2016

Ukraine needs a grand strategy—a set of overarching and realistic goals to serve as a road map for its geopolitical, economic, and cultural development in the next 20 years. The ongoing war with Russia has amply demonstrated that Ukraine can no longer assume that things will just work themselves out. Nor can it try to pursue good relations with everyone. Russia's invasion of Crimea and eastern Donbas means that Ukraine must start choosing—not so much sides as courses of action that promote its own long-term interests.

History holds several lessons for Ukraine. Since the collapse in the thirteenth century of the Kyivan Rus state, the territory of today's Ukraine has been subjected to waves of imperial expansion by aggressive neighboring states. The list includes the Mongols, Lithuanians, Poles, Muscovites, Ottomans, Austrians, Germans, and Russian Bolsheviks. Each invasion destroyed political and social institutions; most also produced enormous human misery. Each aggression ended for good only after the empire concerned was either dismembered, defeated, or transformed into a bounded nation-state.

With one exception—today's Russia. Despite the historical discontinuities with tsarist Russia and the Soviet Union, in size and expansionist inclinations, today's Russia is virtually identical to both. The preference for expansion may be the product of unchanging geopolitical realities that have driven Russian policymakers for centuries. Or it may be the product of Russia's past and present imperial drives. As far as Ukraine is concerned, both possibilities lead to the same conclusion: that Russia is, and will remain, a threat to its security and survival, whether the country remains geopolitically large and insecure or geopolitically large and imperial—even after the era of Russian President Vladimir Putin ends and Russia resumes its transition to democracy. Russia will be an existential threat until it becomes a fully consolidated and stable democracy at ease with itself and the world.

History holds another lesson for Ukraine: that the West or, more specifically, Europe views Ukraine as a target for exploitation (Germany in both world wars) or as an object of indifference (the European Union and its predecessor, the European Economic Community, for most of Ukraine's independence). Yet Ukraine is a strategic interest of vital importance to Europe's security, stability, and survival. Ukraine's existence guarantees that Russia's insecurities and imperial appetites will always fall short of Europe proper. The incapacity to comprehend this elementary geopolitical reality stems from the still widespread western European view of eastern Europeans, even those within the EU, as politically immature "near Europeans." The western European attitude toward Ukraine tends to be even more condescending, generally resting on the conviction that the Ukrainians will never be quite "like us."

History also suggests that Ukraine should be skeptical about Europe's ability to act as a unified body when it comes to Russia. Disunity is the historical norm for Europe—whether at the time of the Holy Roman Empire or during the incessant Franco-German competitions or over the course of numerous tensions among the continent's small states. Even if the European Union bears up under the latest round of pressures, it is likely that it will eventually emerge as a different kind of entity. It will have the ability to make decisions if it is smaller; it will have a hard time doing so if it remains large. Neither Europe will be the same entity of which Ukraine currently desires to become a member: a tightly knit Franco-German club may have little use for anybody, whereas an extremely loose commonwealth may be of little use to anybody. This doesn't mean that Ukraine should abandon its European aspirations (European values and dedication to rule of law will remain worthy aspirations in all circumstances). But it does mean that joining Europe may mean something very different five or ten years from now.

Finally, history suggests that the United States' attitude toward Ukraine will largely be a function of U.S.–Russian relations. When those relations are good, Ukraine recedes from the U.S. agenda. When those relations are bad—as today—Ukraine acquires strategic importance for Washington. The United States, inevitably, is a "bad weather" friend of Ukraine.

The overriding geopolitical realities confronting Ukraine today and in the foreseeable future are thus threefold: the continuing existential threat posed by Russia, the continuing unreliability of Europe, and the continuing subordination of the United States' Ukraine policy to U.S.–Russian relations. Ukraine's grand strategy must be formulated to the challenges and opportunities these realities pose.

First and most obvious, Ukraine must have armed forces that are strong enough to deter any Russian attack short of a full-scale nuclear war. Ukraine's army must be restructured to meet that threat, and it must be armed well enough to ward off any massive tank or air attack as well. Central to this issue is the question of whether Ukraine's security needs are best served by a large conscription army or a small professional force and by a series of stationary fortifications or a mobile defensive strategy. Expert opinion, in Ukraine and the West, suggests that a highly professional mobile force is Ukraine's best bet. Such an army would be expensive.

Second, Ukraine must have an economy that can both sustain such a massive armament effort and provide Ukraine's long-suffering population with a requisite living standard. Ukraine must take advantage of Russia's economic warfare, including embargoes on a raft of Ukrainian products, and reduce its economic ties with Russia to a minimum while opening up its economy to the world to a maximum. In particular, having drastically reduced since 2014 gas imports from and defense cooperation with Russia, Ukraine must make sure never again to become dependent on Russia for its energy and security needs.

Third, Ukraine must counter Russia's use of soft power to subvert Ukraine. Key to Russia's soft-power assault is the notion that there is a "Russian World" consisting of all Russians and Russian speakers, whom the Kremlin is obligated to protect. There is only one way for any country trapped in this "Russian World" to break out of it: by gradually reducing Russian-language use and replacing it with native-language use. So, too, Ukraine must, like the Baltic states, attempt to make Ukrainian and English the languages of everyday public discourse and reduce Russian to a household tongue increasingly confined to an aging population. Such a shift can be introduced without violating human or cultural rights by effectively making Ukrainian the sole language of the armed forces.

Ukraine's foreign relations will have to be structured around these three geopolitical realities. Since Russia will always be a threat and Europe will likely remain unreliable, Ukraine should focus its efforts on building alliances with those countries that face equally unpalatable geopolitical choices. Belarus, Estonia, Latvia, Lithuania, Moldova, Poland, and Romania have long been sandwiched between Germany and Russia and subjected to their imperialist aspirations. But now, Germany is benign. Although expansionist, Russia is economically and politically weak, resting on the deeply corrupt and unstable fascistoid regime constructed by Putin. Meanwhile, the states in between have for the most part constructed stable political and economic institutions and armies. In the early 1990s, then Ukrainian President Leonid Kravchuk championed the vision of a Baltic to Black Sea Alliance. It never materialized because Ukraine's western neighbors understandably opted for EU and NATO membership. That vision has recently been resuscitated as the Intermarium project as a result of Putin's aggression and the West's anemic response. Ideally, the Intermarium states would also include Turkey.

Naturally, Ukraine must continue to maintain the best possible relations with Europe, Russia, and the United States. Diplomacy will always matter. But no amount of Ukrainian diplomacy will transform Russia into a friendly neighbor. As history suggests, only Russia's transformation into a smaller or nonimperial state will do that. Nor will Ukrainian diplomacy persuade western Europe that Ukrainians are as worthy of a European future as the Germans or French. Only a rich and powerful Ukraine can do that. Ukrainian diplomacy toward the United States therefore becomes all the more important. Ukraine should focus on promoting the deepest possible economic and cultural ties with the United States and on reminding Washington that Russia's existential threat to Ukraine is a strategic threat to the United States.

Political, economic, and cultural divorce from Russia, integration with the world, and alliance building with eastern Europe, Turkey, and the United States are the three components of a grand strategy that could ensure Ukraine's security and survival in the next two decades. When the Putin regime ends, Russia possibly collapses, and the dust from this time of trouble settles, Ukraine may need to rethink its grand strategy. Until then, its priority must be the one foisted on it by Putin—divorce.

The Dutch, Kyiv, and Reform, *World Affairs Journal*, April 7, 2016

The Dutch referendum is not the end of the world for Ukraine. As one smart and sober Ukrainian analyst points out, it changes very little in Ukraine's relationship with the European Union. In a word, Ukraine need not panic.

That said, Ukraine needs to draw several conclusions from the decision by some 20 percent of Holland's electorate to reject the EU's Association Agreement with Ukraine.

First, that percentage of nay-sayers roughly corresponds to the percentage of citizenry in all EU states who actively reject "European values." These are the supporters of extreme right-wing parties, many of which of late have attained 20–30 percent of the vote in various elections. These are the people who disagree with the following passage in the Preamble of the Charter of Fundamental Rights of the European Union:

> Conscious of its spiritual and moral heritage, the Union is founded on the indivisible, universal values of human dignity, freedom, equality and solidarity; it is based on the principles of democracy and the rule of law. It places the individual at the heart of its activities, by establishing the citizenship of the Union and by creating an area of freedom, security and justice.

These people will never support Ukraine or many other bilateral and multilateral relationships.

Second, probably as many if not more Europeans view European values in the same manner that former German Chancellor Gerhard Schröder and a lot of his comrades in the German social-democratic party do: they're fine, as long as they're not inconvenient. If rights imply inconvenience or if indifference to rights entails profit, then who needs rights? Schröder, in case you've forgotten, finagled a cushy job with the Russian mafia-like state firm, Gazprom, while still in office. And he's been lobbying for Vladimir Putin, apologizing for his imperialism, and lining his pockets with rubles ever since.

The European Schröders will support Ukraine only if it's profitable and convenient.

The rest of the Europeans—a third, maybe more—sincerely believe in European values. These are the people who believe in the EU, believe in NATO, support sanctions against the mafia in the Kremlin, and largely welcome Middle Eastern refugees regardless of the cost or inconvenience that their arrival in Germany entailed.

These Europeans will support Ukraine, but only if no other, more pressing human rights issues require their immediate attention.

EU officials break down into these three categories as well, though the set of true believers in Eurovalues is probably greater than in the population at large.

The lessons for Ukraine are several:

First, it cannot count on Europe to do the right thing. Appeals to human rights, common European values, the sacrifices Ukrainians have made to join Europe—all this will fall on mostly deaf ears in about two-thirds of the population. So is the fact that thousands of Ukrainians have died defending Eurovalues against Russian imperialism.

Second, regardless of what the Europeans do or say, Ukraine should continue to do everything it can to join Europe and adopt Eurovalues. Western political and economic institutions do work—even if those of the EU may not—and Western values (such as human rights, democracy, and rule of law) are far better than those promulgated by the Putins of the world.

Third, Ukraine must realize that its progress toward Western institutions and values depends almost exclusively on itself. Europe won't go out of its way to help it; neither will anybody else, including the United States—if Ukraine's doesn't start measuring up to western governance and rule of law standards. Ukraine must become a strong, rich, democratic country by adopting policies that promote strength, wealth, and democracy.

Fourth, once Ukraine is strong, rich, and democratic, Europe—including the Eurovalue nay-sayers and the Schröder-like opportunists—will come knocking on its door.

Fifth, for Ukraine to become strong, rich, and democratic, its elites must finally get their act together and govern like mature elites and not children.

What the Dutch did is shameful: they betrayed decency and Ukraine. But what Ukraine's squabbling, incompetent, self-serving, shortsighted elites are doing is even worse: they're destroying Ukraine and its people.

*

Ukraine's New Cabinet, *World Affairs Journal*, April 21, 2016

How should we evaluate Ukraine's just-completed process of forming a new coalition and cabinet?

For starters, coalitions and cabinets are routinely changed in democracies. Devious presidents, devious prime ministers, and devious parliamentarians are also business as usual. So, too, are horse trading, smoke-filled rooms, shady deals, opportunistic bargains, and outrageous demands. Although these things usually dismay and demoralize non-politicians like most of us, their presence signifies that a democratic process is taking place.

That said Ukraine isn't a run-of-the-mill democracy. It's a transitional democracy mired in economic crisis and war. While other elites can squabble to their hearts' content, those in Ukraine have a political and moral obligation to set aside personal ambitions and animosities and, in the national interest, find effective solutions quickly. When time is of the essence, one can't waste two months, as the Ukrainians just did, trying to come up with a new coalition and cabinet. That's criminal.

Blame President Petro Poroshenko for trying to exercise excessive control over the government. True, the conflict between president and prime minister is built into Ukraine's parliamentary-presidential system, but a wise leader would not have provoked a crisis he could not immediately resolve. Blame former Prime Minister Arsenii Yatseniuk for pathetically clinging to office even when he and everyone else knew he was doomed. And blame opposition leaders Yulia Tymoshenko and the preposterous demagogue, Oleh Lyashko, for stoking the flames and Andrii Sadovy for refusing to help put them out.

In sum, all of Ukraine's political elites failed to act responsibly.

Unsurprisingly, a recent poll shows that Ukraine's president, cabinet, and parliament have abysmally low ratings. Only 17 percent of Ukrainians support or "tend" to support Poroshenko, while 75 percent do not. The cabinet gets the following ratings: 7 percent for and 89 percent against. The Rada's numbers are: 5 percent for and 88 percent against.

The new cabinet with Prime Minister Volodymyr Hroysman can't do worse.

Predictably, Ukraine's chattering classes are already gleefully dooming the cabinet. But their expectations may be premature. The 38-year old Hroysman was an excellent mayor of Vinnytsia. He did well as speaker of the parliament for the last two years. The development and adoption of Ukraine's ambitious decentralization plan was, in large part, to his credit. And, in conducting negotiations for the composition of the cabinet, he demonstrated that he had backbone and was not, as many charge, Poroshenko's lap dog. Not bad for a young guy who could be my student. He may fail, of course, but then again he may not. In any case, the jury isn't out. Indeed, it hasn't been assembled.

The other key appointment in the cabinet is the finance minister, Oleksandr Danyliuk. The English-speaking Danyliuk has impressive credentials: he worked as senior consul-tant at McKinsey and Company in London, has an MBA from the University of Indiana, and helped initiate the National Anti-Corruption Bureau. True, he also served in some advisory capacity in the Yanukovych government, but that neither disqualifies him nor suggests he's incompetent.

Not surprisingly, Hroysman's and Danyliuk's critics are pretty much the same people who insist that "nothing has changed" in Ukraine. That's nonsense, of course, as I've repeatedly pointed out. But, if true, then Ukraine's nattering nabobs of negativism have no logical grounds for criticizing the new cabinet and making unflattering comparisons between Danyliuk and his predecessor, Natalie Jaresko. If "nothing has changed," then Jaresko is to blame as much as anyone else. If Jaresko's departure is unfortunate—and it is—then something may indeed have changed.

Either way, the above-mentioned poll shows that only 14 percent of Ukrainians approve of Jaresko and 64 percent do not. In contrast, the loudmouthed Radical Party leader Lyashko received 23 percent for and 69 percent against. Decide for yourself what these numbers say about polls as measures of reform.

So, how will the Hroysman cabinet do?

We'll know it's doing well if the nabobs insist months from now that "nothing has changed."

*

Why Slow and Steady Wins the Race: A Case for Patience in Post-Maidan Ukraine, *Atlantic Council*, May 13, 2016

The aftermath of revolutions is always disappointing. Expectations of immediate transformation come up against intractable reality and a deep and debilitating disappointment usually sets in among much of the population. But not among radicals, who typically demand a thoroughgoing renewal of the elites deemed responsible for "betraying" the cause. In France, which set the pattern for many subsequent revolutions, the Jacobins under Maximilien Robespierre called for a republic of virtue to be brought about by terror.

Post-Maidan Ukraine has yet to acquire the dangerous "fever" described by Crane Brinton in his *Anatomy of Revolution*, but some signs are already pointing in that direction. Increasingly, Ukrainians decry their government as illegitimate. Many hope for a third Maidan that will violently settle scores. They obsessively uncover every infraction policymakers commit. Not surprisingly, after twenty-five years of corrupt rule, Ukrainians want their rulers to be saints.

Many a Ukrainian blogger could have written Robespierre's terrifying words:

> Now, what is the fundamental principle of the democratic or popular government—that is, the essential spring which makes it move? It is virtue ...

> [W]hen, by prodigious efforts of courage and reason, a people breaks the chains of despotism to make them into trophies of liberty ... then if it does not climb rapidly to the summit of its destinies, this can only be the fault of those who govern it ...

> [N]ow in this situation, the first maxim of your policy ought to be to lead the people by reason and the people's enemies by terror.

> If the spring of popular government in time of peace is virtue, the springs of popular government in revolution are at once virtue and terror: virtue, without which terror is fatal; terror, without which virtue is powerless. Terror is nothing other than justice, prompt, severe, inflexible; it is therefore an emanation of virtue; it is not so much a special principle as it is a consequence of the general principle of democracy applied to our country's most urgent needs.

Yes, of course, Ukraine's elites are deeply corrupt and their commitment to eliminating that corruption leaves much to be desired. Yes, of course, Ukraine needs better elites, purer elites, cleaner elites. Yes, of course, Ukraine needs more competent, more effective, more professional elites.

But, as former President Leonid Kravchuk used to say, "We've got what we've got." Ukraine's existing elites won't get better if Ukrainian civil society, the media, and the West insist they are irremediably corrupt and need to depart the scene. Sure they are, and sure they should, but, before Ukrainians cry, "Off with their heads!", which saints will replace them?

The obsession with moral purity misses the point. Saints are called saints precisely because they are exceptions to the rule. Most people—and most policymakers—lean more toward the side of sinners. That's as true of crummy democracies such as Ukraine, malfunctioning democracies such as today's America, post-totalitarian democracies such as Konrad Adenauer's Germany, authoritarian democracies such as Charles de Gaulle's France, illiberal democracies such as Viktor Orban's Hungary, and benign democracies such as Justin Trudeau's Canada. Western policymakers and media are especially hypocritical to insist on moral standards for Ukrainians that Americans and Europeans (who provide a welcome home for the ill-gotten gains of Ukrainian corruptioneers and oligarchs) routinely violate.

Robespierre's Jacobin followers in today's Ukraine are dead wrong about virtue. It's not, and never has been, a precondition of systemic change. If it were, we'd all still be living in caves. But if sinful men and women slowly, patiently, imperfectly, and agonizingly change institutions, systems will change and virtuous behavior can result.

Virtue, like successful change, is the product of hard work—not of guillotines.

*

25 Years of Ukraine's Independence, *World Affairs Journal*, July 25, 2016

Ukraine's biggest achievement since independence in 1991 is to have confounded its critics, ill-wishers, and the Kremlin by surviving as a democratic state. Many expected Ukraine to be short-lived. And many others expected it to follow in the footsteps of its post-Soviet neighbors and abandon democracy. Instead, 25 years after independence, Ukraine survives as a democratic state, albeit an imperfect one.

Its survival and consolidation as a democracy can be largely attributed to the fact that, from 1991 to 2014, Ukraine had the good fortune to exist in relatively benign geopolitical circumstances. Russia, the only existential threat to Ukraine, was in disarray during the Boris Yeltsin era. And, until 2014, Putin's Russia, while far from being a good neighbor, had resisted direct intervention. Europe in general and Eastern Europe in particular were stable and prosperous during this period: NATO enlarged and the EU did so in its wake. The United States remained committed to its leadership role in the region, and the West's relations with Russia were mostly constructive. And, finally, Ukrainians—or, more precisely, Ukrainian civil society—consistently challenged government corruption and incompetence and promoted accountability, democracy, tolerance, and transparency.

Despite these years of relative stability, Ukraine's elites failed to reconstruct the nation or set it on a path that would ensure the development of its enormous potential. Instead, their rule was defined by incompetence, corruption, and rapaciousness. The apogee of elite criminality and state dysfunctionality occurred in the three years of Viktor Yanukovych's misrule, 2010–2014.

The Euromaidan Revolution fundamentally upended this status quo. First, by asserting the right of people to choose their leaders, the movement provoked the Kremlin to execute a military land grab in Crimea and the Donbas. Second, the Kremlin's breach of international law and the subsequent Russo-Ukrainian War compelled the West to stand with Ukraine. Third, the Revolution and War profoundly enhanced Ukrainian national consciousness by forcing Ukrainians, for the first time since 1991, to take sides: with Ukraine or with Russia. Most chose Ukraine.

Ironically, Putin forced Ukraine's political elites to finally get serious about systemic reform. It is small wonder that Ukraine has changed more in the two years since the Euromaidan Revolution than in the 23 years that preceded it. The political elites have performed well, or well enough, introducing significant economic, political, and cultural changes. They may even have begun to address issues of corruption and rule of law. That most Ukrainians refuse to recognize the reality of these changes—in large part because corrupt elites now removed from power have escaped justice and revenge—does not change the empirical fact of these changes.

Although the Revolution and War have had a positive effect on Ukraine's trajectory by forcing Ukraine's elites, finally, to make difficult choices, they have also confronted Ukraine's elites and civil society with an unprecedented challenge: outright Russian imperialism. Back in the 1990s, the Yeltsin administration was disturbingly worried about the condition of Russians and Russian speakers in the so-called near abroad. Until the Putin regime turned fully fascist by the late 2000s, it generally expressed its distaste of Ukrainian sovereignty by weaponizing its energy resources. The gloves came off and the diplomatic niceties ended with Putin's invasion of Ukraine in late February 2014.

Almost miraculously, Ukraine managed to field a genuine army, generate thousands of volunteers, and stop the Russian assault. The current stalemate in eastern Ukraine—despite costing the lives of innocent Ukrainian soldiers and civilians—is a major victory for Ukraine. It stopped one of the world's largest armies and most vicious dictators. That is an achievement that most Europeans would be hard-pressed to repeat. And yet, it is a short-term victory.

To be able to deter a Russian attack permanently, Ukraine must grow economically. Ukraine must become an East European tiger with double-digit growth rates. Failing that, Ukraine's economy will not be able to sustain a long-term security effort to stop Russian imperialism. Economic reform is thus indispensable to political and national survival. And inasmuch as rapid economic growth is impossible if corruption remains unaddressed, the fight against corruption is also indispensable to Ukraine's survival.

As Ukrainian soldiers die on a daily basis in the occupied Donbas, the questions Ukrainians must address as they embark on their next 25 years are these: Will economic reform and the struggle against corruption be easier with or without the occupied Donbas? Will economic reform and the struggle against corruption be more effective with or without the occupied Donbas? Can economic reform and the struggle against corruption be sustained with or without the occupied Donbas? Will political and national survival be more likely with or without the occupied Donbas? The future of their country depends on the correct answers to these questions.

For the first time since 1991, Ukraine has the opportunity to break out of Russia's orbit and to transform itself into a genuinely self-reliant, democratic, and prosperous state. It would be a shame, and a tragedy, if Ukrainians sacrificed their statehood, nationhood, and prosperity on the altar of some imagined "sacred" territorial unity and thereby returned into Putin Russia's imperial fold.

*

Ukraine's Next 25 Years, *Foreign Affairs*, September 25, 2016

As Ukrainians celebrate the 25th anniversary of their independence this year, they would do well to remember that the next 25 years will be far more important—and difficult—than the last.

Ukraine declared independence on August 24, 1991, in exceptionally favorable geopolitical circumstances: the Soviet empire was disintegrating; its Russian successor state was democratically inclined and militarily weak; the United States, the world's sole superpower, was determined to promote democracy around the world; NATO had proved its mettle and was soon to expand; and Europe was brimming with the self-confidence that would culminate in the formation of the European Union.

Under such benign conditions, Ukraine could neglect fundamental systemic reform and simply get by, as it did for many of its 25 years.

This period of fair weather has ended, and the approaching storm clouds will require Ukraine to cope with far more challenging, as well as existentially threatening, conditions. In order to survive, Ukraine will need to do more than muddle along. It must pursue, with unwavering resolve, a clearly defined set of priorities.

Consider the changes that have taken place in Ukraine's geopolitical environment.

President Vladimir Putin is actively pursuing hegemony in Russia's "near abroad." Hoping to reestablish a militarily dominant Russia in central Eurasia, Putin has expended an enormous amount of resources in upgrading Russia's armed forces and weapons arsenal; engaged in relentless saber-rattling and occasional land grabbing; routinely violated international norms and the post-war European security order; vastly strengthened Russia's internal security apparatus; dismantled the country's democratic institutions; and constructed a despotic, hypernationalist regime centered on his cult of personality. In the process, Putin has managed, by means of bluster and propaganda, to persuade most Russians, and many Westerners, that he is acting in their interests.

At the same time, Putin's Russia is a brittle regime that is in the throes of advanced decay. It is hyper-centralized, corrupt, inimical to introducing systemic reform, and incapable of changing itself. Although Putin himself is wildly popular, the ossified regime he leads is not, as his decision to form a powerful National Guard and the dismal turnout in the recent Duma elections suggest. A regime that is so dependent on the erratic judgment of an increasingly aging leader is inherently prone to strategic errors that, sooner or later, could embroil it in destabilizing misadventures at home and abroad. Putin's invasion of Ukraine in 2014, for instance, not only alienated Kyiv but also the near abroad and the West. Meanwhile, it brought Russia nothing that it did not already have, such as de facto control of Ukraine's pro-Russian Crimea and the Donbas.

The failing Russian state is increasingly fragmented between its center in Moscow and the periphery, elites and non-elites, and Russians and non-Russians. Its unreformed economy is in secular decline, while its pell-mell effort to modernize its armed forces and take strategic initiative has revived NATO, terrified Russia's formerly pro-Russian neighbors, and put off much of the world. The longer Putin stays in power, the greater the likelihood that Russia will collapse, with untold consequences—from civil war to mass refugees—for its neighbors.

The United States' superpower status remains unquestioned, but its willingness to engage with the world declined significantly in the aftermath of the Afghanistan, Iraq, and Syria debacles. Making things worse, Republican presidential nominee Donald Trump's inflammatory and knee-jerk rhetoric will likely infect U.S. discourse with greater isolationist tendencies regardless of who wins the presidency this November.

NATO, which had lost its sense of mission after the end of the Cold War, has been revitalized by Putin's aggression in Ukraine, but the alliance's military capabilities are woefully inadequate to meet the growing Russian threat. As Western policymakers know, were Putin to test NATO by invading Estonia, the alliance would be hard-pressed to defend it. It would take years for NATO to meet such a challenge.

Finally, the European Union is beset with troubles, from Brexit to the continued flow of refugees to the rise of an anti-democratic and pro-Putin right in France, the Netherlands, and, most alarming, Germany. As Europeans turn inward and as the possibility of pro-Russian political forces coming to power grows, the EU's capacity to sustain a united front against Putin will decline.

Regardless of how these trends play out, chances are that some combination of them will characterize Ukraine's geopolitical neighborhood for the next five to ten years. The worst-case scenario for Ukraine would be a United States distracted by its internal troubles and external failures, a weak Europe, and either a strong, aggressive Russia or a disintegrating one. The best case would be a strong, engaged West, which would make whatever transpires in Russia less threatening. Unfortunately, that seems less likely than the worst case.

Given these uncertainties, Ukraine's policymakers need a strong set of principles to guide them.

First, Kyiv must make its own survival as an independent, democratic state its overriding strategic priority. All other concerns should be subordinate. That means, above all, shifting policy attention from Crimea and the occupied Donbas to state and nation building in free Ukraine. This need not mean recognizing Russia's annexation, but Kyiv should live with the temporary loss of these regions, or their quasi-reintegration on confederal terms, in order to focus on the difficult but long overdue restructuring that is needed to make Ukraine's Westernization irreversible and its vulnerabilities to Russian aggression minimal.

Second, Ukraine must understand that it alone is responsible for its survival. Although Europe and the United States should recognize that Putin's Russia has become an existential threat, no Western country is currently ready to abandon its hopes of rapprochement and fight Russia on Ukraine's behalf. That may change, especially if Putin strikes again, but probably not in the foreseeable future.

Third, Ukraine's survival rests on four interconnected pillars: a strong military, a strong economy, a strong democracy, and a patriotic population. One cannot stand without the others. Only a strong military can deter further Russian predations and thereby offer the conditions for economic and democratic institutions to develop and thrive. A growing economy is a precondition for a strong military, a vital democracy, and a patriotic population; an open, democratic society ensures a dynamic economy and a supportive population; and popular support is necessary for a strong military and a strong democracy.

Among these, however, Ukraine must make economic growth its immediate priority. Its army and democracy are strong enough for the time being, and popular patriotism is at a high as well. But these three pillars will weaken if Ukraine's economy fails to grow at near-double-digit rates. Ukraine currently spends five percent of its GDP on its armed forces, an enormous strain on a poor country. Democracy requires a growing middle class—as a counterweight to powerful political and economic elites, as a guarantor of private property, and as a repository of liberal values. But, at present, the middle class is declining in Ukraine. And patriotism is hard to sustain under punishing economic conditions. A strong economy will also enable Ukraine to pursue a more confident foreign policy and imbue its current government with greater legitimacy.

Fourth, although Ukraine should do everything possible to eradicate corruption, the key to generating rapid and sustainable economic growth is small and medium-sized entrepreneurship. Ukraine has vast reserves of impressive human capital that could, if permitted by the right combination of economic incentives, produce as much growth as its highly-developed information technology sector. Unless that human capital is put to productive use, Ukraine's economy will always languish. As nineteenth-century Europe and the United States, and today's Brazil, China, and India, demonstrate, if human capital is mobilized, corrupt economies can and do grow at very high rates. Even corrupt Ukraine enjoyed seven to eight percent growth rates and significant inflows of foreign capital in the recent past. Foreign direct investment in Ukraine dried up over the last two years not because of some sudden spike of corruption but because of the war with Russia.

Ukraine has adopted an impressive raft of economic reforms since the Euromaidan Revolution of 2014, and the result is that two years of significant negative growth have translated into one to two percent growth in 2016. But it needs to do more. Among other things, Kyiv must sell its state-owned enterprises, privatize its land, cut the government apparatus while raising salaries, radically simplify procedures for establishing businesses, and find some form of modus vivendi with the oligarchs and their overseas accounts. If these and other measures—such as preventing outright seizures of property by oligarchs, state officials, and organized crime—are adopted, and the war in the east remains in a stalemate, foreign investors will return and, together with Ukrainian entrepreneurs, significantly expand the economy.

For its first 25 years as an independent nation, Ukraine survived mostly because no one threatened its existence. That has changed for good, and Ukraine must learn to live with a permanent Russian threat and the likelihood of growing Western indifference. Above all, Ukraine must become an Eastern European economic tiger. If it does not, it may not live to see its 50th anniversary as a sovereign state.

PART THREE
RUSSIA'S WAR AGAINST UKRAINE

A Russian Threat to Ukraine? *World Affairs Journal*, October 28, 2011

Who's right about the threat Russia poses to its neighbors—the distinguished American historian Richard Pipes or the distinguished Russian analyst Dmitri Trenin?

According to Pipes, the Russians "do pose a threat to their ex-republics. They have no problem with Central Asia, because those [states] are rather docile. But they can't reconcile themselves to the loss of the three Baltic Republics [Estonia, Latvia, and Lithuania] and Ukraine and Georgia. I feel fairly confident that if Georgia or the Ukraine were to join NATO, as they would like to, the Russians would invade and destroy their independence."

According to Trenin, "Russia's remarkable disinterest in its former empire has been paralleled by the other former Soviet republics distancing themselves from the former imperial center. Several have proclaimed a European vision or vocation. Others reaffirmed Muslim roots and focused on their neighborhoods. A couple have gone into isolation."

So, who's right—the Harvard historian or the director of the Carnegie Moscow Center? If Pipes is right, then the Ukrainians should be building a Maginot Line on their eastern frontier. If Trenin is right, they should be pulling out the corks and drinking to Mother Russia's eternal health.

The answer is: neither. Pipes's mistake is to suggest that Russia has the capacity to invade a country the size of Ukraine. It doesn't. Trenin's mistake is to suggest that Russia no longer has the desire to in-gather its former imperial lands. It does.

The reality is both simpler and more complex. Russia is a post-imperial state with post-imperial aspirations and post-imperial capacities. On the one hand, many Russian policymakers and significant segments of the Russian public continue to think of their country as unjustly robbed of their empire and would be happy to correct that perceived wrong. On the other hand, the Russian-led Soviet Union wouldn't have fallen apart if it had been a strong state, and the post-Soviet Russian Federation, having inherited many of the USSR's weaknesses, is as incapable of reestablishing full imperial control as the Soviet Union was capable of maintaining it.

This Janus-faced quality in contemporary Russia accounts for the continued nervousness with which non-Russians—from the Poles to the Ukrainians to the Estonians to the Georgians to the Kazakhs—have in dealing with it. The non-Russians know Moscow isn't going to send tanks across their borders in a blitzkrieg, but they also know that some not uninfluential Russian imperialists are itching to do just that, and that many other Russians understand that Russian pipelines, investment, churches, spies, and criminals can just as easily deprive the non-Russian nations of their hard-won, and still tenuous, sovereignty.

Viktor Yanukovych and his fellow Regionnaires are a case in point. After tripping over each other in their declarations of love for Mother Russia for much of 2010 and 2011, they are now waking up to the realization that Russian political, religious, cultural, and economic elites regard their bailiwick—you know, that big, flat place called Ukraine—as, well, Little Russia, and regard them—the big, bad Regionnaires—as push-overs and non-entities. Small wonder that Yanukovych has been making overtures to the West: he has no other place to go.

Past Ukrainian presidents knew that Russia's love for Ukraine was a mixed blessing and therefore pursued a "multi-vector" policy of balancing Russia with the West. Viktor Yushchenko was never the rabidly anti-Russian president his opponents made him out to be. He just decided to be a bit more pro-Western and immediately experienced Moscow's wrath for his supposed betrayal of Russo-Ukrainian friendship. Leonid Kuchma claimed to be more pro-Russian initially, but quickly learned that you can suffocate in the bear's embrace and felt impelled to write a book, *Ukraine Is Not Russia*. Leonid Kravchuk agreed to the Commonwealth of Independent States, while keeping Ukraine at arm's length of the beast.

Trenin's vision of Russia's amity with its non-Russian neighbors will finally set in if (or when) Russia abandons all forms of imperialism—military, political, religious, cultural, and economic—and accepts its neighbors as fully sovereign states. If Trenin were president of Russia, and Pipes were his prime minister, that would happen in a jiff. With Vladimir Putin and his sidekick Dmitri Medvedev pulling the strings for the foreseeable future, the rapprochement may take a while longer.

*

Soft and Hard Power Threats to Ukraine, *World Affairs Journal*, March 16, 2012

Ukrainians like to blame their country's ills on "Moscow and the Muscovites," but the UK's highly respected Royal Institute of International Affairs (a.k.a. Chatham House) has just provided good grounds for thinking that their paranoia may be justified.

Take a look at the January 2012 briefing paper, "A Ghost in the Mirror: Russian Soft Power in Ukraine," by two Kyiv-based analysts—Alexander Bogomolov and Oleksandr Lytvynenko. Bogomolov is president of the Association of Middle East Studies, while Lytvynenko is director of research projects at the Foreign and Security Policy Council. Neither is a "nationalist hothead." Both are sober establishment men.

Here are the bullet points of their argument:

- "For Russia, maintaining influence over Ukraine is more than a foreign policy priority; it is an existential imperative. Many in Russia's political elite perceive Ukraine as part of their country's own identity."

The problem with existential imperatives is that they are "zero-sum games." If Russia's existence truly depends on Ukraine's nonexistence, then compromise is impossible, at least as long as Russia's rulers perceive Ukraine as part of Russia's identity.

- "Russia's socio-economic model limits its capacity to act as a pole of attraction for Ukraine. As a result, Russia relies on its national myths to devise narratives and projects intended to bind Ukraine in a 'common future' with Russia and other post-Soviet states."

Russia's Putinist model is more accurately termed "fascistoid," an ugly word that captures the wretched nature of Vladimir Putin's brand of authoritarianism plus charismatic strongman rule. The good news is that, since no right-thinking non-Russian elite would presumably want to adopt such a model, even Ukraine's doltish Regionnaires may want to resist Russian soft-power blandishments if they recognize that they are a cover for the hard-power brutality of Putinism.

- "These narratives are translated into influence in Ukraine through channels such as the Russian Orthodox Church, the mass media, formal and informal business networks, and non-governmental organizations."

Here's the bad news for Ukraine. Its elites can, in principle, easily say no to Putin and Putinism, but how does one say no to religion, language, and culture?

- "Russia also achieves influence in Ukraine by mobilizing constituencies around politically sensitive issues such as language policy and shared cultural and historical legacies. This depends heavily on symbolic resources and a deep but often clumsy engagement in local identity politics."

- "Russia's soft power project with regard to Ukraine emphasizes cultural and linguistic boundaries over civic identities, which is ultimately a burden for both countries."

The last two points are especially bad news for Ukrainian and Russian liberals committed to interethnic tolerance and amity. If Russian soft power is focused on creating "disloyal minorities" with intolerant identities, then the ultimate effect will be to promote racism, chauvinism, and intolerance both within Ukraine and Russia and between Ukraine and Russia.

According to the two analysts, the root of the problem is that

> the very idea of a Ukrainian nation separate from the great Russian nation challenges core beliefs about Russia's origin and identity. Ukraine hosts the most valuable symbols constituting the core of Russia's national identity—the mythological birthplace of the Russian nation and the cradle of the Russian Orthodox Church along with its holiest places. ... From this perspective, the collective goods that bring the majority of Ukrainians together as a nation ... appear to be meaningless, second-rate or blasphemous to a large number of Russians. Generations of Russian intellectuals have turned belittling of the Ukrainian language and culture into a part of the Russian belief system alongside anti-Tatar and anti-Muslim stereotypes. But whereas the latter are built around national

229

differences, what makes Ukraine stand out in this list is a dismissive attitude to any assertion that national differences exist. This coexistence between friendship for a "kindred *people*" and hostility to the Ukrainian *nation* is what gives relations between Ukraine and Russia their distinctive quality.

More than distinctive, the quality of Ukrainian–Russian relations is, given such a mindset, necessarily going to be conflictual. Worse, if such dismissive attitudes are part and parcel of Russian identity, then there is no solution short of a fundamental transformation of Russian identity—something that, even in the best of circumstances, will take a long time.

*

Spy vs. Spy in Ukraine and Russia, *World Affairs Journal*, May 3, 2013

The spies have been in the news these last few months. On February 14th, Russia's president, Vladimir Putin, spoke at an expanded board meeting of the Federal Security Service (FSB). Then, on March 25th, Ukraine's president, Viktor Yanukovych, addressed the Security Service of Ukraine (SBU) on the 21st anniversary of its founding. Putin's website ran his entire speech; Yanukovych's—only a brief excerpt.

Putin made three key points:

- The priority of terrorism: "The most important aspect of your work is forestalling and preventing terrorism. It is necessary to protect people, and young people in particular, from being drawn into terrorist groups and the criminal underground. The direct link between extremist and terrorist groups is clear."

- The impermissibility of outside interference in Russia's internal affairs: "no one holds a monopoly that gives them the right to speak on behalf of all Russian society, especially the entities managed and financed from abroad as they inevitably serve others' interests. ... Any direct or indirect interference in our internal affairs, any form of pressure on our country or on our allies and partners, is unacceptable."

- The permissibility of FSB interference in its neighbors' internal affairs: "Recently we have heard a number of, to be perfectly honest, nervous, angry statements regarding integration processes within post-Soviet space. ... Close integration is an objective, global process which cannot be stopped—including on our territories—by shouting and criticizing. Nevertheless, we can expect—and as you know we are indeed faced with—various attempts to impede our integration efforts by employing a number of instruments of pressure, including the so-called mechanisms of soft power. I want to emphasize that Russia's sovereign right and that of our partners to build and develop our integration projects must be duly protected. I would ask you to work closely with your colleagues and partners from Belarus, Kazakhstan, and other countries involved in various integration processes in this respect."

That Putin sees no contradiction between his second and third points and between his view that integration is both "objective" and in need of presumably subjective "integration projects" and "efforts" is doubtless due to his many years' practice in dialectical reasoning as a KGB agent.

Yanukovych, in contrast, spoke in generalities, almost as if he had no idea of what a security service is supposed to do—or that, at least, is the impression the official press release creates. Here's Yanukovych on the SBU:

The organs of law and order, and in the first place the Security Service of Ukraine, must be a reliable shield that defends our national interests against any interference under conditions of the complex challenges of the contemporary world. Ukraine must be strong, modern, and efficient, inasmuch as only then will it be able to defend its national interests. The Security Service is the key link in the sector of security and defense and it bears this important task. Our joint responsibility is to ensure order, maintain civic peace, and continue with the effective reform of all the country's spheres of vital activity.

Who could disagree? I'd like to think Yanukovych said a bit more to Ukraine's spies, especially about the FSB's mandate to promote "integration processes" among Russia's neighbors, but it is not, alas, inconceivable that he's oblivious, or perhaps even welcoming, of Putin's intentions.

Fortunately, the same day as Yanukovych greeted the SBU, its press service provided more detail on the SBU's activities. Besides fighting drug trafficking, corruption, and terrorism, the SBU is engaged in counterintelligence:

In the last year alone in Ukraine a stop was put to the espionage of 8 foreign spies and over 20 agents of foreign secret services, who were attempting to acquire illegally information about promising developments and technologies used above all in the military-industrial complex, the space sector, and the aviation industry. A court sentenced three citizens of the Asian-Pacific region to 5 to 8 years' imprisonment for attempting to acquire illegally secret documents.

Since Russian capital already has a strong presence in, and arguably knows everything about, Ukraine's military-industrial complex, space sector, and aviation industry, the eight spies and 20 agents are probably from the "Asian-Pacific region," and not from Russia. The current SBU head's background also suggests he may be disinclined to view the FSB's integrationist efforts with alarm. Appointed to this office on January 9, 2013, Major General Oleksandr Yakymenko was born in Estonia, served in the Soviet Armed Forces from 1982 to 1991, and spent most of the last 20 years in security-related positions in Crimea and Donetsk Province. In other words, he may be infected with Regionnaires' Disease. The man he succeeded, Igor Kalinin, was an out-and-out Russian KGB agent of many years' standing.

That said, there may be a smidgeon of potentially good news here. The SBU's press service does speak of the "need to reform the SBU within the framework of the new Strategy of National Security of Ukraine and above all with regard to intensifying the counterintelligence and analytical sectors of the Ukrainian security service's activity." The convoluted sentence structure suggests that the SBU needs more than just good analytical skills, but the bit about counterintelligence may be grounds for hope that Yakymenko's service in the front lines of Putin's "integration processes" may have actually sensitized him to their destabilizing impact on Ukraine.

*

Russia's Trade War Against Ukraine Will Backfire, *World Affairs Journal*, August 27, 2013

Stupidly, if not unexpectedly, the Putin regime has declared a trade war on Ukraine in order to force it to turn away from an Association Agreement with the European Union and, instead, join the Customs Union consisting of Russia, Belarus, and Kazakhstan. The war will be painful for Ukraine, but its expected effect is highly unlikely to happen, demonstrating, once again, just how little Russia's elites understand Ukraine and Ukrainians.

On August 14th, Ukrainian exports to its northern neighbor came to a halt after Russian authorities imposed onerous border procedures on vehicles transporting Ukrainian goods. Since 25 percent of Ukraine's exports go to Russia, a prolonged blockade could cost Ukraine as much as $2.5 billion in 2013. The Kremlin (which, as a recently leaked document appears to suggest, apparently has developed a ramified neoimperialist strategy vis-à-vis Ukraine) obviously expects these numbers to persuade the Yanukovych regime that the Customs Union is its least worse option.

That expectation is misplaced for several reasons.

First, the Yanukovych regime has amply demonstrated in the last three years that the well-being of Ukrainians is the least of its concerns. Ukrainian living standards could drop catastrophically as a result of Moscow's actions, and President Yanukovych and his entourage wouldn't lose a wink of sleep.

Second, since the Yanukovych regime's number-one priority is its own well-being, Russia's trade war, inasmuch as it erodes some of that well-being, will only lead Yanukovych, his Family network, and their many cronies to view their erstwhile ally with mistrust, suspicion, and disdain. The very last thing they'll now want to do is join the Customs Union and thereby put themselves and their wealth in a position of permanent dependence on Moscow's whims.

Third, Yanukovych and the Regionnaires pride themselves on being tough. Some, like the president himself, have a criminal background; others, like the pogromchiks who periodically attack the democrats with fists, are just street thugs; all of them refuse to be bullied and pushed around. Like American mafiosi, they want, above all, respect. The Kremlin's obvious belief that it can treat the Yanukovych regime as a bunch of lily-livered punks is the ultimate insult to the "goodfellas" running Ukraine.

Fourth, Ukrainians are tired of being pushed around—by their own government and by outsiders. Even though most of the population (in both east and west) views Russians quite positively, they resent being treated as second-class citizens, younger brothers, Little Russians, uncivilized savages, and the like. Part of that resentment has been directed at the hypocrisy of the European Union's effort to make travel for ordinary Ukrainians so difficult while simultaneously insisting on Ukraine's adherence to EU norms. Much of that resentment will now be redirected toward the Putin regime, whose punitive economic measures are obviously intended to affect Ukrainians' already fragile lives.

Fifth, Ukrainians appear to be increasingly committed to the integrity and viability of their own state. According to a recent study conducted by the Ukrainian Institute of Social Research and the Social Monitoring Center, 61 percent of Ukrainians would vote for independence in a referendum today. That may not seem like much, until one considers that the number was 56 percent in 2001, when the Ukrainian economy began to recover from a decade-long depression, and 47 percent in 2011, after five years of Orange mismanagement. No less significantly, opponents of independence comprised 28 percent in 2001 and 2011, and 21 percent in 2013. Another survey, by the "Rating" Sociological Research Group, indicates that a surprisingly high 46 percent say they'd defend Ukraine with arms. Clearly, three years of Regionnaire mismanagement have led Ukrainians to value what they still have: a country. If so, then Russia's neoimperialist aspirations and inability to acknowledge Ukraine's difference will only stiffen their resolve to remain in-dependent—and outside the Customs Union. As one Russian-speaking Ukrainian com-mentator wrote: "If you have enemies, that's bad. If those enemies are idiots, that's good."

Take all these factors together and you may conclude that President Yanukovych will soon discover his "deep" and "unwavering" love of Ukraine and wrap himself in the Ukrainian flag. As a pro-Russian stance can appeal to no more than 21 percent of the population and, more important, undermine his Family's wealth, what else is there to do but turn toward one's people and claim to be their national champion? As Samuel Johnson said in 1775, "Patriotism is the last refuge of the scoundrel." Who knows? Perhaps Europe will turn out to be the last refuge of Ukrainian scoundrels.

*

Deconstructing Putin on Ukraine, *World Affairs Journal*, September 11, 2013

President Vladimir Putin's September 4th interview with Russian state broadcaster Channel One and the Associated Press cast a bright light on the incompetence of his public relations office and on his own antediluvian notions about Ukraine.

Whoever translated the official Kremlin transcript showed a striking ignorance of the English language—the translation is wooden—and of elementary political-historical terminology. Several sentences stand out, both because the translation is shockingly bad and because, when dissected, they reveal a great deal about Putin's mind-set.

In response to Channel One correspondent Kirill Kleymenov's question about Russia's relations with Ukraine, Putin says the following (my translation from the Russian): "You know, regardless of what happens and where Ukraine goes, we will still meet sometime and somewhere. Why? Because we are one people." Here's the official English translation: "You know, no matter what happens, and wherever Ukraine goes, anyway we shall meet sometime and somewhere. Why? Because we are one nation."

Putin explicitly says "people" (*narod*), and not "nation" (*natsia*). As an ex-KGB officer well-schooled in Leninist dialectics and Stalinist nationality policy, he knows that the Russian and Ukrainian nations cannot constitute a nation. But they might constitute a "people," a lower-level, ethno-cultural agglomeration that doesn't have all the objective characteristics of a nation as defined by Stalin in 1913. Back in Soviet days, Russians, Ukrainians, and all the other nations were supposed to be "drawing together" to form a "new community of people"—the "Soviet people." Since the language and culture of the Soviet people were essentially Russian, non-Russian dissident critics of Soviet policy argued, not incorrectly, that the Soviet people was just a smokescreen for a policy practiced by the tsars—Russification.

Putin is not only drawing inspiration from Soviet theory and practice, he is also explicitly basing his views on those of Russia's reactionary tsarist forces. As he told Kleymenov in reference to the bloody Civil War between anti-Bolsheviks and Bolsheviks in 1918–1921 (according to the official translation): "Both the White movement and the Red one were fighting against each other to death, millions of people died during the civil war, but they never raised the issue of separation of Ukraine. Both the Reds and the Whites proceeded from the integrity of the Russian state." Indeed, they did. Some left-leaning Sovietologists used to insist that Lenin and the Bolsheviks supported the liberation struggles of the non-Russian nations, but Putin is quite right to say that the only thing the Reds had in common with the Whites was the continued maintenance of the Russian imperial state.

The line immediately following the one ending with "from the integrity of the Russian state" is especially revealing. My literal translation from the Russian reads as follows: "As far as this part, Ukraine, is concerned, it is a land and we understand and remember that we were born, as I said, within a common Ukrainian Dnipro [River] baptismal font, Rus was born there, and we all come from there." Putin's translator wrote the following: "As far as this part of Ukraine is concerned, it is a territory and we understand and remember that we were born, as I said, from the unified Ukrainian Dnieper baptistery, Russia was born there and we all come from there."

The nuances require some elucidation. First, it's clear from the grammatical structure of the above two sentences that Putin is saying "As far as this part [of the Russian state],

Ukraine, is concerned" and not "As far as this part of Ukraine is concerned." Willfully or not, Putin is claiming that Ukraine is a part of the Russian state. His translator kindly removed that undiplomatic sentiment from the English version.

Second, Putin says Ukraine is a "*krai*"—purposely avoiding the Russian word for country, *strana*. I've translated it as "land"—which is the way it frequently appears in patriotic Russian verse or songs—while the translator prefers "territory," which, while more prosaic, also conveys the non-state quality of Ukraine. Either way, Putin comes across as believing that Ukraine is just a place, populated by people who resemble Russians, and not an independent state with a national identity of its own.

Finally, Putin knows that the state whose capital was ancient Kyiv and which adopted Christianity 1,025 years ago was known as Rus. As a Soviet-era apparatchik, he would never have called it Russia, as the translator did (and as some historically challenged Western scholars still do), although he obviously believes that, since Russians were "born" there, so too Russia, the state, must be able to trace its lineage to that political entity. (By the way, the Russian version of Russia—*Rossiya*—shows that Russia's seeming terminological derivation from Rus is apparent only in English.) While many Ukrainians also trace the lineage of their statehood to Rus, the fact of the matter is that Rus is to Ukraine and Russia as ancient Rome is to Italy and France. While all four countries can trace their roots to their respective big states, none can claim to be identical with them, even though Italy and Ukraine can insist on some geographic priority by virtue of having the same capitals as those states.

By the same token, even though the French and the Italians can trace their origins to the "baptismal font" in ancient Rome, no one would suggest that they are therefore the same people or the same nation. Nor would the French claim that Italy is a borderland or territory of France.

So what's the bottom line? Putin should fire his translators for making him sound like a wild-eyed Russian chauvinist. He's not. He's just a run-of-the-mill neo-Red, neo-White neo-imperialist.

*

Russia's Revisionist Claims on Ukraine and Moldova, *World Affairs Journal*, October 11, 2013

Is President Vladimir Putin readying the rhetorical groundwork for a full-scale attack on international norms regarding the inviolability of borders and state sovereignty? Could be, if the recent comments of two of his closest advisers are any indication of what the Kremlin is thinking.

In early September, Russia's Deputy Prime Minister Dmitri Rogozin told the Moldovans that Moldova "would lose Transnistria, if Moldova continues moving toward the European Union." Then, in a sudden onrush of poetic sentiment, Rogozin added: "Moldova's train en route to Europe would lose its wagons in Transnistria." Transnistria is the breakaway part of Moldova, sandwiched between Ukraine and the Dniester River, that declared independence in 1990 and enjoys Russian military and diplomatic backing.

Then, later in S eptember, P resident P utin's a dviser o n economic integration, Sergei Glazyev, took part in the 10th annual summit of the Yalta European Strategy, a non-governmental group founded and funded by the westward-leaning Ukrainian oligarch Viktor Pinchuk. Here's how the *Times* of London reported Glazyev's comments:

> Russia has threatened to support a partitioning of Ukraine if it signs a landmark co-operation agreement with the European Union in two months' time. Sergei Glazyev, one of Vladimir Putin's top advisers, said that Ukraine's Russian-speaking minority might break up the country in protest at a move that European, Russian, and Ukrainian politicians see as a shift away from Moscow's influence. He said that Russia would be legally entitled to support them.

Take both sets of comments together and what have you got? A not-too-veiled threat to revise Europe's post-war borders—in violation, by the way, of United Nations principles and the Helsinki Accords. Significantly, both Rogozin and Glazyev are close to Putin; their sentiments may therefore be interpreted as reflecting his. Until now, the only people who expressed such destabilizing views tended to be loony demagogues such as Vladimir Zhirinovsky. No more. Neo-imperialist, revisionist rhetoric has clearly become mainstream, at least within Putin's regime.

When I visited Kyiv last summer, a German colleague expressed concern that Russia might stage a provocation in order to annex parts of Ukraine as payback for Kyiv's pursuit of integration with Europe. As we kicked around possible scenarios, we ended up agreeing that, if such an event were to take place, it would resemble the infamous "Gleiwitz incident," which served as Adolf Hitler's pretext to attack Poland. Here's the Wikipedia account of how the Nazis staged a provocation in the city of Gleiwitz (today's Gliwice), which lay just to the west of the German Reich's border with Poland:

> On the night of 31 August 1939, a small group of German operatives, dressed in Polish uniforms and led by Naujocks, seized the Gleiwitz station and broadcast a short anti-German message in Polish (sources vary on the content of the message). The Germans' goal was to make the attack and the broadcast look like the work of anti-German Polish saboteurs. To make the attack seem more convincing, the Germans brought in Franciszek Honiok, a German Silesian known for sympathizing with the Poles, who had been arrested the previous day by the Gestapo. Honiok was dressed to look like a saboteur; then killed by lethal injection, given gunshot wounds, and left dead at the scene, so that he appeared to have been killed while attacking the station. His corpse was subsequently presented as proof of the attack to the police and press.

Change the year to 2014 and the setting to a place such as Sevastopol or Luhansk. Russian secret-police operatives dressed as rabid Ukrainian nationalists and chanting patriotic Ukrainian slogans and waving the blue-and-yellow Ukrainian flag attack some peaceful Russians, perhaps housewives standing in line outside a grocery store. Blood is spilled. A few women lose their lives. The supposed Ukrainians parade their triumph in the streets, threatening to destroy all Russians. (The Soviet secret police, by the way, staged just such provocations in the aftermath of World War II, in its efforts to destroy the Ukrainian underground resistance movement.)

If this happens in Sevastopol, locally based Russian sailors will obviously have no choice but to rush to their compatriots' defense. If the setting is Luhansk, "spontaneously" formed militias will suddenly appear. Both will claim to be resisting crude violations of human rights by dastardly Ukrainians. They'll appeal to Moscow for help. Kyiv will appeal to Brussels and the United Nations for intervention. What choice will the Kremlin have but to save its brethren from genocide by fascists? The European Union and the UN will, in the meantime, dither over the meaning of the words they'll use to express their concern. Luhansk and Crimea will request annexation by Russia. Moscow, reluctantly, but in full awareness of its sacred commitment to humanity, will agree.

To be sure, both scenarios are premised on a pretty big If, but that If no longer seems all that iffy in light of Rogozin's and Glazyev's comments.

The following joke used to make the rounds in Soviet times:

> A Frenchman, a Brit, and a Russian are captured by some tribe in Africa and are about to be killed. The chief asks them if they have any last requests. The Frenchman asks for a glass of wine and gets it. The Brit asks for a cigar and gets it. The Russian asks for a punch in the nose and gets in. Thereupon he removes a gun from his pocket and shoots the chief. The Brit and the Frenchman are astounded. "If you had the gun all along," they say, "why didn't you use it immediately?" The Russian smiles: "We are never the aggressor."

In Ukraine and Moldova, they're not laughing.

*

A Russian Threat to Ukraine? *World Affairs Journal*, February 7, 2014

Let's start with the alarming question many people are now asking and then consider other forms of possible Russian intervention in the ongoing Ukrainian Revolution. It was on January 31st that Vladimir Putin's former adviser, the economist Andrei Illarionov, shocked Ukrainians with his claim that the Kremlin has already developed several scenarios ranging from "control over all of Ukraine" to "control" over several provinces. His views might have been dismissed as alarmist were it not for the fact that Ukrainians have been expecting a more forceful Russian response to the ongoing revolution for weeks.

Imagine two possible scenarios: (1) a full-scale invasion of all, most, or much of Ukraine and (2) a limited invasion of one or two provinces of Ukraine. In both instances, the point would presumably be annexation, occupation, or longer-term control.

Now let's ask several sub-questions: (1) Does Russia have the military resources to pull off such operations? (2) Would they succeed? (3) Would they make sense strategically? (4) Would the external and internal consequences be acceptable? We'll then ask whether Vladimir Putin would be likely to make such moves. Let me state at the outset that, while the answers to (1) and (2) are positive, the answers to (3) and (4) are not. The good news is that Putin would have to be deeply irrational to embark on the kind of full-scale or limited interventions Illarionov has in mind.

As stated, the answer to the first question is an unqualified yes. The Russian armed forces, at about three-quarters of a million troops, are several times larger than the Ukrainian army; their budget allocations are much larger, their weapons more modern, their training better. As their travails in Chechnya have shown, the Russian armed forces are not world-class, but they're improving, while the Ukrainian army appears to be in terminal decline. Obviously, Russia couldn't mobilize all its troops in some putative attack on Ukraine, but, whatever the number, they would be more than adequate to defeat Ukraine's. Russia could also rely on Cossack and other "volunteers" to do some of its dirty work.

The answer to the second question—would such operations succeed?—is less obvious. The Ukrainian military consists of some 150,000 poorly armed, poorly trained soldiers. Would they even fight? Some would, some wouldn't: those from Luhansk might welcome Russian troops; those from Lviv might shoot back. Chances are, though, that the Russian army would win hands down, especially in a limited invasion of one or two provinces. Would its losses be acceptable to Russians back home? Probably, though that, too, would depend on how protracted and widespread the fighting would be. A more complicated issue is whether the Russian military would have the stomach to deal with the guerrilla resistance that is sure to follow a Ukrainian defeat. A quick, grand, and glorious victory might just lead to cheering in the streets of Moscow and St. Petersburg. A long slog in a huge country might turn into a disaster back home and undermine Putin's rule. Clearly, a full-scale invasion bears significant risks. A limited invasion would be far more manageable for the Kremlin.

Would either a large-scale or limited invasion make sense strategically? Would either advance Russia's geopolitical interests? If a large-scale invasion were successful, Russia would presumably come to control Ukraine's ports, energy grid, and economic resources (as well as, quite possibly, a very disgruntled population). At most, that would be a very mixed blessing. Ukraine's economy is a mess, its coal and gas reserves are nothing compared to Russia's (though its potential shale-gas reserves might be large), and its ports need modernization. It's not immediately clear just how Russian ownership of these resources would enhance Russia's interests. Owning Ukraine's aging gas pipeline would be nice—though bringing it up to snuff would cost billions—but it's not quite as imperative now that Russia has poured, or is planning to pour, billions into constructing the North and South Stream pipelines that bypass Ukraine.

A more significant concern relates to Russia's internal difficulties with terrorism in the North Caucasus, a region that has pretty much escaped Moscow's control. Wouldn't starting a major conflagration with Ukraine mean diverting security personnel from the volatile North Caucasus? Wouldn't such a Ukrainian adventure encourage Islamic resistance movements to accelerate their campaigns within the Russian Federation? Does Russia really want to fight a two-front war? Here, as with the second point, the risks drop appreciably with a limited incursion into one or two provinces.

Finally, what would the international consequences of a large-scale invasion be? Remember: such a move would mean a crass and blatant violation of every single international norm regarding state behavior. Ukraine poses no threat to Russia. It possesses no weapons of mass destruction and houses no anti-Russian terrorists. An invasion would be just that—an invasion, a blatant aggression, an imperialist land-grab. In violating United Nations norms, the Helsinki Final Act, the standards of the Organization for Security and Cooperation in Europe, and every other post-war accord, Russia would be declaring itself a rogue state. Its ability to play a great-power role as an international mediator would be shot. Its relations with China, Turkey, Europe, and the United States would go into nosedive. A cold war would be likely. North Korea might cheer, and the some on the American left might develop elaborate pro-imperialist justifications, but most of the world would condemn Russia. The rogue state would inevitably become a pariah state.

A limited invasion of one or two provinces—presumably those populated by Russian minorities "clamoring" for "salvation" from "cutthroat bands of Ukrainian fascists"—would have far fewer negative international consequences, and it would certainly be far more doable. But it could also have nasty consequences for the Kremlin's plans to in-gather former Soviet republics. What would Kazakhstan's President Nazarbayev say if Putin annexes Russian-populated Ukrainian territories? How would President Lukashenka of Belarus react? Northern Kazakhstan is inhabited by Russians and Russian speakers; most of Belarus consists of Russian and Russian speakers. If Putin can in-gather Ukraine's Russians with impunity, why should he stop there? One thing's for sure, under conditions such as these, Putin's playthings—the Custom's Union, the Eurasian Union, and the Russian World project—would die.

But let's imagine Putin does opt for a limited intervention—perhaps by Russian Cossacks and irregulars pining to deal a mortal blow to the greatest threat to world peace, some non-existent Ukrainian fascism. Which provinces might he want to annex? Well, there's Crimea, of course, except that Russia de facto controls most of it anyway. Sevastopol, where the Russian Black Sea Fleet is based, is a Russian city that pretty much does what it likes. De jure control of Crimea or Sevastopol might be nice, but would it be worth the bother and risk? Maybe, maybe not. The other two provinces with large Russian populations in need of potential liberation from cutthroat Ukrainian fascists are Luhansk and Donetsk. The Donbas is the unredeemable Ukrainian rust belt, a post-industrial economic cesspool that would require trillions in investment to bring it into the 21st century. Does Putin need such a drag on the stagnating Russian economy at precisely the time that his gas weapon has become blunted due to the shale gas revolution?

In sum, the strategic costs of any kind of invasion could be very high and the strategic benefits are at best uncertain. If Putin is a rational statesman motivated primarily by considerations of Realpolitik and geopolitics, he would not invade. If Putin is a fascistoid leader who needs imperial talk to legitimate his rule, the outcome is somewhat less certain, but with one important qualification. Imperial talk and chest beating are one thing, and Putin is a master of both. Chest beating does not, however, necessarily translate into war making. It can—as we know from Hitler—but, more often than not, it just results in saber-rattling, scowling, and an eventual return to one's cave.

I conclude from the above that—if we assume that Putin is motivated by geopolitical rationality—a large-scale invasion of Ukraine is too risky and, thus, highly unlikely, while a small-scale intervention is unnecessary and, thus, highly unlikely. Not impossible, mind you, just highly unlikely. Dictators the world over, and especially machismo-inspired fascistoid dictators, are prone to strategic mistakes, and one cannot exclude the possibility that even the cold-blooded Putin might experience a frisson of excitement from imagining his troops planting the Russian tricolor in the smoking ruins of Lviv.

If not an invasion, then what? Far more in Putin's interests is a weak and pliant Ukraine. If you can advance all your interests by kicking around a 99-pound weakling, why not do so? Why pummel him to death? Ukraine already is weak and pliant. The Ukrainian Revolution is unlikely to make it stronger anytime soon. (A democratic Ukraine may become an economic powerhouse sometime in the next decade, but that's a very long time in the world of politics.) If the Yanukovych regime cracks down, initiates a bloodbath, and sparks a civil war, Russia could be "dragged into" a conflagration with all the risks mentioned above. A huge failed state on its southwestern border cannot be construed as stabilizing and security-enhancing by any rational Russian policymaker. A smashing victory for the democratic opposition would also be undesirable. It's far better for Russia for the Ukrainian Revolution to result in some kind of negotiated solution, with or without Yanukovych.

*

Should There Be One Ukraine? *World Affairs Journal*, February 14, 2014

As the criminal Yanukovych regime's violence, terror, and repression are driving Ukraine to armed conflict and, possibly, fragmentation, it may be worth asking whether Ukraine might not be better off without some of its southeastern provinces.

First let's consider the bad reasons for a breakup—Ukraine's diversity in general and the regional, ethnic, confessional, and cultural divisions between its "West" and "East", in particular. A good place to start is a recent article by Orlando Figes, professor of history at Birkbeck College, University of London, "Is There One Ukraine?" Figes, who should know better coming from the UK, writes about Ukraine's divisions as if they were unique and as if diversity alone justified or led to breakup. He's wrong on both counts. Ukraine's diversity is pretty much the norm for all stable states everywhere.

Is there one United States or are the divisions between North and South and Red and Blue states indicative of many Americas? Try telling the Quebeckers that there is only one Canada. Is there one Germany—or two (East Germany and West Germany) or several (Bavaria, the Rhineland, Berlin, and the rest)? Needless to say, there are many Russias—one centered on the Moscow-Petersburg axis, another in Siberia, yet a third in the Far East. And that's not even counting the non-Russian regions of the Russian Federation. How many Turkeys are there? I can name at least three: secular Istanbul, conservative Anatolia, and the Kurdish east. China? Go tell the Tibetans and Uighurs they're Han Chinese. India? Let's not even go there. Austria? Vienna, as anyone who's been to the country knows, is a world apart from the Tyrol. Perhaps Italy is one country? Take a train from Milano to Palermo and then answer the question. Surely France is one? *Mais, non*—as the Bretons, Basques, Provençals, Parisians, and many others can tell you. Isn't Israel a homogeneously Jewish state? Only if you disregard the Arabs and the enormous distinctions between secular and religious, Sephardic and Ashkenazy Jews. And so on and so forth. The only country that may be "one" country is, possibly, Japan, and that may be because it's an island state.

Here's another question. Has any country ever been "one" country—especially twenty-odd years after its establishment? The United States was a loose agglomeration of former colonies—and, oh, yes, there was that slavery thing between the North and the South. Canada? Ditto. Otto von Bismarck's Germany? Mazzini's Italy? Ditto, ditto. And how about the country Figes studies—Russia? It's always been a multinational empire marked by enormous regional, ethnic, and confessional diversity, as Figes knows.

Now, I don't know whether diversity is, as the conventional wisdom insists, a source of strength. But I do know that it's a fact of life—for countries, for universities, for corporations, for everybody. In this sense, Ukraine is normal and anything but atypical. (By the way, the same applies to Ukrainians: they're neither better nor worse, neither more nationalistic nor less nationalistic, neither more generous nor less generous, neither more anti-Semitic nor less anti-Semitic, neither smarter nor dumber than any other people.)

What *is* unusual about contemporary Ukraine is that it's exploited by a criminal gangster regime—Yanukovych's— in cahoots with another criminal gangster regime—Putin's. Many countries have the misfortune of being misruled by homegrown camarillas. Many countries have the misfortune of being dominated by predator states. Ukraine has the double misfortune of being misruled at home and "mis-dominated" abroad.

That's why Figes's suggestion—"Ukraine ought to consider applying a precedent from elsewhere in eastern Europe: deciding the country's fate by referendum"—wouldn't work. Personally, I have no doubt that Ukraine without its southeast would be much stronger, more stable, and more prosperous than Ukraine with its southeast. The southeast's rust-belt economy needs either to be shut down entirely or to be refitted at the cost of trillions of dollars of non-existent investments. Moreover, the statistics plainly show that Kyiv subsidizes the Donbas, and not vice versa. The southeast also has a low birth rate, a high death rate, low life expectancy, high energy consumption, and high AIDS and crime rates. Last but not least, the southeast is home to the ruling Party of Regions and the Communist Party. Remove the southeast and Ukraine's treasury experiences an immediate boon; its demographics, energy consumption, and health improve; and its politics automatically become more democratic and less corrupt.

Although lopping off the Donbas would benefit the rest of Ukraine, Yanukovych's mafia regime desperately needs Ukraine to be whole. If Luhansk and Donetsk were to split away, their rust-belt economy would collapse without Kyiv's financial support and the Regionnaires, trapped in their polluted bailiwick, would have nothing to steal. And what would Yanukovych's multibillionaire pal, Rinat Akhmetov, do without easy access to Ukraine's resources? A similar logic holds for Putin. What would he do with a rotten slice of Ukraine—a kind of mega Transnistria? Subsidize its dead-end economy? Spend valuable time and resources on jailing the corrupt Regionnaires and the troglodyte Communists? No, a weak Yanukovych regime in a weak Ukraine serves Putin's interests perfectly.

So, forget a referendum. No Regionnaire-controlled regime will ever agree to it and, were one to take place, Donbas-based Regionnaires would do everything possible to guarantee an anti-secession vote. The Regionnaires need to be in Ukraine; more than that, they need the threat of secession to compel spooked democrats to make concessions. But the threat is hollow, precisely because Ukraine would be much better off without the Donbas and Regionnaires. The sooner the democrats realize this, the better.

The moral for the democrats is simple. When they return to power, the democrats should call the Regionnaires' bluff. Next time the Regionnaires threaten to leave, the democrats should point to the door, and say, "Don't call us. We'll call you."

*

Putin's Play, *Foreign Affairs*, March 1, 2014

A week ago, I wrote that Russian President Vladimir Putin would have to lose "all his geopolitical marbles" to try to "break off bits of Ukraine," such as Crimea. If this weekend's events are any indication, he has. Russian troops have invaded Crimea, and Putin has declared his right to keep them "on the territory of Ukraine until social-political conditions in that country normalize." In other words, Putin claimed that he can send Russian armed forces anywhere in the country, not just Crimea, and that he may leave them there until his definition of normalization is met—which might be never.

The international community, caught off guard by Putin's move, must now try to grapple with why he did what he did, and with what comes next. The question of why he invaded Crimea is complicated. Just before the move, experts had been skeptical about his resolve. By marching into Ukraine, the thinking went, Putin would be initiating a new Cold War with the West, precisely at a time when Russia (and its stagnant economy) needs good ties with the world. And annexing Ukraine's southeast, in particular, would mean taking ownership of an industrial rust belt and hundreds of loss-producing coal mines. Even more, it would invite Crimean Tatar resistance and could lead to the subsequent radicalization of some within that community. Finally, unilateral annexation of Russian-inhabited territories in Crimea could provoke similar moves against Russia. China, for example, might be interested in those sections of the Russian Far East that have large Chinese migrant populations.

In other words, destroying or dismembering Ukraine serves no country's interests, least of all Russia's. After all, it is in Russia's interests to have a stable, prosperous, and friendly Ukraine on its borders. The only thing the move could serve is the megalomaniacal Putin. Like other empires that collapsed at the peak of their power, today's Russia is still coming to grips with the humiliation of losing its imperial holdings and superpower status in 1991. Putin is a charismatic strongman who has systematically dismantled Russia's democratic institutions while legitimizing his rule through neo-imperialist promises to reclaim Russia's place in the sun by "reintegrating" non-Russian states. He has consistently questioned Ukraine's legitimacy as a sovereign state, disputed Ukrainians' separate identity from Russia, and claimed that pro-Western Ukrainian democrats are really fascists in the pay of Western imperialists. And now he has turned his words into action, hoping to enhance his legitimacy and teach the unruly Ukrainians a lesson.

For Ukrainians, the question of what comes next mainly centers on whether Putin's aggression will be confined to Crimea. Soon after he arrogated the right to deploy armed forces anywhere in Ukraine, there were reports that Russian troops were out in force in Zaporizhzhya Province, just to the northeast of Crimea, and Kharkiv Province, on Ukraine's northeast border with Russia. Donetsk, Dnipropetrovsk, and Mykolaiv—eastern cities in which pro-Russian activists have seized government buildings, hoisted the Russian flag, and called for Russian assistance—could well be next. If Putin heeds their calls and moves into those regions, he might not stop until Kyiv. Ukraine has already placed its military on call and Ukrainian policymakers have called for a mass mobilization, but it is unclear whether they could stop a determined Russian assault. To be sure, it may seem overly alarmist to speak of the possibility of an attack on Kyiv (and, one hopes, it is). But, given Putin's past statements and the leeway he has afforded himself now, Ukrainians cannot ignore what could be a direct threat to their state's survival.

The other puzzle is what the West will do next. U.S. President Barack Obama warned Putin that "there will be costs for any military intervention in Ukraine," but failed to specify just what that might entail. Europeans have enjoined Russia to respect Ukraine's sovereignty, but have not made specific plans for enforcing it. And the UN Security Council is holding an emergency session to discuss the crisis in Ukraine. Given Russia's veto, however, the body will probably be unable to respond to the crisis in any meaningful way.

Although getting involved in a Russo-Ukrainian war cannot be appealing to the West, Western leaders must appreciate the fact that Putin has fundamentally challenged the international order. At the very least, the West should convey to Russia that it will suspend business as usual until Russian troops exit Ukraine. In addition, the West can make symbolically important gestures to support Ukraine. Obama might say that the United States is considering sending a small contingent of U.S. troops to protect the Kyiv airport. U.S. Secretary of State John Kerry, like his European counterparts, could board a flight to the Ukrainian capital and express solidarity with Ukraine. European policymakers could call for Ukraine to begin discussions over accession to NATO. And both the United States and the EU could vow to impose severe travel and economic sanctions on Russian officials responsible for the aggression.

Instead, the West has not done much more than express vague criticism. And so Ukraine is alone. If it tries to fight Russia's superior armed forces to retain Crimea and its southeast, it will be defeated. Worse, armed conflict with Russia could spark a bloody civil war nationwide, one that could easily result in atrocities. Given the thuggish recent displays of some Putin supporters in Ukraine's southeast—in Kharkiv, they beat up one of Ukraine's best poets, Serhii Zhadan—it is easy to imagine a massive campaign of ethnic cleansing intended to rid Russian-occupied territories of all pro-Western Ukrainians.

If Russian troops advance into Ukraine proper, Kyiv's only course of action may be to state, unilaterally, that Crimea and the southeast are no longer parts of Ukraine and then deploy its army to the borders of those eastern provinces that are solidly pro-Ukrainian. In this kind of worst-case scenario, a desperate Ukraine might just succeed in holding the line or, if the road to Kyiv is clear, the West might finally intervene forcefully to protect the international order. One must hope that Putin appreciates that an attempted Anschluss would result in a bloody war, the costs of which would be inordinately high. He was "mad" to try to annex any part of Ukraine; he'd have to be madder still to march on Kyiv; and he'd have to be positively insane to send his tanks all the way to Ukraine's eastern border with Poland and thereby threaten NATO. Unfortunately, by invading Crimea, Putin can no longer be interpreted in exclusively rational terms.

Putin's geostrategically irrational muscle-flexing might enhance his legitimacy at home and stabilize the system he built for a while. But, over time, it will be Putinism's undoing. Imperialist behavior will make Russia a rogue state and Putin *persona non grata*. Boris Nemtsov, a liberal Russian politician, described the consequences of Putin's folly well on a Facebook post. "This bloody madness," he wrote, "will have high costs for Russia and Ukraine: once again young boys from both sides will die, mothers and wives will weep, and children will become orphans. Billions, tens of billions of rubles will be taken from senior citizens and children and thrown at war, and afterwards still greater resources will be needed to sustain the criminal regime of the Crimea." But that, Nemtsov continued, is just what Putin desires. "He cannot hold on to power any other way. The vampire needs war. He needs the people's blood."

Today, the international community, the European Union, and the United States face the greatest threat to world peace since the Cold War. After all, if Putin can get away with Ukraine, why would he stop there? If the West will not respond forcefully to such imperialism in a country as large as Ukraine, it is unlikely that it would be ready to stop him on behalf of tiny Estonia and Latvia. The world should have learned from World War II that stopping aggression before it spreads is the best way to prevent geopolitical and humanitarian catastrophes. The West cannot close its eyes to fascistoid imperialism. It must express its full support of Ukraine and tell Putin, in no uncertain terms, that only an immediate withdrawal of all Russian troops can forestall Russia's transformation into a rogue state.

*

Will Putin's Invasion Backfire? *World Affairs Journal*, March 3, 2014

Back in the early 1990s, when the Russian chauvinist Vladimir Zhirinovsky first reared his loony head, analysts began discussing the "Weimar Russia" scenario. Accordingly, the chaos of the late-Gorbachev period (Weimar) would be followed by the emergence of a strong man à la Adolf Hitler (Zhirinovsky), who would impose order, consolidate the nation, and lead it to some imagined form of glory.

The scenario didn't work for crazy Vlad, but it turned out to be useful in understanding subsequent developments in Russia. The chaotic period of Boris Yeltsin's presidency in the 1990s proved to be similar to Weimar Germany in the 1920s: in both cases, imperial collapse, economic hardship, and political humiliation were blamed on democracy and the democrats. And Vladimir Putin turned out to be Russia's version of the Führer. Both came to power legally, developed cults of the personality, dismantled democracy and made the trains run on time, employed chauvinism and neo-imperialism to legitimize their rule, remilitarized their states and promised to make them great powers, and made it their mission to in-gather ethnic brethren in neighboring states.

I've been writing for several years now that Putin's system has all the features of a "fascis-toid" state. I had defined fascism as a non-democratic, non-socialist political system with a domineering party, a supreme leader, a hyper-masculine leader cult, a hyper-nation-alist, statist ideology, and an enthusiastically supportive population. And I had argued in the March 2010 issue of the *Harriman Review* that, "although Putin's Russia possesses many of the defining characteristics of fascism, it does so only to a greater or lesser extent. Having emerged haphazardly, these characteristics have not yet assumed the form of a consolidated political system; nor is it clear that they are here to stay. In that sense, Russia today resembles Germany in 1933 or Italy in the early-to-mid–1920s. Russia could follow in their footsteps, or it could falter and find its way back to some form of democracy or authoritarianism. Located somewhere between authoritarianism and fascism, today's Russia may therefore be termed fascistoid."

You can judge for yourself whether Putin's Russia has become more or less fascist since 2010.

I had also concluded that:

> All fascist states scare their neighbors and provoke them to defend themselves against perceived threats emanating from the behavior and bluster of fascist

leaders. In that sense, fascist hyper-nationalism becomes a self-fulfilling prophe-cy—effectively creating the very enemies it invokes as the reasons for its justifica-tion. The soldiers and policemen who run fascist states have a natural proclivity to toughness and weaponry. The hyper-nationalism, state fetishes, and cult of hyper-masculinity incline fascist states to see enemies everywhere. The cult-like status of leaders encourages them to pound their chests with abandon. And the population's implication in its own repression leads it to balance its self-humili-ation with attempts to humiliate others. Unsurprisingly, Russia has taken to as-serting its "rightful" place in the sun by engaging in energy blackmail vis-à-vis Ukraine, Belarus, and the Baltic states, cyber-wars against Estonia, a war against Georgia, Polar land grabs, saber-rattling in Crimea, and other forms of aggres-sive behavior.

Putin's invasion of Ukraine fits the above pattern all too neatly. The only question is: is the invasion comparable to Hitler's annexation of German-inhabited Sudetenland, to Hitler's Anschluss of Austria, or to Hitler's attack on Poland? In the first case, Putin might go no farther than Crimea. In the second, he might try to occupy all of Ukraine. In the third, he'd settle for eastern Ukraine.

Whatever Putin's choice, he'll have to expend enormous resources on pacifying a hostile population. According to a public opinion survey conducted in mid-February by the Kyiv International Institute of Sociology, support for unification with Russia stands at only 26 percent in Ukraine's east and 19 percent in the south. In Crimea, supposedly a hotbed of Russian irredentism, only 41 percent want to join Mother Russia.

The Crimean invasion may turn out to be the greatest strategic blunder of Putin's career. Indeed, it could even lead to the end of Putinism.

If Putin knew his history, he'd know that nothing consolidates post-revolutionary re-gimes like invasions. Some counter-revolutionaries join the invaders, but most people put aside their differences and rally around the flag. The threat of existential annihilation strengthens post-revolutionary states, invigorates national identities, and encourages leaders to adopt radical change. The ongoing Ukrainian response to Putin's invasion fits this bill to a tee: even the country's top oligarchs, all Russian speakers, have condemned the invasion and rejected partition. When the crisis ends, Ukraine will be stronger and its diverse population may finally possess all the features of a modern nation. Ironically, Putin might accomplish what Ukraine's elites have thus far failed to achieve: effective state building and genuine nation building. And that Ukrainian state and that Ukrainian nation are as unlikely to regard him with affection as they are certain to want good rela-tions with a democratic Russia rather than Putin's.

Putin's naked aggression has also outraged the international community and, in particu-lar, the United States and European Union. (In this respect, the Weimar Russia scenario does not, fortunately, hold: the democracies have not responded to Putin's aggression with Munich-like appeasement.) Ordinary Russians will suffer as a result, even as Putin persuades them that his chest-beating is an adequate substitute for a good life.

Although some two-thirds of Russians currently support Putin, that number could drop precipitously if body bags arrive in Moscow and the stagnant Russian economy creaks under the burden of military adventurism. Wars and occupations are expensive, especially for states with declining reserves of energy-generated easy money. How will Russians react? By happily dying for a dictator or by taking to the streets? How will Russian elites react? By supporting an irrational leader or by jumping ship? Russia's Führer would do well to remember that the Argentine invasion of the Falklands brought down the military junta in Buenos Aires.

*

The Dangers of the Putin Doctrine, *Al Jazeera*, March 5, 2014

In occupying Ukraine's southernmost province, the Autonomous Republic of Crimea, Russian President Vladimir Putin has simultaneously invaded a neighboring country that poses no security threat to Russia, unilaterally declared that he has a carte blanche to invade any country with a Russian population and even invited rogue states to develop nuclear weapons.

This new Putin Doctrine threatens to undermine the entire global order. His insistence that he is entitled to violate international law for the pursuit of his own ends is nothing less than a megalomaniacal claim that could, if implemented systematically, produce a world war.

Putin justified his invasion of democratic Ukraine on two counts. First, he claimed that Russians were being threatened by Ukrainian extremists and that their lives were in danger. There is no shred of evidence of such a threat. Quite to the contrary, Ukraine's Russians have repeatedly stated that they do not need Putin's protection. Indeed, even Putin's own Human Rights Council concluded on March 2 that there "were no victims and wounded among the civilian population and soldiers" of Crimea.

Perhaps because the grounds for an intervention were preposterous, Russia then argued on March 3 that it intervened because Viktor Yanukovych, Ukraine's former president, requested that it do so. Russia continues to recognize Yanukovych, even though he lost all his legitimacy in the course of four years of mercilessly exploiting Ukraine and its population (the Ukrainian Treasury is empty, and the country is bankrupt, thanks to Yanukovych), committed crimes against humanity during the mass violence against the demonstrators in Kyiv (almost 100 civilians were killed) and abandoned his office when he fled the country.

Even more destabilizing than the invasion of Crimea was Putin's claim that he had the right to march into "the territory of Ukraine" in defense of Russian citizens. Here's the entire statement of his request to Russia's Council of the Federation, which immediately granted him his wishes:

> In connection with the extraordinary situation that has developed in Ukraine and *the threat to citizens of the Russian Federation, our compatriots*, the personnel of the military contingent of the Russian Federation Armed Forces deployed on the territory of Ukraine (Autonomous Republic of Crimea) in accordance with international agreement; pursuant to Article 102.1 (d) of the constitution of the Russian Federation, I hereby appeal to the Council of Federation of the Federal Assembly of the Russian Federation to *use the armed forces of the Russian Federation on the territory of Ukraine until the social and political situation in that country is normalized.* (emphasis added)

The logic at the base of this extraordinary claim, which stands in violation of every international norm, enables Putin to invade not just Ukraine but any state with a Russian population. And since it is up to Putin to define a "threat" to Russians and to determine when the "situation" is "normalized," he has in effect given himself a carte blanche to send troops to Georgia (where he intervened in 2008 on behalf of South Ossetia and Abkhazia), Estonia, Latvia, Lithuania, Belarus, Moldova, Armenia, Azerbaijan, Kazakhstan, Kyrgyzstan, Uzbekistan, and Tajikistan—in other words, into any country of the former Soviet space. Small wonder that Estonian officials have reacted with special alarm. They know their country, with a Russian population that accounts for almost a third of the total population, could easily be next.

Finally, by invading and occupying Ukraine, in violation of the 1994 Budapest Memorandum on Security Assurances, Putin has signaled to rogue states with nuclear ambitions that they are free to develop them in violation of international norms. In that agreement, Ukraine gave up its nuclear weapons in exchange for guarantees of its territorial integrity by the United States, the United Kingdom and Russia. By violating Ukraine's territorial integrity, Russia has effectively denounced the Budapest Memorandum and its broader message that the nuclear powers will protect states that willfully disarm. As a result, there is no reason that a rogue state with nuclear aspirations should take the threats or assurances of nuclear states seriously.

The Putin Doctrine places Russia and Russia's interests above those of the international community and world peace. In effect, it has transformed Putin's Russia into a rogue state that should be treated accordingly. Every state near or bordering Russia must recognize that its security and integrity could be on the line if Putin gets away with his assault on Ukraine. By the same token, the international community must recognize that the structure of international relations could collapse if Putin succeeds. If the international community fails to act, it will be inviting further expansion, further aggression, and quite possibly war—by Russia and by states emboldened by Putin's impudence. Russia's violations of the international order should be of particular concern to the post-colonial states of Africa and Asia, which, like Ukraine, suffered decades of imperial rule and understand quite well the importance—as well as the fragility—of internationally accepted principles of nonaggression, sovereignty and inviolability of borders.

Although the Security Council cannot take forceful measures due to the certainty of a Russian veto, the United Nations General Assembly has the authority to act. As Humboldt University's Christian Tomuschat points out:

On 3 November 1950, the General Assembly adopted resolution 377 A (V), which was given the title "Uniting for Peace" ... The most important part of resolution 377 A (V) is section A which states that where the Security Council, because of lack of unanimity of the permanent members, fails to exercise its primary responsibility for the maintenance of international peace and security, the General Assembly shall seize itself of the matter ... To date, 10 emergency special sessions have been convened. The first one took place on the occasion of the 1956 war between Israel and Egypt and the British-French attack on the Suez Canal zone; the 10th emergency special session, dealing with the Israeli occupation of Palestinian territory, started in 1997 and has not yet come to its end ...

As Tomuschat notes, the resolution empowers Third World states:

The seventh emergency special session on Palestine (1980–1982) was in fact initiated by Senegal, the eighth emergency special session on Namibia (1981) goes back to a request by Zimbabwe, and the 10th emergency special session was solicited by Qatar as the chair of the Group of Arab States at the United Nations. It stands to reason that in such instances the overwhelming weight of Third World countries can manifest itself to its full extent.

In other words, the international community need not sit idly on the sidelines and watch Putin destroy the foundations of international order. It can consider taking important measures within the U.N. framework to stop Russian aggression before the crisis leads to war in Ukraine, resulting in thousands of dead, and before Russian land grabs in the former Soviet republics destabilize Eurasia.

*

Is Losing Crimea a Loss? *Foreign Affairs*, March 10, 2014

By the end of this month, it is likely that Vladimir Putin's Russia will fully control Ukraine's Crimean Peninsula. And it is clear that he aspires to much more. Although a tense calm has settled over Crimea since thousands of Russian troops poured in a week ago, the chance for a Russian military push deeper into Ukraine increased markedly on March 4, when Putin declared at a press conference that he was "not worried" by the prospect of war with Ukraine. In a line that shook Ukrainians to their core, he continued that, if Russia decided to fight, it would be to "to protect Ukrainian citizens." And it would be impossible, he hinted, for Ukrainian troops to do anything about that: "Let's see those troops try to shoot their own people with us behind them—not in the front but behind. Let them just try to shoot at women and children!" In one fell swoop, Putin had broadened his intentions in Ukraine from "protecting" Russian citizens (his rationale for invading and occupying Crimea) to "protecting" all of Ukraine and made clear that he would use Ukrainian civilians—women and children—as a shield for invading Russian forces.

It is time to imagine what once seemed impossible: Putin attacks and partitions Ukraine and, in addition to Crimea, annexes the southeastern Ukrainian provinces that are generally regarded as most susceptible to conquest—Donetsk, Kherson, Luhansk, Mykolaiv, and Zaporizhzhya, which contain much of Ukraine's ethnic Russian population and form an arc along the Black Sea and Sea of Azov from Mykolaiv, just northwest of Crimea, to Luhansk, which is farther northeast. (On March 8, there were already some reports that Russian troops had advanced from Crimea into a narrow isthmus that is part of Kherson Province.) In such a scenario, Russia would be the immediate winner and Ukraine the immediate loser. But in the medium to long term, Ukraine would end up ahead.

Ukraine's initial losses are obvious: defeat in a land war, surrender of territories and populations, and the sacrifice to violence of thousands—perhaps tens of thousands—of Ukrainians. Once the war is over, however, Ukraine would emerge more compact, more homogeneous, and more unified in purpose: Along with its eastern territories would go much of the electorate that routinely votes for the Communist Party and for former President Viktor Yanukovych's Party of Regions. As a result, anti-Ukrainian and anti-Western sentiments would decline. The new Ukraine's government could confidently proceed with a radical political and economic reform program (a more solidary population would be more likely to accept the belt-tightening that reform entails) and pursue rapid integration into European and international structures. Unburdened of some of its most unprofitable rust-belt industrial sectors, Ukraine's economy would be more open to foreign direct investment and could be poised for takeoff. Without Crimea and its southeastern provinces, Ukraine would be smaller, but it would survive and, in all likelihood, be much stronger.

Russia's gains are also obvious: victory in a "grand and glorious" war and the annexation of territory. But the hypernationalism generated by the war and the enthusiasm over territorial expansion would soon fade as the sobering reality in these provinces sinks in and Russians realize just whom and what they have annexed.

For starters, Russia is fooling itself if it believes that Ukraine's southeastern population will gladly go along with annexation. According to a mid-February 2014 public opinion survey conducted by the respected Kyiv International Institute of Sociology, the overwhelming majority of Ukrainians—even in the southeast—reject "unification" with Russia. Crimea was least opposed, with 59 percent against. In Donetsk, the number was 66.8 percent. In Luhansk, it was 75.9 percent. In Kherson and Mykolaiv, more than 95 percent of respondents were opposed. And a full 83.3 percent of those in Zaporizhzhya said no. In short, annexation will bring an extremely disaffected population into Russia's fold. The people could passively resist Russian rule. They could also take up arms.

Popular disaffection will make it difficult for Putin to walk away. Tens of thousands of Russian troops will have to remain as occupiers for a long time to come—an expensive proposition that could run into billions of dollars annually. And Russia will not be able to neglect the region's economy, since doing so would only increase disaffection and resistance.

In their search to maintain control, Russians would quickly discover that they are in possession of economically unviable provinces that cannot survive without massive infusions of rubles. According to a detailed Ukrainian study of how much Ukraine's provinces paid into and received from the central budget in the first half of 2013, Crimea, Donetsk, Kherson, Luhansk, Mykolaiv, and Zaporizhzhya represented an enormous drain on Kyiv's resources: 22.82 billion hryvnia (around $2.5 billion, or 90 billion rubles). And that is only for the first six months of the year. Multiplied by two, the deficit amounts to 45.64 billion hryvnia (about $5 billion, or 180 billion rubles).

In 2014, Russia expects its budget revenues to be around 13.6 trillion rubles (around $375 billion); its expenditures are supposed to total 14 trillion rubles ($380 billion). That amounts to a deficit of 400 billion rubles ($11 billion). Even without extra development funds or the costs of an occupation, annexing Ukraine's southeast will raise Russia's deficit by 45 percent.

The bad news gets worse for Russia. Luhansk and Donetsk provinces are home to Ukraine's loss-making coal industry. Kyiv spends between 12 and 14 billion hryvnia (around $1 billion–$1.5 billion, or 47 billion–55 billion rubles) annually to support these mines. Will Russia back these enterprises even as they compete with more economically produced coal from Russia's Kuzbass? It will have to: As Kyiv knows from experience, firing thousands of coal miners could spark massive civil unrest. Moscow will also have to pay them their wages on time. In 2013, wage arrears reached a total of 135 million hryvnia (about $15 million, or 530 million rubles) in Donetsk and Luhansk.

Prospects for Crimea are even worse. In 2013, the region hosted 5.9 million tourists, 25 percent of whom were from Russia and 70 percent of whom were from Ukraine. Ukrainians will likely avoid, or be prohibited from traveling to, an annexed Crimea. And Russians will probably prefer less restive playgrounds, such as Sochi or Turkey. Very quickly, Crimea's famed beaches could go into steep decline. And since tourism accounts for the largest chunk of the peninsula's economy, living standards there would plummet. Crimeans could also face disruptions in electricity, gas, and water supplies, for which they are completely dependent on mainland Ukraine.

These depressing numbers might not matter were it not for the fact that the Russian economy is expected to see subpar performance in the decades ahead. After almost a decade of strong GDP growth, the Russian economy is expected to expand by only 2.5 percent in 2014 and 2.8 percent in 2015. (Previous estimates were around 3 percent and 3.1 percent respectively.) Even worse, Russia's Economic Ministry has revised its long-term growth forecasts for Russia, predicting only a 2.5 percent growth in GDP annually through 2030. The global rate is expected to be roughly 3.5 percent. Imperial "overreach" can quickly turn into imperial collapse if the money to sustain occupation is missing.

Putin was lucky. When he came to power some 14 years ago, energy prices rose and money was abundant. The boom enabled him to flex his muscles and build a fascistoid state, in which he and his cronies could acquire fabulous wealth and still have enough left over for raising his people's living standards. The next decade will be especially difficult economically for Russia. Although the easy money has vanished, elite corruption and popular expectations remain high. And now there could be the added expense of occupying and ruling Ukraine's money-draining southeast. All these rubles will ultimately have to come from the Russian people and the corrupt elites. It is unlikely that they will accept a significant decline in living standards in exchange for the fleeting glory in Ukraine's rust belt.

Ukraine and Ukrainians will be fine. But Russians should be very worried.

*

Why Ukraine Should Risk It All, *Foreign Policy*, March 13, 2014

Tensions continue to rise ahead of Crimea's vote to join the Russian Federation, scheduled to take place on Sunday. Russian troops are massing along the Ukrainian border, and a spokesman for the government in Kyiv has warned of a possible "full-scale invasion from various directions." Meanwhile, President Vladimir Putin has added fuel to the fire by reportedly questioning whether Ukraine's exit from the USSR was legal. Fortunately, there's a simple way to defuse the Russo-Ukrainian conflict once and for all. Forget a single-province referendum in Crimea: Ukraine should ask the United Nations or some other neutral international organization to hold a vote on secession in all the southeastern provinces with significant Russian and Russian-speaking populations.

If that sounds outlandish or foolhardy or even politically impossible, just consider what it would accomplish. Russia insists these southeastern populations are being threatened by the "neo-Nazis" and "fascists" in Kyiv. Putin insists he has the right to employ mili-tary force to defend them. Kyiv—along with most Western observers—reasonably rejects these claims, but being right makes little difference when Moscow has the force of might on its side. According to acting Ukrainian Defense Minister Ihor Teniukh, Russia has positioned 220,000 soldiers, 1,800 tanks, 400 helicopters, 150 planes, and 60 ships along Ukraine's eastern border. By contrast, Ukraine's infantry consists of 41,000 soldiers, of whom only 6,000 are battle-ready. In other words, if Putin were to launch an attack on Ukraine, it would swiftly succeed, although it could conceivably

Since the relative force capability precludes a successful military defense of Ukraine by Kyiv—and a Western military intervention is unlikely as long as Russia's aggression is confined to the southeastern provinces (all bets are off if Russian tanks advance on Kyiv or Lviv)—Ukraine's government really has only one option: to remove the pretext for a possible invasion. Since Russia insists that any intervention would be motivated solely by a desire to help threatened countrymen, Ukraine should act immediately to determine just how many of its southeastern residents do in fact feel threatened enough to want independence.

The provinces in question would be, from west to east: Odessa, Mykolaiv, Kherson, Zaporizhzhya, Donetsk, Luhansk, and Kharkiv. Ideally, Crimea would be added to the mix.

An internationally-conducted referendum would give the residents of these provinces the chance to speak for themselves. The organization overseeing the vote would have to be acceptable to Ukraine, Russia, and the West; the United Nations or the Organization for Security and Cooperation in Europe come to mind. Guided by international conventions, that organization should determine how high the percentage of pro-independence votes would have to be to trigger legal secession: 50 percent plus one, 60 percent, or some other figure. The referendum should be held as quickly as possible, so as to keep tensions from rising as a result of divisive campaigning. To guarantee a peaceful environment, U.N. peacekeepers should be temporarily deployed to the provinces in question. Three-person teams of international observers consisting of one European or American, one Ukrainian, and one Russian could monitor the voting. The results should be binding on both Ukraine and Russia. The question could be as simple as this: "Do you support X province's independence from Ukraine and annexation by the Russian Federation?" Since both Russia and Ukraine insist that the local populations support them, a referendum would call their bluffs.

There is a precedent for this kind of procedure in recent Soviet history. On March 17, 1991, Soviet voters were asked to vote on the following question: "Do you consider necessary the preservation of the Union of Soviet Socialist Republics as a renewed federation of equal sovereign republics in which the rights and freedom of an individual of any nationality will be fully guaranteed?" Seventy-one percent of Ukrainians voted yes. Ukrainian voters were also asked: "Do you agree that Ukraine should be part of a Union of Soviet sovereign states on the basis of the Declaration of State Sovereignty of Ukraine?" Eighty-two percent said yes. Although the referendum proved inconclusive—the August putsch followed soon thereafter, Mikhail Gorbachev effectively lost power, and Ukraine declared independence on August 24—it is certainly still remembered in Ukraine and could serve to legitimate a new vote.

The results of a referendum in Ukraine's southeastern provinces should be acceptable to Russia, but it's a gamble. The will of the people will have been heard, and if, as Moscow insists, it is pro-Russian, the Russian Federation will have the opportunity to annex a few territories. If it is not pro-Russian, then Moscow will have to recognize that its claims of persecution are unfounded.

Ukraine should also be satisfied with such a procedure, both because a Russian invasion of mainland Ukraine looks more likely with every day and because mid-February polling data suggest that none of the southeastern provinces has more than a third of its voters supporting unification with Russia.

If these provinces choose to stay, then Russia will no longer be able to claim that they are oppressed. If pro-Russian sentiment grows exponentially in the immediate future and some provinces choose to leave, then Ukraine's stability and security will only be enhanced by the departure of regions with fifth columns that exceed 50 or 60 percent of the population and that, as a result, could not be defended from Russian aggression.

The referendum could be capped with a broad treaty between Russia, Ukraine, the European Union, and the United States in which all sides agree to respect the referendum's results in perpetuity. Russia and Ukraine would also agree to respect each other's sovereignty, independence, and territorial integrity, to provide for minority rights (especially in the disputed southeastern provinces), to refrain from threatening actions, and to respect each other's choice of domestic policies and international orientations.

The results would insulate Ukraine from further Russian aggression—and they should satisfy Putin that large numbers of southeastern Ukrainians aren't being held hostage against their will. Unless Putin intends to swallow all of Ukraine and thereby declare war on the entire post-war international order, he should appreciate that only such a referendum would produce legal and legitimate outcomes, and not internationally unrecognized statelets and frozen conflicts at best, and a land war, a lengthy occupation, and the certainty of protracted conflict at worst.

*

Putin's Terrifying Warmongering, *World Affairs Journal*, March 14, 2014

On March 8th, some 15,000 women and children lined the roads of Crimea, and Kherson Province to its north, in protest against Russian President Vladimir Putin's invasion of Ukraine. The Crimean Tatar and Ukrainian women didn't come out in force just because it happened to be International Women's Day. They were also responding to Putin's threat to implicate them and their children in further acts of war against Ukraine.

Putin had put the women—and the world—on alert at his March 4th press conference, where he declared that he was "not worried" by the prospect of war with Ukraine and that, were he to decide to attack, he intended to use women and children as a shield for Russian troops.

Here's how the official Kremlin website translated Putin's terrifying exchange with a Russian-speaking woman journalist:

> QUESTION: [...] Are you concerned that a war could break out?
>
> VLADIMIR PUTIN: I am not concerned, because we do not plan and we will not fight with the Ukrainian people.
>
> QUESTION: But there are Ukrainian troops, there is the Ukrainian army.
>
> VLADIMIR PUTIN: Listen carefully. I want you to understand me clearly: if we make that decision, it will only be to protect Ukrainian citizens. And let's see those troops try to shoot their own people, with us behind them—not in the front, but behind. Let them just try to shoot at women and children! I would like to see those who would give that order in Ukraine.

The translation of the first question doesn't do justice to Putin's alarming views. Here's a more literal translation that retains the structure of the original Russian:

QUESTION: [...] That war could begin, that does not worry you?

V. PUTIN: That [i.e., that war could begin] does not worry me, because we do not intend and will not fight with the Ukrainian people.

Putin did not say, as the official translation suggests, that he is "not concerned" by war. The word "concern" connotes a general indifference. Instead, he used the Russian word "*besspokoit*," which is more accurately translated as "worried" or "perturbed." When the journalist asked, "that doesn't worry you?" the "that" in her question referred to the clause "that war could begin." Putin, in his response, therefore said "[that war could begin] does not worry me."

The qualifier that immediately follows that statement only made things worse: "because we do not plan and we will not fight with the Ukrainian people."

As Putin knows, wars are not fought between an army on the one hand and a civilian population on the other. Wars are fought between armies. Whether or not Putin plans to "fight with the Ukrainian people" is therefore completely irrelevant to whether or not he plans to launch a war against Ukraine and its armed forces. The journalist caught him in that contradiction and promptly said: "But there are Ukrainian troops, there is the Ukrainian army."

At that point, Putin made things still worse. Watch the video clip. He bears down on the journalist, raises the forefinger of his right hand, and proceeds to lecture her.

For starters, he says, "If we make that decision, it will only be to protect Ukrainian citizens." Recall that Putin explained his aggression in Crimea on the grounds that "Russian citizens" needed protection. The logic of that claim would have justified a Russian attack on Estonia, Latvia, Belarus, Moldova, and Kazakhstan, all of which have large Russian populations. The logic of the claim that he might start a war with Ukraine to "protect Ukrainian citizens" goes much further: it justifies a Russian invasion of any country. Poland, Hungary, Romania, Mongolia, and China should take note.

And then, when it seems barely possible for Putin's warmongering to get any more ter-rifying, it does. As he explicitly states, he intends to "protect Ukrainian citizens" by po-sitioning the Russian army *behind* them—not in front of them, as a genuine desire to protect people from an assault would appear to dictate. In effect, Ukrainian "women and children" would serve as a shield in any armed conflict that he chooses to initiate. Putin dares the Ukrainian side to fire first, but conveniently ignores that "women and children" would agree to serve as a shield for his troops only if coerced to do so by those very same troops. In other words, Russian troops would in fact not "protect Ukrainian citizens," but cow them into submission and then force "women and children" to protect Russian soldiers. Whether he means this literally or figuratively, I leave to your imagination, but he is clearly blackmailing Ukraine with a thinly veiled threat that resistance will mean that "women and children" will die.

I cannot think of a single world leader—other than Adolf Hitler—who would have so explicitly, so callously, and so casually declared his indifference to mass human suffering. Especially worrying is that Putin made these statements at a press conference. He was, in other words, not just speaking to Russians or Ukrainians. He was placing the international community in general and the West in particular on notice: If he chooses to start a war, large numbers of civilians will die. They may be Ukrainian, but they may also be anybody he resolves to "protect."

Unsurprisingly, Ukrainians are terrified by Putin's warmongering. A friend in Lviv, which is as far as one can be from Ukraine's eastern border (or is it front?) with Russia, tells me that "people are petrified and believe war is inevitable." So are Crimean Tatars, whose ancestral land has already been occupied by Putin's troops and who remember Stalin's genocidal policies in 1944, when the entire Tatar population was deported to Central Asia and half died. What if Crimean Tatars, who have already begun forming self-defense units (and some of whom have begun talking of an anti-Russian jihad), take to the streets after Putin wrests Crimea from Ukraine? How will Putin respond? His warmongering statements suggest that mass internments of Crimean Tatars in concentration camps, ethnic cleansing, and even genocide are no longer inconceivable.

*

Putin Won't Stop at Crimea, *CNN*, March 17, 2014

As Crimea held a bogus referendum on independence under the watchful eye of Russian occupation force on March 16, I confess that my mind and heart were elsewhere.

I have never experienced war or the threat of annihilation. But now, thanks to the Internet, like thousands of other Ukrainian-Americans I am living at the edge of an existential abyss. The violence—the war—that threatens Ukraine does not threaten me. I am in New York and Ukraine is thousands of miles away. But war will threaten my friends, colleagues and family in Ukraine. We Ukrainian-Americans must now live with the very real possibility that their lives could be extinguished if Russian President Vladimir Putin chooses to do so. Indeed, Ukraine could even disappear as a state, if he chooses to make it disappear.

The Internet has inserted the reality and possibility of mass death into our lives. We watch events unfold in real time. And we watch these events unfold all day, every day. There is no respite. There is no pause.

Ukrainians in Ukraine must live with the tangible threat of physical annihilation. We must live with the virtual threat. Their fears are palpable. The consequences for them of war and violence are real: destruction and death. The consequences for us are virtual: We are witnesses to tragedy and mass killings. We watch, our eyes glued to our computer screens, and we imagine the horror.

Our empathy is not abstract: Our friends, colleagues and relatives are real people. Neither is our feeling of impotence abstract: It gnaws at our insides and reminds us that we, too, are dying, albeit spiritually.

For three months, starting in late November, when the mass pro-democracy demonstrations began in downtown Kyiv, and ending on February 21, when Ukraine's version of Papa Doc Duvalier, Viktor Yanukovych, fled and people power triumphed, we had been witnessing daily regime violence punctuated by a few killings in January and mass killings just before the regime collapsed.

Every morning, turning on my computer, I wondered whether this was the day the criminal Yanukovych regime would crack down, as it continually threatened to do. If all that happened that night was a disappearance or two, a few savage beatings and fire-bombings of cars, we Ukrainian-Americans breathed a sigh of relief. You see, we had gotten used to daily terror. We, like the demonstrators in Ukraine, could live with that. After all, they had been living with the violence and predations of the Yanukovych regime since 2010.

On Tuesday, February 18, about 16 demonstrators and 10 police officers were killed. We were shocked and mourned their deaths, while hoping and expecting the violence to ebb. On Wednesday, February 19, nothing happened and our hopes appeared to be justified. On Thursday, February 20, the regime ordered snipers to shoot randomly at demonstrators. Scores died. And, thanks to the Internet, we saw them being mowed down. The violence had come home. The criminal regime had insinuated itself into our lives.

After Yanukovych fled and a democratic government assumed power, we rejoiced. Finally, we thought, Ukraine would be able to become "normal"—free, democratic, liberal and Western. We were euphoric. The death of the country had been averted.

Except that, exactly one week later, on Friday, February 28, that euphoria was replaced with the deepest of fears. Vladimir Putin's Russia invaded and occupied Crimea. That was bad enough. Far worse was yet to come. On Saturday, March 1, Putin claimed to have the right to "defend" "Russian citizens" anywhere in Ukraine, thereby giving himself carte blanche to invade any part of Ukraine he chooses. Which province would be next?

On Tuesday, March 4, our existential angst got worse. At a revealing press conference, Putin claimed he had the right to go to war with Ukraine in defense of "Ukrainian citizens." Putin also said if he made the decision to go to war, "women and children" would act as a shield for Russian troops.

Many Ukrainians in Ukraine now believe that a Russian invasion of mainland Ukraine is inevitable. If it happens, war will break out and thousands will die.

It's hard to believe that Putin will stop with Crimea. Putin's former economic adviser Andrei Illarionov, who resigned in protest after a bloody hostage crisis, believes Russian armies will march on Kyiv.

Putin's ideological mentor, Aleksandr Dugin, insists that Russia's goals go beyond Ukraine into Europe—a reunification of the Slavic peoples. Meanwhile, Russian troops and tanks are massing on Ukraine's borders. Terrified realists that we have become, we suspect the worst: that they will soon be attacking a country that dared say no to Putin.

As the clouds of a massive land war appear to approach Ukraine, we watch our screens with horror and hope against hope that Russian bombs will not begin to fall on our friends, colleagues, and family in Ukraine.

*

Ukraine Prepares for War, *CNN*, March 28, 2014

When Russian Minister of Defense Sergei Shoigu stated that the Russian troops along Ukraine's borders were only conducting "training exercises" and have no "intention to cross Ukraine's borders or to engage in any aggressive actions," Ukrainians rolled their eyes.

And when President Vladimir Putin told Ukrainians "Don't believe those who terrify you with Russia, who shout that other regions will follow Crimea. We do not want Ukraine's division. ... We want Ukraine to be a strong, sovereign, and self-sufficient state," Ukrainians shrugged.

The problem is, even if Putin and Shoigu were being sincere, Moscow has lost all credibility among most Ukrainians and the international community. After three weeks of aggressive Russian behavior and the possibility of existential annihilation, Ukrainians, like Israelis, prefer to think in terms of worst-case scenarios. After all, they blithely assumed Russia would never attack—and then Russia seized Crimea.

They never imagined that Russian officials would treat their country as an object of abject scorn. They never suspected that thousands of Russians would chant anti-Ukrainian war slogans in the streets of Moscow. In each instance, Ukrainians' working assumption of a friendly Russia proved dead wrong.

They also never imagined that the Yanukovych regime had so thoroughly permitted Ukraine's defensive capacity to deteriorate, by sacrificing Ukrainian security on the altar of the Yanukovych family's untrammeled accumulation of power and embezzlement of state funds.

A political scientist at Kyiv's elite Mohyla University has stated that he is not "not optimistic about Ukraine maintaining the integrity of even its mainland territorial borders" until the end of March and has evacuated his family from the capital.

A friend in Lviv tells me that "an invasion and war are unavoidable." An American businessman in Kyiv writes: "I believe we are closer to World War III than we have ever been." In many parts of the country, Ukrainians have taken to preparing little suitcases with all the necessities—just in case they have to flee at a moment's notice.

Ukrainians' jitters are perfectly understandable. Ukrainian officials say that 80,000 Russian troops and heavy armor are amassed on Ukraine's borders. Putin claims to have the right to intervene anywhere in Ukraine if and when he deems that Russian citizens are being threatened.

He and myriad Russian policymakers routinely insist that Ukrainians are really Russians and that Ukraine is an artificial entity. Thus far, Moscow refuses to recognize the democratic government in Kyiv and claims that it is no longer bound by the 1994 Budapest Memorandum on Security Assurances.

Because of Russia's occupation of Crimea and Putin's militarist rhetoric, many Ukrainians are certain that war is inevitable. Prime Minister Arsenii Yatseniuk warned Moscow on March 20 that Ukraine's response to a Russian invasion would be vigorous.

Kyiv has already begun improving its defensive capabilities. On March 17, the Ukrainian Parliament allocated 6.9 billion hryvnia—about $684 million—to defense. In the last few weeks, Ukrainian armed forces, tanks and other defensive weapons have been deployed along the country's border with Russia. The number of border guards along Ukraine's southeastern borders has also increased. Kherson Province is planning to build a 20-kilometer long ditch along its border with Crimea.

A National Guard has been formed, and its ranks are to consist of 20,000 troops. The Ukrainian Security Service appears also to have become more active in Ukraine's vulnerable southeastern provinces. No less important, the population is determined to resist and sales of guns have far outstripped supply.

Thinking in more long-term categories, former Minister of Foreign Affairs Volodymyr Ohryzko has even suggested that Ukraine exit the Nuclear Non-Proliferation Treaty and initiate the "process of uranium enrichment." American provision of non-lethal military equipment and advisers would also go a long way to improving Ukraine's deterrent capacity.

Kyiv's defensive efforts may or may not be enough to stop a possible Russian attack, but they would certainly make it far more difficult, risky, and bloody—which may be enough to deter Moscow. Alternatively, these efforts may just induce Russia to seek less frontal modes of undermining Ukraine. After all, any potential Russian assault on mainland Ukraine would rest on three pillars: an invasion by the army, the agitation by pro-Putin "fifth columns" within Ukraine, and the diversionary activities of Russian secret agents and special forces tasked with sowing panic, sabotaging transportation and communica-tions, and attacking military bases and arms depots.

Although Ukraine appears to have the capacity to neutralize internal threats, a concerted long-term Russian effort at stoking instability could lay the groundwork for a later inva-sion or, at the very least, divert Kyiv's attention from the pressing cause of economic and political reform.

While Ukraine's security may or may not be enhanced by most of these measures, the irony is that Russia's will not be—at least in the medium to long term. Putin's seizure of

Crimea may have provided him with the opportunity to beat his chest before adoring Russian crowds, but it will eventually undermine Russian security.

Ukraine is and will remain too weak to be a threat. And on its own, no country in Russia's "near abroad" can pose a threat. Even taken together, the non-Russians will be weaker than Russia. But Putin's land grab will make all of them inclined to regard Russia as a potentially land-grabbing foe and to promote their own security independently of Russia and outside of any Russian-led blocs or unions. Expect the Central Asians and Azerbaijanis to turn increasingly to China and Turkey, and the Georgians, Moldovans, Ukrainians, and even the Belarusians to head for the West. Also expect the Russian Federation's non-Russian autonomous republics and regions to press for greater autonomy from Moscow.

If Putin could just put aside his hypernationalist neo-imperialism and think straight about what's good for Russia, he'd try to nip the problem in the bud. A sober Russia would then withdraw all the forces that are engaged in "exercises" along Ukraine's borders and agree to a significant force reduction in Crimea.

A sober Russia would also explicitly state that it recognizes the Budapest Memorandum and the current Ukrainian government. That last point is essential. As long as the Kremlin insists that the Kyiv government is illegitimate, it will always be able to claim that its behavior toward Ukraine's Russian minority is also illegitimate and, hence, liable to correction by means of Russian intervention.

Seen in this light, annexing Crimea must be one of Putin's worst strategic blunders. Had the province become "independent," there would still have been a theoretical possibility of finding some accommodation with Kyiv. After annexation, any dialogue with the Ukrainian government—and, thus, any resolution of the Russo-Ukrainian conflict—becomes significantly more difficult. It's perfectly possible that Putin wants the conflict to remain unresolved, on the assumption that it will undermine Ukraine. The problem is that an unresolved conflict will also undermine Russia.

As Ukraine and Russia's other non-Russian neighbors are compelled by Moscow's aggression to enhance their security, Russia may soon face a nightmare of its own creation—non-Russian encirclement. When Russians wake up to the reality after the euphoria of Crimea's annexation wears off, Putin may very well discover that his own security and stability as President are in danger.

*

Experts on Ukraine Still Getting It Wrong, *World Affairs Journal*, March 31, 2014

When the West's leading experts get elementary facts about Ukraine wrong, blithely encourage Russian expansionism, or make illogical arguments, I worry. As should everybody. After all, these are presumably the people influencing or making policy in the United States and Europe.

The latest two examples are Jacques Attali, the founding president of the European Bank for Reconstruction and Development, and Ian Bremmer, president of the New York–based consultancy, Eurasia Group.

Attali's views on Crimea, Ukraine, and Russia are alarming, indeed, irresponsibly so. Bremmer's rest on definitional ambiguity and faulty logic.

Here's Attali's interpretation of what just transpired in Crimea: "a majority vote from a Russian-speaking province, part of Russia for centuries, attached in 1954 to another province of the Soviet Union on the whim of the secretary general of the Communist Party at the time, Nikita Khrushchev."

No word of the Russian invasion, of the gangsters running Crimea, of the Crimean Tatars inhabiting Crimea "for centuries" before Russia grabbed it in 1783, of the 1944 ethnic cleansing and genocide of the Tatars, of the bogus referendum conducted recently in the shadow of tanks, of the public opinion survey showing that only 41 percent of Crimeans supported unification with Russia, of the mass settlement in Crimea of Russian veterans after the expulsion of the Tatars. And the bit about Khrushchev's whim is too precious. Doesn't Attali know that the USSR was always run on the whims of its leaders?

Then there's this:

> Crimea and Russia chose to use the chaos born of the arrival in Kyiv of a strongly anti-Russian government to reunite. Why does it bother us? Why should the Crimean population be denied the will to choose their destiny against the view of the country of which they are a member? After all, aren't we preparing to allow the Scots to vote on exactly the same issue in Great Britain? Don't the Catalans intend to do likewise in Spain? ... And what will happen if Moldova, Belarus, or the Russian-speaking part of Kazakhstan ask to become attached to Russia? We will interfere? On what grounds? ... What about Czechoslovakia splitting up into the Czech Republic and Slovakia?

Does Attali really believe that referenda in Scotland, Catalonia, and Quebec, and the break-up of Czechoslovakia, are in any way comparable—procedurally—to Russia's military occupation of Crimea and the subsequent bogus referendum? Does he really believe that the government in Kyiv is "strongly anti-Russian"? Heaven help us all, if he does.

But Attali's rhetorical questions—"And what will happen if Moldova, Belarus, or the Russian-speaking part of Kazakhstan ask to become attached to Russia? We will interfere?"—are nothing less than an invitation to Putin to invade these territories. By the way, what if Russian-speaking Nice, Berlin's Charlottenburg, or the high-end parts of London ask "to become attached"?

Attali appears to be blithely unaware of the consequences of such land grabs. Ukrainians, Moldovans, Belarusians, and Kazakhs will resist. There will be war in much of Eurasia, along with tens of thousands of casualties and hundreds of thousands of refugees. And every country on Russia's borders will promptly engage in a military buildup. "What do we have to fear from Crimea returning to Russia?" Attali asks. "That Russia calls the Russian-speaking part of the Baltic states part of Russia and thus a prime target for an-nexation? Come on! These countries are in the European Union and in NATO! Therefore, they have nothing to fear." That "therefore" comes a bit too quickly to be reassuring. If Europe is willing to ignore a Russian attack on its neighbors and pursue Russia's inte-gration despite its aggressions, Estonians and Latvians would be fools to think Europe would sacrifice integration for the sake of two tiny countries.

Attali is dangerous; Bremmer is just wrong. His key premises are twofold: "Ukraine is far more important to Vladimir V. Putin than it is to America"; "Mr. Putin's policy, including whether to seize more of Ukraine, will be informed overwhelmingly by national security interests, not near-term economics."

Although he insists "the United States needs to see the Ukraine crisis from Russia's view-point," Bremmer doesn't tell us what that viewpoint and what Russia's national securi-ty interests vis-à-vis Ukraine are. Like every state, Russia is entitled to want a friendly government in Ukraine. Is it also entitled to invade Ukraine? That m ight be "Russia's viewpoint," but is Ukraine's destruction a Russian national security interest or in any other way valid? How about committing genocide against the Crimean Tatars? Also a valid interest? See the problem. By leaving Russia's national security interests undefined, while extolling its right to pursue them, Bremmer must, like Attali, justify any Russian policy—including war and genocide.

Bremmer also ignores the West's national security interests. Surely, it's in the West's in-terest not to have untrammeled imperialist expansion in Eurasia, to avoid a major land war on Europe's eastern borders, and to maintain the post-World War II international order. Notice how Bremmer focuses only on the economic costs of sanctions:

> ... if Russia pushes farther into Ukraine, America's attempt at tougher Iran-style sanctions, coordinated with allies, will ultimately fail. Indeed, if Mr. Putin pur-sues a broader military campaign, a similarly robust response from both America and Europe is unlikely. Russia's energy exports, its commercial power and its sheer size make the costs of ignoring it prohibitively high for Europe.

But the West, like Russia, has both economic *and* national security interests (and some economic interests are also national security interests). Bremmer does logic a disser-vice by juxtaposing undefined Russian national security interests with narrowly defined Western economic interests.

Bremmer believes that "sharp rhetoric from the West could push Mr. Putin to be even more aggressive. That's because he does not believe that the West would ever treat Russia like Iran and implement robust sanctions that would cut off vast areas of Russia's econo-my from the West."

Now, that just doesn't make sense. If, as Bremmer argues, "Mr. Putin's policy, including whether to seize more of Ukraine, will be informed overwhelmingly by national security interests," then why should he buck the West? To annoy it? To demonstrate his tough-ness? But just what does that have to do with Russia's national security interests—unless those encompass imperialism, war, and genocide? In which case, nothing can stop Putin and nothing can "push" him to "be even more aggressive." He'll just keep going until he's stopped.

*

Could Russia Occupy Ukraine? *World Affairs Journal*, April 7, 2014

A Russian invasion of mainland Ukraine continues to worry Ukrainian and Western policymakers, despite statements by Russian President Vladimir Putin and Foreign Minister Sergei Lavrov that Moscow has no such intentions. The illegal occupation of Crimea serves as one source of disbelief in Russian sincerity; a second source is Moscow's refusal to recognize the Ukrainian government or the forthcoming May 25th presiden-tial elections. A third is the continued placement of Russian troops along Ukraine's bor-ders. Estimates of their number have ranged widely, from 30,000 to 220,000, with most falling in the 50,000–80,000 range. (On April 4th, however, Ukraine's first vice prime minister stated there were 10,000–15,000 Russian troops along Ukraine's borders and another 22,000 in Crimea.)

Ukrainian policymakers are right to assume that Putin's intentions are not benign. That said, could Russia actually occupy Ukraine? How many troops would Russia need to hold Ukraine—especially under conditions of a Ukrainian insurgency?

A 2008 study by US Army Major Glenn E. Kozelka provides some tentative answers. According to Kozelka:

To determine a historical gauge for planning force levels in a COIN [counterinsurgency] environment, this study provides a quantitative and qualitative analysis of two successful COIN case studies, the British-led Malaya Emergency and the US-led Operation in Iraq. Quantitative analysis of the case studies is used to compare the security force size employed to the population size. ... Although each situation is unique and a fixed ratio will not guarantee success, there is a strong correlative relationship between force levels and success. ... The case studies show that the closer force levels approach the ratio of 20 security forces per 1,000 population, the greater the possibility the COIN force will reach the tipping point to success.

Kozelka also cites a 1995 RAND Corporation study by James Quinlivan who "promulgates a continuum of force density levels, based on three levels of violence or threat intensity."

Low violence (police operations): 1–4 security forces per 1,000 of population

Medium violence (civil unrest): 5–10 security forces per 1,000 of population

High violence (insurgency): 10+ security forces per 1,000 of population

Kozelka emphasizes that many local demographic, geographic, political, cultural, and economic factors can affect these numbers. They should therefore be viewed as general indicators, and not as precise measures.

I've combined Kozelka's numbers with Quinlivan's to produce a rough estimate of how many troops Russia would need to occupy Ukraine. Since the quality and counterinsur-gency experience of Russian troops are probably much lower than those of British and American forces, I've used the high-range estimates: Quinlivan's 4 per 1,000 in condi-tions of low violence, Quinlivan's 10 per 1,000 in conditions of medium violence, and Kozelka's 20 per 1,000 in conditions of high violence. I've also provided calculations for three clusters of Ukrainian provinces: low, medium, and high violence for Donetsk and Luhansk, which are most pro-Russian, but which also have significant pro-Ukrainian support and may therefore be unpredictable; medium and high violence for the other five southeastern provinces—Kharkiv, Kherson, Mykolaiv, Odessa, and Zaporizhzhya—where civil unrest or insurgency, or both, is likely. And only high-violence estimates for the remaining provinces, where insurgency would be greatest.

Province	Population (2012 estimate)	Low violence (police operations): 1–4 security forces per 1,000 of population: estimate for 4/1,000	Medium violence (civil unrest): 5–10 security forces per 1,000 of population: estimate for 10/1,000	High violence (insurgency): 10+ security forces per 1,000 of population: estimate for 20/1,000
Donetsk	4,403,178	17,612	44,031	88,062
Luhansk	2,272,676	9,090	22,726	45,452
TOTAL		**26,702**	**66,757**	**133,514**
Kharkiv	2,742,180		27,421	54,842
Kherson	1,083,367		10,833	21,666
Mykolaiv	1,178,223		11,782	23,564
Odessa	2,388,297		23,882	47,764
Zaporizhzhya	1,791,668		17,916	35,832
TOTAL			**91,834**	**183,668**
Cherkasy	1,277,303			25,546
Chernihiv	1,088,509			21,770
Chernivtsi	905,264			18,105
Dnipropetrovsk	3,320,299			66,405
Ivano-Frankivsk	1,380,128			27,602
Khmelnytsky	1,320,171			26,403
Kirovohrad	1,002,420			20,048
Kyiv (plus city)	4,533,816			90,676
Lutsk	1,038,598			20,771
Lviv	2,540,938			50,818
Poltava	1,477,195			29,543
Rivne	1,154,256			23,085
Sumy	1,152,333			23,046
Ternopil	1,080,431			21,608
Vinnytsia	1,634,187			32,683
Uzhhorod	1,250,759			25,015
Zhytomyr	1,273,199			25,463
TOTAL				**548,587**

Source: http://www.geohive.com/cntry/ukraine.aspx

The results are not encouraging for proponents of a Russian invasion.

- In order to occupy Donetsk and Luhansk provinces alone, Russian would have to deploy somewhere between 26,702 and 133,514 troops.

- A "land bridge" from Crimea to Transnistria would mean occupying Kherson, Mykolaiv, and Odessa provinces—which would entail somewhere between 46,497 and 92,994 soldiers.

- Occupying all seven southeastern provinces would require between 118,536 (26,702 for Donetsk and Luhansk and 91,834 for the others) and 317,182 (133,514 for Donetsk and Luhansk and 183,668 for the others).

- If Russia decides to conquer all of Ukraine, it would need an additional 548,587 troops—for a grand total of 667,123 to 865,769 troops.

- Kyiv city and Kyiv Province alone would require 90,676 occupying soldiers.

In light of Russia's estimated current force levels on Ukraine's borders (50,000–80,000), the best Russia could do under low- and medium-violence assumptions would be to invade a few southeastern provinces. If those assumptions are changed to medium or high, only one or two provinces would be within its grasp. These conclusions assume that an invasion would entail no force deterioration as a result of the Ukrainian army's resistance. Change that assumption, and Russia's capacity to occupy southeastern Ukraine declines even more.

In sum, Kyiv is right to worry about an invasion of all or part of its southeast—but only if Russia makes optimistic assumptions about the extent of resistance. Accordingly, Ukraine's immediate goal should be to strengthen its southeastern defenses—preferably with American help—so as to deter a focused attack or, at the very least, to make such an attack so costly as to raise the conditions of expected violence in individual provinces. (Ukraine's medium-term priority should of course be to develop a full-scale defensive capacity.) But, unless Putin decides to deploy most of Russia's armed forces (which number about 750,000) against Ukraine and thereby place all of Russia on a war footing, readying bomb shelters in Kyiv may not be a Ukrainian priority.

*

The Weakness of Eastern Ukraine's Pro-Russian Separatists, *Al Jazeera*, April 10, 2014

On Sunday, April 6, pro-Russian separatists captured government buildings in Kharkiv, Luhansk and Donetsk in Ukraine's mineral-rich eastern regions. In the siege of Luhansk's security services headquarters, the radicals took some 60 hostages. The next day, pro-Russian activists in Donetsk seized another security services building and declared the creation of an independent Donetsk Republic. Their comrades in Kharkiv followed suit by creating a Kharkiv People's Republic.

The latest turn of events in Ukraine's five-month-long turmoil testifies to Russia's continued determination to stoke unrest as well as Kyiv's continued vulnerability to Russian subversion. At the same time, Ukrainian authorities are not quite as weak, and the separatists are not quite as strong, as they are believed to be. Following the seizures, Ukrainian authorities successfully pushed back, retaking the security services building in Donetsk on April 7 and the state administration building in Kharkiv on April 8 (during the latter operation, they arrested 70 extremists). On April 9, the Luhansk radicals released 56 hostages after the authorities engaged them in negotiations and called on them to surrender.

The plotters expected mass outpourings of support, but those never came. They probably also expected some local elites to defect to their side, but that, too, never happened. Instead, and contrary to popular belief, a significant number of eastern Ukrainian political elites—including those generally affiliated with former President Viktor Yanukovych's Party of Regions—support the country's independence and territorial integrity. Even Ukraine's richest oligarch, the Donetsk-based Rinat Akhmetov, who financed the Yanukovych regime, called on the Donetsk separatists to come to their senses.

In a word, the coup attempt failed. Four days after the seizures of provincial administration buildings, the separatists in both Luhansk and Donetsk remain completely isolated and reduced to the status of violent extremists. At this point, the choice they face is to surrender peacefully or be ousted forcefully.

The unsuccessful coup has shown just how weak radical separatist sentiment is in eastern and southern Ukraine. A public opinion survey conducted by Baltic Surveys and Gallup last month showed that only 4 percent of residents in Ukraine's east and 2 percent in the south favor Ukraine's division "into several countries." Fifty-three percent of easterners want it to remain a "unitary country," while 26 percent favor a federal arrangement. In the south, the numbers are 69 percent for unitary status and 22 percent for federal. A similar poll by the Institute of Social Research and Political Analysis, meanwhile, showed that 65.7 percent of Donetsk residents favor living in Ukraine, while only 18.2 percent desire unification with Russia.

Donetsk Governor Serhii Taruta claims that separatists in the region, the Donbas, make up about 0.01 percent of the total population and lack a "broad platform that could inspire the broad masses." Taruta says that the radical separatists number about 200 and that their supporters are paid to "play their roles." The total number of pro-Russian extremists in Kharkiv, Luhansk and Donetsk provinces may not exceed three times the Donetsk number.

The upside of these seizures for Kyiv is twofold. First, the separatists are far weaker than they, and Moscow, imagined. And second, the pursuit by central and local authorities of both negotiation and targeted coercion has, thus far, worked.

The downside for Kyiv is, of course, that the coup attempts took place—which testifies, above all, to the fact that the local militia units have been far too desultory in their defense of the government. Some critics accuse the militia of lacking loyalty, a not implausible interpretation in light of the fact that many were recruited during the Yanukovych years.

Taruta is more generous, recognizing that there were "problems with the effectiveness" and "adequacy" of the militia response, while attributing these shortcomings to a "post-Maidan syndrome." During the popular protests that led to Yanukovych's ouster, the militia was accused of "going against the people." In the aftermath of the uprising, the militia has failed to distinguish between those who oppose them and those who support them—and largely remained inactive.

Putin's options

So what's next for Ukraine's eastern provinces?

A popular uprising on behalf of separatism appears to have no future—at least for the time being. If Russia continues to foment instability and hopes to annex all or parts of the Ukrainian southeast, Vladimir Putin now has two options.

The first is to instruct the pro-Russian separatists to engage in what frustrated radicals the world over do: terrorism. Now that they know just how deeply isolated they are, the separatists have only one course of action open to them—to sow unrest by means of targeted bombings and killings, possibly of government officials or even average citizens. Many of the separatists appear to be armed, and, if need be, Russian intelligence can always smuggle armaments and explosives to them. Terrorism would not endear the separatists, or Russia, to the average eastern Ukrainian, but it could deflect Kyiv from reform and disrupt the May 25 presidential election. While those might well be Moscow's targets, terrorism will ultimately fail. Kyiv is likely to crack down hard, and the people of the Donbas would rally around the forces of law and order.

Putin's second option is to invade. But that, too, is risky. On the one hand, even he realizes that an out-and-out invasion, without even the appearance of some local popular support as in Crimea, might put a strain on his credibility among die-hard supporters who want to believe that their "brethren" in Ukraine desperately need their assistance. On the other hand, an invasion would force the West to impose ruinous sanctions on Russia and produce significant popular resistance among the population in the Donbas, which Putin would be claiming to liberate. Russia's invasion of eastern Ukraine would therefore require a very large commitment of forces and a prolonged period of pacification, with the attendant casualties for the occupying Russian troops.

Still, just because terrorism will be of limited utility and intervention will be costly does not, alas, mean that Putin will not try them. In the past few weeks he has shown that he is willing to take chances and buck international opinion. But he is not reckless, either. While Ukraine's southeast will long remain the target of Russian attempts at subversion, time is on Kyiv's side—and Putin's chances of successfully undermining Ukraine diminish with every passing day.

In Eastern Ukraine, Terror from Pro-Kremlin Outsiders, *World Affairs Journal*, April 23, 2014

For three years now, I've been providing a small scholarship to a little girl in the city of Druzhkivka (population: 65,000) in eastern Ukraine's Donetsk Province. Her mother, G, has sent me several brief on-the-ground reports of events in Druzhkivka (the translations below, from Ukrainian, are mine). They convey better than any analysis just what average Ukrainians are experiencing as a result of Vladimir Putin's promotion of terrorism in eastern Ukraine.

Bands of outsiders have been terrorizing the city since February 22nd, the day after the triumph of the democratic Euro Revolution in Kyiv and the collapse of the criminal regime of President Viktor Yanukovych. On Saturday, April 12th, armed pro-Russian terrorists seized the Druzhkivka district administration building. Since then, the city has been at the mercy of the pro-Kremlin extremists.

Note a few important points.

G emphasizes that the troublemakers are outsiders, and not residents of the city—a point that journalists and the Ukrainian authorities also make. It's virtually certain that some of them are Russian intelligence agents and *spetsnaz* special forces.

She also states that Druzhkivka's troublemakers, like those of many other provincial cities, enjoy the support of the local mayor. These officials, all members of the pro-Yanukovych Party of Regions, are clearly hoping to use the provocations as a means of holding on to power and escaping prosecution for corruption and other forms of wrongdoing during the years of the Yanukovych regime.

Finally, G underlines that the *agents provocateurs* are all invoking Vladimir Putin's bogeyman, the long-deceased Ukrainian nationalist Stepan Bandera, who headed a Ukrainian national liberation movement, the Organization of Ukrainian Nationalists, in the 1930s–1950s. Significantly, as G notes, no one has ever encountered Bandera supporters in Druzhkivka. Their absence in the rest of Donetsk Province is just as striking. In a word, the terrorists are sowing fear of a non-existent foe to keep an uninformed population on edge.

*

February 23, 2014 (two days after Viktor Yanukovych's flight from Kyiv):

Long live Ukraine, Alexander!

I'm happy for Kyiv, proud of western Ukraine, and ashamed of Donetsk Province. What's taking place in our city today is simply horrible.

On February 22nd, at 12 noon, on the central square of the city, near the eternal flame, there collected several civilians and one person wearing a Don Cossack uniform. They were holding the flag of the Russian Federation. They also had the black and yellow flag of the Romanov dynasty.

They were asked who they were, what they were doing, what sort of flags they were carrying, and what their plans were.

The one on the Don Cossack uniform said that they were defenders of the homeland from the "Banderites." They were, he said, all members of a Don Cossack organization that was registered in the city. Their general was the city mayor, Valery Hnatenko. They supported the introduction of Russian troops into Ukraine and the annexation of our state by Russia.

In the night of February 22nd–23rd, starting at 10 p.m., groups of 3–4 unknown persons trawled the city's streets, throwing plastic bottles, causing a ruckus, and loudly shouting Long Live Ukraine and that Bandera has finally arrived. There were a few such brigades, and they were evidently drunk. It was clear that they were the little Cossacks headed by our mayor. Another 2,000 people gathered; they were disorganized, drunk, and very aggressive. Some people thought they were defending their town from western Ukrainian "gangs." Many, mostly older people, came to honor the memory of those who had died [during the Euro Revolution in Kyiv]. They were attacked with eggs. The militia asked that they hide the Ukrainian flag, lest the aggressively inclined participants of the gathering be provoked.

February 23rd:

Apologies for the convoluted description ... The people who supported the ideas of the Maidan no longer feel safe in their own land. What a horror.

March 2nd (two days after Russian troops occupied Crimea):

I don't know if you have the opportunity to acquire reliable information about what is currently taking place in eastern Ukraine. As a simple person from the Donbas, I wish to inform everyone I know that unknown people have appeared in many cities of Donetsk Province. They are not residents of these cities, but enjoy the support of local mayors and their machines. They're attempting to promote separatist ideas and to terrify the population with non-existent western [Ukrainian] extremists whom no one has ever seen.

April 14th (two days after terrorists seized the building of the Druzhkivka district administration):

Alexander, they will kill us ...

*

I haven't heard from G since that last note. Although I'm sure she and her family are safe, I still shudder at the thought of how terrified she must have been to have expected death—for nothing more than her identity as a Ukrainian in the unremittingly hostile environment created by Putin's deliberate attempt to create havoc in her country.

*

Separatists Terrorizing, Kidnapping, Beating Citizens in Ukraine, *World Affairs Journal*, May 13, 2014

Several weeks ago, I had written of a woman, G, from the town of Druzhkivka, in Donetsk Province, who had noted in her last e-mail to me: "Alexander, they will kill us." In turn, I had ended my blog post with the comforting words: "I haven't heard from G since that last note. Although I'm sure she and her family are safe, I still shudder at the thought of how terrified she must have been to have expected death—for nothing more than her identity as a Ukrainian in the unremittingly hostile environment created by Putin's deliberate attempt to create havoc in her country."

I was wrong. G and her family are not safe. Their lives are in danger from pro-Russian terrorists precisely because they are Ukrainian patriots.

I just received two more e-mails from her, translated by me from the Ukrainian and reprinted below in full.

From Saturday, May 10th, 8:42 a.m.:

> Dear Alexander: a terrible misfortune has befallen my family. Molotov cocktails were thrown at my parents' house; my parents, my husband, and I were threatened; and then armed commandoes shot at my parents' house. The press and the Internet wrote about this. Here's one report: Yevhen Shapovalov's building was shot at from a jeep, then it was broken into and ransacked, and all the valuables were taken. The neighbors called the militia, but they didn't even go inside; they took some photographs of the outside and said they'd lay a trap. A few days ago they threw three Molotov cocktails at Yevhen's building; miraculously, it didn't catch fire; there was a small child inside, about which everyone in the neighborhood knew. Today, the terrorists attacked an empty building, as the entire family had fled. Yevhen Shapovalov is the head of the Oleksa Tykhy Society of Donetsk Province (a branch of the Prosvita Society) [Tykhy was a prominent Ukrainian dissident; the Prosvita Society concerns itself with the promotion of Ukrainian language and culture]. For the terrorists, Yevhen, like all Ukrainian patriots, is the class enemy. PS. Yevhen is also a member of our civic organization. We are currently in hiding. H and my other daughter are with me. Horrible things are taking place around us ...

From Sunday, May 11th, 6:53 a.m.:

> Dear Alexander: I've changed my e-mail address because the thugs are after my

husband and me. They seized three young girls in Kramatorsk today for organizing the delivery of food to Ukrainian soldiers stationed near Sloviansk. One of them is my colleague; we had been talking just a day ago. One of the girls was released with broken ribs and torn-out hair; she was ordered to come back tomorrow with money ... What are we to do? These fascists are just like the NKVD, even worse. I'm constantly on edge, while my mother had a heart attack. What have peaceful people like us done to deserve this? We're hiding in difficult circumstances, the children are ill, H isn't going to school. That's what our life looks like. ... We pray, but we're losing hope.

What's next for G and her family? Serious physical harm, including death, at the hands of Putin's gangsters is no longer out of the question. Call me irrational, but if G and her family lose their lives I will hold Russia's fascist president and his Western apologists (from Gerhard Schröder to Helmut Schmidt to Henry Kissinger to Stephen F. Cohen) morally responsible. They may not have thrown the Molotov cocktails, but in justifying Putin's aggression they share in his guilt for whatever atrocities Putin's commandoes commit.

The political message of this persecution should be obvious. Putin's terrorists are committed to cleansing the Donbas of Ukrainian patriots—which is to say, of Ukrainians—as in their twisted understanding of identity anyone who speaks Ukrainian is necessarily their enemy. Such an attitude deserves to be called what it is: supremacism, racism, and hate. These, then, are the fruits of Putin's aggression.

As Europeans and Americans contemplate what to "do" about Putin, they should remember that he and his minions stand for everything the civilized world rejects. The United States and the European Union hope that Druzhkivka will be confined to eastern Ukraine. Unless they act more forcefully to stop Putin and his terror troops, the Putinite values on display in Druzhkivka may one day come to Europe.

*

How Kyiv Can Keep the Donbas, *Al Jazeera*, May 15, 2014

On April 30, Ukraine's acting President Oleksandr Turchynov may have been dissembling when he stated that Kyiv had lost control of the country's rust-belt eastern region, the Donbas. At first glance eastern Ukraine does indeed still appear to be as much in the hands of pro-Russian forces as at any time in the past few weeks. Anti-Ukrainian militias still occupy buildings in several cities, including Luhansk and Donetsk, the largest in the Donbas. On May 11, separatists held poorly planned referenda in Luhansk and Donetsk provinces under unfair and unfree circumstances. Despite an absurdly low turnout, they immediately claimed victory, declared independence and asked Russia to annex their regions.

Upon closer view, the situation is less favorable for the militants and their sponsors in the Kremlin. For starters, a day after Turchynov's statement, Ukraine's security forces launched a large-scale "anti-terrorist operation" in which Ukrainian security and armed services engaged pro-Russian extremists in firefights. The Kyiv units dismantled guard posts and recaptured buildings in some of the more than 10 Ukrainian cities where militants have tried to assert control. Ukraine is continuing its offensive, nibbling away at areas controlled by militants and imposing significant casualties on their forces.

In the face of well-armed and well-trained professional pro-Russian rebels, Ukraine's armed forces—decimated by four years of former President Viktor Yanukovych's intentional neglect—have performed quite well in the counterterrorism offensive. In addition to providing the Ukrainians with combat experience—which may come in handy if Russia decides to invade—the fighting has improved Ukrainian morale. The militants, who appeared to be on a roll until late April, are clearly not unstoppable.

More important, last week's pseudo-referenda revealed that the pro-Putin commandos are isolated from the people they claim to represent and have no endgame short of annexation of the Donbas by Russia. In turn, their predicament has placed Vladimir Putin, who has remained silent about the ballots and their implications, in a difficult position.

The militants have shown they are adept at seizing buildings, kidnapping opponents, terrorizing the population, instigating pogroms and making bold statements. But they have also demonstrated that they are dreadful administrators. Local economies are grinding to a halt, the proliferation of weapons and the impotence of local police forces have led to exponential increases in crime, and the population is increasingly impatient about the militants' inability to answer the question "What's next?"

Meanwhile, Putin must decide on the militants' request to annex Luhansk and Donetsk provinces. Given the farcical nature of the referenda and the militants' terrorism, sending Russian troops to "liberate" the Donbas could not be justified with appeals to putative popular will. Putin happily thumbed his nose at international law and annexed Crimea, invoking a nonexistent historical "Russianness" and pointing to the jubilant crowds greeting his invading troops. But after the human rights council affiliated with the Russian president's office said the turnout for the Crimean referendum was only 30 percent, or one-third of what Putin claimed, and that only one-half, or a mere 15 percent of the population, voted for annexation, Putin must now have qualms about using another set of sham referenda to invade more of Ukraine. Moreover, any Russian invasion would likely be met with firm resistance by Ukrainian forces and possibly debilitating Western sanctions. Besides, as shown by reliable public opinion polls, most Donbas residents have no desire to join Russia.

At the same time, Putin knows he cannot sit idly by and watch his commandos in eastern Ukraine suffer defeat and lose popular support. Some of the militants are Russian intelligence agents with explicit orders to sow unrest. Many others, with origins in Ukraine, believe that Putin is their savior. By acting wisely and avoiding war, Putin risks losing the exalted status he enjoys among his commandos in eastern Ukraine.

Kyiv's Options

However unexpectedly, the tide may have turned in Kyiv's favor. Expect the government to pursue a divide-and-conquer policy premised on divisions among the militants and to employ a wide range of sticks and carrots at its disposal.

The demands of pro-Russian rebels are as varied as their composition. In Donetsk and Luhansk, some want independent republics; others want Putin to invade. Many militants, together with most Donbas residents, want greater autonomy or a better life in Ukraine. Some are criminals on the payroll of local elites, Moscow, Donbas oligarchs and Yanukovych. Two cities in Donetsk Province, Slovyansk and Kramatorsk, are under partial control of Russian-trained extremists, Russian intelligence agents and Russian *spetsnaz* special forces. Rebels in Luhansk and Donetsk appear to be divided between a more radical "street" and a more moderate cohort that occupies buildings. Even the building occupiers in both cities are split between radicals and moderates.

Seizing on these divisions, Kyiv should try to separate the locals with legitimate grievances from the Russian agents, pro-Russian extremists and paid criminals. It can initiate negotiations with the former while continuing its anti-militant operations against the latter. Kyiv can then offer the more moderate elements among the militants concessions on self-rule, language and referenda.

Ukraine's east wants "federalization." No one really knows what that means, except that eastern Ukrainians, together with all Ukrainians, want to run their own affairs. Kyiv is already committed to a radical "decentralization" of authority that should placate the call for greater self-rule. But words matter. It's imperative that Kyiv frame the administrative reforms just as residents of the Donbas want them to be called—federalization.

Many in eastern Ukraine want Russian to become a second state language. Kyiv should counter with two proposals. First, Russian can be the second state language of any province that demands it. Second, Ukraine's genuine commitment to language equality would entail that all state employees in all of Ukraine demonstrate fluency in both Ukrainian and Russian. The east wants referenda. Kyiv should accede and let provinces decide how much decentralization they want.

The Donbas still has a good chance of being reintegrated into Ukraine. The militants are isolated, Putin may be in a pickle and Kyiv has shown that it can conduct successful anti-terrorist operations. The stakes are high. If Kyiv fails, the Donbas could easily become a "warlordistan." Corruption, instability, subversion and economic collapse in the Donbas would then radiate in all directions, producing a disaster for the rest of Ukraine, for the wider region and for Russia.

*

The End of the Donbas? *World Affairs Journal*, June 11, 2014

As Ukrainian army units battle it out with Putin's terrorist commandos in eastern Ukraine, we should remember that, regardless of the outcome, the Donbas is probably dead. That may be good news for some and bad news for others, but the bottom line is that this uniquely regressive Ukrainian-Russian rustbelt region will never be the same.

Putin's terrorists—both homegrown and imported from Russia—will almost certainly be defeated by forces loyal to Kyiv. Terrorists and separatists usually lose, especially under steppe-like conditions in which guerrillas do not thrive, and there's no reason to think that Putin's commandos will have any different fate from that of their counterparts in other countries. The only question is: how long will it take for their defeat to be final? For the longer it takes, the more unalterably different—and ruined—will the Donbas become.

As one resident of Donetsk recently wrote in a blog post:

> No one believes that the people who live here are needed by anybody. We've been cast off, and Donetsk has become a cage, a prison, from which one can still escape if one abandons everything—apartment, property, work, hopes and plans for the future—so as to survive, which is the most important thing. Everyone understands that this will go on for a long time. That things will get very, very bad. That many will die. Just as the city will die.

Such words as terror, violence, and instability barely convey the reality of what living in a protracted war zone must be like for the residents of the Donbas. As violence becomes part of the fabric of everyday reality, physical survival becomes the average citizen's primary, and perhaps only, concern. Compounding that concern is a collapsing economy. As stores close, plants and factories shut their gates, goods become scarce, and prices skyrocket, the black market booms, unemployment goes through the roof, wages aren't paid, and crime takes off. People who long for normality will run: ethnic Ukrainians will probably head for Ukraine; ethnic Russians will head for Russia. The young, the talented, and the rich will be the first to go. The old, the weary, and the poor will be the last.

In the words of the Donetsk blogger:

> Almost no one wants to leave, but everyone understands that flight will be necessary, because the city is doomed. No one believes in a happy or quick end. Neither do I. ... Those who could flee have already left. Some people have evacuated their families from Donetsk. Many are getting ready to leave. Those who stay will be people who simply cannot leave. Or who still believe that things won't be as bad as they are now.

Already, some 10,000 to 15,000 residents of Donetsk (population 982,000) appear to have fled; in Slovyansk (population 130,000), the site of widespread terrorist predations and heavy fighting, the number may be as high as 50,000. After the water supply was disrupted in early June in five cities—Druzhkivka, Dzerzhynsk, Kostyantynivka, Kramatorsk, and Slovyansk—the flow of refugees from them is sure to increase.

As infrastructure decays and people flee, institutions cease to function. Universities, research centers, the media, and other forms of intellectual activity will dry up as a result of the brain drain. Existing political and business elites will also disappear. The Party of Regions and the Communists—two political forces that have defined the Donbas and been defined by it—will become irrelevant as society unravels. Rinat Akhmetov, Ukraine's richest man, could easily lose his shirt—and his clout.

The longer the fighting takes, the more likely will Donetsk and Luhansk provinces come to resemble a Hobbesian state of nature. As Thomas Hobbes put it:

> In such condition, there is no place for industry; because the fruit thereof is uncertain: and consequently no culture of the earth; no navigation, nor use of the commodities that may be imported by sea; no commodious building; no instruments of moving, and removing, such things as require much force; no knowledge of the face of the earth; no account of time; no arts; no letters; no society; and which is worst of all, continual fear, and danger of violent death; and the life of man, solitary, poor, nasty, brutish, and short.

When the dust finally settles, democratic Ukraine will have to deal with a de-industrialized, depopulated, and de-modernized region. Under such conditions, all talk of federalism, decentralization, and language rights will sound quaint to people who want only to live.

How many refugees will return? Probably not too many. And how many of the survivors will be able to engage in entrepreneurship, innovation, and self-rule? Perhaps even fewer. How many lives will have been destroyed by Putin's terrorist schemes? How many livelihoods? You can be sure that neither he nor his Western fans care or are counting.

Amid this possible doom and gloom, there may be a sliver of a silver lining. Putin's criminality will have also destroyed the Soviet-era institutions, the Soviet-era mentality and political culture, and the Soviet-era economy that have conspired for decades to retard the Donbas's integration into the modern world. Ironically, by destroying the Donbas, Russia's neo-fascist dictator may pave the way for the Donbas's eventual revival as an integral part of a thriving Ukrainian democratic state. The Donbas could stop being a problem for Kyiv precisely because, thanks to Putin, it could stop being.

*

Putin's Zugzwang: The Russia-Ukraine Standoff, *World Affairs Journal*, June 17, 2014

The choice of outcome in the Russia-Ukraine standoff is largely Vladimir Putin's. Ukraine and the West are not powerless, but they can at most anticipate, prepare for, and deter what might be Putin's next move. This does not mean that they are victims of superior statecraft, however. His admirers may regard Putin as a master strategist, whose petulance and unpredictability give him the upper hand in relations with the West and Ukraine. In fact, the opposite is true. Putin has maneuvered himself, and Russia, into a position of *Zugzwang*—a chess term denoting a condition in which any possible move will worsen the player's position.

Putin has twisted himself into policy as well as rhetorical knots as a result of his absurd insistence that Ukraine's post-Yanukovych government is unconstitutional. Thus, even though Ukraine's two unreservedly pro-Russian parties, the unreformed (formerly ruling) Party of Regions and the Communists, fielded candidates for the May 25th presidential ballot, Moscow declared the elections illegitimate well in advance and, with its sponsorship of terrorism in eastern Ukraine, indicated that it would do all it could to sabotage them. But wouldn't fair and free elections diminish the existential threat Putin claims Russians face in Ukraine? And wouldn't unfair and unfree elections just prove his point that the Kyiv government is illegitimate? Even more illogically, Moscow demands constitutional reform from Kyiv, while continuing to insist the government is unconstitutional. But how can an unconstitutional government implement constitutionally valid constitutional change?

Far from indicating a master strategist at work, Putin's twisted logic and contradictory rhetoric have created a web of preposterous claims that, together with his imperialist policies, have forced him and Russia into a dead end with no easy way out. A would-be strongman who rips off his shirt to the delight of adoring Russian crowds, he dares not look or sound weak, while being hard-pressed to pursue policies that benefit Russia. Worse, uncertainty about Putin's moves will force the West and Ukraine to pursue policies that oppose Russia's interests. Since Putin is both unpredictable and dangerous, the world must prepare for the worst in its dealings with Moscow, causing Russia and the Russian people to suffer.

If Russia continues to rattle sabers, threaten to invade, and foment unrest in Ukraine's southeast, there will be cold war. If, instead of promoting instability, Russia merely refuses to recognize Ukraine's democratic government and alter Crimea's status, while simultaneously promoting terrorism and bogus referenda in eastern Ukraine, there will be cold peace. If Russia acts on the bogus referenda and invades more of Ukraine, there could be a hot war. If Russia recognizes Kyiv and "de-annexes" Crimea, warily neighborly relations—or a hot peace—will be possible. Which of these outcomes is Putin's preference? No one, including quite possibly Putin himself, knows. Putin has become what Winston Churchill once called Russia under Joseph Stalin: "a riddle wrapped in a mystery inside an enigma." Given Putin's unpredictability, the best we can do is prepare for any of these outcomes.

The least likely of the above four outcomes is a hot peace. Russia has made it amply clear that its annexation of Crimea is permanent. Since this *Anschluss* has become the basis of Putin's appeal to Russia's hyper-nationalists, he cannot easily embark on de-annexation, even if he wanted to. Whatever the Kremlin's justifications for the occupation—Crimea was always Russian (not true), the ethnic Russians were being persecuted (not true), Crimea is no different than Kosovo (not true), the referendum was a genuine exercise of the popular will (not true)—the brute fact is that Russia's imperialist landgrab violated every international norm in the book and threatens world peace. The United Nations, the Organization for Security and Cooperation in Europe, the Parliamentary Assembly of the Council of Europe—along with the United States, the European Union, the North Atlantic Treaty Organization, the Group of 7, and a slew of European and other countries (including, importantly, Turkey)—had no choice but to declare the annexation illegal. Russia's relations with the West and Ukraine will remain "non-neighborly" for as long as Russia insists its imperialist adventure is legitimate.

None of this means that détente is impossible, but it does mean that rapprochement is extremely unlikely for as long as Putin remains in power. Western businesspeople may push covertly for sacrificing security for the sake of prosperity, and former German Chancellor Helmut Schmidt may call the Crimea landgrab "completely understandable," but the reality of imperialism on Europe's doorstep, and the possibility of Russia's expansion to the EU's borders, limits the degree to which economic interests can determine Western strategy. Even pro-appeasement types like Schmidt might find Russia's occupation of northeastern Estonia, which is inhabited by Russians, less than *verständlich*.

Permanently tense relations with what is acknowledged to be a rogue Russia need not result in hot war: that could come about only if Putin wills it. A hot war will always remain possible as long as Russian troops remain amassed on Ukraine's borders and Putin retains the right, granted by the Federation Council (the upper house of the Russian Parliament) on March 1st, to intervene wherever he believes "Russians" are threatened. That said, a hot war would be a high-risk undertaking for Putin, involving significant Russian casualties, a bloody long-term occupation, and enormous financial costs—as well as Western sanctions on Russia's banking, energy, and armaments sectors and the likely provision to Ukraine of military hardware by the West. Occupying Crimea was a cakewalk; occupying Ukraine, or parts thereof, could be another Afghanistan.

The most likely long-term outcomes are, thus, cold war or cold peace. Here, too, it is Russia that, ironically, is in Zugzwang. Because the central rationale of Moscow's occupation of Crimea was the defense of supposedly threatened Russians, Putin and his minions must continue insisting that Ukraine's Russians are under threat and that their rights are being systematically violated. But since there is absolutely no evidence of persecution, whether partial or total, Russia's charges are as irrefutable as the beliefs of rabid anti-Semites who insist that Jews run the world: the very absence of evidence is ultimately employed as proof of the vast extent of the conspiracy.

Russia must keep its troops stationed along Ukraine's borders for as long as it claims Russians there are being threatened. And Moscow will claim that Russians are being threatened for as long as it insists that the democratic government in Kyiv is unconstitutional and that Viktor Yanukovych remains Ukraine's legitimate president. It matters little to Putin's twisted logic that the criminal Yanukovych regime had violated its social contract with the Ukrainian people, thereby enabling them to assert their natural democratic rights, in the exact same manner as the drafters of America's Declaration of Independence did in 1776. Nor does he blush, as he should, at the idea of delivering lectures about constitutionality when, in 2004 and 2012, he prevailed in unfair and unfree presidential elections and thereby violated Russia's Constitution. Putin's devotion to constitutionality is selective: the outrage he expressed at Yanukovych's ouster was decidedly absent when, in 2010, President Kurmanbek Bakiyev was driven from power in Kyrgyzstan and replaced by a (pro-Russian!) interim government headed by opposition leader Roza Otunbayeva.

Putin's twisted logic, militarist rhetoric, and neo-imperial ambitions may doom Russia to cold war, even though the benefit Russians would derive from being on a constant war footing is nil and the costs increasingly high. Those costs include loss of prestige and influence, capital flight, declining foreign direct investment, the loss of the Ukrainian market, and growing isolation from the international community and the West. None of this may matter to Putin and his fans in the short run, as his popularity soars; but over time Russia's economy will decline further, it will be more isolated from global structures, and will feel the full weight of hostility from those disgusted by Russian imperialism.

Putin and his acolytes rationalize Russia's growing isolation in terms of a civilizational clash between a declining West and a resurgent Russia. They are delusional to believe that the West is in decline and Russia is on the rise. Russia's rise is illusory and contingent. The society is physically ill (with widespread diseases, high alcohol use, and low life expectancy and birth rates) and, thanks to the imperialist hysteria unleashed by the regime, psychologically unstable, while the state is over-centralized, inefficient, and corrupt. The army is large, but no match for a world-class power or even probably for the armies of Germany, France, and the United Kingdom. And with the shale gas revolution, Russia's energy reserves will no longer provide Putin with the vast wealth to grease his cronies, enrich himself (to the tune of some $45 billion), and keep the population docile. The West has serious problems, but Russia is a paper tiger whose roar is bigger than its bite. Even many Putinites must realize that a long-term confrontation with the West will result in Russia's humiliation.

A cold peace would be the most advantageous of the four courses open to Russia—as well as the most advantageous to Ukraine and the West—but Putin's rhetoric and bluster make it impossible in the short run. In the medium term—say, in a year or two or three—it's not impossible to imagine Putin coming around. Ukraine is planning to decentralize authority in a way that would radically transform the architecture of the Ukrainian state. Kyiv could easily meet eastern Ukrainian demands for enhanced status of the Russian language, already the status quo: the government need only place its imprimatur on the existing state of affairs and call it a concession. Finally, presidential and parliamentary elections in Ukraine will take place in 2014; both ballots should be fair and free and produce a legitimate government. If so inclined, Putin could use these linguistic and constitutional results to claim victory, asserting that, since Ukraine "finally listened" to Russia's sage advice and adopted the changes it deemed necessary, the illusory threat to ethnic Russians has disappeared, thereby obviating the need for a Russian troop presence along Ukraine's border. The only sticking point between Russia and the West and Ukraine would be the *Anschluss* of Crimea, which could slip into the status of a noxious but acceptable *fait accompli* if all other things become "normal."

For now, however, hot war, cold peace, and cold war will remain possible until Putin makes up his mind which course to choose. Some analysts claim he is captive to an all-encompassing imperialist ideology pushing him to continual expansion and war. Others argue that, although he may have a vision of a globally powerful Russia, he is also motivated by geopolitical interests and personal goals. Statements he has made offer little insight into his thinking, since so many of them were misleading or mendacious in the past. In sum, although we do know he has spun a rhetorical web in which he is trapped, we *cannot* know what Putin's intentions vis-à-vis Ukraine and the world are.

If states cannot calculate how an adversary will behave, they have no choice but to hope for the best and prepare for the almost-worst and the worst: the almost-worst is Russia's full embrace of a cold war, while the worst is a hot war. Ukraine and the West must assume that Putin is unreliable, unpredictable, and dangerous—and plan accordingly. For now, Ukraine's short-, medium-, and long-term priorities are threefold.

First, it must safeguard its own security. International agreements such as the 1994 Budapest Memorandum on Security Assurances can be violated, as Russia did by annexing Crimea, or not enforced, as the United States and the United Kingdom did by acquiescing in this *Anschluss*. Ukraine must look to itself and develop a credible army at all costs. Ukraine need not be able to defeat Russia; it need only deter it and crush the terrorist assaults that form a large part of Putin's strategy to keep Ukraine unstable and thus pliable.

Second, Ukraine must jump-start its economy with radical economic reforms. A strong economy is the only long-term guarantee of a strong military, which is the *sine qua non* of Ukraine security. Russia's aggression in Crimea, its support of terrorist commandos in eastern Ukraine, and its permanent threat of hot war should consolidate Ukrainians around painful reforms that enhance their security. Transferring many state functions downwards will reduce corruption: central bureaucrats will have fewer opportunities to demand bribes, while local bureaucrats will have to temper their thievery or face the ire of their neighbors.

And third, to remain democratic in a tough neighborhood dominated by a neo-fascist bully, Ukraine will have to embed itself in the West. Membership in the European Union is the ultimate prize, but any form of affiliation that promotes the deeper Westernization of Ukraine's culture, education, laws, and institutions will help ensure survival.

Looked at from the West's perspective, a strong and democratic Ukraine is its own best defense against an imperialist Russia. That's why doing everything possible—*immediately*—to help Ukraine build a strong military, a dynamic economy, and a Western-oriented democracy is crucial. Loans are fine, but the West must go the next step and provide its military with hardware, training, and advisers as a way of making cold peace more attractive than cold or hot war. The West should not be content with threatening Russia with draconian sanctions if its imperialism goes too far: that's an invitation to Putin to test the "decadent" West. Instead, the United States and Europe should impose painful sanctions immediately and offer to withdraw them only in exchange for good behavior. The West's third line of defense consists of promoting strong non-Russian states, especially Moldova, Belarus, and Kazakhstan, where large Russian minorities could invite Russian imperialism.

These harder-line policies presuppose a strategic shift in the West's thinking—from the illusory belief that Russia will cooperate in resolving the issues it has inflamed to a hard-headed realization that Putinism threatens world peace. As difficult as it may be for Germany, France, and the United Kingdom to sacrifice lucrative economic ties with Russia, they—and especially Germany, whose social-democratic elites have an incomprehensible love affair with a dictator who resembles Adolf Hitler in both word and deed—must understand that, if Putin continues to call the shots, the EU's security, stability, and survival will be at risk. *Der Spiegel* editor Christian Neef's advice to Berlin is right on the money and applies to Germany's allies as well: "If we don't finally take a sober look at Russia, one that is erased of all romanticizing and historical baggage that distorts our view of Putin's world, then we will never succeed in finding a reasonable strategy."

Over time, some combination of cold war, cold peace, and hot war will transform Ukraine into a South Korea, Taiwan, or Israel. Ukraine will have to live with the permanent threat of Russian aggression, but that threat could have a silver lining: compelling it to become a vigorous democracy with a strong economy and a strong army.

Russia's future is less clear. If Putin stays in power for another twenty years, it could become an impoverished garrison state such as North Korea. If Putin departs well before he becomes an octogenarian, Russia could become a second China. More likely than not, Putin will keep on posturing, and Russia will remain an ossified and increasingly unstable petro-state like Saudi Arabia.

*

A Day with Ukraine's Volunteer Fighters, *Al Jazeera*, June 26, 2014

Turmoil in eastern Ukraine has continued despite Ukrainian President Petro Poroshenko's offer of a cease-fire to pro-Russian rebels, with both sides accusing each other of violating it. At least 11 Ukrainian soldiers have been killed since the June 23 cease-fire. Perhaps alarmed by the prospect of punitive sanctions by the United States and the European Union, on June 25 the Russian parliament at the request of President Vladimir Putin rescinded the March 1 resolution that authorized him to intervene militarily in defense of Russian speakers in Ukraine and other non-Russian states.

Putin's actions may also have been motivated by the Ukrainian armed forces' successful counterattacks. After several early setbacks, Ukraine's counterterrorism operations in recent weeks have squeezed the insurgents into an area of about one-third of the Donbas region and regained control of much of the border with Russia. Self-defense units comprising volunteers from the region, who have thrown in their lot with Ukraine in the ongoing struggle against pro-Russian rebels, have been instrumental in that offensive. The volunteers come from diverse religious and ethnic backgrounds (including Ukrainians, Russians, Jews and many others), possess a sincere commitment to a democratic, pro-Western Ukraine and share a remarkable interethnic Ukrainian patriotism.

One such unit is the Donbas Battalion.

Last week I had the opportunity to visit the battalion's training camp outside Kyiv as part of a small group of opinion-makers and experts on a three-day study tour sponsored by the NATO Information and Documentation Center in Kyiv. The visit brought home several points. First, Ukrainians are determined to fight and retain their sovereignty. Second, residents of the Donbas, generally considered indifferent to Ukraine, can be as patriotic as western Ukrainians. Third, the interethnic patriotic sentiments suggest that Ukraine is witnessing the emergence of an all-inclusive polity. These developments bode well for Ukraine's future and portend a sad end for Putin's imperialist adventures in the mineral-rich eastern region.

'Glory to Ukraine'

The camp was located about 12 miles north of Ukraine's capital, on the grounds of a National Guard base, about a mile south of former President Viktor Yanukovych's lavish estate, now a popular museum that serves as a reminder of the vast scale of his regime's corruption, venality and bad taste.

Guards met us at the gate and provided us with passes. They asked that we refrain from photographing the soldiers: They would not be wearing masks, we were told, and a carelessly taken photo could jeopardize the safety of their families, who remained in the Donbas. Our guide, a Russian-speaking adviser to Ukrainian Minister of Internal Affairs Arsen Avakov, took us past Ukrainian-language billboards and several training grounds. We reached a dusty clearing amid a pine forest where the battalion was assembled. Several hundred men, ranging in age from their early 20s to mid-50s, stood at ease, wearing combat boots and various military fatigues. They watched us gather around their legendary commander, an ethnic Russian businessman turned guerrilla fighter from Donetsk known by his *nom de guerre*, Semyon Semenchenko. I had seen photographs of him before, but he was always wearing a balaclava mask. This time his face was fully exposed, and, expecting a formidable fighter, I was struck by his regular-guy appearance.

Avakov's adviser said 800 people had volunteered for the battalion a few weeks ago. But only 462 (including fewer than 20 women) had passed muster and been accepted into the unit. They were now being trained and would shortly return to the Donbas to fight pro-Russian militants. Avakov's adviser then turned to the soldiers, thanked them for their patriotism and sacrifice—all in Russian—and assured them that, once the "terrorists" were defeated, they would all have jobs in the reconstituted and reformed Ministry of Internal Affairs.

A commander shouted, "*Slava Ukraini!*" ("Glory to Ukraine!"), and the soldiers responded with a thunderous "*Heroyam slava!*" ("Glory to the heroes!"). These greetings were employed by the Ukrainian Insurgent Army, the anti-Soviet nationalist underground (largely confined to Ukraine's western provinces), during and after World War II. They were also widely used by the Euromaidan demonstrators during the protests that climaxed in February and have now become part of everyday discourse throughout the country.

We were encouraged to go and speak to the soldiers. I approached a unit of 20 to 30 men and talked to them for about 15 minutes. When I switched from Ukrainian to Russian, several assured me that they understood both languages. "We speak Ukrainian, too," said one of the soldiers. "Why doesn't the West do more to help Ukraine?" some of them asked. "Doesn't Europe understand that Putin is a threat to the world? Don't the Europeans care about Putin's assault on democracy in Ukraine?"

I told them that Europeans cared more about cheap energy from Russia. "But," I continued, "at least the Americans understand what your struggle represents." If that's so, several responded, why doesn't Washington provide them with real weapons? "We don't need American soldiers here," said one of them. "We can fight. We will fight. We need equipment. We need guns."

Another soldier, this time a Ukrainian speaker, continued, "Tell Obama we need M-4 and M-5 rifles."

As our group walked over grassy fields, I asked the soldier next to me where he was from. Fox, a pseudonym, was an ethnic Russian from the city of Mariupol on the Sea of Azov, liberated from rebel control earlier this month.

"Back in 1991," he told me in Russian, "independence just fell on us, and no one understood what it meant. It was only after Russia started a war against Ukraine that I realized that this is my country—that I love it. The same happened to the other guys."

Fox's wife and daughter are still in Mariupol. "You know," he said, "I raised my daughter as a Ukrainian. This is where you live, I told her, this is your home." He paused. "When she asked me one day just why it's dangerous for her to go outside in an embroidered Ukrainian blouse, I decided to join the battalion."

"So this is a national liberation struggle for you and the others?" I asked.

"*Da*," he replied. "We are all Ukrainian citizens, and this is our homeland. We're not fascists, as the Russians say. We are fighting for our homeland. We're Russians, Ukrainians, Greeks, Jews and many others."

It occurred to me that I was in the presence of something Ukraine had never had: a Ukrainian nation whose identity and allegiance were based not on ethnicity but on patriotism. A little later I saw a soldier in a skullcap leading Ukrainians and Russians in a training exercise.

"We all agreed on a dry law," Fox told me about his troops' exemplary discipline, "and everyone knows that drinking will be punished severely."

As we entered his tent, I saw more than a dozen soldiers lounging about on their cots, their Kalashnikovs at their sides. Fox introduced me as a professor from New York, but not one with two f's, jokingly alluding to Yanukovych's inability to spell "professor" correctly.

Fox then pointed to a soldier on his left: "This one is a Ukrainian Bandera" (a reference to the controversial leader of the interwar nationalist movement, Stepan Bandera). "And I'm a Russian Bandera, and that one is a Jewish Bandera." He explicitly used the term "*zhido-bandera*" in reference to his Jewish comrade, the preferred self-designation of the Jewish Ukrainian oligarch and Dnipropetrovsk Province governor, Igor Kolomoisky.

"We're not fascists," the Jewish Bandera said. "We fight fascism."

As we parted ways, Fox gave me a child's crayon drawing of their camp, with "*Heroyam slava!*" emblazoned along the top. Another soldier, who looked like a teenager, gave me a moving Russian-language poem about the vigilance of the Donbas Battalion. A third soldier—a Russian speaker—handed me a black-and-red Ukrainian nationalist flag with a caricature of Putin sporting black hair and a small square mustache, which read "Putler Kaput."

What does one say to volunteer soldiers who will soon be deployed to eastern Ukraine and could be killed in a few days? I was tongue-tied, moved and confused. But I was certain of one thing: Putin's mercenaries would stand no chance against people who are defending their families, their homes and their newfound country.

*

How Putin Compelled NATO to Help Ukraine, *Al Jazeera*, July 7, 2014

The North Atlantic Treaty Organization is back, thanks in large part to Russian President Vladimir Putin. His invasion and annexation of Crimea and his sustained aggression against eastern Ukraine have revived NATO, imbuing the bloc with the sense of mission it lost after the collapse of the Soviet Union and the end of the Cold War. Ukraine is the primary beneficiary of this revival. In effect, Putin, an inveterate NATO opponent, has walked into a strategic trap of his own making.

In 1947, when NATO was formed to provide collective defense for its members, the threat was clear: the Soviet Union. And the need for U.S. leadership was not in doubt either. World War II battered the Europeans, but the United States emerged from the fighting a global superpower. By 1992, however, the Soviet Union was no more. The Russian Federation formally succeeded the USSR, inheriting its United Nations Security Council seat and nuclear weapons, but Russia was still in the throes of a systemic breakdown that lasted more than a decade. As the threat from the Soviet Union disappeared, NATO's core mission also appeared less relevant. Why maintain the alliance if there is no enemy?

By the mid–1990s, Europe was no longer the impoverished place that emerged from the war. While the Soviet collapse made United States the world's sole superpower, the Europeans quickly acquired enough wealth and began questioning the necessity of U.S. leadership.

In the last two decades, NATO has searched for alternative missions, shifting its focus toward the fight against terrorism and deployments outside Europe. The realignment worked, but only up to a point, as Europe's participation in the wars in Afghanistan and Iraq proved desultory and spotty. The central problem was obvious: How Americans and Europeans defined threats differed. As a global economic and military power, the U.S. faced global threats. As a regional economic power, the European Union did not necessarily agree that its core interests were also at stake.

NATO essentially became an alliance without a purpose.

Russia's annexation of Crimea changed all that. By violating the post-war international order and unilaterally annexing foreign territory, Putin reconstituted Russia as a threat. By vowing to protect all Russians living abroad, Putin repositioned Moscow as a menace to Europe. Estonia and Latvia, both NATO members, have significant Russian populations, and Russia has enormous economic interests across Eastern and Western Europe.

Collective Defense

By supporting anti-Ukrainian militants in eastern Ukraine, Putin effectively arrogated the right to wage war in a Europe, where it had been considered unthinkable. Why, then, shouldn't he wage war against other members of NATO's Partnership for Peace, such as Moldova and Georgia? With Crimea's economic collapse and possible transformation into a major Russian military base, Moscow has signally affected the balance of power in the Black Sea region, potentially threatening NATO members Bulgaria, Romania, Turkey and Greece.

"Changing borders with military means is what alarms us," a highly-placed NATO official told me recently. "I think it's astounding to see people close their eyes and pretend the dinosaur doesn't exist."

With collective defense against a resurgent Russia once again its *raison d'être*, NATO is beginning to flex its muscles. NATO officials, including its Secretary-General Anders Fogh Rasmussen, have been vocal in supporting Ukraine and condemning Russia. At a recent briefing for a civilian expert group at NATO headquarters, one of NATO's leading Ukraine-Russia analysts dismissed a suggestion that both Russian and Ukrainian narratives be taken into account in developing policy toward eastern Ukraine. "[There are] no two competing narratives," the NATO analyst said. "The situation is black and white, and we shouldn't be afraid to say it."

NATO is developing mechanisms for helping Ukraine. A 20-person Crisis Action Team Ukraine has been set up to monitor the Russian intervention and provide daily analyses to key NATO policymakers. Several trust funds intended to bolster key aspects of Ukraine's security are in the process of being established. NATO's focus will be Ukraine's communications and information systems, cybersecurity, logistics and standardization, and the retraining and resettling of former soldiers. NATO expects still unspecified lead nations to provide the initial funding and hope to funnel some unspent money from the current budget into those funds.

NATO might also be considering more hands-on approaches to bolster Ukrainian security. One NATO official at the briefing with the group of civilian experts was tight-lipped about the specifics, repeatedly saying she "had nothing to say" about what NATO was doing. While still unclear, such measures may involve sending military advisers to Ukraine. During a visit to a camp near Kyiv where Ukraine's all-volunteer Donbas Battalion was stationed, soldiers told me that they received training from Bulgarians, Georgians and Israelis.

NATO's ace in the hole remains Putin. The only way to undo the enormous damage to his and Russia's reputations is to return Crimea to Ukraine—and that, obviously, will not happen anytime soon. He could help improve relations with the West by ending his support for the militants in eastern Ukraine, but that too would be difficult, as it means enabling Kyiv to reestablish control over territories he has labeled "New Russia." Given these realities, his rhetorical support of peace and negotiations appears hypocritical.

That is not all. Putin continues to meddle in the affairs of his non-Russian neighbors. As Lithuanian President Dalia Grybauskaite recently revealed, Russia proposed reducing the price of oil and gas for Estonia and Latvia if they left NATO. Putin's offer demonstrates a complete lack of understanding of Baltic sentiments toward Russia. The Balts would rather die than exchange the West for Moscow.

Last but not least, by engaging their country in war, Putin has imbued Ukrainians with a remarkable solidarity and unprecedented patriotism.

The greatest irony is that Putin is driving Ukrainians to embrace the West. A public opinion poll conducted from April 23 to 25 by the Razumkov Center in Kyiv showed that more than half of Ukrainians "favor steering Ukraine's foreign policy toward the European Union."

The survey also showed favorable sentiments about NATO. Traditionally, more than half of Ukrainians opposed joining NATO and only 10 to 15 percent supported membership. But in the latest poll, 36 percent were in favor of NATO membership (with 42 percent opposed).

Ukraine's membership in NATO is still many years away, but thanks to Putin, it's now on the table. Although he continually invokes NATO as a military threat to Russia, the fact is that NATO has no army, and its ability to deploy forces is wholly dependent on member nations' willingness to supply them. But NATO has political authority, and its voice does not go unheard. As a vast bureaucracy, NATO can act as a powerful pro-Ukrainian lobbyist within Europe's corridors of powers. Although NATO's anti-Russian stance is more outspoken than that of most European countries, it roughly coincides with the views of the United States. It helps—both NATO and Ukraine—to have the world's only superpower on your side.

PART THREE: RUSSIA'S WAR AGAINST UKRAINE

War Comes to Ukraine, *Foreign Affairs*, July 17, 2014

Yesterday afternoon, by most accounts, pro-Russian separatists shot down Malaysia Airlines flight 17 over eastern Ukraine. The attackers ostensibly thought that the Boeing 777 was a Ukrainian plane about to enter Russian airspace. Soon after the attack, Igor Girkin, the self-styled commander of the Donetsk People's Army, bragged on his website that "We just shot down an AN-26 plane near Torez; it's scattered somewhere around the Progress mine. We warned them not to fly in 'our sky'." Soon after, RIA Novosti, a Russian news agency, seconded Girkin's claim.

After it became apparent that the plane was not Ukrainian, Girkin erased his post and Aleksandr Borodai, the prime minister of the self-proclaimed Donetsk People's Republic, tried to put the blame for the attack, which killed 295, on Ukrainian authorities. Later in the day, Russian President Vladimir Putin stated that it was "unquestionable that the state over whose territory this took place is responsible for this terrible tragedy."

The atrocity comes three days after Russian militants shot down a Ukrainian transport plane fl ing over Krasnodon district in Luhansk Province and one day after a missile—which Ukrainian authorities believe was fired by Russia—brought down a Ukrainian SU-25 jet over Donetsk Province.

This week also saw a major escalation of Russian military involvement in Ukraine; in the early morning hours of Sunday, July 13, about 100 Russian armored personnel carriers and other vehicles crossed from Russia into Luhansk Province in Ukraine. Unlike earlier Russian deployments into Crimea and eastern Ukraine, these carriers were openly adorned with Russian insignia and flags. The flow of Russian tanks and soldiers into the area has since continued, and Ukrainian authorities estimate that up to 400 additional "little green men" (a term coined during the Crimea invasion for Russian troops without insignia) have infiltrated into eastern Ukraine's Donbas.

Until yesterday, that escalation had gone relatively unremarked in Western media. But now, no matter who fired the missile, things are set to change. The downing of a civilian plane may conceivably qualify as a war crime, since it entailed the unwarranted militarily destruction of a civilian target. At any rate, it was certainly an atrocity and an act of terrorism. And if Girkin—an ethnic Russian who hails from Russia and who, by some accounts, is still an officer in the Russian military intelligence service, which would make him officially subordinate to Russia's president—really was involved, Putin might arguably be politically responsible for the crime.

Politically and economically, that couldn't be worse news for Putin, who launched a charm offensive just last week at the World Cup in Rio de Janeiro. Putin, worried about the Ukrainian army's rapid advances on insurgent positions, met with German Chancellor Angela Merkel and convinced her to agree to negotiations with the insurgents. His efforts—presumably deemed insincere by Washington—collapsed on Wednesday when the Obama administration imposed new financial sanctions on several important Russian banking and energy institutions, including Gazprombank, Novatek (an independent natural gas producer), the Rosneft Oil Company, and the VEB Bank for Development and

Foreign Economic Affairs. Hours later, the Russian stock market took a nosedive and the ruble fell.

Putin might have managed to muddle along. Although most of the West has been deeply critical of Russia and its support for separatist groups in eastern Ukraine, European and American policymakers have been hesitant to impose the most severe sanctions and have seemed ready to move on to other foreign policy issues, such as Iraq and the war between Israel and Hamas. Even the Obama administration's recent round of sanctions was not as far-reaching as many critics of the president would have liked.

But the Malaysia Airlines crash will force both the United States and Europe to come to terms with unpleasant realities. First, Russia has effectively embarked on a war against Ukraine. Kyiv is no longer fighting homegrown insurgents and separatists; it is fighting Russian soldiers and Russian military equipment under Russian military command. War, unthinkable in Europe for so long, has truly come to the continent. Second, Russia also apparently believes that Donbas, the region over which the Malaysian flight was travelling, is Russian territory and that terror is a perfectly justified means for keeping control of it. As a new Amnesty International report has made clear, Russian forces have systematically engaged in human rights abuses against civilians in the eastern Ukrainian regions they rule.

In a word, even before yesterday, Donbas was well on its way to becoming Ukraine's Bosnia—with Putin playing the part of Serbian leader Slobodan Milosevic, Russia playing the part of Serbia, and Putin's Donbas supporters playing the part of Bosnian Serb irregulars. Once Bosnia became a killing field, Europe and the United States could no longer turn a blind eye. NATO forces intervened in September 1995 with Operation Deliberate Force; two months later, the war ended with the signing of the Dayton Peace Agreement.

A direct Western military intervention in Ukraine remains unlikely. But other military assistance has now become possible for the simple reason that, if it did down the plane, Russia has already crossed the very red line that Washington had feared a more robust response in Ukraine would lead it to transgress. The United States, for its part, has ample military equipment in Iraq and Afghanistan, which could easily be diverted to Ukraine.

This week's tragedy could remove any last shred of hope that Putin could be a valuable interlocutor in the Ukraine crisis. It is not impossible that he will realize that continued war with Ukraine is a lose-lose proposition and decide to use the crash as an opportunity to reinvent himself as a peacemaker who can pressure the separatists in Ukraine, hammer out some deal with Ukrainian President Petro Poroshenko, and declare victory. That doesn't seem likely. But if he doesn't, Russia's cold war with the West could warm up considerably.

*

PART THREE: RUSSIA'S WAR AGAINST UKRAINE

'Strike Him with an Axe', *Foreign Policy*, July 18, 2014

With each passing hour it looks increasingly likely that pro-Putin militants are responsible for shooting down the Malaysian airliner over eastern Ukraine. (President Obama said today that the missile that destroyed the plane came from "territory controlled by the Russian separatists.") This really shouldn't come as a surprise. The pro-Russian fighters have already shown that they're utterly ruthless in their efforts to subvert the Ukrainian state.

A recently released report by Amnesty International charges the rebels with "savage beatings and other torture meted out against activists, protesters and journalists in eastern Ukraine over the last three months." Ukrainian officials accuse the separatists of using local civilians as "human shields" and of shelling apartment buildings. Pro-Russian militants have also firebombed vehicles as well as blown up bridges, mines, and refineries.

Such tactics are not random excesses. To the contrary, they are entirely premeditated—as one can see from a handbook for insurgents recently published by one of the leaders of the self-proclaimed Donetsk People's Republic, as the leading separatist group in eastern Ukraine refers to itself. Pavel Gubarev, the self-styled "governor" of Donetsk and the leader of the Novorossiya (New Russia) movement, recently posted the manual, entitled "Methodological Guide for Struggle Against the Junta," on his personal website. (The "junta" is the separatists' name for the Ukrainian government in Kyiv.) There is no reason to doubt the authenticity of the document.

Gubarev begins the manual by admonishing those who take up the fight against the government in Kyiv to maintain maximum operational security. He then outlines how to form a group, train, and obtain weapons and cash.

"Cops have always had a lot of informers, and you won't be able to just go and recruit volunteers," Gubarev warns, urging his followers to recruit no more than four supporters. "These should be people you know and believe or those who have bloody debts to the junta." He cautions would-be recruiters against ubiquitous "informers," and to remember that they themselves will be regarded as such by potential volunteers for the cause. "Winning people's confidence will not be easy."

The next step is to find money, transport, reliable communications, and weapons. Robbing banks is dangerous, says Gubarev, so smashing ATM machines is the way to go. Access to a large number of used cars and throwaway cell phones is also advisable. As for weapons, "the best way is to acquire them from criminal acquaintances." He bemoans the fact that "idealists well-disposed toward the partisan movement are not likely to have such acquaintances." And he warns that "there are many informers among the criminals, even at the top levels of the criminal hierarchy."

Attacking and disarming Ukrainian police forces is risky, he observes, as is buying weapons from Ukrainian soldiers. The most practical approach is to "rob weapons depots. This is also a risky and serious operation, but at least the chances of success are higher."

Of critical importance, according to Gubarev, is that all this be done under the strictest secrecy. "The stable forces of the regime are all around," he counsels. "Your group is in danger." So he offers a series of prescriptions, including use of pseudonyms, abstinence from alcohol, and the concealment of identifying marks, including tattoos: "Attract no attention to yourselves; wear gray." Home computers and personal cellphones should never be used for operational purposes. Identifying documents should never be carried. Details of military operations should never be discussed on phones or in front of family members. Identifying documents should never be carried. Details of military operations should never be discussed on phones or in front of family members. Gubarev also advises that fellow partisans should wear gloves to hide their fingerprints. "If time permits," he adds, "read books and watch films for tips about self-concealment. In the USSR and Eastern Europe in the 1940s–1960s these things were well illustrated in films."

Gubarev then recommends three primary forms of action: Liquidating individual enemy fighters, shooting at cars, and random acts of terror.

As for the first, these are, in essence, "simple killings." A rebel who happens to see one or two government soldiers leaving their base should shoot them, then "get in your car and run." One particularly effective way of killing soldiers is to target them as they're tending to their natural needs in the bushes: "Many people have been killed, captured, or robbed in this manner. You don't have to shoot the man; you can strike him with an axe, with almost no resistance on his part. But it's better not to use cold steel until you've killed a few men: it could be risky if you're not morally prepared for such an action and your hand hesitates."

Gubarev devotes a brief paragraph to the topic of "shooting at cars," by which he means, essentially, "ambushes" against enemy forces. Acts of terror, meanwhile, are of far greater interest to him. They should, he emphasizes, be directed against "bands of nationalists," "little Nazis," and sundry other civilian supporters of the Maidan uprising and the central government in Kyiv. "Use your car to approach these people quickly and suddenly, and open fire on them through the windows of your car. Crush those who try to hide and those who are wounded." Indeed, he advises, "shoot without hesitation, even minors and girls. They aren't dealing with you in the same manner only because they're stupid; remember that they wouldn't spare you." (This section of Gubarev's manifesto earned him a rebuke from United Nations human rights chief Navi Pillay. "Such blatant incitement to violence is utterly reprehensible and a clear violation of international human rights law," she said in a statement issued earlier this month.)

The actions touted by Gubarev have three goals. Fighters should "weaken the rear of the Ukrainian armed forces, the National Guard, and the paramilitary formations, all of which will help the fighters in the East." (Interestingly, elsewhere in the document he advises fellow rebels to abstain from attacking police or Interior Ministry troops, since these are "potential allies in the future"—perhaps alluding to groups such as the Berkut paramilitary police, who were accused of killing pro-democracy demonstrators during the uprising against former President Viktor Yanukovych.) Next, the rebels should conduct operations "aimed at destabilizing political conditions in the region." And finally, they should aim at "the physical destruction of the fighters of the junta and its leading personnel." In pursuing these goals, fighters are encouraged to engage in outright provocations: "Don't pass up any opportunity to engage in some atrocity that can be blamed on the junta's fighters."

Gubarev ends his manual with an upbeat epilogue. Fighting, he notes, has already broken out in cities such as Kharkiv, Dnipropetrovsk, and Odessa. "The process has begun. The former Ukraine is bankrupt. It won't survive for long: within a year, or possibly until the New Year, it definitely won't exist in its current boundaries."

Is compromise possible with the likes of Gubarev? Probably not. He detests Ukraine and Ukrainians, and his agenda consists of little more than terrorism. Can Russian President Vladimir Putin control him? That, too, is by no means clear: fanatics such as Gubarev are, by definition, uncontrollable.

If so, the Poroshenko government may have no choice but to attempt to crush Gubarev and his militant groups. The bad news, for Kyiv, is that Gubarev is implacable and is willing to die. The good news is that his manual clearly, if unintentionally, reveals that the militant groups are isolated, on the run, and in constant fear of exposure. His open admission that "[w]inning people's confidence will not be easy" hardly reflects deep popular support. As the document stresses, the terrorists cannot trust the local population, not even the local criminals who in the early days of the insurgency comprised a significant portion of the fighters. Nor can they rely on their own comrades to remain silent, if captured, for more than a "few hours."

Moreover, their worries about money, arms, transport, and communications are never-ending. Gubarev devotes a large part of the manual to the weary task of replenishing supplies after a terrorist act has been carried out—and have no easy solutions. Worst of all for Gubarev, the Ukrainian security forces appear to be strong, alert, and relatively immune to corruption: "Your chances are slight, and there's a high probability that the SBU [Ukrainian Security Service] or the cops will eliminate you."

It would be naïve to think that Putin does not know who his proxies in eastern Ukraine are or what sort of means they routinely employ against civilians and soldiers. While the airline shootdown is almost certainly the handiwork of the pro-Russian thugs in eastern Ukraine, ultimate responsibility for the atrocity must lie with Putin. While the airline shootdown is almost certainly the handiwork of the pro-Russian thugs in eastern Ukraine, ultimate responsibility for the atrocity must lie with Putin. After all, Russia has been providing the separatists with the very money, arms, transport, and communications they so desperately need. In the week before the shootdown, the Kremlin escalated its intervention in Ukraine to the point that "war" is the more accurate term for Russia's aggressive activities. Given such a context, it's hardly surprising that the rebels have declared war on everything Ukrainian—or on everything, such as the Malaysian plane, they thought was Ukrainian.

*

How Much Are Ukrainian and Malaysian Lives Worth? *World Affairs Journal*, July 18, 2014

When Vladimir Putin's proxies shot down a Malaysian Airlines jet with close to 300 passengers over eastern Ukraine on July 17th, I was shocked.

But I wasn't shocked on July 15th, when the former head of the Ukrainian General Staff stated that 330 Ukrainian soldiers had died in the course of Kyiv's anti-terrorist operation in eastern Ukraine, while the press liaison of the National Security and Defense Council said the correct number was 258. Both numbers were immediately wrong, as some 10 soldiers were killed that day.

The sad fact is that I'm getting used to Putin's killing spree.

I still remember when the first demonstrator was killed on the Maidan back in January. What a shock that was. And then the mass sniper shootings in late February. What an outrage. The victims came to be known as the Heavenly Hundred and memorials to them still dot the area around Kyiv's Independence Square.

Now, I read of another 5 or 10 or 15 soldiers being killed and I shrug. Is it 258 or 330? Do they have names? Did they ever have lives? Will they be remembered?

In the meantime, Putin's commandoes keep on killing. To what end?

The Russian militants in eastern Ukraine have lost the battle for the hearts and minds of the local population. The formerly pro-Russian populations that the Ukrainian army recently liberated have been genuinely relieved to be free of Russian rule. Unsurprisingly, Putin's standing in the Donbas, a region that traditionally had regarded him with admiration, has plummeted.

What can continued Russian escalation of the bloodshed accomplish? It can inflict harm on the Ukrainian army and volunteer forces—and only increase Ukrainian soldiers' resolve to fight. It can increase the physical destruction of the Donbas—and only further alienate civilians. It can encourage the militants to engage in more human rights abuses and atrocities—and thereby outrage the international community. It could even impel the morally desensitized Europeans to impose genuinely painful sanctions on Russia.

And just what does Russia gain from continued escalation? It could establish control over parts of the Russo-Ukrainian border and save its proxies from total defeat. That would permit Putin to save face with his cronies and a Russian population that's been whipped up to a hyper-nationalist frenzy. But this victory would at best be Pyrrhic. Would Russia annex the territories it devastated? Would it eventually retreat? Neither option qualifies as a strategic victory.

The fact is that Putin has maneuvered himself and Russia into a dead end.

Having seized Crimea and provided the insurgents in eastern Ukraine with personnel, advice, money, and arms, Putin has only succeeded in galvanizing Ukrainians—both

Ukrainian and Russian speakers—against himself and imbuing them with a sense of unity, purpose, and patriotism that had previously eluded them. Ukrainians know that their survival, as a country and as a nation, is on the line: they have no choice but to fight. At this point, nothing short of Kremlin-sponsored genocide and ethnic cleansing would end Ukrainian resistance.

Meanwhile, despite the growing numbers of Ukrainian deaths, France insists that it will go ahead with the sale to Russia of two Mistral-class assault ships. No matter that Russia has invaded Ukraine. No matter that war—remember: it used to be "unthinkable" in Europe—has come to Europe. No matter that Europeans are dying every day. The sale must go on. After all, 1,000 jobs are at stake.

If you figure that, thus far, about 100 Ukrainians lost their lives on the Maidan and another 100 civilians and 275 Ukrainian soldiers have been killed in the war with Russia, then, all told, about 500 Ukrainians have died for "*liberté, égalité, fraternité.*" Which translates into one Ukrainian life for two French jobs—or exactly 166.66 lives per inspiring word. At the rate things are going, one Ukrainian life will soon be worth far less than one French job. In a year or two, it might even go for the price of a *steak frites* on the Boul' Mich. The good news is that, unless Putin's proxies shoot down more Malaysian airliners, the value of one Malaysian life will remain constant at 3.33 French jobs.

Putin recently called Nazi propaganda chief Joseph Goebbels a "talented person" who was "achieving his goals."

So, evidently, is Putin.

So who's next? Estonia, Latvia, or Delta?

*

Putin Is Transforming Mother Russia into a Rogue State, *Al Jazeera*, July 25, 2014

It is now almost certain that pro-Russian separatists in eastern Ukraine shot down Malaysia Airlines Flight 17 using a Russian-made missile. As some of the initial shock begins to wear off, it may be worth it to step back and consider what the incident means for Russia's place within the international system.

Let's start with what is not unusual about this incident. First, the practice of loosely organized nonstate actors—terrorists, guerrillas, revolutionaries, militants and other irregular fighters—harming civilians is not new. The 9/11 attacks against the United States forever altered international relations. There have also been exceptionally deadly terrorist attacks in scores of other countries, including Russia, Israel, India, Pakistan, Turkey, Spain, England and the Philippines.

Second, these rogue actors have always received refuge and material support such as supplies, money and armaments from states looking to use proxies to subvert their adversaries. The Cold War is replete with examples of both the Soviet Union and the United States supporting foreign guerrillas to fight their respective ideological battles. Communist East Germany supported the terrorist Red Army Faction in West Germany in the 1970s and 1980s. From 1979 to the early 1990s, the U.S. supported the contras to fight the Sandinista regime in Nicaragua. Iran currently supports Hezbollah against Israel, while Israel, the U.S. and Turkey have all been accused of arming rebels to fight Bashar al-Assad's regime in Syria.

The main difference in the tragic MH17 incident is that a state—Russia—provided extremely powerful surface-to-air missiles to its terrorist proxies in another state. By doing so, Russia violated informal norms among states on permissible forms of subversion. Such actions threaten to upend the entire international security system.

The rationale for supporting irregular fighters is typically to annoy, destabilize and subvert neighboring states. A sponsoring state keeps the rival population on edge, diverts its government's attention away from local reforms, drains the country's resources and foments internal discontent to engineer a regime change through an internal coup or popular rebellion. However, such outside attempts at subversion often backfire—strengthening the government by stoking national unity. For example, the U.S. support of the Bay of Pigs invasion in 1961 only helped consolidate Fidel Castro's fragile regime in Cuba. But the mixed success rate of outside subversion has not deterred states from pursuing such a strategy.

'Rational Sponsors'

Until now, states have not provided subversive proxies with advanced armaments. Although all states fear that terrorists could acquire nuclear, chemical or biological weapons, established states—even those considered rogue by the international community—have avoided supplying terrorists with such weapons. President George W. Bush accused Iraq's Saddam Hussein of this transgression, but his accusations later proved unfounded.

States usually avoid such behavior for two reasons. First, the sponsoring states fear getting embroiled in international and regional instability once their proxies acquire the means to destabilize and destroy entire populations or states. Weakening adversaries may be a desirable end, but your proxies going out of control, destroying adversaries and creating chaos in the process are not. Second, there is no guarantee that proxies would spare their sponsors in the future when interests diverge or that they won't sell the weapons to forces fighting their sponsors. After all, terrorists are fickle allies. The U.S. certainly learned both lessons in Afghanistan and Iraq, even though the armaments it supplied to Iraqi and Afghan insurgents were far short of high-tech weapons.

Rational state sponsors of terrorism have historically avoided violating this logic. In other words, states want subversives to cause trouble in neighboring states, but they do not want those proxies to gain the capacity to eventually threaten their sponsors. States that are guided by relentless pursuit of national interests would be as opposed to such weapons

294

proliferation as those that are guided by devotion to international norms.

Moscow defied this logic by supplying missiles that could shoot down airliners fl ing at 33,000 feet to pro-Russian terrorists in eastern Ukraine. Russia's irresponsible behavior may now encourage terrorist groups around the world, signaling that Moscow is open for business. Terrorists could now approach Russia with shopping lists for advanced weaponry, including the radar-guided SA-11 or Buk missile, which was apparently used to down the MH17 airliner.

Once the ongoing international investigation is completed, states and institutions such as the United Nations will likely react with outrage to Russia's transgression of accepted behavior. Ukraine and the U.S. have already accused Russia of complicity in the crime. In order to minimize future irresponsible transfers of destructive weapons to nonstate actors, the international community will likely target Russia by strengthening control over Russian weapons production, increase espionage against terrorist groups and their connections to Russia and pay especially close attention to Russian intelligence agencies.

In the longer run, the sheer scale of the human tragedy caused by Moscow's reckless actions, as well as international efforts to curb future transfers of such weapons to terrorists, will move Russia further away from the international community into rogue state territory.

Putin has already pushed Russia far in that direction. Under his rule, Russia engaged in wanton destruction of civilians during its war against Chechen and other militants in the northern Caucasus region, dismembered Georgia in 2008, invaded Crimea and eastern Ukraine in 2014, and aided and abetted terrorists in the destruction of a civilian airliner. The downing of Flight MH17 may even qualify as a crime against humanity or a war crime, precisely because it took place within the context of a massive Russian escalation of the terrorist war against Ukraine. Significantly, on July 22, the Red Cross made a confidential legal assessment that Ukraine was officially in a war, opening the door to prosecutions for war crimes, such as, possibly, for the destruction of Flight MH17. Whatever the exact designation, Putin, who hosted the Sochi Olympics to world acclaim only a few months ago, has been transformed into a rogue leader who could, if he refuses to change his ways, even morph into an international outlaw. A similar process is transforming his country from Mother Russia into the Wicked Witch of the East.

Under such conditions, more states will likely reduce their political and economic engagements with Russia and its leaders. If that happens, Russia's economy will atrophy and the regime will resort to more repression to cling to power. In the longer term, such a scenario could facilitate Putin's downfall through either a popular rebellion or an internal coup led by disgruntled elements of the elite.

Putin thumbed his nose at the world and got away with it in Crimea. In denying any responsibility for the downing of MH17, he is thumbing his nose again. This time he may not get away with it.

Loose Cannons and Ukrainian Casualties, *World Affairs Journal*, August 27, 2014

So now the number of dead Ukrainian soldiers is 722. The number of wounded is 2,625. The Ukrainian army keeps on making slow but steady advances; the pro-Russian terrorists appear to have suffered heavy losses; Russian regular forces are openly engaged in the fighting; Russia's "humanitarian convoy" apparently looted some Ukrainian armaments factories on its way back home; and, on August 25th, Russian tanks crossed into Ukraine just north of the Sea of Azov.

All is definitely not quiet on the eastern front.

German Chancellor Angela Merkel visited Kyiv on August 23rd, where she expressed support of Ukraine. Some Ukrainians were unhappy that her support wasn't stronger, but they should remember that her very presence in Ukraine on the eve of its Independence Day celebrations was a powerful message to Russia's unconstitutionally elected president, Vladimir Putin.

Whether or not Putin chooses to heed that message is another matter. If he's smart, he will. No country can take on the whole world. The United States, when it was still a "hyper-power," tried, and you know how that ended. A "Belgium with the bomb" and lots of gas to sell is acting stupidly if it thinks it can get away with playing the world's bully.

Putin, unfortunately, looks more and more like a loose cannon, an irrational leader who responds to his own internal demons and not to anything resembling logic or national interest. Significantly, when a German interviewer **asked** Merkel to explain just "what Putin wants," she couldn't answer, providing instead an elaborate argument for the need for a political solution.

Take that "humanitarian convoy." Just what did it prove? That Russia can intervene in Ukraine? But it's been doing that for two months, and everyone knows it. That Russia is humanitarian? But if it is, why all the subterfuge? That Russia is tough? But if it is, then why all the humanitarian rigmarole? The one thing the convoy didn't prove is that Russia is reliable. Instead, the whole convoy business made Russia and Putin look like conniving SOBs.

The Russian terrorists in Ukraine look more and more like Putin, too. On Sunday, August 24th, they marched a column of Ukrainian prisoners down the main street in Donetsk. **The amateur video I saw** (subsequently "removed by the user") showed a crowd of several hundred or several thousand people avidly jeering. "On your knees!" was one constant refrain. Well, marching the soldiers through this "corridor of shame," as the terrorists call it, was bad enough (Human Rights Watch suggested it was a violation of the Geneva Convention), but heck, they're showing off their booty. They're trying to project strength. That's quasi-understandable.

What was unforgivable—and terrifying—was what happened after the column passed. Several sanitation trucks followed in their wake, spraying water on the street. The loudspeaker announced that they were cleaning up after "the filth." The crowd cheered. Obviously, it occurred to no one that the terrorists had adopted Nazi practices, having transformed the captured Ukrainians into "dirty Jews." Nor did it occur to the terrorists or their admirers in Donetsk that they had just engaged in a weird inversion: the Nazis had the dirty Jews clean the sidewalks; the terrorists in eastern Ukraine cleaned the streets after the dirty Ukrainians had passed.

So what does Putin want? No one knows. How do you negotiate with someone who won't tell you what he wants and keeps on acting as if he wants to destroy you? Merkel is right to want a political solution to the war. But politics, as she practices it, is about give-and-take, while politics, as Putin practices it, is about domination. For Merkel, other Western leaders, as well as President Poroshenko of Ukraine, politics is a positive-sum game, in which all can be winners. For Putin, it's a zero-sum game, in which there can only be one winner: him. Worse, it's not even clear what Putin sees as victory.

All we really know is that Putin and his forces are doing two things: killing Ukrainians, both armed and unarmed, both ethnic Ukrainians and ethnic Russians, and destroying the infrastructure and economy of the Donbas— not as collateral damage, but intentionally. Since his original goal—stated way back in late February, remember?—was to protect Russian speakers in Ukraine, all one can say is that Putin's got a strange way of showing his love.

Speaking of Ukrainian deaths, I must mention one soldier in particular: the Ukrainian-American Mark Paslawsky. The 55-year-old West Point graduate and former investment banker had joined the volunteer Donbas Battalion and been killed on August 19th in a battle near Donetsk. I mention Paslawsky for two reasons.

I actually met him in mid-June when I had the privilege of visiting the camp outside Kyiv where the Donbas Battalion was in training. None of the soldiers introduced themselves with their real names, so I had no idea who he was. We spoke briefly, and I asked him how he came to speak such excellent English. He said he was Ukrainian, but had lived in New Jersey for many years. In a subsequent column, I noted that I felt odd talking to soldiers who might soon be dead: "What does one say to volunteer soldiers who will soon be deployed to eastern Ukraine and could be killed in a few days? I was tongue-tied, moved, and confused." I meant that in the abstract. I never imagined that the genial, gray-haired man with the loping stride would be one of them.

The second reason I mention Paslawsky is that he was, after all, a Ukrainian American. In killing him—and make no mistake about it: Putin killed him—Putin has taken on, in addition to the entire world, the Ukrainian American diaspora. He probably thinks it's a joke. But in killing a Ukrainian American, he's made the war in Ukraine personal for Ukrainian Americans. Their intellectual, material, and political resources are far greater than Putin can imagine. Be forewarned, Vlad: diasporas have long memories. And this one will give you and your apologists in Russia and the West no rest.

*

Putin's Trap, *Foreign Affairs*, September 1, 2014

By now, most observers of the ongoing conflict between Russia and Ukraine assume that Russian President Vladimir Putin aims to annex the Donbas region of Ukraine and, possibly, other parts of the country's southeast, which his regime has taken to calling "New Russia." But that leaves open two questions: First, why didn't Putin invade Ukraine immediately after he seized Crimea in early March; and second, why, if he intends to hold the Donbas, would he allow his proxies to shell cities, kill civilians, and destroy mines, plants, schools, and other infrastructure?

In a recent interview with Marat Gelman, a political commentator for the liberal Russian publication *Novoye Vremya,* Vladimir Lukin, a veteran policymaker who served as Putin's human rights commissioner from February 2004 to March 2014 and who represented Russia in the West's negotiations with Ukrainian President Viktor Yanukovych and the democratic opposition on February 20, offered some answers.

According to Lukin, the Donbas isn't the goal at all: "No one in the Kremlin needs the Donetsk People's Republic, the Luhansk People's Republic [the self-styled secessionist entities in the Donbas], or New Russia," he said. Indeed, "to win the Donbas and to lose Ukraine would be a defeat for the Kremlin." When pressed further about the purpose of the Kremlin's agitation in the region, Lukin responded that one should "forget the Donetsk and Luhansk People's Republics. The goal is to demonstrate to [Ukrainian President Petro] Poroshenko that he cannot win." Russia, he said, would "introduce as many [troops] as necessary to persuade Poroshenko that he must negotiate with whomever Putin chooses." In his commentary about the interview, Gelman went on to explain that, according to Lukin, both Donetsk and Luhansk will serve "as guarantees of [Ukraine's] nonmembership in NATO." After all, "any referendum on joining any bloc would have to take place in every region, and if only one were against, then the country could not join." The Kremlin's ideal outcome, according to Lukin, is that "everything should go back to as it was under Yanukovych, but without Yanukovych."

When asked how long the violence would continue, Lukin explained, "We're in no hurry. [Poroshenko] is the one who needs to hurry. Or else the girl with the braid"—former Prime Minister Yulia Tymoshenko—"will eat him up. Poroshenko's chair is on fire beneath his butt, not ours." But people do not need to continue to die. "It was because of the false certainty of the Ukrainians that they could win that they proceeded so actively with the Anti-Terrorist Operation," Lukin explained. Now, "everyone sees they cannot win" and so "the most militarily active stage has passed."

Lukin's statements make some sense. First, they provide an answer to the question of why Putin didn't seize the opportunity to invade Ukraine earlier in the conflict. The Ukrainian government and army were completely disorganized after the Maidan revolution, and a quick strike could have won Putin Kyiv. If Lukin is right, an invasion may never have been in the cards. Instead, Putin may have placed his hopes on the secessionist movements that formed the Donetsk and Luhansk People's Republics as a way to get him what he wanted at lower cost. When those failed to win a decisive victory and to prevent a Ukrainian rollback, Putin intervened. In the last few days, he seems to have halted and partially reversed the Ukrainian advance.

Second, Lukin's talking points explain the mass destruction. As a result of separatist rule and the ensuing war, several thousand civilians have been killed and wounded, and hundreds of thousands have fled their homes. In addition, industrial production in Donetsk Province has fallen by 29 percent. In Luhansk, it has crashed by 56 percent. Taken together, both provinces have experienced a 46 percent decline in light industry, a 41 percent drop in the chemical industry, a 34 percent crash in machine building, a 22 percent fall in construction materials, a 19 percent decrease in pharmaceutical production, a 13 percent loss in metallurgy, and a 13 percent drop in the coal industry.

If the proxies' goal was to "liberate" the Donbas and its Russian residents, then why destroy the territory and make life impossible for the residents? But if, as Lukin suggests, the goal was to ensure that the Donbas remains within Ukraine to thwart integration with NATO and to provide Russia with leverage over Kyiv, then maximal devastation would go a long way toward promoting Russia's political goals. A devastated region would be an economic drain on Kyiv's scarce resources and a source of never-ending political instability. It would also invite continued Russian offers of humanitarian aid, particularly for the region's reconstruction, which would enable the Kremlin to continue influencing politics in Ukraine without having to try to swallow the whole country.

Seen in this light, defeating the pro-Russian rebels and the Russian regular forces (estimated to number between 5,000 and 15,000) could be impossible, and accommodating them would be counterproductive. Even if Ukraine liberated the region, as it promises, it will be saddled with a devastated, unstable, and permanently insecure rust belt that will continue to do what it has done since independence in 1991: serve as a channel for Russian influence on Ukraine's internal affairs and a home to political forces—whether among the separatists or among Yanukovych's formerly dominant Party of Regions—that oppose reform and integration with the West.

If that is the case, then Kyiv's best way out of Putin's trap may be to withdraw from the Donbas territories controlled by Russian troops and separatists. The goal would be to turn them not into autonomous federal units within a weak Ukraine, as Putin desires, but into an independent entity, as he pointedly does not. Having turned the tables on Putin, Kyiv could then request Western assistance for enhancing its military's defensive capacities, including building fortifications along its new frontier with Russia and the rump Donbas. Russia and its proxies would then have to clean up the mess they made in the Donbas, Ukraine would be free to pursue integration with the West and the world, and the United States and Europe could breathe a little easier, knowing that the bloodshed had come to an end.

Of course, all this assumes that Lukin really does know Putin's mind and was honest in his exchange with Gelman. There is evidence to support both assumptions. On August 31, Putin called on Kyiv to begin "substantive, content-filled negotiations about the ... political organization of society and the state in southeastern Ukraine," suggesting that the goal of the recent Russian invasion of eastern Ukraine was to lure Kyiv into agreeing to some form of federalization for the Donbas. But even if Lukin's account was inaccurate, Kyiv would still have to realistically assess its chances of retaking those parts of the Donbas controlled by Russia—and of trying to rule those territories afterward. If it decides that its chances of success are small and declining, and that the territories would be impossible to manage, formally abandoning the Donbas and attempting to rebuild a Western country may permit Ukraine to snatch victory from the jaws of defeat. By the same token, saddling Putin with two economic sinkholes—Crimea and the Donbas—could only hasten his regime's decline.

Understandably, Ukrainians—and especially their ambitious political leaders and courageous volunteer battalions—will be unwilling to accept such a solution, arguing that soldiers' and civilians' lives weren't sacrificed for the satisfaction of Putin's imperial designs and that calls to withdraw from the Donbas enclave controlled by Russia are tantamount to treason. Morally, they will be right. And Putin, no doubt, is banking on such morally uncompromising views to influence Ukrainian policy as well. Considering the alternatives, however, Ukrainians might be wise to refuse to play the game on his terms and focus only on what is best for them and their country. If they come to believe that the choice is between constant war, a return to things as they were "under Yanukovych, but without Yanukovych," or genuine independence within manageable frontiers, they may decide that abandoning an ungovernable stretch that was always Ukraine's odd man out would be a stunning example of Ukraine's commitment to real sovereignty.

And who knows? When Putin eventually exits the political stage and Russia tires of Putinism's misdeeds, the Donbas and perhaps even Crimea may come knocking on Ukraine's door. If they do, Ukraine could readmit them on its own terms, not on the Kremlin's.

*

West's Refusal to Arm Ukraine Invites Guerrilla War, *World Affairs Journal*, September 8, 2014

If Russia launches a full-scale invasion and Ukraine is unable to defend itself with its armed forces, the result will be a "people's war" entailing enormous casualties and millions of refugees. Ukrainians, like the citizens of other countries on Russia's borders, know that Vladimir Putin is an existential threat to their survival as a people. They also know they have no choice but to respond to continued Russian aggression with mass popular resistance.

Such a war—involving a partisan movement with widespread civilian participation—will be extremely costly. Hundreds of thousands of Ukrainians will die; streams of refugees will head west. In addition, Putin will have learned that he can have his way with the United States and Europe. Aggressors everywhere will have been emboldened.

If, however, Ukraine's military has the military equipment needed to deter a Russian invasion, people's war will not take place, a humanitarian catastrophe will be prevented, Europe will not be inundated with refugees, and the international order might not be toppled.

There are six arguments against the West's arming Ukraine, and none of them is persuasive.

1. Arming Ukraine will provoke Russia to escalate. The argument is moot, and wrong, as Russia has been steadily escalating since March, despite the fact that Ukraine has received no armaments from the West.

2. Arming Ukraine will lead to war. This argument is also moot, and equally wrong, as Russia launched a war in late August (if not earlier), despite the fact that Ukraine has received no armaments from the West.

3. Arming Ukraine will lead to an arms race with Russia that the West will lose. This is the intellectually strongest argument and deserves extended and detailed attention to its flaws. The thinking behind this argument, beloved of "realist" academics and policymakers, goes as follows. Russia has a larger stake in Ukraine than the West; as a result, Russia will always be willing to up the ante, and any armaments supplied by the West will always be matched or exceeded by Russia. As a result, escalation will occur and the likelihood of war will increase. No less important, at some point, the West will lose its appetite for escalation and give in without having achieved anything other than an escalation of the conflict.

For starters, note that the part of the argument claiming that Western armament supplies will lead to an escalation of the conflict and war is moot and wrong, for the reasons mentioned above.

More important, this argument has two fatal flaws.

First, it assumes that Western and Russian appetites for providing arms are constant. It is true that the West might lose its appetite for arming Ukraine if it believes that Russia's aggression against Ukraine is a local affair. But it is also true that the West might not lose its appetite for arming Ukraine if it believes that Russia's aggression against Ukraine is a European affair. In the late 1930s, the European democracies initially had no appetite for countering Hitler's aggression in Austria and Czechoslovakia. After the invasion of Poland, however, the democracies discovered that appetite and went to war against Germany. There is, in sum, no a priori guarantee that appetites—whether Western or, for that matter, Russian—will remain constant. There is, thus, also no reason to think that Russia will always outbid the West. One can easily imagine perfectly realistic circumstances—an economic collapse, a popular uprising in Moscow, the death of Putin—that would undermine this assumption.

Second, this argument misunderstands just what the point of Western armament supplies to Ukraine is. It is not to match the military capacity of Russia or to provide Ukraine with military superiority. If it were, the argument might be right to suggest that the West will always be outmatched by Russians determined not to face an existential threat from

Ukraine. (Or, as I argued above, the argument might be wrong…) The real point of arming Ukraine is to make it capable of defending itself: of enabling it to deter a Russian attack or to make Russia pay a high price for any attack. If so, even a small amount of defensive armaments can enhance Ukraine's defensive capacity—even if Russia ups the ante in response.

Here's an example. Imagine that Country U has no anti-tank weapons and that Country R has 10 tanks. R can easily overrun U. Now imagine that U receives 10 anti-tank missiles from abroad, W, and that R increases its number of tanks to 20. R can still overrun U, but it will lose 10 tanks in the process. Will R be willing to accept such a loss? Maybe yes, maybe no. Assume now that R ups the ante to 50 tanks and that the weapons supplier W provides U with only 10 more anti-tank missiles. U remains outgunned (50 tanks to 20 anti-tank missiles) and would lose any encounter. But will R be willing to lose 20 tanks? Maybe yes, maybe no. Uncertainty enters the picture, and as R calculates its risks, it may decide that 10 or 20 tank losses are too many. Uncertainty thereby translates into a slightly enhanced Ukrainian ability to deter a Russian attack.

4. *Arming Ukraine will make things worse for Ukraine.* As my critique of arguments 1 and 2 showed, things have gotten worse for Ukraine in the absence of any armaments from outside. As my critique of argument 3 showed, things can only can better—even if only marginally—if it has an enhanced ability to deter aggression.

5. *Arming Ukraine will drag the West into a war with Russia.* This danger exists if and only if the West loses all sense of reality and decides to match all Russian armaments buildups with its own, up to and including Western troops. Rational Western leaders committed only to enhancing Ukraine's defensive capacity will presumably not be that irrational. Western caution about providing Ukraine with armaments suggest that Western leaders are anything but reckless.

6. *Arming Ukraine would create the impression that the Russo-Ukrainian conflict can be solved militarily.* German Chancellor Angela Merkel just made this argument, but it is wrong precisely because it assumes that the West will engage Russia in an endless spiral of armaments deliveries. If, alternatively, the West is committed only to enhancing Ukraine's defensive capacity in the manner described in my critique of argument 3, it would in fact be creating the impression that the conflict *cannot* be solved militarily.

The choice is the West's: either provide Ukraine with the capacity to defend itself against Russian aggression or start building refugee camps and preparing expressions of outrage at Putin's genocide against Ukrainians.

*

Ukraine to Wall Out Putin, Literally, *World Affairs Journal*, September 15, 2014

Ukrainian President Petro Poroshenko announced on September 10th that he intends to build an extensive set of fortifications along Ukraine's frontier with Russia and the Russian-occupied enclave of the Donbas. Called "The Wall," the defensive line would consist of a ditch, a "no-man's land," an actual wall, and watch towers.

Although the name brings to mind the Berlin Wall, Poroshenko actually compared Ukraine's planned fortifications to the Mannerheim Line, the Finnish defense against the Soviet Union, clearly suggesting that he sees today's Ukraine as interwar Finland and Putin's Russia as Stalin's USSR. That reference alone underscores just how profoundly Putin's aggression against Ukraine has changed Ukrainian attitudes to Russia. The formerly big and intrusive strategic partner has become a mortal enemy akin to the Soviet empire under its genocidal dictator, Stalin.

More important than the symbolism is the fact that The Wall is an excellent idea with significant implications. It's high time for Ukraine to do the only sensible thing it can do vis-à-vis its far stronger, imperialist neighbor: switch from offense to defense and build up a defensive capacity that would deter Putin even in his wildest dreams from embarking on a further aggression. It's important to realize that Ukraine will never be stronger than Russia militarily. Calls for wars of liberation of Crimea, or the Donbas enclave occupied by Putin and his proxies, are just demagogy.

That being the case, a Ukrainian withdrawal to strategically defensible positions is in order. Thereafter, those positions must be made sufficiently strong to prevent any Russian leader from expanding westward into Ukraine. "Sufficiently strong" means that the costs in terms of Russian soldiers' lives would be high enough for Putin or his successor to think twice about an invasion. Were Putin determined to throw the entire Russian army against Ukraine and send tens of thousands of Russian soldiers to their deaths, no Mannerheim Line could stop him. The underlying logic behind any defensive line is thus that all leaders, even those that seem irrational, have some sense of the costs of Pyrrhic victories.

A ditch, a no-man's-land, a wall, and watch towers may keep out small numbers of aggressors, but deterring a massive land attack by tanks, aircraft, and infantry will obviously require that Ukraine supplement the line with the requisite armaments. It's clear that, among other things, armaments will need to include anti-tank missiles and limited-range surface-to-air missiles. Neither weapon could be construed by Russia as being offensive; both would inflict enormous damage on attacking Russian tanks and planes. Poroshenko would be well advised to collect a group of Western defense experts to advise Ukraine on just which armaments it does and does not need to fortify The Wall. And the sooner, the better.

The Wall has important political implications. By cutting itself off from Russia and the Donbas enclave controlled by Putin and his proxies, Ukraine will effectively be freezing the conflict and declaring that the enclave is Russia's responsibility. Naturally, the Kyiv government will insist otherwise. But don't be fooled by declarations of implacable determination to win back lost territory. A wall will keep the Russians out of Ukraine, but it will also keep Ukraine out of the Donbas enclave.

A frozen conflict will be to Ukraine's benefit. The enclave, which is where much of the region's population and industry were concentrated, is in ruins. Hundreds of thousands of middle-class professionals have fled and will not return. Industry is shrinking. Infrastructure has collapsed. All these negative tendencies will accelerate, as Putin's terrorist proxies, remnants of the (formerly ruling) Party of Regions and the Communist Party, the Kremlin, the Donbas oligarch Rinat Akhmetov, and the Russian Orthodox Church duke it out over influence. In a word, the Donbas enclave is finished, and, as deindustrialization continues, depopulation will proceed apace. Whoever inherits the mess caused by Putin and his proxies will have a ball and chain on his leg. Fortunately for Ukraine, it doesn't—and in all likelihood will not anytime soon—control the enclave. Rightly or wrongly, justly or unjustly, legally or illegally, the burden of control, and the burden of governance, will fall on Putin. Bully for him. The day is not far off when the economic disaster that is Crimea and the Donbas will burden Putin, and he will be hard-pressed to claim that his imperialism has served Russia well.

So, sure, let Kyiv proclaim that it will never ever give up its sovereign territories. But then let Kyiv build The Wall, beef up its defenses, and get down to the business of fixing the country. Kyiv has time on its side. As I've frequently suggested, Putin's fascist regime is doomed. Let it choke on the Donbas and Crimea. Let it degenerate into an exclusively repressive regime. Let its economy decay thanks to Western sanctions. And let it remain isolated from the rest of the world and Ukraine. And then, when Russians reestablish a democracy, as one day they surely will, The Wall can come down.

*

Enthusiasm for Separation and Reform Weakens in Ukraine, *World Affairs Journal*, October 3, 2014

Three recent news items deserve our attention.

First the good news. According to the Russia-based Sociological Service of the Anti-Corruption Fund, the overwhelming majority of residents of Odessa and Kharkiv provinces support Ukrainian statehood and oppose Vladimir Putin's New Russia (Novorossiya) project. A telephone survey of 1,000 people conducted on September 8th to 17th revealed the following attitudes:

- 87 percent stated they want "their region to remain a part of Ukraine," as opposed to 3 percent who opted for membership in Russia and 2 percent who preferred New Russia.

- 34 percent want "Ukraine's future" to be "tied to Europe," 17 percent want it to be tied to Russia, and 17 percent wanted Ukraine to be "independent."

- 43 percent said they didn't understand, accept, or want to comment on the term "Novorossiya"; 14 percent said it was "bad"; 9 percent called it "nonsense" or a "figment"; 2 percent said it was "criminal" or "illegal"; and 13 percent identified it as a term for those regions that want to join the Russian Federation.

- 50 percent have a negative attitude toward Putin; 12 percent have a positive attitude; those who tend to the positive and those who tend to the negative are both at 6 percent.

In a word, the Novorossiya project is dead in Ukraine, and Odessa and Kharkiv are firmly in the Ukrainian camp.

Now for the not-so-good news. As the *Ukrainian Weekly*'s Kyiv correspondent, Zenon Zawada, points out in an e-mail distributed to his friends and colleagues, the current self-styled "kamikaze" government of Ukrainian Prime Minister Arsenii Yatseniuk hasn't pushed through any reforms. Zawada poses several disturbing questions to Yatseniuk that both he and Ukrainian President Petro Poroshenko need to answer:

1. Why aren't any constitutional reforms in the pipeline, as part of the Feb. 21 agreement to resolve the political crisis in Ukraine? (They were supposed to be *completed* by September.)

2. Why isn't there a new election law, as agreed to in the Feb. 21 agreement and as promised by President Poroshenko?

3. Why hasn't the investigation on the Euromaidan crimes been completed? ... Why haven't there been any criminal convictions of the Euromaidan's persecutors?

4. Why is the National Guard being commanded by Stepan Poltorak, the head of the Kharkiv police academy who dispatched internal army soldiers to disperse the Euromaidan?

5. Why do Russian banks continue to operate in Ukraine, financing the separatist groups?

6. Why did you claim a special fund will be created and supported by oligarchs and international donors to finance the Donbas self-governance zones if the Sept. 16 legislation create[d] a line-item from the state budget?

7. If the war continues for months or years, will you keep blaming it for the lack of reforms?

8. Why haven't you begun any structural reforms at all, such as cutting unnecessary taxes (which you've been promising to do for the last several months) or restructuring and eliminating corrupt schemes from [the state energy

firm] Naftogaz (rather than continuing to pour money into it with state-issued debt)?

War does excuse the Yatseniuk government of some of its initial reform inertia, but—when you consider that structural economic reform is the precondition of Ukraine's ability to wage war and thus to survive—war cannot excuse it all. Indeed, the longer the war lasts, the lesser the excuse. The better than not-so-good news is that Poroshenko delivered a powerful speech on September 25th, in which he outlined a bold vision of simultaneous structural reforms that, if adopted, would amount to a "Big Bang."

And now for the outrageous. Germany's Foreign Ministry recently released an internal report that concluded that Russia "has under President Putin developed into an authoritarian state in almost every respect." Most serious analysts detected the strong whiff of authoritarianism back when Putin and his cadre began speaking of "managed democracy" some 15 years ago. Hopefully, the stark reality check Putin provided with Russia's invasion of Ukraine has cleared the vision of Germany's policy elites. Better late than never, I suppose, though Germany's economic entanglements and interdependencies will prejudice Berlin's better judgment for years to come. At this rate, Berlin will declare Putin's aggression against Ukraine a "war" sometime in 2029.

The really outrageous news concerns another German entity, the tourist agency, Hansa Touristik GmbH. Here's what the Kharkiv Human Rights Protection Group had to say about its recent antics:

> On Sept 17 "Ocean Majesty," a Greek luxury cruise liner operated by the German tourist agency Hansa Touristik GmbH flouted the international embargo and sailed from Sochi in Russia into the Crimea, arriving in Yalta at around 8.30 Kyiv time. While the FSB [the Russian Security Service] carried out an 11-hour search of the Mejlis [the Crimean Tatar Parliament] and men with machine guns raided a Mejlis member's home, a major Crimean Tatar charity, and the Mejlis's newspaper Avdet, 500 German tourists basked in the Yalta sunshine.

Shame on Hansa Touristik. Even greater shame on those 500 "ordinary" Germans, whose immoral behavior makes them complicit in Russia's crimes against the Crimean Tatars.

*

Ukraine Must Reform to Save Itself, *World Affairs Journal*, October 17, 2014

Will NATO Save Ukraine from Russia? I'm surprised by how many people, especially in Ukraine, believe the answer is yes. And I'm no less surprised by how many Western analysts and Russian policymakers claim that that's exactly what NATO hopes to do—and, by implication, will do. Naturally, Russians describe NATO's presumed intentions as offensive and not defensive.

PART THREE: RUSSIA'S WAR AGAINST UKRAINE

It's time to wake up and smell the espresso in Brussels.

First, NATO has no army. As an institution, as a bureaucracy located in two complexes in and near the capital of Belgium, the alliance does not have troops. It can cajole, persuade, bluster, and the like, but the troop-sending is done—if it is done at all—by NATO member states on behalf of NATO member states or, more problematically, in out-of-area missions. Second, most Europeans have slashed their defense budgets way below the limits they have publicly agreed to sustain. The United States is the only significant exception to this general rule. To put it mildly, Europe has passed the military buck to America, while insisting on the right to kvetch about Washington's occasionally unwise use of armed force.

When Europeans say that war has become unthinkable on the European continent, what they really mean is that they don't want to think about it. Unsurprisingly, most Europeans have been, and still are, extremely reluctant to commit large numbers of soldiers to battle. It took genocide to move them to action (sort of) in Bosnia. And even genocide failed to mobilize them, or the United States, in Rwanda. Would a Putin-directed genocide of Ukrainians incline Europeans to intervene? With their mouths, yes. With their weapons, less likely. Same goes for the case of further military aggression.

But what if Ukraine became a member of NATO? Then, surely, NATO member states would rush to its aid, right? Don't bet on that either. The famed Article 5 is the nub of the matter. Here's the relevant text:

> The parties agree that an armed attack against one or more of them in Europe or North America shall be considered an attack against them all and consequently they agree that, if such an armed attack occurs, each of them, in exercise of the right of individual or collective self-defense recognized by Article 51 of the Charter of the United Nations, will assist the party or parties so attacked by taking forthwith, individually and in concert with the other parties, such action as it deems necessary, including the use of armed force, to restore and maintain the security of the North Atlantic area.

Most commentators cite the first few lines, which appear to promise a determined response to aggression. But keep on reading and you'll come to that cop-out clause: "such action as it deems necessary, including the use of armed force." First of all, that line means that a member state's response is made individually, by itself, and not collectively, by NATO, and that the response should accord with the state's estimation of what it "deems necessary." In theory, a state would be perfectly entitled to conclude that doing nothing is what it deems necessary. Second, "armed force" is only one possible permissible response. A state could conclude that convening an international peace conference would be the better way to go.

Being a NATO member is, thus, no guarantee against aggression—especially if the target of Russian aggression is a geopolitically "insignificant" state, such as any of the Balts. Back in 2008, I wrote **an article** asking whether NATO would defend the Estonian city of Narva. My conclusion then, as now, is no. Poland, Lithuania, and Latvia might send troops, and it's possible that President Obama was serious when he said, "If you mess with the NATO country, then there will be a military confrontation," but Germany and France are another matter. The Balts know this, of course—as do, I suggest, the Russians.

It's preposterous to think the Kremlin is unaware of the fact that NATO is riddled with the above weaknesses. (Think of all the Russian spies in Brussels.) It's just as preposterous to take Putin at face value when he insists that NATO is a threat to Russia. (He once justified the Crimean invasion as an attempt to forestall Ukraine's turning Sevastopol into a NATO base; that's either crude pandering to the peanut gallery in Russia, complete ignorance of how NATO functions, or a deep paranoia.) How could an alliance that wouldn't defend its own members from Russia be a threat to Russia? Western analysts who repeat the myth of Russian sensitivity to NATO expansion are just naively buying into the Kremlin's conscious or subconscious myth-making.

Forbes columnist Paul Roderick Gregory exposes this myth by imagining a scenario in which Russia launches a "hybrid war" against Latvia in order to destroy NATO. Russia takes control, the Europeans and Americans huff and puff, and Putin wins the day: "Putin has called NATO's bluff, and the world has seen that NATO is an empty shell. There is no more NATO. Putin is king of the roost. It is he who decides who will be spared and who will be punished." Gregory is right to imply that, contrary to his public statements, Putin knows that NATO is bluffing.

What, then, should Ukraine do? Obviously, closer ties to NATO can't hurt—especially as a bargaining chip with delusional Russians. But far, far more important is the condition of Ukraine's own army. Only Ukraine can defend itself. To do that it needs, as the military analyst Yuri Butusov rightly **says**, to develop a complex, long-term strategy, modernize its armed forces, develop an adequate force structure, procure the requisite armaments, and raise its level of organizational competence. And for all that to become possible, Ukraine must grow economically. Ukraine's security and survival are thus ultimately, and intimately, dependent on economic reform.

During the Maidan Revolution, demonstrators chanted "freedom or death." Today's Ukraine should be chanting: "Radical economic reform or death."

*

Ukraine Should Abandon the Donbas Enclave, *World Affairs Journal*, October 21, 2014

Ukraine has two nonnegotiable priorities in its ongoing war with Russia: survival and reform. Ukraine must survive as a sovereign democratic state in the short term if it is to reform, and it must reform itself in the medium term to survive and become a prosperous and secure sovereign democratic state in the long term. Both goals can be best advanced if Ukraine washes its hands of the enclave of the Donbas region that Russia and its proxies now control.

Europe's foremost priority is inextricably connected to Ukraine's. Europe's two key pillars—the European Union and the North Atlantic Treaty Organization—must survive as effective institutions, but they can do so only if Ukraine survives and reforms. If Ukraine, a geopolitically pivotal country in the heart of Europe, falls to Russia or becomes a European Zimbabwe, Europe will be hard-pressed to remain functional, prosperous, and stable.

Ukraine's priorities are, therefore, Europe's—and by extension America's. The only difference—and the only source of policy disagreement—is on the time frame. Ukraine needs to survive immediately, and it must reform itself as soon as possible. If it fails to do so, Europe's survival will come into question, but only in time—a prospect that enables some Europeans to hope that things will somehow work themselves out in the future.

Ukraine's survival is predicated on one simple goal: stopping Putin.

Stopping Putin means two things. First, the West cannot abate its sanctions or recognize Russia's illegal occupation of Crimea and the Donbas. If sanctions are rolled back and the occupations are deemed legal, Putin will be told that imperialism pays. No one knows what he wants, but it's clear that his minimal goal is to keep Ukraine unstable, poor, and on the verge of collapse. His maximal goal may be all of Ukraine or, as he told Ukraine's President Petro Poroshenko, "If I want to, Russian troops can be not only in Kyiv in two days, but also in Riga, Vilnius, Tallinn, Warsaw, or Bucharest."

Second, Ukraine must have the defensive capacity to deter a further Russian invasion. Kyiv has already adopted a plan to build extensive fortifications along its border with Russia and the Donbas enclave. Ukraine must now do everything possible—preferably with Western help—to strengthen its army and acquire the force structure it needs to stop Russian tanks and aircraft. Since vast amounts of Western military assistance are unlikely, the burden of security will fall on Ukraine, which will be able to sustain it only if its economy begins to grow briskly.

Ukraine's adoption of painful systemic reforms requires political will on the part of the political elite, a willingness by the population to endure hardship, and a clear road map. For the first time since independence in 1991, all three components are in place. The post-Maidan democrats understand that reform is unavoidable; the majority of Ukrainians want change and know that reform can make life only marginally worse; and the EU Association Agreement provides Ukraine with a clear vision of the concrete steps it must take.

But systemic reform will be next to impossible if Kyiv's attention and resources remain focused on the Donbas enclave. Under the worst-case scenario, if fighting continues or intensifies, increasingly scarce resources will flow eastward and reform will be delayed until peace finally comes. Under the best-case scenario, if some form of peace arrives and holds, while Kyiv continues to devote its attention to integrating and, ultimately, financing the reconstruction of the region, reforms will be tabled because the Donbas enclave will, as Putin knows, obstruct westward-oriented change and promote Russian influence in Ukraine's internal affairs.

The enclave's population has been and may still be unremittingly anti-Ukrainian and anti-Western. Its elites—whether the old guard in the Party of Regions and the Communist Party or the new guard in the self-styled Donetsk and Luhansk People's Republics—are political and economic reactionaries. The enclave's chief oligarch and corruptioneer, Rinat Akhmetov, is still uncertain about his loyalty to Kyiv. And the enormous economic and human destruction wrought by Russia and its proxies will require massive amounts of subsidies that Kyiv can obtain only by raiding the coffers of Ukraine's other provinces.

In sum, reintegrating the Donbas enclave into Ukraine will retard and prevent reform and, thus, undermine Ukraine's survival. In contrast, keeping it at arm's length will free Ukraine to pursue reform and consolidate its sovereignty.

There are several ways in which "keeping it at arm's length" may be interpreted. Ukraine could cut the enclave loose and tell it to determine its own future. It could, as Poroshenko's current peace plan does, grant them a special status within Ukraine that effectively amounts to independence, especially if Russia's proxies run the enclave. Or Ukraine could "freeze" the status quo, turn inward and westward, and "wash its hands" of the region.

Whatever Ukraine's choice, it—and the West—must understand that their future ultimately hinges on what happens to the enclave. The Donbas was probably the single most important obstacle to Ukraine's adoption of reforms in the last 23 years. It would be a tragedy if, through Kyiv's and the West's unwillingness to recognize Ukraine's priorities, the enclave continued to play this dubious role in the future.

*

Leave Putin His Scraps, *World Affairs Journal*, October 24, 2014

Would territorial retreats whet Vladimir Putin's imperialist appetite?

I'd be rich if I had a hryvnia for every time I've heard that question answered in the affirmative. Accordingly, if one concedes an inch to Putin, he'll take a mile. And, naturally, that mile will only be the prelude to many more miles. In sum, you can't concede an inch—or else.

Critics of Ukrainian President Petro Poroshenko's "peace plan" for the Donbas enclave controlled by Russia and its terrorist proxies generally make this argument. Providing the enclave with a special status and effectively conceding Russian control of the territory isn't just a "capitulation." It's an invitation to further Russian aggression.

Let's unpack the arguments for inches becoming miles.

Supporters of this view—let's call them pessimists— generally assume several things. First, that Putin desires to grab all of Ukraine and as much of Europe as he can. Second, that every territorial concession is a valued prize for Putin. Third, that Putin has the capacity to absorb enormous amounts of territory. Fourth, that Ukraine and other target countries have no influence on Putin's appetite. And fifth, that Putin is immune to pain in his quest for empire. Let's call the people who question some or all of these assumptions optimists.

The first assumption gets at the question that's been obsessing analysts for years: just what the heck does Putin want? If you're an optimist, you're likely to believe that Putin wants hegemony over Ukraine and glory for Russia. If you're a pessimist, you probably think Putin, like his ideological twins Aleksandr Dugin and Vladimir Zhirinovsky, wants to capture Lisbon and nuke Tallinn. I submit that this question is unanswerable. We just don't know, and we can't even be sure that Putin knows. That said, given the stakes, we would be wise to agree with pessimists and assume the worst.

The second assumption rests on the view that all territorial acquisitions are equally valuable and, hence, equally desirable. But that's obviously false. Imperialists generally want prize real estate and eschew barren deserts. Seen in this light, neither Crimea nor the Donbas enclave is much of a prize: the former is turning into an economic mess, the latter has been reduced to a hell hole by Russian predations. True, both regions represent gains for Putin inasmuch as they are (still) home (sort of) to ethnic Russians supposedly pining for annexation to Russia. On the other hand, any further move into Ukraine will entail more destruction and increasingly fewer Russian "piners," with the value of additional real estate thereby falling accordingly.

The third assumption rests on the view that seizing territory is easy. But, *pace* the ease of the Crimean annexation, most annexations are, like the Donbas annexation, extremely messy affairs, entailing military campaigns, human losses, economic distress, and enormous financial costs. And then there's the problem of administering the occupied territories. For one thing, the occupier must eliminate the inevitable resistance. For another, the occupier must divert resources from the homeland to the occupied territories. Does Putin really want to be fighting Estonian, Latvian, Lithuanian, Polish, Ukrainian, and many other partisan movements—and thereby repeat the bloody experience the USSR had with these nations after World War II?

The fourth assumption rests on the view that countries willing to make territorial adjustments will always accede to countries insisting on territorial adjustments. But why should they? As the above paragraph suggested, a further invasion of Ukraine or Eastern Europe will definitely produce resistance. If so, why shouldn't potential invadees do everything possible to prevent invasions? Such as build defensive fortifications, arm and train their armies, and develop alliances? And why shouldn't those defensive measures suffice to prevent expansionist countries from taking additional territory?

The answer to that last question leads straight into the fifth assumption: that Putin is immune to pain. According to pessimists, Putin will keep advancing regardless of the losses Russia incurs in his march to the Atlantic. How likely is that? If Russia suffers enormous pain, it may become objectively incapable of marching to Lisbon, even if Putin wants it to. (Remember that Hitler's will proved powerless to stop Nazi Germany's defeat.) And how

311

likely is Putin to remain unaffected by Russia's pain? If he's completely bonkers, the answer is completely. If he has a twinge of rationality in him, then, sooner or later, the pain will make a difference in his calculations—not because he's a humanitarian, but because he'll see that a weak Russia will never reach Lisbon.

These are not just abstract reflections. They concern Crimea, the Donbas enclave, and perhaps more of Ukraine. It is probably true that the ease of Russia's conquest of Crimea led Putin to believe that he could just as easily take another bite out of Ukraine. But the Donbas war has been anything but a cakewalk for Russia and its terrorist proxies. Ukraine has fought back and stopped the Russian advance. "The result," according to Russian analyst Konstantin Gaaze, "was a dirty, bloody tie."

Will Putin's experience in the Donbas further whet his appetite or will it curb it? Three of the above five assumptions don't hold for the Donbas enclave: the territory is no prize, the Ukrainians have fought hard, and Putin has paid a high price. Will the pain associated with these factors influence Putin? If he's rational, yes. If he's irrational, then Lisbon better prepare for a Russian assault.

But the really important question is this: Will Putin be emboldened if Ukraine accepts the enclave's frozen status and uses the breather to build fortifications, reform its army, strengthen its arsenal, and enhance its ability to inflict pain on Russian invaders? I don't see how those actions could possibly *increase* Putin's appetite. They may not dull it—if he's irrational—but even then, an objectively improved defense could stop Putin even if he believes otherwise. On the other hand, if absolutely nothing can stop Putin, then Europe and Russia are doomed, regardless of whether territorial retreats whet his imperialist appetite or not.

What, then, are the implications for rational policymakers? That's easy. Regardless of whether you're an optimist or a pessimist, the mere possibility of Putin's unleashing a war against European civilization should be enough for rational European policymakers to appreciate that stopping Putin in the Donbas is infinitely preferable to stopping him farther west.

*

The Ukraine Crisis According to John J. Mearsheimer: Impeccable Logic, Wrong Facts, European Leadership Network, October 31, 2014

John J. Mearsheimer, R. Wendell Harrison Distinguished Service Professor of Political Science at the University of Chicago, has written a controversial analysis of the ongoing crisis in Ukraine, which neatly reveals why "realism" fails when applied dogmatically and without an adequate knowledge of the facts. The article, entitled "Why the Ukraine Crisis is the West's Fault," appeared in the September/October 2014 issue of *Foreign Affairs*.

"Putin's actions should be easy to comprehend," writes Mearsheimer. Ukraine is a "huge expanse of flat land that Napoleonic France, imperial Germany, and Nazi Germany all crossed to strike at Russia itself." Since Ukraine serves as a "buffer state of enormous strategic importance to Russia ... no Russian leader would tolerate a military alliance that was Moscow's mortal enemy until recently moving into Ukraine." By the same token, no "Russian leader [would] stand idly by while the West helped install a government there that was determined to integrate Ukraine into the West." After all, "great powers are always sensitive to potential threats near their home territory."

The argument is marred by two fatal flaws. First, by invoking past invasions, Mearsheimer goes beyond the analytical framework of realism, which assumes that "objective" threats would be recognized as such by any rational observer, and invokes Russian historical memory, ideology, and political culture—or perceptions. Once perceptions enter the picture, we leave the realm of realism's logical rigor and introduce factors that contradict the objectivity and rationality assumption of realism and implode Mearsheimer's theoretical framework. After all, the power of realism resides in its claim that all rational observers, regardless of nationality, would assess national interests and power relations in approximately the same way. If they do not, because values, norms, ideas, and the like get in the way, then realism amounts to the banal observation that power somehow matters in our assessments of international relations. Who could disagree?

The second problem with the argument is that is it based on non-facts or twisted interpretations of real facts. For starters, Napoleon crossed today's Belarus, not Ukraine; imperial Germany couldn't have crossed Ukraine to strike at Russia, because Ukraine in 1914 was part of Russia; Nazi Germany attacked not Russia but the Soviet Union in general and Soviet Ukraine and Soviet Belarus in particular, when its forces launched Operation Barbarossa on June 22, 1941. Mearsheimer might counter that this kind of criticism is picky and that his point is that three powers crossed Ukraine—"a huge expanse of flat land"—to attack Russia. But that image of Ukraine (and Belarus) is precisely the problem. Europe never consisted of aggressive states in the west, a powerless Russia in the east, and a "huge expanse of flat land" in between. Sometimes Russia incorporated that huge expanse; sometimes that huge expanse had a non-Russian political identity; and never was Belarus identical with Ukraine.

These elementary factual mistakes set the tone for the rest of the article. Thus, NATO is anything but an "impressive military alliance," and everyone—from NATO, to the United States, to Europe, to Russia—knows it. Ever since NATO lost its *raison d'être* with the end of the cold war and the collapse of the USSR, the alliance has been floundering, seeking a new rationale for its existence (and arguably finding it only after Russia invaded Crimea). Meanwhile, while American defense spending has remained high, that of the Europeans is declining, and almost no one in Europe or the United States can imagine the Europeans engaging in a concerted military action. Indeed, as I learned during a visit to NATO headquarters in June 2014, NATO officials make no secret of their fear that, if a member state such as Estonia were to be invaded, no other member state would rush to its assistance and the famed Article 5, which only encourages member states to respond militarily, would be revealed as hollow.

It may be useful to look more closely at NATO Treaty's Article 5, which states that in case of an armed aggression the Allies "will assist the Party or Parties so attacked by taking forthwith, individually and in concert with the other Parties, such action as it deems necessary, including the use of armed force". The key element is the last line, which means two things: first, that a member state responds to an armed attack based on its own estimation of what it "deems necessary." Second, doing nothing or convening a conference could be what it deems necessary. Given European insistence that war is "unthinkable," given declining European defense budgets, and given the unlikelihood that any NATO country would commit troops to the defense of a strategically insignificant country such as Estonia, it is hard not to conclude that NATO is a paper tiger.

A strict application of realist logic should lead rational Russian leaders to reach the above conclusion about NATO. After all, if NATO is a paper tiger, what difference would its "moving into Ukraine" make? Russia's prestige might be affected, but that, too, shouldn't matter in a strictly realist account. Due to this failing, Mearsheimer must bring perceptions into the argument by the back door: NATO enlargement matters, not because NATO matters as an impressive military alliance, but because the memory of NATO's role in the cold war matters to Russians suffering from an ideologically and culturally twisted version of reality. Besides contradicting himself (and contradiction matters greatly to realists, who pride themselves on their logical rigor), Mearsheimer effectively opens the door to an alternative explanation of Russia's behavior that emphasizes great-power ambitions—and which he regards as "wrong."

Is it true that the West has been determined to incorporate Ukraine into NATO? Has Ukraine wanted to join the alliance? The answer to both questions, as Ukraine experts know, is a resounding no. Neither NATO nor any major NATO country has ever stated that Ukraine should be incorporated immediately into the alliance. And for good reason: they understood that no NATO member state would invoke Article 5 and rush to Ukraine's assistance in case of an attack by Russia. True, the North Atlantic Council stated the following at its Bucharest summit of April 3, 2008: "NATO welcomes Ukraine's and Georgia's Euro-Atlantic aspirations for membership in NATO. We agreed today that these countries will become members of NATO [...] We will now begin a period of intensive engagement with both at a high political level to address the questions still outstanding pertaining to their Membership Action Plan applications". The first line is about as squishy an endorsement of Ukrainian membership as one can imagine. But the second—"We agreed today that these countries will become members of NATO"—is profoundly non-committal, employing the future tense ("will become") without any specificity whatsoever. I submit that no rational leader, or analyst, could possibly interpret these words as a ringing endorsement of Ukraine's immediate membership in NATO. All the more so as Ukraine has never acceded to the Membership Action Plan. While all pre-Yanukovych Ukrainian governments have cooperated with NATO's Partnership for Peace program—never eliciting more than a yawn from Moscow—only President Viktor Yushchenko tried, and failed, to have Ukraine accede to the MAP in 2008. Since then, Ukraine's relationship with NATO has been on the back burner. Under the three years' reign of Viktor Yanukovych, it disappeared altogether from the policy agenda of both Ukraine and the West. Indeed, Yanukovych even signed a law in 2010 affirming Ukraine's non-aligned status. Public opinion surveys in Ukraine consistently showed that no more than a fifth of the population ever desired NATO membership. That changed only after the outbreak of Russia's war with Ukraine in 2014.

Is it at least true that the West was "determined to integrate Ukraine into the West"? Until the Maidan Revolution broke out in late 2013, Western policy toward Ukraine had been characterized by "fatigue" since about 2008, when the reformist energy of the Yushchenko government fully dissipated. Even before that, there was never any talk in Western policy circles of including Ukraine in the European Union. Indeed, the EU's development of its Eastern Partnership program and its offer of an Association Agreement to Ukraine were precisely intended to address that policy lacuna without promising Ukraine even the prospect of membership in the EU. Indeed, the striking thing about the EU has been its reluctance for the last two decades to state that Ukraine could, even at some time in the distant future, become an EU member.

Is it, finally, even true that the West was determined to transform Ukraine into a pro-Western democracy? Mearsheimer cites two bits of evidence for this: the United States has given Ukraine more than $5 billion of technical assistance since 1991 and the National Endowment for Democracy "has funded more than 60 projects aimed at promoting civil society in Ukraine." Disregard the fact that $5 billion over 23 years is not an impressive amount, or that civil society projects, in Ukraine and elsewhere, have done little to promote actual civil society. Far more distressing, and remarkable, for a realist, Mearsheimer ignores the actual state of relations between the United States and Europe and Ukraine. The West did nothing as the Leonid Kuchma regime slid toward authoritarianism in the late 1990s, as the Yushchenko government abandoned its democratic reform agenda and focused only on internecine squabbling, and as the Yanukovych regime rolled back civil rights and established an authoritarian regime. True, some Western policymakers rhetorically supported the Maidan Revolution and insisted that Yanukovych seek a compromise with the democratic revolutionaries; but many more did not. None provided any material assistance to the Maidan. And no Western presidents or prime ministers called on Yanukovych to step down during the revolution. Once he abandoned his office, many Western policymakers welcomed his move—but that was after, and not before, the fact.

Amazingly, Mearsheimer believes the West tried to turn Ukraine into its "bastion." This would be news to Ukrainians, who have consistently accused the West of doing little to nothing to advance Ukraine's integration into Western institutions. Pro-Russian Ukrainians, like Putin, will agree with Mearsheimer, but they do so not because the facts are on their side, but because their historical memories, political culture, ideological predispositions, and Soviet-era perceptions incline them to misread the facts and see threats where there are none. Unsurprisingly, Mearsheimer fails to mention that Putin explicitly abrogated the 1994 Budapest Memorandum on Security Assurances in justifying his annexation of Crimea.

Inasmuch as some—and only some—Western policymakers are arguing for turning Ukraine into a Western bastion today, it is due to the fact that Russia annexed Crimea and unleashed war in eastern Ukraine. Mearsheimer is wrong to suggest that Western outrage is due to a "flawed view of international politics" based on "such liberal principles as the rule of law, economic interdependence, and democracy." In fact, Western elites who resolutely oppose Russian aggression are acting on strictly realist principles, recognizing that Russia's invasion of Ukraine poses a direct threat to Western security and stability.

Despite being wrong, Mearsheimer's analysis does offer a potential approach to solving the crisis: "There is a solution to the crisis in Ukraine, however—although it would require the West to think about the country in a fundamentally new way. The United States and its allies should abandon their plan to westernize Ukraine and instead aim to make it a neutral buffer between NATO and Russia, akin to Austria's position during the Cold War."

Mearsheimer thinks his solution would require a change in the West's thinking about Ukraine. In reality, since the United States and its allies never had a "plan to westernize Ukraine," there is nothing for them to abandon. Since "Western leaders" have comfortably coexisted with every Ukrainian administration, there is no reason to think that they would "support an anti-Russian regime" in Kyiv. Since Ukraine's governments have always sought good relations with both Russia and the West—Mearsheimer's ignorance of the fact that no Ukrainian government has ever been anti-Russian is shocking—Ukraine has been, is, and will be amenable to some form of neutral or non-bloc status, as long as its security is guaranteed. Ukrainians' skepticism about any such status derives primarily from the fact that they believe, correctly, that Russia—and especially Putin—cannot be trusted. Since Putin tore up the Budapest Memorandum, it's obvious to Ukrainians that no document could possibly suffice to provide security guarantees. Hence their current interest in NATO membership. Hence their belief that Ukraine must enhance its own armed forces as the only long-term guarantee of its security.

Mearsheimer's plan requires little change in the West's and Ukraine's thinking. But it would require Putin to think differently and abandon the very predilection Mearsheimer pooh-poohs: his "long-standing desire to resuscitate the Soviet empire." Whether or not Putin can do so will be the test of realism's persuasiveness as a theory and the major challenge for the West's ability to cope with Russian imperialism.

*

Kyiv Cuts Subsidies to Separatist-Controlled Enclaves, *World Affairs Journal*, November 14, 2014

Even as Putin's proxies in the Donbas enclave are preparing a major assault on the Ukrainian army, they are also evidently panicking. And all thanks to the Ukrainian government's recent wise decision to stop funding enclave political institutions and providing pensions and other social benefits to enclave residents. All of sudden, the Russia-sponsored separatists appear to understand that the territory they control will soon become ungovernable.

Here's the evidence. On November 12th, the press center of the so-called Donetsk People's Republic (DNR) issued a statement supposedly crafted by the "society" of the DNR in which said "society" chides Kyiv for cutting off social payments "to our veterans, pen-sioners, invalids, and mothers," all of whom are "citizens of [Kyiv's own] country residing in the Donbas."

One has to blush at the DNR's chutzpah. First these Kremlin-sponsored thugs seize public buildings, intimidate and terrorize thousands of citizens, declare independence from Kyiv, stage bogus elections, establish a new government with themselves as its leaders in defiance of Ukrainian and international law, conduct a war against Ukraine, violate human rights, commit war crimes, shoot down an airliner, and threaten to attack Kyiv. Now they insist that they deserve funds from the very country they denounce as fascist and whose sovereignty they reject! Worse, the same individuals who deny the Holodomor of 1932–1933, in which 3–4 million Ukrainians died in Stalin's genocidal famine, call Kyiv's withdrawal of subsidies to an avowedly enemy entity a "social genocide."

The separatists are right to panic. No subsidies from Kyiv means no money for them and the people they pretend to govern. How will the proxies fund their terrorism? How will the civilians feed themselves? Might some DNR supporters soon have second thoughts about life under Putin's proxies? Might work stoppages be ahead in the few enterprises that are still functioning? Does social unrest or resistance loom ahead? A November 12th press report described a deadly strike by pro-Ukrainian enclave partisans against a group of terrorists. If social, economic, and political conditions in the enclave worsen, might partisan activity increase?

There's another reason for the panic. The enclave is an economic mess, having expe-rienced dramatic drops in GDP and employment and rises in business closures, food shortages, and inflation. And conditions will get much, much worse as subzero winter temperatures envelop the enclave. People will die not only from the fighting, but also from hunger and cold. Even Nikolai Levchenko, the young Regionnaire hotshot from Donetsk who distinguished himself a few years ago by insulting the Ukrainian language, brazenly flaunting his ill-gotten wealth in Jakob Preuss's documentary film *The Other Chelsea*, and preposterously claiming to have read Leo Tolstoy's *War and Peace* seven times, says he's worried: "More than 3.5 million people who have remained in the zone of direct conflict will suffer from the cold and will be placed on the verge of survival under conditions of a wintry humanitarian collapse."

Recall that this same Levchenko's supremacism and corruption made the terrorists and the looming humanitarian catastrophe in the Donbas enclave possible. His are croco-dile tears. And he probably knows it, as his suggestion that *both* sides adopt a cease-fire reveals: after all, it's precisely the separatist refusal to honor the cease-fire declared in Minsk in early September that has forced Kyiv to cut funding. And yet, the humanitar-ian problem Levchenko notes is real. I doubt that the proxies will be especially troubled if their citizens starve and freeze, but the enclave's growing ungovernability will surely undermine their war effort. How do you conduct a war against the fascists in Kyiv if your home base is literally becoming a cold Somalia?

Putin and his proxies chose war, and their supporters in the West excused it. With war comes suffering—not only of the Ukrainian fascists, but also of the very population Putin, his proxies, and their Western supporters claimed to be liberating. There is no easy solution to the looming humanitarian disaster. The separatists and the Kremlin have had their way. As long as they maintain their control over the Donbas enclave, Ukraine will rightly refuse to support them—just as President Lincoln refused to negotiate with and support the secessionist Confederacy.

Continued war, and especially a full-scale terrorist attack on Ukraine, will make things even worse for the enclave's population. Will Putin and his proxies subordinate their war-mongering to humanitarianism? Don't bet on it. They are likely to push ahead. Blood and iron have become their self-justification—their *raison d'être*. The war will continue, and the innocents will die. And the West? The West will draw red lines and express "concern."

*

Time for a Hybrid War Against Russia? *World Affairs Journal*, November 25, 2014

Should Ukraine embark on a "hybrid war" against the Donbas enclave controlled by Russia and its proxies? One of Ukraine's best military analysts, Yuri Butusov, the Russian-speaking editor of the Censor.net website, effectively argues that the answer is yes.

Hybrid war is the term analysts apply to what many believe is Russia's new way of war-making in southeastern Ukraine, one that employs a variety of means—propaganda, subversion, outright aggression, support for proxies, and the like—while remaining undeclared or denied.

Butusov believes that the recent G-20 summit in Australia confronted Russia's illegitimately elected president, Vladimir Putin, with a "new reality of world politics" and "an anti-Putin front." Butusov is therefore "99 percent certain" that Russia will refrain from attacking Ukraine, because Putin now understands that "any further escalation" will result in "new packets of sanctions much more quickly. And Russia is already paralyzed by the drop in world prices for raw materials."

Moreover, Ukraine's current focus on an exclusively defensive strategy isn't sustainable in the long run. "We cannot," writes Butusov, "construct rows of trenches and fill them with soldiers along the whole line of the front." As a result, the Russian militants are always able to take the initiative, strike unexpectedly wherever they want to, and inflict casualties on the Ukrainian army. Such attrition is both demoralizing and destabilizing.

Butusov therefore suggests that Kyiv change its tactics—from playing defense to playing offense, but with "a scalpel." Ukraine needs a "new concept of military activities."

It is imperative that quick-response strike forces be created on the basis of existing formations and that systematic work be conducted toward liquidating the knots of resistance and the units of the adversary. Our defense should be proactive. The enemy should not remain in peace. We need a war of diversionary groups, howitzers and mortars, large armored units, and well-defended convoys.

In a word, Butusov is recommending that Ukraine adopt hit-and-run tactics against the Russian proxies, engage in surgical strikes against strategic targets, both on the front line and in the occupied Donbas, and thereby force the terrorists to dig in, anticipate, and lose the initiative. Ukraine's offensive actions would therefore mirror Russia's hybrid war. Ukrainian "little green men" and diversionary units would strike at vulnerable targets in the rear, while lightly armed commandoes enjoying the support of mobile artillery units would harass the Russians and their proxies along the whole length of the front.

Here are the two key elements of Butusov's plan:

1. We can drive out the Russian Federation from the Donbas, but for that we need to conduct a genuine war—without flags, without PR, without advertising. Without any large attacks or maneuvers. Instead, locally, surgically, and fatally.

2. There should be one goal of the war: to inflict maximal casualties on the armies of the occupiers.

First, Kyiv would neither discuss what it is up to nor admit to having a Ukrainian military presence behind enemy lines. Like Moscow, Kyiv would adamantly insist that the attacks are being launched by local resistance to the proxies. Second, the goal of the offensive would not be to win back territory—at least not immediately—but to impose unacceptable casualties on Putin's forces.

Would Butusov's plan work? It's obviously premised on the inability or unwillingness of Putin to launch a full-scale attack on Ukraine. If he does not or cannot, Ukraine's hands are free. If he does, hit-and-run tactics may still be useful, but Ukraine's primary task would then be to defend its territory. As I've written many times, we have no idea what Putin will or will not do. In that case, either you may agree with Butusov or you may not.

But there would be two ancillary advantages to Butusov's strategy. First, localized strikes would not offer Russia the option of claiming that it must launch a full-scale attack in response to a Ukrainian offensive. Since Ukraine would purposely eschew "large attacks or maneuvers," Russia would be placed in the same position Ukraine has been in for much of 2014: continually facing small-scale attacks that, individually, never quite merited a massive response.

Second, thanks to Kyiv's cut-off of government subsidies, social unrest in the Donbas enclave has noticeably increased, with locals demanding that the proxies provide them with money and goods. The unrest is sure to intensify as the temperatures drop in the months ahead. Butusov's plan would both build on and contribute to such unrest. Seen in this light, disrupting separatist rule behind the lines could turn out to be the best way of weakening separatist forces on the front lines.

Who Will Save the People of the Donbas? *World Affairs Journal*, December 4, 2014

The answer, as is becoming increasingly obvious, is no one. Having ruined the economy of the Donbas enclave they occupy and caused a humanitarian catastrophe, neither Russia nor its terrorist proxies will come to the population's rescue. Western powers reluctant to confront Vladimir Putin certainly aren't going to open their wallets to the tune of billions of dollars. And Ukraine, which continues to proclaim that the territories are "temporarily occupied," lacks the financial and military capacity to liberate the area. That leaves the enclave's people isolated and, ultimately, completely dependent on themselves.

As many residents of the area now realize, the self-proclaimed leaders of the Donbas and Luhansk republics are more inclined to destroy than to create. As long as they're around, the enclave will be unsalvageable, and it looks like they'll be around for a while.

Russia has the money to make a difference, but it appears determined to let the population suffer. Putin enjoyed playing the role of the bull in the china shop. Now that the china is all broken, Putin should pick up the tab. He's the guilty one, and he should atone for his crimes. He won't, of course.

Andrei Kortunov, a liberal Russian international relations expert who may be privy to Kremlin debates, stated on November 25th that Russia has no intent to annex the enclave territories. Why?

First, it's very expensive to incorporate them into Russia. Second, if you annex them, you have to assume responsibility for their future. But, as you know, these are very complex territories with many criminals and radicals who would pour into Russia and the Russian political space. I don't think Russia is ready for that.

Kortunov is right. It would be senseless for Russia to annex that much trouble.

But so, too, would it be senseless for Ukraine.

Tetyana Chornovol, an investigative reporter who was savagely beaten by former President Viktor Yanukovych's goons back on December 25, 2013, and is now a parliamentary deputy, agrees with Kortunov's logic. "I believe," she stated on November 26th, "that the occupied part of the Donbas must be separated from Ukraine. That's the most optimal variant for the state." Why? Because a long-term war means defeat for Ukraine. Chornovol would even cut off gas supplies to the enclave: "Why should we give gas to territories that Putin controls? Let Putin give them gas."

The upshot of these two complementary, though competing, logics is a standoff. And a standoff means a "frozen conflict," a territory that remains disputed and ruled by the insurgents. That's the worst-case scenario for the proxies. Left to themselves, they'll drive the Donbas enclave deeper into depression, hasten population flight, and stoke criminality and radicalism.

Kyiv appears to agree with Chornovol. Although no Ukrainian policymaker could say that "the occupied part of the Donbas must be separated from Ukraine," Kyiv's decisions to build an armed perimeter around the enclave, cut off subsidies to its governing agencies, curtail pensions and other social payouts, close down ATMs and mail service, reduce rail traffic to the area, and remove the region's key universities to Ukraine all point to a withdrawal of Ukraine's institutional presence from the enclave.

Who then will save the enclave's population? Keep in mind that a significant portion does not wish to be saved, believing that the self-proclaimed republics are just fine. Some of these folks may change their minds as winter settles in and misrule becomes the order of the day. They may then join those who wait for liberation.

Unfortunately, their waiting will be in vain.

Putin's victims will have to realize that only they can free themselves. Will they rise up against the illegal occupying forces? That's the sixty-four thousand dollar question.

In the meantime, the enclave's inevitable drift toward "frozen conflict" status has important implications for Kyiv. If it's serious about ending the fighting and reestablishing semi-normal relations with Moscow, Kyiv will have to insist that the status of the enclave remain indefinitely frozen in any possible peace deal. Kyiv could give up its NATO aspirations—which will not be consummated in the foreseeable future anyway—and it could agree to eternal love of Russia, but if it agrees to take back the enclave, all hope for reform in a European Ukraine will be dead. And Putin knows it.

*

Decoding Putin's State of the Union Speech, *World Affairs Journal*, December 9, 2014

Vladimir Putin's December 4th "state of the union" address to Russia's Federal Assembly once again explained why he annexed Crimea. This time, his explanation reached new ideological heights, while again confounding academic realists, who continue to insist that Russia grabbed Crimea in response to an aggressive West. Here are Putin's words:

> [The annexation of Crimea] has special significance for our country and our people. Because our people live in Crimea, and the territory itself is strategically important; because it is here that is found the spiritual source of the formation of a multifaceted but monolithic Russian nation and a centralized Russian state. It was here, in Crimea, in ancient Chersonesus or Korsun, as ancient Russian chroniclers called it, that Grand Prince Vladimir was baptized and then baptized all of Rus.
>
> In addition to ethnic similarity, a [common] language, common elements of material culture, a common territory unmarked by stable borders, and nascent common economic activity and princely rule, Christianity proved to be a powerful spiritual unifying force that helped include very different blood tribes and

tribal unions of the extensive eastern Slavic world in the formation of a single Russian nation and the creation of common statehood. And it was on this spiritual soil that our forefathers for the first time and forever became conscious of themselves as a single people. And this gives us the grounds to say that Crimea, ancient Korsun, Chersonesus, and Sevastopol have enormous civilizational and sacral importance for Russia. Like the Temple Mount in Jerusalem is for those who believe in Islam or Judaism. And that is how we will relate to it from now and forever.

There's no mention of NATO, the United States, American imperialism, and the like. Instead, we're told that Crimea is sacred Russian land. Forget Putin's ignorance of Russia's own history (as I've written before, Russia is to Rus as Romania is to the Roman Empire—i.e., Rus is not ancient Russia, just as the Roman Empire is not ancient Romania). Disregard the fact that putative sacredness is the worst possible reason for territorial adjustments. Focus on the fact that Putin is intentionally invoking Islam and Judaism to underline that today's Russia is bound to ancient Rus by means of Christianity. (Hence Putin's obscenely close relations with the Russian Orthodox Church and its ex-KGB patriarch, Kirill.) This is nothing more than a rehashed version of the Muscovite imperial notion of Moscow as the Third Rome. This is crazy stuff, especially in the 21st century, but the good news is that, when dictators seek legitimacy in religion, it usually means they know they're weak and need succor from outside.

There's another important aspect to this passage. Lest it go unnoticed, it should be pointed out that the list of unifying forces Putin mentions at the beginning of the second paragraph are a restatement of Joseph Stalin's famous definition of the nation. Putin is using that definition in order to make the point that it was then, in 988 AD, when Kyivan Rus was baptized, that "a single Russian nation" came into existence. Putin specifically says nation, and not people—an important semantic distinction that is supposed to connote a far greater degree of identity and solidarity for the former. This is a fundamental revision of the standard Soviet and Russian ideological line, according to which Kyivan Rus was the birthplace of three "fraternal" *peoples*—the Russians, Ukrainians, and Belarusians. There's no mention of the latter two in Putin's speech. It follows, according to Putin's logic, that Kyivan Rus was a Russian nation state. That'll be news to scholars, who generally agree that nation states are relatively recent political entities. Putin's version of eternal Russia has been a nation and a state since time immemorial.

Contrast these sentiments with Putin's March 18th speech to an assembly of Russian policymakers in which he gave his first justification for Crimea's annexation:

Literally everything in Crimea is suffused with our shared history and pride. Here was ancient Khersones, where the saintly Prince Vladimir accepted baptism. His spiritual feat of turning to Orthodoxy determined the common cultural, value-based, and civilizational foundation that unites the peoples of Russia, Ukraine, and Belarus.

Crimea is a unique blend of different peoples' cultures and traditions. This makes it similar to greater Russia, where not a single ethnic group has disappeared or vanished in the course of centuries. Russians and Ukrainians, Crimean Tatars and people of other peoples have lived side by side in the Crimean land, retaining their own identity, traditions, languages, and faith.

Putin said nothing about Kyivan Rus as home to a Russian nation. Quite the contrary, he emphasized "the peoples of Russia, Ukraine, and Belarus" and the multiethnic nature of Crimea. And no word of the sacredness of Crimea for the Russian nation.

So, what does this all mean?

First, international relations specialists of the "realist" school should finally acknowledge the obvious truth that has escaped them thus far: Putin wasn't thinking of NATO or the West when he ordered his troops to occupy Crimea. Only once, on July 1st, did Putin ever mention some putative NATO threat. Contrast that one sentence—"we could not allow NATO forces to eventually come to the land of Crimea and Sevastopol, the land of Russian military glory, and cardinally change the balance of forces in the Black Sea area"—with the hundreds of words justifying the land grab in ideological or historical terms.

Second, Putin either knows very little about his own history or is manipulating and distorting it shamelessly. The first possibility is probable, given his KGB background. The second is equally probable, given his KGB background. Either way, Russia is ruled by a neo-fascist leader who is either shamefully ignorant of his country's history or cynically promotes a distorted version of it to Russians. Little surprise there.

Third, Putin has clearly decided to adopt a Russian supremacist line. Apparently, the Ukrainians, Belarusians, and Crimean Tatars no longer have a place in his visions of the Russian future. At best, they're irrelevant to the project of constructing a Fourth Rome, the Putinite successor to Muscovy's third version. At worst, they're obstacles that must be removed. That's bad news for the Tatars and the Belarusians. Ukrainians may breathe a bit more easily, knowing that they've managed to stop the ongoing Russian assault.

Fourth, and this is the good news, Putin appears to know that Russia is alone. The rest of his speech makes that point over and over again. His new Moscow will be the center of a Fortress Russia, and there's at least a possibility that the fortress will be too busy building walls to trouble its neighbors.

By the way, if Putin knew Kyivan Rus's history a bit better, he might abandon his insistence on Russia's continuity with that state. Kyivan Rus fell victim to internal divisions and external attacks and disappeared as a state in the 13th century.

*

The Surrealism of Realism: Misreading the War in Ukraine, *World Affairs Journal*, January 5, 2015

Most general readers following events in Ukraine may not be aware that much of the debate and many of the policy prescriptions among "experts" have been dominated by a school of thought in international relations scholarship known as "realism." In a nutshell, realists have argued that US policy toward the Russo-Ukrainian conflict should be driven by pragmatic American interests and by the realities of Russia's regional great-power status—two propositions few would disagree with. Realist arguments become more controversial, however, when they go on to insist that Russia's behavior toward Ukraine is a reasonable response to Western attempts to wrest Ukraine from Russia's sphere of influence and that the culprit behind the ongoing Russo-Ukrainian war is, thus, the West in general and the United States and NATO in particular.

Realists can be found on the right (Henry Kissinger and Nikolas K. Gvosdev), on the left (Stephen F. Cohen and Michel Chossudovsky), and in the center (John J. Mearsheimer and Stephen M. Walt). At first glance, it may be most surprising that leftists should have embraced a Realpolitik view of the world. But only at first glance. Recall that Lenin, Stalin, Mao, and a host of other Marxist leaders were no less realist in their conduct of foreign policy than Winston Churchill and Richard Nixon. It is no surprise that many policymakers come into office with grand ideals, discover that the realities of power militate against their easy transformation into policy, come to appreciate that politics is, indeed, the "art of the possible," and embrace realism as the worldview of the sadder but wiser.

Realism rests on the astonishingly bold claim that all states always pursue their own national interests and struggle for power. Underlying this empirically unprovable tenet are several key assumptions. First, that states are rational actors. Second, that their rationality concerns maximizing material self-interest and minimizing material risk. And third, that all states share pretty much identical rationality "functions" that reasonable individuals, such as realists assume themselves to be, can easily divine and interpret. If states are irrational, or their self-interest is non-material, realism implodes. After all, the power of realism lies precisely in its claims about objective rationality and objective interests. Any concession to subjectivity (such as leaders who assess interests based on their historical memory, political culture, or ideology) opens the door to realism's theoretical antithesis—"idealism"—and its theoretical nightmare—"constructivism," which claims that rationalities and interests are "socially constructed" and, hence, fluid, unstable, and anything but objective. A Theory of Everything such as realism can be either right or wrong: there is no gray in between. As a result, if they concede any ground to their idealist and subjectivist competitors, realists can no longer claim possession of the intellectual Rosetta stone that explains everything all the time.

When it comes to the Russo-Ukraine conflict, the important dichotomy is not between realism and idealism but between the theory of realism and the empirical knowledge generated by Ukraine studies. For many Ukraine specialists, realist commentary on the Russo-Ukrainian war appears to be so utterly and completely divorced from reality as to be surreal. Most Ukraine specialists would probably agree that there are three reasons for realism's striking irrelevance to the current Ukrainian context.

First, realists may believe that the ongoing Russo-Ukrainian war is a matter between two states, but Ukraine experts, in both Ukraine and the West, know that the war is no less the result of important domestic developments within Ukraine and Russia. Ukraine has been in turmoil since at least 2004, when the Orange Revolution reversed Viktor Yanukovych's first attempt to seize power illegally. The Revolution in Dignity—a.k.a. the Maidan or Euromaidan—that followed in 2013–14 entailed the "people power" of millions of Ukrainians who, in late February, succeeded in effecting Yanukovych's flight from Ukraine. As Ukraine experts know, both pro-democracy uprisings were the products of domestic factors and had absolutely nothing to do with Western agendas.

Just as Ukraine underwent these signal changes, so, too, did Russia—but in an opposite direction. Almost immediately after coming to power in 1999, Vladimir Putin began dismantling democratic institutions and civil liberties, seizing control of the media and economy, amassing enormous power (and wealth) in his own hands, reviving a neo-imperial rhetoric and agenda, and instituting a cult of personality centered on his machismo image. Regardless of what one calls the resultant regime, it marked a radical rejection of the inchoate democratic ethos that characterized Russia under President Boris Yeltsin and a bold leap toward authoritarianism, empire building, and possibly even fascism. As Ukraine was rejecting the authoritarianism of Presidents Leonid Kuchma and Viktor Yanukovych, Russia was embracing it under Putin. Realists are entitled to believe these disparate trends are irrelevant to understanding the ongoing war, but Ukraine experts suggest that downplaying or ignoring these developments is foolhardy.

Second, focusing as they do on "interests," realists also prefer not to take ideology, culture, and norms into account, while Ukraine experts do not see how ignoring these matters can possibly enhance understanding of the conflict. Putin's neo-imperial ideology, his stated determination to make Russia great again, his conviction that all Russian speakers are Russians deserving of the Russian state's protection, and his belief that Ukraine is an artificial state with no right to exist appear to be part and parcel of his pursuit of authoritarianism and empire and his adoption of a hegemonic policy toward Russia's "near abroad." The realist case for ignoring ideology would be stronger if Putin's ideological message were not so openly rooted in Russia's cultural heritage. As his high popularity ratings suggest, Putin's ideology resonates with, and may even be a product of, Russian political culture.

Realism's disregard of norms also leads it to misunderstand the Revolution in Dignity. That, Ukraine experts will insist, was overwhelmingly about self-respect and self-empowerment. Participants assert that they took part in the mass marches or manned the barricades because they objected to the Yanukovych regime's daily assaults on their humanity and identity. Economic issues were irrelevant to their struggle. Today as well, most Ukrainians will insist that their struggle against Russia is not about the economic advantages of being associated with the European Union but rather about their right to self-determination, both as individuals and as a people.

Once again, in ignoring ideology, culture, and norms, realism appears to be ignoring the two most important developments within Russia and Ukraine. The former abandoned democratic norms at precisely the time that the latter embraced them. Can these parallel and intersecting movements be considered as irrelevant to the war?

Finally, Ukraine experts are not so sure about the bedrock assumption of the realists that states—or, more precisely, their elites—always act rationally. Yanukovych seemed determined to undermine his own power and did little to promote Ukraine's state interests. Putin appears obsessed, sometimes bizarrely so, with Russian state interests, but it's not at all clear just how annexing Crimea made Russia stronger. Nor is it clear how destroying one-third of the Donbas in eastern Ukraine benefited Russia or Putin. Nor, finally, is it clear just how Russia's interests have been enhanced by the imposition of Western sanctions. If this is rationality, then the term is evidently so broad as to encompass self-destructive behavior.

Another salient factor of realism's flawed approach to the Russo-Ukrainian war is this: ignorance about Ukraine.

Realists are not the only scholars who have been, or are, ignorant about Ukraine. That ignorance is wide and deep, affecting virtually every aspect of American—and more generally Western—intellectual life. Knowledge about Ukraine has been, and to a large degree still is, confined to a small coterie of specialists, almost none of whom specializes in international relations theory or is committed to the realist worldview.

Until recently, realists had good reason to ignore Ukraine. After Kyiv gave up its nuclear weapons in 1994, Ukraine became at best a second- or third-rate power in the shadow of the significantly larger, richer, and more powerful Russia. Russia was interesting to realists, all the more so as it had nuclear weapons and posed a threat of sorts to the United States. Ukraine was boring—at least until Russia's invasion of Crimea in March 2014 and the outbreak of war a few months later. As soon as Ukraine became a security issue for Russia, it also became a security issue for realists.

The war confronted realists with an explanatory and policy task for which they were wholly unprepared. Few could read Russian; my guess is that none knows Ukrainian. The number of realists with an adequate understanding of Ukrainian history, politics, culture, and economics could probably be counted on the fingers of one hand—if that. Nonetheless, there was a need to stake out a position concerning its conflict with Russia that affirmed the realist position.

As a result, realists evinced a woefully embarrassing ignorance about elementary facts regarding Ukraine. Consider the following, from Henry Kissinger's March 5th op-ed in the *Washington Post*:

> The West must understand that, to Russia, Ukraine can never be just a foreign country. Russian history began in what was called Kievan-Rus. The Russian religion spread from there. Ukraine has been part of Russia for centuries, and their histories were intertwined before then. Some of the most important battles for Russian freedom, starting with the Battle of Poltava in 1709, were fought on

Ukrainian soil.

Any Ukraine expert could have told Kissinger that Russian history did not begin only in Kyivan (or Kievan) Rus. It began in many places, including Russia itself. The Russian religion did not spread from "what was called Kievan-Rus." What spread was Orthodox Christianity, and it spread from Constantinople. True, Ukraine "has been part of Russia for centuries," but it has been no less a part of the Mongol empire, the Grand Duchy of Lithuania, the Polish Commonwealth, the Habsburg Empire, and the Ottoman Empire. The Battle of Poltava was fought by two empires, the Swedish and Russian, and had nothing to do with "Russian freedom" or independence.

In addition, realists grasped at prefab analytic approaches to Ukraine. Two examples will convey the point. Ukraine is allegedly "deeply divided" into two irreconcilable and homogeneous blocs: western Ukraine speaks Ukrainian, supports the West, and detests Russia; eastern Ukraine speaks Russian, detests the West, and supports Russia. That there are gradations, shadings, and nuances in these divisions is irrelevant. That "deep divisions" must be politically decisive is also taken for granted.

Another bromide is that Ukraine is "artificial," consisting of territories and populations that were cobbled together in the course of several decades. Just what makes Ukraine more artificial than France, Italy, Germany, the United States, Russia, or Great Britain remains unarticulated. Just why Ukraine's ethno-cultural and linguistic diversity should be more of a problem than any other country's also remains unexplored in realist accounts.

Stephen F. Cohen nicely illustrates both clichés in a *Nation* article about "fallacies" concerning Ukraine:

> Fallacy No. 2: There exists a nation called "Ukraine" and a "Ukrainian people" who yearn to escape centuries of Russian influence and to join the West.

> Fact: As every informed person knows, Ukraine is a country long divided by ethnic, linguistic, religious, cultural, economic and political differences—particularly its western and eastern regions, but not only. When the current crisis began in 2013, Ukraine had one state, but it was not a single people or a united nation. Some of these divisions were made worse after 1991 by corrupt elite, but most of them had developed over centuries.

Unlike realists who come out of international relations, Cohen should know better. He's a lifelong student of the Soviet Union and Russia; he speaks Russian. Alternatively, it may be his lifelong "Russocentrism" that blinds him to the Ukrainian side of things.

Finally, given their ignorance about Ukraine and inability to read its native texts, and given their susceptibility to bromides as a substitute for knowledge, realists naturally tend to accept the "narratives" of the country they believe matters most in the Russo-Ukrainian conflict—Russia. Thus, realists generally accept at face value Russian claims that NATO is a threat to Russia. Just how a feeble alliance that lost its sense of purpose after the end of the Cold War and that consists of countries that have slashed their defense budgets, cannot imagine going to war anywhere, and would almost certainly never send troops to save Estonia, say, from a Russian takeover could be a threat to anybody is unclear. Faced with that obvious objection, most realists say that, although the alliance may not be objectively threatening, the Russians perceive it differently and their perception is itself a reality.

To illustrate this point, consider John Mearsheimer's empirically preposterous claims, in a recent issue of *Foreign Affairs*, about why Ukraine is "the West's fault" when he says that "the taproot of the trouble is NATO enlargement, the central element of a larger strategy to move Ukraine out of Russia's orbit and integrate it into the West." What larger strategy? Western policymakers have certainly been open to Ukraine's efforts to move westwards, but they have at best been consistently noncommittal about Ukraine's joining any key Western institutions such as the European Union and NATO.

Mearsheimer goes on to claim that "the EU's expansion eastward and the West's backing of the pro-democracy movement in Ukraine—beginning with the Orange Revolution in 2004—were critical elements, too." Ask Ukrainian democrats and they'll tell you that the West's "backing" of Ukrainian democracy has been lackadaisical and spotty. Who in the West refused to cooperate with President Kuchma when he turned authoritarian? Who in the West denounced the criminal Yanukovych regime? And who in the West did not succumb to Ukraine fatigue after 2008—precisely the period when Ukrainian democracy most needed Western support?

Mearsheimer doesn't stop there. "Since the mid–1990s," he writes, "Russian leaders have adamantly opposed NATO enlargement, and in recent years, they have made it clear that they would not stand by while their strategically important neighbor turned into a Western bastion." Bastion? Can Mearsheimer be serious? Ally or partner perhaps. But bastion?

He continues: "For Putin, the illegal overthrow of Ukraine's democratically elected and pro-Russian president—which he rightly labeled a 'coup'—was the final straw. He responded by taking Crimea, a peninsula he feared would host a NATO naval base, and working to destabilize Ukraine until it abandoned its efforts to join the West." The ignorance in these two sentences is simply astounding. For starters, democratic theory—and especially its Lockean variant, which served as the justification for the American "coup" against the British crown in 1776—easily justifies popular rebellions against dictators. "Coups" are never the handiwork of hundreds of thousands of people, as every political scientist should know: they are the results of secret plots by small cabals, usually based in the military. As any Ukraine expert could tell Mearsheimer, there was no such thing in Ukraine. Most disturbing is the second sentence, which reveals Mearsheimer's ignorance of elementary facts about NATO. How could NATO establish a base in Crimea when Ukraine is not a member of NATO—and has zero chances of becoming one anytime soon?

Finally, realists engage in the worst kind of evidentiary cherry-picking, citing only those Russian claims that support realism, while ignoring the many others that do not. Most egregious is their misinterpretation of Putin. As the above quotation from Mearsheimer demonstrates, realists insist that Russia's annexation of Crimea was a defensive reaction to the West's attempts to transform Ukraine into a bastion. But Putin, in all his explanations of the annexation, has consistently emphasized first, that Crimea is historically Russian; second, that it holds a revered place in Russian memory and culture; and third, that the Russian population in Crimea was under direct threat from the "fascists" who had engineered the "coup" in Kyiv and therefore needed protecting. Indeed, Russia's Federation Council explicitly authorized on March 1st the use of force in defense of Russians and Russian speakers anywhere. Are Putin's anti-realist justifications delusional? Is he really a realist, as the realists insist, who doesn't know it? Or is he, as Ukraine experts would claim, being frank about his imperial intentions and aspirations to reestablish Russian glory?

The reason realists feel that they have the authority to pronounce on a country like Ukraine, with which they are only slightly acquainted, lies in their belief that realism holds the answers to all inter-state relations in all places and at all times—from Thucydides to today. As a Theory of Everything, realism doesn't need to know the unique facts about countries and their people. All it needs to know is what it assumes to be *a priori* true: that all states are rational actors pursuing their materially defined national interests and no contrary fact about Ukraine or Russia could possibly place that assumption in question.

Not surprisingly, realists and Ukraine experts differ on what Western policy toward Ukraine and Russia should be. And their disagreements are anything but academic. Realists generally reject all appeals to justice, fairness, liberation, and the like and insist that Russia will and should have its way in a struggle that affects its immediate national interests more than it does those of the West. As a result, the West should seek to accommodate Russia and convince Ukraine to accept some form of subservience to its neighbor. As Mearsheimer's writing partner, Stephen Walt, wrote for *Foreign Policy* in March:

> It's easy to understand why Ukraine wants to jump in bed with the European Union and NATO; what is not so obvious is why sharing the covers and pillows with Ukraine is something we should want to do. A country with a bankrupt economy, modest natural resources, sharp ethnic divisions, and a notoriously corrupt political system is normally not seen as a major strategic asset.

> Furthermore, the fact that US courtship of Ukraine happens to make Russian President Vladimir Putin angry is not a good argument for embracing Kiev either—simply put, Russia is the more important country. And a long-term squabble isn't in Washington's or Moscow's long-term interest.

Such a statement is diametrically opposed to the assumptions of Ukraine experts, who generally emphasize that the roots of the conflict lie in the clash between Russian and Ukrainian regime types, and their history, culture, ideology, and values; that Russia's regime, imperial ambitions, and ideology pose a threat to the West as much as they threaten Ukraine; and that Russia cannot be accommodated—not because that's normatively bad, but because doing so would upend the world order and affect the security and survival of the West. Russia can only be stopped, by means of the West's support of Ukrainian independence, security, and stability—not because that's the morally right thing to do, but because it's easier to stop Russia in the Donbas than in Silesia.

The choice for policymakers is simple: Whom should they trust more—area specialists who claim to know their country of interest well or grand theoreticians who believe that their theory is, was, and always will be right? The megalomania of realism should caution policymakers against hewing too closely to a Theory of Everything that rests its boastful claims of omniscience on empirical knowledge of nothing. Theory should inform and enlighten; it should suggest new ways of seeing and understanding. But it can be useful if and only if it is grounded in facts. Assumptions about reality cannot trump knowledge of reality.

*

Putin's War on Civilians Defines Terrorism, *World Affairs Journal*, January 30, 2015

Russian President Vladimir Putin is rapidly cementing his reputation as a sponsor of terrorism in Ukraine. One could, with some stretch of the imagination, have qualified the earlier violence perpetrated by his proxies in eastern Ukraine as mere "separatism." In a blog post on April 14, 2014, however, I suggested that it qualified as terrorism, and that Putin's Russia was therefore a state sponsor of terrorism. I then provided the definition of terrorism found in Section 2656f(d) of Title 22 of the United States Code:

> (1) the term "international terrorism" means terrorism involving citizens or the territory of more than one country;

> (2) the term "terrorism" means premeditated, politically motivated violence perpetrated against non-combatant targets by subnational groups or clandestine agents; and

> (3) the term "terrorist group" means any group practicing, or which has significant subgroups which practice, international terrorism.

The recent bombings of purely civilian targets in Kharkiv, Odessa, Donetsk, and Zaporizhzhya provinces are terrorism, pure and simple. When bombs are intended to kill regular folk and then do so, the civilized world denounces such barbaric behavior as terrorism and rightly condemns its perpetrators as criminals. Or, at least, it should—even if the perpetrator runs a huge state with nuclear weapons and bank accounts in the West. If it fails to do so, it loses the right to condemn terrorism and terrorists anywhere.

The perpetrators of Putin's terrorism are welcome to call themselves "partisans," and their leader, "Rudolf," insists they are acting on their own initiative. That's about as believable as Russian Foreign Minister Sergei Lavrov's repeated statements that there are no regular Russian forces in the Donbas. Just as the Donbas proxies are creatures of the Russian security services and armed forces, so too the only possible rational working assumption must be that the terrorists in southeastern Ukraine are the creatures of Putin. Given his ruthless mendacity and duplicity, it would be absurd and naïve to assume otherwise.

"Rudolf" claims that the terrorists number 10,000 in Odessa Province, 12,000 to 15,000 in Kharkiv Province, and 5,000 in Zaporizhzhya Province. The numbers are obviously greatly inflated. There could be that many sympathizers, in which case the actual number of active terrorists is probably in the hundreds. That makes them a tiny minority within populations that overwhelmingly reject everything the terrorists and Putin stand for. But terrorists always are small minorities who know that they don't stand a chance in an open political competition and therefore need to terrorize.

The emergence of a Russian-sponsored machine expressly intended to kill Ukrainian civilians has several important implications—for Ukraine, the terrorists and their Kremlin sponsors, and the world.

Ukraine will have to get used to the fact that it has become the Israel of Eastern Europe. Terrorism will remain a threat to the security of its people as long as Putin rules the Kremlin. To live that way is terrible, but Ukrainians may console themselves with the fact that Israel has thrived despite terrorism.

The terrorists and Putin will fail to achieve their goals—whatever they happen to be. Terrorists may cause mayhem, but in the long term they rarely destabilize the states they attack. Rather, their pursuit of terror reliably creates a strong counter-terrorist security service and police force in the targeted countries. Ukraine's security forces, which have already begun to crack down on the terrorists, will get better at their job as time passes. Just as Putin's aggression in eastern Ukraine has led Ukraine to acquire a real army, so too his proxies' bomb-throwing is leading Ukraine to acquire a real security apparatus.

Finally, it is time for the world and the West in particular to recognize that Putin is not just a warmonger and imperialist, but also a terrorist—no different than Muammar Qaddafi, Saddam Hussein, Bashar al-Assad, or Osama bin Laden. They all kill civilians with abandon; they all engage in "premeditated, politically motivated violence perpetrated against non-combatant targets." Russia should be declared a state supporter of terrorism, and Putin should be shunned by every democratic leader who believes in the intrinsic value of human life. Anything else is to tolerate and encourage the barbarian in the Kremlin.

*

The Case for Arming Ukraine, *World Affairs Journal*, February 9, 2015

No one could make the case *against* supplying weapons to Ukraine better than my good friend Rajan Menon, a professor of political science at City College of New York. So, if his best shot falls short, then it's safe to say that there is no sound argument against America's provision of military hardware to Ukraine.

That best shot appeared last week as an op-ed in the *Los Angeles Times*. And it falls far short of what it sets out to be—a persuasive critique of a report released by the Atlantic Council, the Brookings Institution, and the Chicago Council on Global Affairs that argues for US supplies of weapons to Ukraine. Here's Menon's first charge:

> The group assumes that sending Ukraine arms will send Russian President Vladimir Putin a clear message. … They assume that Putin will recalculate and wind down the war once he sees that the United States is serious about backing Ukraine and that victory will be costlier, bloodier, and more uncertain than he'd anticipated. Well, that's one possibility. But it's not the only one. Putin's main defense for his war has been that the West is actively undermining Russia's security by drawing into its orbit what from the Russian standpoint is a critical country. Arming Ukraine, therefore, probably would prompt Putin to scale up the war. He would send the secessionists more troops, advisors, and arms.

Ironically, Menon agrees that it's possible for Putin to "recalculate and wind down." How could Menon disagree? The argument that leaders respond to negative incentives—higher costs, more blood, greater uncertainty—is conventional wisdom among policymakers, diplomats, and academics. Only fanatics impervious to any kind of cost-benefit analysis would push ahead with suicidal behavior, and Menon is not calling Putin a fanatic. Menon mistakenly says: "The presumption that Putin will back off once Kyiv gets US weaponry is not based on evidence but hope. And hope is not a strategy." In fact, this "presumption" is based on a history of effective deterrence in geopolitics accompanied by academic studies. Menon's protestations to the contrary, the outcome anticipated by the report is perfectly possible, especially given Menon's implicit assumption of the primacy of geopolitical interests.

So why does Menon lean toward the possibility that Putin would "scale up the war"? Because, in the Kremlin's view, Ukraine is a "critical country." Disregard the obvious riposte: that Ukraine is also a "critical country" for the United States and Europe, assuming the West intends to preserve the global post-war security architecture that Putin's aggression threatens to dismantle. Rather, focus on Menon's claim that "Putin's main defense for his war has been that the West is actively undermining Russia's security." That's just not true. The war against Ukraine began with the Kremlin's occupation of Crimea, from where it spread to the Donbas. From the start, Putin has been unequivocal about his reasons for attacking Ukraine: the need to defend Russians and Russian speakers from the "fascist junta" that replaced President Viktor Yanukovych in Kyiv and the imperative to reclaim sacred and historically Russian territory. Which makes sense, as Putin's war was a response to Ukraine's democratic Maidan Revolution, which enshrined people power and posed a direct threat to his rule. Domestic and ideological rationales have always overshadowed invocations of some Western threat in his pronouncements—which also makes sense, as NATO's supposed interest in "drawing" Ukraine into its "orbit" is nonexistent (and only an ideologically driven Putin could not know that).

Menon says that US weapons supplies would lead "Putin to scale up the war. He would send the secessionists more troops, advisors, and arms." But Putin has relentlessly committed "more troops, advisors, and arms" since his annexation of Crimea! When the West and Ukraine did nothing in response, he escalated. When the West imposed minor sanctions, he escalated. When the Ukrainians took a beating in September, he escalated. When the Minsk cease-fire occurred, Putin escalated. Whatever the West and Ukraine do, Putin escalates. As Menon rightly says, "There's not a shred of evidence that Putin has changed course in Ukraine. To the contrary. Moscow's backing for the separatists has increased, enabling them to regain some of the land lost to Ukraine's counteroffensive." Quite. Giving Ukraine arms won't be the thing that makes Putin escalate whenever he does so again.

Menon's next argument relates to the supposed absence of a Plan B. As he says, "There's a basic axiom in war: Don't take a big step (or even a small one) without having thought hard, and planned for, what you will do if it doesn't have the intended effect."

Ignore the fact that Menon has no Plan B, and that, logically, his response to all further Russian aggression would have to be: do nothing, lest the Russians escalate. Here's the more important problem with this thinking: Military assistance to Ukraine is more like a Plan D. Plan A was for the West and Ukraine to protest. Putin escalated in response. Plan B was sanctions. They're destroying the Russian economy, but, once again, Putin escalated. Plan C was the Minsk cease-fire—and Putin escalated. Military assistance is not an alternative to current policy; it's a logical outgrowth of the failure of Western policy to stop the Russian aggression. And it's an approach that is rooted in the conventional wisdom of the foreign policy establishment in both the West and Russia. The only thing that could stop Putin is some combination of soft and hard power—of diplomacy, economic pressure, and military threats. The West's mistake has been to embark on these actions serially, and not simultaneously. By arming Ukraine, the United States and its allies would finally be in the position to engage in effective diplomacy and bring about a peaceful solution to the war.

Menon's final argument is this: "But here's the plan's biggest flaw. Imagine that a Ukrainian army beefed up with American weaponry suffers serial defeats. ... What then? ... We would have to retreat or wade in deeper."

This argument is far too simple. Why should the Ukrainians necessarily suffer serial defeats if, as every Ukrainian policymaker who knows Ukraine can't beat Russia will tell you, the point of getting US weapons is to *deter* the Russians and prevent them from making further territorial gains? Even if the Russians escalate in response—and they escalate regardless of what the West does—why does Menon assume that they'd be willing to throw all caution to the wind and escalate so severely? Why does Menon assume that supplies of arms must be so huge as to transform Ukraine into a strategic threat that Russia feels impelled to nip in the bud? Why does he assume that US policymakers are irrationally incapable of recognizing their own country's interests and simultaneously saying yes to Ukrainian self-defense and no to war with Russia?

Assumptions, like hope, are not a strategy.

The West Should Arm Ukraine, *Foreign Affairs*, February 10, 2015

Before the United States can decide how it might want to support Ukraine in that country's war with Russia, Washington needs to decide just how Ukraine fits into U.S. strategic interests and, more generally, those of the West. In a recently released *National Security Strategy*, the White House failed to do either, stating only that Russian aggression should be resisted and that the Ukrainian people should be supported "as they choose their own future and develop their democracy and economy."

That all sounds fine. But what does "support" mean? Former National Security Adviser and Secretary of State Henry Kissinger was less obfuscatory at a January 29 hearing of the Senate Committee on Armed Services. Ukraine "should be maintained with its existing borders and Russian troops should be withdrawn as part of a settlement." The "outcome," he continued, "must be a free Ukraine" and it "may include military measures as part of it. But I am uneasy when one speaks of military measures alone without having a strategy fully put forward."

Kissinger seems right to say that Ukraine should remain free, but why? Answering that question requires an overarching strategy that proceeds from hard geopolitical realities. Some analysts argue that Russia is far more important to the United States than Ukraine because of its size, oil, economy, and military. Others suggest that Ukraine is equally important, not least because its citizens yearn to fully join the West. In fact, both camps are right. Both are also wrong. Depending on whether Russia is a strategic asset or a strategic threat to the United States, Ukraine could be either strategically unimportant or critical.

Ukraine's Worth

In a geopolitical vacuum (or "other things being equal," as academics might put it), Ukraine matters little to the United States in terms of security, stability, prosperity, and democracy. As long as Ukraine remains a militarily and economically weak state with no strategic resources, its ability to affect the United States in any way will remain marginal at best.

In contrast, Russia matters much more than Ukraine, regardless of whether it, Russia, is weak or strong, friendly or hostile. Although its economy is in shambles and its population is in decline, Russia is a regional power that is actively enhancing its military capabilities. It is a territorially huge state that occupies a pivotal position between Europe and Asia. It has a seat on the United Nations Security Council and possesses a vast array of nuclear weapons. It also possesses large reserves of two of the world's most important strategic resources, oil and gas.

Under normal circumstances, when Russia's relations with the West are friendly—and, despite Russian President Vladimir Putin's beliefs to the contrary, a strong and friendly Russia is in the West's best interests—it makes eminent sense for the United States and Europe to place greater strategic importance on Russia than on Ukraine. But we live in an abnormal world.

When relations with Russia deteriorate somewhat—to the point that Moscow interferes with the West's pursuit of its interests—Ukraine takes on potential tactical importance for the West. The United States and Europe can then use Ukraine to counterbalance or, more precisely, to signal their displeasure with Russian behavior by including Kyiv in Western peacekeeping missions or in diplomatic initiatives in the United Nations, OSCE, and other international or regional institutions. When relations with Russia deteriorate to the point that a hostile Russia becomes a strategic threat to the West, Ukraine acquires immediate strategic importance for the United States and Europe. Under such conditions, Ukraine is not just a useful counterbalance to Russia but a central component of the West's strategic defense against Russia. Ukraine's importance to the West is thus a function of U.S. and European relations with Russia. In this case, the West would regard Ukraine as an ally similar in strategic importance to West Germany during the Cold War.

Russian Roulette

How should the West interpret its relations with Russia and the place therein of Ukraine? In the last 24 years, Russia has progressively moved from being weak and friendly under President Boris Yeltsin (Ukraine matters little strategically) to weak and hostile under the first few years of Vladimir Putin's rule (Ukraine still matters little) to strong and hostile since Ukraine's Orange Revolution in 2004 and Russia's war against Georgia in 2008 (Ukraine starts to matter strategically). In 2014, with Moscow's annexation of Crimea and the aggression in Ukraine's Donbas region, Russia moved from simple hostility to the West to an outright assault on it and its values, institutions, and interests (Ukraine becomes a strategic asset). Putin's drift into hostility was not the product of some supposed Western desire to wrest Kyiv from Russia and to incorporate Ukraine into NATO—besides, only a small minority of Ukrainians ever wanted to join NATO before 2014—but, rather, of Putin's establishment in the mid–2000s of a fascist-type regime that made imperial revival and the reestablishment of Russia's place in the sun the core of his legitimation strategy.

Putin therefore sees Russia as being embroiled in a civilizational clash with the West. In his view, Russia stands for authoritarianism, conservatism, and moral vitality, whereas the West represents chaotic democracy, rampant liberalism, and moral decay. Putin's aggression in Ukraine challenges the entire post-war security architecture, as well as the relevance of its institutions—NATO, the European Union, the OSCE, and, ultimately, even the United Nations. Finally, Putin appears determined to weaken the West economically, to split it politically, and to establish Russia as the hegemonic power on the European continent.

Putin's actions thereby threaten the West's security, stability, prosperity, and democracy. War in Europe has become both thinkable and real, and Putin's saber-rattling along Europe's perimeter suggests that he may be interested in expanding his aggression beyond Ukraine. In addition to destabilizing Europe, Putin is also lowering living standards there, by forcing the continent to countenance spending more on defense at a time of economic decline. Finally, by promoting his aggressive authoritarianism and cultivating supporters thereof in Europe, he is undermining European democracy and European values.

Putin's war against Ukraine is thus a war against Europe. As such, Russia has become a strategic threat to the United States. And now, as a result, Ukraine's geopolitical position between Russia and the West has made it into a critical component of the West's defense against Putin's Russia. It will also be a strategic asset should Putin's corrupt, ossified, authoritarian state implode. In this case, a strong Ukraine would defend the West—not against Russian aggression but against Russian instability.

Armed Allies

Ukraine's newfound strategic important to the West has several implications for Western policy toward Ukraine. Ukraine can defend the West against Russia only if Ukraine can defend itself against Russia right now and has the economic and political capacity to generate a political system that can defend itself against instability in the long term. In other words, Ukraine needs to have an army strong enough to deter further Russian attacks and it needs to have an economy strong enough to sustain a strong military. As former U.S. Secretary of State Madeleine Albright said at the January 29 Senate hearing, "Our support for Ukraine must enhance its security capabilities and support the new government's ambitious reforms, because Ukraine will need to restore security and implement dramatic economic changes to emerge from the current crisis."

Providing Ukraine with both military and economic assistance as part of a larger Western defensive strategy against a hostile Russia rests on two assumptions. First, that it is in the West's and Ukraine's best interests for Russia to be strong and friendly, as only such a Russia can be a reliable partner in maintaining a stable and just international order. And, second, that Putin is concerned with Russia's interests—security, stability, and prosperity, if not democracy—and is rationally responsive to positive and negative incentives. If Putin is determined to continue escalating the war (as he has, relentlessly, since his annexation of Crimea), destroy Ukraine, and march on Europe regardless of cost, treating Ukraine as a Western strategic asset would have no impact on his intentions, but it would objectively hinder their execution. If, alternatively, Putin is a rational Russian patriot, then a stronger Ukraine—and a strong and friendly Ukraine is in Russia's best interests—would lead him to de-escalate and to seek a negotiated solution to the war. We have no way of knowing which Putin is the real one, but a stronger Ukraine has the same positive strategic consequences in both scenarios.

The task for the United States and the rest of the West is thus clear. Policymakers need not be "uneasy when one speaks of military measures," precisely because a strategy justifying such measures exists. Putin's Russia is strong and exceedingly hostile to everything the West stands for, and a strong Ukraine can help stop Russian aggression against the West. Neither Western boots on the ground in Ukraine, nor NATO membership for Ukraine would be necessary. Ukraine should be strong enough militarily to prevent further Russian expansion. To achieve that end, Kyiv needs real-time intelligence, sophisticated communications, and anti-tank missiles. The challenge for the West is greater economically and could entail as much as the $50 billion in aid that the investor George Soros suggests is imperative.

If Putin becomes genuinely conciliatory and the war in the Donbas ends, the West's commitment to Ukraine would focus only on economic assistance. If he continues, irrationally, to escalate, the West will have increased Ukraine's, and its own, defensive posture. Whatever his response, the United States and Europe must never lose sight of the fact that their Ukraine strategy is only part of a larger Russia strategy whose goal must be a strong and friendly Russia. As assistance to Ukraine is ramped up, therefore, the West must also redouble its diplomatic efforts, which work best when appeals to reason are backed by economic and military incentives.

If and when Russia abandons its hostility and becomes friendly toward the West, which could take months or years, Ukraine's strategic importance would fall away and the West could regard Ukraine as just another stable, secure, and pro-Western state enjoying normal relations with a strong and amicable Russia. In the meantime, defending Ukraine's strategic interests—security, stability, prosperity, and democracy—is the best way to defend the West's own strategic interests.

*

Five Fatal Flaws in Realist Analysis of Russia and Ukraine, *The Monkey Cage*, March 3, 2015

The standard realist narrative regarding the Russo-Ukrainian War generally runs something like this. The West—the United States, the European Union, and NATO—attempted to expand its influence into Eastern Europe and wrest control of Ukraine from Russia. In turn, Russian President Vladimir Putin responded by defending his country's vital security interests by seizing Crimea and attempting to annex eastern Ukraine. Western arms deliveries to Ukraine would only lead to further escalation by Putin, because Russia's interests in Ukraine far outweigh the West's. Indeed, every Western escalation—whether by means of sanctions or by means of arms supplies—will always produce an equal and opposite Russian response, regardless of the cost to Russia's economy, polity, and society.

There are five fatal flaws with this argument.

First, there is no empirical evidence for the West wanting to wrest control of Ukraine from Russia at any time since Ukraine became independent in 1991. The United States lost interest in Ukraine strategically after Kyiv signed the Budapest Memorandum on Security Assurances in 1994 and agreed to give up its nuclear weapons. The European Union has never expressed even a rhetorical interest in Ukraine's membership. And NATO failed to include Ukraine in its Membership Action Plan in the only year, 2008, that some minor rapprochement between NATO and Ukraine took place. True, the North Atlantic Council said at its Bucharest summit of April 3, 2008 that "NATO welcomes Ukraine's and Georgia's Euro-Atlantic aspirations for membership in NATO. We agreed today that these countries will become members of NATO." But the first line is about as ano-dyne an endorsement of Ukrainian membership as one can imagine, while the second is intentionally noncommittal, employing the future tense ("will become") without any specificity whatsoever. In fact, since 2007, Western attitudes toward Ukraine have been characterized by "Ukraine fatigue."

Second, the claim that NATO enlargement in 1999 and 2004 posed an objective security threat to Russia cannot be substantiated. NATO has lacked a sense of purpose since the end of the Cold War, and its member states have radically reduced defense expenditures. How a "paper tiger" such as this could have posed a security threat to anyone is unclear. At this point, realists usually say that, while it may be true that NATO is no genuine se-curity threat, the fact is that Russians perceive it as such. Fair enough, but in arguing in this manner, realists are contradicting their own premises. Realism assumes rationality, and it assumes a particular kind of material-centered rationality that is more or less the same from country to country and, as such, is open to analysis by realist scholars. In opening the door to Russia's perceptions, realists adopt a constructivist understanding of interests and thereby undermine their own rationality assumption. Anti-realists are perfectly comfortable with arguing that Putin's paranoia and imperial imperative lead him to see enemies where there are in fact none. But if paranoia and Russian imperial ambitions are "rational," then so, too, is Hitler's belief that Jews posed a mortal threat to Germany's security.

Third, Putin's own justifications of the seizure of Crimea always emphasize the need to protect Ukraine's Russian and Russian-speaking population from the "fascist junta" in Kyiv and to bring historically Russian, "sacred" territory back into the fold. If he men-tions Western intentions at all, it's always after emphasizing the domestic reasons for the land grab. Realists cannot ignore Putin's own rhetoric; instead, they must explain why a realist leader such as he is purported to be should not openly invoke the threat of the West in his explanations for the Crimean annexation. Putin may be lying or he may not understand the "real" realist reasons for his land grab. Whatever the "true" reason for his odd behavior, realists need to explain just why a rational leader would rationally lie about something that needs no lying about or just how someone could be motivated by realist concerns without being aware of them.

Fourth, the assumption that Russia's interests in Ukraine are greater than those of the West's can only be justified in constructivist terms. Geopolitically, Ukraine is as close to Europe as it is to Russia, and, if it matters to Russia economically, politically, and militarily, it matters also to Europe (and the United States). But realists never confine their claims of criticality only to realist considerations. Instead, they invariably invoke Russia's close historical, cultural, and religious ties to Ukraine. Even disregarding the fact of equally close such ties between Ukraine and the West, the obvious problem with such a claim is that it invokes socially constructed perceptions of closeness and not hard realities. Once again, the realists contradict themselves.

Fifth, the argument against arms deliveries to Ukraine assumes that Putin will escalate regardless of the costs involved. Such a relentless, single-minded pursuit of something, regardless of the costs and benefits involved, is what we generally characterize as fanaticism or, possibly, as a psychological disorder. In any case, such behavior is anything but rational in the realist sense of the term.

Part of the realist problem with Ukraine is empirical. Because Ukraine never ranked high on any list of objective (and not constructed!) geopolitical power, less is known by many analysts about Ukraine and Russia's relations with Ukraine than should be. But the larger problem is logical. Realists want to have it both ways—arguing for and against rationality in general and in the Russian context in particular. Consistency can be reestablished, but only if realists finally agree that Putin is or is not rational and stick to one, and only one, interpretation.

*

A Stalemate Ukraine Can Win, *Foreign Policy*, March 4, 2015

The crowing began before the battle of Debaltsevo had even concluded. During the ceasefire negotiations in Minsk, Vladimir Putin reportedly boasted that 500 Ukrainian soldiers would be killed and 2,000 taken prisoner. After the Ukrainians had withdrawn, he <u>taunted</u> them by saying that they had been defeated by "yesterday's tractor drivers." Perhaps inevitably, Western media reports picked up on the irresistible alliteration and began referring to the "Debaltsevo debacle."

In contrast, Ukrainian government officials claimed that the withdrawal had been planned and orderly. Some Ukrainian soldiers and analysts disagreed; others substanti-ated Kyiv's claims. One policymaker even suggested that Debaltsevo was a win, calling it "a colossal signal of Russia's impending failure." The truth lay in between. Kyiv had in fact planned and, to a large degree, effected an orderly withdrawal. The Ukrainians had fought hard and well, apparently inflicting high casualties on the Russians and their proxies. Reliable Ukrainian sources estimate that, in the month before the Ukrainian army withdrew, Ukraine had up to 260 dead or missing soldiers, while Russia lost 868, for a "kill ratio" of 1:3.3. In short, for the Ukrainians, Debaltsevo was anything but a rout.

But neither was it a victory. Indeed, the Debaltsevo battle exposed serious weaknesses in the Ukrainian army, highlighting the need for immediate reform. Much attention has focused on the fact that weapons and supplies are insufficient and frequently obsolete. Arguably more serious is poor top-level leadership, inadequate inter- and intra-agency coordination, and a lack of strategic and tactical planning. Serhii Pashynsky, head of the parliamentary committee on national security and defense, is unsparing in his criticism. The Ministry of Defense, the General Staff, and the military-industrial sector—charac-terized by "an absolutely primitive bureaucracy, lack of responsibility, and non-profes-sionalism"—do not communicate effectively with each other and are unable to coordi-nate their actions, he said.

The consequences of these shortcomings are clear. Debaltsevo was the third time in half a year that large numbers of Ukrainian soldiers were encircled by Russian forces. The first was the disastrous battle of Ilovaisk, in August, where Kyiv lost up to 1,000 men and much heavy equipment. The second was the four-month battle for Donetsk airport, where Ukraine's so-called "cyborgs" held on to their bit of a terminal until their opponents blew up the remnants of the structure—and the Ukrainians with it—in January. In all three instances, the Ukrainian General Staff was determined to hang on to territory even after it had become obvious that the positions were indefensible. The top-notch Ukrainian military analyst, Yuri Butusov, puts the blame squarely on the head of the General Staff, General Viktor Muzhenko, whom he accuses of gross incompetence and an inability to break with outdated Soviet military thinking that emphasized heavy artillery, wars of position, and the impermissibility of tactical retreats.

Since Muzhenko is President Petro Poroshenko's protégé, criticism of the former trans-lates into criticism of the latter. Equally harsh critics of Poroshenko and the General Staff are found among the commanders of Ukraine's volunteer battalions, which frequently occupy front-line positions and bear the brunt of the fighting. Accusing the high com-mand of ignorance of facts on the ground, their leaders have recently agreed to coordi-nate their activities, implying that they may do so independently of Kyiv. The threat these battalions pose to the stability of the Ukrainian government has been grossly overstated, and their commanders are anything but warlords. But Kyiv's failure to integrate them fully into the formal armed forces means that their potential to act as loose cannons will always remain a danger, especially if the government adopts policies they reject.

Ukraine has three reform priorities: eliminating corruption, fixing the economy, and transforming its army into a modern fighting force. Like the first two, the third will not be easy. Every Ukrainian government has neglected the military since 1991, when Ukraine inherited some 780,000 troops from the Soviet Union. The decay was especially rapid under Viktor Yanukovych's rule from 2010 through 2013, as he assiduously divert-ed resources to the Internal Ministry, which offered his regime protection.

Since then, there have been substantial improvements. As Pashynsky suggests, there is no comparison between the army of today and the ragtag force that called itself an army when Putin seized Crimea without firing a shot a year ago. Ukraine plans to double the size of its army to 250,000 soldiers; the 2015 budget foresees a significant rise in military expenditures, to 5 percent of GDP. (Compare that to the less than 2 percent spent by most NATO members.) Thanks to a massive volunteer effort and some Western assistance, the army's physical infrastructure, basic equipment, food provisions, and medical supplies have improved. Ukraine's defense industry, which was the world's fourth largest arms ex-porter in 2012, has been manufacturing and repairing the requisite heavy (mostly Soviet-era) equipment and is slated to ramp up production in 2015. And Ukraine's soldiers have demonstrated that they can hold their own against a more modern Russian adversary.

But much more needs to be done for Ukraine to defend itself against further Russian aggression. As Butusov and other analysts argue, the General Staff and the lower levels of the command structure must be revamped, replacing old Soviet-era cadres with officers who have experienced real battle in the last year. The Ministry of Defense and

"Ukroboronprom," the state agency responsible for military production, must be streamlined. An up-to-date grand strategy identifying Ukraine's friends and enemies and stating how Ukraine's security can best be pursued under current conditions must be developed. The implications of such a plan for tactics, force structure, and weapons procurement must also be spun out. Finally, the armed forces themselves, currently consisting of some 130,000 conscripts and 35,000 battle-ready troops, have to be restructured. A smaller, leaner, and meaner army consisting of mobile units with the ability to deliver targeted firepower is just what Ukraine needs to meet its only real strategic threat, that emanating from Russia. All these changes will take time and money.

Still, even if the General Staff is fixed, competent commanders are appointed, coordination is improved, the army is reformed, and the requisite armaments are increased, Ukraine's armed forces will be no match for Russia's in a head-on collision—which, for what it's worth, even Putin says would be an "apocalyptic scenario" that is "virtually impossible." Although Russia's armed forces, as the military analyst Pavel Felgenhauer notes, could not win a war against a modern opponent such as the United States or NATO, they are, and will remain, much stronger than Ukraine's, if only because of the size difference. But victory means different things for Ukraine and Russia.

The unspoken assumption of much Western commentary on the Russo-Ukrainian war is that Ukraine needs to have the capacity to "beat" Russia, but in fact Ukraine's military doesn't have to be stronger than Russia's for Ukraine to win. It just must be strong enough to keep Russia from winning: that is, from embarking on a massive land war or compelling Ukraine by means of a costly war of attrition to reintegrate the Donbas enclave. Neither of those options is easy for Russia. Attempted conquest of Ukraine would be a bloody, risky, and expensive proposition that would unleash partisan resistance, lead to a prolonged occupation, and could start World War III. In addition, although the Minsk-2 agreement envisions Ukraine's paying for the Donbas enclave's reconstruction, Kyiv is highly unlikely ever to accept financial responsibility as long as the anti-Ukrainian sepa-ratists run the region and continue violating ceasefires.

The challenge before Ukraine is to acquire as quickly as possible the force structure and armaments it needs to sustain a potentially long war of attrition. Changing the force structure is intrinsically difficult and time-consuming; acquiring the appropriate weaponry is not, being primarily a function of money and political connections. Russia has a huge advantage over Ukraine in terms of aircraft and tanks: 1,571 combat aircraft and 392 helicopters to Ukraine's 231 and 139, as well as 2,750 tanks, plus an additional 18,000 in storage, to Ukraine's 1,150, plus 1,435 in storage. Given this disparity, it's unsurprising that Kyiv is prioritizing the acquisition of surface-to-air and anti-tank missiles, real-time intelligence, and advanced radar systems.

Russia's conundrum is arguably greater than Ukraine's, because Russia already has ownership of the disputed territories. Continuation of the status quo will only reinforce the eastern Ukrainian enclave's status as an impoverished, unstable, and desperate Russian protectorate, increasingly free Kyiv to pursue reform in the rest of the country, and tax the Russian economy, which has already gone into a tailspin as a result of Western sanctions and falling oil prices. Putin's strategic miscalculations—and starting a war without knowing how to finish it must be the greatest of them—have maneuvered him and Russia into a dead end with no easy escape. The recent increase in terrorist bombings of civilian targets in Odessa and Kharkiv may be a last-ditch effort by Putin's proxies to maintain the heat on Ukraine despite the emerging stalemate and frozen conflict.

Ukrainian policymakers have no illusions that Western weapons would change the balance of power in eastern Ukraine. But they expect that a stronger Ukrainian military would compel Putin to think twice about further escalations, and especially a massive one. As Kyiv sees it, Putin initiated the war by invading Crimea, as punishment for the Maidan Revolution (a view corroborated by a recently leaked, and apparently authentic, high-level Russian document). And he has escalated since then, despite the fact that the West never courted Ukraine (indeed, it suffered from "Ukraine fatigue" since 2007) and has done nothing to undermine his control of Crimea and the eastern Donbas. His consistently aggressive behavior suggests that escalation is a function, not of aggressive Western actions, but of equally consistent Western *inaction*.

Seen in this light, the stalemate in the Donbas is the result of Ukraine's being strong enough to stop Putin. Accordingly, it was Ukraine's strong-enough performance at Debaltsevo—and not Western pleading—that brought Putin to the table at Minsk-2. Continued stalemate—or even a lasting ceasefire—is therefore dependent on Ukraine's remaining strong enough for the foreseeable future. Since Russia will escalate in the face of weakness, maintaining the stalemate means enhancing Ukraine's military capabilities just enough to keep Russia at bay. Then, and only then, as Kyiv sees it, would peace be possible.

*

The Myth of the West's Threat to Russia, *Atlantic Council*, March 5, 2015

Much Western thinking about the causes of the Russo-Ukrainian War is rooted in a myth. It posits that the West—or, more specifically, NATO—attempted to wrest Ukraine from Russia's sphere of influence, thereby forcing Vladimir Putin to defend Russia's legit-imate strategic interests by going to war with Ukraine.

The logic is impeccable. The only problem is that there isn't a shred of truth to this claim.

Was the West determined to integrate Ukraine into its institutions? Until the Maidan Revolution broke out in late 2013, Ukraine "fatigue" had characterized Western policy since about 2008, when the government of then-President Viktor Yushchenko lost the reformist zeal it had inherited from the 2004 Orange Revolution. Even before that, Western policymakers never talked of including Ukraine in the European Union. Indeed, the EU's Eastern Partnership program and its offer of an Association Agreement to Kyiv were supposed to placate Ukraine without promising it even the distant prospect of membership in the EU. The reluctance to offer that prospect remains unchanged.

Has NATO Been Active—or Passive?

Was the West determined to transform Ukraine into a pro-Western democracy? The United States and Europe pumped several billions of dollars into Ukrainian civil society projects since 1991, while remaining indifferent to the Leonid Kuchma regime's slide toward authoritarianism in the late 1990s, the abandonment by Yushchenko's "Orange government" of its democratic reform agenda, and Viktor Yanukovych's establishment of a full-fledged authoritarian regime in 2010–2013. Some Western policymakers supported the Maidan Revolution rhetorically and insisted that Yanukovych seek a compromise with the democratic revolutionaries; but most did not. No Western state provided any material assistance to the Maidan. And no Western presidents or prime ministers called on Yanukovych to step down during the revolution: quite the contrary, they travelled to Kyiv in late February 2014 with the express purpose of saving him. Once he abandoned his office, many Western policymakers welcomed his move—but that was after, and not before, the fact.

Did NATO ever push Ukraine to join the alliance? The answer is no. And for good reason: It was (and still is) unready to make the commitment, under its Article 5, to rush to Ukraine's assistance in case of an attack by Russia. Three months after the Yushchenko government formally requested a "membership action plan" as a first step toward joining NATO, the alliance's North Atlantic Council in April 2008 issued the vaguest "welcome" possible of "Ukraine's and Georgia's Euro-Atlantic aspirations for membership." While NATO declined to repudiate the "Open Door" principle it had declared a decade earlier (with the less vulnerable and more viable Poland and Czech Republic in mind), it also dampened the Yushchenko government's ardor, declining to issue the requested membership plan and promising instead to talk about it.

Did Ukraine ever come close to joining NATO? Of course, not. The alliance's polite and vague 2008 "welcome" effectively slow-walked the idea until, two years later, Yanukovych won election in Ukraine. He quickly reduced Kyiv's stated ambition from "membership" to a maintenance of its existing "partnership" with NATO. The alliance just as quickly agreed, and Ukraine's relationship with NATO disappeared altogether from Kyiv's policy agenda. Public opinion surveys in Ukraine consistently showed that no more than a fifth of the population ever desired NATO membership. That changed only after the outbreak of Russia's war with Ukraine in 2014, when the percentage of NATO supporters quickly exceeded half.

Putin's Real Motive

Did Putin seize Crimea because of the West's desire to transform Ukraine into its bastion? From the start, Putin has explained the seizure in terms of some putative need to protect Russians from the "fascist junta" in Kyiv and to bring "sacred" Russian territory back into the fold. He began invoking the Western threat only after war with Ukraine had broken out and the West chose to support Kyiv. The fact is that Putin unleashed war against Ukraine for the same reasons that Saddam Hussein unleashed war against revolutionary Iran in 1980: to prevent revolutionary contagion, to punish the revolutionaries, and to take advantage of their weakness to make territorial gains.

Supporters of the view that NATO enlargement provoked Russia are right about one thing. Enlarging NATO in 2004, just as Putin was consolidating his authoritarian regime and developing visions of imperial expansion, created an impossible security conundrum for Ukraine. NATO enlargement effectively sent Russia an unmistakably strong signal: that Ukraine was outside the West's security interests and thus was fair game for Russia.

The West's deep and long-lasting indifference to Ukraine's security—and, in 2008, to Georgia's security—encouraged Putin's aggression. By the same token, the West's commitment to Ukraine's security—whether by means of economic or military assistance or both—can only discourage Putin's aggression, by conveying to him in no uncertain terms that Ukraine matters to the West.

*

Russia Expected to Escalate War in Ukraine Soon, *World Affairs Journal*, April 2, 2015

That's what a number of prominent experts think. Andrii Parubii, the vice speaker of Ukraine's Parliament and former national security adviser, stated on March 27th that there is a "high risk" of a "full-scale military operation" in the next few weeks. An expert team led by Wesley Clark, a retired US Army general and former NATO supreme allied commander, informed the Atlantic Council in Washington on March 30th that "Ukrainian forces expect [an] attack within the next 60 days. This assessment is based on geographic imperatives, the ongoing pattern of Russian activity, and an analysis of Russian actions, statements, and Putin's psychology to date." Finally, Russia' premier military analyst, Pavel Felgenhauer, said on March 31st that the next "Russian offensive campaign" is "highly likely to begin soon."

Heightened fears of major Russian escalations—up to and including air strikes and a massive land assault—have occurred every one-to-two months since Russia's invasion of Crimea in February 2014. Russia has confounded these expectations by escalating slowly, steadily increasing its supply of arms, money, irregular forces, and regular troops—while always stopping short of a full-scale war.

No one knows why. Has Vladimir Putin been skittish about the risks involved? Did he just make a mistake and fail to seize the best opportunity to attack—i.e., anytime in the first few months after the Maidan Revolution? Or has he been developing fiendishly clever plans and sharpening his knives?

To launch a truly big war now would be a huge strategic mistake for Russia. Ukraine has a functioning government, police force, and army, and the latter has shown that it can dole out serious punishment to Putin's commandoes in eastern Ukraine. According to official Ukrainian sources, the Russian separatists have lost 14,600 men since the spring of last year. In comparison, Ukraine's armed forces incurred 1,232 deaths in 2014 and 2015. (If the number were to include soldiers who are missing in action, and probably dead, it would probably be 2,500–3,000.) That's a kill ratio of 1:4 or 1:5 in Ukraine's favor. The kill ratio in the Battle of Debaltsevo, in mid-January, was similar, putting the lie to the claim that it was a rout for Ukraine.

Russia has more soldiers and better equipment and it could defeat Ukraine in a massive land war, but the cost to Russia would be extremely high, especially as victory on the battlefield would not immediately translate into control of the country. Ukraine has a vast volunteer movement, an active civil society, a newly found sense of national solidarity, while Ukraine's population overwhelmingly supports Ukraine's territorial integrity and sovereignty. Resistance would be fierce, and a Russian occupation could easily turn into a strategic defeat.

As Felgenhauer argues: "There will in all likelihood be no drive toward Kyiv or Lviv, up to the Polish boundary. It won't happen because Russia lacks the forces. In order to occupy Ukraine and place 45 million people on their knees, it is necessary to have many human resources and the army should consist of no fewer than a million. Seizing Kyiv is much easier than controlling it ... We don't have the capacity."

Worse for Russia, a major escalation in the next few months would torpedo Moscow's carefully calibrated attempts to split the European Union and convince Brussels to drop its sanctions. War—and the certainty of thousands of civilian deaths and hundreds of thousands of refugees fleeing westward—would consolidate the Europeans and probably lead to an intensification of sanctions. Even the Obama administration would feel impelled finally to arm Ukraine with lethal weapons, as the only argument against provisions—that they would provoke an escalation—would fall away in the face of Putin's unprovoked escalation. Stephen F. Cohen, North Korea, Marie Le Pen, and Germany's *Russlandversteher* might cheer Putin's aggression, but that would be small consolation for the Kremlin.

Still, Putin just might be irrational—or ill—enough to do something profoundly stupid and inhuman. Power-hungry dictators presiding over crumbling regimes and fearful of their own physical decay have been known to sacrifice millions for the sake of their manias.

The West must understand that Ukrainians will fight and that Putin's war, if he launches it, will not be a cakewalk for Russia. Ukraine and Russia could be destabilized. If they are, Europe will be next. The EU's favorite mantra—that there is no military solution to the war—can come to pass only if Ukraine has the capacity to stop a Russian assault. And that means provisions of lethal weapons.

Here's what the Clark team recommends:

1. strategic imagery and other electronic/communications intelligence detailed and timely enough to be able to provide warning of an impending attack;

2. long-range, mobile anti-armor systems, as well as the shorter ranger Javelin

system, both equipped with thermal imagery;

3. secure tactical communications down to vehicle level;

4. long-range, modern counter battery radars able to detect firing positions for long range rockets;

5. sniper rifles with thermal or night vision sights for counter sniper teams;

6. modern intelligence collection and EW [electronic warfare] systems effective against Russian digital communications; and

7. whatever counter UAV [unmanned aerial vehicle] systems can be made available on a near-term basis.

Most important, the West must act immediately. "At the minimum," concludes Clark, "a palletized, emergency assistance package consisting of as much of the lethal components as possible should be assembled and pre-deployed for strategic airlift upon commencement of the Russian offensive."

As the Romans said, "If you want peace, prepare for war."

*

Meet Motorola, Self-Confessed War Criminal of the Donbas, *World Affairs Journal*, April 10, 2015

The latest entry into the Donbas enclave's Pantheon of heroes is one Arsenii Sergeevich **Pavlov**, a slight 32 year-old Russian from Russia who sports the *nom de guerre*, Motorola.

Why Pavlov chose this ridiculous moniker is unclear. Was his first cell phone a Motorola? Is he even aware that Motorola was a telecommunications firm founded in a country he detests almost as much as Ukraine—America?

The Russian Spring website, which serves as a cheerleader for Putin's separatist commandoes in Ukraine's Russian-occupied territories, refers to Pavlov as "legendary." And indeed he is. The guy's fought in all the major battles in eastern Ukraine and earned a name for himself as the commander of the Sparta battalion.

He's also a self-declared war criminal.

Here's what Motorola told the *Kyiv Post* on April 3 after being asked to comment on eyewitness testimony that he had murdered a Ukrainian prisoner of war on January 21:

> I don't give a f**** about what I am accused of, believe it or not. I shot 15 prisoners dead. I don't give a f****. No comment. I kill if I want to. I don't if I don't.

Ukrainian human rights activists were outraged. As was Amnesty International's Europe and Central Asia Deputy Director Denis Krivosheev, who asked: "The new evidence of these summary killings confirms what we have suspected for a long time. The question now is: what are the separatist leaders going to do about it?"

Krivosheev is missing the point.

Criminality is at the very core of the separatist movement in eastern Ukraine. The separatist leaders are not just not going to do anything about it. They positively need criminality to be who they are. Criminality is their *raison d'être*. To Motorola's credit, he was open and honest about it. You can accuse Pavlov of many things, but pussyfootin' ain't one of them.

Remember: these are the guys who've managed, in just under a year, to bring about a humanitarian catastrophe in the Donbas enclave. These are the guys who are actively involved in stripping the region of its few remaining assets. These are the guys who shot down a Malaysian airliner last summer. These are the guys who are threatening to bring more destruction to Ukraine.

True separatists would be actively building—a nation, a state, whatever. All these guys do is actively destroy.

But that should come as no surprise to anyone who knows they're Putin's puppets. After all, Herr Putin is Russia's dictator. He's the man who transformed a potential democracy into a full-fledged fascist state. He's the man who promotes hate with his vast propaganda machine. He's the man who's managed to persuade some 85 percent of Russians that war is peace, hate is love, democracy is fascism, and fascism is democracy. If that sounds like George Orwell's 1984, that's because it is. No, wait: it's more like Adolf Hitler's 1939.

The Donbas enclave that the Motorolas of Russia have invaded is just an outgrowth of Putin Russia proper—a thuggish little protectorate that like, Ramzan Kadyrov's Chechnya, serves as model of Putin's regime style.

Putin, after all, has been a man of violence and criminality all his life. The KGB was his natural home, and fascism is his natural worldview. Motorola is just Putin writ small.

The problem for Ukraine is that there are thousands of crazed Motorolas running around the Donbas enclave and many thousands more in Russia, willing and able to pick up the killing. Worse, there are probably hundreds of thousands of enclave residents who think Motorola's a great guy.

Does Ukraine really want to reintegrate a territory awash with fascist thugs and their morally obtuse collaborators? Cut them loose, I say. Renounce the enclave, build a deep moat, and surround it with the Great Wall of China.

You can't build a decent country with war criminals.

Funding Ukraine's Recovery, *World Affairs Journal*, April 24, 2015

Ukraine needs 60–100 billion euros in investment in the next 10 years in order to rebuild its economy and reach the GDP level it had in 2013, according to **Gunter Deuber**, an analyst at Vienna's Raiffeisen Bank International. One half will have to come from the European Union and the United States; the other half from private investors.

The numbers look fantastically large, but they're not. The United States and the EU have provided Afghanistan with about 100 billion euros worth of aid in the last 10 years, while the USA has invested at least 60–70 billion euros in Iraq. Romania has received 20 billion euros from the EU, while Poland has received 80 billion. Although the costs of rebuilding Ukraine are, as Deuber says, "substantial," the implied economic transformation is "plausible." The same holds true for the necessary 30–50 billion of private investments, which are "not utopian." The bottom line is that the EU "has a vital interest in the success of Ukraine's economic modernization," as the risk-filled alternative would be "mass emigration and political radicalization."

The catch, according to Deuber, is that several preconditions be met.

1. Ukraine needs to have a "functioning economic model that entails deep reforms and cooperation with the EU and the Eurasian Economic Union" led by Russia.

2. Ukraine must fulfill all IMF requirements, as only that will persuade skittish European investors to sink their money into the Ukrainian economy.

3. Ukraine must reduce corruption and makes its institutions capable of productively absorbing incoming monies.

4. Ukraine needs to adopt a market mentality.

5. Ukraine needs to stabilize its security situation and deal with the Donbas.

With respect to point 1, Russian President Vladimir Putin can block, and has blocked, Ukraine's economic relations with the Eurasian Economic Union, but the EU is not without leverage, especially with regard to Russian energy exports, and could probably work out a deal that promotes everybody's economic interests. Kyiv seems committed to points 2 and 3. The IMF looks happy with Ukraine's progress, but the problem is that long-term austerity risks producing social discontent and weakening Kyiv's resolve. With respect to corruption, so far, so good—sort of. Kyiv is cracking down on some forms of low-to-high-level corruption and has recently appointed a young, and presumably incorruptible, head of an anti-corruption bureau. As to point 4, my sense is that most Ukrainians have assimilated a market-oriented approach to life, if only because they've been forced to do so.

That leaves point 5, where Ukraine appears to be completely hostage to Russia. The conventional wisdom is that the war will continue as long as Putin wants it to continue, and the Donbas will remain a cancer as long as Putin wants it to be one. Technically, that's true. At the same time, the war will stop, if not formally end, when Ukraine has the military wherewithal to stop any Russian or proxy attack short of an all-out invasion or nuclear assault. In fact, Ukraine is close to achieving that capability and, with every day, comes closer.

Moreover, the West and Ukraine can take the initiative and mold conditions in their favor.

The West can decrease the likelihood of an escalation by making it very clear to Putin that the costs of such a move will be very high: exclusion of Russian from the SWIFT international banking system and the massive provision of lethal weapons to Ukraine. In the meantime, providing non-lethal equipment, intelligence data, and training can only bolster Ukraine without in any way alarming Russia or its apologists in the West.

Kyiv, meanwhile, can hasten the Donbas enclave's transformation into a "frozen conflict" by renouncing the liberation of the region by military means. Yes, that also means renouncing the Donbas enclave, but, as I have argued before, that can only benefit Ukraine and its reform prospects.

Deuber expresses the same sentiment in the circumspect language of economists:

> It is worth considering from the economic point of view whether deep reforms as well as a sustainable reconstruction would not be easier to achieve without the Donbas. This would be especially true if [Ukraine's] relations with Russia do not improve markedly, Ukraine's orientation on the West continues, and if a cooperative "economic model" with the EEU is not realized.

If you're still unpersuaded, ask yourself this: Would *you* invest in the Donbas enclave? And if you would, might I interest you in the Brooklyn Bridge?

*

On Donbas Autonomy—Again, *World Affairs Journal*, June 12, 2015

Foreign policymakers and analysts intone "autonomy" for the Russian-occupied Donbas enclave with tedious regularity, almost as if they were in possession of some magic formula. One of the latest to join the chorus was NATO General Secretary Jens Stoltenberg.

In fact, invocation of autonomy is at best an evasion, at worst meaningless.

For starters, the Donbas, like Crimea, effectively enjoyed vast autonomy since Ukraine's independence in 1991. Local political elites—their latest manifestation was Viktor Yanukovych's Party of Regions—ruled Luhansk and Donetsk provinces in cahoots with organized crime and oligarchs, foremost among them being the multibillionaire Rinat Akhmetov. Kyiv had almost nothing to say about their political, economic, and social policies. Russian language and culture reigned supreme, while Ukrainian language and culture were absent from the public realm, a fact that pro-autonomy proponents of "protecting" Russian from nonexistent Ukrainian "nationalist" assaults conveniently overlook.

In any case, while more regional autonomy is a good idea for all of Ukraine, the Donbas weakens the case for decentralization, suggesting that it leads to the formation of regional clans that exploit people, steal like mad, whip up chauvinist passions, and promote war for their own nefarious ends.

But the main reason for viewing autonomy as a bogus solution for the occupied Donbas enclave is that it means completely different things for the parties involved—Kyiv and the separatists. Implementation of the Minsk accords has made little progress beyond the ratty cease-fire, partly because the separatists and Russia violated the agreement from day one and mostly because there is no way that Kyiv and the self-styled Donetsk and Luhansk "people's republics" can agree.

Understandably, Kyiv insists on the region's de-militarization and on fair and free elections to determine who will run things. To agree to anything less would be to abandon all pretense of Ukraine's statehood and sovereignty. After all, states are supposed to have a monopoly of violence; they cannot countenance the presence on their territory of armed militias. By the same token, sovereignty means that states set the rules according to which elites and sub-elites are chosen. Kyiv has stated that, if the current separatists are elected in fair and free elections, it would recognize them. But for sovereignty to have any content, Kyiv must insist on elections held according to its rules.

No less understandably, the separatists insist on retaining their militias and on remaining in power—demands that are diametrically opposed to, and irreconcilable with, Kyiv's minimal requirements. To make matters worse, Vladimir Putin's proxies simultaneously maintain that they are already independent and that they would be happy to remain within Ukraine's fold under maximally autonomous conditions. That's nonsense: you cannot be independent and not independent at the same time.

How can this circle be squared?

It can't. Kyiv must insist that Ukraine is a sovereign state, while the separatists must insist on remaining in power. Which is why I've been suggesting with no less tedious regularity that Ukraine would do well to freeze the conflict and let the enclave drift away. That way, Ukraine doesn't recognize the people's republics, while effectively enabling the separatists to run them into the ground, with, presumably, minimal negative effects for Ukraine proper. This won't stop the fighting, at least not immediately. Even though Kyiv rejects using force to win back the enclave, Russia's proxies still say they have the right to "liberate" at least all of the Donbas. Over time, however, the continued decay of the en-clave will, or should, erode the separatists' war-fighting ability. In any case, since Russian Foreign Minister Sergei Lavrov believes the enclave should be part of Ukraine, we can be certain that keeping it out is the right thing to do.

Of course, mine is a halfway measure. If Kyiv were bold, it would countenance giving the occupied territories the independence that its separatist leaders say they want or have.

Think about it. If Kyiv took the initiative, it could, in one fell swoop, establish clarity in its east. If the enclave were independent, all talk of "civil war," autonomy, and "economic blockades" would cease, and the only issue would be the Russian war against Ukraine proper. The West would be happy to see the problem of the Donbas go away, and, with the conflict reduced to its stark Russo-Ukrainian dimension, a diplomatic solution might be easier to find. In the meantime, Ukraine and the enclave could establish whichever relations they like, but only if both sides found them mutually profitable.

Sounds great, except that this approach would outrage Ukraine's hyper-patriots and the pro-Kyiv eastern Ukrainians who've been fighting for their homeland in the Donbas. Populist mobilization and popular discontent could even lead to a march on Kyiv or, heaven forbid, a third Maidan.

So are we back to square one or might this particular circle be squared?

A prominent democratic western Ukrainian policymaker, the 50-year-old Taras Stetskiv, has recently suggested just how the impossible might happen. He recommends holding a binding plebiscite in the occupied territories, with the choices being unification with Ukraine or independence. But here's the rub. Even though chances are the enclave would opt for independence, it's not at all clear that the separatists would let the ballot go ahead. After all, to do so would be to accept Kyiv's rules, which they reject *a priori*.

And that brings us back to square one: keeping the enclave at arm's length (and, as a side benefit, poking Lavrov in the eye). In time, the separatist-controlled territory is likely to acquire the accoutrements of independence, while Ukraine, bathed in blissful indiffer-ence to the enclave, continues on its path toward the West. A few years from now, "auton-omy" would be moot, as Ukraine and the enclave will have drifted so far apart as to exist in different worlds. Sort of like Putin and the West.

*

Should Kyiv Blockade the Donbas Enclave? *World Affairs Journal*, June 18, 2015

Ever since the Poroshenko Bloc's leader, Yuri Lutsenko, stated that the "President of Ukraine believes the cancerous tumor should be subjected to a blockade," Ukrainians have been heatedly debating whether Kyiv should sever all ties with the Russian-occupied Donbas enclave.

The argument for a blockade, which would entail a total cutoff of economic relations as well as deliveries of electricity, gas, and water, is straightforwardly strategic. Ukraine is at war with Russia and its puppets. The Kremlin started the war and seems to have no intention to end it. Putin's puppets engage in continual aggressions, systematically vio-lating cease-fires, and openly stating that they intend to conquer at least all the Donbas. Kyiv knows it can't win on the battlefield, but is hoping to be able to stop further Russian expansion. If Ukraine is to prevail, Kyiv needs to do everything possible to weaken the Kremlin's proxy war machine. A blockade would hasten the Donbas enclave's economic decline and make the region ungovernable. The blockade would do the trick.

The argument against a blockade rests on humanitarian and political concerns. A blockade would hurt the enclave's citizens—Ukrainian citizens who don't deserve to suffer for the misdeeds of the separatists. Abandoning these people would not only be cruel, but counterproductive, as it would turn them completely against their mother country, Ukraine. Moreover, cutting off all economic ties to Ukraine would only drive the region into Russia's arms and thereby seal its loss to Ukraine.

Both arguments are compelling, and both arguments entail painful trade-offs, but I find the one for a blockade to be more persuasive. Which side you choose depends on what you believe Ukraine's top priority is. For me, that's easy: it's the war, which is killing soldiers and civilians, undermining Ukraine's national economy, threatening its stability and its prospects for survival, and hampering reform. The war must either end or be frozen, and the sooner the better. If a blockade promotes that goal, then it's justified.

Would the people of the enclave suffer as a result? Yes, but remember this. The choice before Kyiv is not who should suffer, but who should suffer more: the 40 million Ukrainians in Ukraine, who are already paying an exorbitantly high price in terms of blood and money for Putin's war, or the 3 million "Enclavians" in the Donbas, who are also paying an exorbitantly high price for their misguided support of the separatist adventure? For me, 40 million who made the right choice beats 3 million who made the wrong choice hands down.

Would a blockade drive the region into Russia's arms? Yes and no. For starters, the overwhelming majority of the enclave's residents detest Ukraine and everything it hopes to become (such as a Western, democratic, rule-of-law, market state). Ditto for the separatists and their leaders. In effect, the region is already lost to Ukraine. At the same time, it's not at all clear that the enclave would therefore join Russia. The Kremlin has made it clear that it wants the enclave to remain in Ukraine. And if you don't believe Moscow's statements, consider its deeds. Russia has constructed a 100-kilometer-long ditch along its border with the occupied Donbas, ostensibly to keep out smugglers. Whether that's the actual intent is unclear, but the mere fact of a long ditch separating Russia proper from the enclave its puppets claim to be liberating obviously does not testify to Russia's desire to incorporate the enclave. And why should it? Rebuilding the region would cost billions, and Moscow is already saddled with the economic mess that is Crimea.

The choice before Kyiv—and it's one that Ukrainian policymakers have assiduously been pretending doesn't exist—is quite stark. Either a reformed, Western-oriented, and prosperous Ukraine without the Donbas enclave or an unreformed, Russia-oriented, and backward Little Russia with the enclave. You can't have both. And if you don't believe me, listen to Yuri Shvets, a former Ukrainian KGB agent now living in Washington: "The Donetsk and Luhansk province territories captured by the aggressor ... are a Trojan horse. Putin created it; let him now feed it. To let that 'horse' into Ukraine is tantamount to political and economic suicide."

PART THREE: RUSSIA'S WAR AGAINST UKRAINE

Ukraine's August Blues, *World Affairs Journal*, August 4, 2015

August is when most of Europe closes down, as people dash to their country homes or head for resorts. Beaches overflow; fun becomes mandatory. A perfect tan is all that matters.

What a wonderful time to forget that the war in eastern Ukraine will continue to rage, perhaps even intensify.

Vladimir Putin's terrorists, commandoes, mercenaries, and troops will keep on violating the Minsk-2 accords by shelling Ukrainian territory and killing Ukrainian citizens and soldiers. Yesterday, four soldiers lost their lives. The day before it was, I think, one. The day before that—none. The day before that: was it two? I forget.

Who's counting anymore? We've all become jaded by the steady trickle of single digits. Remember the shock everyone felt during the Maidan Revolution, when the first demonstrators were killed? No more. Putin has achieved nothing with his aggression except one thing: to inure us to death.

And just why are they dying? Ah, yes: for that lovely bit of Ukraine called the Donbas.

Germany's "iron chancellor," Otto von Bismarck, famously quipped that the "Balkans aren't worth the bones of a single Pomeranian grenadier." Since Prussians regarded Pomeranians as a backward folk, his remark was doubly derogatory.

Just how many Ukrainian grenadiers is Luhansk worth? Or Donetsk?

Most Europeans willingly suspend their commitment to European values when the lives of non-EU members are at stake. Aren't the Ukrainians defending Europe and everything it supposedly stands for? Sure, whatever; pass the sunblock, please, and let's have another beer.

How many Ukrainians would be willing to become Pomeranian grenadiers? Or let their sons or husbands join that distinguished category? There'll be lots of time to answer those questions. The war shows no signs of ending, even as the pointlessness of the shelling and killing becomes more obvious with every day.

Putin thinks he can wear Ukraine down. He's wrong.

Time is on Ukraine's side, not Russia's. With every day, Ukraine's economy strengthens, its state apparatus becomes a tad less dysfunctional, its army a bit more battle-ready, its institutions a little more consolidated. And with every day, Putin Russia moves, steadily but inexorably, in the opposite direction. Russia still has an advantage, for another six months or so. After that, Ukraine's existence should be pretty much assured.

All that Putin is sure of achieving is more death, more destruction, and Russia's collapse. Naturally, Putin doesn't quite see things this way. What's not to like about more death, especially of those pesky Little Russians? As to Russia, it's as eternal as he is.

Like all autocrats, Putin has become so predictable. His hubris blinds him to the obvious: he's doomed to join the lost list of dictators who went down in flames and dragged their countries along with them.

Poor Russia: the time of troubles that awaits it may make the Donbas war look like a cakewalk.

Poor Europe: if it forgets that the only thing that makes it worth having is European values and that Ukraine is defending those values more assiduously than the Europeans, the EU won't survive. After all, how many Pomeranian grenadiers is the euro worth?

Poor Ukraine: it'll have to lose many more lives before it realizes that the Russian-occupied Donbas enclave isn't worth the toe of a single Ukrainian grenadier.

*

Anti-Donbas Sentiment Growing in Ukraine, *World Affairs Journal*, August 21, 2015

Is Ukrainian public opinion turning toward getting rid of the Russian-occupied Donbas enclave?

The evidence is beginning to look persuasive. A year ago, the suggestion that Ukraine would be better off without the Russian-occupied bits of Luhansk and Donetsk provinces provoked cries of treason. No more. The view has become legitimate, and it may even be winning the day.

A May 2015 public opinion survey by the Sofia Center for Social Research showed that 61.8 percent of Ukrainians would be willing to give up the occupied territories in exchange for peace. Only 22.9 percent supported continuing military operations until the region's full liberation. (The survey was not conducted in Crimea or the occupied territories.)

My own conversations—with experts, family members, friends, and colleagues—in June and July in Ukraine revealed only one die-hard supporter of Ukraine's holding on to the enclave at all costs: a young television journalist. Indeed, I was struck by the prevailing view: people were tired of war, shocked and saddened by the killing and dying, and repulsed by the Russian separatists and their many supporters within the enclave's population. I'm not exaggerating when I say that the Ukrainians I spoke to felt zero loyalty to it.

Now two highly authoritative voices have joined the growing chorus of anti-enclave sentiments.

On August 3rd, Volodymyr Lanovy, the liberal economist who served as vice prime minister and minister of the economy in 1992, argued that, by maintaining economic relations with the enclave, Kyiv was effectively financing the enemy that was daily killing its soldiers. According to Lanovy: "At present, Crimea and the Donetsk-Luhansk enclave have de facto stopped being internal regions of Ukraine." Given that Russia controls the border, the "occupied lands of Crimea and the Donbas have provisionally entered the political and economic space of the aggressor country"—Russia. Given also that the Ukrainian authorities hold no sway in the enclave, it follows that "all talk of trade, subsidies to the coal mines, salaries to state employees, state-funded pensions according to Ukraine's norms are simply out of place."

Then, on August 17th, independent Ukraine's first president, Leonid Kravchuk, stated the following:

> We should finally make an important political decision. We should state that the line of demarcation in the Donbas is the provisional line of separation between the occupied territories of Luhansk and Donetsk provinces and Ukraine. We [should] sever all economic and political relations with these regions controlled by the militants and Russia. They seized power by force. I believe we should give them the opportunity to administer these territories, and life will then test their talents.
>
> All talk of the fact that our people live there and that they should be helped must be removed from the order of the day. This humanism and tears in general give Ukraine nothing. Today, as a result of Russia's influence, a cancerous growth has formed on this territory. This growth can be eliminated only by surgery and nothing else.

These are strong and unambiguous words. No less important, their author is Kravchuk. Is the architect of Ukraine's independence and the Soviet Union's dissolution in 1991 speaking only for himself? Could be. But nothing is ever quite that simple in Ukraine, especially as Lanovy served as Kravchuk's economy minister. Are the two coordinating their messages? Are they speaking for some faction in the government?

Their statements are either trial balloons or a harbinger of things to come. Either way, the enclave's days as a cancer in Ukraine's body may be limited.

*

A Cautionary Note: Reintegrating the Donbas, *World Affairs Journal*, October 16, 2015

The fighting in the Donbas may be winding down, but Ukraine's war with Russia will continue as long as Vladimir Putin believes that Ukraine must become his subject.

Now more than ever Ukraine's survival as a democratic Western state depends on the continued strengthening of Ukraine's military capability and the acceleration of reform.

An ostensibly peaceful Russia wedded to imperial expansion is no less of a military threat to Ukraine than an openly hostile Russia wedded to imperial expansion. The West is too preoccupied with its own problems and too indifferent to Putin's destruction of the post-war international order to save Ukraine.

Only Ukraine can protect itself from further Russian predations by acquiring a first-class military able to deter all but the craziest of Russian leaders. Meanwhile, a first-class military is impossible without a strong economy, which in turn is impossible without serious, sustained reform.

As difficult as introducing reform has been, it's about to get much harder—for two reasons.

First, the seeming end to fighting will incline some Ukrainian policymakers to conclude that the Russian threat has waned and that they can relax.

Second, it now looks like Ukraine may have to reintegrate the Donbas enclave sometime in the near future. I've been arguing ad nauseam that Ukraine would be infinitely better off by keeping the enclave on the other side of a high wall. Alas, my argument may be about to become moot, as—or if—Minsk-2 is implemented.

Signed in February 2015, the Minsk-2 accords propose a series of steps—a cease-fire, an exchange of prisoners, a constitutional amendment regarding the Donbas enclave's status, Russian withdrawal, local elections, and Ukrainian control of the enclave's border with Russia—that are supposed to end the war and usher in peace. The problem with the deal is that Ukraine expects Minsk-2 to lead to its reassertion of sovereignty, that Russia expects it to produce Ukrainian subservience, and that the separatists expect it to reinforce their rule.

It's therefore perfectly possible that Minsk-2 will break down, as all sides realize there is no way to finesse their incompatible demands. The result could be a frozen conflict, with the added advantage that Russia might be reluctant to renew hostilities and incur sanctions. Were that to happen, Kyiv should formally declare that the Donbas enclave is occupied territory that falls under the purview of the occupying power, Russia.

If Putin's proxies are less strategically daft than he is, they might push for reintegration and thereby put Ukraine in the hot seat. As absolutely everyone knows, the enclave—and indeed the whole Donbas, even the part occupied by Ukrainian forces—has been and still is ruled by criminal clans, criminal oligarchs, criminal mafias, and—the latest twist—criminal separatists and criminal warlords. Most of the population is unremittingly hostile to everything the new Ukraine stands for. The economy is in ruins.

If anyone knows how Ukraine is supposed to reintegrate this cancerous region without infecting itself in the process, please tell me.

The challenge would be enormous even if Ukraine defeated the Russian separatists and occupied the territory. And Ukraine has not defeated the rebels. Nor will it ever occupy the enclave and impose its will without reigniting the war.

Instead, Ukraine will have to reintegrate an unreconstructed and unreconstructable region. That's what Minsk-2 mandates. And that's been the declared goal of the Ukrainian political establishment.

As they say, be careful what you wish for. It may come true.

There's only one way for a potentially reintegrated Donbas enclave to wreak minimal damage on Ukraine.

Kyiv should quarantine the territory and its thugs by giving it, and them, almost complete sovereignty within a confederal relationship with Ukraine.

Neither Kyiv nor the enclave would interfere in each other's internal or external political affairs. Both sides would pursue their own economic policies, refrain from subsidizing each other, keep all the taxes they collect, and pursue trade with whomever they desire. Each side would be responsible for law and order, speak whichever language it desires, remember what it wants to remember, and honor whomever it wants to honor. Other issues would be stickier (Would there be one army or two? Would the enclave pursue its own foreign policy? Would there be one president or two?), but not immune to creative solutions.

Russia and its separatist thugs—along with France, Germany, and the United States—would be hard-pressed to say *nyet* to such a deal, while Kyiv and Ukraine's hotheads could claim victory and declare that Ukraine is whole again.

Do confederations work in the medium to long term? Rarely, unless, as in the case of the Swiss, there are special circumstances that overcome the centrifugal forces built into them.

If the Ukrainian confederation works, great. Ukraine proper will reform, while the enclave goes to the hell of its choice. If the confederation doesn't work and both sides agree to go their own way—perhaps like the Czechs and the Slovaks—what's not to like?

*

Why the Realists Were Wrong About the War in Ukraine, *Atlantic Council*, November 2, 2015

The ongoing ceasefire in eastern Ukraine may or may not lead to a lasting peace, but it has already had one important consequence: it has undermined both Russian and realist interpretations of the Russo-Ukrainian war.

On August 29, Russian President Vladimir Putin, French President Francois Hollande, and German Chancellor Angela Merkel agreed that a ceasefire should take place in eastern Ukraine on September 1. And indeed, on that day, most guns fell silent. Since then, the ceasefire has largely held.

The separatists stopped firing not because of anything Hollande or Merkel said, but because Putin instructed them to do so. In short, Putin stopped the war. Consider what this fact means for explanations of the war proposed by Putin and realists.

Putin has usually explained the 2014 invasion of Crimea and eastern Ukraine as a defensive measure necessitated by the "fact" that Ukrainian fascists had seized power in a coup, and that the rights and lives of Ukraine's Russians and Russian speakers were in danger. Russia had no choice but to come to their aid.

On September 1, 2015, however, the very same Ukrainian "fascists" were still in power in Kyiv. Indeed, they now have an army of over forty thousand battle-hardened patriotic troops, supplemented by former volunteer battalions that the Kremlin has never failed to call fascist as well. If Russians and Russian speakers were right to fear for their lives in 2014, they have even more reason to fear for their lives today.

Russian and Western realists have also explained the 2014 invasion in light of two supposed facts. First, the United States allegedly staged the Euromaidan, thereby attempting to wrest Ukraine from Russia's legitimate sphere of influence. Second, NATO had relentlessly expanded its boundaries and was determined to incorporate Ukraine in the aftermath of the CIA-inspired Euromaidan, directly threatening Russia's security. Naturally, Russia could not simply watch as the West encroached upon its interests, so it responded as any great power would: by flexing its muscles and showing that it would not tolerate more Western expansion.

On September 1, 2015, however, the US commitment to Ukraine, as well as its presence and interests there, were much greater than they had been in early 2014. So, too, were NATO's. Indeed, the Alliance had beefed up its military presence in Eastern Europe and adopted a variety of measures to incorporate Ukraine in its planning and procedures. In brief, if the West was a threat to Russia in 2014, it was an even greater threat to Russia in late 2015. And yet, Russia—that is, Putin—mandated a ceasefire.

According to the logic proposed by Putin as well as Russian and Western realists, Russia and the separatists should have continued, and perhaps even intensified, the fighting in eastern Ukraine in the last few months. Instead, Putin has deescalated, despite the fact that all the alleged reasons for the war were still in place.

Realists might reply to this critique by suggesting that the real reason for the ceasefire in Ukraine is perfectly obvious: Putin had decided to go to war in Syria, and Ukraine was thereby relegated to the strategic backburner.

That may be true, but the explanation does nothing to enhance the credibility of realism. After all, if Syria was strategically more important than Ukraine on September 1, 2015, then it should have been strategically more important in the last few years of the Syrian civil war, when Russian ally President Bashar Assad was on the defensive and the terrorist group ISIS threatened Russian interests. Indeed, how could a rational Russian leader have decided to go to war with Ukraine—supposedly a strategically less important issue—while far more important Russian interests were being threatened in Syria?

One could explain Russian behavior as either an example of irrationality or a case of changed perceptions. But if Putin acted irrationally, then realism's rationality assumption becomes false and the theory's relevance to the Russo-Ukrainian war disappears. Alternatively, if Putin perceived Syria to be a greater threat than Ukraine at Time B as opposed to Time A, then realism morphs into constructivism by implicitly adopting the latter's claim that national interests are not objective or stable, but continually constructed and reconstructed by elites. That concept may or may not be true, but it is certainly not realism.

Whichever explanation of Russia's wars one chooses, one must assign a central role to Putin, rather than to internal conditions in Ukraine or external threats from the West. At the core of the explanatory model may be Putin the man or Putin the psychopath. Or it may be Putin the machismo-obsessed leader of a highly centralized, institutionally weak, authoritarian system that requires militarist chest beating and imperialist saber-rattling for its, and his, legitimacy.

What is clear is that Putin started the war and only Putin can end it. Russia and its supposedly objective national interests, like Ukraine and its alleged capture by fascists, are pretty much irrelevant. Western policymakers would do well to keep the centrality of Putin in mind as they attempt to construct a lasting peace in Ukraine. It's not Russia, Ukraine, or the West that must change for peace to be possible. It's Putin.

*

When Ukraine Lost Donetsk, *Foreign Affairs*, November 22, 2015

If the leader of the self-styled Donetsk People's Republic (DNR) has anything to say about it, the current cease-fire in eastern Ukraine will never translate into permanent peace. Nor will it lead to the separatist territories' reintegration into Ukraine. Alexander Zakharchenko's statements before and after the guns went silent on the first of September reveal a continued rejection of Ukraine, a commitment to Donbas independence, a strong determination to acquire more territory, and a radical division of people into friends and enemies. Small wonder that separatist violations of the cease-fire have increased significantly since early November.

It is impossible to say whether Zakharchenko's militancy is the posturing of a desperate man or the vision of a ruthless leader. Either way, it suggests that the DNR's interests are incompatible with Ukraine's and that the Minsk-2 accords will fail to achieve their intended goal of reintegrating the DNR and its sister entity, the Luhansk People's Republic (LNR). Even if Russia pressures the DNR to make substantive concessions—and that is an extremely big if—its leader will resist.

In effect, peace in eastern Ukraine is dependent on two willful, demagogic, unpredictable, and militaristic men—Russian President Vladimir Putin and Zakharchenko. Putin claims to be a bystander in the war, whereas Zakharchenko insists that he is in charge. The reality is more complex. As the September 1 cease-fire showed, Putin's is the decisive voice. He started the war, and he can sue for peace. But Zakharchenko isn't just a puppet. He has ideas, ambitions, and plans of his own, and his acquiescence will ultimately determine whether any deal holds.

Zakharchenko, a 39-year-old former electrical mechanic, first entered politics in 2010, the year Viktor Yanukovych was elected president of Ukraine. As head of the Donetsk-based pro-Russian and pro-Soviet organization, *Oplot* (Bulwark), he actively opposed the Euromaidan Revolution of 2013–14, was one of seven armed men who seized the Donetsk city administration building on April 16, 2014, and was an active combatant in subsequent fighting with Ukrainian armed forces. In August 2014, he was elected DNR premier. A few months later, he was elected head of the DNR. Zakharchenko has dominated the area's political landscape since then.

The DNR is not, he has routinely insisted, Ukrainian territory. It is an independent state. "Children," he says, "must understand that they live in a different country." Whereas Ukraine is in the grip of a fascist junta and "outspoken Nazis," the DNR is democratic and committed to the commonwealth. That there is dissent and disagreement within the DNR is "normal," says Zakharchenko. "After all, we are not Ukraine!"

Zakharchenko insists that Kyiv exists in a "parallel, virtual reality." Indeed, he believes "Ukraine itself has become a virtual reality under their leadership," suggesting that both the state and the nation are fictitious. One may dispute Zakharchenko's characterization of Kyiv's reality as virtual, but he is right to call it parallel. Post-Maidan Ukraine stands for everything he, and by extension the DNR, reject, just as Zakharchenko and his statelet stand for everything post-Maidan Ukraine and the West reject. There appears to be no room for compromise.

In turn, any attempts by Ukraine to retake the Donbas are, in effect, invasions. On September 7, just a few days after the cease-fire went into effect, Zakharchenko compared the Kyiv government and army to the invading Nazis: "In 1941 a vicious, perfidious, and powerful enemy came to our land. ... In 2014 an enemy again came to our land," he said. "They failed to force the Donbas to its knees in 1941. They also failed in 2014–2015." On another occasion, he accused Kyiv of committing "genocide against our people." Naturally, all of Ukraine's aggressions against the DNR have the backing of nefarious Western forces, including Doctors Without Borders. But woe to Ukraine if it decides to join NATO (a prospect Zakharchenko appears to believe is possible in the immediate future). As he said on September 25, "If Ukraine starts preparing a referendum on NATO membership or other procedures, the DNR will immediately abandon the Minsk agreement and proceed with cleansing all the territory of the Donbas of the Kyiv occupation."

Zakharchenko intends to win back the rest of the Donbas even if Ukraine makes no move to join NATO. "I have stated many times that I consider the territory of the Donetsk People's Republic to be the entire territory of the former Donetsk Province. And I do not renounce those words," Zakharchenko said on November 5. He sees two possible scenarios of the DNR's expansion. If Kyiv resumes fighting, Zakharchenko will seize the Donbas by force. If the Minsk peace process continues, the territory will be retaken through political negotiations.

Zakharchenko was even more outspoken in an August 27 interview. The DNR's minimum goal is recapturing all of Donetsk Province. His maximum goal is "a Great Novorossiya," or New Russia, which would encompass all of southeastern Ukraine. How to attain that goal will be decided "when we're victorious." In the meantime, "there's no need to sit and wait" with respect to "the rest of so-called Ukraine." Whoever "wants to be rid of an illegal government, destroy the fascists, and stop Ukraine from being a spineless puppet in the hands of American puppeteers should evince a more active position."

Zakharchenko's radicalism manifests itself in his attitude toward refugees from and residents of the DNR. Those who fled to Ukraine and opposed the DNR will not, "to put it mildly," be welcomed. To be sure, "we won't shoot returnees," but they will have to prove their "usefulness" and make amends. Open enemies will "possibly be tried." As to those who stayed in Donetsk, Zakharchenko admits that "many" remained, not out of ideological conviction but because "they simply couldn't flee." That makes them no different from the refugees.

Zakharchenko also minces no words about who will rule his state: "those who defended the Republic with weapons in their hands or who, under fire, helped rebuild our industry, economy, and infrastructure." Kyiv's recommendations for conducting local elections in the Donbas are thus divorced from reality, as Zakharchenko puts it, since they entail the participation of "those parties that created the political cover for the punitive operation in the Donbas." Since all of Ukraine's democratic parties supported military action against the DNR, the local elections mandated by Minsk-2 would in effect feature only one set of candidates—Zakharchenko's elite.

Some of this bravado must cheer Russia. In Zakharchenko, Putin has a fanatical opponent of Ukrainian statehood, a man who will, under no circumstances, compromise with Kyiv and the West. But Zakharchenko's fanaticism must also be a source of concern. On November 5, the DNR leader insisted that the "fate of the Donbas" is decided in the Donbas, and not in Moscow, Washington, Berlin, or Paris. Zakharchenko's next sentence had to worry the Kremlin: "I personally do not intend to be a puppet in anyone's hands."

Zakharchenko is best viewed as a regional Russian warlord who, like Chechnya's Ramzan Kadyrov, will be reluctant to play the role of Putin's toady. The recent increase in DNR violations of the cease-fire demonstrates the inherent tensions between Putin and Zakharchenko. Attacking the Ukrainian armed forces is an excellent way of raising the morale of the DNR's dispirited fighters, many of whom appear to feel abandoned by Russia. But the escalation and possible collapse of Minsk-2 would not be advantageous to a Russia worried about Western sanctions and poised to increase its involvement in Syria. Zakharchenko needs Putin, but Putin also needs Zakharchenko—a fact the wily DNR head no doubt knows.

Unless Zakharchenko's words are insincere, there is no way he could possibly agree to implement any version of the Minsk-2 accords. Whatever its own intentions, Russia may be able to twist his arm up to a point, as it did by imposing a cease-fire on his forces on September 1, but it is highly unlikely to force him to follow Moscow's orders blindly.

Minsk-2 thus has two possible outcomes. Most probable is a "frozen conflict" along the lines of Transnistria, the breakaway region of Moldova. Ukraine would be spared the pain of having to integrate a region that cannot be integrated, while Zakharchenko and his elite would be able to continue building their statelet. The West would be happy with any outcome that stops the guns from firing. Even Russia might acquiesce, however grudgingly. It would still have to spend billions on the DNR economy, but it would be able to claim that it saved the Donbas from the "fascists."

Less likely is a very loose confederation of Ukraine and the DNR-LNR, in which the breakaway republics enjoy complete political, cultural, and economic autonomy, receive no financial subsidies from Kyiv, and have no authority to meddle in Kyiv's affairs. Although all parties could claim victory in this scenario, the arrangement would be intrinsically unstable and would probably revert to some form of frozen conflict after a few months or years.

There is a third, less likely alternative, but one that Putin and his parent organization, the KGB, have effectively practiced. A loose cannon such as Zakharchenko may easily lose his usefulness to the Kremlin and become a serious problem. The DNR's leader may thus want to keep in mind the sad fate of another Alexander—Litvinenko—the FSB officer who was poisoned and died in London in 2006.

*

Why Reintegrating the Donbas Is Suicide for Ukraine, *World Affairs Journal*, February 25, 2016

If you're wondering why the Minsk peace process isn't leading to peace, look no further than a recent interview with Vladislav Inozemtsev, a highly respected Russian economist and director of the Center for the Study of Post-industrial Society in Moscow. The bottom line—surprise, surprise!—is this: Vladimir Putin doesn't want peace. He wants to make Ukraine into a permanent backwater state dependent on the Kremlin.

How? By forcing Kyiv to reintegrate the now occupied, politically poisoned, and economically ravaged Donbas into Ukraine, knowing full well that this region, now forever crippled by Putin's proxies, will condemn Ukraine to being a permanently bankrupt puppet of the mafia state next door. This would be suicide. Tragically, although many Ukrainian policymakers understand it makes no sense for Ukraine to infect itself with this cancer, the power of Ukrainian patriotic rhetoric—"The Donbas is eternal Ukrainian land!"—may wind up saddling the country with a burden so heavy that it will crush its sovereign-ty and its democracy, move it decisively away from Europe and the world, and succeed in achieving what Viktor Yanukovych failed to do: transform Ukraine into a backward hinterland of a backward imperialist petro-state.

Is Moscow planning to annex the separatist Donbas enclave? Here's Inozemtsev:

> It's not. ... Perhaps the Kremlin considered this option at the start of the shocks in April-May 2014, but now, after the war, when we have become witness to enormous destruction, a dysfunctional system, and the region's transformation into an economic wasteland, obviously Russia will not annex it. ... Much there has been destroyed, much has been stolen, removed to Russia and resold. I believe this region represents no special economic advantage. More than that, consider what it used to have: the coal and metallurgical industries. Metallurgy remains in Mariupil, which is, thank God, under Ukrainian control, while the coal industry is very unprofitable. Ukraine's budget subsidized the Donbas for many years. ... Russia knows this industry is unprofitable and has no intention of supporting the east of Ukraine. ...

So Moscow wants the so-called Donetsk and Luhansk People's Republics to rejoin Ukraine?

> All of Russia's policies after the collapse of the Soviet Union—and not just Putin's—have aimed at creating a mess somewhere and leaving it in that condition. They tried to use Transnistria to undermine Moldovan statehood, but Transnistria turned out to have no benefit for Russia, while annexing it was undesirable as it would have facilitated Chisinau's road to Europe. The same happened in Georgia. Now it's Ukraine's turn. Moscow doesn't need the Donbas or a strong Ukraine. The Kremlin wants to saddle Kyiv with permanent problems. So that Ukraine won't be able to join the EU and NATO due to its territorial conflict. So that the so-called DNR and LNR will conduct Moscow's line in Ukraine's parliament. That's the hook on which Ukraine should hang.

Economist Anders Aslund is quite right to argue that Ukraine shouldn't pay for the Donbas:

> Who should pay for the restoration of the Donbas? The obvious answer is the aggressor, Russia. In a just world, Ukraine would add a demand to the Minsk negotiations for some $20 billion in war reparations from Russia for the Donbas. In reality, however, only losers pay war reparations.
>
> For the foreseeable future, it is unrealistic to expect that Ukraine will be able to finance the restoration of the Donbas. Nor can the already overindebted country borrow money to do the job. It would have to leave much of the Donbas' urban territories as industrial wastelands, which would make it arduous to reintegrate the population.

I fully agree with Aslund's policy recommendation, but can't imagine that it'll happen anytime soon:

The only sensible solution is for the European Union and the United States to put up substantial grant assistance to Ukraine for the restoration and reintegration of the Donbas. For the sake of stabilizing a former war-ravaged area in Europe, $20 billion is no great amount. Just compare it with the $300 billion the European Union has spent on the Greek financial crisis.

If Russia and the West won't pay for Russia's criminal devastation of the DNR-LNR-controlled territories, then Ukraine will get stuck with the bill. And that'll kill any hope that Ukraine will become a viable and modern democratic state.

Kyiv must find the courage to refuse the suicide option, declare the Donbas enclave Russian-occupied territory, and wash its hands of the mess.

*

Time for Ukraine to Take the Initiative, *World Affairs Journal*, March 23, 2016

Vladimir Putin's maneuverings with the West and Ukraine are often compared to a game of chess. The comparison is spot on, with one qualification. Contrary to the image of grandmaster he prefers, the Russian president more closely resembles a loudmouthed barroom player who slams pieces against the board. The effect is intimidating at first, but the best way to beat him is to take a deep breath, stick to your strategy, and play a consistently offe sive and defensive game.

Unfortunately, President Obama isn't very interested in playing chess with Putin. Maybe the State Department and the Pentagon are, but they're hamstrung by Obama's apparent indifference. The European Union, almost by definition, doesn't play well. Indeed, its member states can't agree on whether the game is chess, checkers, or soccer.

Putin's bullying and the West's non-play give Ukraine's leaders considerable room for maneuver. If Kyiv had a vision of its future, it could stop reacting to events and attempt to settle the war in eastern Ukraine on its own terms. By announcing bold initiatives, Kyiv could take the initiative and shock Washington and Europe out of their complacency or denial.

Consider the stalemate over the Minsk accords. France and Germany are pressuring Ukraine to hold elections in the occupied Donbas even as the Kremlin negates its end of the bargain by violating the ceasefire, arming Putin's proxies, repressing freedom of speech and assembly, and controlling the Ukrainian-Russian border. The elections would be a violation of every value France and Germany claim to stand for and only ensure that Russia would become a permanent cancer on Ukraine's body politic.

Rather than play the endless point and blame game, Kyiv could simply state that it has temporarily suspended its sovereign right to the Donbas enclave and will defer the elections to an appropriate international body. The OSCE or the UN would organize, conduct, and supervise the elections from beginning to end. For its part, Ukraine will accept the results as long as independent international monitors declare that the election process was fair and free.

Better still, President Poroshenko could announce that he supports granting the occupied Donbas the status of a fully sovereign region within a confederal Ukraine. The enclave would have its own government, its own budget, its own police, its own economy, its own laws. Kyiv wouldn't subsidize the enclave, and the enclave wouldn't subsidize Kyiv. All that would bind them would be some largely symbolic institution, perhaps a powerless council of elders that would periodically meet, sing songs, and be merry.

Putin and his proxies would be cornered. Putin wants the Donbas to weaken Ukraine. If you isolate the Donbas with a confederacy arrangement, the Kremlin's ability to infect Ukraine will be nullified. And the proxies couldn't say no: Ukraine would be giving them far more autonomy than they want. In the end, Ukraine would have a bankrupt criminal state on its border rather than a bankrupt criminal region inside its borders.

If that's too radical, consider a third way to take the initiative: Poroshenko could declare that Ukraine has "suspended" all efforts to reintegrate the occupied Donbas for, say, ten years. No Minsk, no military, no diplomacy—just freeze the status quo. After ten years, the OSCE or UN would oversee a referendum on self-determination in the occupied Donbas allowing the citizens to choose to return to Ukraine, remain independent, or join Russia.

Each of these three variants has the inestimable advantage of giving Ukraine the initiative. Kyiv would propose bold solutions that are consistent with human rights and democratic norms, and Russia and the West would have to respond.

Ukrainian elites must seize the initiative. If they don't counter Putin's poor chess play with their smart game, they'll lose.

*

Sick of the Ukraine Crisis? Then Arm Ukraine, *Atlantic Council,* March 29, 2016

Western policymakers who believe the Minsk accords would work if only Ukraine made the requisite constitutional and electoral concessions are missing a key point: that they, and Russia, forced Ukraine to make security its priority by violating the 1994 Budapest Memorandum on Security Assurances.

Russia brazenly invaded Crimea and eastern Ukraine in complete violation of the memorandum. But the United States and the United Kingdom were also complicit in the breakdown of Budapest: their assurances of Ukraine's sovereignty and territorial integrity proved hollow. Sanctions are nice, but hardly an adequate response to Russian imperialism.

The violation and non-enforcement of Budapest underpins Ukraine's approach to the Minsk accords and, indeed, to any peace deal. As constructed, Minsk institutionalizes Russia's invasion and permanent meddling in Ukrainian affairs. It doesn't matter whether Ukrainians do or do not make constitutional changes providing the occupied Donbas with autonomy, and it doesn't matter whether fair and free elections are held in the region. All that matters is that Minsk guarantees that Russia's proxies will remain in control of the occupied Donbas, and that Russia will remain in control of the Russo-Ukrainian border and will use whatever arrangement exists to infringe on Ukrainian security, stability, and sovereignty.

Needless to say, Ukraine cannot accept such an outcome. It's one thing for Ukraine to live in the shadow of Russia or to be mindful of Moscow's security concerns—as it was for the last twenty-five years. It's quite another for Ukraine's security and survival to be permanently hostage to an imperialist power that routinely invades its neighbors and has annexed Ukrainian territory.

Since the failure of Budapest means that formal international security assurances are effectively meaningless, Ukraine's first priority must be preserving its own security. No one can or will guarantee it, and even if they did, Ukraine would be crazy to believe a second Budapest.

Even if Putin were to sign a document guaranteeing Ukraine's security with his blood, Ukraine could not accept his word. Mendacity has become business as usual for Russia's President. But neither could Ukraine accept the West's word. Its long-standing indifference to independent Ukraine's security does not inspire confidence that this time the United States and the United Kingdom will really mean it.

Membership in NATO won't do the trick either, both because it's not in the cards for Ukraine anytime soon, and because Article 5 is squishy. The first part sounds bold: "The Parties agree that an armed attack against one or more of them in Europe or North America shall be considered an attack against them all." But the second part adds a qualifier ("as it deems necessary") that undermines the resoluteness of the first part: "They agree that, if such an armed attack occurs, each of them, in exercise of the right of individual or collective self-defense recognized by Article 51 of the Charter of the United Nations, will assist the Party or Parties so attacked by taking forthwith, individually and in concert with the other Parties, such action as it deems necessary, including the use of armed force, to restore and maintain the security of the North Atlantic area."

In a word, Ukraine will be secure only if it can guarantee its own security.

Since nuclear weapons are out of the question, Ukraine's security can be assured only if Ukraine has the requisite armed forces to guarantee its own security. Ukraine must have the capacity, not to defeat Russia, but to deter it from further imperialist encroachments on Ukrainian territory.

Once Ukraine is certain that its security is assured, all manner of negotiations and compromises become possible. Indeed, the Minsk accords become potentially workable. A strong and secure Ukraine might even countenance neutrality.

The implications for the West are obvious. Only a secure Ukraine will put its name to grand bargains crafted by Russia and the West. And a secure Ukraine can only be a militarily strong Ukraine. No Western deal with Russia can possibly work if it fails to take Ukraine and its justified security concerns into account.

Ukraine has already made enormous progress since the spring of 2014 when it had no more than 6,000 battle-ready troops to face Putin and his proxies. Even though the very imperfect "ceasefire" mandated by Minsk is routinely violated by Russian troops and results in daily Ukrainian deaths, it represents a tactical victory for Ukraine's army. Despite its defeats in several key battles, Ukraine has actually won the war—at least thus far—by stopping Russia's armed forces and Putin's 35,000 proxies.

Now Ukraine needs to gain the capacity to stop a full-scale Russian invasion. Although a massive land war would produce savage Ukrainian partisan resistance and lead to enormous losses for Russia, it would be far better to deter Russia than to embroil it in a costly quagmire. And for Ukraine to deter Russia, it needs to have the clear ability to stop Russian air power and tanks.

Arming Ukraine—building up its military to the point that it can defend itself, but not threaten Russia—is the only way to secure a durable peace there. The sooner the West learns this lesson, the sooner Budapest will fade as a bad memory—and the sooner Minsk or its successor will have a realistic chance of resulting in peace.

*

Dying for the Donbas? *World Affairs Journal*, May 16, 2016

Just about every day, soldiers die. Sometimes, it's as many as three or four. Sometimes, it's two or three. Usually, it's only one.

Only one young life snuffed out—for what?

For the Russian-occupied Donbas enclave. That is to say, for nothing.

I can understand, intellectually, at least, dying for your family or friends, for your country or city or community, for democracy or peace or your nation.

But dying for a piece of crummy land populated by 3 million inhabitants, most of whom hate Ukraine and everything it stands for? That makes no sense.

Most Ukrainian policymakers and most Ukrainian people appear determined to win back the Donbas territory occupied by Vladimir Putin's troops and proxies. At the same time, they appear to be equally determined to lead normal lives, as if the war—and make no mistake, it is a war—were taking place in some distant land.

As Ukraine's restaurants and cafés are abuzz with customers, as policymakers squabble over irrelevant minutiae, as Ukrainians gripe about the declining value of the hryvnia, soldiers who never asked to be sent to the front are dying or, if they're lucky, only losing their legs.

For what? For the 35,000 thugs in Putin's proxy army? For the broken-down industries and bankrupt coal mines? For the devastated cities and ruined infrastructure?

Or perhaps they're fighting and dying for Ukraine? For Europe? For democracy? For human rights?

The supreme irony is that Ukraine can survive only without the occupied Donbas. Europe couldn't care less about the Donbas. And Ukraine's democracy and commitment to human rights can flourish only if the reactionary occupants of that increasingly Putinized region are kept at arm's length.

The sad truth is that these poor young men are being sacrificed for nothing.

Ukrainians should ask themselves two questions.

Are they willing to throw away 5-to-10 human lives per week every week for the next twenty years—or even longer? And if they are willing to throw away 250-500 lives every year, would they be just as willing to augment that number by sending their sons and daughters—and grandchildren—to the front?

Ah, many Ukrainians will say, "We need to keep the Donbas, because, if we let it go, Putin will be emboldened to take more territory."

No, he won't. He would be emboldened if he defeats the Ukrainian armed forces and does so in a cakewalk. He would not be emboldened if the Ukrainian army engages in a strategic disengagement that strengthens Ukraine's ability to resist a Russian onslaught. He would be emboldened if the occupied Donbas were an economic boon for Russia. He would not be emboldened if, as is the case, it is, and remains, a massive drain on Russia's resources.

Sacrificing young lives for the defense of a strategically vital redoubt whose loss would spell defeat would make hard-nosed geopolitical sense. Sacrificing young lives for the defense of a strategically irrelevant cesspool of decay and corruption makes absolutely no sense.

Which brings us back to the ultimate rationale invoked by Donbas-integrators: "It's sacred Ukrainian territory and we won't give it up."

Fair enough, but then go to the front yourself and take your sons and daughters with you.

Just don't let others do the dying for you.

Answering the Critics: Donbas Disengagement, *World Affairs Journal*, May 24, 2016

What should Ukraine do about the occupied Donbas enclave?

As readers of this blog know, I have long been arguing for disengagement. Critics of my view generally emphasize some or all of the following three points:

First, won't disengagement help promote Vladimir Putin's strategic goal of destroying Ukraine?

Second, doesn't Ukraine have a moral obligation to reannex this territory and its citizens?

Third, what exactly does disengagement entail and how would it be brought about??

All three are serious questions that deserve serious answers. I'll address the first two questions in this blog and the third in the next one.

Regarding the first, let's assume, not unreasonably, that Putin's goal is the destruction of the Ukrainian state. Let's also recognize a fact of life: Russia is and will remain, at least for the foreseeable future, a far stronger country than Ukraine, both militarily and economically. It follows that Ukraine cannot defeat Russia in any full-scale war. But Ukraine can, with the right mix of armed forces, strategy, and tactics, deter and/or withstand a Russian attack by making it too costly for Russia to undertake such a move under all conditions short of a nuclear assault.

If you agree with this conclusion, then the questions before Ukraine are: does attempting to win back the Donbas enclave strengthen or weaken Ukraine's capacity to deter a Russian attack? And: does disengaging from the enclave strengthen or weaken Ukraine's capacity to deter a Russian attack?

I submit that the answer to the first question is a resounding NO: attempting to win back the enclave and defeating its 35,000 heavily armed thugs only exposes Ukraine to a debilitating Russian counterattack and thereby increases the likelihood of a full-scale Russian assault on Ukraine. And even if Ukraine were, miraculously, to defeat Putin's 35,000 proxies, attempting to occupy and control an economically devastated region inhabited by a population of dubious loyalty to Ukraine would force Ukraine to expend scarce resources on the Donbas and thereby weaken its ability to resist further Russian aggression.

The answer to the second question is a bit more complicated. If Putin's imperialist appetite is insatiable and unstoppable—i.e. if Putin is preprogrammed to expand regardless of conditions and costs—then he will expand and attack Ukraine regardless of whether it holds on to the enclave or not. Giving it up will no more encourage him to expand than retaining it will deter him from expanding. Alternatively, if Putin's imperialism is opportunistic and, thus, somehow responsive to costs and benefits, then the important question is whether disengaging from the Donbas will increase the costs or benefits of Putin's continued aggression.

I submit that disengagement enhances Ukraine's ability both to forestall aggression and to raise its costs. The reason is simple. The occupied Donbas enclave is an economic black hole that drains enormous resources and provides marginal if any economic benefit to its owner in the foreseeable future. Whoever controls the enclave is, by definition, in a weaker position precisely because the region is a drain on resources and will continue to be so for many years to come. Forcing Russia to bear all the costs of the occupation is Ukraine's single most effective weapon in the war with Putin. Complete disengagement, which would entail cutting off all social and economic subsidies to the region and its inhabitants, would only raise the costs to Russia and thereby enhance Ukraine's relative capacity to forestall or withstand an attack.

Just why Putin would be encouraged to attack when the costs of the campaign and occupation would rise and Ukraine's ability to withstand an attack would grow is unclear. To be sure, he might attack simply because he's preprogrammed to do so, but, if so, Ukraine's relative capacity to survive would be enhanced by virtue of Russia's having to shoulder all the costs of the Donbas occupation.

In sum, disengagement enhances Ukraine's capacity to stop Russia regardless of whether Putin is driven by an imperial impulse or is merely responding to opportunities to expand.

It's important to realize that disengagement will not stop Putin's proxies from continuing to fire on Ukraine and kill its citizens and soldiers. Only Putin can do that. But disengagement does open the door to more possibilities to resolve the conflict diplomatically and politically. As long as Ukraine claims the Donbas enclave, it will be involved in a zero-sum game with the proxies and Russia. Once Ukraine says 'no' to the enclave, it can explore imaginative solutions to the conflict precisely because it no longer claims sovereign control over it.

Won't disengagement violate Ukraine's moral obligation to the citizens of this benighted region? The answer to this question is simple, and it entails answering the following question: Which is the greater obligation—to 3 million individuals who have demonstrated by their behavior since 1991 that their loyalty to Ukraine is at best questionable or to the 40-plus million Ukrainians in Ukraine who have demonstrated that their loyalty to Ukraine is unquestionable? In an ideal world, policymakers would devote as many resources to one citizen as to all citizens. In a less than ideal world of limited resources, policymakers have to choose and opt for the greater good for the greater number. Seen in that light, promoting the life chances of 40-plus million loyal Ukrainians—by introducing reform, raising living standards, and consolidating democracy and human rights—is by far the greater good than sacrificing lives for a population that may not want to be liberated by Kyiv anyway.

As to what disengagement might look like, stay tuned for my next blog.

*

Ukraine's United Future Depends on Leaving Donbas in Its Divided Past, *World Affairs Journal*, June 8, 2016

Before Ukraine can disengage from the occupied Donbas, it must know just what disengagement means. Consider disengagement's opposite—engagement. If we are engaged, we are psychologically concerned about, ideologically committed to, and politically involved in some issue. Disengagement entails psychological indifference, ideological withdrawal, and political non-involvement with respect to that issue.

Disengagement is especially useful with respect to issues that lie beyond the powers of the actor concerned. The war in the Donbas will continue as long as Vladimir Putin wants it to continue, and Ukraine—and the West—must accept that fact. Nothing, short of Ukraine's capitulation or collapse, will assuage Putin. Ukrainians will continue to die as long as he wants them to die.

While the unnecessary deaths will and should preoccupy Ukrainians, the occupied Donbas should not. They cannot change the status quo, and they have far more important things to do at home—such as reform. After all, reforming the economy and transforming Ukraine into a powerful state is the *sine qua non* of its ability to withstand Putin's current or future aggressions. Simply put, no reform, no Ukraine.

Seen in this light, the occupied Donbas has cost too much in wasted lives and time. Focusing on it psychologically, ideologically, and politically only diverts Ukrainian energies and resources from the only thing that matters—Ukraine's survival as a strong, democratic, prosperous, and consolidated state. Disengaging from the occupied Donbas psychologically, ideologically, and politically is, thus, imperative.

It is also difficult. Ukrainians need to stop thinking of the occupied territories as "theirs." They need to stop viewing them as vital to Ukraine's nation- and state-building efforts. They need to stop devoting so much of their politics to finding solutions to the war. They need, in sum, to think about the occupied enclave as a foreign entity, which, thanks to Putin, is exactly what it is rapidly becoming.

The longer the war lasts, the longer the Donbas enclave known as the DNR-LNR continues to exist, the more likely will Ukraine become divided, willy-nilly, into two distinct and separate entities. Putin already directs the region's political, military, and economic affairs. The enclave has become a de facto province of the Russian Federation. Ukraine must recognize and accept that fact—and do nothing to change it. Inasmuch as the Minsk accords cannot force Putin to hold fair and free elections in the enclave and surrender control of the Russo-Ukrainian border, their preprogrammed failure as a viable peace-making process is in Ukraine's best interests.

The status quo in the Donbas is thus Ukraine's best-case scenario. The war is, despite the continued fighting and dying, for all purposes frozen. Ukraine should accept the frozen nature of the conflict, continue to support the Minsk process wholeheartedly, let Putin sustain the enclave on his own, and move on.

Ukrainians must let go of the Donbas enclave and concentrate on the priority that lies plainly ahead—its survival as a democratic and prosperous Western nation. Let the Donbas work itself out at another time—when Ukraine is strong, Putin Russia is weak, and the Donbas population realizes the dreadful mistake it made in siding with the Kremlin's dictator.

*

The Dangerous Perspective of Theo Sommer, *Atlantic Council*, June 27, 2016

This time, Theo Sommer has outdone himself. After closing his eyes to the mass murders of the Soviet regime in an article published on May 31, the editor-at-large of Germany's prestigious *Die Zeit* newspaper has now demonstrated in a just-published piece an alarm-ing ignorance not just of Ukraine but of elementary strategic logic. The former is scandal-ous, given Ukraine's prominence in the news. The latter is dangerous and could destroy Europe.

Sommer defends German Foreign Minister Frank-Walter Steinmeier's recent claim that NATO has been engaging in "saber-rattling and warmongering" vis-à-vis poor Vladimir Putin. Steinmeier's alarming inability to distinguish between cause and effect—after all, it was Putin's invasion of and continued aggression against Ukraine that terrified Russia's neighbors and mobilized NATO—is either a serious cognitive failing or an instance of spineless appeasement.

Here's what else Sommer gets dreadfully wrong in his article.

- His attitude toward Germany's neighbors—the Baltic states and Poland—is insulting. He speaks of their "historically explicable, though actually much exaggerated" fears of being threatened by Russia as if they were grounded in irrational emotions which, naturally, he and his colleagues stand above. That's just an arrogant unwillingness to countenance the possibility that these countries' presence on the front line with Russia may endow them with greater knowledge of Putin's true intentions.

- Unsurprisingly, given Sommer's disregard for his Eastern European EU and NATO neighbors, his attitude toward Ukraine is even worse than demeaning. In fact, Ukraine doesn't figure into his discussion of Western policy toward Russia at all. "The West has a trump card in its hand," writes Sommer. "It could recognize [Russia's] annexation of Crimea if Putin were to offer enough in return." And what of Ukraine? Would its voice matter? Evidently not. In Sommer's vision of the world, Ukraine doesn't exist—as it doesn't in Putin's. That this attitude is classically colonial goes without saying. Worse, it's coun-terproductive. Does Sommer seriously believe any agreement with Russia will stick if Ukraine isn't involved?

Very well, so Sommer's attitudes toward Eastern Europe are identical to those of Putin, imperial Germany, and—dare I say?—Nazi Germany. They may not be politically correct, but is that all there is to his views?

Unfortunately, Sommer also misunderstands the fundamentals of strategy—and that could destroy Europe. He hopes to assuage "exaggerated" Eastern European fears by telling Poles and Balts that "Article Five of the NATO Charter—an attack on one is an attack on all—obviously applies to them as well." Then, after criticizing NATO troops' stationing in the Baltic states, Sommer writes: "The deterrence of Russia does not depend on a few more or less battalions stationed in Lithuania, Latvia, Estonia, and Poland, but in the final analysis exclusively on the nuclear deterrence potential of the Americans and the credibility of their willingness to use" the weapons.

These few lines are absolutely terrifying. For starters, Sommer has either failed to read all of Article Five or failed to understand it. It states explicitly that, while, yes, an attack on one will be regarded as an attack on all, states will determine on their own just how they will respond. Armed force is not the primary response.

So in a situation of Russian aggression against the Baltic states, Germany could call a peace conference, France could stage a demonstration, and the United States could protest at the UN—none of which would actively repel Russian troops. Small wonder, then, that the Balts want NATO troops in their countries now. They know full well that the only way their NATO brethren might intervene against Putin's aggression is if their own soldiers serve as a trip wire and lose their lives. As the war in eastern Ukraine has shown all too well, Western Europeans and Americans will not sacrifice their own lives for Eastern Europeans.

Far more worrisome is Sommer's fatuous claim that the security of the Balts depends on America's willingness to defend them with nuclear weapons. This statement makes sense only if Sommer welcomes America's employment of such terrible weapons in case Russia attacked Estonia. If he doesn't welcome such an intervention, then he shouldn't speak so lightly of the nuclear deterrent in the first place. If this isn't warmongering and saber-rattling, I don't know what is.

At the same time, Sommer must know that America would never respond to a Russian aggression in the Baltic states with a first strike against Russia—and I doubt that any rational person would want it to. He is therefore being naïve, disingenuous, or mendacious in his endorsement of nuclear deterrence, and the Balts and Poles surely know that.

Since his defense of their sovereignty rests on an impossibility, it therefore amounts to a sellout. Sommer is telling his Eastern European neighbors that nothing should be done in case of Russian aggression. Europe will respond to a Russian invasion of Estonia with as much vigor as it did to Russia's invasion of Ukraine. A few sanctions, a lot of tut-tutting—followed by Steinmeierian calls for cutting grand deals with Russia. One can imagine that Sommer will then write of the trump card in the West's hand: the recognition of Russia's annexation of the Narva region of northeastern Estonia.

It should be obvious that this attitude could destroy Europe. It heralds a German-Russian condominium—shades of the Molotov-Ribbentrop Pact of 1939—that will destroy NATO and EU unity and thereby force the Eastern Europeans to struggle to guarantee their security in the uncomfortable space between Russian imperialism and German indifference. Russian paranoia and German arrogance will only be strengthened by the go-it-alone behavior of the Eastern Europeans, thereby leading to the spiral of escalation that Steinmeier and Sommer so fear.

*

Kremlin Tightens Grip on Devastated Donbas, *World Affairs Journal*, August 4, 2016

Mykhailo Pashkov, co-director of the Foreign Policy and International Security Program of the highly respected Razumkov Center in Kyiv, has written an exceptionally timely, sober, and important report on current conditions, as well as an astute **analysis** of the future of the Russian-occupied Donbas. It should be required reading for all Ukrainian policymakers. Once translated into English, it should also be required reading for Western policymakers.

Pashkov has no illusions about the occupied enclave's return to Ukraine anytime soon. He has even fewer illusions about the likelihood that the Minsk accords will lead to anything. After all, the key stumbling block is Russia, whose "maximally simplified position vis-à-vis regulating the Donbas amounts to this: we will continue killing your soldiers until you change your Constitution according to our wishes."

The most important part of Pashkov's analysis concerns the occupied enclave itself, where the Russian Federation has established "a militarized puppet pseudo-state totalitarian formation," a "nano-Russia administered by the militants but controlled by the Russian security services." As a result, there has emerged in this "anomalous zone" a "political-ideological, social-cultural reality that is hostile to Ukraine."

The self-styled Donetsk People's Republic alone has 20 ministries, and a raft of "all-powerful" people's councils, councils of ministers, procuracies, central banks, and supreme courts, as well as a variety of trade unions. The DNR has seven television stations, four radio stations, and 13 newspapers, overseen by the Ministry of Propaganda consisting of 120 employees and possessing a budget far in excess of Ukraine's Ministry of Information Policy. All these agencies consistently denounce the Kyiv "junta," the Kyiv "butchers," the "Ukrainian fascists," as well as "everything Ukrainian."

The DNR is also extending its tentacles into society. The "social organization" known as the Donetsk Republic consists of 140,000 members. DNR propagandists are writing a history of the republic. One museum, in Horlivka, features a section dealing with the "atrocities" perpetrated by the Ukrainian army. The Luhansk People's Republic has a children's magazine that recently featured a story about the evil Fasciston (Washington) and his assistant, Gnuland (Victoria Nuland), and how they were defeated by the valiant Papa, a Putin look-alike.

At the same time, Pashkov reports that the DNR and LNR are rapidly integrating with Russia. In September 2015, the regions adopted the Russian ruble. The militants are reportedly paid 15,000 rubles per month, and Moscow supplies the DNR with a monthly subsidy of 2.5 billion rubles, while distributing Russian passports to ever larger numbers of people. In May alone, 35,000 passports were distributed to enclave residents. The enclave's remaining higher educational institutions are completely tied to Russia's system of education. The Russian Ministry of Defense, the security services, and the Ministry of Internal Affairs control the enclave's 35,000-man army, while the Russian government runs the enclave's finances, taxes, infrastructure, transport, and energy resources via an inter-departmental commission supervised by Putin's advisor, Vladislav Surkov.

The consequences of Russian rule have been catastrophic for the Donbas enclave. According to Pashkov, the region's coal, chemical, and machine-building industries are in ruins. Some 40,000 small and medium-sized businesses have closed down. Infrastructure has been destroyed on a massive scale. The Donetsk airport, which cost $1.5 billion, is a ruin. The militants purposely destroyed several power stations and gas and water lines. About 30 percent of the occupied region's industrial capacity was moved to the Russian Federation. Agriculture and banking are also a mess, while experts calculate that it would take many billions of hryvnia and 10-15 years to remove the mines that have been planted in 7,000 sq. kilometers.

Can the Ukrainian economy cope with such a mess? Pashkov's question is rhetorical. And, he adds, taxpayers would be justified in asking why they should pay for the destruction caused by Russia, in a region now wired to oppose Kyiv. Even if Russia were suddenly to withdraw, Ukraine would have to "quarantine" the territory before it could reintegrate it.

Unsurprisingly, Pashkov concludes that the "best variant" today is a freezing of the conflict, consisting of "a ceasefire, the withdrawal of both sides, and the creation of a 400-kilometer buffer zone along the whole line of the front, necessarily under international control." Pashkov recommends a series of other political and diplomatic measures, but his bottom line is this: "real, tangible European integration, regardless of the internal situation in the EU... is the most effective instrument of defending against the Russian threat."

Pashkov's final observation is spot-on: "this is possible only if effective internal reforms are introduced and, in the first place, if corruption is brought under control." Kyiv, take notice.

*

Let It Go, *Foreign Policy*, August 12, 2016

Although the Russo-Ukrainian war appears to have been largely forgotten in the West, it still continues, claiming lives every day. Indeed, the last two months have seen a major escalation by Russia and its proxies, leading some analysts to expect a full-blown war.

That being the case, it's all the more unfortunate that Ukraine's policy toward its occupied eastern Donbas region, which has been held by pro-Russian separatists since early 2014, is stuck in a dead end. Kyiv lacks the power to defeat Russia and its Donbas proxies and cannot accept reintegrating the region on President Vladimir Putin's terms. But, in the name of preserving national sovereignty and checking Putin's aggression, Kyiv insists it must continue to fight for the region. Never mind that the Russian president's willingness to invade, attack, or escalate appears to have little to do with what Ukraine does (or indeed, with any rational strategy).

What, then, should Kyiv do? The answer won't be easy, particularly since, unsurprisingly, Ukrainians are extremely sensitive to the dismemberment of their country. Ukrainians must ask themselves whether they want to expend their very scarce resources on themselves or on the occupied territories. In an ideal world, there would be no need to choose. But in the very real world of economic crisis and Russia's existential threat, Ukraine must let go of the Donbas psychologically, economically, and, perhaps, even politically if it wants to survive and thrive.

This choice is informed by three basic considerations.

First, Ukraine cannot roll back Russia militarily and any attempt to do so would only increase its vulnerability. Although Ukraine has effectively won the limited conflict by fighting Russia to a draw, Kyiv cannot defeat Moscow in a full-scale war. Russia would probably be unable to prevail against widespread partisan resistance, but any large-scale conflict would, even in the best of circumstances, have deadly consequences for Ukraine and its people.

Second, possession of the occupied Donbas is an economic drain on whoever controls it. The occupied enclave's economy is in free fall. Using nighttime electricity usage as a surrogate for GDP, three Western economists have calculated that "the economic activity in the Donbas region has ... dropped in economic terms to 30 to 50 percent of the pre-war level for the big cities and to only a tenth of the pre-war level for some smaller cities." The region's educated professionals have fled and are unlikely to return. Health conditions may be on the verge of catastrophe; investment is non-existent. And without Russian aid, which amounts to about 2.5 billion rubles per month, the economy and society would, in all likelihood, collapse. Russia is already feeling the pain of maintaining the occupation, even though its economy and resources are far larger than Ukraine's. Were Ukraine suddenly to come into possession of the occupied territories, it would be unable to sustain them or itself economically.

Third, reintegrating the occupied Donbas on Russia's terms—with Russia controlling the national border and the Russian proxies who currently misrule the enclave still in place

—would mean suicide for Ukraine. The proxies would demand scarce resources, obstruct reform, halt Ukraine's political movement toward Europe, and provide a base of support for the return to power of the parties, oligarchs, and criminal elements that have governed the region since Ukraine's independence in 1991.

It follows from these three points that Ukraine is more secure and more capable of reform without the occupied Donbas than with it, and that Russia is weaker and more overextended with the occupied Donbas than without it.

What, then, should Ukraine do? How can letting go of the occupied Donbas become a realistic and politically palatable policy choice?

Above all, Ukrainians must psychologically dissociate themselves from the Russian-occupied territory. They must become as indifferent to the Donbas enclave as they are to the Ukrainian-inhabited territories in the Russian Far East or in Canada. This will take time, but the longer the Russian occupation of the Donbas continues, the easier it will be for Ukrainians to stop identifying with lands that are effectively Russian or anti-Ukrainian. Naturally, the growing number of deaths in the conflict—a total of 623 Ukrainian soldiers died or were wounded in the first half of 2016, a remarkably high number that may not be sustainable in the long run—could just as easily convince some Ukrainians that they must be avenged, and the territories never abandoned.

At the moment, public opinion is divided. According to a February 2016 poll, "ending all ties between Ukraine and the uncontrolled Donbas territories" found support among 64 percent in Ukraine's west, 51.5 percent in the center, 24.2 percent in the south, and 32.9 percent in the east. At the same time, "separating these territories from Ukraine" was supported by 27.6 in the west, 24 percent in the center, 12.1 percent in the south, and 22.9 percent in the east. These figures suggest that Ukrainians are willing to loosen ties with the enclave, but that there is still some way to go before a majority would support outright disengagement. That said, Ukraine's overflowing cafes and restaurants also suggest that many Ukrainians have succeeded in compartmentalizing the war and leading their lives as if the Donbas didn't matter. That few Ukrainians from outside the region have ever visited it and most know little about it will, over time, only deepen their estrangement.

Central to psychological disengagement is abandoning the ideological notion that the Donbas is essential to the vitality of the Ukrainian nation and state. It has become clear in the last two years—during which Ukraine has survived, stabilized its economy, and embarked on serious reform—that Ukraine can do just fine without the enclave. Ukrainians must also develop an alternative national "narrative" that does not identify the occupied Donbas as sacred, eternally Ukrainian territory. That will be harder, but, ironically, Russia's Donbas proxies are promoting Ukraine's ideological disengagement by developing their own historical narrative and anti-Ukrainian identity, establishing their own political institutions, and integrating economically, culturally, and militarily with Russia.

Like Ukrainian public opinion, Ukraine's political elites are divided over the occupied enclave. The notion of disengaging from the Donbas has already become a legitimate topic of public discussion, no longer provoking immediate cries of treason as it did two years ago. But no political force has yet been willing to make a forceful case for disengagement. The politically disreputable Opposition Bloc, a pro-Russian entity consisting of former Viktor Yanukovych supporters, argues for reintegration, albeit on Russia's terms. Nationalist parties such as Svoboda and the Right Sector and populists within Oleh Lyashko's Radical Party and Yulia Tymoshenko's Fatherland party continue to emphasize the indispensability of the occupied region to the integrity of the nation and state.

Implicitly, however, the current government of President Petro Poroshenko and Prime Minister Volodymyr Hroysman has adopted a de facto strategy of disengagement, con-fining its calls for reintegration to rhetoric and taking no practical steps towards this end. Disengagement will become a respectable political option for mainstream, pro-Western parties only if the political forces that explicitly or implicitly favor it become identified with reform and good governance. Thus far, the Poroshenko-Hroysman government's record is mixed, though there are signs that it may be getting serious about combating corruption. Once Ukrainians see that their country can thrive without the Donbas, the ideology of re-annexation should lose its appeal.

In the meantime, Ukraine should make the best of the status quo. The Minsk agreement, which governs the effectively non-existent ceasefire between Ukraine and Russia, rep-resents everyone's second-best option: As long as Minsk continues, Ukraine retains its sovereignty, Russia gets to meddle, and the separatists can play at independence. This equilibrium could last a while.

As a result, Minsk gives Ukraine the time it so desperately needs to enhance its military capacity, continue reforms, and contemplate the precise mechanisms of disengaging. Since Ukraine is effectively cut off from an increasingly foreign and hostile Donbas enclave anyway, the psychological, ideological, and political burdens of disengagement should gradually become lighter. Meanwhile, Ukraine would be wise to reduce or eliminate its economic dependence on resources, such as coal, that are mined in the east, encourage the remaining pro-Ukrainian population in the Donbas to resettle in Ukraine, establish a defensive perimeter that will reduce contraband and attacks by Russian diversionary groups, clearly state that it has no intention of reconquering the enclave militarily, and officially declare the territory as being under Russian occupation. In isolating itself from the Donbas enclave, Ukraine would be shifting all the costs of and formal responsibility for the occupied territories and their population onto Russia and freeing itself to pursue reform.

These measures won't end the war, which will continue until Putin decides he wants to end it. But his decision to disengage can come only after Ukraine realizes it has no stake in the region and has become economically, politically, and militarily strong. And for Ukraine to become stable and strong, it must isolate itself from the occupied Donbas, perhaps not forever, but certainly for the foreseeable future.

Kyiv must choose between its strategic interests and its psychological and ideological attachment to a region it has already lost. Given its precarious position, the choice is clear.

What Ukraine Can Learn from Germany's Cold War Divisions, *Foreign Policy*, October 3, 2016

Ukraine has been fortunate in its misfortune. Russian leader Vladimir Putin has annexed Crimea formally and the eastern Donbas informally, and thousands of Ukrainians have died in the conflict. But most of the West has rallied to Kyiv's side, imposing sanctions on Russia and supporting reforms. Ukraine has become stronger, more stable, and more secure since 2014.

But the path Kyiv must walk remains precarious—not least because there is an inherent contradiction between pursuing reunification with its breakaway regions and implementing pro-western reforms. Not only does Ukraine not know what to do with the 35,000 heavily armed separatists who currently control the eastern Donbas, but the occupied territories are also home to pro-Russian elites and populations who would have blocked reforms if they had remained within Ukraine.

Maneuvering between these contradictions will be easier if Kyiv models its policies on those of post-war West Germany. The similarities are striking. Like post-war Germany, Ukraine is divided into western-oriented and Russian-occupied zones, needs to rebuild its state, society, and economy, and lies on the fault line between a democratic West and an authoritarian East. Most importantly, just like Kyiv today, Bonn had to make difficult trade-offs between reunification and building a pro-western state—and it did so successfully, in the end attaining both.

No historical analogy is perfect. The divided Germany had just lost a war, while Ukraine emerged from the ruins of an empire 25 years ago. West Germany was actually occupied by the western Allies, whereas Ukraine only enjoys their support. And East Germany was a real state, while the eastern Donbas and Crimea are contested territories.

Nevertheless, the German experience can teach Ukraine how to pursue its own development while temporarily ceding control of part of its territory to an outside power. A good approach is to consider how three key West German chancellors—Konrad Adenauer, Willy Brandt, and Helmut Kohl—led their country down this difficult road.

From Konrad Adenauer, who became chancellor shortly after the war, Ukraine can learn why accepting the loss of its territory—in the short and medium term—will help it in the long run. Adenauer firmly believed that West Germany faced a choice between unity and freedom. A free and pro-Western Germany, he thought, could never be unified with the Soviet-controlled east. And although he remained fully committed to ultimate reunification and to the indivisibility of the German nation, he recognized as early as 1945 that "the Russian-occupied part is lost for Germany for an indeterminate time."

Because Adenauer made the western choice, West Germany received Marshall Plan aid, joined the European Coal and Steel Community and NATO, rearmed, and benefitted from the "economic miracle" of the 1950s. These policies came at a cost. By turning to the west, Adenauer paid the price of enabling East Germany to acquire the features of statehood, allowing the German nation to drift part.

Just as Adenauer was right to choose freedom when Germany needed desperately to re-build, so, too, must Kyiv's priority be to survive as a western-oriented state in the face of Russian hostility. Ukraine would therefore be wise to abandon its rhetoric of reunification and formally declare that Crimea and the eastern Donbas are under Russian occupation, thereby keeping anti-Ukrainian elites and populations in these regions out of its affairs and transferring all responsibility for their welfare onto Moscow. Kyiv should then focus on developing its political, military, economic, and cultural institutions to make them fully compatible with, and integrated in, those of the West.

Ukraine can learn another practical lesson from Willy Brandt, who served as chancellor in the early 1970s. During his tenure, the United States and Soviet Union were seeking to improve relations and reduce their nuclear weapons arsenals, and East Germany had become a fact of life. Brandt came to realize that West Germany's policy of cold-shouldering East Germany was bringing few practical benefits.

His new policy of Ostpolitik normalized relations with the USSR, Poland, and Czechoslovakia, accepted the inviolability of post-war borders, and extended formal diplomatic recognition to East Germany. This approach offered new ways of influencing East Germany and therefore of promoting larger German national interests.

Like Brandt, Kyiv may someday have to consider the currently unthinkable: negotiating directly with the separatists and the Crimean authorities. The current exclusion from Ukraine's politics of sizable local anti-Western elites and publics is advantageous for Ukraine, enabling it to adopt pro-Western reforms. But once Ukraine becomes sufficiently Western to appreciate that continued fighting and dying serves no larger purpose, Kyiv will need a Brandt-like Ostpolitik to end the conflict. The German example suggests that the war cannot be stopped without some accommodation with the separatists as genuine interlocutors in peace negotiations. This could even go as far as some form of quasi-recognition.

The final and most hopeful lesson comes courtesy of Helmut Kohl, who provides a useful case study of how Ukraine might eventually win its territories back—by winning the social and economic competition between its system and the Russian system, not by direct military force.

By the 1980s, many Germans had concluded that German reunification was impossible. The new status quo seemed set in stone—until Soviet leader Mikhail Gorbachev's reforms, and his declaration that errant socialist states would not suffer Soviet intervention, destabilized the satellite regimes and subverted the *raison d'être* of the East German state.

East Germany drew legitimacy from its status as a socialist alternative to its capitalist cousin; once socialism began to disintegrate, the game was up. The mass protests of October 1989 and the flows of East Germans westward further delegitimized the regime. Two weeks after the Berlin Wall fell, Kohl articulated his vision for reunification. By late 1990, that vision became reality—not because Bonn had pursued it with any vigor, but because the East German regime had fallen apart, its economy was on the verge of collapse, most East Germans wanted reunification, and the Soviet Union was too weak to stop it.

Like Kohl's Germany, Ukraine must think of reunification as a distant prospect that will materialize only when the success of a reformed, westernized Ukraine can be contrasted with life in a weak and isolated Russia. Ukraine can successfully pursue reunification not by defeating Russia and its proxies militarily, but by winning the competition between two rival systems. Like West Germany, Ukraine can win that competition hands down if it remains committed to the western path.

PART FOUR
THE DECLINE OF PUTIN RUSSIA

Putin's Black Eye and Yanukovych's Beauty Sleep, *World Affairs Journal*, December 16, 2011

Regardless of how the current post-election protests in Russia turn out, the many thousands of ordinary Russians who took to the streets to demand their rights deserve three big cheers. Their courageous behavior has dispelled a few myths about Russia and sent a powerful signal to all post-Soviet dictators.

Big Cheer No. 1: The mostly young and middle-class demonstrators have effectively squashed the regnant view of Russians as having a culturally coded predisposition to quiescence and a strong hand. Obviously, many Russians are authoritarian. Just as obviously, many are not. Some are conservative; some are liberal. Some are religious; some are secular. Here's the shocking news: Russians are like everybody else. Naturally, they want peace and quiet. Who wouldn't, given Russia's turbulent history? Naturally, they want to live well. Who are we to tell them they shouldn't? But, just as naturally, they want to be treated as human beings, and not as chattel. Why should that surprise anyone? If colored revolutions were possible in Georgia, Ukraine, and Kyrgyzstan, then why not in Russia?

Big Cheer No. 2: The demonstrators have also delivered a *mega* black eye to Russia's "man in black"—Vladimir Putin. (The nickname comes from my colleague at Columbia University, Catharine Nepomnyashchy.) The percentage of Russians expressing confidence in him had already dropped from the low 70s in 2010 to the high 50s today, but the spectacle of thousands of Russians chanting "Russia without Putin" across the country clearly suggests that this may be, as Vladimir Kara-Murza puts it, the "beginning of the end" for the black-belt dictator in the Kremlin. And even if it's not, even if Putin bounces back and manages to hold on to power for a few more years, the Putin mystique has been shattered, once and for all. There's just no denying that a dictator with a black eye looks ridiculous.

Big Cheer No. 3: These two accomplishments would be enough for the history books, but the Russian demonstrators have also struck a big blow for democracy in the non-Russian states. Putin's Russia was always the model for would-be dictators in the "near abroad." The place looked stable and strong, and the dictator seemed to be firmly in control. Well, now that those impressions have been rendered delusional, Putin Russia looks like a regime that's set to join what the Soviet used to call the "garbage heap of history." Some model, that.

So what's a non-Russian dictator to do? The Central Asians are likely to scramble and insist that their authoritarianism is rooted in the "ancient" traditions of their nations. That may work for a while, but Central Asians—being human beings with a desire for dignity, after all—are unlikely to buy that line for long. Belarus's embattled Aleksandr Lukashenka has no such traditions to point to and will be especially vulnerable to his growing numbers of critics at home and abroad. A hockey player, he can be expected to start swinging wildly with his stick, eventually losing his balance and falling on his backside.

And what about Viktor Yanukovych? No more beauty sleep for Ukraine's first, and last, sultan. Putin's current travails are a nightmare for Viktor and the Regionnaires. After all, Putin's Russia wasn't just their theoretical model. It was the regime that provided the rationale for their anti-Ukrainian policies internally and their pro-Russian policies externally. Yanukovych could not have appointed a Russian supremacist as minister of education were it not for Putin's hostility to Ukrainian identity. Yanukovych could not have thumbed his nose at NATO, ceded Sevastopol to Moscow, and imprisoned Ukraine's female version of Mikhail Khodorkovsky were it not for his belief that Putin's Russia was Ukraine's "elder brother."

Putin's Russia also provided Yanukovych and the Regionnaires with hope. If the "thieves and crooks" to the east could get away with murder, then why shouldn't their counterparts in Ukraine? If a corrupt dictatorship could hold on to power in Putin's Russia, then why not in Little Russia? By the same token, if even Putin's big-time mobsters are under assault, then Yanukovych's small-time Regionnaire thugs, who can now say good-bye to winning next year's parliamentary elections without massive fraud, had better start packing their bags.

The excellent Luhansk-based analyst Konstantin Skorkin puts it well: "We are witnessing the smashing of the Putin model; its life span, like that of any regime based on repressing civil society, is proving to be limited. Let's hope that our power holders are smart enough to turn away from this destructive path ... and that all of us have enough strength and perseverance to defend our freedom."

So, a very big *spasibo* to Russia's anti-Putin demonstrators, who have banged another— very big—nail into Yanukovych and the Regionnaires' political coffin. If the Ukrainian president follows Skorkin's advice, he'll try to hang on to dear life in the only way possible: by embracing democracy and rejecting supremacism.

Or, to put it in terms Yanukovych is more likely to understand: Mister President, let Tymoshenko be an ex-con like yourself and just sock Tabachnik in the nose.

*

Fascistoid Russia: Whither Putin's Brittle Realm? *World Affairs Journal*, February 28, 2012

The massive demonstrations that rocked Russia in the aftermath of the Duma elections of December 4, 2011, surprised everyone, including most Russians. But they shouldn't have. The conditions for such an upheaval have been ripening as a result of the growing power and decrepitude of Putinism. It is likely that popular mobilization will continue, and that the regime's days may be numbered.

Observers generally agree that the fraudulent elections, in which the pro-regime United

Russia party won 49.3 percent of the vote, sparked the countrywide demonstrations on December 10th and December 24th, in which, respectively, an estimated thirty to fifty thousand and eighty to one hundred thousand people participated in Moscow alone. They also agree that President Dmitri Medvedev's September 24th announcement that he and Prime Minister Vladimir Putin would swap places via the March 2012 presidential elections set the outrage in motion. And finally, they agree that the leading role in the demonstrations belonged to Russia's middle class and youth.

Although this story is correct, it is incomplete. The roots of the Russian uprising are found in the nature of the regime Putin constructed and in its inherent brittleness and ineffectiveness. Too many Western and Russian observers took the regime's claims of stability at face value, causing them to miss the fact that Putin had built a profoundly unstable political system, one that was likely to decay, decline, and possibly even crash. As the early warnings of the December protests suggest, this may be starting to happen.

It was during Putin's first run as president in 2000 that the question of whether Russia was a "managed democracy" or a "competitive authoritarianism" first arose. For those who thought it was a flawed democracy, the modifier hinted at authoritarian imperfections. For those who considered it a flawed authoritarian state, the modifier hinted at residual democracy. Either way, Russia was supposed to be a "hybrid" political system combining elements of both democracy and authoritarianism. For a while, the emphasis on hybridity made some sense—especially after Medvedev, the ostensible liberal, replaced Putin as president in 2008. Medvedev's liberalism rapidly proved to be illusory, however, while his connivance with Putin to transform the March 2012 presidential elections into a sham put an end to notions that Putin's Russia was anything other than an authoritarian state.

Except that that designation isn't quite accurate either. Authoritarian states are typically ruled by faceless bureaucrats or dour generals. Putin, in contrast, has charisma and he *is* popular. This factor makes Russia sufficiently different from run-of-the-mill authoritarian states to qualify it as "fascistoid"—an ugly word indicating that its hybridity quickly shifted from some combination of democracy and authoritarianism in Putin's early years in power to some combination of authoritarianism and fascism today.

Like authoritarian systems, fascist systems lack meaningful parliaments, judiciaries, parties, and elections; are highly centralized; give pride of place to soldiers and policemen; have a domineering party; restrict freedom of the press, speech, and assembly; and repress the opposition. (Consider in this light the similarities between Pinochet's Chile and Mussolini's Italy.) But unlike authoritarian systems, fascist systems always have supreme leaders enjoying cult-like status, exuding vigor, youthfulness, and manliness. And unlike authoritarians, fascist leaders are charismatic individuals who promote a hyper-nationalist vision that promises the population, and especially the young, a grand and glorious future—usually echoing past national glories—in exchange for their subservience. (Consider the differences between Pinochet and Il Duce.) Unsurprisingly, full-blown fascist systems, being the instruments of charismatic one-man rule, tend to be more violent than average authoritarian states.

"Fascistoid" captures nicely the hybridity of the wretched system Putin has created, in which authoritarian institutions serve as a platform for a charismatic leader who is committed to Russian greatness, hyper-nationalism, and neo-imperial revival and who serves as the primary source of regime legitimacy and stability. The term also suggests why the regime is intrinsically weak, and why Putin's attempt to ratchet up the system's fascistoid characteristics by manipulating both the parliamentary and presidential elections drove hundreds of thousands of Russians into the streets.

How and when will the regime end? Accurate predictions are impossible, but good bets are not. The regime could break down overnight or decay for years. Either way, Putin's Russia is a terminal case.

The obvious place to start diagnosing its sickness is the supreme leader himself. The key weakness of any leader-centered system is that cults of vigor cannot be sustained as leaders inevitably grow old or become decrepit. Sooner or later, supreme leaders lose their aura of invincibility and, when they do, their fans and followers fall away. In addition to the depredations of mortality, we know from Max Weber that charisma is hard to sustain, becoming "routinized" over time. Twelve years ago, Putin appeared to be an outstanding politician who could do no wrong. Today, he looks like a crafty politician who's trying to hang on to power by martial arts exhibitions and shirtless location pics. Even if he manages to slog through what may become two six-year terms after March 2012, his youthfulness and charisma will wither away as inexorably as did the Marxist vision of the state.

While it might seem that extreme centralization of power in the hands of a supreme leader would ensure coordination and submission among the elites, the exact opposite occurs, as elites compete for the boss's favor, pass the buck and shirk responsibility, avoid cooperating with their colleague-competitors, and amass resources as they form mini-bureaucracies of their own. Just this happened in such hyper-centralized regimes as Nazi Germany, the Soviet Union, and Communist China—not despite, but because of, hyper-centralization. Leader-centered regimes are thus brittle, and when supreme leaders falter—as they always do, especially during times of crisis—or leave the scene, their comrades usually embark on cutthroat power struggles to assume the mantle of authority. Succession crises are especially destabilizing in all such regimes because the pressures they create cannot be ventilated by institutional mechanisms such as elections.

Finally, supreme leaders are prone to making strategic mistakes—a point first noted by Aristotle and proved repeatedly ever since. They are responsible for everything, but physically and intellectually incapable of making the right decisions all the time. Subordinates become toadies unable to act on their own, solidifying their own positions by always passing the boss good (and therefore inaccurate) news—a point recognized by Karl Deutsch back in the 1950s. Forced to make critical decisions without accurate information, the big leader will make big mistakes, especially if he already has an obsessive ideological vision.

Putin's involves his deeply rooted desire to achieve an in-gathering of the former Soviet territories, as manifested in the "gas wars" with Ukraine, the real war with Georgia, and the creeping takeover of Belarus. While his integrationist "Eurasian Union" project provides him and his rule with legitimacy—and many Russians, understandably distressed by the Soviet empire's ignominious collapse and Russia's transformation into an "Ivory Coast with the bomb," support their country's return to a place in the sun—it will at best distract Russia from its problems and at worst turn its non-Russian neighbors against Russia, thereby intensifying those problems. The fact is that, while neo-imperial projects serve all authoritarian and fascist leaders well at first, they invariably get them and their countries in serious trouble, as Argentina's military leaders discovered after their ill-fated invasion of the Falkland Islands.

The global financial crisis and its impact on Russia's economy will only intensify elite infighting and competition for scarce resources and erode Putin's aura of omnipotence, especially if living standards continue to decline. The next few years will be particularly difficult for Russia, as Putin tries to remain firmly in control of a hybrid system while the mounting problems of the global economy challenge his claims to charismatic authority. Chances are that Putin will place the blame for his failure to modernize Russia on Medvedev, who, in turn, will blame Putin. Sooner or later, however, Putin will have to accept responsibility for the system's failures, thereby admitting that the emperor has even fewer clothes than he wears on his topless photo ops.

Like every dictator, Putin hopes to make the trains run on time, but introducing marginal efficiencies will not modernize Russia. As George Soros, drawing on Karl Popper, reminds us, modernity requires open societies. Since economic change undermines political systems that cannot adapt to it, modernization and authoritarianism are incompatible—unless populations are rural, uneducated, and provincial, and thus incapable of active political involvement. If populations are urban, educated, and informed, as in Russia, authoritarian states are caught in a race against time.

They may succeed in industrializing agrarian societies—Bismarck's Germany, Stalin's Russia, and Mao's China come to mind—and they may be able to promote extensive economic growth and supervise planned economies, as in Communist states, but they cannot foster entrepreneurship, risk-taking, openness, and engagement, which are at the core of any fully modern society. Worse, if such entrepreneurial forces do emerge, they invariably threaten the legitimacy of the regime precisely because authoritarian regimes lack the institutions to accommodate them and their participatory aspirations. The late Samuel P. Huntington had it right when he noted, "The stability of any given polity depends upon the relationship between the level of political participation and the level of political institutionalization."

In Russia, as in all modernizing societies, these participatory qualities are associated with the middle class. The rise of a social grouping committed to private property, rule of law, and greater involvement in the political process is thus an obvious challenge to the stability of the Putin state. Even if the Kremlin follows in China's footsteps and succeeds in converting affluent and educated Russians to hyper-nationalism and neo-imperialism— and thereby deflecting their attention from internal problems—a self-confident entrepreneurial class is unlikely to allow itself to be bought off for long. Putin, like today's Chinese Communists, will attempt to square the circle by trying to co-opt the middle class into existing authority structures, but that strategy will necessarily fail since authoritarian institutions are, by definition, incompatible with democratic strivings.

389

Complicating things for Putin, as for all autocrats, are students. It is at first glance remarkable that Russia's many students have been so quiescent for so long. Like Americans and Europeans in the 1950s, they may have been responding to past economic insecurity and current economic prospects by focusing on their educations and careers. But they are also like their American and European counterparts in the 1960s, in that they can now take some prosperity for granted and translate their self-assurance and sophistication into critical thinking and social protest.

Russia is tailor-made for two types of social protest—one resulting from "relative deprivation," or the disappointment, frustration, and anger that follow when hopes are suddenly, and unexpectedly, dashed; another resulting from a sense of injustice that boils over into anger and rage and spurs people to rebel against an illegitimate order, as during Ukraine's 2004 Orange Revolution.

Relative deprivation is generally the product of rapid economic growth followed by a sudden economic downturn. Russia's energy-fueled economic growth may turn out to be similar to China's and last for several decades or, rather more likely, it may—as a result of price drops, supply disruptions, regional tensions, or political crises—suddenly fall and remain low for some time. The economy is already growing less than before. If a significant downturn occurs, especially after a self-confident middle class and a vocal student body have emerged, both groups are likely to become restive.

A smoldering sense of moral outrage, at the transgressions of public trust Putin has committed in his effort to retain and expand power, is already present and was what drove the demonstrators on December 10th and 24th. Russians expected fair and free elections. Instead they got two slaps in the face: the first, when Putin and Medvedev announced that the former would be president; the second, when results of the Duma elections were falsified. They also expected Putin, whose popularity had fallen some twenty percentage points in the last few years, to act with greater self-restraint instead of greater arrogance.

Unsurprisingly, as middle-class entrepreneurs and students chafe at authoritarian controls, they insist that the state is unjustly violating their rights. Just as social science theories would lead us to expect, everyone—from entrepreneurs to students to average Russians—has become angry at the all-pervasiveness of the Russian ruling elite's corruption and cynical indifference to popular well-being. We may expect that, as younger generations begin to ask tough questions about the Soviet Union's criminal past, they will, like young Germans who fifty years ago were incensed about Nazism, want to know why their government has refused to complete the condemnation of Stalin's crimes and even subtly and subliminally sought to reinforce continuities with his rule.

What then does the future hold for Putin's Russia? As social protests mount, tensions within the elites will multiply. As the system becomes fragmented and ineffective, factions within the central elites will begin to look for alternatives and reach out to oppositions and "the people" for support. If the tide begins to turn and the democrats look stronger than the authoritarians, "people power" and "color revolutions" can gain critical mass as ever larger numbers join what appears to be a sure bet. Russia's situation is far more volatile than the Putinists would have us believe. Democratic opposition looked marginalized and weak in the summer of 2011. It may be premature to say that it's now on the march, but there's no denying that it has since presented its birth certificate in the streets. Prospects for the democrats look much better now than they did in the recent past, and they will improve if the authoritarian elites continue to appear confused or weak—recall how Romanian dictator Nicolae Ceausescu's momentary show of weakness on television turned the tide against him in 1989—and if popular perceptions of stability and legitimacy continue to decline.

Putin obviously believes that Russia's vast oil and gas reserves will save the authoritarianism he created. Energy resources have fueled Russia's economic development, but easy money has also transformed Russia into a "petro-state" that has become an impediment—some would say the *greatest* impediment—to further economic development and political stability. When easy money promotes corruption and outright theft and inclines elites to use the state as a source of patronage, the state itself becomes an obstacle to modernization. The worst-case scenario for Russia would be ending up like Nigeria or the Shah's Iran. It's only somewhat less alarming that at best it could end up like Saudi Arabia or Hugo Chávez's Venezuela.

In a word, Putin's Russia is in decay. Putin's hybrid authoritarian-fascist system is intrinsically brittle, susceptible to elite fragmentation, and incapable of sustaining modernization, coexisting with the middle class, and preventing rising discontent. Like a very sick person, its condition could easily become critical—especially if some catalyzing incident hastens the disintegrative process. Putin becoming ill would be one such event; another would be some overcommitment on the part of the Kremlin to a costly misadventure in the near abroad—another quick, glorious little war, for instance, along the lines of the one with Georgia. Still another catalyst could be a sudden drop in the price of oil, a secular decline in Gazprom's ability to produce gas, or a recession.

If things were to get out of hand and Russia's non-Russian regional elites began claiming power, Russia could even turn into competing, if not quite warring, principalities. Whatever the outcome, the global effects of Russian turmoil would be substantial. These could include disruptions in energy production and supplies, the revival of the "loose nukes" problem, the emergence of full-fledged guerrilla and terrorist movements in Russia's provinces, and the inability of Russia to play any kind of role in global affairs. If Russia's problems spill over into the near abroad, some of the more fragile non-Russian states could follow in its footsteps, thereby compounding all the threats emanating from Russian instability.

What can the world do to forestall such a scenario? Very little. Russia's well-wishers can reduce the risk of the worst kind of turmoil by encouraging Putin to fix his problems at home and not overextend himself with ill-advised, neo-imperial schemes. They can also minimize the likelihood that Russia's turmoil will spill over into its neighbors by propping up the non-Russian states and enabling them to deal with their own sources of instability. Seen in this light, Germany's foreign policy toward the former Soviet Union is a textbook case of what *not* to do. On the one hand, Berlin encourages Moscow to assert its regional primacy by means of the North Stream pipeline. On the other hand, Berlin has done little to help such pivotal states as Ukraine to strengthen their sovereignty.

Such shortsightedness also encourages Russia's neighbors to imitate Putin's authoritarianism. But consider this. If the scenario I have sketched out holds for Russia, then it holds no less for Lukashenka's Belarus, Yanukovych's Ukraine, Nazarbayev's Kazakhstan, and a score of other non-Russian states. Serial crashes cannot then be discounted, especially as both the Communist breakdowns of 1989 and the Arab Spring of 2011 suggest that even seemingly stable authoritarian states can, amazingly, crumble overnight.

*

Preparing for Russia's Upcoming Collapse, *World Affairs Journal*, February 15, 2013

A just-published report by Russia's premier political analyst, Lilia Shevtsova, has important implications for the post-Soviet states in general and Ukraine in particular. Titled "Russia XXI: The Logic of Suicide and Rebirth," the report was released by the Moscow Carnegie Center in January 2013. Shevtsova, who together with democratic reformer Grigory Yavlinsky shares the distinction of having been born and raised in the West Ukrainian city of Lviv, chairs the center's Russian Domestic Politics and Political Institutions Program and is the author of, among many other books, *Putin's Russia and Russia—Lost in Transition*. When Shevtsova speaks, Western policymakers and academics listen—and post-Soviet dictators should listen.

The "Russia XXI" report has good news for democrats and well-wishers o f Russia: Vladimir Putin's days as Russia's dictator are numbered. According to Shevtsova, "The Russian system is beginning to decay. It cannot sustain the crumbling status quo, nor can it be certain of finding a new incarnation for itself. The only real questions are what stage of decay the system is in, whether the agony of its demise has already started, and, if so, how long it will last. To be sure, the system still has some resources, if not to revive itself, then to draw out its death, and that survival instinct could take a nasty, even bloody, form."

That last sentence suggests that the demise of Putin's fascistoid regime could take on nasty forms with profoundly deleterious consequences for Russia and Russians:

> The system no longer has adequate resources to manage society through means of mass coercion and force; the resources required for that are being quickly depleted. By opting for harsher management instruments, the regime will significantly truncate its own support base. By suppressing the relatively moderate opposition, which is trying to express itself openly and constitutionally, and by rejecting constitutional rights and freedoms, the Kremlin itself will breed a radical and destructive opposition that will act clandestinely and opt for violent methods. It is the Kremlin that is shoving these differences of opinion and opposing viewpoints into a revolutionary niche.

In its attack on pluralism, the regime is not only radicalizing the conflict and accelerating the political cycle, it is also reducing the chances of reaching an agreement between the opposition and a part of the ruling elite. As it tries to shift responsibility for the use of force to all of the elite, the Kremlin impairs the chances for the formation of a pragmatic wing ready for a peaceful exit from the Russian system.

No less serious is the fact that the current ruling elite, feeling that is has been cornered and apparently beginning to understand the nature of the challenges, has started to consciously pursue a policy that will deepen the degradation of society, preserve its atomization, and provoke ethnic and social hatreds. This is the goal of the Kremlin's propaganda and policy: to prevent society's consolidation against the authorities and to provoke conflicts and tensions that make the authorities the arbitrator. If this policy is successful, Russia is doomed.

In order to forestall such a dire outcome, says Shevtsova, it is imperative for the democratic opposition to get its act together as soon as possible:

The agenda for the upcoming political season contains a few objectives. One of them is consolidating the opposition and formulating an agenda that is responsive to the challenges posed by a more repressive regime. Another objective is integrating political and socioeconomic demands. Yet another is uniting all of the opposition factions and the moderates within the system ready for change under the banner of universal democratic demands and the peaceful transformation of the system.

The fast-paced events of the day and the degradation of the system may call for some ad hoc changes to the agenda, but one objective remains paramount under any circumstances: the pledge by all participants in the political process to renounce personalized power and to step down from positions of power in case of electoral defeat. This has never happened in Russian history. If Russia finally manages to do it, it will have reached its "end of history" and the beginning of a new one.

Note that Shevtsova's analysis could be applied, word for word, to Ukraine, Belarus, Kazakhstan, and several other dysfunctional post-Soviet authoritarian regimes. Just as these regimes emerged from similar political and economic circumstances that may loosely be termed the "Soviet and post-Soviet legacy," so, too, these regimes are likely to break down, collapse, or crack up for the same reasons, the primary one being their systemic unsustainability. Moreover, just as these regimes emerged pretty much at the same time, so, too, they are likely to vanish at the same time. Indeed, one can easily imagine that the collapse of any one of them—and especially of Putin's regime—will immediately have spillover effects in the others, producing a chain reaction of regime breakdowns similar to the collapse of communism that swept East Central Europe in the course of six months in 1989. Domino theory redux, anyone?

As Shevtsova warns us, Russia's collapse could be peaceful and lead to democratic consolidation or it could be bloody and spell Russia's doom. Exactly the same outcomes face post-Yanukovych Ukraine, post-Lukashenka Belarus, and post-Nazarbayev Kazakhstan. It is conceivable that we'll witness, within the next five or so years, a wave of democratic transitions in the entire post-Soviet space or a wave of bloody breakdowns. The former scenario would be wonderful, but, as Shevtsova says, it can happen if and only if the democrats prepare for it accordingly. The latter scenario—breakdown—would be a disaster for everyone concerned. Its consequences—instability, economic collapse, refugees, bloodshed—would spill over into East Central Europe and, despite the iron curtain set up by the Schengen-zone countries, into the core of the European Union as well. Smart Western policymakers might consider asking themselves whether they're doing enough to prevent that doomsday scenario from happening. The wrong way to proceed is to try to prop up doomed regimes, even if they export gas. The right way is to start working with the democratic oppositions in preparation for the day the dictators disappear.

It's too late for the regimes in Russia, Belarus, and, probably, Kazakhstan to change: they've been around for too long and they're too entrenched. It may not be too late for the significantly younger and less entrenched Yanukovych regime to try to change its spots and avoid an ignominious end. All Yanukovych need do is free Yulia Tymoshenko and Yuri Lutsenko, sell his palatial estates outside Kyiv, tell his son Sasha to go back to dentistry, fire the thuggish Minister of Education Dmitri Tabachnik, and retire before the 2015 presidential elections. Oh, and read Shevtsova's excellent report now, when he could learn a thing or two about survival—and not several years from now, when he's in the slammer or on the lam.

*

Is Putin Rational? *Foreign Affairs*, March 18, 2014

Ukrainians are waiting to see whether Russian President Vladimir Putin, having wrested Crimea from Ukraine, will continue his advance. The outward signs point to yes. Tens of thousands of Russian troops and hundreds of tanks and other armored vehicles are amassed along Ukraine's borders. The Kremlin insists that they are conducting military exercises, but that seems unlikely. Ukrainian armed services have caught Russian agents, tasked with gathering military intelligence and fomenting unrest, in several of Ukraine's southeastern provinces. And border guards have stopped thousands of armed Russian "tourists" from entering Ukraine. Pro-Putin militants have seized government buildings and violently attacked peaceful demonstrators outside of Crimea, in Donetsk and Kharkiv. Meanwhile, Russia's state-controlled channels whip up anti-Ukrainian hysteria as Putin and the Kremlin insist that the government in Kyiv illegitimate.

No one can fully know Putin's intentions. One's best guess depends on one's assumptions of his rationality. If he is irrational—unable to correctly judge the costs and benefits of invading Ukraine because he is in thrall to some ideology or the pursuit of power—then it is safe to assume that he will continue on his current course. **Lilia Shevtsova**, a liberal

Russian analyst, and Andrei Illarionov, Putin's former economic advisor, make that case. "He believes that he is chosen by divine providence to punish liberated Ukrainians," Illarianov writes, "He believes that now there is a unique historical situation: Ukraine is in [a] state of severe crises, its authorities and institutions do not function effectively. He dreams that providence demands him to fulfill this mission." If Illarionov and Shevtsova are right, nothing can stop Putin from launching a massive land war against Ukraine, regardless of how much it would cost in human life, property, and prestige. Such a Putin could conceivably keep marching up to the Atlantic, as Aleksandr Dugin, a Russian political scientist and Putin's ideological mentor, believes Russia must. "If we win," he recently wrote, "we will begin the expansion of liberational (from Americans) ideology into Europe. It is the goal of full Eurasianism—Europe from Lisbon to Vladivostok. Great Eurasian Continental Empire."

If, alternatively, Putin is rational—and thus capable of weighing costs and benefits and associating effects with causes—then there is reason to hope that he will stop somewhat short of destroying Ukraine and the world order. To make such an assumption is not to suggest that Putin is a benign leader. Quite the contrary, he probably possesses all the qualities he was trained to have as a KGB agent: ruthlessness and arrogance. But that doesn't mean he can't understand risk or won't respond to punishment. In this telling, the occupation of Crimea was a grand and glorious little war that raised Putin's popularity with hyper-nationalists in Russia, cost no lives, and transpired quickly and relatively inexpensively. It might have turned Russia into a rogue state, but Putin could reasonably argue that "Russian glory" was worth that price, the full effects of which would not be felt immediately but sometime in the future.

Seen in this light, a full-scale assault on all of Ukraine—or even on Kyiv—would be extremely risky and costly. And it would offer few or no tangible benefits to Putin or to Russia. The Ukrainian army, newly formed National Guard, and militias would put up a fight, and it is by no means certain that Russia could easily advance in Blitzkrieg fashion. A subsequent occupation would entail the deployment of several hundred thousand troops, who would be the targets of a popularly supported resistance movement. And the West would be livid. It could provide significant military assistance to Ukrainian partisans, and it would certainly impose sanctions on the Russian economy as it searches for immediate alternatives for Russian energy. Russian casualties would likely reach the thousands, and the hyper-nationalist hysteria in Russia would diminish as the body bags start arriving home. Dugin might not be fazed by these prospects, but a rational Putin should be.

Less risky and possibly less costly would be the annexation of one or more of Ukraine's southeastern provinces. They border Russia, they're smaller than all of Ukraine, and they've been the targets of agitation and subversion by Russian special forces, "tourists," and thugs for months. But even that occupation wouldn't be as easy as invading Crimea. Ukrainian armed forces with tanks and heavy weaponry are already positioned along the eastern border. There would be fighting and Russian casualties could be high. The occupation would be less costly, but resistance would still be likely and pacifying the population would require a long-term commitment. All in all, these provinces would be an enormous drain on Russia's economic resources.

In all likelihood, Putin is motivated by some combination of Duginite ideology, geopolitical interest, and self-interest. All leaders in all countries are. The ideology provides a set of ultimate goals (freedom, democracy, socialism, Lebensraum) and informs policy choices. But it rarely serves as the sole motivating force. Lenin, for instance, believed in world communism but agreed to a peace with imperial Germany to save the revolution. Stalin went even further, abandoning world revolution for "socialism in one country" in 1925 and becoming an ally of Nazi Germany in 1939. Putin might want to teach Ukraine and the West a lesson even as he remains responsive to Western and Ukrainian behavior.

For its part, Kyiv has beefed up its armed forces and border defenses and started to crack down on Russian special forces in Ukraine. The United States and European Union have imposed ever more painful political and economic penalties on Russia and its leaders. None of these measures may convince Putin to abandon his long-term dreams in Eurasia, but they should encourage him to search for face-saving alternatives to costly wars that bring little benefit to him or to Russia. The United States could tip the scales in rationality's favor by agreeing to supply the Ukrainian armed forces with military assistance. Armaments need not be on the table just now. Trucks, jeeps, uniforms, food, fuel, and medical supplies would suffice to send a strong signal of the United States' seriousness about Ukraine's security.

At the same time, the West should be ready to talk with Russia at any time, any place. On March 17, the Russian Ministry of Foreign Affairs issued a statement about forming a Group for Assisting Ukraine that would consist of Russia, the United States, and Europe. Its job would be to help Ukraine overcome what the ministry calls the "deep crisis of the Ukrainian state" in accordance with certain principles and policy goals, most of which are not intrinsically offensive. (One point, that "the right of Crimea to determine its fate in accordance with the results of the free expression of the will of its population in the March 16, 2014 referendum will be acknowledged and respected," is a nonstarter.) Leaving aside the irony of Putin lecturing anybody on constitutional norms and human rights, the statement does not sound like the sort of thing an ideologically driven irrational leader would issue. Why pussyfoot with the West when it is so much easier to send tanks toward Kyiv?

Ukraine, the United States, and Europe should take up the ministry's offer and propose a series of high-level meetings at which the issues raised by the Russians—as well as issues to be raised by Ukraine and the West—would be discussed. Ukraine and the West could reasonably insist that such discussions could not be held in good faith as long as Russian troops were within striking distance of Ukraine and Russian special forces were fomenting trouble in the southeast. Ukraine could also withdraw its troops from the eastern border, and United Nations peacekeepers could be invited to patrol the territories. The negotiations might turn out to be a bust, but they would at least force everybody—and especially the Kremlin—to take a deep breath and survey the situation with some measure of calm. As the diplomats talk, there's a chance that Putin will come to his geopolitical senses, the war hysteria in Russia will cool down, the sabers will stop rattling so loudly, and Ukraine will get some breathing space. Peace might then appear to be the win-win solution.

PART FOUR: THE DECLINE OF PUTIN RUSSIA

Is Putin Next? *World Affairs Journal*, March 26, 2014

Here are a few trick questions. Who was elected democratically—Viktor Yanukovych or Vladimir Putin? Who violated his country's Constitution? Who enjoyed popular legitimacy? Whose rule was unstable?

The answer to the first question—Who was elected democratically?—is obvious. That was Yanukovych, back on February 7, 2010, in elections that were roundly considered to be fair and free. Putin, in contrast, was elected democratically in 2000, semi-democratically in 2004, and non-democratically in 2012.

Here are excerpts from three Final Reports of the Election Observation Missions of the Organization for Security and Cooperation in Europe's Office for Democratic Institutions and Human Rights (OSCE/ODIHR):

Russian election of March 26, 2000:

> In general, and in spite of episodic events that sometimes tested the system's capacity to uphold principles of fairness and a level playing field, the presidential election was conducted under a constitutional and legislative framework that is consistent with internationally recognized democratic standards, including those formulated in the OSCE Copenhagen Document of 1990.

Russian election of March 14, 2004:

> While on a technical level the election was organized with professionalism, particularly on the part of the Central Election Commission (CEC), the process overall did not adequately reflect principles necessary for a healthy democratic election. The election process failed to meet important commitments concerning treatment of candidates by the State-controlled media on a non-discriminatory basis, equal opportunities for all candidates and secrecy of the ballot. Essential elements of the OSCE commitments for democratic elections, such as a vibrant political discourse and meaningful pluralism, were lacking.

Russian election of March 4, 2012:

> Although all contestants were able to campaign unhindered, the conditions for the campaign were found to be skewed in favor of one candidate. While all candidates had access to media, one candidate, the then Prime Minister [Putin], was given clear advantage in the coverage. State resources were also mobilized in his support. On election day, observers assessed voting positively, overall; however, the process deteriorated during the count due to procedural irregularities. ...

> There was ... a general lack of confidence among many interlocutors in the independence of election officials at all levels, mostly due to their perceived affiliation with local administration and the governing party.

> There was an evident mobilization of individuals and administrative resources

in support of Mr. Putin's campaign, which was observed by the OSCE/ODIHR. In several regions, participants in campaign events reported that they had been ordered to take part by their superiors. Various levels of public institutions instructed their subordinate structures to organize and facilitate Mr. Putin's campaign events. Local authorities also used official communication, such as their institutional websites or newspapers, to facilitate Mr. Putin's campaign.

Contrary to the legal requirements, the broadcast media did not provide balanced coverage of all candidates. Mr. Putin dominated the campaign in the media with frequent appearances. While newscasts on television channels monitored by the OSCE/ODIHR covered the daily activities of each contestant, they were outweighed by lengthy items about him, both as Prime Minister and as candidate, and by a series of documentaries praising his achievements. This created unequal conditions for the candidates, giving Mr. Putin a clear advantage. ...

[P]rocedural irregularities were observed. The process deteriorated clearly during the count, which was assessed negatively in nearly one-third of polling stations observed due to procedural irregularities.

Who violated his country's Constitution? That's easy: both Yanukovych and Putin, repeatedly and brazenly, in systematic efforts to dismantle democratic institutions, constrict civil liberties and human rights, and structure the rules of the game in their favor. Naturally, each violated his Constitution "constitutionally"—by manipulating legislative elections, creating legislative majorities, and then shamelessly using those majorities to rewrite the rules.

Who enjoyed legitimacy? Not Yanukovych—precisely because he was elected democratically and precisely because he promised to be a democrat and promote the people's interests. When Yanukovych shifted gears almost immediately after becoming president and then proceeded to amass wealth, stifle democracy, and humiliate the people, his legitimacy plunged—thereby setting him up for the democratic Euro Revolution that led to his flight and abandonment of the presidency.

In contrast, Putin promised to restore Russia's power and greatness, and he delivered, at least outwardly—by flexing his muscles in Transnistria, Chechnya, Georgia, and Crimea. Small wonder that the hyper-nationalist Russian masses have consistently supported and conferred legitimacy upon him. Yanukovych tripped up because he could not deliver on democratic legitimacy. Putin has succeeded because he delivered on neo-imperialist legitimacy.

Whose rule was, or is, unstable? Yanukovych's, obviously: the sultanistic regime he built was hyper-centralized, inefficient, and corrupt. It survived only as long as the people acquiesced in its existence. Once the mass demonstrations of November 2013 turned into a popular revolution, the regime quickly dissolved and Yanukovych was left on his own, without the support of either the masses or the elites. His systematic violations of the Constitution and his illegitimacy automatically conferred legitimacy on the people power from which he fled.

But here's a surprise perhaps: Putin's rule is equally unstable. His regime is also hyper-centralized, inefficient, and corrupt. It—and Putin with it—can survive and enjoy neo-imperialist legitimacy only because it's been the beneficiary of loads of free money derived from higher energy prices. Thanks to a vast increase in state wealth, Putin could buy popular legitimacy and still have enough to accommodate regime inefficiency and corruption. That's about to change. Energy revenues are declining and will almost certainly continue to decline, as the West develops energy alternatives (shale gas, liquefied natural gas, and energy from other suppliers). With declining revenues, Putin will soon be exposed as a corrupt dictator unable to deliver neo-imperialism to the masses and embezzlement to the elites. Add to that the growing costs of his Crimean misadventure, and, sooner rather than later, Putin could become Russia's Yanukovych.

*

Putin's Russia as a State Sponsor of Terrorism, *World Affairs Journal*, April 14, 2014

Putin's Russia has become what the US Department of State calls a "state sponsor of terrorism."

Here's how: After the Anschluss of Crimea, Putin had three options. He could invade all or parts of Ukraine, or hope that pro-Russian demonstrators would flood Ukraine's streets and assert their "people power." The first option has not been pursued, perhaps because it's too risky. The second failed, as most of Ukraine's southeastern citizens have remained indifferent or opposed to unification with Russia.

That left utin with one remaining option: terrorism.

Here's why Putin's Russia qualifies as a state sponsor of terrorism. According to Section 2656f(d) of Title 22 of the United States Code:

(1) the term "international terrorism" means terrorism involving citizens or the territory of more than one country;

(2) the term "terrorism" means premeditated, politically motivated violence perpetrated against non-combatant targets by subnational groups or clandestine agents; and

(3) the term "terrorist group" means any group practicing, or which has significant subgroups which practice, international terrorism.

There is overwhelming evidence of Russia's direct and indirect involvement in the violence that rocked several eastern Ukrainian cities on April 12–13. Russian intelligence agents and *spetsnaz* special forces are directly involved; the weapons and uniforms worn by the terrorists are of Russian origin (a point made by the US ambassador to Kyiv, Geoffrey Pyatt); and the assaults on government buildings in Slavyansk, Mariupol,

Makiivka, Kharkiv, Yenakievo, Druzhkivka, Horlivka, Krasny Lyman, and Kramatorsk were clearly coordinated by Russian intelligence. As EU High Representative Catherine Ashton delicately put it in a statement yesterday:

> I am gravely concerned about the surge of actions undertaken by armed individuals and separatist groups in various cities of Eastern Ukraine.... I reiterate the EU's strong support for Ukraine's unity, sovereignty and territorial integrity and call upon Russia to do so as well. To this end, the Russian Federation is urged to call back its troops from the Ukrainian border and *to cease any further actions aimed at destabilizing Ukraine.* (Emphasis added.)

Former NATO Supreme Allied Commander Europe Wesley Clark was more blunt, stating that the attacks were not spontaneous and represented the second stage of Russia's plan to occupy Ukraine (the first being the occupation of Crimea).

Does the behavior of the pro-Russian forces in eastern Ukraine involve "premeditated, politically motivated violence perpetrated against non-combatant targets"? Obviously. Does this violence involve "citizens or the territory of more than one country"? Yes, it does. The violence therefore qualifies as international terrorism, and its perpetrators are obviously "terrorist groups." QED.

By the way, the European Union's far more detailed definition of "terrorist acts" should dispel any lingering doubts one may have had that the violence in eastern Ukraine qualifi s as terrorist:

> "Terrorist acts" mean intentional acts which, given their nature or context, may seriously damage a country or international organization and which are defined as an offence under national law. These include:
>
> - attacks upon a person's life which may cause death;
>
> - attacks upon the physical integrity of a person;
>
> - kidnapping or hostage taking;
>
> - causing extensive destruction to a Government or public facility, a transport system, an infrastructure facility;
>
> - seizure of aircraft, ships or other means of public or goods transport;
>
> - manufacture, possession, acquisition, transport, supply or use of weapons, explosives, or of nuclear, biological or chemical weapons;
>
> - participating in the activities of a terrorist group, including by supplying information or material resources, or by funding its activities in any way, with knowledge of the fact that such participation will contribute to the criminal activities of the group.

In order for these acts to constitute terrorist acts, they must be carried out with the aim of seriously intimidating a population, or unduly compelling a Government or an international organization to perform or abstain from performing any act, or seriously destabilizing or destroying the fundamental political, constitutional, economic or social structures of a country or an international organization.

In light of Russia's direct and indirect promotion of international terrorism in eastern Ukraine, Russia obviously qualifies as a "state sponsor of terrorism" and, after formally being declared as such, must be immediately subjected to the sanctions the United States is legally bound to impose on state sponsors of terrorism. (Naturally, the EU should fol-low suit.) Here's the State Department:

> Countries determined by the Secretary of State to have repeatedly provided support for acts of international terrorism are designated pursuant to three laws: section 6(j) of the Export Administration Act, section 40 of the Arms Export Control Act, and section 620A of the Foreign Assistance Act. Taken together, the four main categories of sanctions resulting from designation under these authorities include restrictions on U.S. foreign assistance; a ban on defense exports and sales; certain controls over exports of dual use items; and miscellaneous financial and other restrictions.

> Designation under the above-referenced authorities also implicates other sanctions laws that penalize persons and countries engaging in certain trade with state sponsors. Currently there are four countries designated under these authorities: Cuba, Iran, Sudan and Syria.

That list should now consist of five rogue countries—unless, of course, both Washington and Brussels prefer to supplement their weak-kneed response to Putin's violation of international norms with an implicit endorsement of terrorism.

*

Putin's Strategy: Good Cop, Bad Cop, *CNN*, April 23, 2014

So, just what is Russia up to now?

On April 17, at the same time Russian President Vladimir Putin snarled at Ukraine and the West at a press conference in Moscow, Russian Foreign Minister Sergey Lavrov signed a conciliatory agreement in Geneva with the United States, the European Union and Ukraine.

On the face of it, the foreign minister seemed to repudiate the President and betray the pro-Russian terrorists in eastern Ukraine.

Whatever Putin and Lavrov's game, the statement signed by Lavrov in Geneva represents a major stand down by Russia. To be sure, given the Kremlin's past mendacity and slipperiness, the agreement is ultimately nothing more than a piece of paper. If Putin could breach the 1994 Budapest Memorandum on Security Assurances (wherein the United States, the United Kingdom and Russia agreed to guarantee Ukraine's security and territorial integrity), he could easily tear up the Geneva statement if it suits him.

In his press conference, true to form, Putin denied the existence of Ukrainians as a separate nation, reserved to himself the right to intervene in Ukraine, and supported the pro-Putin armed commandos who have caused havoc in eastern Ukraine.

Here's Putin on Ukrainians as really being Russians: "The desire to get Russia and Ukraine to quarrel, to divide what is essentially a single people has been an object of international politics for centuries." It gets worse. Putin says the fanatical Bolsheviks and their reactionary White opponents agreed on one thing only: that Ukraine and Russia were a "part of a common, united space and a single people." And, he adds, "They were absolutely right."

Ukrainians, naturally, beg to differ. And they worry. If Ukraine has no right to exist as a separate nation, then why shouldn't Putin bring Ukrainians "home" whenever he chooses to follow in the footsteps of the Bolsheviks and the Whites?

Here's Putin on the right to intervene to "help" Russians and "Russian-speaking citizens" in Ukraine:

> But we know exactly that we ought to do everything to help these people defend their rights and independently determine their fate. This is what we will fight for. Let me remind you that the Federation Council of Russia gave the president the right to use armed forces in Ukraine. I very much hope that I will not have to exercise this right and that, through political and diplomatic means, we will be able to resolve all the acute, if not indeed very acute, problems in Ukraine today.

Unsurprisingly, Putin's insistence that he has a right to aid Ukrainian citizens spooks Ukrainians, especially as his invocation of that right is coupled with the continued massing of thousands of battle-ready Russian troops along Ukraine's borders.

Finally, here's Putin on the pro-Russian commandos who have terrorized southeastern Ukraine in the last week and thereby compelled Kyiv to try to regain control of the region:

> Now we hear of calls (by the West) to the people in the southeast to lay down their arms. ... But then (the Ukrainian authorities should) pull back the army from the civilian population. ... All right, the east will disarm, all right, let's assume the army will withdraw—why have the (Ukrainian) nationalist groups not been disarmed yet?

One of the central points of the Geneva statement undermines Putin's concerns: "All illegal armed groups must be disarmed; all illegally seized buildings must be returned to legitimate owners; all illegally occupied streets, squares and other public places in Ukrainian cities and towns must be vacated." Geneva made it clear that all groups should be disarmed and all buildings and streets be vacated—immediately. There is no talk in the statement of one side's disarming first and then the other's disarming next.

Because virtually no Ukrainian armed groups are in Ukraine, nor are they occupying buildings—the groups have been disarmed in the last few weeks—the statement applies almost exclusively to the Russian-supported, Russian-funded, and Russian-directed commando-terrorists.

Lavrov also signed the following statement: "Amnesty will be granted to protesters and to those who have left buildings and other public places and surrendered weapons, with the exception of those found guilty of capital crimes."

This is, indirectly, a recognition of the Ukrainian government's legitimacy, something that Putin repeatedly denied at his press conference.

After all, who is to capture the terrorists and determine if they committed capital crimes? The Ukrainian Ministry of Internal Affairs, the procurator's office, and the Ministry of Justice, of course. If the government is illegitimate, then so, too, they are illegitimate. Conversely, if they are legitimate, then so, too, is the government.

President Obama was absolutely on the mark to be skeptical of Russian intentions. "Our strong preference would be for Mr. Putin to follow through on what is a glimmer of hope coming out of these Geneva talks," he said. "But we're not going to count on it until we see it. And in the meantime, we're going to prepare what our other options are."

Even so, the Geneva document is important. It represents a standard against which the reduction of terrorist activities in eastern Ukraine and Russia's behavior toward them can be measured.

Thus far, the evidence is neither encouraging nor discouraging. Russia insists the Ukrainians have to move first, the extremists in Sloviansk and Donetsk have insisted the agreement does not affect them, and their comrades in Kramatorsk have seized more buildings. On the other hand, extremists in Yenakievo abandoned the buildings they had occupied and the Donetsk separatists have promised to vacate two floors and the conference hall of the state province administration building.

Regardless of the desultory response by Russia and its supporters, both the United States and Ukraine have, correctly, insisted that Russia stick to the agreement and convince its supporters in eastern Ukraine to surrender their arms and abandon the buildings they seized.

Kyiv has also agreed to an amnesty for those extremists who did not, as the document insists, engage in capital crimes. And Yulia Tymoshenko, the former prime minister-turned-political prisoner who is now running for president, has used the agreement as the basis for calling on the extremists to engage in roundtable discussions.

The next week or two will demonstrate whether Russia is or is not serious about the Geneva agreement. If the terrorist groups do not abandon buildings and give up their arms, and if Russia does not stop infiltrating Russian intelligence agents into Ukraine, then Putin and Lavrov will effectively be declaring that they cannot be trusted and that their intentions in Ukraine are aggressive.

Alternatively, if they adhere to the agreement, the document could lead to further forms of de-escalation, perhaps even including a permanent withdrawal of Russian troops from Ukraine's borders.

Are Lavrov and Putin playing good cop–bad cop, hoping to convince the United States, the European Union, and Ukraine that Russia really is reasonable and has no aggressive intentions? If so, is this just a ploy to win time while war preparations continue? Or is their routine indicative of Russia's finally coming to its senses?

Has Putin realized that invading or destabilizing Ukraine will bring him and Russia nothing except painful Western sanctions and the possible arming of Ukraine's military?

Whatever the answer, it seems obvious that the West's consistent expressions of support for Ukraine and condemnation of Russia's illegal annexation of Crimea, along with Kyiv's decision finally to resist Russian aggression, played some role in convincing Putin to have Lavrov make nice.

The moral is clear: Talk tough and act tough, and Putin may just possibly listen.

*

Why Germans Are Smitten with Putin, *World Affairs Journal*, May 23, 2014

The German liberal newspaper *Die Zeit* recently shed a bright light on the German population's odd love affair with Russian President Vladimir Putin. Germans profess a love of democracy and human rights; Putin has done everything in his power to destroy democracy and human rights. Germans stand for peace; Putin has unleashed war on Ukraine in 2014 (and on Georgia in 2008).

"Why do so many German citizens judge the crisis in Crimea in a completely different way than politicians and the media?" asks Bernd Ulrich. "Unless surveys are misleading, two-thirds of German citizens, voters, and readers stand opposed to four-fifths of the political class." The former either approve of or are indifferent to Putin's aggression in Ukraine. The latter are aghast. (With some significant exceptions: e.g., former socialist chancellors Helmut Schmidt and Gerhard Schröder. Schmidt defended Putin's Anschluss of Crimea, while Schröder recently invited Russia's version of the "good Hitler" to his 70th birthday bash.)

Ulrich identifies five reasons for this divide.

The first is the perceived arrogance of the West (read Washington) since 9/11. "Many are now saying that limits need to be placed on" Washington's highhandedness, and if

German Chancellor Angela Merkel "can't do it, then maybe Vladimir Putin can."

The second is the perceived arrogance of the "Euro machine": "Putin claims that the EU backed him into a corner with its association agreement for Ukraine. One could bet that the vast majority of people within the EU were just as surprised by the fact that yet another country was supposed to be associated to it ... the majority seems to feel this ominous mix of foreign presumptuousness and personal powerlessness not only toward Washington, but also toward Brussels."

The third is the perceived arrogance of the media: "When the vast majority of media make arguments along the same lines, as is the case with Ukraine, it is anything but easy—even for well-intentioned readers—to discern whether what we are dealing with here (a) is once again an instance of hype, (b) is a tacit measure to educate the populace, or (c) is a case of deep-seated convictions concerning democracy and human rights."

The fourth is the suspicion that the West is unwilling and unable to engage in military solutions:

> The entire discussion about Russia and Putin is being poisoned by the presumption that, to some people, this is about much more than Crimea and Ukraine. ... We are less and less willing to intervene, and arms expenditures are declining, even in the US now. In Germany, this development is proceeding in a particularly rapid and radical fashion. People haven't properly come to terms with the disappointment of Afghanistan, and Germans said "no" to both war in Iraq and intervention in Libya. The respective reasons for staying on the sidelines were of a kind that makes it difficult to even imagine any major military intervention in which Germans would participate.

The first three reasons are situational (they depend on post-9/11 developments) and, thus, could change. The fourth may reflect an attitudinal disposition that appears to be taking root today. It, too, could change (and if it doesn't, Germany's eastern European NATO partners had better watch out).

Ulrich's fifth reason is rooted in German political culture:

> For us, the post-war period was characterized by wrestling with suppressing or accepting the Holocaust, by the German guilt for having murdered 6 million Jews. But other types of guilt have lingered behind that, including that for killing millions of Russians. ... This is one of the main reasons why there now appears to be significant willingness here in Germany to concede a "zone of influence" to the Russians. The thinking here is: Haven't they already been hurt and penalized enough by the loss of their Soviet empire? Should we Germans, of all people, argue with them over Ukraine?

This view, of German guilt for Russian deaths, is extremely widespread. German intellectuals, policymakers, and average citizens speak of World War II as the "*Vernichtungskrieg gegen Russland*" (the war of destruction against Russia); accordingly, the millions of civilian and military casualties were suffered by "*die Russen*." The terminology goes back to the war, when the Nazi regime characterized its enemy in exactly the same terms.

The reality was quite different. Nazi Germany devastated, above all, Poland, Belarus, and Ukraine—and not Russia. This is not a question of who suffered most, but, quite simply, of setting the historical record straight. Which Ulrich, to his credit, does:

> Today, with a view to German guilt, the right to self-determination of another people—Ukrainians—is once again being disputed. Should they not be allowed into the EU because Germans justifiably have a guilty conscience vis-à-vis Russians? The fact that Germans and Russians are once again making decisions about the fate of Ukraine would be a perverse lesson to learn from history for this country, which suffered under both nations like no other. The Soviet Union and Nazi Germany killed millions upon millions of people on Ukrainian territory with planned famines, pogroms, and extermination campaigns. During the years when Stalin and Hitler were in power, more people died here than anywhere else in Eastern Europe. Likewise, millions of the "Russians" that German soldiers killed during World War II were actually Ukrainian citizens of the Soviet Union. The current debate ignores the havoc that Nazi and Soviet imperialism wreaked in this country. In today's crisis, the price is being paid for the fact that Germans have not yet arrived in their collective memory at a place where they can view the fate of Ukrainians as Ukrainians.

That last sentence is key. Ukrainians, like Belarusians, do not exist in the German consciousness. During the war, they were *Untermenschen* (subhumans). At present, they are, for most Germans, not even worth the disdain that the modifier *unter* conveys. How convenient for German defense contractor Rheinmetall, which has been happily training Russian troops. And how convenient for the German public: if Russia invades Ukraine and kills thousands of Ukrainians, Germans will be able to assuage their guilt by shedding a tear for poor Putin.

*

Enough False Rhetoric from Putin, *World Affairs Journal*, June 2, 2014

I have one request to Russia's fascistoid leader: stop lecturing Ukraine and the world.

I've been listening to you for close to 15 years now and, frankly, I'm tired of your half-baked views and cockamamie opinions. I know you think you know a lot about the ways of the world, Volodya, but permit me to let you in on a secret that everyone besides you knows: You don't.

Just what makes you think that a career in the KGB qualifies you to speak authoritatively about anything—and, especially, about constitutions, democracy, and legitimacy? Indeed, former members of criminal organizations might be better advised to keep mum about the very things they spent their entire careers trying to destroy.

But it gets worse. After all, we know you plagiarized your dissertation:

> According to official sources, Russian President Vladimir Putin holds a degree of candidate of economic science (incorrectly described on the English-language version of his website as a "Ph.D in economics"), awarded by the St. Petersburg Mining Institute in 1996. Putin never actually attended the institute, however, and the topic of the dissertation he submitted and defended was one in which he had no previous background. With the aim of exploring the mystery, Brookings [Institution] researchers Clifford Gaddy and Igor Danchenko in 2005 obtained a copy of the previously inaccessible dissertation and examined its contents. On March 30, 2006, ... they also presented evidence of extensive plagiarism in the dissertation.

We also know that yours is a particular brand of ruthlessness. There is very strong evidence to suggest that you were in on the plot to bomb two apartment buildings in Moscow in September 1999, in which 300 Russian citizens were killed and several hundred others were wounded. As Amy Knight, a specialist on the KGB argues:

> The evidence provided in [John Dunlop's] *The Moscow Bombings* makes it abundantly clear that the FSB of the Russian Republic, headed by Patrushev, was responsible for carrying out the attacks. ... Yet it is hard to imagine that they would have gone so far as to order bombings that they knew would kill so many innocent people. The more likely possibility is that the FSB was told by Yeltsin's inner circle that violent acts were needed to destabilize Russia but that no specific instructions were given to blow up apartment buildings. The FSB, including its top leadership, responded by seizing the initiative. What, then, was the role of Putin, who was prime minister at the time, and also secretary of the Security Council? ... as Dunlop demonstrates, ... it is inconceivable that [this terrible act] would have been done without the sanction of Putin.

In October 2002, you crushed a Chechen seizure of the Dubrovka Theater in Moscow by killing 40 Chechens and 130 Russian hostages. Then, in September 2004, you crushed a Chechen takeover of a school in Beslan by killing a few dozen militants and 334 Russian citizens, including 156 children. And with a record like that, you have the temerity to accuse Kyiv of failing to negotiate with the terrorists you've sponsored and sent into east-ern Ukraine. And you have the unmitigated gall to accuse Ukraine of being indifferent to civilian casualties!

You claim to have built up Russia's economy, Volodya, but everyone knows you had nothing to do with sparking rapid GDP growth. All the credit goes to a huge spike in the price of oil and gas that, happily for you, coincided with your coming to power. Now that energy prices have leveled off and the shale gas revolution has taken place, let's see you get the declining Russian GDP going again. I'm betting you'll fail. Not that you won't keep taking a big piece of the shrinking Russian economic pie. Just how much have you squirreled away in Western banks, Volodya? Is it $45 billion or $75 billion?

But, heck, if you want to destroy Russia and bamboozle the Russians, who am I to stop you? What really gets me is your moralizing Ukraine and the rest of the world about constitutions, democracy, legitimacy, and stability. You know, as well as everybody, that you've systematically violated Russia's Constitution since 1999. You also know that you've dismantled every single democratic institution in Russia. You know that your legitimacy rests exclusively on your ability to pay off your cronies with your ill-gotten loot and buy off he population with promises of imperial grandeur and quick infusions of easy money. And you know that the major reason for instability in much of the post-Soviet world is your interminable meddling, and not the internal difficulties of the countries concerned. Stop infiltrating terrorists into Ukraine, Volodya, and I bet eastern Ukraine will quickly settle down.

Some people are impressed by your statecraft, but I'm not. You happen to have been at the right time in the right place. Just as Russia remains an Ivory Coast with a bomb, so, too, you remain a Yanukovych with gas. If it weren't for all that filthy lucre that's rained down on you, you would have long since been voted out of office by Russians. If it weren't for your genuine skill at talking tough, democratic policymakers would have long since realized that your bare-chested bluster is just a cover for your policy incompetence.

So, Volodya, stop lecturing Ukraine about constitutions, democracy, legitimacy, and stability. Indeed, stop lecturing us about anything. Except, perhaps, on the mechanics of mendacity, death, destruction, and destabilization. Do everyone a favor, Volodya: please shut up.

*

How Putin Lost Ukraine, *World Affairs Journal*, June 19, 2014

Half a year ago, in the fall of 2013, Ukraine was well on the way to becoming an authoritarian vassal state of Russia. Now, thanks to Russia's neo-fascist dictator, Vladimir Putin, Ukraine is well on the way to becoming a democracy and a full-fledged member of the international community.

How did Putin snatch a humiliating defeat from the jaws of surefire victory? How could he have walked into a strategic trap of his own making? In a word, how did he lose Ukraine?

And make no mistake about it: it was Putin, and no one else, who lost Ukraine. He had it. He could easily have kept it. But now he'll never have it again. And he has no one to blame but himself.

Putin has never understood Ukraine. For him, as for all too many Russians, it's a historical mistake: a part of Russia that's been swayed from the path of righteousness by a few dastardly fascist imperialist cigar-chomping bourgeois nationalists in cahoots with the CIA. If you treat a bona fide country with a bona fide people with a bona fide identity as your dirty backyard, don't be surprised if you slip in the mud and fall on your face.

Putin's first major slip was during the 2004 Orange Revolution, when, stupidly, he backed Viktor Yanukovych. That disaster taught Putin nothing, and, nine years later, he made the same mistake during the Euro Revolution. How could a supposedly smart leader back the same loser—not once, but twice? How could that same supposedly smart leader still insist that the loser remains Ukraine's legitimate president—even after a fair and free election gave a huge mandate to Petro Poroshenko? The sad thing is that, after 15 years in power, Putin still doesn't "get" Ukraine.

Putin's most egregious blunder was to coerce Yanukovych into rejecting the Association Agreement with the European Union last fall. That strategic error led to the demonstrations in Kyiv, Yanukovych's downfall, the emergence of a pro-Western, democratic Ukraine, and Russia's transformation into a rogue state and sponsor of terrorism. That's bad enough. Worse, Putin's move was premised on his belief that the agreement would remove Ukraine from Russia's sphere of influence. Sure, it would have provided Ukraine with a foothold in Europe, and, yes, it would have diminished Ukraine's international isolation in the long run, but a Yanukovych-misruled Ukraine would have remained firmly ensconced in Russia's backyard for a long time to come.

After all, with the Association Agreement as his main claim to fame, Yanukovych would have probably been reelected in 2015; the penetration of Kyiv's government by agents of the Kremlin would have remained high or gotten higher; and the presence of Russian propaganda, business, and other forms of "soft power" would have only grown. Meanwhile, Ukraine's military would have continued to decay, Ukraine's foreign policy would have remained unremittingly pro-Russian, and a large segment of the Ukrainian population would have stayed ambivalent about Ukraine's independence. The Europeans, meanwhile, and Germany in particular, would have remained indifferent to Ukraine. What's not to like from the Kremlin's point of view? A smart Russian president would have *encouraged* Yanukovych to sign the agreement with Brussels.

Alas, when it comes to Ukraine, Putin's IQ takes a nosedive. Having sparked the Euro Revolution, having destroyed his pal Yanukovych, having embarked on the idiotic Crimean adventure, and having supported terrorism in the Donbas, Putin has forced Ukraine to become independent, democratic, and pro-Western. He's forced it to develop an army and security apparatus. He's forced the population to take sides and discover its Ukrainian identity—and pride. He's forced the government to streamline the state apparatus. He's forced elites to embrace democracy. And he's forcing them to embark on radical economic reform and administrative decentralization. Faced with Putin's aggression, Ukraine has no choice but to embody all the qualities—democracy, rule of law, tolerance, a functioning market economy—that Putin systematically destroys.

Worse still for Putin, his imperialism is driving Ukrainian elites to seek refuge in Western security institutions. Half a year ago, the elite and popular consensus in Ukraine was distinctly anti-NATO. The West, meanwhile, was suffering from "Ukraine fatigue" and had little interest in Ukraine as a strategic partner. Now, everything's changed. Ukraine is the darling of the West, and Ukrainian public opinion on NATO is shifting.

Amazingly, Putin appears to think that, by supporting terrorism in eastern Ukraine, he can compel Ukraine to back away from the West. The effect, as any schoolboy confronted by a bully could have told him, is just the opposite. Faced with a hostile Russia, Ukraine has no choice but to turn westward. And, thanks to Putin's treachery and mendacity, a democratic Ukraine will never again be the close, and fawning, partner of Russia that it was until a few months ago. Since Putin cannot be trusted, whatever deal Kyiv eventually signs with Moscow will at best establish a condition of formally peaceful relations between hostile neighbors ("cold peace") or informally belligerent relations between hostile neighbors ("cold war"). Warily peaceful relations following a "de-annexation" of Crimea and recognition of Kyiv ("hot peace") will be impossible as long as Putin remains in power.

For the time being, most Russians are still too bedazzled by Putin's Tarzan yells to realize that he's lost Ukraine irrevocably—and may be in the process of losing Russia. When they wake up to the reality of his "harebrained" blunders, Putin will discover that his sky-high ratings are as ephemeral as his swings on the vine are a pathetic pose.

*

Bawdy Lyrics Mock Putin in Ukraine, *World Affairs Journal*, June 25, 2014

Ukrainians have taken to fighting back against Russia's fascistoid dictator, Vladimir Putin, with obscenities and humor. A Ukrainian psychiatrist I recently saw on Ukrainian TV calls such behavior psychologically healthy during periods of "extreme stress"— an understatement for the savage war Putin and his terrorists have unleashed against Ukraine. The American social scientist James C. Scott might call both obscenity and humor "weapons of the weak." Whatever you call them, they're spreading like wildfire across Ukraine.

The case in point is a song or, more exactly, a chant that goes like this:

Putin khuylo
La-la la-la la-la la-la

"*Khuylo*" is the extremely vulgar Ukrainian term for penis. Its equivalents in English are well known (and, for the sake of my more sensitive readers, will go unmentioned). The words have been translated as "Putin is a d—khead" or as "Putin is a d—k," but I prefer "Putin is a pr—k." "D—khead" and "d—k" connote stupidity; "pr—k" connotes nastiness. And, I suspect, most Ukrainians view Putin as a nasty piece of work.

Soccer fans apparently first sang the chant on March 30, 2014, in Kharkiv, during a match between Kharkiv Metalist and Donetsk Shakhtar. Since then, the chant—whose lyrics and melody are readily accessible to all of Putin's detractors, regardless of their

410

musical abilities—has gone viral. If anything is a barometer of Ukrainian attitudes toward the man and his war-mongering, this, obviously, is it. A shorthand, more modest version of the lyrics has even entered the popular discourse. If you want to express your views of Putin, all you need do is say, "la-la," and everything's quite clear. One Ukrainian wit has even incorporated the two-word text into the Russian national anthem, a move that transposes his feelings about Putin to—gasp—Mother Russia (the implicit gender bending should appeal to postmodernists).

The democratic national deputy, Oleh Lyashko, who ran for president on May 25th and received over 8 percent of the vote, actually sang the song at a mass rally in Ternopil. That incident didn't seem to annoy the Kremlin. But when Ukraine's acting minister of foreign affairs, Andrii Deshchytsia, stated at a June 15th anti-Russian rally in Kyiv that he agreed that "Putin is a *khuylo*"—contrary to media reports, Deshchytsia never sang the chant—Moscow exploded, with calls for Deshchytsia's resignation coming from his Russian counterpart, Sergei Lavrov, and the head of the Duma's Committee on International Relations, Aleksei Pushkov.

The target of Ukrainian invective remained silent, but one can imagine that Putin—whom Hillary Clinton has called "thin-skinned"—must have been boiling mad.

Russia's strongman obviously knows how to dish it out—remember that this is the man who called on chasing down Chechen terrorists "even in the outhouse"—but just as obvi-ously can't take it, especially when his hyper-masculine image is questioned.

Here's Celestine Bohlen of the *New York Times*:

> Asked by two French journalists on June 4 about [Hillary Clinton's] comparison of Russia's seizure of Crimea to Hitler's aggression in the 1930s, Mr. Putin scoffed. "It's better not to argue with women," he said. "When people push boundaries too far, it's not because they are strong but because they are weak. But maybe weakness is not the worst quality for a woman."
>
> Leaving aside the blatant sexism, Mr. Putin strayed into what for him is potentially dangerous territory. If pushing boundaries too far is a sign of weakness, then what to say about Mr. Putin's own policies in Ukraine? When Russia annexes Crimea, when it gives tacit support to attacks by pro-Russian separatists on Ukrainian border posts, isn't that—literally—about testing the frontiers of a neighboring sovereign state? Does that make it muscle-flexing by a weak man? ...
>
> Mr. Putin's behavior with other leaders is often seen as a clue to the quality of his personal relationships with them. In theory, he and Chancellor Angela Merkel of Germany should have an excellent rapport; each speaks the other's language, and the two countries have strong economic ties. And yet twice (most recently in the thick of the Ukrainian crisis), well aware of Ms. Merkel's deep-seated fear of dogs, he let his big, black Labrador Koni into the room with her, even sniff her legs, and watched with a peculiarly passive expression.
>
> On the occasions when he and Mr. Obama have sat together for photographers,

the chill has been almost visible. Mr. Obama denies that he has a bad relationship with the Russian president, but it is clearly not a good one. For one thing, relations between the United States and Russia are strained. For another, Mr. Obama is a good six inches taller than Mr. Putin, an advantage probably not lost on someone who seems to put such stock in projecting an image of power.

This is odd behavior for a wannabe world statesman. Walking around bare-chested while holding big guns is embarrassing enough (although I don't doubt that it goes well with the pre-Freudian ladies in Omsk), but purposely insulting strong women—whose strength, evidently, challenges his masculinity—takes the cake. Russia's premier literary critic, Tatyana Tolstaya, recently referred to "little men with Napoleonic complexes" on Russian TV. Quite.

Putin's "blatant sexism" may go some way to explaining his hatred of an independent Ukraine. In much Soviet propaganda, which Putin knows all too well, Ukraine was often represented as a peasant woman, while Russia was represented by a working-class man. In Putin's world, Ukraine, like women, should stay quiet. And if they don't? Obviously, you're perfectly entitled to smack them around.

*

Contradictions Define Kremlin Apologists, *World Affairs Journal*, July 10, 2014

According to the conventional wisdom, Vladimir Putin and his Western supporters propagate a uniform message throughout the world. At its most extreme, this view sees Russia as having a formidable propaganda machine that is running roughshod over the Western media and public.

In fact, Putin and his supporters and apologists often disagree. One reason may be that the machine just isn't as formidable as it's made out to be. Another may be that the Kremlin's supporters make mistakes when interpreting or anticipating the frequently contradictory or incomprehensible statements of the Delphic oracle that is Putin. A third may be that they have difficulties bridging the growing gap between reality and Putin's oftentimes shifting views. The Putinite interpretation—one that I won't even bother refuting—is that disagreement is the foundation of vigorous democracies such as Putin's Russia.

Consider three recent texts: Putin's July 1st speech to the Conference of Russian ambassadors and permanent representatives in Moscow; Andranik Migranyan's June 28th article in the *National Interest*; and Katrina vanden Heuvel and Stephen F. Cohen's May 19th article in the *Nation*.

Putin is Russia's unconstitutionally elected president; Migranyan is director of the Institute for Democracy and Cooperation in New York, a Kremlin front; vanden Heuvel, editor of the *Nation*, and Cohen, her spouse, are Putin's cheerleaders on the American left.

Before looking at discrepancies, consider the most striking similarity: all four see the current crisis in Ukraine as the product of US intrigues (echoes of Jeane Kirkpatrick's "Blame America First" speech many years ago).

Putin: "The events provoked in Ukraine became the concentrated expression of the notorious policy of containment."

Migranyan: "Pushing Kyiv towards decisive pro-NATO and pro-EU actions, Washington in effect pushed the country into civil war."

Vanden Heuvel and Cohen: "the Ukraine crisis was instigated by the West's attempt, last November, to smuggle the former Soviet republic into NATO."

What's missing? Ukraine and Ukrainians, of course. None of the texts sees Ukrainians as agents with a voice: they are marionettes, following the dictates of Washington. That this view is completely at odds with what happened on the Maidan should be obvious. Far worse, denying Ukrainians agency and a voice is just an old racist trick. Obviously, blacks wouldn't have demanded civil rights if some outside agitators hadn't incited them. The women's movement? A feminist plot. Ukrainians demonstrating in Kyiv? Stooges of the CIA.

Putin and Migranyan probably can't see that this is racism. Vanden Heuvel and Cohen, who rightly rail against racism on the pages of the *Nation*, should know better. Shame on them all.

Now consider the differences between these three texts.

Putin sees NATO as a threat: "In the past 20 years, our partners have been trying to convince Russia of their good intentions, their readiness to jointly develop strategic cooperation. However, at the same time they kept expanding NATO, extending the area under their military and political control ever closer to our borders. And when we rightfully asked: 'Don't you find it possible and necessary to discuss this with us?' they said: 'No, this is none of your business.'"

So do vanden Heuvel and Cohen: "twenty years of NATO's eastward expansion has caused Russia to feel cornered."

Migranyan disagrees with both Putin and the *Nation*, arguing that NATO is a failure: "With regard to the Ukrainian crisis, a serious topic of conversation is the net benefit to the West (and to the new countries) of NATO's inclusion of the Baltic States, Poland, and some Balkan countries. As it turned out, strategists who advocated the endless expansion of NATO never dreamt that it would come at a cost. ... In this regard, we need only recall the recent scandalous statement by Polish Foreign Minister Radek Sikorski, who ... noted that no matter how much Poland tried to bend to US interests, it would only receive the illusion of security and stability in return. Today, it is clear to all that the strategic line followed by [President] Clinton on Russia and the former Eastern Bloc, as well as a string of strategic decisions by the Bush Jr. administration, were a total failure."

No less embarrassing is the incoherence of the three texts' defense of Russia's Crimean landgrab. Here the authors both agree and disagree.

Putin: "What did our partners expect from us as the developments in Ukraine unfolded? We clearly had no right to abandon the residents of Crimea and Sevastopol to the mercy of nationalist and radical militants; we could not allow our access to the Black Sea to be significantly limited; we could not allow NATO forces to eventually come to the land of Crimea and Sevastopol, the land of Russian military glory, and cardinally change the balance of forces in the Black Sea area. This would mean giving up practically everything that Russia had fought for since the times of Peter the Great, or maybe even earlier—historians should know."

Putin used to argue the invasion was necessary to save Crimea's poor Russians from Ukrainian fascists. Now, everything but the kitchen sink seems to matter. Can any serious European statesman really believe that NATO forces would have been stationed in Crimea *before* Ukraine became a member of NATO (an eventuality that is highly unlikely in the short term and possibly longer)? Even more worrisome is how Putin links his imperialism to imperial Russia's and himself to Peter the Great. Is that a sign of historical manipulation or megalomania?

Vanden Heuvel and Cohen: "the West's jettisoning in February of its own agreement with then-President Viktor Yanukovych brought to power in Kyiv an unelected regime so anti-Russian and so uncritically embraced by Washington that the Kremlin felt an urgent need to annex predominantly Russian Crimea, the home of its most cherished naval base."

Putin invokes a phantom NATO threat, radical militants, and Russian imperialism. The *Nation*'s daring duo reduce Putin's annexation to some bizarre (and physiologically painful!) "urgent need" and an irrational love for, of all things, a naval base!

Migranyan, meanwhile, has nothing coherent to say about Crimea. Except that even his incoherence rests on a contradiction. Thus, he insists that "Washington did not take into account the fact that Moscow had had no plans to take over Crimea or split Ukraine." But then his language belies that claim: such phrases as "after Crimea's *return* to Russia" and "the *reabsorption* of Crimea" (my emphasis) clearly suggest that he views Crimea as a natural part of Russia, which was merely "reabsorbing" what had always belonged to it.

Do these absurdities and contradictions matter? Personally, I'd like to think that coherence goeth before the fall.

*

PART FOUR: THE DECLINE OF PUTIN RUSSIA

What's Rong with Wrussia? *World Affairs Journal,* July 16, 2014

Everything, according to some. Many things, according to others. Nothing, according to many Russians.

Back in 2004, two US academics, Andrei Shleifer and Daniel Treisman, wrote a controversial piece for *Foreign Affairs* in which they argued that statistics proved that Russia was a "normal country." Since they focused on mostly economic parameters, such as GDP, income distribution, and the like, they had a point.

What Shleifer and Treisman overlooked was the politics. Do "normal" countries normally invade their neighbors, lop off bits and pieces of foreign territory, support unconstitutionally elected, power-obsessed strongman leaders, distrust the world and continually whine about their lost glory, take the crudest Goebbelsian government propaganda at face value, export terrorism, call democrats fascists and fascists democrats, and approve of profoundly corrupt, deeply inefficient, hyper-chauvinist, and blatantly imperialist fascist states?

In a word, what's rong with Wrussia is not that it's backward, but that it's got so many important things backwards.

The depth of one's pessimism about Russia is largely a function of which part of that long-suffe ing country strikes you as irredeemably wrong.

If you think Vladimir Putin is the problem, you're an optimist. After all, if all that's rong with Wrussia is Putin, then his departure—which even his acolytes must agree is inevitable—will solve Wrussia's problems. Naturally, if, like Patrick Buchanan, Stephen F. Cohen, Gerhard Schröder, Aleksandr Dugin, and Marine Le Pen, you think Vlad is the cat's pajamas, then nothing's wrong with the place and we can all sleep soundly.

If you believe the system Putin built—or, possibly, the system that spawned Putin—is the problem, then you're well on the way to being a pessimist, though not yet of a hopeless kind. I call that system fascist, because, while possessing all the features of run-of-the-mill authoritarian regimes, it also has a charismatic, hyper-masculine strongman leader who employs chauvinism, supremacism, and imperialism as means of reaching out to the public and underpinning his own legitimacy. If the term, fascist, bothers you, fine: call it something else. Call Russia a Putinist authoritarian dictatorship. Call it democratic populist authoritarian. Call it a hyper-managed hybrid post-democratic democracy. Go to town with the modifiers that make you feel better. Just remember that, whatever you call it, it walks and talks like the systems built by Mussolini in Italy and Hitler in Germany.

If the system is what's rong with Wrussia, then Putin's inevitable departure, whether from life or from politics, may not change it—or, possibly, it may only transform it into a run-of-the-mill authoritarian regime. Would such a Russia be less inclined to act like a bully internally and externally? Probably not, at least in the short run. Will such a regime outlive Putin? Quite possibly yes.

It's at this point of any analysis that the depth of one's pessimism about Russia is tested. If you think that the real problem with Russia is neither Putin nor the house he built, but the Russian people—or, more precisely, their political culture, which, as many Russians and non-Russians argue, is authoritarian and, thus, can countenance only dictatorial rule—then your pessimism is pretty much hopeless. Can Russian political culture change? Sure. But it's in the nature of culture to change slowly—which means that Russians have the fascist system and the fascist ruler they "deserve." Even if the ruler goes and the system collapses, both will likely be succeeded by stable authoritarian variants.

Many Russians, along with Putin, Buchanan, Cohen, Schröder, Dugin, and Le Pen, disagree with this diagnosis. That is to say, they don't disagree that the ruler, regime, and culture are, er, not quite democratic. They just happen to believe that's a good thing. To them, all I can say is: If you want to destroy democracy, undermine liberalism, and adopt a paranoid foreign policy that has turned Russia into a rogue state, go right ahead. Just keep your proclivities to yourself and don't export your ruler, regime, and culture to countries that reject fascism.

Which, obviously, brings me to Ukraine and its neighbors in the "near abroad" (a term that only a Russian imperialist pining for the good ol' days of empire could love). Like everyone else, they don't know how Russia will or will not change in the next few years. Unlike everyone else, they have to live next door to this hulking, sulking Cyclops of a country.

What do you do if the guy next door is a loud, rude, vulgar, aggressive, violent, thuggish, and heavy-drinking drug dealer and you can't move out? You reinforce your wall, install several locks, put metal sheeting on your door, lift weights, practice karate, ignore him—and hang out with those neighbors who don't have awful habits.

That's why Ukraine's signing the Association Agreement with the European Union on June 27th was arguably the most important thing to have happened to the country since independence. It means that Ukraine and Ukrainians may finally be able to live in peace—not immediately, as their neighbor turns up his boorishness in response, but eventually and permanently, once he collapses in a drunken stupor. (Unfortunately, many western Europeans are so hooked on Russian oil that they are willing to sell their ideals for a fix.)

When Wrussia becomes Russia—note the "when": I believe that Putin and his regime will soon alight the ash heap of history—Ukraine and its neighbors should extend the long-suffering Russian people a helping hand. Until then, they have no choice but to avoid Wrussia and its rongs like the plague.

As former President Leonid Kravchuk put it: "We must learn to live with a country that will permanently engage in provocations. ... We can't change Russia, but we can learn to live together against Russia. There's no alternative."

Or as a Russian-speaking Donetsk native recently said about the Russians: "My relatives and I, along with millions of Russian-speaking and Russian people in Ukraine, will never again call you our brothers ... we want to protect ourselves from you with a three-meter-thick wall ..."

PART FOUR: THE DECLINE OF PUTIN RUSSIA

Putin, Just Evil Enough, CNN, July 25, 2014

Vice President Joe Biden recently confided a sensational bit of news to the New Yorker magazine: In a 2011 meeting with Vladimir Putin, he had actually told Russia's then-prime minister that he had no "soul." Even more remarkable was Putin's response. "And he looked back at me, and he smiled, and he said, 'We understand one another.'"

Many people—in Ukraine, Europe, America and even Russia—probably share Biden and Putin's estimation of the Russian president's spiritual condition. In saying Putin has no soul, it means he seems to lack both the capacity to feel emotions and to show empathy.

Russia's leader certainly has a long record of inhumanity. He was an agent of the Soviet secret police, a criminal institution with a record that goes back to the purges of Stalin, a record more bloody than that of the Nazi SS.

John Dunlop of Stanford's Hoover Institution wrote in "The Moscow Bombings" that there is strong evidence to suggest that Putin was in on the plot to bomb two apartment buildings in Moscow in September 1999, in which 300 Russian citizens were killed and several hundred others were wounded. He says the bombings were blamed on Chechen rebels as a pretext to invade Chechnya.

Putin has funded, promoted, supplied and aided and abetted the Russian and pro-Russian terrorists in eastern Ukraine. And by invading Crimea, he created the conditions of war, hatred and fanaticism that led to the destruction of 298 innocent lives aboard Malaysia Airlines Flight 17 on that day of infamy, July 17.

Is Putin evil? His actions certainly are, if by evil we understand behavior that willfully, consciously and purposely destroys human life. Perhaps we can call his actions undeniably evil and Putin himself "evil enough." Evil enough for what? Evil enough for condemnation by people of good will.

If Putin is "evil enough," what are the implications for policy-makers?

First, they should openly state that they condemn Putin's behavior. Because silence implies approval, policy-makers must understand that their moral standing, like that of the countries they represent, is on the line. Evil is indivisible. If they refuse to condemn this instance, they effectively surrender the right to condemn any instance of evil.

Second, they should refuse to shake his hand, engage in chitchat, attend photo ops with him and in any way create the impression that they accept his behavior as a socially acceptable. German Chancellor Angela Merkel would not hobnob with a German neo-Nazi; President Barack Obama would not have drinks with the head of the Ku Klux Klan. By extension, neither of them should hobnob with Putin at World Cup soccer games.

Third, policy-makers should avoid doing anything that aids and abets Putin's proclivities. Since those proclivities largely rest on his ability to employ armaments to cause death, any form of assistance to Putin's war machine or repressive apparatus is the moral equivalent of supplying barbed wire and bullets to Auschwitz. Two examples will illustrate this point.

The Düsseldorf-based German defense company Rheinmetall is manifestly abetting Putin's evildoing by continuing to insist that it has "to meet its contractual obligations with Moscow and finalize a combat simulation center where up to 30,000 soldiers could be trained annually." Since Rheinmetall signed the contract with Russia in 2011, when Putin's record was already on full display to the world, it cannot claim ignorance of Putin's evil intentions.

France's continued determination to supply the Putin war machine with two Mistral-class assault ships is no less of a moral outrage.

As Robert C. O'Brien, a former U.S. representative to the United Nations, argues, "With the downing of Malaysia Airlines Flight No. 17, it should now be clear to all observers that Russia is fully intent on subjugating and intimidating its former Soviet constituent states and Warsaw Pact allies, and will do so with the most advanced weapons in its inventory."

"There is no reason to believe that the Mistral-class warships, once in the Russian Navy, will not also be used in the Black Sea, Baltic and Pacific to further increase the pressure on Russia's neighbors. Given its recent history, Moscow should not be handed another military tool of the Mistral-class magnitude."

This does not mean that morally concerned policymakers should refrain from talking to him entirely. As professor Walter Clemens, an associate of Harvard's Davis Center, argues in a fascinating paper, "Can—Should—Must We Negotiate with Evil?": "If a cruel dictatorship is willing to negotiate security arrangements likely to limit arms competition and make war less likely, democratic governments should engage and seek verifiable arrangements."

So, yes, according to this logic, talk to Putin about making "war less likely" in eastern Ukraine and talk to him about limiting "arms competition." Otherwise, shun him and everything he stands for.

Such countries as France and Germany, which have extensive economic relations with Russia, face a difficult moral choice. They must ask themselves whether Putin is evil or evil enough. If they decide his killing spree in eastern Ukraine is neither evil nor evil enough, they must explain—to themselves and to the rest of the world—just why they believe the destruction of Ukrainian, Russian, Malaysian, Dutch and other lives is not a form of evil behavior.

If, alternatively, Putin's behavior strikes them as evil, they must either act on that conviction, in the manner suggested above, or explain to themselves and the rest of the world just why their enhancing Putin's war-making proclivities is not wrong.

Ultimately, France and Germany, as well as all countries that aid and abet Russia's destructive capabilities, have to decide whether they care more about values or about money. Dictatorships can answer that question easily: Their leaders are indifferent to values.

Prosperous capitalist democracies, and especially prosperous capitalist democracies that are part of a self-styled community of values called the European Union, cannot take the easy way out and pretend values do not matter. In the final analysis, the willingness of France, Germany and all the other states making up the European Union to respond to Putin's evil doing will determine the moral fate of the EU. If they sacrifice morality to arms contracts or gas, the EU will have lost its *raison d'être*. Worse, like Putin, it will be without a soul.

*

Recriminations and Denials after Putin, *World Affairs Journal*, August 6, 2014

One of these days Russians will wake up from what they now think is a dream and realize that it was a terrible nightmare. They'll realize that Vladimir Putin—their current hero and demigod—is really a loser and a thug who's brought ruin to their country, ruin to their people, ruin to their ethnic brethren in Ukraine and other non-Russian states, and ruin to the world. They'll realize that Putin is a criminal, that the regime he created is fascist, and that his policies are paranoid, delusional, destructive, and self-destructive to the point of being suicidal.

And that's when the recriminations and denials will begin. There'll be lots of finger pointing. "Blame it all on my neighbor," many Russians will say, "He's the collaborator. He's the flag-waver. He's the one who voted for Putin and attended all those mass rallies. And he did it voluntarily too."

Most will insist they "knew nothing." The war against Ukraine? "Gosh, there were rumors to that effect." The destruction of Russians and Russian-speaking Ukrainians in the Donbas? "Lord, had we only known!" The billions that Putin and his pals purloined from the Russian Treasury? "More rumors!" The tens of thousands of Chechen deaths? The thousands of Ukrainian deaths? The hundreds of Russian deaths? "Rumors, rumors, rumors."

Some Russians will realize that such denial is uncomfortably reminiscent of post-war German reactions to Hitler and his crimes. Death camps? The gassing of Jews? The destruction of Poland, Belarus, and Ukraine? The starvation of Leningrad? "Never heard of it! And believe me, had I only known, had I only known—I would've fought that criminal Hitler regime for sure! By the way, wasn't Hitler really Austrian?"

A few brave Russian intellectuals will feel shame, guilt, and responsibility and call for lustration and trials. Most Russians will prefer to put the past behind them: "let bygones be bygones, let's all be pals again." What to do with Putin and his closest entourage will be a bit of a problem. Naturally, people will blame everything on him—their former hero and demigod. "He's the criminal, he built the system, he started the wars, he bamboozled us: we're innocent." But putting him on trial could be inconvenient: Putin might spill the beans and reveal just how deeply popular he, his system, and his policies were.

Not putting a world-class war criminal on trial could be equally inconvenient. After all, Moscow is the Third Rome. Oh, if only Putin would make a run for Belarus, Kazakhstan, or China! Alas, that's not likely: it would be too humiliating for him to seek refuge in a vassal state or among the overbearing Chinese. South America? Too far; besides, isn't that where Nazis go to hide? Perhaps Germany or France? That just might work. Putin's got some mighty powerful friends in the former and he received the Legion of Honor decoration from the latter. A Putin-Schröder Peace Institute funded by all those purloined billions in Berlin? *Warum nicht?* Residence in Baby Doc Duvalier's former villa in France? *Pourquois pas?*

Germany and France will be as eager to forget Putin's crimes as most Russians. Ukrainians and other non-Russians will be less quick to do so. Victims of aggression, war, and genocide tend to remember the pain. Whom will they blame? Putin and his system, definitely. But millions of fingers will also be pointed at Russians. "Why did our self-styled brothers enthusiastically support Crimea's annexation and the war in eastern Ukraine? Why did they look the other way as Russian forces and Russian proxies killed thousands and destroyed the Donbas? Why did no one protest? How could they believe that our efforts to establish a democracy were anti-Russian? How could they possibly believe that we were ever anti-Russian?" Expect Ukrainians to insist on reparations. Expect Russians to shrug in response.

Ukrainians will look back at the 2014 Russo-Ukrainian War as their third bloody encounter with Russia in the last 100 years. Russian Reds and Whites crushed Ukrainian independence in 1917–1921. Soviet Russians then crushed the Ukrainian liberation movement in Western Ukraine in 1945–1954. Then, in 2014, Putin's Russians and their proxies tried to crush independent Ukraine.

And failed.

Putin's failure is as evident now as are his crimes. He's lost Ukraine. He's destroyed the Donbas. In a word, he's lost. The most he can do now is kill more Ukrainians and destroy more cities.

One day, when they finally wake up and realize their hero was a ruthless dictator, Russians will understand just how enthusiastically complicit they were in his evil—up to the very end.

*

Hitler and Putin: A Tale of Two Authoritarians, *World Affairs Journal*, August 21, 2014

Will Russia's unconstitutionally elected president, Vladimir Putin, unleash a full-scale land war against Ukraine?

I can give you ten reasons for every possible answer to this question. Which is to say that, like everyone else trying to divine Putin's "mind," I don't know.

But there is one thing that I do know. Suddenly, we are all talking about war in Europe. The one thing that was supposed to have become "unthinkable" and "unimaginable" after the end of the Cold War and the rise of the European Union has become perfectly thinkable and quite imaginable.

And all thanks to Putin. If tomorrow's headlines scream "RUSSIA INVADES ESTONIA," we'd be shocked, but would we be surprised?

Don't blame the thinkability and imaginability of war on the Ukrainians. All they did was remove a corrupt dictator and embark on building a democracy. The Ukrainians didn't invade Crimea. Nor did they arm separatist republics with Russian soldiers and weapons. That was Putin's doing and only Putin's doing.

There's a lesson here, and it's not either of the ones that are usually drawn: that Putin is a power-hungry madman, if you're his critic, or that Putin is a shrewd statesman motivated by *raison d'état* and Realpolitik, if you're his backer. The real lesson is that dictatorships, especially fascist dictatorships built on the ruins of collapsed empires, are prone to do bad things, such as engage in imperialist wars.

I've made the comparison many times before (starting in the late 1990s, by the way), but it's worth reminding ourselves just how similar Russia's and Putin's trajectories are to those of post–World War I Germany and Adolf Hitler. The point is not to score easy debating points or to shake Germans' assumptions about the uniqueness of Nazi evil, but to demonstrate that there are deeper structural reasons for Putin's aggressiveness and indifference to international norms.

Both Germany and Russia lost empires and desired to rebuild them. Both Germany and Russia suffered economic collapse. Both Germany and Russia experienced national humiliation and retained imperial political cultures. Both Germany and Russia blamed their ills on the democrats. Both Germany and Russia elected strong men who promised to make them grand and glorious again. Both strong men employed imperialist arguments about "abandoned brethren" in neighboring states, remilitarized their countries, developed cults of the personality, centralized power, gave pride of place in the power structure to the forces of coercion, constructed regimes that may justifiably be called fascist, and proceeded to engage in re-annexing bits and pieces of lost territory before embarking on major landgrabs. Both strong men demonized friendly nations. Germany's strongman ended up starting a world war. Russia's strongman—well, we don't know what he'll do, but please do notice that a rigorous pursuit of the comparison does not bode well for peace in Europe or the world.

Democracy matters. Dictators are more prone to war precisely because they can manipulate public opinion and ruthlessly pursue whatever warped visions they have without much resistance from institutions and elites. Democratic presidents don't have that luxury—as a rule of course. That's why democracies plod along. That's why they muddle through. That's why they're the worst form of government, as Winston Churchill observed, except for all the others.

Ukraine's democracy has at best been crummy and creaky for the last two and a half decades. It's done far too little about reform and it's been much too enamored of corruption. As a result, Ukraine has muddled along, sometimes muddling up, sometimes muddling down. Change is imperative, and, thanks to the Maidan Revolution, everyone in Ukraine finally knows it. Stasis is bad, possibly unsustainable, probably destructive. And yet, and yet: Ukraine remains a democracy, far more so now than just a few months ago. It's searching for answers to complex questions, balancing far too many interests and sensitivities, moving much too slowly to satisfy proponents of breakthroughs (and that includes me).

But do take note of one very important fact. Amid all this democratic sludge, independent Ukraine has been pacific for the entire time of its existence. At the same time, when provoked, as in the past few months, democratic Ukraine has also demonstrated that it can fight to defend itself and its values.

Which goes to show two things: that, except for the likes of Vladimir Zhirinovsky, Stephen F. Cohen, Marine Le Pen, and Aleksandr Dugin, even a crummy Ukrainian democracy is preferable to an efficient Russian dictatorship and that a war initiated by democratic Ukraine really is unthinkable and unimaginable.

*

Will Putin's Successor Be Worse? *World Affairs Journal*, September 22, 2014

Who will succeed Vladimir Putin when he falls? Will things get better or worse? Those are the intriguing questions posed by Benjamin Bidder, Moscow correspondent for the German news weekly *Der Spiegel*.

Bidder concludes that the democrats have little chance of replacing Putin and that his successor is likely to be worse.

It takes little fantasy to imagine Putin's political end. He cannot be voted out of office like his friend Gerhard Schröder. Two scenarios are possible: either the current political elite in the Kremlin installs a successor or the Russians get rid of Putin and his minions….

And then what? The fear is that someone could seize control of the Kremlin who thinks and acts more radically than Putin. The president created the preconditions of such a possibility with his own failed policies. If the Kremlin insiders want to find a successor, they will have to recruit him from the immediate circle of the current president. But Putin has reinforced hard-liners and pushed out the liberals.

The revolution scenario is no less disheartening. Power could be seized by forces from the extreme right and left. The boundaries between both are vague in Russia, as the name of such groups as the "National Bolsheviks" suggests.

Given his analysis, Bidder's conclusion is logical:

> Putin's fall would be no solution for Russia or for Europe. ... What follows therefrom? There is only the choice between bad alternatives. NATO must therefore discuss arming itself, if only to protect itself against what may come after Putin. But the West must also turn to Moscow as soon as possible, speak with it, and propose compromises. Not because Putin deserves it, but because Russia's isolation creates more problems than solutions.

Unfortunately, Bidder's analysis of who may succeed Putin is at best flawed, at worst dead wrong.

First, it's premised on the view that it's possible to be worse than Putin. That's true, if you think of him as a run-of-the mill authoritarian. That's not true, or not as true, if you think of him as a full-fledged fascist who has transformed Russia into an anti-modern, repressive, belligerent, imperialist rogue state.

Second, it's theoretically possible for an even greater fascist to replace Putin. But how likely is it that Aleksandr Dugin or Vladimir Zhirinovsky would fill that role? Not at all. And if Putin's replacement comes from within his inner circle, he's likely to be a hard-liner who comes to power under conditions that militate against an even greater radicalism and fascism. Remember: when extremely powerful and charismatic dictators leave office, they always leave an institutional mess and a power vacuum behind them. Power struggles invariably result, precisely because there are no rules for finding a successor, and contenders for power have to woo support. In other words, Putin's successor will first have to spend some time—months? years?—consolidating power before he can promote his own agenda.

Third, don't discount the democrats. For one thing, Viktor Yanukovych's downfall should, if nothing else, caution us against assuming that seemingly powerless political forces really are powerless. For another, the Russian democrats managed to organize massive demonstrations in Moscow just a few years ago. Putin's supporters have never come out in equivalent numbers, and if the democrats establish themselves as a strong political force in the capital, that may suffice to tip the balance of succession in their favor. Finally, in times of crisis, the "street" often has greater influence on politics than the elites. Bidder mistakenly assumes that the insiders who make policy today will make policy after Putin leaves. Don't be so sure.

Neither Russian, nor Soviet, nor world history supports Bidder's view that bad dictators are followed by worse ones. Russian tsars and tsarinas came and went, with bad succeeding good, good succeeding bad, and mediocrities succeeding both. Soviet history is even less supportive of Bidder's claims. True, the awful Lenin was succeeded by the dreadful Stalin, but Stalin was followed by the pretty good Khrushchev, the pretty good Khrushchev was replaced by the worse (though by no means Stalinist) Brezhnev, who in turn was replaced by the pretty good Gorbachev. And Gorbachev, after he fell in 1991, handed over power to the not bad Yeltsin, who was replaced by the awful Putin.

Last, consider world experience. Who was worse—the Shah or the Ayatollah? Papa Doc Duvalier or Baby Doc Duvalier? It's a toss-up. But there are very many examples—from Greece to Spain to Portugal to Brazil to Argentina to China—of lousy dictators being replaced with decent democrats or less lousy dictators.

In the final analysis, Bidder's assessment amounts to an unwitting justification of dictatorial rule, repeating the self-serving claim that all dictators make: *après moi, le déluge*. In fact, world experience and both Russian and Soviet history suggest that Russia is likely to experience a better future if and when Putin finally goes. Getting rid of him, as quickly as possible, is a bet worth making—both by Russia and the West.

*

Ukraine's Commitment to Values Ensures Its Independence, *World Affairs Journal*, November 4, 2014

At the moment, Russia has lots of hard power and very little soft power, while Ukraine has lots of soft power and little hard power. Russia's determination to exclude soft power will ultimately be suicidal. In contrast, Ukraine's future is bright, but only if it manages to hold on to its soft   ower while building up its reserves of hard power.

Power is generally understood as the capacity to induce others to do your bidding. The central components of hard power—armies and economies—either coerce others to bow to your will (by force or the threat of economic sanctions) or encourage them to accept it (by the promise of economic rewards). Soft power, a fuzzy concept first developed by Harvard University's Joseph Nye, is about your attractiveness and the attractiveness of your policy goals. Realist international relations analysts who live in a world of money and bombs don't quite know what to do with soft power thus defined, but its utility is obvious to any other political scientist or analyst. If other countries view you as worthy of emulation, respect, and trust, you'll need to expend far less hard power to get them to do your bidding. They'll want to be on your side. By the same token, if other countries view your policy goals as attractive—to them, that is—you'll also need to expend less hard power to get them to do your bidding. Once again, they'll want to be on your side—not because they "like" you, but because they view your behavior as reassuring and your policy goals as advantageous. In a word, soft   ower is cheaper than hard power.

These considerations matter, both domestically and internationally, since all states have limited amounts of resources. Machiavelli suggested that it's better for a prince to be feared then to be loved, but that may be true only if the prince is absolutely certain that he has and always will have the requisite means to induce fear and suppress rebellion. You can't be a great power without hard power, but you can't be a great power for long without soft power. The European Union has tons of soft power, but little hard power: it is, thus, no great power. The United States is a superpower that recently squandered much of its soft power: it's still a great power, but it's clearly struggling, as the hard-power costs of remaining a great power have grown relative to its diminished soft-power reserves.

Back in 1991, Russia had lost most of its hard power, while possessing, as a new democracy committed to joining the international community, a fair amount of soft power. Under Putin, Russia's reserves of hard power have grown considerably; its soft power probably peaked during the 2014 Winter Olympics. Since invading Ukraine, Russia's soft power has pretty much evaporated: no one, except perhaps for North Korea, admires Russia, and no one, except perhaps for Western European neo-fascists and American leftists, shares Putin's policy goals or is persuaded by his propaganda. For much of the world, Russia has become a rogue state.

The United States got into trouble in Iraq and Afghanistan, even though its economy and military were significantly larger than Russia's and its soft-power attractiveness as a "beacon of democracy" and the site of the "American dream" has always been, and remains, strong. Putin's Russia is slated for far greater trouble, possibly even collapse, especially as it's decided to take on the entire developed world. Putin must now hope to compel compliance with a military that is no match for America's, China's, Britain's, France's, and Turkey's and with a petro-state economy that is comparatively small and doomed to secular decline for the foreseeable future. You don't need to be a realist geostrategist to see that this is a losing proposition. A country with relatively modest reserves of hard power such as Russia can only throw its weight around if it begins to experience phenomenal economic growth rates (which, as a corrupt petro-state, it can't and won't) or if it decides to build up its reserves of soft power (which Putin has precluded). Most states and most policymakers realize that Russia is acting like a bully; most also know that its chest-beating is mostly unsustainable bluster. What looks like success is just the shock felt by Europeans and Americans at the brutish stupidity of Russian policymakers.

Contrast Russia with Ukraine. Ukraine's people elicit admiration from much of the world; their dedication to freedom and democracy and their government's commitment to democratic procedure and human rights draw accolades from the international community. Its policy goals—independence, stability, security, integration with the West and the world—are shared by many other countries. Ukraine arguably has never had this much soft ower in the 24 years of its independent existence.

Hard power is another thing. The army and economy are a mess. But the former is improving, while the latter may be on the verge of a breakthrough if the pro-reform president, parliament, and government adopt the radical reforms they say they will adopt. The challenge before Ukraine is to pull off radical reform and remain attractive. That means following in the footsteps of the Baltic states, Poland, and other East Central European countries. The precedent is there. The Poroshenko-Yatseniuk government need only mimic its western neighbors. But the West has an important stopgap role to play, too. The United States and the European Union—along with the International Monetary Fund and the World Bank—must increase Ukraine's reserves of hard power in the short term. And that means military assistance and financial aid, preferably of a massive kind, to enable Ukraine to make that great leap forward toward democracy, rule of law, and the market.

If Ukraine succeeds—and all indicators suggest that it will—watch its relationship with Russia change. Russia's bullying will only dry up its hard-power reserves. Sooner or later, it'll degenerate to the level of a North Korea—an impoverished pariah state with lots of guns and bombs. With some luck and Western assistance, Ukraine could become the next Poland.

*

Is Russia Artificial? *World Affairs Journal*, November 7, 2014

Most people would unthinkingly answer: of course, not! Just look at all the Russians inside and outside Russia. Just look at the Russian state. They're real, aren't they? They're organic. How could one possibly suggest Russia might be artificial?

If you subscribe to these views, take a deep breath and hold on to your seat. The fact is that the Russian state is completely artificial, while the Russian nation is completely fragmented. Both are historically contingent. They're as real—or unreal—as any non-Russian nation or state or as any recently constructed post-colonial state.

Whether or not Russia is artificial matters because Vladimir Putin and his Western apologists justify Russia's aggression against Ukraine in terms of Ukraine's supposed artificiality. The larger principle they're invoking is that "artificial entities may be dismembered." That principle is dangerous nonsense. No less important, if applied consistently, it leads to Russia's dismemberment.

On October 24th, Putin told the Valdai Club that "Ukraine is a fairly compound state formation," apparently comparing Ukraine to a compound sentence consisting of two or more clauses joined by a conjunction. "The history of Ukraine's formation in its current borders is a rather complex process." He then invoked the inclusion of supposedly Russian territories in Soviet Ukraine in 1922, the addition of western Ukraine after World War II, and Khrushchev's "illegal" transfer of Crimea from Russia to Ukraine in 1954.

Putin's ignorance of history is alarming. Back in 1922, when the Soviet republics were being formed, Soviet Russia was created on the basis of imperial Russia's former boundaries and not on the basis of some ethnic majoritarian principle. Western Ukraine's annexation to Soviet Ukraine was the result of Soviet imperial expansion, but it involved the transfer of territories that were largely ethnically Ukrainian. In any case, there were lots of significant border adjustments—think of Germany and Poland—in the aftermath of the war, and only Nazi revisionists would find them disturbing. Finally, Khrushchev did not seize Crimea and "give" it to Soviet Ukraine. The transfer, like so many other Soviet border adjustments, was sanctioned by the USSR Supreme Soviet and was as legal—or illegal—as anything the Soviets did.

So forget Putin's twisted invocation of Soviet history. Was Ukraine's state formation, as Putin implies, more complex than Russia's? Look at any map of Muscovy's expansion from a tiny statelet in the 14th century to the Russian Federation of today. There was nothing simple or natural or preordained about the process. Successive Muscovite princes and tsars fought incessant wars, killed foreign peoples, destroyed foreign cultures, and seized foreign territories. Today's Russia is the "compound" product of relentless imperial expansion, war, and destruction.

Unsurprisingly, today's Russia consists of 27 regions (republics, districts, and provinces) that have the status of autonomous non-Russian political entities. That's 32 percent of the total number of regions, and about 40 percent of the Russian Federation's territory. According to Putin's logic, each of these units has the right—and obligation—to secede from Russia.

Things get even worse when one takes a closer look at the Russian "nation." The Russian state, though artificial, at least exists. But is there anything resembling a coherent Russian nation? Don't be so certain that the answer is yes. For one thing, Russians aren't sure whether they're *rossianie* or *russkie*. English makes no difference between these two designations, but, as the rough equivalent of British vs. English, they stand for very different self-perceptions. For another, there are vast differences, in mentality, history, identity, and language, between—just to take three examples—European Russians centered on St. Petersburg and Moscow and those Russians living in Siberia, the Far East, and southern Russia. Siberian Russians have an identity as *sibiryaks*. Far Eastern Russians resent the intrusiveness of Moscow. Southern Russians sound more like Ukrainians—substituting H for G—than Muscovites and Petersburgers.

Things get even more complicated when one looks at Russian attitudes toward their history. Some Russians view Soviet history as Russian history and the Soviet Union as a Russian state. Others violently disagree with what they consider to be a Soviet deformation of true Russian values. Some Russians view themselves as Western, others as Asian, still others as Eurasian. Most Russians trace the history of their state to Kyivan (Kyivan) Rus, the huge polity that dominated Eastern Europe in the 9th–13th centuries, but there is as much continuity between Rus and Muscovy as there is between ancient Rome and Romania. Rus was established by Viking marauders who settled among the Slavic tribes near Kyiv. Muscovy was the product of Muscovite elites and Finno-Ugric tribes. Rus was destroyed by the Golden Horde; Muscovy was promoted by the Golden Horde. At Rus's heyday, Moscow was a tiny village. At Muscovy's heyday, Rus no longer existed. In time, imperial Russia developed the myth of its continuity with Kyivan Rus and insisted that Kyiv (Kyiv) was "the mother of Russian cities." The rulers of early Muscovy saw no continuity with Kyiv, so much so that no Muscovite prince or Russian tsar has ever borne the name of a Rus grand prince. Contrast that with any other European dynasty and their innumerable Henry's, Louis's, and Otto's.

In a word, the Russian nation is as artificial as the Russian state. Should both therefore be dismembered—say, by the Chechens, Bashkirs, Yakuts, Tatars, Ukrainians, and Chinese?

Should Germany lay claim to Kaliningrad (the former Königsberg)? Should the Crimean Tatars—or perhaps even the Turks—claim Crimea and boot out the Russians? Should the Kazakhs drive out the Russians in the north of their country? If you believe Putin, then the answer must be yes. If you're a rational policymaker or decent human being who suspects that endless border adjustments are a recipe for incessant wars, you may decide that the answer is no. After all, the bottom line is that all nations and all states are artificial historical constructs.

Either way, the issue may be moot. Having opened a Pandora's Box of territorial revisions, Putin may have dealt a death blow to the artificial Russian state and fragmented Russian nation. In the years ahead, expect the Russian Federation's many nations, autonomous regions, and large neighbors to test Putin's commitment to state dismemberment.

*

The Sources of Russian Conduct, *Foreign Affairs*, November 16, 2014

As the West searches for an adequate policy response to Russian President Vladimir Putin's ongoing aggression in Ukraine, American and European policymakers would do well to reread George F. Kennan's famous "X" article, published in the July 1947 issue of *Foreign Affairs*. Compelling then, Kennan's case for containing Russia makes just as much sense now.

Kennan's central claim was that "the political personality of Soviet power as we know it today is the product of ideology and circumstances." On the one hand, there was messianic Marxism, which rested on a Manichean view of the world and promised victory over capitalism to the socialist proletariat. On the other hand, there was a genuine belief that the rest of the world was hostile—antagonism that justified Russia's pursuit of absolute power at home.

The policy consequences of "ideology and circumstances" were twofold. First, Soviet Russia would have to expand, as its ideology dictated. But, second, it was under no compulsion to expand immediately and unconditionally. Quite the contrary, Kennan emphasized. He wrote, "Its political action is a fluid stream which moves constantly, wherever it is permitted to move, toward a given goal. Its main concern is to make sure that it has filled every nook and cranny available to it in the basin of world power. But if it finds unassailable barriers in its path, it accepts these philosophically and accommodates itself to them."

In his article, Kennan drew the logical consequences of Soviet behavior for the West. For one thing, Western policies should be "no less steady in their purpose, and no less variegated and resourceful in their application, than those of the Soviet Union itself." In particular, "the Soviet pressure against the free institutions of the Western world is something that can be contained by the adroit and vigilant application of counterforce at a series of constantly shifting geographical and political points, corresponding to the shifts and maneuvers of Soviet policy, but which cannot be charmed or talked out of existence."

Indeed, containment, Kennan emphasized, was not only about "counterforce." What we would today call soft power also mattered: the United States, he wrote, should "create among the peoples of the world generally the impression of a country which knows what it wants, which is coping successfully with the problems of its internal life and with the responsibilities of a world power, and which has a spiritual vitality capable of holding its own among the major ideological currents of the time."

Ultimately, Kennan concluded, a combination of internal Soviet weaknesses and containment would "promote tendencies which must eventually find their outlet in either the breakup or the gradual mellowing of Soviet power. For no mystical, messianic movement—and particularly not that of the Kremlin—can face frustration indefinitely without eventually adjusting itself in one way or another to the logic of that state of affairs."

Although Kennan's article purported to address the sources of Soviet conduct, it's clear from the text that he equated the Soviet Union with Russia, Soviet leaders with Russian leaders, and Soviet conduct with Russian conduct. And that is why, unsurprisingly perhaps, his analysis holds up remarkably well when applied to Putin's Russia.

To be sure, the ideology is different today. No one in Putin's regime believes in Marxism. But the superiority of Russia and Russian civilization are still closely held values, as is the belief that the West is hostile and that the country needs a strong leader, Putin, to assert Russia's greatness and combat Western influence.

The quest for absolute power at home is also familiar. Ever since he first appeared on the Russian political stage in 1999, Putin has been assiduously constructing a highly centralized authoritarian regime with himself at the center. Putin's cult of personality emphasizes his hyper-masculinity and his control over a worshipful public. Putin's is no longer a simple authoritarian regime run by a non-charismatic ruler with little sex appeal and no overarching ideology. In its structure and, increasingly, tone, Russia's current regime resembles those of the fascists of yore.

Like the Soviet Union, Putin's Russia fosters antagonism to the West, and, like the Soviet Union, it feels impelled to expand, but not "immediately and unconditionally" or against "unassailable barriers." It is under no real threat: NATO has been in decline, Europe has been cutting its defense budget, and the United States has been distracted by the Middle East and domestic priorities. Instead, Putin's neoimperial ideology and his standing as Russia's all-powerful leader require him to gather former imperial territories.

The implications for the West of Kennan's analysis are no less relevant today. For starters, the United States and Europe must understand that "there can never be on Moscow's side any sincere assumption of a community of aims between the Soviet Union and powers which are regarded as capitalist." Second, Putin's Russia "can be effectively countered not by sporadic acts which represent the momentary whims of democratic opinion but only by intelligent long-range policies on the part of Russia's adversaries." It's high time, in other words, for the West to abandon its illusions about Putin and his regime and develop a serious, steady, long-term policy response to Russian expansionism.

And that, of course, means containment. In today's terms, the front lines of containment are the non-Russian states in the potential path of Russian expansion. Seen in this light, a divided Ukraine occupies the same role in today's containment strategy as a divided Germany did in yesterday's. Ukraine should therefore be the recipient of similar financial, political, and military assistance. Finland, Sweden, Estonia, Latvia, Lithuania, and Moldova—as well as, possibly, Belarus and Kazakhstan—must also figure as points where counterforce, in the form of enhanced military assistance, will have to be applied. The goal in all these cases is not to roll back Russian power but to stop its penetration of the non-Russian post-Soviet states.

Central to today's containment policy is constraining Russia's ability to use energy as a weapon. Halting the building of the South Stream pipeline, reducing Europe's dependence on Russian oil and gas, and helping Ukraine reform its energy sector will be key. Last but not least, sanctions—as forms of minimizing Russia's economic power—must be maintained and possibly intensified.

The United States and Europe must also work on their soft-power appeal. If they claim to stand for democracy, human rights, and "European values," then they should actively promote them—especially in those places into which Russia seeks to expand. It is there that Western values can be made to mean something essential to their very existence— or, if inconsistently applied, can be revealed to be utterly hollow.

Last but not least, the West should always be ready to provide Putin with a face-saving exit from his aggressive behavior: "it is a *sine qua non* of successful dealing with Russia," Kennan wrote, "that the foreign government in question should remain at all times cool and collected and that its demands on Russian policy should be put forward in such a manner as to leave the way open for a compliance not too detrimental to Russian prestige." In sum, counterforce plus soft power plus a willingness to compromise make for the best form of containment, whether in 1947 or in 2014.

The West's face-saving measures could range from welcoming Putin as an equal interlocutor in international negotiations to seeking Russian cooperation in conflicts such as the one in Iraq and Syria to agreeing to possible limits on NATO enlargement. Naturally, the West could harbor no illusions about "any sincere assumption of a community of aims" and would have to insist on verifiable quid pro quos in return for its olive branches. That may be a challenge. In light of Putin's violation of the 1994 Budapest Memorandum on Security Assurances, his contradictory explanations of the annexation of Crimea, and his continued denial of a Russian troop presence in eastern Ukraine, the West will have to insist that only measurable changes in behavior will warrant Western consideration of Russia's desires.

Kennan's optimism about the future can also be applied today. Thanks to Western sanctions and the general Russian economic stagnation, Putin's Russia is rapidly approaching irreparable decay. The fascistic regime Putin built suffers from the pathologies of all such states: vast corruption, overcentralization, inefficiency, ineffectiveness, and bureaucratic empire-building. With containment, such decline—or, as Kennan suggested, genuine reform—could be accelerated.

Putin's inevitably waning cult (after all, aging leaders cannot sustain hyper-masculine charisma) will set in motion, as Kennan also predicted, a power struggle: "It is always possible that another transfer of preeminent power may take place quietly and inconspicuously, with no repercussions anywhere. But again, it is possible that the questions involved may ... shake Soviet power to its foundations." A wise, sustained, steady policy of containment redux could ensure that, when Putin's regime is shaken to its foundations, the outcome will be favorable for Russians, their aggrieved neighbors, and the world.

*

Sex, Politics, and Putin, *World Affairs Journal*, January 5, 2015

If you'd like to know one of the reasons for Vladimir Putin's phenomenal popularity in Russia, pick up Clark University Professor Valerie Sperling's excellent new book, *Sex, Politics, and Putin: Political Legitimacy in Russia*.

Putin's actual accomplishments are few. He dismantled democracy and muzzled the media. He constructed a fascistoid regime and perverted the very notion of truth. He marginalized the democratic opposition and, at least until recently, crushed the North Caucasus independence movements. He annexed Crimea and doesn't know what to do with it. He started a war in eastern Ukraine and, once again, doesn't know what to do next. The bottom line is that Russia remains a Belgium with a bomb and a profoundly corrupt petro-state incapable of technological innovation and sustained economic growth, while having become, under Putin, a rogue state.

These are the accomplishments of a profoundly mediocre leader, one whose popularity ratings should be around 20 percent at most—and not the breathtaking 85-plus that he routinely garners. As Sperling explains in her well-written and well-researched book, an important reason for Putin's popularity is his careful manipulation of gender and sex as a means of sustaining his political legitimacy: "his variant of masculinity (including strength, sobriety, decisiveness, and attractiveness to women) was met with popular approval, reinforcing his position of power and authority."

There are several complex reasons, or what Sperling calls "multiple opportunity structures," for the success of Putin's strategy, and I shall list only their sound-bite versions:

- The "weakness of the Russian women's movement" meant that there were few people "to draw critical attention to public sexism."

- "As commercial capitalism was introduced to Russia in the 1990s," it "commodified and objectified women's bodies." In turn, "the sexualization of economic products lay the groundwork for the sexualization of political products."

- "The 'Russia needs a strong leader' myth has never been dissolved."

- Russian culture is characterized by "sex-based discrimination and misogyny."

- "Putin's macho image accompanied a broader strategy to 'remasculinize' the country domestically and internationally," in the aftermath of the USSR's humiliating collapse.

In sum, Putin has imposed his retrograde views on Russians, but Russians have also been highly receptive to his message.

Sperling's analysis has important implications for the stability of the regime.

First, the older Putin gets—and he is already 62 years old—the more difficult will it be for him to project a macho image. Look at today's Putin and compare him to the Putin of 2000. Then, he resembled a sleek killing machine. Today, his face is puffy, his features are distended, and he looks like he's been a one long binge. Several years ago, it was plausible for two sexy Russian ladies to sing, "I want a man just like Putin." Today, that sentiment would sound bizarre coming from anyone but the septuagenarian crowd.

The inability to project machismo matters precisely because, as Sperling underlines, it is central to Putin's political legitimacy. Worse for Putin, machismo has become so large a part of his supremacist ideology and anti-Western bluster that it would be hard for him to abandon hyper-masculinity and focus only on ideology and chest-beating. Inasmuch as Putin is central to the Putin regime, the inevitable decline in his legitimacy automatically translates into the decline of the regime.

Second, Sperling's analysis suggests that the 20-plus point increase in Putin's popularity in the aftermath of Crimea's annexation—from the low 60s to the high 80s—may be due less to the Russian public's endorsement of imperialist landgrabs and more to its enthusiasm for the tough-guy posturing the landgrab permitted Putin to engage in. The war in eastern Ukraine can't have the same effect, partly because Putin denies that Russian troops are involved and mostly because the fighting has produced significant numbers of Russian casualties (possibly as many as several thousand). Victorious Russian troops in the streets of Sevastopol enhance Putin's macho image. Body bags from the Donbas do not. If so, a wider war with Ukraine will not enhance Putin's machismo. Incessant saber-rattling throughout the world will.

Third, Russia will remain a retrograde society when it comes to gender relations for many years to come. If the problem were just Putin, Russia could become a nice place as soon as Putin departs the scene. But since, as Sperling implies, the problem is also Russia, then Putin's departure won't change things. Expect disillusioned Russian liberals to head for the West and for comparatively more tolerant places such as Ukraine. Since this cohort is likely to be best educated, their departure will also condemn Russia to decades of economic backwardness.

Poor Russia: thanks to its leader's 19th-century machismo, it may soon be catapulted back to the 1850s.

*

What to Expect from Russia, Ukraine in 2015? *World Affairs Journal*, January 16, 2015

What should we expect from Ukraine and Russia in 2015?

My guess is: more of the same. And that's both the good news and the bad news.

Ukraine will consolidate its democratic institutions, while Vladimir Putin's Russia will consolidate its fascist regime. Although Ukrainians will complain more than Russians, their country will be getting stronger, while the hypercentralized state structure centered on Putin's cult of the macho personality gets weaker. Democratically ruled peoples whine publicly; dictatorially ruled peoples whine privately. The fact that 80-plus percent of Russians are likely to continue to support Putin won't mean that 80-plus percent are happy with life in Putin's crumbling realm.

Economically, both countries will be in for trying times. Ukraine's GDP will contract, unemployment will rise, and inflation will increase—but for the right reasons, as Kyiv embarks on reforms that, while not quite as radical as most economists would wish, will be radical enough to begin the long and arduous task of transforming Ukraine into a genuine market economy. Russia's GDP will also contract, unemployment will also rise, and inflation will also increase—but for the wrong reasons, as the ossified Putin regime pays heavily for having not diversified or developed its doomed economy. Energy prices, the ruble, its gold reserves, and foreign and domestic investment will collapse as Russian capital takes flight and pressure from Western sanctions continues. The economies of both the Russian-occupied Donbas enclave and Crimea will contract even more, making life increasingly unbearable for their inhabitants, who will continue to flee both eastward and westward, thereby pushing both regions closer to literal no-man's-lands.

Socially, both countries will see a rise in popular activism. Ukrainians will take to the streets to protest against radical reforms that inevitably lower their already low living standards. Russians, even those who continue to dote on Putin, will take to the streets to protest against empty store shelves, government corruption, and the steady flow of body bags from the occupied Donbas. As Putin's repressive apparatus responds with more arrests and head-crackings, expect a determined minority—perhaps Russians, almost certainly non-Russians—to respond with acts of terrorism.

The war in eastern Ukraine will go on, despite the best efforts of the West and Kyiv to reach a negotiated settlement. For one thing, Putin's proxies in eastern Ukraine are out-of-control warlords for whom war has become their only *raison d'être*. For another, Putin will want no permanent peace, as that would only stabilize Ukraine. A large-scale military assault aimed at capturing all of Ukraine, or even establishing a corridor from Russia to Crimea, is probably out of the question, as the Ukrainian armed forces are strong enough to deter it. But low-level fighting of the kind that has characterized the Donbas for the last few months seems a sure bet. Equally likely is a continuation of terrorist attacks within Ukraine, which Ukraine will survive while Putin's reputation as an exporter of terrorism will only grow.

Ukraine will continue to insist that the Russian-occupied territories are occupied only "temporarily," and Russia will continue to insist that its war against Ukraine is only an internal Ukrainian squabble, but the result of Russia's continued occupation of both the Donbas enclave and Crimea will be the continued, if uneven, consolidation of Russian rule. Faced with tough economic circumstances at home, Kyiv will continue to reduce its economic relations with, and financial subsidy of, the occupied territories. The burden of supporting the increasingly desperate inhabitants will fall on Russia, which will have to decide whether it prefers to make hay from a humanitarian catastrophe of its own making or to help save the victims of its imperialist policies. My guess is that Putin the great humanitarian will opt for catastrophe.

All in all, barring some unexpected *deus ex machina*, Ukraine's state, society, and army should get stronger, while its economy should be on the mend. Russia's state and economy will weaken, its army will discover the limits of its strength, and its society will grow more troublesome for Putin. Ukraine and Russia will be moving in diametrically opposed directions. Time is on Ukraine's side, and decidedly not on Russia's, because time favors democracy and not fascism.

Under conditions such as these, the Putin regime could disintegrate. Russia's foreign minister, Sergei Lavrov, has recently accused Western leaders of wanting "regime change" in Russia. They don't. But they should. Replacing Putin's fascism with democracy as soon as possible would be the greatest thing for Russia, Ukraine, and the world.

*

When Putin's Brittle Regime Implodes, Our Protection Will Be a Stable Ukraine, *Atlantic Council*, January 26, 2015

Although "regime change" has become a dirty phrase, the best thing that could happen to Russia, its neighbors, and the world would be a change from Vladimir Putin's brand of strongman authoritarianism to some form of democracy.

Putin's regime is oppressive at home and imperialist abroad. Power is concentrated in the hands of Russia's dictatorial leader, who routinely violates human and civil rights and quashes all opposition, while legitimizing his rule by appealing to Russian dreams of erstwhile glory and great-power status and systematically engaging in military adventures in supposed defense of Russian minorities in Russia's "near abroad." Putin's cult of personality centers on his hyper-masculine image as a tough leader willing and able to stand up to real and imagined internal and external foes.

Russian rights and democratic aspirations will continue to be stifled, and non-Russian states will continue to be invaded, as long as Putin's regime stays in place.

Putin Is Expanding, Not Negotiating

Western hopes of resolving the Russo-Ukrainian war in eastern Ukraine by means of negotiations are therefore misplaced. Whatever Putin agrees to—even Ukraine's agreement never to seek NATO membership—will be at best a temporary retreat from his expansionist foreign policy. And Putin's choice of countries to pressure is large, extending from the Baltic states to Belarus, Moldova, and Ukraine to Armenia, Azerbaijan, and Georgia to the five Central Asian states. Russians or Russian speakers inhabit all these states and can, in principle, be used to justify Moscow's strong-arm tactics.

The only effective short- to medium-term solution to this expansionism is the capacity of Russia's neighbors to withstand Putin's imperialism. The key state in any such emergent *cordon sanitaire* is, of course, Ukraine. But Belarus and Kazakhstan, both of which have very sizeable Russian-speaking populations, are a close second. If all three could be denied Putin, his imperialist proclivities would be effectively contained.

The only effective long-term solution to Putin's expansionism, however, is regime change. Putin and his fascistoid regime will always be prone to repress Russians and oppress non-Russians. The Putin regime's removal is thus the precondition of a freer and more neighborly Russia.

Naturally, no Western state will pursue regime change in Russia. Despite Russian claims to the contrary, Western policymakers have not done anything, are not doing anything, and are unlikely to do anything to make Putin and his regime go.

Putin's Brittle Regime

For better or for worse, however, they need not do anything, as the regime is fast crumbling and could easily collapse in the coming months or years. Hyper-centralized states with leader cults are extremely corrupt and ineffective forms of rule, and Russia is no exception. Thanks to high energy prices, Putin's regime could engage in massive theft and still have enough for social and military needs. Those days are over, for good, and continued regime theft   ill now come at the cost of the population.

Russia desperately needs reform, but leader-centered states such as Russia can at best engage in business as usual and exhortations to the population to work harder. The leaders of such states are also prone to make huge strategic mistakes: convinced of their infallibility and lacking any institutional counterweight, they can pursue their madcap visions to the detriment of their country and, ultimately, themselves. Putin's annexation of Crimea, for instance, has worsened Russia's economic, military, and diplomatic standing and transformed Putin into an international pariah. Finally, the legitimacy of Putin's regime depends directly on his ability to project a hyper-masculine image of vigor and vitality. That ability is rapidly crumbling, as Putin visibly ages and comes to resemble what he is—an old man pretending to be young.

Continued Russian adventurism in the non-Russian states is the worst thing for such an ossified, corrupt, and near-bankrupt state. As Russian commitments exceed its capacities, as they very soon will, the economy and polity will come under increasing strain. At some point, a relatively small shock—a riot, a killing, a death—could easily spark an uprising, a putsch, or even civil war.

Ironically, the West is likely to face the prospect of regime change in Russia even though it desperately prefers not to think about such an eventuality. There is nothing that Western states can do to manage the inevitable decay of Putin's regime in Russia. But they can do a great deal to limit the damage that regime change will bring about by actively supporting Ukraine and other non-Russian states and thereby containing the instability to Russia.

*

Goodbye, Putin, *Foreign Affairs*, February 5, 2015

The longer the Russian war against Ukraine continues, the more likely it is that President Vladimir Putin's regime will collapse.

Despite Putin's bluster, the authoritarian regime he has constructed is exceedingly brittle. At the center stands Putin; surrounding him, the power-hungry loyalists he has folded into his inner circle. Some, called the *siloviki*, belong to powerful institutions such as the secret police or the army. Others, formally affiliated with various government agencies, are loyal only to Putin. In such a system, sycophantism is rewarded above good governance, empire-building runs rampant, policy loses its effectiveness, and corruption becomes routine.

The neo-tsarist ideology of Russian imperialism, Orthodox revival, and anti-Western Slavophilism that Putin has constructed has limited appeal to the cynical men who help him run Russia. Therefore, Putin's ability to retain their loyalty rests primarily on his control of the country's financial resources. Thanks to the record-high energy prices that accompanied his assumption of power in 1999, Putin could personally purloin some $45 billion and still have enough money to raise the country's standard of living, strengthen the Russian military, and keep his cronies happy. No longer. Oil prices have collapsed and are likely to stay low; Western sanctions are hitting hard; and the Russian economy is on the downswing.

Sooner or later Putin will be forced to make some cuts, but it is hard to know where that money will come from. Given the ongoing war in Ukraine and his anti-Western ideological crusade, reducing military funding will be unfeasible. And Putin's popularity would take a serious hit if he were to roll back support to the lower classes. The only option, therefore, may be to stop his cronies from dipping into state coffers, even if doing so will alienate them.

For 15 years, Putin's record of success won him enormous public support. He crushed the Chechen rebellion, presided over military reforms, built infrastructure, improved the lives of ordinary Russians, and regularly outwitted the West. And then, just after the Sochi Olympics, he blew it all. The Crimean annexation has been an unmitigated economic disaster. The Russian war in eastern Ukraine has killed Russians by the thousands. Ukraine, which was well on its way to becoming a Russian vassal state under former President Viktor Yanukovych, has turned against the Kremlin. The ruble, along with the Russian economy, is in free fall, as Western sanctions bite. Putin, Russia's "Man of the Year," is now routinely compared to Adolf Hitler.

Beyond his policy mistakes, Putin also has an image problem. Fifteen years ago, Putin could pass himself off as a charismatic leader who, despite his diminutive size, was man enough to chase down Chechen rebels—in his own words—"even in the outhouse." That tough-guy image was essential to Putin, who claimed that he could reestablish Russia's imperial glory and needed to look the part. Now 62 years old, Putin looks tired, his face distended, and it's hard to imagine that the two leggy singers who once sang, "I want a man just like Putin," would still feel that way today.

Putin knows he's in a tough spot. He started the war in Ukraine, and now it's up to him to bring about some satisfactory conclusion, even though it's clear from his erratic behavior that he lacks a strategy. He has no way to crush Ukraine without unleashing a global conflict. He has no way to erode Ukraine's economy without simultaneously destroying Russia's. Ironically, the one thing Putin could do easily—declare victory in the Donbas and withdraw his troops—is off limits for him, not because it's politically unfeasible (most Russians would be delighted to get out of this mess), but because his own cult of personality forbids him from blinking.

Ousting the President

All signs point to the eventual collapse of Putin's regime.

Although 85 percent of Russians currently support the president, an Orange Revolution in Moscow—a city that has seen a series of mass anti-Putin demonstrations in the past few years—is not out of the question. Such a movement need not encompass the entire country to be effective. Demonstrations in the capital, like past displays of "people power" in Cairo, Kyiv, and Manila, can effect regime change.

A coup d'état is another possibility. The *siloviki*, like all Praetorian guards, are a mixed blessing. They can keep him in power by crushing political opposition, but they can also stage a coup should they conclude that Putin's policies are undermining their own security and wealth. Putin knows that he replaced Boris Yeltsin (and that Leonid Brezhnev replaced Nikita Khrushchev) in just this fashion.

Even if Putin is not ousted by popular revolution or by a coup, he will be crippled by unrest in Russia's non-Russian regions. Much of the North Caucasus, for example, has already spun out of Moscow's control, as the recent terrorist attacks in Chechnya and the continued violence in Ingushetia and Dagestan demonstrate. As the regime visibly decays and Putin loses his sheen, militant non-Russians may emulate Putin's invocation of Russians' right to self-determination in southeastern Ukraine and pursue their own separatist agendas—with mass protests when possible, and violence when necessary. The Crimean Tatars, whose frustration with increasingly oppressive Russian rule in their homeland is growing, could be the first to act out violently. The Volga Tatars and Bashkirs, both of whom have large reserves of oil in their regions, could easily follow, as they did in the 1990s, with demands for greater autonomy or independence.

Russia after Putin

Will Russia and the world be better off without Putin? Yes, but only if Putin's successor ends the war and comes to a rapprochement with the West.

Putin's successor, whenever he takes power, is likely to be a hardliner; even so, his first priority will have to be to clean the mess created by Putin. Chances are that the new president will be more inclined to end the war and more likely to adopt a conciliatory tone vis-à-vis the rest of the world.

If Putin's successor is not a hardliner, those chances will be even better. This is a small but real possibility: Russia's democrats might just be able to take control of the country at a time of chaos and instability, especially if they succeed in forging coalitions with the increasingly disgruntled Russians whose sons are dying in Ukraine and with non-Russian minorities, as Boris Yeltsin did in the waning days of the Soviet Union. Besides, if history is any indication, Russia's next leader is anybody's guess. The awful Lenin was succeeded by the dreadful Stalin, but Stalin was followed by the decent Khrushchev, who was replaced by the worse Brezhnev, who was succeeded by the good Gorbachev. And Gorbachev handed over power to the pretty good Yeltsin, who was ousted by the dreadful Putin.

In the meantime, the West should do all it can now to support Ukraine and encourage Putin to deescalate the war. The West can also limit the fallout from a possible regime collapse by supporting Russia's neighbors—especially Belarus, Kazakhstan, and Ukraine—economically, diplomatically, and militarily. When the rotten Russian dam breaks, as it inevitably will, only strong and stable non-Russian states will be able to contain the flooding, shielding the rest of the world from Putin's disastrous legacy of ruin.

Trusting or Containing Putin? *World Affairs Journal*, February 13, 2015

Now that the first step toward a negotiated settlement of the Russo-Ukrainian war may have been reached in Minsk, the question of Russian President Vladimir Putin's reliability as a negotiating partner should be on everyone's mind.

In a word, can he be trusted with anything? The answer, unfortunately, is no—for several important reasons.

First, by invading and annexing Crimea, Putin violated the 1994 Budapest Memorandum on Security Assurances, in which Russia, the United States, and the United Kingdom agreed to respect Ukraine's territorial integrity in exchange for Ukraine's adherence to the Treaty on the Non-Proliferation of Nuclear Weapons. Putin's subsequent justification—that the Maidan Revolution ushered in a new Ukrainian state that was not a signatory of the memorandum—was a preposterous claim that, if generalized, would subvert every treaty ever signed. Subsequently, Putin also violated the April 17th Geneva accords and the September 5th Minsk Protocol, both of which outlined specific steps toward defusing the conflict.

Second, by instigating and arming the separatist rebellion in eastern Ukraine, as well as by deploying thousands of regular Russian troops in the occupied Donbas enclave (whose presence there he continues to deny despite indisputable photographic evidence), Putin has launched a unilateral attack against a neighboring country, thereby violating the spirit and letter of every post-World War II agreement on international norms.

Third, Putin has shown himself to be in thrall to an imperial Russian ideology that clouds his ability to make rational judgments about Russia's genuine interests. He has repeatedly justified the Crimean annexation in terms of the peninsula's supposed "sacredness" to Russia and centrality to Russian perceptions of grandeur. In fact, the adventure—along with the subsequent invasion of eastern Donbas—has led to international condemnation and isolation and crippling sanctions that have contributed dramatically to Russia's current economic free fall. Putin wants Ukraine to remain in Russia's orbit. Yet, by waging a war of aggression in the Donbas, he has assured and accelerated Kyiv's westward movement and taken Ukraine-Russia relations to their lowest point in memory. Just a year ago, Ukraine was well on the way to becoming a Russian vassal state with no army, a confused identity, and an unreformed economy. Today, thanks to Putin, Ukraine is an independent state with a functioning army, a reforming economy, and a strong sense of national identity that had eluded the population until the Kremlin and its proxies decided to wage war.

How should Kyiv and the West stop the fighting in eastern Ukraine, if the other side is led by a man who is mendacious, untrustworthy, and consumed by ideology?

The West's current set of approaches—negotiations and sanctions—must be supplemented with a third, one whose effectiveness does not depend on the trustworthiness of Putin: containment. Negotiations with Putin should be pursued, even though no document that Putin signs will be meaningful—or more meaningful than the 1994 Budapest

Memorandum. Sanctions should be maintained and, possibly, even increased, but they will not soon force the hand of a leader whose strategic priorities are driven by an obsession with an ideology that blinds him from his self-interests. If and when sanctions and continued low energy prices bring the Russian economy to a standstill, even Putin may see that he's driven Russia to the brink of collapse, but that could take years.

That leaves only one option: containment. The Romans built fortifications along sections of their boundary with the barbarians. The Chinese built the Great Wall. The West should try to keep Putin east of Ukraine and Belarus, while Kyiv should keep the Donbas enclave east of Ukraine.

The West should treat Ukraine as the contemporary equivalent of West Germany and help transform it into a stable, secure, democratic, and prosperous state. That means, above all, economic and military assistance. A more ambitious form of containment would regard Belarus—whose authoritarian president has recently changed his country's course from its formerly pro-Russian direction to a more pro-Ukrainian and pro-Western direction—as another key state in need of Western aid.

Ukraine should pursue containment vis-à-vis the separatist Donbas enclave that, according to the February 12th Minsk agreement, is supposed to enjoy a level of autonomy within Ukraine. Personally, I would have preferred a sanctioned separation of this corrupt and backward region, but since Kyiv agreed to make an effort at reintegration, so be it. But, in that case, Kyiv must now work to restrict the nefarious influence the region will otherwise have on the rest of Ukraine and its efforts to establish a politically and economically reformed and coherent society. Let the separatists have all the autonomy they want. Let them misrule the place to their hearts' content. In return, let them have as little influence on Ukraine's movement toward democracy, the market, the West, and the world. Squaring that circle will be hard, but Kyiv may be able to offer maximal autonomy in exchange for maximal non-interference. And if, at some point in the future, Ukraine's reactionary "Deep South" chooses to separate, Ukraine should oblige.

Will containment resolve the problem of Russia's illegal annexation of Crimea or bring a quick end to Putin's imperialism? No, but it will throw a wrench into Putin's expansionist designs and thereby weaken his claim to being Russia's savior. By undermining his legitimacy, containment will accelerate the decay of the Putin regime and its ability to be a bull in Europe's china shop. In time, the result may even be a Russia that is once again willing to be a fully respected member of the international community.

*

Has Putin Lost Germany? *World Affairs Journal*, March 9, 2015

A recently released German documentary about Vladimir Putin—*Mensch Putin!*—paints a decidedly unflattering picture of Russia's leader. He is, according to the film, a disturbingly insecure man with a deeply rooted need to compensate for his inadequacies with manifestations of physical prowess and the exercise of power.

"So what else is new?" Putin's many critics might ask. The answer is: the film is German, produced by none other than the venerable ZDF, or Germany's equivalent of BBC or PBS. That makes the film a touchstone of changing German attitudes toward Putin. The film updates former Chancellor Gerhard Schröder's characterization of Putin as a "*lupenreiner Demokrat*" ("flawless democrat") to something closer to Russia's version of Hitler lite. What other German leader was a disturbingly insecure man with a deeply rooted need to compensate for his inadequacies with manifestations of physical prowess and the exercise of power? Germans will get the implied comparison, even if it remains unarticulated in the documentary.

Unsurprisingly, the film has caused an uproar in Germany. A recently established self-styled media watchdog, Die Ständige Publikumskonferenz der öffentlich-rechtlichen Medien (which translates as "The Standing Public Conference on Public-Legal Media"), has formally charged ZDF with misrepresenting the reality by falsely depicting Putin's residence in Dresden and citing a questionable eyewitness. The group's head, Maren Müller, is a 54-year-old leftist from Leipzig and its primary target appears to be mainstream reporting that challenges the Kremlin's worldview.

Contrary to Müller's charges, *Mensch Putin!* is a serious piece of investigative reporting. The film draws on intelligence documents and the testimony of a wide range of impressive Russian and Western experts including Masha Gessen, Nina Khrushcheva, Ben Judah, and Erich Schmidt-Eenboom. Its only fault, to my mind, is to fail to identify one of its interviewees, Aleksandr Dugin, as a Russian fascist.

It's obvious why Müller is upset. The film contrasts today's sleek, hyper-masculine, clean-cut Putin with the Putin of the 1980s, when he was a slovenly, heavy-drinking, womanizing, overweight minor Russian spy in Dresden. The entire film is worth watching just to catch a glimpse of two remarkable photographs of a decidedly portly Putin (at 15:35 and 17:11 minutes). A reliable source also states that she knew that Putin regularly beat his wife, Lyudmila—which seems disturbingly credible in light of the film's suggestion that Putin continually needs to demonstrate his power over others. It's hard not to conclude that Putin's war against Ukraine is a form of wife-beating writ large. The man demands submission to his will. Ukraine—often depicted in Soviet and Russian propaganda as a wide-eyed young girl—says no. The result is violence.

Especially interesting is the extraordinary claim that Putin has been the object of five assassination attempts: in London, Moscow, St. Petersburg, Tehran, and Baku, the capital of Azerbaijan. The distribution of cities is revealing. Putin clearly has enemies everywhere, in the West, in Russia, in the non-Russian "near abroad," and in the rest of the world. Small wonder that his style of politics rests on paranoia, which, in his case at least, is to some degree justified. Was the Boris Nemtsov murder the Putin regime's latest agonized expression of this paranoia? And will the assassination of Russia's leading democrat radicalize Putin's opponents and, in the long tradition of Russian radicalism, move some of them to try a sixth assassination attempt?

Notwithstanding these reports, the most important aspect of the documentary is that it was produced by ZDF, an independent nonprofit station. Until recently, Germany's political culture—and politics—were distinctly, even embarrassingly, pro-Russian and pro-Putin. But no more. Chancellor Angela Merkel says Putin "lives in another world." The majority of Germany's intellectuals and pundits are increasingly critical of Putin and his wars. And the ZDF documentary (as well as another, reportedly in production, that features Putin's war in Ukraine) demonstrates that, while Putin may have gained the hearts and minds of German leftists, he has lost Germany. And that means that he has lost the European Union.

*

What the Bolsheviks and Nazis Can Teach Us about Russia Today, *The Monkey Cage*, March 16, 2015

Back in the late 1980s and early 1990s, the concept of empire entered Soviet and post-Soviet studies, as scholars attempted to place the end of the Soviet multinational state in an appropriate comparative framework. A variety of excellent books was the result, including edited volumes by Bruce Parrott and Karen Dawisha, Barnett Rubin and Jack Snyder, Richard Rudolph and David Good, and Karen Barkey and Mark von Hagen. No less important, the concept of empire entered the post-Sovietological discourse and, as such, lost its former association with Cold War political platforms. Empire, in a word, became respectable, so much so that the term is now used far more loosely with reference to the USSR and Russia than most rigorous scholars of empire would prefer.

Oddly enough, while many of Vladimir Putin's policies toward the Russian "near abroad" have often been termed imperial or neo-imperial, very little effort has been made to connect Putin's current imperial aspirations to the obvious fact that the Soviet empire collapsed and that imperial collapse presumably had some impact on Russia's subsequent trajectory. Although Mikhail Gorbachev's perestroika weakened the sinews of the empire, the USSR remained intact until 1991, when, within the space of several months, the entire imperial system disappeared and was replaced by independent—or nominally independent—states.

Movements, parties and individuals committed to imperial revival have existed in all post-imperial metropoles. And of course, they have also existed in post-Soviet Russia, with the most obvious example being Vladimir Zhirinovsky and his bizarrely named Liberal Democratic Party, who have been explicitly promoting imperial revival since the early 1990s. But the urge for reimperialization is especially strong in metropoles that survive imperial collapse—or the sudden, rapid and comprehensive dismantling of the core-periphery ties that defined the empire. Metropoles that emerge from decaying empires, those that lose territory over centuries or decades, generally reconcile themselves to the loss of empire and rarely embark on full-scale attempts at imperial revival. In contrast, post-collapse metropoles still retain imperial ideologies, discourses and cultures, while the economic, institutional and social ties that once bound peripheries to cores generally continue to exist, even after the formal core-periphery relationship has been dismantled. Under conditions such as these, there are strong grounds for imperial revival to acquire policy prominence among post-collapse core elites.

There are three good examples of post-collapse cores pursuing imperial revival after their empires collapsed. The Russian Bolsheviks drew on imperial ideologies and took advantage of continuing structural ties and succeeded in reestablishing most of the former Russian empire in 1918–1922. The German Nazis drew on similar ideologies and structural connections, but they failed to reestablish the German Reich in the 1940s. And post-Soviet Russian elites, both in the 1990s, when the imperial discourse first enjoyed a revival among Russian policymakers and intellectuals, and in the period since Putin came to and consolidated power, have progressively encroached on the sovereignty of their non-Russian neighbors. Russian elites have pursued reimperialization in the form of economic schemes intended to bind non-Russian economies to Russia's, the use of "soft power" propaganda of the indivisibility of the so-called "Russian world" and the cultivation of Russians and Russian speakers in the "near abroad," and by means of hard power, as in Georgia in 2008 and Ukraine in 2014–2015.

It is with imperial collapse and revival in the analytical background that comparisons of Weimar Germany and "Weimar Russia" become apposite. Both experienced collapse. Both experienced terrible economic hardships in their aftermath. Both blamed the collapse and the economic hardships on democrats. Both sought succor in the imperial traditions and cultures of their nations. Both experienced the coming to power of right-wing nationalists and strong men who promised to reestablish the glory of the nation and its imperial grandeur. And both embarked on soft- and hard-power attacks on their neighbors.

Two observations flow from this analysis. First, it attributes the ongoing Russo-Ukrainian War almost exclusively to Russia's internal post-imperial dynamics—culture, ideology, discourse, economic and institutional structures—and not to external factors, such as real or perceived threats from the post-collapse core state's neighbors. Seen in this light, although the Treaty of Versailles may have been punitive, it was not responsible for the Nazis or Hitler's aggression. Similarly, NATO and the West may have annoyed the Russians, but Putin's turn to the right and his wars against Georgia and Ukraine are the products of Russian imperial collapse, the nature of his strongman regime and systemically generated attempts at imperial revival.

Second, the outcome of Putin's attempts at imperial revival is still unclear. Will he succeed like the Bolsheviks, or will he fail, even if at great cost to everybody, like the Nazis? The factor that may decide the outcome today, just as it did in Russia in 1918–1922 and Europe in 1939–1945, is the degree to which other powers get involved in the conflict between post-collapse metropoles and peripheries. In the Russian case, they stayed out, and the Bolsheviks were able to regain much of the empire. In the Nazi case, the great powers got involved and the result was the collapse of the Nazi imperial project. What is striking about today's Russo-Ukrainian War is the extent to which the great powers—the United

ALEXANDER J. MOTYL: UKRAINE VS. RUSSIA

States, Germany, France and the United Kingdom—have sided with Ukraine. That suggests that Putin's imperial project will fail, though just when that will happen and how many lives will be lost in the process remains unclear.

*

Is Putin's Russia Fascist? *Atlantic Council*, April 23, 2015

A growing number of Russian analysts, in Russia and abroad, have taken to calling Vladimir Putin's regime "fascist." And they don't use the term casually or as a form of opprobrium. They mean that Putin's Russia genuinely resembles Mussolini's Italy or Hitler's Germany.

One of the most recent examples was Mikhail Iampolski. According to the Russian-born NYU professor, "the appeal of quasi-fascist discourse was predictable" as the Russian economy tanked. Moscow rejects "[a]nything that could be seen as a sign of weakness or femininity," including liberalism and homosexuality, and then projects these qualities onto the enemy. Consequently, "Ukrainians are systematically accused of fascism, while Russian fascism is displaced by a false idealization of one's own image."

In March, Moscow commentator Yevgeni Ikhlov charged Putin with introducing a "left fascism" that, while "anti-market and quasi-collectivist," is "fascism because it is a form of a militant and most primitive philistinism." In January 2015, Andrei Zubov, fired from the Moscow State Institute of International Relations for opposing Putin's Ukraine policies, argued that Russia's President was building "a corporate state of a fascist type packaged in Soviet ideology, the ideology of Stalinism," resulting in a Russia that closely resembles Italian fascism with its "nationalism and union with the church." Moscow-based analyst Aleksei Shiropaiev claimed that Russia was moving toward fascism "at a galloping pace." Russian fascism "has become a FACT," "mass Russian consciousness remains absolutely imperialist and chauvinist," and most Russians have "ACCEPTED fascization and are ready to agree to even massive political repressions."

But are the analysts right? The evidence is compelling. Fascist regimes have charismatic dictators with hyper-masculine personality cults. These regimes generally evince a hyper-nationalist ethos, a cult of violence, mass mobilization of youth, high levels of repression, powerful propaganda machines, and imperialist projects. Fascist regimes are hugely popular—usually because the charismatic leader appeals to broad sectors of the population. Putin and his Russia fit the bill perfectly.

In calling Putin's Russia fascist, Russian critics have proven to be far bolder than their non-Russian counterparts in the West, who remain wary about the F-word. Some Westerners genuinely believe that Putin's brand of dictatorship differs from past fascist regimes. They often locate the differences in the historical conditions that gave rise to Hitler, Mussolini, and Putin, and not in the actual characteristics of their regimes.

444

But doing so confuses the origins of similar things with their essential features. No one would say that America is not democratic because the origins of American democracy lay in revolution and not, as with Britain, in historical evolution.

But many Westerners fear the implications of calling a spade a spade. If Putin's Russia is fascist, then it is comparable to Hitler's Germany and Mussolini's Italy and, thus, certifiably evil. And that means that calls for understanding Putin amount to calls for understanding evil. So it's better to pretend that Russia isn't fascist. Hence the popularity of abstruse designations like managed democracy and sovereign democracy or terms—such as Putinism—that only state the obvious.

If the past is any guide to the future, Western skittishness about the F-word will evaporate. In the 1980s, Russian critics of the USSR described it as totalitarian, even as Western scholars shunned a term that had been vilified as anti-Communist. Western analysts feared its critical implications at a time of détente and preferred anodyne terms like authoritarian or non-democratic. Once Russians showed them that totalitarian was an accurate, and politically correct, designation for the Soviet regime, some Westerners got on the bandwagon. Those who did realized that the USSR's transition from totalitarianism to democracy was going to be far more difficult than a transition from authoritarianism to democracy. Unfortunately, the epiphany came too late to affect policies formulated in the end of history euphoria of the early 1990s.

A similar conceptual change is likely to take place with fascism. As the chorus of Russian voices using the F-word grows, Western policymakers who <u>insist</u> that we should listen to Putin and understand his point of view will have no choice but to listen to and understand his critics.

Calling Putin's system fascist will mark a conceptual breakthrough in Western attitudes—and perhaps policies—toward Russia. Viewing his state as evil does not necessitate rattling sabers. Soft power and diplomacy will remain no less important than hard power. But the conceptual shift would recognize that Putin and his regime are the problem, and that the problem will go away only when he and his regime go away. In a word, there are no quick fixes to the Putin problem. The West is in for a long, hard slog involving economic and military support for Ukraine and its neighbors, the containment of Russian imperialism, and support for anti-fascist elements within Russia. The good news is that, now as then, democracy will win.

*

Expanding Putin's Black List, *World Affairs Journal*, June 5, 2015

European Union officials are outraged by the Kremlin's "black list" of European officials denied entry into Russia. The president of the European Parliament, Martin Schulz, called it "unacceptable." Federica Mogherini, the EU high representative for foreign affairs, issued the following statement:

In the past few months several EU politicians have been denied entry when arriving at the Russian border. The Russian authorities justified these refusals by referring to the inclusion of these individuals on a confidential "stop list."

After each of these refusals, the EU and the Member States whose nationals were affected had repeatedly requested transparency about the content of this list.

The list with 89 names has now been shared by the Russian authorities. We don't have any other information on legal basis, criteria and process of this decision. We consider this measure as totally arbitrary and unjustified, especially in the absence of any further clarification and transparency.

The 89 names hail from Estonia, Latvia, Lithuania, Poland, the Czech Republic, Bulgaria, Romania, Germany, France, Denmark, Sweden, Finland, Belgium, the Netherlands, Great Britain, Spain, and Greece. Kudos to these countries. And shame on Slovakia, Hungary, Austria, Portugal, Luxemburg, Italy, and the rest for failing to make the grade.

For the fact is that inclusion on the list is an honor, akin to a formal acknowledgement of one's official status as an enemy of Hitler, Stalin, Pol Pot, or some other vile dictator. Anna Maria Corazza Bildt, a Swedish member of the European Parliament, got it just right: "Those who try to censor us and make us scared for standing up for values deserve even more criticism. For me it's about being very committed to standing up for peace and freedom in Ukraine. I'm more proud than scared and this gives me more determination to continue. ... If the Kremlin takes me and my colleagues seriously it means we're doing a good job."

The list is not, as Mogherini said, "totally arbitrary and unjustified." It makes perfect sense for a fascist state such as Vladimir Putin's Russia to keep out anti-fascists. The real problem with the list is that it's much too short. I can think of many policymakers, intellectuals, and professionals who have been far more outspoken in their criticism of Putin's regime than some of the people on the list. Just about all my friends and colleagues belong on it. Heck, *I* belong on it! (I hate to bother you, Mister Putin, especially as you're preparing for more war, but is there any way of applying for inclusion? Would letters of recommendation from Stephen Cohen, Gerhard Schröder, and Gérard Depardieu and a 200-word personal statement do the trick?)

Come to think of it, every decent person belongs on the list. Which raises an important ethical question. Should a decent person travel to a fascist state? Or should a decent person avoid all unnecessary contact with such a state?

The argument against travel is simple: travel financially supports and morally legitimizes the regime. The argument for travel is also simple: travel provides moral support to embattled democrats. The argument against is unconditional: every dollar or euro you spend in Russia supports Putin, regardless of what you do or say while in the country. The argument for is conditional: your presence in Russia may provide moral support to embattled democrats if and only if you articulate that support—boldly and publicly.

If these ethical principles persuade you, then simple tourism to Russia is out. If you want to experience Russian culture, visit the Russian émigré colonies in Europe and North America. If you want to visit Slavic countries, go to Ukraine, Poland, or the Czech Republic. If you want to get a taste of post-Soviet life, visit the Baltic states.

How about academics, policy analysts, and other intellectuals? Should they travel to Putin's fascist realm? Only if they openly side with the democratic opposition and risk being thrown out. Won't their mere presence help the democrats? Hardly. The last thing courageous Russian democrats need to see is hypocritical Westerners who feign concern for Russian human rights but won't speak out against Putin's tyranny outside their comfortable offices.

*

Putin Destroys Tons of Food Imports. What's Next? *World Affairs Journal*, August 19, 2015

Russian President Vladimir Putin's wanton destruction of hundreds of tons of Western food products has provoked a storm of criticism.

The outrage is justified, but, no less important, his bizarre behavior gives us an opportunity to test some of the theories that have been applied to Russia's behavior in the last two years.

Start with realism, the theory of geopolitics, national interests, and hard facts, as preached by John Mearsheimer, Henry Kissinger, and Stephen Cohen.

Realism explains Russia's annexation of Crimea and war in eastern Ukraine as a defensive measure made in response to NATO enlargement and American instigation and/or support of Ukraine's Euromaidan revolution. The West supposedly tried to wrest Ukraine from Russia's legitimate sphere of interests, and Russia had no choice but to defend itself by playing hardball in Ukraine.

As I've written, realism gets the facts wrong and mixes causes with effects—NATO was and still is a paper tiger and Western mobilization in support of Ukraine happened after Russia's intervention—but no matter. The logic of the theory is clear enough, and, when taken on its own terms, not unpersuasive. Unfortunately, it's incapable of making any sense of Putin's anti-food measures. One would have to think of the food that Russia destroyed as a Western form of geopolitical aggression for realism to have any traction. That, obviously, makes little sense. So, forget realism.

Theories that explain Russia's aggressive behavior in terms of Putin's need to pander to the Russian people also fall flat. No people looks at the destruction of precious foodstuffs with equanimity, and the Russians are no exception. Ditto for theories that explain

Putin's warmongering in terms of some putative need to pander to special interests. Russia's food producers may have greeted the destruction, but they play no role in the decision-making process in the Kremlin, and it would make no sense for Putin to act bizarrely on their behalf.

Theories that focus on the hyper-centralized nature of the Russian political system fare much better. If you think of Russia as a deeply authoritarian (or, as I suggest, fascist) sys-tem with all power concentrated in the hands of the dictator, we would expect Putin to be prone to tactical and strategic mistakes. Hyper-centralized authority structures encour-age kowtowing behavior by elites, distort the flow of information to the leader, place an enormous decision-making burden on his shoulders, and thereby make blunders inevi-table. Seen in this light, the Crimean annexation, the attack on the Donbas, and now the destruction of food are all part of a chain of bad decisions on the part of an overextended and informationally challenged autocrat.

Naturally, the theories that do best in explaining the food destruction are those that claim that Putin has from the start been acting irrationally, perhaps as a result of the de-mands of his office, perhaps as a result of his personality, biography, or psychology. Seen in this light, perhaps the destruction of food is just the latest link in a chain that goes back to Putin's childhood and the sense of inadequacy he felt as a youth.

So where do these reflections leave us?

The good news is that Putin's regime may be on its last legs. There was at least some ideo-logical benefit from annexing Crimea. Destroying food is just plain stupid. If Putin has truly lost touch with reality, the system he's constructed is doomed.

Alas, there is also bad news, and the bad news could be very bad. A leader who is irratio-nal enough to do something as dumb as destroy food could be irrational enough to bomb Kyiv, attack Estonia, or try to test NATO's war-making resolve.

*

The Fool, Russia, and Ukraine, *World Affairs Journal*, September 22, 2015

With *The Fool* (*Durak*), 34-year-old Russian film director Yuri Bykov has officially be-come his country's Cassandra.

The *New York Times* says the film is about corruption in a squalid Russia. Bykov's 2014 film is about much more than that. *The Fool* is an obvious allegory of the rottenness—and coming collapse—of Vladimir Putin's Russia.

Dima Nikitin, a plumber, notices that a building occupied by the dregs of society in his hometown has a large crack running from top to bottom and concludes that, since the foundation is shifting and the building is tilting some 10 percent, its collapse is inevitable.

He tries to mobilize the city mayor and her council to take action. At first determined to do something, they realize that their theft of state funds has depleted the treasury and made evacuating the building impossible. Besides, there's no place to put the 800-plus inhabitants. The mayor and one of her advisers then decide to do nothing, hatching a plan to blame any later calamity on the heads of the fire and housing departments. Meanwhile, Dima decides to save the building's inhabitants on his own. He runs from apartment to apartment shouting that the "building is collapsing." Once everyone leaves, and the building fails to fall, the people turn on him. The last scene shows him lying in the snow, unconscious or dead.

Obviously, the building stands for Putin's Russia. Everybody is on the take—from the people who live in the building to the mayor and her chums to the governor who gets a 50 percent kickback from the city budget. The police chief says, "I'm Russian. How can I not take bribes?" However, Bykov's central concern is not corruption *per se*, but its destructive impact on Russia—on the building. "Leave," Dima's father tells him, "this place will never change. Never." Dima tells his wife that "we live and die as swine, because we treat one another as nothing." The mayor asks Dima when the building will collapse. "It's already falling," he replies.

Just like Putin's regime.

The film reminded me of Andrei Zvyagintsev's *Leviathan*, also released in 2014, which depicts one man's hopeless battle against corrupt city officials in Russia's North. Not only does he lose. He also loses his wife and best friend and is thrown into jail, to boot.

More important, *The Fool* is very reminiscent of *Little Vera*, Vasili Pichul's 1988 film that depicted the squalor and corruption of late Brezhnev Russia. Some three decades later, nothing has changed. The population lives in misery, while the elite drink champagne. *Little Vera* presaged the USSR's collapse. *The Fool* predicts Russia's downfall. Whether it's the country's or the regime's, you can decide for yourself.

I hope *The Fool* gets widely distributed in Ukraine. Unfortunately, there is all too much about the film that applies with equal force to Ukraine. Viewers will have no trouble realizing that both Russia's and Ukraine's buildings are in trouble.

There are two key differences, however. Thanks to the Orange and Maidan Revolutions, Ukrainians know they need to fix their home fast. Russians are still in denial. Indeed, Putin seems intent on adding other decrepit buildings to his existing collection, while Russians cheer him on and turn on their Cassandra.

That may be the key difference between Ukraine and Russia. Ukraine has hope. Russia is hopeless.

*

Putin's Misguided Move in Syria, *World Affairs Journal*, September 25, 2015

Russia's incompetent bully of a leader, Vladimir Putin, has just committed his latest blunder. He's decided to prop up the dying Assad regime with weapons and soldiers. Good luck! The USSR's fiasco in Afghanistan and America's in Iraq have clearly failed to deter the Kremlin's serial bumbler from committing his latest strategic mistake.

The mortar shell that struck Russia's embassy compound in Damascus on September 20th is a foretaste of things to come. As Russian troops intervene in greater numbers—as they surely will to prop up a doomed regime—Russian casualties will mount. Eventually, ISIS will engage in its usual barbarism and beheaded Russian soldiers will appear on television. At that point, Western commentators, who've mostly interpreted Putin's intervention as a devilishly clever move, will start saying that Russia stumbled into a conflict it cannot win.

Putin watchers shouldn't be surprised by the Russian dictator's latest blunder.

His mistakes started with his unwillingness to use the enormous windfall from rising energy prices to modernize the Russian economy. Instead of building an open society, Putin constructed a "fascistoid" political system and kept Russia as a petro-state. That Russia's economy is now contracting as a result of falling energy prices is Putin's fault. So is the fact that educated professionals and money are leaving the country in droves.

Putin stupidly supported Ukrainian President Viktor Yanukovych in 2004, thereby accelerating that country's drift toward the West. Even more stupidly, he opposed Ukraine's Association Agreement with the European Union in late 2013, thereby sparking the Euromaidan Revolution that led to Yanukovych's flight. Putin then invaded Crimea and the Donbas—provinces that he already controlled—thereby turning Ukraine against Russia, destroying the occupied regions' economies, and saddling Russia with the bill. All this, while sanctions accelerated Russia's economic decline, smothered foreign investment, and increased capital flight.

Meanwhile, Russia's violation of the post-war security order in Europe galvanized a demoralized NATO, turned the United States and Europe against Russia, led to traditionally Russophile Germany's adoption of an anti-Russian stance, forced Putin to grovel before an indifferent China, and transformed Russia into a rogue state whose closest ally now appears to be mighty North Korea.

Russians used to joke that Mikhail Gorbachev's perestroika was a CIA plot to destroy the Soviet Union. I'm beginning to think Vlad Putin is a sleeper agent of the Company. A few more years of his bumbling, and the Russian state may become history.

The bottom line is that Russia's security and strength are significantly worse off today than they were two years ago. And Putin, whom Russians adore, is to blame.

To top it off, Putin has decided to jump from the frying pan into the fire by intervening in Syria.

Not just with weapons, but with actual troops. The Assad regime is either doomed, or it can be saved only with massive outside intervention. Wisely, neither the West nor the Arab states want to send in troops. Russia will have to, increasingly. Will Russia be able to defeat ISIS? Probably not. Even if it does, the price it'll pay in lives and money will be high. You'd think that Putin might have learned from the USSR's misadventure in Afghanistan and America's in Iraq. Evidently not—which is exactly what you'd expect from a paranoid, narcissistic, solipsistic fascist leader who doesn't understand that a declining economy is a brake on foreign interventions.

Meanwhile, ISIS isn't Putin's only problem. The National Coalition of Syrian Revolution and Opposition Forces condemned Russia on September 12th:

> With this aggressive move, Russia has moved from a stage of supporting a criminal regime that carries out genocide in our country to a stage of direct military intervention alongside a crumbling illegitimate regime. The direct Russian military intervention places the Russian leadership in a position of hostility towards the Syrian people, and makes its forces on Syrian soil occupation forces. ... We present these facts to the international community, to the UN, to the Arab League, and especially to the Russian people—we do not wish upon them in Syria a repeat of their experience in Afghanistan—because Syrians will not remain silent over the occupation of their land and the spilling of their sons' blood.

Putin's Syrian idiocy makes Ukraine the big winner. Having effectively abandoned his proxies in the Donbas, Putin has made a frozen conflict there almost inevitable. The terrorists, thugs, and mercenaries misruling the Russian-occupied Donbas enclave won't agree to reintegrate into Ukraine on Kyiv's terms, and Kyiv can't agree to reintegrate them on theirs. The resulting stalemate will keep the Donbas hellhole out of Ukraine, force Russia to keep paying millions to sustain it, and free Ukraine to focus on internal reforms and external Westernization.

Russians are the big losers. They will have to pay with their lives for Putin's megalomania and their own moral blindness.

Also in the running are Western realist scholars.

They've been arguing that Russia attacked Ukraine because of some mythical NATO plot to incorporate it. Wrong: NATO was a paper tiger and, while Kyiv did not seriously pursue Ukraine's membership until after Russia invaded, NATO has remained skittish about the prospect even today.

They've also been arguing that Ukraine is an existential interest of Russia, and that Moscow would defend it to the finish. Wrong again: No rational leader abandons an existential interest to engage in crazy overseas adventures.

Finally, they've been arguing that Putin is a rational ruler who wants to maximize Russia's power and security. Wrong, wrong, wrong: Putin is rational only if rationality is tantamount to paranoia, hyper-nationalism, imperialism, and supremacism.

Morality, Pragmatism, and Orwell in Rhetoric and Policy, *World Affairs Journal*, November 10, 2015

We've all gotten very familiar with Vladimir Putin's Orwellian logic, according to which peace is war, intervention is non-intervention, democracy is fascism, and fascism is democracy. His latest comments at the Valdai discussion club just reinforced, if any reinforcing were still necessary, the point that the man is a master of mendacity.

We generally don't expect equally bizarre ethical or logical standards from Western commentators. And yet they do occur, especially with regard to Putin, Russia, and their war in Ukraine.

On October 20th, Professor Mark Galeotti of New York University argued that the "West has lost the right to lecture Putin." According to Galeotti:

> This is not simple "whataboutism," that classic trick of deflecting criticism through raising the other side's real or alleged flaws. Rather it is to note that Washington is currently seeking to have its cake and eat it. It can choose to base its foreign policy on strict moral principles or geopolitical pragmatism.

> At present, it seems happy to act pragmatically but think morally. Thus it genuinely considers Putin not simply an antagonist, but an immoral one.

> This is dangerous and foolish. ... Castigating [Putin's Russia] on moral grounds, without behaving in an unimpeachably moral way, is simply going to alienate Moscow, undermine Western credibility, and create a wholly false series of assumptions on which to base policy.

> The uncomfortable truth is that in Syria, as in so many other ways, Putin is simply ruthlessly exploiting and expanding precedents already set by the West.

Galeotti's suggestion that the choice before policymakers is either "strict moral principles" or "geopolitical pragmatism" is absurd. The fact is that Western democracies do indeed attempt to combine both principles; they do not just "act pragmatically but think morally." True, Western democracies as often fail to combine both principles as they succeed. But 100 percent success is not the point. Instead, the point is to try to be both pragmatic and moral—no easy task.

In this respect, Western democracies differ fundamentally from authoritarian dictatorships, fascist states, and autocracies such as Putin's Russia. Putin makes no effort whatsoever to combine morality with pragmatism. Indeed, he twists morality as need be to pursue his ends. A guilty conscience is thus impossible in Putin's warped moral universe, while guilty consciences are built into the very fabric of Western thought. When the West criticizes others for their misdeeds, it effectively criticizes itself. Although the West is frequently hypocritical, its hypocrisy is testimony to the fact that it does have ethical standards, even, or especially when, it violates them. As a result, the West doesn't just have the right to criticize Putin: It has the obligation to do so.

Take Galeotti's argument to its logical conclusion, and you'd have to claim that only a saint should dare to express ethical reservations about anything or anybody.

Even more bizarre standards are found in a commentary by Bloomberg columnist Leonid Bershidsky, who believes that the recently released "MH17 crash report shows no side was innocent." According to Bershidsky, while it's true that "the Buk missile that destroyed the plane must have been launched from rebel-held territory," Ukraine "failed in its duty by allowing passenger jets to fly over the conflict area." To be sure, says Bershidsky, "while there can be no moral equivalency between arming or protecting the perpetrators of that crime, and failing to close the skies, the uncomfortable truth laid bare by the report is that both sides in the conflict were glaringly incompetent."

Come again? The rebels or the Russians commit a heinous crime by deliberately shooting down a plane, and that's mere incompetence? Even if they believed it was a military plane—which may be unlikely, given the high altitude at which MH17 was flying—the fact is that they deliberately decided to shoot it down. Meanwhile, the Ukrainians fail to imagine that the rebels or Russians would shoot down passenger planes and they, too, are as incompetent as the rebels or Russians who commit the crime?

Competence or incompetence is not the issue here, just as it is not the issue in any crime. The only relevant questions are: Was a crime committed and who committed it? And the answers to both questions are: Yes, a crime was committed because a plane was deliberately shot down, and the Russians or their proxies fired the missile that destroyed the plane.

Bershidsky doesn't take his argument far enough. Logically, he should also accuse the pilot of MH17 and its passengers of being equally incompetent and hence indirectly complicit. After all, who but an incompetent would decide to fly over a war zone? Who but an incompetent would fail to determine beforehand whether the plane would be flying over contested territory?

The questions are as obscene as the moral standards of Putin and his apologists.

*

Putin vs. ISIS: Which Threatens the West More? *World Affairs Journal*, December 9, 2015

President Vladimir Putin's December 3rd address to the Federation Council, the upper house of Russia's national legislature, was an exercise in chutzpah, trying to present Russia as a victim of barbarism and a defender of peace:

> Russia has long since been on the front lines of the struggle against terrorism. It's a struggle for freedom, truth, and justice. For the lives of people and the future of our civilization.

Disregard the fact that Putin's Russia has been on the front lines of promoting terrorism, at home and in Ukraine. Disregard the fact that Putin's regime is the antithesis of freedom, truth, and justice. And disregard the fact that Putin has declared war on civilized norms of international behavior.

Consider only Putin's offer of an anti-ISIS alliance with the West. As Western policymakers consider such a possibility, they would do well to first ask just who the greater threat to world peace is—the Islamic State or Putin's Russia? The question is of fundamental importance. While no one would dispute the utility of coordinating the Western assault on ISIS with Russia's, an anti-terrorist *alliance* with Russia presupposes that ISIS poses a greater threat to the West and its interests than Russia.

Although the barbarism of ISIS inclines us to believe that the Islamists are a greater threat than the Putinists, that conclusion would be a mistake. In fact, Putin's Russia is a greater threat to the West—both because Putin's ruthlessness borders on barbarism and because he has the will, capacity, and desire to undermine the international order that made the West possible.

Start with barbarism. Although ISIS's cruelty is extreme and its destructiveness is wanton, they barely exceed those of Putin's Russia. During Putin's campaign to exterminate Chechen separatists, Russian bombs leveled Chechnya's capital city, Grozny, while Russian soldiers killed many thousands of innocent civilians. In 1999, three Russian apartment buildings were blown to bits, and all the evidence points to the Russian secret police, of which Putin was then head, as the perpetrator. Since mid-2014, some 8,000 Ukrainians and Russians have lost their lives in Putin's war against Ukraine. Russian troops do not behead their prisoners, as does ISIS, but Russia's proxies have executed Ukrainian prisoners of war in the Russian-occupied Donbas. ISIS boasts of destroying a Russian plane, while Putin still denies any complicity whatsoever in the downing of Malaysia Airlines Flight 17 on July 17, 2014. Indifference to civilian casualties has also characterized Russia's ongoing bombing campaign in Syria.

Dead Parisians may shock us more than dead Chechens, dead Russians, or dead Ukrainians, but if human lives are equally valuable, then Putin has surely destroyed his fair share.

But barbarism is not the issue. Barbarism shocks and terrifies us, but it does not threaten international peace. What does? Above all, rogue states like Russia—and not radical movements like ISIS.

Despite its name, ISIS is not yet a genuine state with all the functioning government institutions that comprise a bona fide state. It's a revolutionary movement that hopes to construct a state. Thus far, its record of state-building has been mixed. It has seized some territory in Syria and Iraq, but its ability to administer the population is uncertain, and its prospects for continued control are even worse. Revolutionary movements can and do defeat their opponents and establish stable state institutions, but only if they have the military capacity and economic wherewithal to do so. In taking on Turkey, Iraq, Iran, Syria, Saudi Arabia, the United States, France, Russia, and many other states, ISIS is almost sure to lose on the battlefield or, at a minimum, surrender much territory. It may survive in the underground and wreak terror throughout the world, but terror, however atrocious, does not, and cannot, threaten world peace. Dead civilians are a tragedy and a crime, but they do not undermine the international order or entail inter-state war.

In contrast to ISIS, Putin's Russia is a state—and a rogue state, to boot. It violates treaties and borders, rejects international norms, and sees war as a legitimate means to its great-power ends. Russia tore up the 1994 Budapest Memorandum that guaranteed Ukraine's territorial integrity and unilaterally revised the borders of Georgia and Ukraine by means of armed force. Putin's Russia views the sovereignty and airspace of its neighbors—from Estonia to Belarus to Armenia to Kazakhstan to Turkey—as anything but inviolate, while insisting that it is perfectly entitled to pursue its imperial interests by means of force.

Russia's hitherto lackadaisical bombing of ISIS may make it a temporary, tactical, short-term partner of the West, but Putin's established hostility to the post-World War II international system that produced the European Union and consolidated peace in Europe precludes Russia's becoming an ally of the West.

Both Putin and ISIS reject the West and everything it stands for. But only Putin has the ability to destroy the West—by progressively undermining the international system that made a peaceful and prosperous West possible. Tactical cooperation with Russia in Syria may therefore be attractive, but it cannot distract from Putin's strategic hostility to the West.

Should the West cooperate with Putin to destroy ISIS? Of course. But the West must remember that Putin's Russia remains an adversary committed to the West's demise. Its support of Ukraine and of sanctions must therefore remain unchanged. Its commitment to NATO must remain firm. And its opposition to Putin's expansionist designs must be unequivocal.

*

Putin Is Steering Russia to Collapse, *World Affairs Journal*, December 30, 2015

As the new year begins, both Ukraine and Russia are making steady progress. The difference is that, while Ukraine is slowly, and more or less surely, adopting a raft of systemic reforms that will make it a normal Western market democracy, Russia is becoming a failed state. If current trends continue, as they probably will, Russia may even disappear.

That's not just my conclusion. It's Dmitri Trenin's, and Trenin is the director of the prestigious Carnegie Moscow Center and a distinguished Russian analyst who, unlike his former colleague, the anti-Putin firebrand Lilia Shevtsova, has often expressed a soft-line interpretation of the Putin regime and its intentions.

In a recently published commentary, however, Trenin takes off his gloves and compares Vladimir Putin's Russia to the tsarist regime on the eve of World War I. If, writes Trenin, Russia doesn't develop a new foreign policy and embark on serious internal reform, "the Russian state could share the fate of the Romanov regime in World War I."

That is, Russia could collapse. In effect, Trenin is comparing Putin to Romanov Russia's last tsar, the hapless Nicholas II, and arguing that he has failed—*completely.*

Here's Trenin:

> The political conflict between Russia and the United States is fundamental. There may be moments when tension eases and cooperation is possible, but there are no obvious options for strategic compromise. Moreover, Russia has entered a phase of mutual estrangement with a large part of Europe; and it has, for the foreseeable future, acquired a hostile Ukraine on its border, whose new foundation for nation-building is based on hostility to Russia. Finally, Russia has been sucked into the permanent theater of conflict that is the Middle East. ...

> In its recent history, Russia has sought to embrace one of two competing overarching foreign policy concepts—but both have shattered. ... Both concepts—we can call them Plan A and Plan B—came into jeopardy in the first half of the 2010s, and were ultimately torpedoed by the Ukraine crisis.

So, what should Russia do?

> The key strategic objective must be to develop a new Russian foreign policy concept—a kind of Plan C. This concept should be based on a balanced understanding of both Russia's need for self-sufficiency and its necessary engagement with the rest of the world. ...

> Yet all this is not the main thing. ... Russians should turn their minds back to 1914, when amid a clash of world powers the old Russian regime came crashing down. If it wants to escape the fate the reform-averse Romanovs endured in World War I, the current ruling elite needs to prioritize domestic change and carry out a comprehensive overhaul of the country's institutions. ... Russia's current political and economic order, if it persists, will sooner or later doom it to a tragic failure as a state.

And there you have it. Unless it changes fundamentally, Russia will fail as a state. Which is to say that Putin has, within a few short years, managed to transform a stable polity into a failing state. How? Above all, by means of an ill-advised, criminal invasion of Ukraine. What was supposed to be a quick, glorious, little war has become a disaster—for Russia. Give the man another year or two and his current grade of C will, as Russia collapses and chaos envelopes its unfortunate population, become an F.

Trenin is being coy when he says that "Russia" got itself into trouble. Although Russia may fail as a state, it's Putin, the man Steven Lee Myers calls the "new tsar," who has failed as a leader and pushed Russia to the brink of disaster.

It's hard to imagine that anyone could be a worse leader than deposed Ukrainian President Viktor Yanukovych. Yet Russia's leader has done just that.

Fortunately, as Trenin implies, the new tsar may soon be Russia's final tsar.

*

Lights Out for the Putin Regime, *Foreign Affairs*, January 27, 2016

Russian President Vladimir Putin used to seem invincible. Today, he and his regime look enervated, confused, and desperate. Increasingly, both Russian and Western commentators suggest that Russia may be on the verge of deep instability, possibly even collapse.

This perceptual shift is unsurprising. Last year, Russia was basking in the glow of its annexation of Crimea and aggression in the Donbas. The economy, although stagnant, seemed stable. Putin was running circles around Western policymakers and domestic critics. His popularity was sky-high. Now it is only his popularity that remains; everything else has turned for the worse. Crimea and the Donbas are economic hellholes and huge drains on Russian resources. The war with Ukraine has stalemated. Energy prices are collapsing, and the Russian economy is in recession. Putin's punitive economic measures against Ukraine, Turkey, and the West have only harmed the Russian economy further. Meanwhile, the country's intervention in Syria is poised to become a quagmire.

Things are probably much worse for Russia than this cursory survey of negative trends suggests. The country is weathering three crises brought about by Putin's rule—and Russia's foreign-policy misadventures in Ukraine and Syria are only exacerbating them.

First, the Russian economy is in free fall. That oil and gas prices are unlikely to rise much anytime soon is bad enough. Far worse, Russia's energy-dependent economy is unreformed, uncompetitive, and un-modernized and will remain so as long as it serves as a wealth-producing machine for Russia's political elite. Second, Putin's political system is disintegrating. His brand of authoritarian centralization was supposed to create a strong "power vertical" that would bring order to the administrative apparatus, rid it of corruption, and subordinate regional Russian and non-Russian elites to Moscow's will. Instead, over-centralization has produced the opposite effect, fragmenting the bureaucracy, encouraging bureaucrats to pursue their own interests, and enabling regional elites to become increasingly insubordinate—with Ramzan Kadyrov, Putin's strongman in Chechnya, being the prime example. Third, Putin himself, as the linchpin of the Russian system, has clearly passed his prime. Since his catastrophic decision to prevent Ukraine from signing an Association Agreement with the European Union in 2013, he has committed strategic blunder after strategic blunder. His formerly attractive macho image is wearing thin, and his recent attempts to promote his cult of personality by publishing a book of his quotes and a Putin calendar look laughable and desperate.

The problem for Putin—and for Russia—is that the political–economic system is resistant to change. Such a dysfunctional economy is sustainable only if it is controlled by a self-serving bureaucratic caste that places its own interests above those of the country. In turn, a deeply corrupt authoritarian system needs to have a dictator at its core, one who coordinates and balances elite interests and appetites. Putin's innovation is to have transformed himself into a cult-like figure whose legitimacy depends on his seemingly boundless youth and vigor. Such leaders, though, eventually become victims of their own personality cult and, like Stalin, Hitler, Mao, and Mussolini, do not leave office voluntarily. Russia is thus trapped between the Scylla of systemic decay and the Charybdis of systemic stasis. Under such conditions, Putin will draw increasingly on Russian chauvinism, imperialism, and ethnocentrism for legitimacy.

Since none of this mess will be resolved anytime soon, Russia appears poised to enter a prolonged "time of troubles" that could range from social unrest to regime change to state collapse. It might be foolhardy to predict Russia's future, but it is clear that the longer Putin stays in power, the worse things will be for the country. Putin, who claimed to be saving Russia, has become its worst enemy. For now, the United States, Europe, and Russia's neighbors must prepare for the worst.

Drivers of Instability

Some analysts dismiss the possibility of massive instability in Russia on the grounds that the opposition is weak, its leaders lack charisma, and Putin's popularity is high. These factors are not as important as they are assumed to be. Most revolutions have come as a result of deep structural crises; few have been made by self-styled revolutionaries. Charismatic leaders emerge during systemic instability as often as they predate it. And country-wide popularity is never as important for a movement or leader as power in the capital city and among key political and economic elites.

Imagine that the three crises noted above continue to deepen, as they in all likelihood will. In that case, nearly every sector of Russian society will get closer to rebellion. As inflation and unemployment rise and living standards fall, dissatisfaction will grow among workers and social unrest will increase. Political and economic elites, too, will grow increasingly unhappy as Russia's three crises deepen. Their status and wealth will increasingly become vulnerable, and their willingness to countenance alternatives to Putin and his system will grow. Urban intellectuals, students, and professionals will likewise rediscover their voices and provide intellectual guidance to the forces of instability.

With more systemic chaos and elite stasis, patriotically-minded elements within the armed forces (army, militia, and secret police) will search for alternatives to Putin and his ruinous system of rule. And soldiers and mercenaries now fighting in Ukraine and Syria may return home and promote radical views throughout the country. Outside Russia, the Russian Federation's 21 non-Russian republics will assert their authority.

For 18 years, Putin could defuse discontent by the three means all elites use to stay in power. He bought popular support with the windfalls from rising energy prices. He strengthened the forces of coercion and repressed discontent. And, by projecting manliness and vigor and promising to remake Russia in his own image, he created ideological incentives to support him and his regime. Thanks to his mistakes and the system's decay, however, Putin no longer has the material resources he once possessed and his image has been greatly tarnished. And thanks to Russia's transformation into a rogue state incapable of defeating Ukraine and increasingly mired in the Middle East, the vision of renewed Russian greatness is losing its appeal. As a result, Putin now relies almost exclusively on the forces of coercion to stay in power and sustain his regime. He thus depends on their willingness to go along with his rule. And Putin, whose regime recently adopted legislation permitting the secret police to shoot protestors, knows it.

Forcing the Forces

Relying on the armed forces could be a dangerous bet. For one, they might be unwilling to employ coercion if they face large numbers of protestors drawn from the general population. This is true for all repressive regimes, which tend to emphasize the elite nature of policing and deploy officers far away from their homes. Given Putin's popularity and the relatively greater difficulty of organizing mass protests in the Russian provinces, the greatest likelihood of such a scenario playing out is in Moscow, which witnessed mass demonstrations in 2011–2012, and in the non-Russian regions such as Tatarstan, Bashkortostan, Yakutia, Dagestan, and Ingushetia, where ethnic solidarity could override orders to use coercion. If women and workers participate in such disturbances, coercive forces would be least inclined to follow orders and shoot.

At present, such a revolution looks improbable; but in mid-2004 and mid-2013, no one was predicting the Orange Revolution or the Euromaidan Revolution in Ukraine. Such revolutions, as Putin probably realizes, are intrinsically unpredictable, because they are the product of inchoate forces of discontent, dissatisfaction, anger, radicalization, and hope. Even so, given the dysfunctionality of the political–economic system and its incapacity to change, the chances of such disturbances will increase with every year. The protests are likely to be sparked by a sudden, unexpected event that outrages people and propels them into the streets. That shock could be anything, from an embarrassing televised slip-up by Putin to an act of brutality by the police to a tragic fire. No one ever predicts such shocks, but, as systems decay, they become more likely.

Another scenario would be if the armed forces are unable to stop elite anti-regime forces from plotting a palace coup or promoting independence in the non-Russian regions. Although Putin has constructed a form of authoritarianism that resembles the regimes of Nazi Germany and Mussolini's Italy, Russia's forces of coercion are not yet, as in Stalin's times, a state within the state capable of monitoring all elite behavior. The loyalty or neutrality of Russia's elites cannot therefore be entirely assured. Russian elites know that, like Mikhail Khodorkovsky, the Russian businessman-turned-opposition figure who incurred Putin's ire and several years' imprisonment for fraud, they could be punished for stepping out of line, but they also know that, in times of troubles, the Kremlin needs them as much as, if not more, than they need the Kremlin.

How likely is a palace coup or regional separatism? Soviet and Russian history is replete with examples. After Stalin's death, his successors killed his secret police chief, Lavrentii Beria, in 1953. In 1964, Nikita Khrushchev was ousted in a coup. In 1998–1999, Putin came to power as the result of a coup-like deal with elites and then President Boris Yeltsin. As to the non-Russians, they made claims on sovereignty every time the state was in crisis—during the Revolution of 1917–1921, during the German occupation of 1941–1943, and during Mikhail Gorbachev's perestroika in 1987–1991. Elite loyalty depends on Putin's ability to pay them off. Just as political and economic elites flocked to Putin during the years of plenty, between 1998 and 2013, so too, will they be tempted to abandon him during the coming years of scarcity. Meanwhile, non-Russian elites—and especially those in oil-rich Tatarstan and diamond-rich Yakutia—may be the first to loosen their ties to Moscow, because they may have nationalist ambitions, and are farther from the center and thus less susceptible to threats. Once elites see that they can get away with criticizing the regime, things will reach a tipping point and anti-Putin bandwagoning could take place. Some may even plot against Putin and try to have him forcibly removed or killed.

The third scenario is that coercion might prove inadequate to quell discontent if the opposition resorts to violence and the armed forces are too weak to respond. Armies that lose wars or experience battlefield humiliation are prone to such weaknesses. The Russian army is currently involved in two wars—in Ukraine and in Syria. Additional incursions, in the Baltic States or in Central Asia, may also be in the offing, as Putin tries to sow disarray within NATO and protect Russia from the Islamic State (also known as ISIS). Despite Russia's formidable advantages, the Russian war against Ukraine has ended, thus far, in the annexation of two economically destitute regions, Crimea and the eastern Donbas, with little hope of rapid recovery. More important, Moscow's New Russia project, which aimed at annexing all of Ukraine's southeast, has failed. In sum, despite several tactical victories, the Russian armed forces have suffered defeat.

Victory in Syria appears equally distant, even as the prospect of additional involvement grows. Sooner or later, Russia's humiliated and defeated soldiers and mercenaries will come home, and their anger is likely to be directed against the regime that sent them into losing fights. Domestic police and armed forces are unlikely to crack down on discontent soldiers. Complicating matters is the growing likelihood of renewed terrorism in Russia. Chechnya could easily blow up if Kadyrov is replaced in a local palace coup or assassinated by the Russian secret service, which reputedly detests him. Much of the north Caucasus is already in a state of half-open rebellion. Russia's Syrian adventure and its open alliance against Sunnis may not only exacerbate tensions with Russia's Sunni population, but also provoke ISIS to engage in terror in Russia proper.

How likely is it that armed forces might prove inadequate to quell discontent? The First Chechen War of 1994–96 demonstrates that the Russian armed forces can be defeated. The Ukrainian War demonstrates that the Russian army and mercenaries can be held at bay by a significantly weaker force. The series of terrorist actions that befell Russia in the early years of Putin's rule show that Russia is vulnerable to violent assaults. It is impossible to say just when anti-regime violence might break out, but the likelihood that it will grows as the political–economic system decays, and as mass disturbances and elite discontent rise.

After the Storm

Russia is on the edge of a perfect storm, as destabilizing forces converge. Under conditions such as these, mass disturbances are highly probable. Revolutions, palace coups, and violence will be increasingly likely. The result could be the collapse of the regime or the break-up of the state. Whatever the scenario, Putin is unlikely to survive.

What should the West and Russia's neighbors do? They cannot stop Putin and they cannot prevent Russia's disintegration, just as they could not prevent the USSR's disintegration. The best option is containing the damage that results from mass instability. In particular, they will have to worry about mass refugee flows, the spillover of violence, and the problem of loose nukes. The non-Russian states will be able to deal with the first two issues only by strengthening their own state borders, armies, police forces, and administrative apparatuses. The West must view them (Belarus, Ukraine, and Kazakhstan, in particular) as allies or client states whose stability and security are vital to the stability and security of the West. After that, the West should support a stable pro-Western democracy in what remains of post-Putin Russia. Western policymakers will be tempted to support the Russian armed forces, especially after mass instability breaks out. That would be counterproductive: In a lost cause, supporting the forces of coercion will only prolong the fighting, bloodshed, and instability and thereby increase the likelihood that loose nukes will fall into the wrong hands.

Sooner or later, Russia's time of troubles will end. After the dust settles, a smaller and weaker Russia and a host of newly independent non-Russian regions-turned-states might make for a more stable world, at least inasmuch as Putin's Russia, which has become a major threat to world peace, will have disappeared and rump Russia may finally abandon the imperial aspirations that enabled Putin to come to power.

Whatever the outcome, the best immediate guarantee of stability and security in the post-Putin, post-Soviet space will be Russia's current non-Russian neighbors, in particular, Ukraine, Kazakhstan, and Belarus. If they are strong, much of the damage will be contained. If they become weak, the damage will spread to the West. The best time to strengthen them is now—before the deluge.

*

Kissinger's Vapid Vision Thing, *Atlantic Council*, February 15, 2016

For more evidence of how badly Russian President Vladimir Putin has damaged the international order, look at former US Secretary of State Henry Kissinger's recently articulated "vision for US-Russia relations." It consists of large swaths of boilerplate language and several disingenuous arguments demonstrating that the architect of détente has no idea how to fix what Putin has broken.

Correctly, Kissinger says, "I do not need to tell you that our relations today are much worse than they were a decade ago. Indeed, they are probably the worst they have been since before the end of the Cold War. Mutual trust has been dissipated on both sides. Confrontation has replaced cooperation."

Heavy-duty boilerplate follows this opening statement, leading to the following utterly anodyne conclusion:

> Any effort to improve relations must include a dialogue about the emerging world order. What are the trends that are eroding the old order and shaping the new one? What challenges do the changes pose to both Russian and American national interests? ... I am here to argue for the possibility of a dialogue that seeks to merge our futures rather than elaborate our conflicts. This requires respect by both sides of the vital values and interest of the other. These goals cannot be completed in what remains of the current administration. But neither should their pursuits be postponed for American domestic politics. It will only come with a willingness in both Washington and Moscow, in the White House and the Kremlin, to move beyond the grievances and sense of victimization to confront the larger challenges that face both of our countries in the years ahead.

These are the kind of content-less recommendations that foundations and Hollywood celebrities like, and that no one in the real world formerly inhabited by Kissinger has much use for.

Worse yet are Kissinger's disingenuous arguments. For example, he says, "At the end of the Cold War ... Russian pride in their role in modernizing their society was tempered by discomfort at the transformation of their borders and recognition of the monumental tasks ahead in reconstruction and redefinition."

Just how the pathologies of central planning and Communist dictatorship represent modernization is unclear. Worse, Kissinger has his history wrong: few Russians were proud of the USSR at the end of the Cold War. Nor did they experience discomfort at the transformation of their borders: the borders that transformed were Soviet. The borders that remained untransformed were Russian.

Kissinger also writes, "The prevailing narrative in each country places full blame on the other side, and in each country there is a tendency to demonize, if not the other country, then its leaders. As national security issues dominate the dialogue, some of the mistrust and suspicions from the bitter Cold War struggle have reemerged. These feelings have been exacerbated in Russia by the memory of the first post-Soviet decade when Russia suffered a staggering socio-economic and political crisis, while the United States enjoyed its longest period of uninterrupted economic expansion."

Just how and why should memory of Russia's travails in the 1990s—which were the product of Mikhail Gorbachev's perestroika and the Soviet collapse it brought about—enhance mistrust and suspicion of the United States today? Kissinger's claim makes sense only if Russian memories are rooted in paranoia: the view that Russia's problems were brought about by the United States. Kissinger suggests that both sides' narratives are equally to blame. That's absurd: Americans may have misjudged Russia, but Russians fundamentally misunderstand the world.

Finally, he states that "Russia's historical experience is more complicated. To a country across which foreign armies have marched for centuries from both East and West, security will always need to have a geopolitical, as well as a legal, foundation. When its security border moves from the Elbe 1,000 miles east towards Moscow, Russia's perception of world order will contain an inevitable strategic component."

This is just plain silly. The last time foreign armies marched across Russia from the East was, well, never. Back in the thirteenth century, the Mongols attacked *Kyivan Rus*. At that time, Moscow was a provincial town and Russia wasn't even in existence. And just which foreign armies marched *across* Russia from the West? Hitler's and Napoleon's tried, but were smashed—by Russians, non-Russians, and the winter. Moreover, they did most of their marching and killing in Ukraine and Belarus. Sweden, Poland, and Lithuania fought Muscovy, but that was hundreds of years ago. Surely, Russian security fears don't extend to modern-day Sweden, Poland, and Lithuania, and if they do, is that evidence of historical astuteness or paranoia? Besides, Moscow dealt with its putative fears quite efficiently, dismembering Poland in 1939 and annexing Lithuania in 1940.

But the most inauthentic part of the whole essay is its studious avoidance of any reference to Putin. Kissinger desperately wants to root the current imperialistic behavior of Putin's Russia in Russian history. Fair enough, but to construct a "narrative" that ignores the man who has completely dominated Russian politics since 1999 is just too much. At the very minimum, it should be abundantly clear that, even if Russian behavior does have roots in history, it also has roots in Putin's will to power.

Small wonder that Kissinger's vision is so vapid. Having purposely elided one of the most important causes of the current troubles between Russia and the West, the best he can recommend is not a vision but, to quote President George W. Bush, a "vision thing." The best one can say about Kissinger's analysis is that it illustrates just how badly the man he refuses to mention has damaged the international security architecture.

*

Two Cheers for Cold War! *Atlantic Council*, March 2, 2016

Russian Prime Minister Dmitri Medvedev's recent suggestion that Russia and the West are embroiled in cold war provoked hasty denials by Western policymakers and commentators.

In fact, Medvedev was right: cold war between Russia and the West does exist. But the West's denials were unnecessary, because cold war is the best possible option for its relations with Russia.

Obviously, cold war is not the Cold War. The latter was waged between two superpowers—the United States and the Soviet Union. A second Cold War is impossible because Russia is an underdeveloped country with the bomb and is no match for the United States. Cold war, in contrast, is being waged and has been waged ever since Russian President Vladimir Putin destroyed Europe's post-war security architecture by invading Crimea and the Donbas in 2014.

Is cold war an ideal condition for the West's relations with Russia? Of course, not. That would be some variant of peace, whether hot or cold. But peace is not an option since Putin went to war in Ukraine. The only realistic alternative to cold war is thus hot war, or widespread armed hostilities between Russia and the West. Those may yet take place if Putin decides to test NATO's resolve in Estonia, provoke Turkey, or launch a full-scale invasion of Ukraine. Compared to hot war, however, the political, economic, diplomatic, and ideological hostility that characterize the current cold war is surely preferable.

And not just for the West. Ukraine, too, is currently enjoying a cold war relationship with Russia. Having stopped the Russian advance in the Donbas, Ukraine has effectively frozen the conflict and brought about a condition that is neither genuine peace nor full-scale war. Russian forces in the Donbas continue to shoot, and Ukrainians continue to die, but Russo-Ukrainian relations have moved from military hostility to political, economic, diplomatic, and ideological hostility.

Unfortunately, neither the West nor Ukraine can do much to move their relations with Russia from cold war to some variant of peace. Putin broke the peace, and only Putin can reinstate it. And there's little reason to believe he's interested in peace. For there to be hot peace, Putin would have to withdraw his troops from the Donbas, return Crimea to Ukraine, and embrace Kyiv, none of which seem likely. For there to be cold peace, Putin would have to recognize the legitimacy of Ukraine's government and stop destabilizing the country. That, too, is unlikely.

All the West and Ukraine can do is reduce the likelihood of Putin's going to war in the Baltic states or Ukraine. And that's exactly what they are doing. The United States and the European Union have imposed sanctions on Russia. NATO is beefing up its presence in Eastern Europe and Scandinavia. Russia's western neighbors are raising their military budgets and seeking to cooperate against possible Russian aggression. And Ukraine has, despite its minimal resources, built up one of Europe's most formidable armies in eighteen months.

Will these measures stop Putin? No one knows. On the one hand, he doesn't seem irrational, having refrained from embroiling Russia in a bloody occupation of Ukraine in the spring of 2014. On the other hand, he stupidly seized Crimea, thereby devastating its economy, and destroyed the Donbas, thereby harming the interests of Russia and the Russians in Ukraine he was claiming to defend. Putin's Syrian adventure doesn't offer any clear-cut evidence for rationality or irrationality either. True, he went in to defend Russia's ally. But that intervention will cost Russia—and Putin—dearly by involving Russian forces in a costly long-term occupation at a time of domestic economic decline, exposing them to the inevitable terrorist attacks, and sacrificing Moscow's relations with two strategically important Middle Eastern countries, Saudi Arabia and Turkey, to prolonging the Assad regime's death throes.

Putin remains a cypher. Worse, he cannot be trusted. Having happily destroyed the postwar security framework that kept Europe stable for so many decades, having threatened to use nuclear weapons to protect his realm, Putin has openly defined himself as a revisionist and a warmonger. Keeping his warmongering inclinations at bay is the best the West can achieve.

So two cheers for cold war! It's far from ideal, but also far better than the only realistic alternative.

*

Putin's Syria Gambit, *World Affairs Journal*, March 18, 2016

All the hullaballoo provoked by Vladimir Putin's surprise announcement of a Russian troop withdrawal from Syria misses two important points.

First, given that even Putin's inner circle in the Kremlin appears not to have known anything about his plans, the episode has reaffirmed the widespread belief that Putin makes all the strategic decisions in the Kremlin. Which is exactly what we would expect from a dictator who models his leadership style on Benito Mussolini's. Unconstrained by institutions or rules, Putin can invade Crimea, the Donbas, and Syria one day and announce a withdrawal from Syria the other. If he wanted to end the war against Ukraine, he could do so by declaring victory over the "Kyiv junta" and withdrawing his troops. That he chooses not to do so is less the result of a rational calculation of the war's costs and benefits for Russia than the product of his whim.

Not surprisingly, Putin keeps surprising the world—and, in all likelihood, himself. That's not leadership, and that's certainly not genius. That's authoritarian conceit.

Second, it's premature to proclaim that the announced withdrawal is a stroke of genius. After all, Putin's recent abrupt decisions have rarely turned out well. Indeed, many look downright stupid. Take, for example, Putin's annexation of Crimea and the destruction of the Donbas. At first, Russians applauded—and some still do. But outside analysts and astute Russians know these foreign adventures have given Russia—and Putin—exactly zero benefits. The contrary is poorer, most of the world regards it as a rogue, and Ukraine has moved westward. What has Russia gained? An impoverished peninsula and 35,000 well-armed proxies in the Donbas.

Likewise, by intervening on Assad's behalf, Putin raised Russia's diplomatic stature in authoritarian circles. And if Assad survives, if the peace talks work, if the Syrian opposition cooperates, and if ISIS refrains from taking advantage of the Russian withdrawal, Putin will look good.

Consider four other ifs. If, as is likely, the peace talks bog down; and if, as is likely, the opposition reinforces its positions; and if, as is likely, ISIS attempts to regain lost ground, trumpets the withdrawal as a Russian humiliation, wins more recruits, and launches terror strikes against Russia; and if, as is likely, Assad's hold on power becomes tenuous once again—then Putin will be forced to re-invade or let Syria collapse. Even his authoritarian admirers will think twice about his smarts.

In sum, Putin's move isn't a checkmate, but an extremely risky rook sacrifice. If everybody plays poorly, he wins. If everybody plays just adequately, he loses—big.

I'm betting that the announced withdrawal will be far less of a triumph than the pundits now predict. Perhaps because they're jaded by the ordinariness of American politics, they are confusing rashness for brilliance.

*

Putin Celebrates Unrepentant Fascist Zhirinovsky, *World Affairs Journal*, April 25, 2016

This time, Vladimir Putin has out-Putined himself.

On April 18, Russia's erratic, though consistently anti-democratic, leader **awarded** the Russian Federation's prestigious "For Service to the Fatherland Order, Class II," to none other than Vladimir Zhirinovsky.

Zhirinovsky, who is the head of the bizarrely named Liberal Democratic Party of Russia, has been an unabashed promoter of Russian illiberalism, fascism, and imperialism since he first made a splash in the Duma elections of 1993, when his party garnered 23 percent of the vote.

Zhirinovsky has never minced his words. To his credit, he's never pretended to be anything but an imperialist and a fascist. Indeed, he's been so brazen, so outrageous, and so unapologetic that not even Putin Russia's most ardent Western apologists apologize for him.

Here's a classic Zhirinovsky statement threatening Eastern Europe with war, from August 2014:

> Poland—the Baltics—they are on the whole doomed. They'll be wiped out. There will be nothing left. Let them re-think this, these leaders of these little dwarf

states. How they are leaving themselves vulnerable. Nothing threatens America, it's far away. But Eastern Europe countries will place themselves under the threat of total annihilation. Only they themselves will be to blame. Because we cannot allow missiles and planes to be aimed at Russia from their territories. We have to destroy them half an hour before they launch. And then we have to do carpet bombing so that not a single launch pad remains or even one plane. So—no Baltics, no Poland.

Not enough? Here's one more, from June 4, 2015, aimed at Odessa Governor Mikheil Saakashvili and Putin's Ukrainian political prisoner, Nadia Savchenko:

We will shoot all your governors starting with Saakashvili, then they'll be afraid, and there will be a different situation in Europe and Ukraine. ... Let's aim at Berlin, Brussels, London, and Washington, then they'll agree and will promise to leave us alone. ... Shoot this Savchenko tomorrow and hang her in Belgrade.

By awarding the honor to Zhirinovsky, Putin not only legitimizes his ISIS-like barbarism, he endorses it. And by awarding the honor for Zhirinovsky's "great contribution to the development of Russian parliamentarism and his active law-making work" (sic!), Putin repudiates liberalism, rule of law, democracy, and every international norm known to the civilized world—openly and unconditionally.

For Putin's critics, this is no surprise. They've never had any illusions about his politics. For Putin's Western apologists, the award is a moment of truth. If they fail to repudiate Putin's celebration of barbarism, they will have effectively endorsed Zhirinovsky and his declaration of war on the West and its values. Both Donald Trump and Germany's foreign minister, Frank-Walter Steinmeier, should remember that their knee-jerk Putinophilia is a rejection of everything the West represents. Russian recipients of the award—many of whom are respectable scholars, artists, and policymakers—face a similar choice.

The award to Zhirinovsky is important for another reason. His inclusion in his "Fatherland's" political pantheon suggests that Russian political culture and geopolitical thinking are perfectly compatible with, and perhaps even supportive of, his extremist views. Zhirinovsky's exaltation may mean that imperialism, illiberalism, and authoritarianism, if not downright fascism, are central to Russia's perceptions of itself and its place in the world.

That's exactly what realists such as former Secretary of State Henry Kissinger and University of Chicago political scientist John Mearsheimer believe. Similarly, Princeton University historian Stephen Kotkin argues that Putin's foreign policy is a continuation of the traditional Muscovite imperial behavior of Peter the Great and Alexander I. Since their Russia will always be imperialist, aggressive, and authoritarian, Western policy can either appease it or go to war.

My own view is that the neo-fascist Putin regime's policies of oppression at home and aggression abroad are the result of his determination to rebuild a Russian empire. The goal of US and Western policy should therefore be to contain Putin the dictator and wait for his regime's inevitable demise. As negative as it sounds, my view is optimistic, resting on the hopeful assumption that Russians can be democratic and that Russia can and eventually will change.

*

Karaganov Shows Pathology of Putin's Realism, *World Affairs Journal*, July 21, 2016

Sometimes, Vladimir Putin snarls and reveals his true self to the world. More often than not, one of his minions shows his teeth. This time, it was Sergey Karaganov's turn to terrify the world with a short interview in the German weekly, *Der Spiegel*.

Karaganov is no bit player. Here's how *Der Spiegel* identifies him: "Sergey Karaganov, 63, is honorary head of the influential Council on Foreign and Defense Policy, which develops geopolitical strategy concepts for Russia. ... Karaganov is an advisor to Vladimir Putin's presidential administration and deacon of the elite Moscow college National Research University Higher School of Economics."

In a word, Karaganov is speaking for Putin. And what he has to say reveals the full and frightening extent of the Putin regime's chauvinism, imperialism, and paranoia.

Large parts of the interview sound reasonable, even if imbued with fundamental misunderstandings of reality. Thus, Karaganov's claims about NATO enlargement could easily have been made by former Secretary of State Henry Kissinger or University of Chicago political scientist John Mearsheimer: "We warned NATO against approaching the borders of Ukraine because that would create a situation that we cannot accept." Indeed, it's no accident that the print version of the interview features a photograph of Karaganov standing next to a prominently displayed copy of Kissinger's *Diplomacy*. The message should be clear: Karaganov, like his boss, is just a hard-nosed realist.

Fair enough, but, while the realism of Kissinger and Mearsheimer is based on logic and a lamentable ignorance of Ukraine and its relationship with Russia, Karaganov's is based on logic, Russian megalomania and paranoia, and a lamentable ignorance of reality. Scratch beneath the polished surface of Karaganov's realism and you encounter a crazy Russian nationalism that threatens world peace while propagating world salvation.

If Karaganov restricted his comments to the claim that NATO enlargement was a threat to Russian security, one could let him slide. But he genuinely appears to believe that NATO wants war with Russia. That's absurd for so many reasons. For starters, that conclusion is based on a profoundly illogical leap—from the claim that NATO is a security threat to the claim that NATO wants war. That's a *non sequitur*, as Karaganov should have learned in high school. Moreover, if anybody knows the true condition of NATO, it has to be Karaganov. He must know that, ever since the end of the Cold War, NATO has been without mission and vision, and that its member states have utterly failed to modernize their armed forces. NATO has about as much ability to mount a war against Russia as Ukraine.

How then is it possible for a hard-nosed realist such as Karaganov to entertain the absurd idea that NATO is ready, willing, and able to embark on war with Russia? Consider in this light Hitler's views of Jews. There is no way that one can rationally argue that Jews posed a threat to Germany. And yet, it is unquestionably true that Hitler sincerely believed them to be a threat. Why? Because of his peculiar psychology and his crazy ideology. So, too, with Karaganov—as with Putin—fear of NATO is grounded, not in any empirical reality, but in the megalomaniac, paranoid perceptions of the current Russian elite.

Hence such statements by Karaganov: "you have to understand that Russia is very sensitive about defense. We have to be prepared for everything." (Everything? Really? Including a nuclear attack by France or an invasion by Finland?) And especially this: "we want the status of being a great power: We unfortunately cannot relinquish that. In the last 300 years, this status has become a part of our genetic makeup. We want to be the heart of greater Eurasia, a region of peace and cooperation. The subcontinent of Europe will also belong to this Eurasia."

Read these lines carefully. On the one hand, Karaganov clearly suffers from a superiority complex, as his talk of great power status being part of the Russian genetic makeup suggests. On the other hand, despite this megalomania, he's absolutely terrified of the world, as his talk of sensitivity reveals.

Both pathologies are manifestly evident in the following exchange:

> SPIEGEL: Russian politicians, including President Vladimir Putin, are trying to convince their population that the West wants war in order to fragment Russia. But that's absurd.

> Karaganov: Certainly there has been some exaggeration. But American politicians have openly said that the sanctions are aimed at bringing about regime change in Russia. That's aggressive enough.

In Karaganov's twisted universe, as in Putin's, mere talk by Westerners of regime change—by ballot, after all, and not by force of arms—in Russia is, evidently, equivalent to a declaration of war against Russia. Note that this equivalence rests on another equivalence: that Putin is Russia.

Small wonder that the West in general and Russia's neighbors are terrified of Putin, Karaganov, and the psychological and ideological pathologies that define them. In effect, Karaganov is promising to subordinate them to Russia's will.

After all, what else but subordination could Karaganov have in mind when he says: "We want to be the heart of greater Eurasia, a region of peace and cooperation. The subcontinent of Europe will also belong to this Eurasia."

Karaganov's greater Eurasia will be Putin Russia writ large, and the subcontinent of

Europe will be transformed into Putin's fiefdom. That is the peace and cooperation of the Gulag.

*

Sloppy Thinking about War Helps No One, *Atlantic Council*, August 2, 2016

How likely is a war between the United States and Russia?

According to Matthew Rojansky, director of the Wilson Center's Kennan Institute, in a recent *World Politics Review* article, "a war between Russia and the United States is more likely today than at any time since the worst years of the Cold War."

That's strong language. If Rojansky is right, we should all be starting to worry.

Except that Rojansky isn't right. More exactly, the point he makes rests on conceptual slipperiness—which means that his argument is incoherent. That matters. Sloppy language breeds sloppy thinking, and sloppy thinking makes for lousy policymaking.

Read Rojansky's article carefully and you'll notice that none of it, absolutely none of it, deals with war—if by war you mean a large-scale military conflict involving thousands of casualties. Indeed, after the above lead sentence about the likelihood of war, Rojansky continues as follows:

> This may sound implausible or exaggerated to policymakers, journalists, and the wider public. Yet the fact remains that increasing deployments by both sides, coupled with severely constrained direct dialogue, mean that dangerous incidents will become far more likely and will be far harder to defuse and deescalate.

As that quotation makes clear, Rojansky is concerned with "dangerous incidents" such as "recent 'near-miss' incidents at sea and in the air, most notoriously in April, when a Russian fighter buzzed the USS Donald Cook in the Baltic Sea, passing just thirty feet above the ship's deck."

Rojansky is probably right to conclude that "it is only a matter of time before more such dangerous incidents between Russian and US or NATO forces occur." And he may also be right to say, "The question then will be how well-equipped both sides are to manage the consequences. Judging by the state of the relationship overall, the answer is not very well at all."

Policymakers in both Washington and Moscow should heed Rojansky's call for better mechanisms for dealing with dangerous incidents. But should they really be worried about war?

The answer, alas, is yes, but for none of the reasons that Rojansky gives.

For starters, it should be obvious that the difference between a dangerous incident and a war is enormous. They are profoundly different things, and to suggest, as Rojansky does, that incidents will automatically escalate into wars is at best disingenuous. At worst, it's egregiously careless thinking that, if heeded, would result in bizarre policies that may put too much attention on incidents and too little on the real reasons for wars.

Incidents don't lead to wars, unless both sides are already bracing for a fight or one side is looking for a pretext to start a fight. Therefore, only one question really matters: are both sides bracing for a real fight, or is one side looking for a pretext to start a real fight?

Is the West in general and the United States in particular bracing for war with Russia? Even if you accept the paranoid Russian view of the world and believe that NATO is a monstrously aggressive, anti-Russian alliance, you'd be hard-pressed to argue that official Brussels or Washington or Berlin or Paris actually wants war with Russia.

Which leaves us with the other question: Is Russia bracing for war or looking for a pretext to start one?

Rojansky repeatedly implies that America and Russia are equally responsible for the lack of mechanisms for managing the relationship. But he obviously knows, or must know, that all the dangerous incidents he referred to were caused by Russian planes, ships, or submarines. That may or may not prove that Russia harbors warlike intentions, but it definitely does not prove that America does.

More important, Russia has initiated two wars in Europe, the region of the world where Russian and American interests most overlap. The first was in Georgia in 2008; the second, still going on, was in Ukraine in 2014.

Even if you believe that both wars were started in response to NATO enlargement and the CIA's manipulation of colored revolutions, the fact is that Russia started both, demonstrating at the very least that Russia is perfectly capable of starting and fighting wars in Europe.

Does this mean that Russia is therefore preparing for a war against America or Europe? Not necessarily. But it does suggest that Western worries about the possibility of a Russian-initiated war are not irrational.

Which brings me to my last point: Putin's rationality and the nature of the Putin regime. Rojansky treats him and his American interlocutors as normal, rational, run-of-the-mill statesmen who should pursue confidence-building and crisis-reduction measures. He also assiduously avoids any mention of the profoundly authoritarian, hyper-centralized, repressive, and possibly fascist system constructed by Putin.

But leaders and domestic systems affect the foreign-policy behaviors of states. Irrationally inclined, hyper-masculine leaders with cults of personality are not particularly known for their pacific behavior. And authoritarian states are intrinsically more inclined to rattle sabers and start wars than democratic ones.

Western leaders should therefore fear war with Putin's Russia. They should do everything they can to reduce the likelihood that dangerous incidents escalate. But, above all, they should do everything possible to contain Putin and bolster the defensive capacity of the frontline states: the Balts, Belarus, Ukraine, Georgia, and Kazakhstan. That may sound like cold war, but it's infinitely preferable to Putin's proven penchant for hot war.

*

Why Peace Is Impossible with Putin, *Atlantic Council*, August 15, 2016

Peace in Europe is impossible as long as Vladimir Putin remains Russia's leader. As both the biggest obstacle to peace and the key source of potential war, Putin has become the main threat to Russia's neighbors and the West. But what, exactly, motivates him?

Analysts are divided over the reasons for Putin's foreign policy moves. Some see them as being grounded in his realist fears of Western strategic encirclement. Others root them in his authoritarian regime and imperialist ideology. Putin's most striking feature, however, is his unpredictability. Were his foreign policy grounded in some discernible logic, his moves would be predictable and *ex post facto* explicable. But his ability to constantly surprise his domestic constituents and the world demonstrates that his moves are not grounded in any one logic or strategy.

To the contrary, they appear to be rooted in his personal whims. As Russia's undisputed dictator, he can do whatever he decides is right, regardless of whether it promotes Russia's interests or harms those of his perceived enemies. In this sense, Putin is the twenty-first century's Hitler—a tyrant who solipsistically defines rationality in terms of his own shifting understanding of the concept.

Russia's recent military build-up and saber-rattling on Ukraine's borders are a case in point. Do they portend war? Are they merely intended to intimidate? No one knows, and every interpretation is pure speculation about what is really going on in Putin's head.

The same holds true for Putin's latest provocation: the supposed neutralization of groups of Ukrainian terrorists in Crimea by the Russian security service. Putin's claim that Kyiv is now resorting to terrorism follows directly from his earlier characterization of Ukraine's post-Viktor Yanukovych democratic government as fascist. Is the provocation a prelude to an all-out attack along the lines of Hitler's after the notorious Gleiwitz incident of 1939, in which German commandos dressed as Poles attacked a German border radio station? Or is it intended to scare Russians into supporting Putin's party in the September parliamentary elections? Or is the provocation a signal to the West and Kyiv that Putin is angry and will lash out? No one knows, and it's not inconceivable that even Putin does not know.

Is Putin rational? The answer depends on what is meant by rationality. If rationality means doing the morally right thing, then Putin is rational only in some twisted, immoral world. If rationality entails finding the best means to enhance one's ends, however disreputable they might be, then Putin must qualify as deeply, disturbingly irrational. After all, has Russia's power and status in the world increased since Putin went on the warpath against Ukraine? Has its economic standing improved? Has his own position become stronger? Putin almost certainly would answer yes to each of these questions (Germany's Führer also believed that final victory was at hand, even as his country was ablaze), but a dispassionate analysis would suggest the opposite is true.

Finally, if rationality entails understanding the relationship between actions and consequences, between causes and effects, then Putin must qualify as irrational—not because he gets that relationship wrong, but because he appears to believe that actions have no consequences and causes have no effects. Hence, his unpredictability.

The comparison with Hitler is strong stuff, of course, but it's high time Western policymakers realize that they are dealing with a man who could blithely start a world war because his position of supreme power for close to two decades has led him to believe that he is Russia. What the eighteenth century Scottish philosopher David Hume once said about rationality applies with full force to Putin: it is "not contrary to reason to prefer the destruction of the whole world to the scratching of my finger." Indeed, the fact that a full-scale military assault against Ukraine, Belarus, or Estonia appears to make no sense is precisely why Putin could do it.

While one must negotiate with irrational leaders, the only thing that can keep them in check—possibly—is preparedness. Their promises are as meaningless as their declarations of peace, and appeasement only whets their appetites. Only a strong military and a determined policy of containment has any chance of keeping them in bounds.

German Social Democrats like to say that security in Europe is impossible without Russia. That may be true. But so, too, is the claim that peace in Europe is impossible with Putin. He will have to go, one way or another, for peace-loving Europeans to breathe easier again.

*

Eastern Europe Must Prepare for the Worst about Trump, *Atlantic Council*, November 22, 2016

President Barack Obama's advice to the world that it shouldn't "assume the worst" about Donald Trump may apply to countries whose existential interests cannot be threatened by the president-elect's policies, but those that face a possible Russian invasion must as-sume and prepare for the worst.

They cannot, as Obama recommended, "wait until the administration is in place" and then "make your judgments as to whether or not it's consistent with the international community's interest in living in peace and prosperity together."

Russian President Vladimir Putin's tanks could be on the outskirts of Estonian capital Tallinn by then.

No one knows what the Trump administration's foreign policy will be. That said, his extreme disregard for the European Union, NATO, NAFTA, the WTO, and international law and his continual trumpeting of American interests suggest that, at best, he may be indifferent to Putin's aggression in Eastern Europe or, at worst, he may even facilitate it by encouraging Russia to establish a sphere of influence.

The Baltic states are the most vulnerable to complete takeover, since they lack the military power to deter Russia and, without American support of NATO, could not rely on the Alliance's intervention in case of a Russian attack. Their only hope is to prepare for an extended occupation and underground resistance along the lines of the anti-Russian nationalist movements that were active in all three states in the aftermath of World War II. Small wonder that Lithuania has recently issued a manual on what to do if Russia invades.

Belarus is next in terms of vulnerability. Russia already has troops stationed in the country and a large portion of Belarus's Russian minority would probably welcome a Russian seizure. Belarusian President Aleksandr Lukashenka has stated that his country would resist, but, lacking combat experience and being of uncertain loyalty, the Belarusian armed forces might not be able to stop a Russian attack. An underground partisan movement modelled after the one that inflicted severe damage on the Germans in World War II is likely and, if coordinated with the Baltic movements, could make for a very costly occupation.

Ukraine is least vulnerable to a conventional attack, because the ongoing war with Russia has enabled Kyiv to build up a serious army that has proven its mettle in the fighting in the Donbas. Russia could launch a full-scale attack against Ukraine, of course, but that would require the mobilization of most of its army and the application of massive air power. Even then, it's hardly clear that Ukraine's soldiers and population would roll over.

Ukraine's real vulnerability is less military than political. Imagine that Trump and Putin agree to the following deal: The United States recognizes Russia's annexation of Crimea and, in return, Russia withdraws its armed forces and economic assistance from the occupied Donbas, essentially bequeathing the devastated territory, its impoverished and alienated population, and tens of thousands of heavily armed separatists to Ukraine. Ukraine would be hard-pressed to say no, especially as regaining the occupied Donbas has been a central feature of Kyiv's official rhetoric since 2014.

Reintegrating such a Donbas would amount to the end of Ukraine's reforms, pro-Western leanings, and democracy. Moreover, it would bankrupt the government, polarize the population, and destabilize the state. Putin, with Trump's assistance, would have succeeded in destroying Ukraine without losing a single Russian soldier in the process.

These worst-case scenarios may not materialize, but Belarus, Estonia, Latvia, Lithuania, and Ukraine do not have the luxury of waiting for the post-election dust in America to settle and then figuring out what to do. They must prepare for the very worst immediately. The Balts and Belarusians must prepare for extended guerrilla warfare. The Ukrainians must develop a Plan B, in case Putin decides to transform the occupied Donbas into a Trojan horse.

Europe, or what remains of the entity in a Trumpian world, must come to grips with the possibility that, within a year or two, Russian tanks could be stationed on the European Union's eastern borders, waves of desperate Eastern European refugees could seek asylum in the EU, and Russia, militarily overextended and economically weak, could be on the brink of collapse.

All thanks to Trump.

PART FIVE
HISTORY, LANGUAGE, AND NATIONAL IDENTITY

Stepan Bandera: Hero of Ukraine? *Moscow Times*, March 15, 2010

Former Ukrainian President Viktor Yushchenko's decision to confer the title of Hero of Ukraine on nationalist leader Stepan Bandera on Jan. 22 has unleashed a storm of outrage inside and outside Ukraine. Critics accuse Yushchenko of whitewashing a Nazi-era fascist and betraying the ideals of the Orange Revolution that brought him to power.

Some hint darkly at a resurgence of fascism in Ukraine.

As always, the reality is more complicated. Just who was Bandera and what does he represent?

Bandera headed the Organization of Ukrainian Nationalists, a nationalist movement that emerged in 1929 and took root in the Ukrainian-inhabited lands of eastern Poland in the 1930s. Neither Bandera nor the Organization of Ukrainian Nationalists was fascist, although both had fascist inclinations—particularly in 1940 and 1941. Fascists run or aspire to run existing nations. Nationalists, in contrast, aspire to create nations. Fascists are always authoritarians and chauvinists; nationalists can be liberals, democrats, Communists, authoritarians, or fascists. Nationalists and fascists sometimes look alike, especially to conceptually challenged analysts, but their differences are greater than their similarities.

Like the Algerian nationalists in the National Liberation Front, the Palestinian nationalists in the Palestine Liberation Organization or the Jewish nationalists in the Irgun, the Ukrainian nationalists were unconditionally committed to national liberation and independent statehood. All four movements had hierarchical structures, authoritarian leanings and strong leaders and engaged in violence and terrorism against their perceived enemies. Bandera was the Ukrainian version of Palestinian leader Yassir Arafat, not Adolf Hitler.

Bandera hoped for an alliance with Nazi Germany against the Soviet Union. But the Nazis failed to oblige, cracking down on the nationalists in mid-1941, imprisoning Bandera in Sachsenhausen and inadvertently saving him and his supporters from a collaborationist and possibly fascist fate. In the years that followed, the nationalists did fight both the Germans and the Soviets, but they also fought and killed thousands of Poles and participated in anti-Jewish actions. The nationalists abandoned their fascist leanings in the mid-1940s and then spearheaded a vicious anti-Soviet struggle through the mid-1950s. Bandera himself was assassinated by a Soviet agent in Munich in 1959.

Soviet propaganda always demonized the nationalists—not for their violations of human rights, of course, but because of their unconditional opposition to Stalinist rule. By the same token, Russians picked up on official cues and frequently insulted Ukrainians who dared to speak their own language or show any signs of nationalist pride by referring to them derogatorily as "Banderas."

When the Soviet Union collapsed in 1991, all the newly independent states began questioning the Soviet historical narrative and constructing their own histories. What Soviet historians had assiduously ignored or distorted became the object of research, discussion and debate. The term Russian chauvinists had used derogatorily—"Banderas"—became a term of praise, much in the way that blacks appropriated the "N-word."

For many Russians, the quest for historical memory meant accepting Stalin and Stalinism as qualified goods. For non-Russians, the quest for historical memory became inextricably connected to the search for an anti-Soviet identity. The former Soviet republics have focused on the violent, forced conditions under which they were incorporated into the Russian Empire or the Soviet Union, as well as the destruction they experienced under Lenin and Stalin, the repression and stagnation they experienced under Nikita Khrushchev and Leonid Brezhnev and the opportunity for freedom they seized under Mikhail Gorbachev.

For Ukrainians, these discoveries were particularly painful. The Communist Party had done a particularly thorough job of destroying Ukrainian historical memory, but at the same time Ukraine experienced astounding human losses in the first half of the 20th century. Unsurprisingly, Ukrainian historians centered on the Great Famine of 1932–1933, the Holodomor, which took some 4 million lives. Although the issue of whether the Holodomor should be classified as "genocide" has always been debatable, the tide has recently shifted. The emerging consensus is that the famine was part of Stalin's deliberate campaign against Ukrainians.

Attention also centered on the villains of Soviet propaganda—Bandera and the nationalists. Most Ukrainian historians are actually quite objective in their treatment of the movement, seeing both its virtues and all too many sins. Contemporary Ukrainian nationalists who lionize Bandera generally do so because he represents an unconditional devotion to Ukrainian independence and rejection of all things Soviet. Putin's attempts to undermine Ukraine's sovereignty only enhanced Bandera's attractiveness among Ukrainian nationalists.

Of course, this brief reading of Ukrainian history is one-sided, and a full account would entail both the good and the bad things that Bandera did. But one-sided readings are not unusual, especially among insecure nations struggling to retain their newfound independence. In their national narratives, Algerians overlook the massacres of French by Algerian nationalists, Palestinians overlook the violence against Israelis, and Israelis overlook the expulsion of Palestinians. Even self-confident Americans remember President Harry Truman for his successful conclusion of World War II, conveniently downplaying the controversial decision to drop atomic bombs on Hiroshima and Nagasaki.

Bandera became especially popular as the noble ideals of the 2004 Orange Revolution were progressively tarnished by the heroes of that revolution, Yushchenko and Prime Minister Yulia Tymoshenko. The more unpopular Yushchenko became, the more he promoted Bandera and the nationalists in the hope that some of their idealistic glow would rub off on him. Unfortunately, Yushchenko's ill-considered conferral of Hero of Ukraine status on Bandera threw a wrench into a more or less even-tempered discussion of the nationalists and their legacy. Yushchenko's critics—among them Putin and other top Russian officials who have indirectly rehabilitated Stalin—added fuel to the fire with their irresponsible accusations of fascism. At this point, a sensible discussion is almost impossible in the highly-politicized atmosphere surrounding Bandera.

The objective, even-handed accounts of Ukrainian historians, who see Bandera in all his complexity, will eventually seep into the public realm, but only after Ukrainian identity is consolidated and Ukrainian fears of a neo-imperial Russia subside. Ukrainian President Viktor Yanukovych could promote this shift by unifying the country around a common identity and history, vigorously protecting Ukrainian interests vis-à-vis Moscow and eschewing Yushchenko's proclivity for provocation. Europe could help by opening its doors to Ukraine, and Russia can assist by rejecting Stalinism. And we should not forget about Western historians in this equation, who can do their part by refraining from simple-minded analyses.

*

Deleting the Holodomor: Ukraine Unmakes Itself, *World Affairs Journal*, September 1, 2010

The first thing Ukrainian President Viktor Yanukovych did after his February 25 inauguration was delete the link to the Holodomor on the president's official Web site. Yanukovych's predecessor, Viktor Yushchenko, had made the Holodomor—the famine of 1932–1933 produced by Joseph Stalin and responsible for the deaths of millions of Ukrainian peasants—into a national issue, promoting what Czech novelist Milan Kundera famously called "the struggle of memory over forgetting" as part of his attempt to move the country toward democracy. That Yanukovych turned his back so dramatically on this movement to rehabilitate Ukraine's tragic past indicated the extent to which the recent election was as much about identity as it was about politics.

This was no accident. Thanks to the 2004 Orange Revolution, Ukrainian national identity has become synonymous with democracy and the West. And thanks to Vladimir Putin's construction of a newly assertive Russian state, Russian identity has unfortunately become associated, as in Soviet times, with authoritarianism and empire. Yanukovych's Party of Regions has its electoral base in Ukraine's southeastern rust belt, the Donbas; the region produced, and is still proud of, both Communist Party leader Leonid Brezhnev and Stalin's favorite proletarian, the coal miner extraordinaire Aleksei Stakhanov. It names its streets after Stalinists, displays statues of the Soviet dictator, and retains its Soviet-era identity as a Russian-speaking enclave with an authoritarian political culture. When president-elect Yanukovych decided to turn back the clock on Yushchenko's Ukraine and reestablish its role as a client of Moscow, it was natural that he should begin by shutting down discussion of what historian Robert Conquest called Stalin's "terror famine."

Yanukovych's assault on Ukrainian identity, newly resurgent following the Orange Revolution, has focused on education, culture, language, and history. Various policy measures have already begun to squeeze the authentically Ukrainian out of public life, education, and media. University rectors have been co-opted into supporting the new, Russocentric regime, while the only two holdouts—from the pro-Western Ukrainian Catholic University in Lviv and the Mohyla Academy in Kyiv—have come under pressure from the authorities. But the central target of the regime's rollback of Ukrainian identity is history. As Yanukovych well knows, all new nations develop identities based on their understanding of history. Foundation myths, heroes, villains, defeats, and victories are identified—and sometimes invented—so as to create "narratives" that have implications for contemporary political movements. Americans glorify the Founding Fathers, while the French lionize their first revolution. Germans moved from sanctifying Otto von Bismarck to admiring Konrad Adenauer after the catastrophe of the Third Reich. So, too, have Ukrainians in the last twenty years been developing a distinctly Ukrainian historical narrative as part of their slow-motion embrace of democracy and the West.

Any attempt to construct a distinctly Ukrainian identity must inevitably address the recent past. Ukraine today remains largely a product of the terror, violence, war, and genocide of Russian tsars, Soviet Communists, and German Nazis. A 2008 study by the Moscow-based Institute of Demography calculated that Ukraine suffered close to 15 million "excess deaths" from 1914 to 1948: 1.3 million during World War I; 2.3 million during the Russian Civil War and the Polish-Soviet War of the early 1920s; 4 million during the Holodomor; 300,000 during the Great Terror and annexation of western Ukraine; 6.5 million during World War II; and 400,000 during the post-war famine and Stalin's campaign against Ukrainian nationalism.

According to Yale University historian Timothy Snyder, "The peoples of Ukraine and Belarus, Jews above all but not only, suffered the most, since these lands were both part of the Soviet Union during the terrible 1930s and subject to the worst of the German repressions in the 1940s. If Europe was, as [Columbia University historian] Mark Mazower put it, a dark continent, Ukraine and Belarus were the heart of darkness." That darkness continued until Stalin's death in 1953. Although everyday violence disappeared and the death camps were disbanded, totalitarianism as a system of pervasive, oppressive rule stayed intact for three more decades, surviving long enough to mold a new type of human being. What Soviet propaganda called "the new Soviet man" is precisely the voter who supports Yanukovych and Putin, yearns for the good old days of Soviet greatness and cheap vodka, overlooks Stalin's crimes against humanity, and cannot imagine Ukraine as having an identity different, or separate, from Russia's.

As the excess deaths suggest, however, the Holodomor's "murder by starvation" remains the single greatest catastrophe endured by Ukraine during Soviet rule. Any attempt to reconstruct a national Ukrainian narrative must take a stand on a trauma of such proportions—especially since all Soviet historians, propagandists, and officials assiduously ignored the famine or dismissed it as an émigré delusion for decades. Unsurprisingly, the first Ukrainians to draw attention to the tragedy of the Holodomor were survivors who had fled to the West. In the mid-1950s, they compiled two major volumes of survivor testimony and other documentary materials called *The Black Deeds of the Kremlin: A White Book*. They were dismissed as rabid anti-Communists and cold warriors by much of the Western political and intellectual establishment. They continued their efforts in the decades that followed, but with very little resonance outside their own immediate émigré communities.

Things began changing by the early 1980s. Soviet studies had discovered the "nationality question," and academic research increasingly shifted to the USSR's non-Russian republics, including Ukraine. At the same time, "revisionist" social historians were reassessing Stalin and investigating the origins of Stalinism in the early 1930s. As the fiftieth anniversary of the famine in 1983 approached, it became impossible for Western scholars not to recognize the tragedy. Some continued to view it as the consequence of Stalin's policy of forced collectivization of the peasantry. Others insisted that it was not just a by-product of agricultural policy gone haywire, but a conscious political act that had to be viewed in the context of Stalin's vicious crackdown on Ukrainian national identity.

In 1986, the Ukrainian Research Institute at Harvard University published Robert Conquest's pathbreaking *The Harvest of Sorrow*, the first systematic scholarly study of the Holodomor as a weapon of Stalin's terror. In 1988, the American historian James Mace, who explicitly argued that the famine was an anti-Ukrainian measure, compiled three volumes of documentation and testimony in the U.S. Commission on the Ukraine Famine, a report delivered to Congress. Conquest and Mace were denounced as anti-Communists, but this effort to marginalize their work was subverted by Mikhail Gorbachev's *glasnost* policy, which exposed many black holes in Soviet history to scrutiny not only by Russians but also by Ukrainians and other non-Russians. Once Soviet historians began examining the horrors of the Soviet past and concluding that Stalin was a monster, the famine could no longer be claimed to be a conspiracy of Western anti-Communists and disgruntled Ukrainian émigrés.

Following Ukraine's independence in 1991, the quest for a distinctly Ukrainian historical narrative and identity took on a new urgency, especially as Ukraine became open to Western intellectual debates and testimony by the remnants of the generation that had survived the famine. As the number of books and articles published in Ukraine about the Holodomor grew exponentially, it became an established historical reality: today almost no one denies that a terrible human tragedy took place and that millions died. But while the issue of whether or not the Holodomor happened was settled, the question of *why* it happened developed into an even more contentious issue argued by two opposing camps. Following in the footsteps of James Mace (who settled in Kyiv, where he continued to write about the Holodomor until his untimely death in 2004), Ukrainian national democrats generally argued that the famine was a genocide. Their pro-Soviet, pro-Russian, and anti-democratic opponents, most of whom eventually grouped around Yanukovych and the Party of Regions, rejected this claim and the idea that the famine had been explicitly anti-Ukrainian in favor of the more anodyne view that, as Yanukovych's minister of education and science, Dmitri Tabachnik, succinctly put it, "the Holodomor of 1933 was a general tragedy of the peoples of Ukraine, Russia, Belarus, and Kazakhstan."

Reflecting the time lag between Ukrainian and Western intellectual currents, Ukrainians began debating the Holodomor-as-genocide thesis just as Western scholars were moving to accept it. A recently discovered 1953 speech by Raphael Lemkin, the Jewish-Polish scholar who coined the term genocide, contributed to the shift in the debate; Stalin's famine, he said, was "not simply a case of mass murder" but "a case of genocide, of destruction, not of individuals only, but of a culture and a nation." According to Lemkin, the Ukrainian genocide consisted of four components: "The first blow [was] aimed at the intelligentsia, the national brain, so as to paralyze the rest of the body." The second was "an offensive against the churches, priests, and hierarchy, the 'soul' of Ukraine. ... The third prong of the Soviet plan was aimed at the farmers, the large mass of independent peasants who are the repository of the tradition, folk lore and music, the national language and literature, the national spirit, of Ukraine. The weapon used against this body is perhaps the most terrible of all, starvation. ... The fourth step in the process consisted in the fragmentation of the Ukrainian people ... by the addition to the Ukraine of foreign peoples and by the dispersion of the Ukrainians throughout Eastern Europe."

Just as the earlier debates in the West over the famine had been politicized, pitting "anti-Communists" against their critics, so too did the debate over the Holodomor-as-genocide thesis in Ukraine become profoundly political. First, it challenged the nature of Soviet reality. Second, it became the centerpiece of Yushchenko's nation-building project after the Orange Revolution. And third, it undermined Russia's hegemony over Ukraine.

On the first point, if the national democrats were right to say that the Holodomor was genocide, then Stalin, Communism, and the Soviet Union were to blame, and the construction of a democratic and pro-Western Ukrainian identity must necessarily entail rejection of all three as comparable in their evil to Hitler and Nazi Germany. So the opponents of the national democrats, whose identity remained pro-Stalinist, pro-Russian, and pro-Soviet, were bound to struggle against such an interpretation. Their battle was fought not only in large abstract arguments but in small linguistic skirmishes. While national democrats began referring to the war against Hitler as "World War II," the Yanukovych camp stuck to the Soviet term, "The Great Fatherland War," with the "Fatherland" being the Soviet Union, and not Ukraine. Since the debate also reflected popularly held attitudes—according to a 2009 InterMedia survey, eighty-three percent of Ukrainians in the west, fifty-eight in the center, twenty-eight in the south, and fifteen in the east accept the genocide thesis—the Holodomor quickly became the main focus of efforts by both national democrats and their opponents to mobilize voters in the recent elections.

Complicating the issue was the fact that Yushchenko had made the Holodomor-as-genocide thesis a central tenet of his nation-building efforts, which mostly consisted of affirmative-action programs for promoting Ukrainian as the country's constitutionally recognized state language, in public education and the thoroughly Russified media. Yushchenko supported the construction of Holodomor monuments throughout Ukraine, introduced the Holodomor into school textbooks, founded the Ukrainian Institute of National Memory to research the Holodomor, built the Holodomor Memorial (down the street from Kyiv's ancient Monastery of the Caves and the Soviet-era complex celebrating the "Great Fatherland War"), initiated a series of celebrations to coincide with the famine's seventy-fifth anniversary in 2008, and sought international recognition of the Holodomor as genocide. Fourteen countries agreed, while the European Parliament stopped short, calling it a crime against humanity.

As the political tussle between Yushchenko and Yanukovych heightened, especially in the run-up to the presidential election of 2010, opposition to Yushchenko translated into opposition to his nation-building project. Besides promoting awareness of the horrors of the Holodomor, that project consisted of several other important historical dimensions. The first was the claim that Ukrainian history included the history of the state of Kyivan Rus, which one thousand years ago was one of Europe's largest and most powerful polities. The second was the rehabilitation of Ivan Mazepa, the Cossack hetman (or leader) whose desire for greater independence from Russia led him to join Sweden's Charles XII against Peter the Great in the disastrous Battle of Poltava in 1709. The third was the reassessment of three controversial leaders of Ukraine's anti-Soviet national liberation struggles during the twentieth century: Symon Petliura, Roman Shukhevych, and Stepan Bandera. Petliura was a democratic socialist and lifelong philo-Semite who happened to head a thoroughly ineffective government in 1918 and 1919, at just the time that terrible pogroms swept the country. Shukhevych and Bandera were both leaders of the interwar Organization of Ukrainian Nationalists, a radical nationalist movement—similar in structure, tactics, and ideology to the Algerian National Liberation Front, the Palestine Liberation Organization, and the Jewish Irgun—that first tried to carve out an independent Ukrainian state with the help of Nazi Germany and then, after Berlin cracked down in 1941, conducted a hopeless struggle against both the Germans and the Soviets.

National democrats argued that Ukrainians could not have a history and an identity if they did not look for their roots in the distant past and come to terms with events and individuals demonized by Russian imperial historiography and Soviet propaganda. Supporters of the Party of Regions and the Communists rejected the whole package of proposed changes, insisting that Mazepa, Petliura, Shukhevych, and Bandera were unmitigated "enemies of the people," "fascists," and "traitors," and that the Holodomor was a generalized human tragedy. When the Ukrainian parliament voted in November 2006 to declare the Holodomor genocide, the votes split predictably: the national democrats voted for the motion, while the Party of Regions and the Communists voted against it.

History and historical interpretation entered the contemporary political dialogue. Yushchenko's opponents understood that in attempting to rewrite Soviet and Russian versions of Ukrainian history, rehabilitate those who had traditionally been seen as proto-fascist, and carve out a distinct Ukrainian identity rooted in a democratic and pro-Western political culture, the president was effectively challenging Soviet and Russian identity as well as Russian claims to political hegemony over Ukraine. As the Kremlin's unofficial Ukraine spokesman, Konstantin Zatulin, noted with alarm in 2010, "A significant portion of Ukraine's citizens has accepted nationalist clichés. These people quite sincerely believe that Ukraine should have a language, history, and heroes that are necessarily separate from Russia's." Russian policymakers were fully aware of the ideological and political implications of what Yushchenko and the national democrats were up to. Putin expressed alarm and the Russian Duma passed a resolution in 2006 denying that the famine was genocide. Russian historians were mobilized to produce textbooks emphasizing Ukraine's common history with Russia and to deny the Holodomor's Ukrainian specificity, and the Kremlin began funneling substantial sums of money to its supporters and intelligence operatives in Ukraine.

It made perfect sense for Yanukovych to delete the Holodomor from the presidential Web site in his first act as president: it was a silent gesture, signifying to both the Kremlin and his own countrymen that his Ukraine, unlike Yushchenko's, would adopt pro-Soviet and pro-Russian stances. The next logical step was for Yanukovych to inform the world of his intentions. While attending an April 26 meeting in Brussels of the Parliamentary Assembly of the Council of Europe, he stated that "it would be wrong and unfair to recognize the Holodomor as an act of genocide against one nation." One day later, at a press conference in Strasbourg, he gave an authoritarian definition of democracy as "order." Once those discursive adjustments had been made, the door was open for Yanukovych and Russia's president, Dmitry Medvedev—who had pointedly refused to attend the national seventy-fifth anniversary observances of the Holodomor in 2008—to visit the Holodomor Memorial in Kyiv on May 17. They were now commemorating an act of God, not an intentional genocide.

The Yanukovych regime has also signaled that it regards genocide discourse as a political act. The minister of education and science has already announced that he intends to purge history textbooks of "delirious hyperbolization" about the Holodomor. The minister of humanitarian affairs has ominously suggested that the Institute of Historical Memory may need to undergo official review. In turn, the newly appointed director of the institute, a Communist sympathizer from the Donbas, has publicly stated that the famine was the "the result of difficult circumstances" and intends to promote "a national memory" that "unites" Ukrainians. The head of Ukraine's Security Service has closed the secret police archives, while another leading official has stated that "people know all they need to know." The Holodomor has thereby been transformed into a touchstone of political *loyalty* and a code for what is permissible in talking about the Yanukovych regime. To maintain that the famine was genocide or an anti-Ukrainian crime is effectively to engage in dissent and declare one's political opposition to Yanukovych. And in Yanukovych's Ukraine, as in Putin's Russia, dissent is risky business.

*

Holodomor, History, and Other Dilemmas, *World Affairs Journal*, December 13, 2010

This year's Holodomor Remembrance Day, the November 27th commemoration of the Stalin-engineered famine of 1932–33 that killed between 3 and 4 million Ukrainians, took place with some interesting background developments.

Two days before, Israeli President Shimon Peres enjoined Ukrainians to "forget history." One day before, Ukraine's President Viktor Yanukovych called the Holodomor an "Armageddon" and asked Ukrainians not to forget it. And in the months preceding the commemoration, the chorus of distinguished scholars who consider the Holodomor genocide acquired two American members.

Peres obviously knows that the creation of Israel would have been impossible without "history"—or, more precisely, historical memory. But he also knows that, just as remembering the past can be indispensable to forming nations, it can also become a source of later problems once nations have established themselves. There can, evidently, be too much of a good thing.

Yanukovych is obviously trying to square the discursive circle. On the one hand, he's kowtowing to the Kremlin's insistence that the Holodomor was just the local variant of a Soviet-wide famine (WikiLeaks shows how Russia pressured Azerbaijan on this point:); on the other, he's hoping to accommodate Ukrainian sensibilities and growing expert opinion that the horror of the Holodomor is best captured by the term *genocide*.

In his 2010 book *Stalin's Genocides*, Norman M. Naimark of Stanford University makes a forceful case for regarding Stalin as a "genocidaire"; the Stalinist system as genocidal; and dekulakization (the bloody process of eliminating "rich" peasants "as a class" from 1929 to 1932, when "some ten million kulaks were forced from their homes"), the Holodomor, and the "murderous campaigns against non-Russian nationalities" (such as Poles, Chechens, and Crimean Tatars) as instances of genocide.

In *Bloodlands* (also published this year), Timothy Snyder of Yale University approvingly notes: "Rafał Lemkin, the international lawyer who later invented the term *genocide*, would call the Ukrainian case 'the classic example of Soviet genocide.'" And with respect to "each of the cases" of mass killings "discussed in this book, the question 'Was it genocide?' can be answered: yes, it was." According to Snyder, "In 1933, Ukrainians would died [*sic*] in the millions, in the greatest artificial famine in the history of the world. This was the beginning of the special history of Ukraine, but not the end. Hitler would seize Ukraine from Stalin and attempt to realize his own colonial vision beginning with the shooting of Jews and the starvation of Soviet prisoners of war. The Stalinists colonized their own country, and the Nazis colonized occupied Soviet Ukraine: and the inhabitants of Ukraine suffered and suffered. During the years that both Stalin and Hitler were in power, more people were killed in Ukraine than anywhere else in the bloodlands, or in Europe, or in the world."

Naimark's and Snyder's claims raise some troubling questions. After all, if Stalin committed genocide, then the individuals who executed, supported, and condoned it must be considered his collaborators.

Russians need to ask whether the Russian Federation's status as successor state to the Soviet Union entails moral responsibility for Stalin's crimes. Is a formal apology necessary? Might reparations be in order? They also need to ask why and how Russians, and their language, culture, and identity, came to be so deeply implicated in, and supportive of, Soviet institutions of oppression.

Both Russians and non-Russians need to ask who among them pulled the triggers, ran the concentration camps, and starved the peasants. Most post-Soviet states have avoided "lustration"—exposing crimes and barring perpetrators from office—on the grounds that it would be destabilizing. The case for not rocking the boat was plausible when the crime wasn't genocide. If it is, can silence still be justified?

Communists, Soviet sympathizers, and fellow travelers in Western Europe and the United States need to ask whether they bear some moral responsibility for Stalin's genocides. They knew of dekulakization, the Holodomor, and the murderous campaigns—and did nothing. Worse, they defended Stalin and the Soviet Union. Are mere mea culpas enough?

Finally, Western policymakers need to explain just how they can justify turning a blind eye to the Kremlin's rehabilitation of Stalin. Reset buttons and cheap gas are important, of course, but perhaps mass murder masquerading as Armageddon matters, too.

Or should one just forget? Too bad President Peres didn't say how.

*

Do Animals Speak Ukrainian? *World Affairs Journal*, February 11, 2011

That's what Oleksandr Shvets, a traffic cop in Odessa, thinks, having recently told a driv-er not to speak that "language of calves." That's also what a male resident of Donetsk Province thinks, having told Christmas carolers in 2009 that he hates their "language of swine." And these are only two incidents that happen to have been captured on video. Ukrainian speakers insist that such behavior is all too typical in Ukraine, and especially in its Russian-speaking southeastern provinces.

Discrimination against the Ukrainian language—and the view that it's the language of dumb brutes—has its roots in the Russian Empire, when the authorities forbade Ukrainian in two notorious decrees, and the Soviet period, when the Communist Party actively promoted Russian chauvinism, tried to transform Ukrainian identity into a museum artifact, and looked the other way when Russian speakers insulted Ukrainian speakers. A frequent refrain in Ukrainian dissident writings was the complaint that fellow citizens would sneer at them when they spoke Ukrainian and tell them to speak "human"—namely Russian.

Language discrimination is a common phenomenon in dictatorial multinational states that attempt to force their subjects to have one set of opinions, one set of behaviors, and one language—that of the dominant ethno-cultural group. The Russian and Soviet empires were no exceptions to this rule. What is exceptional about the Soviet and contemporary Ukrainian experience is the visceral hatred of Ukrainian that some Russian speakers have. Polls show that the vast majority of Ukrainians are either tolerant of or indifferent to language issues—they have other things, such as a dysfunctional economy, growing authoritarianism, and rampant corruption, to worry about—but there is a vocal minority that becomes positively apoplectic when it hears Ukrainian. Most of them are probably Stalinists; many, alas, probably support Viktor Yanukovych and the Party of Regions.

Viewing Ukrainian as a bestial language doesn't make sense. Look around the world and you'll see that people generally refuse to speak the language of the group they perceive as their oppressor. They then insist on speaking their own language as a sign of resistance and pride. They may hate the oppressor and they may hate the oppressor's language as the language of oppression, but they don't usually conclude that the language itself is inhuman. Quite the contrary: It is all too human precisely because it is the language of the all-too-human oppressor.

Ukrainian-haters can't possibly view Ukrainians as oppressors, if only because Ukrainians have been powerless and stateless for most of their history. Status explains some of the disdain, as Ukrainians have traditionally been the "country bumpkins" viewed as social inferiors by Russian-speaking "city slickers." Nationality doesn't quite do the trick either, as Russian chauvinists generally regard Ukrainian as an absurd dialect of Russian and Ukrainians as misguided closet Russians. Obviously, something else—something psychological—must be going on here.

Consider that the two Ukrainian-haters captured on video were Ukrainian. Shvets is a common Ukrainian name, and the gentleman in Donetsk Province identifies himself as a Ukrainian. Why would they think of Ukrainian as the language of animals? In all likelihood, the language reminds them painfully of their own diminished status. They obviously chose to acculturate into Russian (which, of course, is their perfect right). As residents of Ukraine's southeastern rustbelt, they almost certainly feel a deep nostalgia for the good ol' days of the Soviet Union, when their language choice enhanced their career prospects, provided them with a sense of superiority vis-à-vis Ukrainian speakers, and promised access to the empire's many goodies. But then the collapse of the USSR transformed them—over night—into losers, several times over. They lost their past, they lost their status, they lost their jobs, and they lost their future. As the present passed them by and their very existential being came into question, they became "lumpenized." Now they have nothing, except for residual pride in their own supremacy, which rests almost exclusively on a language choice that promises little more than continued entrapment in a decaying region. They are, in sum, "lumpen supremacists."

And, of course, they are deeply resentful. One of their more articulate spokesmen is Oles Buzyna, a Russian-speaking Ukrainian columnist for the Kyiv-based newspaper *Segodnya*. He recently posted a psychologically fascinating video blog—an address to Ukraine's democratic "grant eaters" (i.e., recipients of US democracy-promotion grants)—in which he sarcastically congratulates them on their ability to live well and travel. What's clear from the blog is that Buzyna is a very angry man, full of resentment at being passed by while others adjust to, and even get to experience, the changing world. In a word, he is the classic loser—and his response, a visceral hatred of all things distinctly Ukrainian, is just what one would expect from a lumpen supremacist whose black-and-white view of the world precludes easy abandonment of the illusions that gave, and still give, his sad life meaning.

The position of Ukraine's lumpen supremacists is tragic. They deserve better. They deserve to live well, have self-esteem, and become winners, regardless of which language they prefer to speak. Unfortunately, Yanukovych and the Party of Regions—which has its fair share of lumpen supremacists—need them to remain losers with resentments that can be manipulated toward authoritarian ends. Were the lumpen supremacists to become winners and develop attitudes of tolerance toward all of Ukraine's many cultures and languages, why would they ever vote for thugs, crooks, and pogromchiks?

*

Was the Holodomor Genocide? *World Affairs Journal,* April 8, 2011

Here's what got me thinking about this issue—again.

A friend and colleague at the Canadian Institute of Ukrainian Studies and I are currently compiling a collection of documents on the Ukrainian famine of 1932–1933, tentatively called *The Holodomor Reader.* We're including survivor testimony, journalistic accounts, documents, legal assessments, scholarship, and literature in what we hope will be a must-have collection aimed at general readers, students, and scholars. With a little luck, the book may be published later in the year.

We take the view that the Holodomor, in which some 3 to 6 million Ukrainian peasants were starved to death during a massive crackdown on the Ukrainian cultural, religious, and political elites, was genocide. The view happens to reflect the views of the founder of the term, Raphael Lemkin:

> perhaps the classic example of Soviet genocide, its longest and broadest experiment in Russification [is] the destruction of the Ukrainian nation. … The nation is too populous to be exterminated completely with any efficiency. However, its leadership, religious, intellectual, political, its select and determining parts, are quite small and therefore easily eliminated, and so it is upon these groups particularly that the full force of the Soviet axe has fallen, with its familiar tools of mass murder, deportation and forced labor, exile and starvation.

We noted in the first draft of our introduction that "although there are scholars and policymakers who dispute that interpretation, it is our belief that expert opinion has now shifted—and continues to shift—toward viewing the Holodomor as genocide." One of the reviewers took issue with the claim, suggesting that the shift is hardly as evident as we made it out to be.

And that's what got me thinking: Is there a shift and is it quite as inexorable as we suggested it might be? I think the answer to both questions is yes, and here's why.

Consider where in the popular consciousness the famine was back in the 1950s. Nowhere. Survivors, refugees, and émigrés wrote about it extensively, but primarily in Ukrainian, and their audience consisted largely of themselves. Although Western journalists had written a great deal about the famine in the 1930s, their focus had shifted to other issues after World War II, while Western scholars ignored the famine almost completely. A Soviet history atlas compiled by the respected historian Martin Gilbert in 1972, for instance, illustrates the "main area of the forced collectivization of over 5 million peasant holdings 1929–1938" and notes that "thousands of peasants were killed when they resisted (some by armed force)."

The famine's status as a non-event at best or an émigré fantasy at worst has changed by 180 degrees. No one, anywhere, today disputes that millions of Ukrainians were starved to death in 1932–1933. No one disputes that the famine was avoidable, and almost no one disputes that it was a crime. Even Viktor Yanukovych calls it an "Armageddon." And a significant, and growing, number of serious non-Ukrainian scholars, journalists, and other opinion makers consider the Holodomor to have been genocide. The shift is remarkable and it is here to stay.

But will the view of the Holodomor as genocide gain the upper hand? I'm betting that the answer is yes because expert opinion is formed on the basis of both evidence *and* the Zeitgeist. As our *Reader* demonstrates, the empirical evidence for viewing the Holodomor as an intentional mass killing is overwhelming. If you're neutral, you'll be persuaded. If you're a die-hard skeptic or have a political agenda, on the other hand, no amount of evidence will do the trick.

But to focus only on evidence is to misunderstand how expertise works. Although scholars deny it, they are swayed as much, if not more, by real-world events as by dry evidence. No one today would deny the importance of women, even though the evidence—women—was always there. It took a women's movement to convince academics to see the obvious. It was only after policymakers and business people began glorifying globalization some two decades ago that academics took notice. And, of course, until the recent pro-democracy Arab revolts, few academics would have written about democracy in the Middle East and North Africa with a straight face.

In sum, experts, like all people, are swayed by life—by the Zeitgeist. And the Holodomor-as-genocide thesis is just such an example of a Zeitgeist-in-the-making. The Holodomor's currently undisputed status as a mass killing will set the norm for future scholars without political agendas. As the die-hards exit, their place will be taken by scholars who view the famine from the perspective of today's norm—and not yesterday's. As the number of experts who view the Holodomor as genocide grows, a tipping point will be reached and scholars, like all rational beings, will accept the genocide interpretation simply because it's the Zeitgeist.

I'm betting that experts with political agendas will also decline in number. There are those who support Vladimir Putin's Russia, a system that draws on neo-imperialism and neo-Stalinism for its legitimacy. When that system collapses—and I belong to those optimists who believe that will inevitably happen—Russian democrats will govern and set the terms of the debate on the Holodomor. Some will still bristle at accepting the genocide thesis; many will not. Some experts also support Yanukovych's version of Ukraine. That system draws on a denial of Ukrainian history for its legitimacy. The house that Yanukovych built is even more decrepit than Putin's, and once it kicks the bucket the door to accepting the genocide thesis will be open wide. That leaves closet socialist scholars, who may be incorrigible. After all, if they still believe in socialism after the collapse of Communism 20 years ago, they may be better off n the closet.

Of course, one could argue that the case for or against the Holodomor as genocide is ultimately irrelevant. All people of good will now recognize the Holodomor as one of the greatest crimes of the twentieth century. Calling it genocide or calling it something else won't change that fact.

*

Ukrainians and Jews and Ukrainians and Jews and ..., *World Affairs Journal*, April 15, 2011

Mossad's apparent involvement in the recent kidnapping of a Palestinian in Ukraine—he was whisked off the Kharkiv-Kyiv train on February 19th—has raised important and awkward questions about the highhandedness of the Israeli security service on the one hand and the complicity, ignorance, or incompetence of the Ukrainian security service on the other. But the subsequent evasions by both Ukrainians and Israelis may be the most interesting thing about this affair. I may be reading too much into the silence, but it's almost as if they were determined not to go *there*—with *there* being the unbearably tangled nature of Ukrainian-Jewish relations.

As students of Ukrainian-Jewish relations know, both sides appear to be trapped in a vicious circle described well by the historian Henry Abramson:

> Students reflecting on the dual genocides that Ukraine endured during the twentieth century cannot avoid the cruel paradigm of Ukrainian-Jewish history, in which each group constructs competing and often mutually exclusive narratives of suffering at the hands of the other. Viewed from afar, the pendulum of abuse and violence seems clear: the Jewish orendars exploit the Ukrainian peasantry, who exact terrible revenge in 1648–49 and the Kolivshchyna; Jewish Russophiles undermine the fledgling Ukrainian state, which is then submerged in the bloody pogroms of 1919. Convinced that the Ukrainian national movement represents a distinct threat both physical and ideological, Jews join the Communist Party, and both engineer and enforce the policies that lead to the Holodomor; Ukrainians retaliate with widespread collaboration with the Nazis in the Holocaust.

Is there any way out of this cycle of mutual recriminations?

Israel's President Shimon Peres suggested one solution on November 25, 2010, when, while on a state visit to Kyiv, he enjoined Ukrainians to "forget history." Taken to its logical conclusion, Peres's proposal would also have Jews forget history, with the presumably happy result that both sides could forge relations on the basis of current concerns and not past memories. Great idea, except for one thing: no one, especially in today's hyper-historicized and information-saturated environment, could possibly follow Peres's advice. And, even if someone could, who would be first to forget?

Another approach might entail stepping back from the mutual recriminations and, by trying to empathize with both sides, hoping to establish common grounds and common assumptions for viewing both Ukrainians and Jews. One possible starting point would be to acknowledge that both nations are, well, human—and, thus, equally rational or equally irrational as well as equally prone to good or equally prone to evil. Another would be that both nations are not monoliths, but agglomerations of individual human beings, with all their strengths, weaknesses, and peccadillos.

Just this search for commonality—heavily laced with attempts at scholarly objectivity—pervades the Ukrainian-Jewish Encounter, a privately funded initiative established in 2008 by Adrian Karatnycky of New York and Alti Rodal of Toronto. The UJE's aim is "to enable the two formerly stateless peoples, sharing memory (from differing perspectives) and space (in the home territory, and in lands of resettlement) to understand each other's historical experience, identities, and narratives, to treat embedded stereotypes, and to more firmly secure the foundation for building modern identities (and interaction) on the basis of greater measures of comprehension and mutual respect." The UJE has already organized several excellent conferences with no-holds-barred discussions of a whole range of painful issues and has planned a series of path-breaking publications. The question, or challenge, facing the UJE, of course, is whether the work of academic conferences can percolate into the popular consciousness.

The same search, but this time imbued with emotional sensitivity, underpins an excellent documentary film, *Three Stories of Galicia*, which hopes to find commonalities by revealing "the intimate stories of three courageous individuals who took it upon themselves to preserve the dignity of the human spirit." The accounts ring true, because the technically expert film avoids both pathos and bathos by letting a Jewish man, a Ukrainian woman, and a Polish priest tell their own stories in their own voices. As the two filmmakers, Olha Onyshko and Sarah Farhat, say, "When we set out to make this film four years ago, we wanted to bring peace to the hearts of the people of Galicia and to their descendants that are now spread all over the world. That is why we decided to reflect the perspectives of the three major ethnic and religious groups that used to live on that land: Jews, Ukrainians and Poles. We wanted all three groups to have a chance to hear the other side's perspective and hopefully feel some sympathy towards people who were formerly perceived as enemies." Once again, the intent is noble, but will groups learn, or want to learn, from the stories of three individuals?

If they don't, one could just seek refuge in the absurd. My own novel, *The Jew Who Was Ukrainian or How One Man's Rip-Roaring Romp through an Existential Wasteland Ended in a Bungled Attempt to Bump off the Exceptionally Great Leader of Mother Russia*, grapples with many of the same issues as the UJE and Onyshko and Farhat by relating the blackly comedic story of a man whose Ukrainian mother was a Nazi concentration camp guard and hates Jews and whose Jewish father was a Stalinist butcher and hates Ukrainians. The hero of the story struggles to find meaning at the intersection of Hitler's

Holocaust and Stalin's Gulag. He doesn't, by the way. Indeed, who could?

Perhaps that question can suggest how to escape the never-ending Jewish-Ukrainian re-criminations. Perhaps the only way out is for both Ukrainians and Jews to take the exact opposite of Peres's advice and to remember history with a vengeance, choke on it until they all turn blue, and then, while spluttering and gasping for air, realize that it may be time to move on and smell the roses. Then, let the historians fight it out. After all, that's what they get paid to do.

*

Regionnaires to Ukrainians: Let Them Eat Red Flags! *World Affairs Journal*, May 12, 2011

The war over symbols continues in Ukraine—this time heatedly and violently—threatening to split the country into warring factions. The immediate pretext was the May 9th Victory Day celebrations, a Soviet-era holiday marking the "Soviet people's" defeat of Nazi Germany.

Why should there be disagreement over something as important as that? Because the Yanukovych regime stupidly and purposely permitted red flags to be included in the celebrations. For some Ukrainians—those primarily in the east and south—the red flag symbolizes both victory in the "Great Fatherland War" and Soviet rule. They're as proud of the former as they are nostalgic for the latter. For other Ukrainians, the flag symbolizes Stalinist totalitarianism, Communist terror, the Holodomor, the Gulag, and the indignities of colonial rule. The analogy with the Confederate flag in the US is not inappropriate: for some American Southerners, it's just a symbol of their identity; for others, especially African Americans, it's a symbol of slavery. An analogy with the Nazi flag is also apposite. Sympathizers of the Third Reich view it as a symbol of Germany's resurgence. Opponents of the Third Reich associate it with Auschwitz.

We know how these disagreements have been resolved in the United States, where the Confederate flag is frowned on in official settings, and Germany, where the Nazi flag is banned outright. Things are more complicated in Ukraine, both because large numbers of people sympathize with Stalinism and communism and because leading members of the Yanukovych regime (such as the supremacist Education Minister Dmitri Tabachnik) have been actively promoting Stalinist agendas. That said, no red flag has ever been officially displayed on Victory Day celebrations in the past 19 years of independent Ukraine's existence: every president, from Leonid Kravchuk to Leonid Kuchma to Viktor Yushchenko, understood that waving it would be needlessly provocative. When the Regionnaire-dominated Parliament recently agreed to permit public displays of the red flag this May 9th, it knew full well that it was endorsing the functional equivalent of showing off swastikas in Israel. Yanukovych—too terrified to sign or veto the Parliament's criminal measure—just hoped the controversy would go away. Naturally, it didn't.

The red flag was displayed in all parts of the country and, predictably, led to violent alter-cations, especially in the western Ukrainian city of Lviv. Instead of unifying the country, the May 9th celebrations divided it. That's stupid, because it threatens to make Ukraine even more ungovernable than it was under Yushchenko, but it's also unsurprising. The Regionnaires know they're bankrupt. The only way they can retain any degree of popu-lar support is by stoking the culture wars, enhancing divisions, and creating a "national-ist" bogeyman to distract attention from their own criminality and Ukraine's economic woes. Significantly, the Regionnaire provocation and Yanukovych's indecision also mean that he has effectively lost control of his own party. How's that for stability?

What could Yanukovych have done differently? Well, for one thing, just as it was per-fectly possible to celebrate the defeat of Nazi Germany without red flags for two decades, so too it must have been possible to do so today. After all, the victory over Hitler was the selfless achievement of common Ukrainians, who died in the millions, and not of Stalin, who killed them in the millions. But even if you think some version of the red flag was imperative, Yanukovych should have insisted that the celebrations feature Soviet Ukraine's blue-and-red flag alongside independent Ukraine's blue-and-yellow flag. That way, both sides might have been mollified, with the national democrats getting the noun, Ukraine, and the color blue, and the pro-Soviet forces getting the adjective, Soviet, and the color red. Of course, Yanukovych would have had to sell the idea to the people and his party. A strong president could have. A weak one who knows his future is tied to a band of desperate thugs wouldn't even try.

But the problem may be more deeply rooted in the general Regionnaire obtuseness re-garding symbols and morality. The mayor of Donetsk, Oleksandr Lukyanchenko, recent-ly stated that his city wouldn't remove its statues of Lenin and Stalin for the Euro 2012 soccer championships. Fair enough, but here's why: "European values do not permit re-moving statues for events. Please excuse me, but why does Germany still have Marx?" Disregard the fact that a Regionnaire's invocation of "European values" is as obscene as a Ku Klux Klanner's invocation of the Declaration of Independence. More important is that Lukyanchenko's comment is breathtakingly idiotic. After all, the continued presence of Marx's statues in Germany just may have something to do with his having been a great political thinker and not the founder of a totalitarian state. Had the good mayor looked at Deutschland more closely, he might have noticed that Hitler's statues came down some time ago.

On the other hand, if Donetsk wants European soccer fans to see its collection of Lenins and Stalins, go right ahead, I say. German burghers will get a kick out of their spooky encounter with East Germany redux; Polish patriots will shake their heads at memorials to the perpetrator of the Katyn massacre; French Stalinists will nod approvingly; while English football hooligans will enjoy relieving themselves at the feet of the great leaders. Oh, and business people seeking rapidly modernizing places to invest in are sure to con-clude, upon hearing Lukyanchenko's commitment to a pre-modern past, that Donetsk is just what they've been looking for. After all, who needs foreign direct investment? Let the proletariat eat red flags!

The Extreme Implications of the Demjanjuk Ruling, *World Affairs Journal*, May 27, 2011

The May 12th sentencing of John Demjanjuk couldn't have come at a better time. Just as Russia and Ukraine are experiencing a rehabilitation of Stalin and Stalinism, the Munich District Court's verdict unintentionally revealed just how morally demanding and politically disruptive the prosecution of real and alleged evildoers can be.

The court sentenced Demjanjuk to five years for being an accessory to the murder of 28,060 Jews in the Nazi concentration camp in Sobibor, in occupied Poland. The former automobile worker from Cleveland and former Soviet POW from Ukraine had already been tried, unsuccessfully, for being the sadistic Treblinka guard known as Ivan the Terrible. This time, German prosecutors claimed that Demjanjuk had been a guard at Sobibor and that the very fact of being a guard in such a setting constituted a crime, even though—or perhaps because—they were unable to prove he had actually committed any specific criminal act. Much of the subsequent commentary has either expressed satisfaction at justice having been done or decried the trial as a farce. Both sides have a point and both sides miss the real point.

What the German court did was to declare that dispositions, not actions, can be criminal. Demjanjuk was found guilty not because he demonstrably killed anybody, but because he had been present, as a guard, in a place that killed people. Since he could presumably have made himself absent, his presence must have been indicative of moral turpitude. According to the court's logic, that moral turpitude—that callousness, that indifference to human suffering—must be treated as a criminal *act*. In other words, one might be punished not for actions but moral intentions, or lack thereof. Consciously or not, the court pursued a line of reasoning that represents an extremist variant of Kantian morality. The court went far beyond Kant's claim that intentions must be judged moral or not and argued that they may in fact be judged *criminal*—a claim that even hyper-fundamentalist Christian sects might consider too radical for their taste.

What makes the court's logic profoundly revolutionary is that it, like Kantian morality, must be universalized and made applicable to everybody—not just Holocaust-era concentration camp guards. That means that *all* guards in *all* prisons and camps in which atrocities have been committed bear criminal responsibility for those atrocities and should be treated accordingly. Thus, given the inherently murderous nature of the Gulag, all Soviet concentration camp guards and secret-police agents are, whether Russian, Ukrainian, Jewish, or some other nationality, necessarily culpable for crimes that are probably as severe as those ascribed to Demjanjuk. Every East German who patrolled the border with West Germany bears criminal responsibility for the people who were shot trying to cross. Every American who guarded the prison at Abu Ghraib is as guilty as the few soldiers who tortured inmates.

But the court's logic is even more far-reaching than this. After all, being a guard in a camp is not essential to the moral claim of criminal liability. The court's moral logic must, by the very nature of the boundlessness of moral claims, extend to anybody who was in the *presence* of crimes and failed to act to prevent them. Accordingly, the Dutch peacekeepers who did nothing to stop the massacre at Srebrenica are accessories to the actual killers. Vladimir Putin, as a career KGB officer, is no less culpable than Soviet concentration camp guards. In turn, Gerhard Schröder and Jacques Chirac must share in Putin's guilt, the former for calling him a "flawless democrat," the latter for granting him the Legion of Honor medal—actions that implicitly whitewashed the KGB's crimes. And Angela Merkel, every time she travels to Moscow, is almost as responsible for the continued incarceration of Mikhail Khodorkovsky as the Kremlin, since she could easily insist that the unjustly imprisoned businessman be released—or else.

Legal theorists will debate whether or not the German court made a mistake in taking the argument for culpability this far, but what's done is done and, if the international community is serious about morality and criminality, it will have to build on Germany's example and pursue justice assiduously. Obviously, such a course will be extremely destabilizing, if only because there must be many thousands of former Communist guards and secret policemen living comfortably in the post-Soviet states, Israel, Europe, Canada, and the United States. Defenders of justice will have to argue that some instability—even if reaches into the highest circles of Russian, German, and other political elites—is as small a price to pay for morality as the temporary financial turmoil caused by the IMF head's recent resignation for alleged sexual misconduct.

Perhaps aware of the destabilizing consequences of its ruling, the Munich court also imposed a sentence that suggests that the price to be paid for justice will indeed be tiny. Consider that Demjanjuk was given five years for allegedly helping to kill 28,060 people. Doesn't 1,825 days seem like a laughably small sentence for such a heinous crime—amounting to one day for 15 victims, or just over an hour and a half per victim?

This is the truly scandalous story behind the Demjanjuk case. After having gone for the über-Kantian high ground and making moral dispositions criminal acts, the Munich District Court appears to have panicked and backtracked, effectively declaring that the dead are practically worthless. Like the court, we still don't know exactly what Demjanjuk did or did not do in Sobibor, or why. But we do know that, after a contradictory ruling such as this, no one need fear German justice. Schröder, Chirac, and Merkel could probably get off with a few minutes' time. Putin might have to serve a few days. And the real Ivan the Terrible, wherever he is, is certainly laughing.

*

Breaking the Myths of World War II's Bloodlands, *World Affairs Journal*, June 9, 2011

Take a look at a fascinating piece published in the May 27th *New York Times Book Review* by Adam Kirsch, a senior editor at the *New Republic*. Kirsch asks: "Is World War II Still 'the Good War'?" His answer is as interesting for what it does not say as for what it does.

Over the last several years, historians, philosophers and others have begun to think about the Second World War in challenging and sometimes disturbing new ways ...

... the British historian Norman Davies begins from the premise that "the war effort of the Western powers" was "something of a sideshow." America lost 143,000 soldiers in the fight against Germany, Davies points out, while the Soviet Union lost 11 million.

And if the main show was a war between Hitler and Stalin, he wonders, wasn't World War II a clash of nearly equivalent evils? ...

Davies's deliberately provocative book had a mixed reception, in part because of the way his account of the war in Eastern Europe seemed determined to minimize the importance of the Holocaust. No such objection can be made to Timothy Snyder's morally scrupulous book "Bloodlands: Europe Between Hitler and Stalin" (2010), which also spotlights Eastern Europe—in particular, the region comprising the Baltics, Ukraine, Belarus, Western Russia and Poland that Snyder calls "the bloodlands," because they were the greatest killing field of the Second World War. This was the site of the titanic battles between the Wehrmacht and the Red Army: it was also the scene of 14 million noncombatant deaths between 1933 and 1945. This figure encompasses 10 million civilians and prisoners of war killed by the Nazis—including six million Jews murdered in the Holocaust—and four million civilians and P.O.W.'s killed by the Soviets.

By grouping German and Soviet casualties together, Snyder is making an implicit point. The Soviet Union was America's ally, Germany our enemy; but both regimes were guilty of killing millions of people for ideological reasons. Weren't the three million Ukrainians starved by Stalin in 1932–1933 deliberate victims of state aggression and ideological terror, no less than the three million Soviet P.O.W.'s starved by Hitler in 1941–1942?

Consider the moral distinction Kirsch draws between Snyder and Davies. Snyder's book is "morally scrupulous" because, in contrast to Davies's, it does not "minimize the importance of the Holocaust" and is thus *balanced*. In other words, moral scrupulousness and balance go together, just as moral unscrupulousness and imbalance go together. It follows that, since a morally scrupulous, or balanced, stance must entail recognizing *both* the Holocaust and the Gulag as comparable (if perhaps not quite equivalent) crimes, histories that minimize the importance of the Gulag are as morally imbalanced, and "unscrupulous," as those that minimize the importance of the Holocaust. Davies may therefore be at fault, but so, too, is several decades' worth of Western historiography that ignored, downplayed, rationalized, or even glorified Stalinism. Indeed, since that historiography set the norm for Western thinking about Eastern Europe for more than half a century, its "cumulative" moral unscrupulousness is incomparably greater than that of a single scholar such as Davies.

Now, it's not as if there was no information on the Gulag, Stalinism, and the sufferings of Stalin's victims. Eastern European émigré communities have been writing and speaking about little else since the 1930s. But no one listened to them because they were the quint-essential "Other"—"clannish" refugees who spoke bad English, had unpronounceable names, and ate unpronounceable foods, didn't look or dress like Americans, were gener-ally religious and anti-Communist, and could easily be dismissed as crazies, right-wing-ers, nationalists, fascists, anti-Semites, Cold Warriors, fanatics, and the like. And be-cause, according to this perverse historical logic, the war in the East was a "sideshow," Eastern Europeans obviously did nothing to fight Nazism, being at best bystanders and at worst collaborators. As bystanders, they had to be morally obtuse; as collaborators, they had to be morally repugnant. Either way, they weren't really *moral* beings: which is to say they weren't really *human* beings. Such a historiography may not have been dehumaniz-ing in intent, but it was surely that in effect—and dehumanization is of course at the core of every form of racism, including anti-Semitism.

Kirsch is wrong to say that "To those who fought World War II, it was plain enough that ... the bulk of the dying in Europe was being done by the Red Army at the service of Stalin." In reality, American GIs had little knowledge of the eastern front and saw the war through the lens of their own experiences. It didn't help that the wartime American media lionized "Uncle Joe" and called every resident of the Soviet Union Russian. Nor did the Cold War contribute to understanding of Eastern Europe: after 1947, the wartime Soviet-American alliance became an embarrassment, Soviet pronouncements on the war were viewed with suspicion, and Americans celebrated their contribution to the libera-tion of *Western* Europe.

It was only after the collapse of the USSR, the emergence of independent Eastern European states committed to pursuing anti-Stalinist identities and anti-Soviet historical narratives, and the opening of Communist archives that Snyder's book became possible. The irony is that its basic thesis—that Eastern Europe was victimized by both Hitler and Stalin—has been the conventional wisdom among refugees from the "bloodlands" for decades. They knew better, because they had lived through the horrors of both totalitari-an empires. Westerners knew worse, but that didn't matter, since they were the ones who wrote the English-language histories and could dismiss their Eastern European critics as anti-Communist loons.

Kirsch concludes his essay by writing: "It is only in retrospect that we begin to simplify experience into myth—because we need stories to live by, because we want to honor our ancestors and our country instead of doubting them. In this way, a necessary but terrible war is simplified into a 'good war,' and we start to feel shy or guilty at any reminder of the moral compromises and outright betrayals that are inseparable from every combat." He should have added that, if it weren't for the Eastern Europeans' insistence on their own humanity, American views of World War II would still be myths.

*

Language Intolerance in Ukraine, *World Affairs Journal*, January 6, 2012

The Ukrainian language is back in the news. The Venice Commission, the Council of Europe's advisory body on constitutional matters, recently ruled on the Regionnaire-proposed draft law, On Principles of the State Language Policy of Ukraine: "the question remains whether ... there are sufficient guarantees ... for the consolidation of the Ukrainian language as the sole State language, and of the role it has to play in the Ukrainian multi-linguistic society" (article 66).

The commission's language is squishy, but diplo-babble always is. In reality, the above remarks represent a severe criticism of the draft law. And rightly so. The Regionnaires have done everything possible to roll back Ukrainian in the last two years. Naturally, they insist they're being evenhanded, even liberal. Indeed, they claim that they're the true Europeans. They say they want linguistic freedom; they say they stand for equality of languages. It's them other guys—the supporters of Ukrainian language and culture—who are imposing their preferences on a reluctant population. Them other guys, meanwhile, insist that all they want is equal time for a language that's been discriminated against for hundreds of years.

Now, the Regionnaire monoglots do have a point: language use should be guided by liberal values. We may doubt their sincerity—after all, these guys wouldn't know a contemporary European value (as opposed to those practiced by European colonialists, racists, and anti-Semites) if it snapped at their jowls—but it *is* true that imposing languages or denying people the right to speak the language of their choice contravenes liberalism and tolerance. Defenders of Ukrainian also have a point. Ukrainian language and culture *have* been subjected to sustained persecution by the tsars and the Soviets and surely deserve to have a significant presence in a country that calls itself Ukraine.

So how do we reconcile both claims?

Consider what the ideal language situation in a liberal and tolerant Ukraine would be like.

Imagine a country in which two languages are spoken by the overwhelming majority of the population. What linguistic skills and values should citizens have if they want the society to be based on contemporary European values and be liberal, tolerant, and functional? That is, if they want all citizens to enjoy freedom of linguistic choice *and* still be able to communicate?

First, everybody should be proficient in both languages. Proficiency translates into the ability to comprehend and speak both languages.

Second, everybody should feel free to use whichever language they want whenever and wherever they want to. The freedom to use whichever language one wants is tantamount to liberalism.

And third, everybody should accept others' use of whichever language they want whenever and wherever they want to. The acceptance of whichever language others use is tantamount to tolerance.

Now imagine two languages—U and R. In ideal circumstances, speakers of U would be proficient in and tolerant of R, while speakers of R would be proficient in and tolerant of U. If a speaker of U and a speaker of R met, they could and would happily speak their own preferred languages, either only U, only R, or each other's languages. The conditions of liberalism, tolerance, and functionality would be maintained.

So how do these reflections apply to Ukraine, where the two key languages are Ukrainian and Russian?

In ideal circumstances, speakers of Ukrainian would be proficient in and tolerant of Russian, while speakers of Russian would be proficient in and tolerant of Ukrainian. If a speaker of Ukrainian and a speaker of Russian met, they could and would speak their own preferred languages, only Ukrainian, only Russian, or each other's languages. The conditions of liberalism, tolerance, and functionality would be maintained.

How does the actual linguistic condition in Ukraine measure up against the ideal?

Not as bad as you might think. The vast majority of Ukrainian speakers are proficient in and tolerant of Russian; when speakers of Ukrainian encounter speakers of Russian, most are more than happy to hear Russian and even speak it. That is as true of Lviv as it is true of Kyiv and Donetsk.

In contrast, the vast majority of Russian speakers do not meet these conditions. Many are not proficient in Ukrainian; some are intolerant of Ukrainian (and consider it the language of animals); and, when speakers of Russian encounter speakers of Ukrainian, few are more than happy to hear Ukrainian and speak it. That is as true of Kyiv and Donetsk as it is true of Lviv.

Ukraine's language condition is thus only half ideal. For the society to be truly European and thus liberal, tolerant, and functional, that part of the population which lacks proficiency in Ukrainian should acquire proficiency in Ukrainian; that part which is intolerant of Ukrainian should become tolerant of Ukrainian; and that part which is unwilling to hear or speak Ukrainian with Ukrainian speakers should acquire the willingness to hear or speak Ukrainian with Ukrainian speakers.

Each of Ukraine's presidents—Leonid Kravchuk, Leonid Kuchma, Viktor Yushchenko, and even Viktor Yanukovych—has in fact behaved according to European principles. Whatever their personal private linguistic or cultural preferences, they have all made a public effort to be liberal and tolerant in just the way described above. The vast majority of Ukraine's national democrats also adopt the above posture. The only political forces that are, in both principle and practice, linguistically illiberal and intolerant are the anti-Russian Svoboda party, the anti-Ukrainian Communists, and the anti-Ukrainian Regionnaires—as well as most of their respective constituents. Illiberal and intolerant Ukrainian speakers probably comprise no more than 5 percent of the total population, while illiberal and intolerant Russian speakers probably comprise about 40 percent. Unsurprisingly, the vast majority of the latter are concentrated in the Regionnaire stronghold in the south and east of the country.

Ukraine, then, still has a long way to go before it'll embody European values and be linguistically liberal, tolerant, and functional. But the only way it'll ever get there is if the Regionnaires abandon their bigoted attitudes and start being liberal toward and tolerant of Ukrainian.

*

Ukrainian Stereotypes in Holland's 'In Darkness,' *World Affairs Journal,* April 6, 2012

Go see Agnieszka Holland's *In Darkness,* both because it's an excellent film about the Holocaust in wartime Lviv and because it demonstrates just how deeply rooted some ethnic stereotypes can be.

The story is simple: an anti-Semitic Polish sewer worker and part-time crook, Poldek Socha, finds himself in the unexpected position of hiding a group of Jews in Lviv's sewers. At first, he does so only for money. In time, he abandons his anti-Semitism and acts with altruism. The film ends with the liberation of Lviv by the Soviets and the emergence of the surviving Jews from the sewers. "These are my Jews!" Socha beams. "These are my Jews!"

In an interview, Holland emphasized what she thought was one of the film's strong points: its avoidance of one-dimensional characterizations. Here's what she says about Socha:

> First of all, the main character, this Polish guy, was ambiguous, both hero and not hero, and a very simple, ordinary man, not very good. What was always interesting for me was not the mystery that people can be terrible. I think humanity has a tendency to be terrible. What always surprises and intrigues me is that in those circumstances somebody acts in a good way, especially somebody who doesn't have deep reasons or preparation to do so.

Socha doesn't think about what will happen, what he will do. He just acts. What I thought was an interesting, dramatic part of the story was that you don't know what he will do. Even to himself he doesn't know. It's like walking on a wire, and at any moment he can slip to one side or the other.

And here's what she says about the Jews hiding in the sewer:

> The Jewish characters aren't one-dimensional angelic, they are full-bodied human beings with anger, sex, weakness, and selfishness, and generosity and love as well. That was another thing that irritates me in English-language Holocaust movies: that in most of them the Jews are turned into some kind of non-living, positive stereotypes. I think that in doing so, in some way you are killing them

again. They become unreal.

Holland is right to state that multi-dimensional portrayals can only enhance our experience and understanding of the Holocaust. Unfortunately, she restricts multidimensionality to Poles and Jews and resorts to straightforward stereotyping when it comes to Ukrainians. That she does so unwittingly just goes to show how "taken for granted" some stereotypes are.

There are three Ukrainian characters in the film. By far the most domineering is a Ukrainian policeman by the name of Bortnyk. He's fanatically pro-German, fanatically anti-Semitic, and fanatically pro-Ukrainian. His eyes glisten when he speaks of hunting down Jews and, naturally, he loves to drink. He appears for minutes on end, arguably being the second most important character in the film. He identifies himself—and is identified as—Ukrainian. And, lest the point escape you that the external appearance of Ukrainians shouldn't mislead you about their internal brutishness, he is, unlike the dumpy Socha, tall, dark, and handsome. Indeed, Bortnyk even comes across as worse than the Germans, who are portrayed only as background brutes. The Ukrainian is a living, breathing embodiment of evil, whereas the Nazis have no personality whatsoever. Not surprisingly, Bortnyk becomes stereotypically "unreal," and the film suffers aesthetically as a result.

Two other Ukrainians make bit appearances lasting a few seconds apiece. One is a peasant woman selling vegetables who expresses regret over the killing of Poles. The other is a worker who helps one of the Jews get through town. Neither of these two characters is identified as Ukrainian, and the only way you'd know they are is if you understand the language. If you don't, you're liable to think they're two of the many more or less nuanced, multi-dimensional Polish characters. And besides, the two Ukrainians appear on screen for a total of about 30 seconds.

Here's how Yale historian Timothy Snyder describes Holland's portrayal of Ukrainians:

> Poldek has a Ukrainian friend, Bortnik, who serves as a chief of the local police. This friendship saves Poldek once, but has its risks, since among the tasks of the police are the discovery and murder of Jews. Bortnik comes to Poldek's house late at night drunk and demands sustenance; Poldek's little daughter, rubbing her eyes in bed, reminds her father that they were saving food for "the Jews." She then realizes what she has done, and convinces Bortnik that by "Jews" she meant her dolls, which, she says, came from the ghetto. In a story of interaction between Poles and Jews, the natural tendency would be to export local evil as much as possible to the third nationality: the Ukrainians. Without at all disguising the horrible local politics of occupation, Holland carefully balances Ukrainian villains with sympathetic Ukrainian characters. One of the Jews in hiding smuggles himself into a concentration camp to see if the younger sister of the woman he loves is still alive. This heroism is enabled by a Ukrainian, who performs the indispensable [sic] logistical work and refuses payment.

Carefully balances, indeed! Imagine a German-language film with multi-dimensional

German characters and three Jews. Two speak Yiddish (which sounds awfully like German to the untrained ear), are never identified as Jewish, and come off positively for all of 30 seconds. The third identifies himself as Jewish, is a fanatical Zionist, is depicted as a blood-sucking banker, and is on screen for 10 to 15 minutes.

I don't doubt that both Holland and Snyder would find the film aesthetically flawed and anti-Semitic.

*

Germany, East Central Europe, and Moral Responsibility for the Holocaust: Part 1, *World Affairs Journal*, June 22, 2012

Since June 22nd marks the day Nazi Germany attacked the Soviet Union in 1941, it's an appropriate time to consider the question posed by Paul Hockenos, an accomplished journalist and political analyst in Berlin, in a recent article in the *Chronicle of Higher Education*: "Can Germany Help Central Europe Confront Its Dark Past?" Unsurprisingly, the answers his interlocutors provide range from "yes" to "no" to "it depends." The yea-sayers generally argue that the truth is the truth and, if Germans can help promote it, so be it. The naysayers insist that the Germans have no right to preach morality in a region they devastated in two world wars. The it-depends camp says that truth-telling is fine—as long as it's done with sensitivity and tact. I come down hard in all three camps.

The problem is obvious. The German Reich and Austria-Hungary brought World War I to Central and Eastern Europe from 1914 to 1918. Twenty-five years later, Nazi Germany and Stalin's USSR dismembered Poland. On June 22, 1941, Adolf Hitler turned on his erstwhile pal and attacked the Soviet Union. In both conflicts, the countries that suffered most from German aggression were Poland, Belarus, and Ukraine, and those that died in largest numbers were Poles, Belarusians, Ukrainians, and Jews.

While there is nothing intrinsically wrong with a German helping East Central Europe "confront its dark past," it's not hard to see why such an effort, however well-intentioned, could easily misfire. Germany and Germans represent power, wealth, and arrogance to Central and Eastern Europe in the same way that America and Americans represent pow-er, wealth, and arrogance to the world. And it doesn't much matter whether the German or American really is powerful, wealthy, or arrogant. Back in 1976, when I was doing a six-month Eurail pass trip through Europe, I spent a month in Frankfurt and Munich. Almost everyone I met held me personally responsible for the Vietnam War, the arms race, racism, and Watergate. Just how a politically ignorant 22-year-old with a shoestring budget could have had so much influence in Washington didn't seem to trouble my inter-locutors, but they obviously knew that, as an American tourist, I necessarily represented American imperialism.

No one likes to be preached to, especially by people, peoples, or states with less than exemplary moral records. Americans like to pontificate about human rights and democracy, and it's not too surprising that many people in the world find such preaching hypocritical, especially as American power often appears to undermine the very human rights and democracy Washington claims to be promoting. The image of the "ugly American" hardly does justice to most Americans, but there are indeed American behaviors that warrant the label. So if you're going to preach, you better make sure that you have a spotless moral record. And if you're not a saint, you may want to pick your words with extra care. That admonition holds as much for self-righteous Canadian scholars and hot-headed German graduate students as it does for opportunistic French politicians and moralizing American heads of state.

Germans shouldn't be surprised that, like Greeks responding to Germany's advice on how to overcome their debt crisis, many East Central Europeans view them with some suspicion. People and countries that preach to others have a moral obligation to practice what they preach. Just how committed has Germany been to democracy, human rights, truth, justice, and the like in East Central Europe? Forget the two world wars and the millions of dead. In 1922, Germany signed the Treaty of Rapallo with Soviet Russia and subsequently provided strategic assistance to the Soviet economy and military. In 1939 came the Molotov-Ribbentrop Pact, followed by two years of enthusiastic support of Stalin. West Germany's postwar policy of Ostpolitik was utterly indifferent to the "captive nations" of East Central Europe, so much so that Bonn even turned its back on Poland's Solidarity movement. Since 1991, Germany has focused all its energies on Russia and Russian gas, prompting former Chancellor Gerhard Schröder to call Vladimir Putin a model democrat at the height of Ukraine's Orange Revolution.

In all these instances, Germany has pursued a policy of ruthless Realpolitik, very much in the manner of the United States, China, France, and Russia. That is Germany's right, and, as some might argue, that is also its imperative. But you see the problem. Practitioners of Realpolitik really shouldn't preach democracy and human rights—especially to countries that they devastated twice. Even the mayor of Luhansk sensed this, when, back in April, he responded to criticism of his city's treatment of dogs by German animal rights activist Maja von Hohenzollern with the comment that "when they say we're bad, let them look at themselves and at what they did during the war."

It gets even more complicated. Before Germany can help East Central Europe confront East Central Europe's dark past, Germans should first confront their own dark past in East Central Europe. But have they? Commendably, Germans have devoted an enormous amount of energy to understanding the Holocaust. Unfortunately, their focus on the Nazi destruction of Jews has also tended to blind them to their own very dark past in what Yale historian Timothy Snyder calls the "Bloodlands." With all the research Germans have devoted to World War II, why did it take an American—and before him, an Englishman, Norman Davies—to point out the obvious: that millions of non-Jews also suffered at the hands of the Nazis? How many German museums devote any attention to the Slavic "*Untermenschen*"? How many Germans still refer to mismanagement and sloppiness as a "*polnische Wirtschaft*" or a "Polish economy"? How many know anything about Ukraine? How many care to know anything? Ignorance may be a right, but preaching based on ignorance probably is not.

Many years ago I had lunch with a German diplomat and his wife who were going to be posted to Kyiv. He had never heard of Ukraine's "national poet," Taras Shevchenko—a faux pas equivalent to a Ukrainian's never having heard of Goethe—and she thought Kharkiv was Kraków. That lamentable ignorance has changed among diplomats and scholars, but the abysmally small amount of attention devoted by the German media to Ukraine probably means that it continues with full force at the level of the population in general. Nobel Prize winner Heinrich Böll's 1949 novel, *The Train Was Punctual*, suggests that this ignorance has deeper roots. The novel describes a young German soldier's return to the front in southern Ukraine. As he travels eastward from his furlough, he traces his route on a map and "visits" various cities, towns, and villages in Ukraine. He speaks of Poles and Jews and Russians in great detail, but doesn't mention Ukrainians once, even though they formed the vast majority of the country and were the people whose farms he and his comrades probably plundered on a daily basis. That German soldier—and Böll arguably with him—didn't *see* Ukrainians even when he looked at them. Imagine a trip through the Jim Crow American South without a single reference to the black population.

*

Germany, East Central Europe, and Morality: Part 2, *World Affairs Journal*, July 2, 2012

Germans view the interwar period and World War II through the lens of Nazism and the Holocaust. Central and East Europeans view the interwar period and World War II through the lens of Nazism *and* Stalinism as well as the Holocaust *and* Communist genocides and atrocities. Their moral issues are infinitely more complex than Germany's, whose can more or less easily be viewed in black and white terms as a struggle of good versus evil and victims versus victimizers. Some Central and East Europeans were unquestionably bad; others were unquestionably good. But the vast majority—and that includes most Eastern European Jews—existed in a zone of reality that was simultaneously black, white, and every shade of gray. Victims were victimizers and victimizers were victims. Heroes could be villains and villains could be heroes. Most important, the vast majority of people were neither heroes nor villains. They simply tried to survive in awfully complex circumstances that usually offered them the choice between a very bad outcome and an extremely bad one. Ask yourself this: What was the right thing for an East Central European to do during the war? Support Stalin against Hitler, support Hitler against Stalin, fight both, collaborate with both, or try to survive both? From what I've seen of the behavior of Western policymakers, pundits, and tenured professors, I don't doubt for a second that the vast majority of them, and certainly those that preach the loudest, would have opted for collaborating with both while insisting that they were actually resisting valiantly.

It is only when Germany and Germans finally come to appreciate their less than altruistic role in East Central Europe and come to terms with their own moral responsibility for that dark past that both Germans and East Central Europeans will be in the position to cooperate fully, and without resentment or rancor, in investigating the entire dark past in the region. It'll help greatly if moral distinctions and complexities are treated careful- ly. In his recent *Chronicle of Higher Education* article, Paul Hockenos quotes a German researcher as saying, with reference to Polish anti-Semitic actions after the German oc- cupation, "The Holocaust didn't end when the Red Army entered Poland in 1944." Yes, it did, in the same way that genocides end when their perpetrators stop killing and wars end when attacking armies withdraw. The Holocaust—the name we give to Nazi Germany's mass destruction of European Jews—was a distinctly Nazi German project and it ex- isted only where Nazi power existed. (That's why Poles rightly insist that Auschwitz be called a Nazi death camp in Poland, and not a "Polish death camp.") To suggest that the Holocaust existed in the absence of Nazi Germany is to make the Holocaust coterminous with the history of anti-Semitism, to deprive the Holocaust of all meaning, to transfer responsibility for it from Nazi Germany to the world, and to engage in a brazen act of, ultimately, Holocaust denial. After all, if every act of anti-Jewish violence is part of the Holocaust, then Nazi Germany's culpability is reduced to zero, Hitler becomes no more responsible than some Ukrainian camp guard, and the tragedy itself becomes diffused throughout all of time.

Just a bit of reflection shows that without Hitler, without Germany's embrace of Nazi rule, and without Nazi Germany's initiation of World War II and pursuit of the Final Solution, there would have been no Holocaust. There would have been anti-Semitism in East Central Europe, there would have been discrimination against Jews, and there may have been pogroms, but there would have been no death camps, no Zyklon B gas, and no mass shootings. The causes of the Holocaust lie within Nazi Germany, the impetus for the Holocaust came out of Nazi Germany, and the moral responsibility for the Holocaust lies with Germany as well. Individual Czechs, Poles, Ukrainians, Hungarians, Lithuanians, Russians, Belarusians, and others collaborated with Nazi Germany, but their collabo- ration and moral turpitude was the situational product of Nazi Germany's aggressive and murderous designs on East Central Europe, and not the cause of them. It would never occur to us to extend the blame for European colonialism to Africans and Asians, even though many Africans and Asians were deeply implicated in colonial institutions. It would never occur to us to blame apartheid on the relatively more privileged "colored" and Indian populations of South Africa. It would never occur to us to blame slavery on the blacks Malcolm X called "house Negroes." And it would certainly never occur to us to place any blame for the Holocaust on the Jewish councils and Jewish police that adminis- tered the ghettos. Collaborators may or may not be odious, but they don't plan or start or serve as preconditions of the wars and genocides in which they are implicated.

Now please "read my lips." My call for moral distinctions is *not* a call for moral absolution or moral relativism. Quite the contrary, it *is* a call for moral responsibility. Let Germans come to terms with their moral failings and let East Central Europeans come to terms with theirs. No one should get off the hook, but let everyone hang on the proper hooks. As I write this, I know full well that readers who prefer their morality served up in the form of Hollywood Westerns will purposely misunderstand me: after all, simplicity is so much simpler than complexity and it's so much easier to believe that you're a hero and everyone else is a villain. And besides, there's nothing like throwing around epithets to end rational discussion and assert moral superiority.

So let me be perfectly clear—again. Central and Eastern Europeans have their own manifold mortal and venial sins to atone for: racism, chauvinism, massacres, and other atrocities, whether committed before the war, during the war, after the war, or today. No nation in the region has a spotless record, and Lord knows the Ukrainians certainly don't. Those East Central Europeans who aided and abetted Nazi Germany in the Holocaust must be held as responsible for aiding and abetting war criminals as those East Central Europeans who aided and abetted Lenin's and Stalin's genocides must be held responsible for aiding and abetting mass murderers. But to make "the Poles," "the Ukrainians," "the Russians," or other Eastern and Central Europeans responsible for "the Holocaust" is to engage in moral relativism, moral shirking, moral buck-passing, and, ultimately, astoundingly bad faith. And the one thing that is sure to transform a well-intentioned German investigator of East Central Europe's dark past into an "ugly German" is bad faith about Germany's contributions to that dark past.

*

Remembering an Erased Western Ukrainian Town, *World Affairs Journal*, July 9, 2012

I recently visited the western Ukrainian town my mother lived in. It's called Peremyshlyany and it's about 45 kilometers southeast of Lviv.

The town is a shadow of what it used to be. Back in the interwar period, Przemyślany (the Polish name) had a population of about 5,000, with Poles and Jews comprising about 90 percent and Ukrainians the rest. A railroad connected it to Lviv, or Lwów as it was then called, and the town appears to have displayed some class despite the difficult economic times. No less impressive was the political, cultural, and religious vibrancy of all three ethnic communities, each of which had a highly exclusionary sense of identity and all of which lived side by side, didn't like one another too much, but more or less got along.

World War II and its aftermath changed everything. First the Soviets killed Poles and Ukrainians. Then the Nazis exterminated the Jews. Then Ukrainians and Poles settled old scores. And, finally, the Soviets came back and drove out the Poles and killed many of the Ukrainians. Within a few years of the war's end, Peremyshlyany had changed completely. Its pre-war Jewish and Polish populations had disappeared, but so too had its pre-war Ukrainian population, most of whom had either died in the war, fled to the West, or been deported to Siberia. Their place was taken by new settlers—from other parts of Ukraine, from the surrounding villages, and from the formerly Ukrainian parts of Poland whose population was expelled in 1947.

Unsurprisingly, virtually all traces of the town's pre-war vibrancy also disappeared as Soviet totalitarianism forced everything, including history and memory, into its institutional straitjacket. Peremyshlyany's civil society was replaced with the Communist Party and its monolithic rule. The railroad that connected the town to Lviv had been bombed during the war and was never rebuilt, and a short commute to a metropolis turned into a complicated trek with unreliable buses. Although the economy grew thanks to some industry in the area, Peremyshlyany turned into a deeply provincial place. Things became worse after Ukraine became independent in 1991. The local economy went into a tailspin, unemployment rose, and large numbers of residents fled abroad to find work and send their meager earnings back home. A sense of listlessness and hopelessness descended on those who stayed, while the town itself became increasingly shabby. Those lucky enough to be receiving remittances from abroad have the money to fix up their houses and buy cars. Everything else, alas, looks gray and neglected and in need of a simple paint job.

Peremyshlyany has been "erased," to use Omer Bartov's term, several times over. The pre-war Jews and their memories are gone. The pre-war Poles and their memories are gone. The pre-war Ukrainians and their memories are gone. And, now, the post-war Ukrainians, with their Sovietized memories, are also going. The town's cemetery is about the only thing that's "alive and well."

That's too bad, as the town generated many remarkable individuals. One is my uncle, Bohdan Hevko. He'd spent some five years in Polish prisons in the 1930s, underwent extensive beatings and torture, was arrested by the Soviets on June 22, 1941, and then killed during the "night of long knives," on June 30th, along with thousands of other western Ukrainian political prisoners. The locals found him at the bottom of a pit, his hands tied behind his back with his underpants and his tongue torn out. Another is my mother's best friend, Fania Lacher, a Jewish girl who survived the Holocaust by finding refuge in a Ukrainian Catholic monastery, converted to Catholicism, became a nun, Sister Maria, and turned into a leading figure in the underground church in Soviet times. The love of her life was a young Ukrainian nationalist, Volodymyr Zaplatynsky, who helped hide her and her parents from the Nazis and took his life during a firefight with the Soviets in 1944. Still another is Father Omelian Kovch, the parish priest who persuaded the local Gymnazium to let my mother finish her studies tuition-free and who, for his efforts to save Jews, was arrested by the Nazis and killed in the Majdanek concentration camp. The street my mother lived on is named after Kovch, who was beatified by Pope John Paul II in 2001. And, finally, there was Adam Rothfeld, the future Polish minister of foreign affairs who survived the Holocaust in a nearby monastery.

Peremyshlyany is a sad and tragic place. I'm drawn to it precisely because so much of its history has been destroyed by the Nazis and Soviets. I'm also drawn to it because so much of that history lies just below the shabby surface and is struggling to get out. One could do worse than to remember Hevko, Lacher, Zaplatynsky, Kovch, Rothfeld, and the many others who were erased.

Santayana and Remembering the Past in Ukraine, *World Affairs Journal*, July 13, 2012

My current visit to Ukraine brings to mind the philosopher George Santayana's famous aphorism, that "those who cannot remember the past are condemned to repeat it," and its commonplace misrepresentation, that "those who forget history are doomed to repeat it."

Let's start with the fact that these two statements are completely different. Santayana is talking about a capacity or facility. That is, if we lack the capacity or facility to remember—i.e., if we cannot remember—we will suffer certain consequences. In contrast, the misrepresentation asserts that, unless we remember—i.e., if we forget—we will suffer certain consequences. To possess the capacity to remember does not mean that we must always exercise it, that we dare never forget. It means only that we are able to remember the past when we want to and, by logical extension, that we are able *not* to remember the past when we want to. According to the misrepresentation, we have no such choice. We *must* remember, we may not forget—*ever*—without suffe ing the consequences.

"Remember, if you desire or need to remember," is the polar opposite of "Never stop remembering!" The former is future-directed; the latter is past-directed. The former is about living one's life "in the moment" and in the moments to come; the latter is about living in the past. The former claim says that there may be lessons in the past that we may want to heed. The latter claim insists that the only lessons worth knowing are the lessons of the past. Santayana's injunction is liberating: it is premised on our freedom and on our freedom to choose how we live, what we remember, and how we cope with the future. The misrepresentation is confining: it is premised on our inability to remember wisely, to exercise choice, and to prepare for the future.

Santayana is right to say that the ability to remember can be useful in avoiding mistakes. Put that way, of course, the claim is hardly as profound as it may at first glance strike us. After all, who would dispute what is ultimately little more than an assertion of common sense? In contrast, the popular misrepresentation is likely to produce the very opposite of what it claims. If all we do is remember and never forget the past, how can we possibly live in the present and anticipate the future? Ironically, never forgetting and always remembering probably dooms us to repeating that which we never forget and always remember.

Which brings me to Ukraine. In Soviet times, the country and its people lacked the capacity to remember. That right was appropriated by the Communist Party and its propaganda machine, which churned out usable versions of a past that rarely corresponded to anything resembling the "real" past. Independent Ukraine seized back that capacity and has been doing little but trying to remember since 1991. Those efforts have produced mixed results. The people who can remember the past are mostly dead, much of the documentary evidence of the past has been destroyed by the Soviets and the Nazis, the magnitude of Soviet distortions of the past far exceeds the capacity of Ukraine's overworked historians to correct them, and the far more institutionalized remembrances of Poles, Russians, and Jews often reduce Ukrainians to bit players, voiceless Others, and brutes.

Has remembering kept Ukraine from repeating past mistakes? Hardly. If remembering were a panacea, Ukraine would be Switzerland, and not Zimbabwe. If we accept as true the claim that non-remembering leads to repetition of mistakes, it does not logically follow that remembering leads to non-repetition of mistakes. So what good is remembering? It may be a great way to build identities and to settle political scores, but remembering is only marginally useful when it comes to solving problems. Look at the Israelis and Palestinians: the more they remember, the less capable they become of solving their problems today. Look at Germany: its commemoration of the Holocaust hasn't prevented it from being supremely indifferent to human rights violations in Russia. Look at the United States: its obsession with the Founding Fathers offers little guidance to fixing the American economy and polity.

These examples suggest two conclusions. First, that remembering and problem-fixing are very different things and the connection between them is hardly as obvious as misrepresentations of Santayana suggest. And second, that the state, as the key problem fixer, should keep a low profile when it comes to remembering.

For one thing, the state is a clumsy and inefficient instrument for remembering the past. If it can't pick economic winners, how can it pick historical winners? More important, the state—and, above all, the profoundly corrupt and self-centered Ukrainian state—has its own interests, and these are, after all, to live well at popular expense. When the state promotes remembrance, cui really bono?

This is not to say that, as the Regionnaires insist, the Holodomor should be erased, that World War II should forever remain the Great Fatherland War, that Ukraine should not accept the historical validity of the anti-Soviet nationalist resistance movement, and so on. After all, the Regionnaires want to turn back the clock and reintroduce Stalinist policies of enforced misremembering. But it is to say that the best form of remembering is societal remembering.

Let people remember. Let historians remember. Let people tell historians what they believe is important. And let historians tell people what they think really happened. And let the state remember to fix the country and itself.

*

A Jewish Diarist in Occupied Ukraine, *World Affairs Journal*, August 31, 2012

Just around the time I was writing a recent blog post on my mother's hometown of Peremyshlyany, I came upon a fascinating diary by Samuel Golfard, a victim of the Holocaust in that very place. (The full bibliographic reference is: Wendy Lower, ed., *The Diary of Samuel Golfard and the Holocaust in Galicia*; AltaMira Press, 2011.)

Don't read the diary for Lower's superficial introduction. Although an impressively productive Holocaust scholar, Lower knows little about Ukraine and even less about Peremyshlyany and simply superimposes a ready-made Holocaust "template" on a complex country and town. But do read the diary for a gut-wrenching glimpse into the heart and mind of an articulate Polish Jew who fled his native Radom after Hitler and Stalin dismembered Poland in September 1939 and, along with more than 2,000 other Jewish refugees, settled in Peremyshlyany, then part of Soviet Ukraine. Golfard's diary was written in Polish and encompasses the period from January 25 to April 14, 1943.

Golfard's friend and fellow refugee, Jacob Littman, describes him as "an urbane, informed, and self-confident man" with "liberal-progressive-leftist convictions." In the months before his death, writes Littman, Golfard "was the only Jew in the immediate territory to land a job with a German firm in charge of collecting scrap metals for recycling… [He] became a garbage collector with no pay but with a tin badge on his chest to prove his special status." That status enabled Golfard to look, to see, and to reflect.

Golfard comes down hard on everybody. He denounces the local Jewish Council in no uncertain terms: "Those bandits have done their duty, have finally recognized that it is time to leave. Instead of arming young people and sending them to the woods, they consigned them until now to camps and a slow agony. They 'saved' Jewry by taking contributions from them, rounding them up for the camps, and deploying the Jewish militia in the massacres, as long as there was no threat to themselves. They sacrificed their people for the price of their own lives. Now, fleeing with their moneybags, they disappear in the nick of time—leaving, at last, the few remaining Jews to their own inevitable fate." Golfard's judgment is rather harsh, but his sense of betrayal and his outrage are perfectly understandable.

About Germans, Golfard speaks like a biblical prophet: "Let the German people be cursed forever. Let the damnation of the murdered mothers, children, and elderly pursue the German people to their own ultimate destruction." However, notes Golfard, "The Germans are not alone guilty of our tragic fate. The English and the Americans who tolerated the acts of the German nation are also guilty. They fattened Hitler and nurtured the present regime in Germany." Oddly, Golfard fails to condemn Stalin, who, as he obviously knew, "fattened" Hitler in 1939–1941.

Golfard's views of Ukrainians are both highly critical and remarkably measured. On the one hand, he says: "The participation of Ukrainians in the murder of hundreds of thousands of Jews is beyond any dispute. To this day they carry out, often ruthlessly, the beastly Hitlerian orders. … In Przemyślany the perpetrators of this were the Ukrainians. Had they been allowed, they would even today take apart the entire ghetto in their passion for plunder." On the other hand, Golfard also notes: "I cannot for a moment equate a people with a bigger or smaller minority of its bandits. They can be found in each nation, even among the Jews."

Poles come across best in Golfard's account. True, he writes that "Poles as well … would rather send helpless ones to death, even when extending some help posed no threat to them." But Golfard also says the following: "In the camps the flower of the Polish nation is perishing. Millions of Poles in Germany do the work of hard labor convicts. Tens of thousands have perished in camps. … The nation in bondage is carrying a heavy yoke. But not for a moment does the nation lose hope that freedom and the fatherland will be restored." Clearly, Golfard's is not the prevalent image of Poles as inveterate anti-Semites.

Naturally, Golfard's views, like those of all diarists and memoirists, must be taken with a grain of salt. He came to Peremyshlyany in mid-1941 and obviously had no time to understand the complexities of the town and its inhabitants. Living on the edge of extinction, while possibly feeling guilty for enjoying "special status," was unlikely to foster moderate views. And, as a left-wing Jew from central Poland, Golfard probably shared many of the stereotypes that characterized Polish views of their eastern borderlands and left-wing views of nationality relations.

In that sense, Golfard was, as one would expect, a man of his times. Like most interwar Europeans and Americans (even those who claimed to be democrats), he believed that "Every nation possesses its innate traits." Thus, "I became convinced that there is no and has never been any racial solidarity among Jews." The innate trait of Poles is "their overly hot temperament and recklessness. With the Ukrainians, it is indisputably their hypocrisy and cruelty." In other words, Jews can't get along, Poles are hotheads, and Ukrainians, like the anti-Semitic image of Jews, are crafty and vicious and have a "passion for plunder."

Like most left-wingers, however, Golfard believes that these traits, though "hereditary," are "by no means constant. They developed in the psyche of the Ukrainian masses as a result of their political situation, always uncertain, and as a response to the methods of ruthlessness and violence that constituted their daily bread in our eastern lands" from the 17th century onward. Indeed, concludes Golfard, class is at the root of all evils: "Despite its nationalistic appearance, the struggle in the eastern provinces has its base in class discrimination with the nationalist factor only as a secondary phenomenon aroused by political parties and foreign forces."

Golfard died in mid-1943 while attempting to shoot a Nazi official. His death was as heroic as his attempt to survive as a scrap-metal collector was not. His comments are as insightful and objective as they are one-sided and extreme. Samuel Golfard was human—indeed, very fallibly human—and he reminds us that World War II and the Holocaust were not scholarly constructs or polemical devices, but enormous human tragedies.

*

Genocide's Definition Revisited, *World Affairs Journal*, October 19, 2012

If you think you know what Raphael Lemkin, the originator of the term *genocide*, thought about genocide, think again. A dissertation-in-progress on Lemkin and the history of the United Nations Genocide Convention by Douglas Irvin-Erickson, a doctoral student in global affairs at Rutgers University-Newark, is likely to change how we think and talk about genocide.

As Irvin-Erickson writes in an article ("The Romantic Signature of Raphael Lemkin") scheduled to appear in the *Journal of Genocide Research*:

> Lemkin used the work of an art historian to define nations as "families of minds." ... Lemkin intended the word genocide to signify the cultural destruction of peoples, which could occur without a perpetrator employing violence at all. In his 1944 *Axis Rule in Occupied Europe*, Lemkin wrote that genocide was "a coordinated plan of different actions aiming at the destruction of essential foundations of the life of national groups, with the aim of annihilating the groups themselves." A colonial practice, genocide had two phases: "One, the destruction of the national pattern of the oppressed group; the other, the imposition of the national pattern of the oppressor."

Genocide, in other words, is not, in Lemkin's understanding, about mass killing per se, but about the destruction of nations qua nations. Mass killing is, thus, a means to the end of genocide, and not its goal.

Lemkin adopted his definition of a nation as a family of minds in the context of his writing on the French genocide against Algeria, where he believed that the French colonial power was breaking the "bodily and mental integrity" of the Algerian people.... The goal of the genocide, Lemkin wrote, was to integrate Algerians into the French Republic and prevent Algeria from emerging from colonial rule.

Keep in mind that here, too, genocide for Lemkin is not the bloody and brutal war fought between France and the Algerians in the 1950s and early 1960s, but the entire French colonial project that attempted to destroy the Algerian "family of mind."

Lemkin believed the political regimes led by Hitler and Stalin both committed genocide.... [T]hese two regimes shared the defining characteristic of attempting to destroy the national patterns of the oppressed groups and replace it with a "Sovietness" or "Germanness." Lemkin argued that the Russian and Soviet attack on the Ukrainians, Poles, Hungarians, Romanians, Jews, the Crimean and Tatar Republics, the Baltic nations of Lithuania, Estonia and Latvia, and the total annihilation of the Ingerian nation, were all genocides, before and during Stalin's reign.

Genocide, Lemkin asserted, was a long-term element of the Kremlin's internal policy and "an indispensable step in the process of 'union' that the Soviet leaders fondly hope will produce the 'Soviet Man,' the 'Soviet Nation.'" Just as the Nazi genocide sought to eradicate the national patterns of the occupied territories and install a distinct "Germanness" to consolidate state control, "the leaders of the Kremlin will gladly destroy the nations and the cultures that have long inhabited Eastern Europe." The Ukrainian genocide was "an essential part of the Soviet program for expansion, for it offers the quick way of bringing unity out of the diversity of cultures and nations that constitute the Soviet Empire."

It follows from the above that, according to Lemkin, the Holodomor—the famine of 1932–1933—was only one of the means employed by the Stalinist regime to Sovietize and Russify the Ukrainian nation. The actual genocide was Sovietization and Russification, processes that were initiated during the Civil War of 1918–1921, revived by Stalin in the late 1920s, and then vigorously pursued by him and all his successors, including Nikita Khrushchev and Leonid Brezhnev, into the early 1980s. It was only under the liberalizing rule of Mikhail Gorbachev that the Russificationist project, and hence genocide, was abandoned.

The genocide was not that Stalin's regime killed so many people, but that these individuals were killed with the purpose of destroying the Ukrainian way of life, an argument in line with his writings on how the French colonial state sought to eradicate Algerian national consciousness through state terror, political disenfranchisement, and poverty…. The most devastating aspect of the genocide for Lemkin was not the death of individuals, but the potential loss of a cohesive group who shared a common belief in their unity through language, customs, art, or even a sense of shared history.

Irvin-Erickson here raises the intriguing possibility that the cultural policies of the current Yanukovych regime would qualify as genocidal in Lemkin's eyes. After all, there is little doubt that their purpose is: "One, the destruction of the national pattern of the oppressed group; the other, the imposition of the national pattern of the oppressor." In this case, "the Ukrainian way of life" would, in the Yanukovych regime's scheme of things, be replaced with the "Donbas pattern of the oppressor"—a way of life that is Soviet, criminal, and Lumpen-Russian. As the pesky Ukrainian "family of mind" gives way to a "family" of, as Czeslaw Milosz might have put it, "captive minds," what's left of Ukrainians as a "cohesive group who shared a common belief in their unity through language, customs, art, or even a sense of shared history"?

Naturally, you needn't reach this conclusion—but only if you disagree with Lemkin's views on genocide.

*

Yanukovych and Stalin's Genocide, *World Affairs Journal*, November 29, 2012

Every November Ukraine commemorates the Holodomor, the famine and genocide of 1932 and 1933. Since 2010, President Viktor Yanukovych has marked the occasion with a formal address to the people. Read in isolation, none of them is terribly interesting. A comparative look at all three speeches, however, reveals some interesting shifts in tone and content that may illuminate Yanukovych's own evolving thinking about the genocide and his regime.

But first a striking continuity. Yanukovych has never called the Holodomor a genocide. He's called it a crime, a tragedy, and an Armageddon, but not genocide. Ironically, he does use the term Holodomor, which means "killing by means of hunger" and, in that sense, is virtually a synonym for genocide. There are indications that this reluctance to call a spade a spade may change.

Back in 2010, during his first encounter with Holodomor Remembrance day, Yanukovych stated (this and subsequent citations are the translations provided on his website):

> I bow to the memory of those innocently killed by the Holodomor.

> Even now, the tragedy of 1932–1933 is difficult to comprehend. It was a real Armageddon, when people were loosing [*sic*] their human essence because of hunger.

> Therefore, this national tragedy that has devoured millions of innocent people, is no subject to oblivion.

Note the reference to "a real Armageddon" and the "millions of innocent people." Note as well, however, that Yanukovych treats the Holodomor almost as if it were a natural catastrophe that somehow befell Ukraine. And he can't resist chiding the Orange government of Viktor Yushchenko for its efforts to commemorate the famine:

> However, when these sad commemorations have begun to resemble a conveyor, when at numerous gatherings and round tables some so-called "scientists" have begun throwing around with ease the numbers of those, who died of starvation—3 million—5 million—7 million and even more, it became a blasphemy. After all, even one person's death is an uncompensated loss not only for the family, but also for the Cosmos. So how can one throw around millions at the abacus as though it is something insignificant? It is an unforgivable sin.

One year later, in 2011, Yanukovych's speech strikes different tones. For one, it's much shorter—94 words as opposed to 336 in 2010, when finger-pointing was the order of the day. For another, Yanukovych clearly implies that the famine had a political cause: totalitarianism.

> Every year, in late November, we pay tribute to the victims of a terrible famine that killed millions of people. The unprecedented tragedy of global scale inflicted an irreparable loss on Ukraine.

> Terrible years of totalitarianism have been a spiritual catastrophe: numerous churches were demolished, hundreds of thousands of peasants, workers, and intellectuals were physically eliminated or sent to the Gulag camps, almost every Ukrainian family suffe ed.

The bravado that characterized the 2010 speech is also gone: after almost two years of power, Yanukovych knew he had little to boast about and ends his speech as follows:

Preserving the sacred memory of our tragic past, the Ukrainian state is confidently moving forward, building civil society on the principles of rights and freedoms, laying a solid foundation for future generations.

In 2012, a further shift is evident. The speech is still short (141 words), but the Holodomor is now a "crime" and crimes always have, as we know, perpetrators. Yanukovych doesn't say who is responsible and he expands the Holodomor to "other countries of the former USSR," but the implication is clear: the totalitarian Soviet regime committed the crime.

> These days it will turn 80 years since trouble has come to our land.

> In the period of 1932–1933, Holodomor covered the territory of Ukraine and other countries of former USSR.

> This crime has changed the history of Ukrainian people forever. It has been one of the severest challenges of Ukrainians. Holodomor not only killed people, but also had the purpose of causing fear and obedience. For decades, any mention of those dreadful events has been banned.

No less important, there is no talk of past or present governments and their failures or achievements: after all, by November 2012 Yushchenko is just a memory and the Yanukovych regime is a complete bust. Instead, Yanukovych acts like a politician in serious trouble and praises the people for their fortitude and strength:

> But Ukrainian people demonstrated tenacity. Due to belief in its power, love to Ukraine, primordial pursuit of freedom and independence we have survived.

> Today, a little candle flame unites us in a prayer for souls of Holodomor victims. We also remember those who shared the last piece of bread and saved lives of compatriots.

Here's a tentative prediction. If the regime continues to decay at its current rate and if the economy tanks, as it's very likely to do, Yanukovych will—hold on to your seats!—utter the word genocide in his Holodomor commemorative address of 2013. If he does, you'll know that he knows his days in power are numbered.

*

Soviet-Style Imperialism and the Ukrainian Language, *World Affairs Journal*, February 11, 2013

An important new book by the distinguished University of Vienna linguist Michael Moser promises to be the definitive account of the anti-Ukrainian language policies of the Yanukovych regime. Entitled *Language Policy and Discourse on Languages in Ukraine under President Viktor Janukovyč, 25 February 2010–28 October 2012*, Moser's monograph is slated for publication as part of the "Soviet and Post-Soviet Politics and Society" series with Ibidem Press in Germany. Professor Moser is the author of eight books and a specialist on the Slavic languages in general and Ukrainian, in particular.

The book begins with a short overview of the Ukrainian language's historical development and treatment by both the Russian tsarist and Soviet regimes. In particular, during the Soviet period:

> The population of Ukraine was increasingly Russified through Russian-language education, Russian-language media, and the prevalent use of Russian in the public sphere. The use of the Ukrainian language was increasingly restricted to intellectual spheres that were under control of the totalitarian system, while the Ukrainian language standard was brought as close to Russian as possible. Apart from the Western territories that became part of the Soviet Union only in 1944, the Ukrainian standard language was rarely spoken in the streets of Ukrainian cities. Owing to widespread Soviet propaganda, those who did so were readily labeled either as country bumpkins or as "nationalists." These tendencies lost momentum only when the Soviet Union was already about to collapse. But while the breakup of the Soviet Union did bring about a revival of the Ukrainian language, Russian never ceased to be widely used or even dominate in many spheres of life.

Given seven decades of forced Russification and de-Ukrainization, the Russian language enjoys exalted status in independent Ukraine. As Moser says, "My main argument is that the Russian language has never been under threat in Ukraine, but on the contrary tends to threaten the Ukrainian language." Worse, the Yanukovych regime and the Party of Regions are doing everything they can to discriminate against the Ukrainian language and promote Russian.

> While President Viktor Janukovyč and many others have routinely declared that Ukraine's language legislation must go along "the European way" ... concrete political actions have had a quite different touch and not led to any actual support [of] Ukrainian prior to the elections of 28 October 2012. Instead, it has only been the Russian language that has been quite efficiently promoted under the slogan of the "human right for the native language." One vehicle of the propaganda has been the insistence on the alleged importance ... of the European Charter for Regional or Minority Languages in Ukraine. This deserves attention inasmuch as Russian, though in fact legally protected by the Charter, does not meet the criteria of a regional or minority language as defined by the Charter itself. In contrast, neither the President nor the party in power have demonstrated any serious efforts for the development of any of the true regional or minority languages of Ukraine—or for the "human rights" of the speakers of those languages. Moreover, virtually nothing has been done to meet the demands of Ukrainophone citizens of Ukraine with regard to spheres where Ukrainian is obviously underrepresented, as in the media.

But that's not all. As I've repeatedly argued in this blog, the Yanukovych regime doesn't just discriminate against Ukrainian language, identity, and culture, it is positively hostile and in fact embraces a discourse and worldview that can best be termed "Russian supremacist," with all the nasty connotations that term conveys. According to Professor Moser: "those representatives of the party in power who take an active part in Ukrainian language policy routinely refer to the Ukrainian language and identity only along patterns that have been well-known since Russian imperial and Soviet times. ... they stick to an image of Ukrainian as an incomplete or 'soiled' language of little or no value as compared to the 'great and powerful' Russian language."

Unsurprisingly, Ukraine's domestic Ukrainophobes have found support in Vladimir Putin's hyper-chauvinist Russia.

> Particularly since 2004, official Russia and other ideologists of Russkij Mir [the Russian World Foundation] have routinely stigmatized the alleged suppression of the Russian language and the Russophone population of Ukraine, while the minority rights of the Ukrainian population, the second-largest minority in the Russian Federation, have increasingly been not only neglected, but even violated during the past two and a half years. Along with that, official Russia has returned to Russian imperialist ideologemes denying the very existence of the Ukrainian nation and language. Moreover, Russkij Mir ideologists in Russia as well as in Ukraine have increasingly depicted any initiatives for the support of the Ukrainian language as "nationalist" or "fascist" and stylized their own attempts to maintain or enlarge the Russian sphere of influence in the post-Soviet space, for which the Russian language plays a crucial role, under the slogan of a struggle against "fascism."

There are several villains in Moser's measured account, but two are worth mentioning. The first is the notorious anti-intellectual thug Vadim Kolesnichenko, who was the driving force behind the anti-Ukrainian language law adopted by Ukraine's Parliament last summer. Here's Moser on Kolesnichenko: "Kolesničenko's discourse perfectly demonstrates the essence of the current struggle for the 'human right for the native language' in Ukraine. The same person who routinely refers to 'European values' and the necessity of the democratization of Ukraine, particularly in the sphere of language legislation, routinely makes statements that present him as a totalitarian politician of a neo-Stalinist type, who has cultivated a remarkable type of post-Soviet new-speak filled with hate rhetoric."

The other villain is, of course, the notorious intellectual thug Dmitri Tabachnik, Ukraine's minister of education, science, youth, and sports. According to Moser: "In the educational sphere, where the dissemination of the Ukrainian language had been most successful until 2010 (although Russophone schools or classes have always remained widespread particularly in the South and the East of the country) ... Tabačnyk has made all possible efforts to cut the use of Ukrainian language and foster the use [of] Russian instead. This concerns preschool, school, and university teaching as well as the production of textbooks or the procedures of entrance exams. Tabačnyk continues to deny the very existence of the Ukrainian nation even as Minister of Ukraine."

Professor Moser's conclusions are not entirely gloomy:

> There is no doubt that language policy as conducted under Viktor [Janukovyč's] Presidency will have a major impact on the history of the Ukrainian language in the years to come, and that this impact will tend to be to the detriment of the state language. In the end, however, the actual impact of this policy depends on factors that are not under the direct control of politics. The decisive factor will

be the reaction of all citizens of Ukraine[:] Those who speak whatever language they wish, but accept the status of Ukrainian as the state language of Ukraine and have a favorable attitude toward it, [a]nd those whose preferred language is Ukrainian and whose loyalty toward their language is of crucial importance.

There are two other reasons for some optimism. First, the Yanukovych regime is dreadfully incompetent, and policymakers who cannot tie their own shoelaces are unlikely to destroy a language. And second, the regime and its supremacist allies won't be around for much longer. Ukrainian language, culture, and identity will.

*

Fixing Ukraine's Villages One House at a Time, *World Affairs Journal*, February 22, 2013

If you've ever been to Ukraine's countryside, you may have noticed that many villages look like holdouts from the late nineteenth century. Dirt roads are the norm, water frequently must be hauled from wells, and outhouses abound.

Don't blame the villagers for that. Put the blame squarely on Joseph Stalin and the Communist Party. Collectivization destroyed Soviet agriculture, while the forced starvation of 1932–1933, known as the Holodomor, destroyed the Ukrainian peasantry. Nazi occupation policies during World War II only made things worse, while continued Soviet neglect of agriculture condemned the peasants to a nether existence up to the end of the Soviet Union. Collective farmers had a third-class status that some analysts even compared to modern-day serfdom.

Independence did little to revive the countryside. The collapse of Soviet central planning led to the collapse of most post-Soviet economies, Ukraine's included. Inefficient collective farms fell apart and were replaced by subsistence farming; villagers headed for the cities or, if possible, Western Europe for work, and the village population, already aged and poor in Soviet times, became even more so. Out-migration also changed the sex balance. Before 1991, the only surefire way of leaving one's village was to be drafted into the army: a trend that favored young men. Nowadays, it's mature women who are most likely to get jobs as global nannies and Euro-housecleaners.

And yet, as a drive through Ukraine's countryside shows, many villages appear to be experiencing a building boom. A big reason is the remittances that Ukrainian labor migrants to Italy, Spain, Portugal, Germany, Great Britain, Russia, and Poland send home. Another reason is that those who've stayed are proud of their villages and want to raise their socioeconomic development. A third is that some provincial governments provide villagers with micro-loans for capital improvements of their homesteads.

For example, take the Lviv Province Fund for Supporting Individual Housing

Construction in Villages, in existence since 2000, which disburses loans as part of the "Your Own House" program. Borrowers only need to live, work, and build housing in rural areas, and, of course, be able to repay the loan according to the terms of the loan agreement. Those are very generous: you can get a loan for up to 20 years at 3 percent per annum, while the banks charge almost 30 percent. Provincial inputs into the fund's budget have grown from 219,500 hryvnia in 2005 to almost a million (or about $123,000) in 2012, while the central government has provided a total of 9.9 million hryvnia since 2000. In that same period, repayment of loans has jumped from 119,500 hryvnia to more than 1.1 million. From 12 to 35 buildings and roughly 1,000 to 4,000 square meters of land are involved on an annual basis: not a crash program, obviously, but the improvements add up. Most important, the improvements are real: houses get fixed, roofs get replaced, homesteads are modernized—and more than 320 families' immediate lives have gotten better. You'll be happy to know that loans are distributed without regard to "nationality, religious beliefs, sex, or family status."

The head of the fund happens to be a good friend of mine, the 59-year-old Zenoviy Drevnyak, who may have learned a thing or two about regional management while on a three-month internship with a Washington, DC, NGO in the early 1990s. "Zenko" is no political activist and no *biznesmen*. He's just a regular guy who wants to make his country work. And if you've been to Ukraine, you'll know that there are thousands of people, men and women, young and old, just like him: low-key patriots who understand that, in the final analysis, they are responsible for Ukraine's future.

Zenko's latest scheme is to revive the tiny village of Sernyky, located about 45 minutes southeast of Lviv. Sernyky encompasses Rehfeld, a settlement founded by German farmer-colonists in the late eighteenth century. They were "repatriated" to Germany by Hitler in 1940, and the village became completely Ukrainian in the aftermath of World War II. Zenko bought a dilapidated house formerly owned by one of the Germans, Adam Lang. He and his wife fixed it up, set up an organic garden, and hold weekly grill parties for friends, neighbors, and relatives. He also helped refurbished a broken-down chapel, established a Sernyky website, and reached out to a website that serves as a meeting place for descendants of German colonists from Galicia. Zenko's hope is to attract German tourists and, at some point, perhaps even convert the village's other run-down chapel into a small museum.

This could all turn out to be what Germans might call a *Schnapsidee* (a crazy idea), but then again: *warum nicht?*

*

Monuments, Ambiguity, and Double Standards, *World Affairs Journal*, May 31, 2013

They're smashing monuments in Ukraine again. In the eastern provinces, it's Vladimir Lenin who's under attack. In the western provinces, it's usually Stepan Bandera, the leader of the interwar nationalist movement. Heads, fingers, and noses are being hacked away, tempers are flaring, activists are outraged. Meanwhile, Europeans and Americans are tut-tutting and wondering why those crazy Ukrainians don't do things their way.

Which way would that be?

On a recent visit to Moscow, John Kerry let himself be photographed near Stalin's bust. Indeed, the State Department released the photo with the following caption: "US Secretary of State John Kerry and Russian Chief of Protocol Yuriy Filatov, with US Ambassador to Russia Michael McFaul behind, walk past Joseph Stalin's tomb in Red Square in Moscow, Russia, on May 7, 2013." What's more disturbing—that Russia still has a Stalin monument in Red Square or that the State Department doesn't see the problem with photographing Kerry near it?

How about Hollywood? Quentin Tarantino's *Inglourious Basterds* and *Django Unchained* are unalloyed glorifications of sadism, violence, and serial killing, performed in living color by good guys (us) against bad guys (them). I dare say most fascists and Nazis would have found Tarantino's sentiments appealing. And yet, both films got decent to excellent reviews and were wildly popular with American and European audiences. Should Ukrainians emulate Quentin?

Or perhaps they should emulate Steven Spielberg's *Lincoln*? Crotchety ol' Abe, as ably played by Daniel Day-Lewis, lies, cheats, violates laws, ignores the Constitution, commits a slew of offences that, today, would guarantee him impeachment, and prolongs a war, thereby sending thousands of men to their deaths (while assigning his war-hungry son to a cushy job with General Grant), and, yet, the consensus among publics and reviewers was that Spielberg's Lincoln was a hero. Would they say the same about Viktor Yanukovych, who has also been known to have, er, liberal attitudes toward Ukraine's laws and Constitution and who treats his offspring with no less solicitude?

The problem is that the people monuments immortalize are always far more ambiguous than the material physicality of the monuments suggests. Everybody, and especially heroes, has skeletons in closets. Everybody has dirty laundry. Everybody has a checkered past. Even saints. St. Paul was once Saul, the persecutor of Christians. St. Augustine was a dissolute young man. Countries, peoples, nations, states, and religions generally commemorate people for what they believe was the good they did. And, at the same time, they turn a blind eye to the bad things or dismiss them as irrelevant to the overall picture.

I once asked my Rutgers University undergraduate students if they could guess who made the following statements:

- "From what I have already seen of the workings of the Soviet government, I can only say that anybody who lifts his hand against it ought to be shot!"

- "They have sung—sing now and will sing his praise—in song and story. Slava-slava-slava—Stalin, Glory to Stalin. Forever will his name be honored and beloved in all lands. In all spheres of modern life the influence of Stalin reaches wide and deep. From his last simply written but vastly discerning and comprehensive document, back through the years, his contributions to the science of our world society remain invaluable. One reverently speaks of Marx, Engels, Lenin and Stalin—the shapers of humanity's richest present and future. Yes, through his deep humanity, by his wise understanding, he leaves us a rich and monumental heritage. Most importantly—he has charted the direction of our present and future struggles. He has pointed the way to peace—to friendly co-existence—to the exchange of mutual scientific and cultural contributions—to the end of war and destruction. How consistently, how patiently, he labored for peace and ever increasing abundance, with what deep kindliness and wisdom. He leaves tens of millions all over the earth bowed in heart-aching grief."

They agreed it had to be some totalitarian monster. Imagine their surprise when I told them it was Paul Robeson, the Rutgers alumnus and renowned African American civil rights activist, who also happened to be a fervent Stalinist. He made the first comment in 1935, as Stalin was destroying his opponents, and the second in 1953, after Stalin's death. Needless to say, if you view the campus display devoted to Robeson—in, naturally, Robeson Hall—these quotations are missing.

Back in 2007, Estonians decided to relocate a monument to the Red Army on the grounds that Stalin's armed forces brought enslavement to their country for more than 40 years. And who could disagree?

A few years later, Israel decided to build a monument to the Red Army and its victory over the Nazis. As Prime Minister Benjamin Netanyahu put it, "About half a million of Jews fought in the Red Army, and many of them are still living in Israel. This memorial is also a tribute to their heroism and contribution to the victory." And who could disagree?

Vienna's monument to the Red Army is still standing, having been built by the Soviet occupation authorities in 1945. It dominates Schwarzenbergplatz, which until 1956 was known as Stalinplatz. Few Viennese regard the Red Army as a force of liberation; and many Austrian and German women remember the mass rapes that Soviet soldiers (among whom there must have been some Estonians and Jews) were encouraged to commit in 1945. Should the Austrians tear down the statue or leave it alone? Should they follow the example of those Bulgarians who painted the figures on their Red Army memorial in Sofia as comic-book superheroes? Should the Estonians have invoked or apologized for the mass rapes in Germany and Austria in arguing for their monument's relocation? Should the Israelis have dismissed or apologized for them in deciding to build theirs?

The answer is that there are no easy one-size-fits-all answers. I'm inclined to suggest that all the monuments in Ukraine be left alone. If some East Ukrainian town wants to be associated with one of the 20th century's greatest mass murderers, let it. If some West Ukrainian town wants to identify with a nationalist leader from the 1930s, let it. I think both could do better—and both will pay the price in terms of tourism, investment, and cultural, political, and social development—but then again I also think Vienna, Moscow, Tel Aviv, Hollywood, and my university could do better. Meanwhile, as Ukrainians try to sort things out, it may be best for European and North American moralists—and especially all of us with ethically challenged personal lives and well-paying jobs in the academic world—to stop their finger-pointing, smirking, and lecturing.

*

On Nationalism and Fascism, Part 1, *World Affairs Journal*, June 10, 2013

Ukrainian "nationalism" has been in the news these last few years. As usually happens with words that have seeped into our daily vocabulary, nationalism in general and Ukrainian nationalism in particular have come to mean just about anything. Its detractors, many of whom believe that Adolf Hitler's National Socialism demonstrates that nationalism and fascism are inextricably connected, insist Ukrainian nationalism is a form of fascism. Its supporters, who often invoke Giuseppe Mazzini, say it's noble and empowering.

Compounding the problem, many of the historians who study Ukraine show little interest in conceptual clarity. How we define things matters enormously, because definitions enable us to group similar things together and explain them systematically. The alternative, a habit of sloppy scholars, is a seat-of-the-pants approach that permits flawed comparisons. So please bear with me, as we go through some conceptual exercises.

Let's start our enquiry by asking what fascism is *not*. Well, for starters, it's not any of the things that casual users of the term appear to mean when they apply it to people they dislike. Intolerance may be a bad thing, but it is not fascism. Violence may be abhorrent, but it too isn't fascism. Nor is conservatism, xenophobia, or racism. Richard Nixon may have been soft on all these features, but it would be absurd to suggest, as many on the left do, that he was a fascist. The term fascist is not and cannot and should not just be shorthand for stuff e don't care for, if only because everybody soon becomes a fascist.

So how do we define fascism? Fascism, I suggest, is best conceived of as a *type* of regime, political system, or state on the same order as democracy, authoritarianism, dictatorship, oligarchy, totalitarianism, and the like. That is, fascism, like other types of regimes, political systems, or states, is fundamentally concerned with *how* regimes, political systems, or states are structured and organized. Fascism is thus "about" the political institutions of regimes, systems, and states.

Fascism may also be conceived of as an ideology or as a movement, group, or organization. Fascism as an ideology is a set of core beliefs that justify and promote fascism as a type of regime, political system, or state, while fascism as a movement, group, or organization is a human collective that shares a fascist ideology. A fascist individual would obviously be someone who believes in such an ideology.

Fascism as a type of regime, political system, or state; fascism as a set of beliefs about the correct organization of a regime, political system, or state; and fascism as a human collective with a fascist ideology all presuppose an existing state that should be transformed into one that corresponds to fascist ideals. Fascism and fascists aspire to change existing non-fascist regimes, political systems, or states into fascist regimes, political systems, or states. Fascism and fascists may aspire to do so legally, democratically, and constitutionally or they may aspire to do so illegally, undemocratically, and unconstitutionally, but their end goal is always anti-democratic.

The type of regime, political system, or state that fascism and fascists aspire to create is generally acknowledged to be a variant of authoritarianism or totalitarianism. Fascist regimes, political systems, or states are thus invariably anti-democratic, but, in contrast to run-of-the-mill authoritarian or totalitarian regimes, political systems, or states, fascist regimes, political systems, or states exalt "the leader." In turn, fascist leaders in fascist regimes, political systems, or states are, or attempt to be, charismatic, and they usually view themselves as spokesmen for "the nation," an entity that fascism treats as a monolith.

As the quintessential fascist, Benito Mussolini was the charismatic leader of a movement with a fascist ideology that proceeded to establish a fascist regime within an already existing Italian state. Adolf Hitler, if you consider Nazism to be an extreme variant of fascism, acted in the exact same manner as Mussolini, the only difference being that the former won power in an election while the latter seized it. Francisco Franco came to power by winning a civil war. Vladimir Putin, whose regime I've called quasi-fascist, came to power both legally and illegally. The way in which fascists seize power may therefore vary, but where they seize it (within an existing state) and what they then do (transform it into an authoritarian state with a charismatic leader) is pretty much constant.

To summarize: Fascism's two preconditions are an already existing state and an already existing non-fascist *type* of regime, political system, or state. Fascists do not build states *de novo*; nor do they build *types* of regimes, political systems, or states *de novo*. Unsurprisingly, it is in fact the case that fascism and fascists are always found in already existing states with already existing non-fascist types of regimes, political systems, or states.

*

On Nationalism and Fascism, Part 2, *World Affairs Journal*, June 14, 2013

In contrast to fascism, nationalism is *not* best conceived of as a type of regime, political system, or state (on the same order as fascism, democracy, authoritarianism, dictatorship, oligarchy, totalitarianism, and the like) for two very simple conceptual reasons. First, a nationalist regime, political system, or state would have to be a set of political institutions that are fundamentally different from those that characterize fascism, democracy, authoritarianism, dictatorship, oligarchy, or totalitarianism. But there is no such distinctly different nationalist regime, political system, or state with its own distinct political institutions. Instead, every supposedly nationalist regime, political system, or state is always just a variant of fascism, democracy, authoritarianism, dictatorship, oligarchy, or totalitarianism.

Second and unsurprisingly, it is in fact the case that *every* type of regime, political system, or state contains some national characteristic—be it the claim that "the nation" is a monolith or the claim that "the nation" is the basis of popular sovereignty or the claim that "the nation" must be embedded in proletarian internationalism. One should resist the temptation to conclude that every type of national regime, political system, or state is therefore "nationalist," since to argue in this manner is to confuse "nationalist" with "national" and thereby to reduce "nationalism" to everything and everybody that somehow entails "the national," thus producing a semantically bleached and utterly meaningless concept.

Now that we know what nationalism is not, what is it?

Nationalism, I suggest, is best conceived of as an ideology or as a movement, group, or organization with a nationalist ideology. Nationalism as an ideology is a set of core beliefs that *sometimes* justify and promote national liberation and the creation of nation-states in general and *always* justify and promote national liberation and the creation of a nation-state for some particular nation. Nationalism, in this sense, is always particularistic and only sometimes universal. Nationalism as a movement, group, or organization is a human collective that shares a nationalist ideology. A nationalist individual would obviously be someone who believes in such an ideology. Nationalism is thus "about" the creation of states, and not about *how* the political institutions of regimes, systems, and states should be structured.

Seen in this light, the popular term "hyper-nationalism" is meaningless. If nationalism is an ideology, then hyper-nationalism would have to be a hyper-ideology. If nationalism is a movement, group, or organization, then hyper-nationalism would have to be a hyper-movement, hyper-group, or hyper-organization. Obviously, such conceptual obfuscation is not useful. What scholars really mean by hyper-nationalism is, quite simply, chauvinism. Appending the modifier "hyper" to the term "nationalism," however, is a convenient sleight of hand that creates a putative connection between nationalism and chauvinism when none such connection need exist, whether conceptually or empirically. After all, the ideological or organizational promotion of national liberation and nation-states is fundamentally different from the hatred of or superciliousness toward other nations—which is what we presumably mean by chauvinism. To define fascism as hyper-nationalism only compounds the problem, reducing fascism either to some sort of incomprehensible hyper-ideology or hyper-collective or, worse, to nothing but chauvinism.

In contrast to fascism as an ideology or as a movement, group, or organization, nationalism as an ideology or nationalism as a movement, group, or organization with a nationalist ideology does not presuppose an existing state that should be transformed into one corresponding to nationalist ideals. As a result, nationalism cannot and does not presuppose an existing type of regime, political, system, or state. Quite the contrary, nationalism presupposes the *non-existence* of an independent state and therefore concludes that the existence, or creation, of such a state is imperative. Like fascism and fascists or communism and communists or democracy and democrats, nationalism and national- ists may aspire to create such a state legally, democratically, and constitutionally or they may aspire to do so illegally, undemocratically, and unconstitutionally.

Th *type* of state that nationalism and nationalists aspire to create can be authoritarian, democratic, liberal, totalitarian, and so on. Unlike fascist states, which are invariably an- ti-democratic, the states to which nationalists aspire are not invariably anti-democratic. Unsurprisingly, nationalisms and nationalists have ranged across all political ideologies, including fascism, and individual nationalists and nationalist movements, groups, or or- ganizations have always displayed a remarkable political flexibility, being able to change their political ideology whenever and wherever the circumstances so demand. This is not, as is mistakenly assumed, opportunism. Nationalisms and nationalists can be so chame- leonic precisely because their ideology is fundamentally indifferent to the type of regime, political system, or state that emerges within the newly created state.

The key distinction among nationalisms and nationalists concerns not the goal (they all agree that national liberation and a nation-state is their goal), but the means. Whereas legally, democratically, and constitutionally inclined nationalists will employ legal, dem- ocratic, and constitutional means, illegally, undemocratically, and unconstitutionally inclined nationalists will employ illegal, undemocratic, and unconstitutional means. That is to say, they will break laws, be conspiratorial, disciplined, and hierarchical, and use violence. This is why sloppy scholars believe that nationalists "look like" fascists. But if the willingness to break laws, be conspiratorial, disciplined, and hierarchical, and use violence makes one a fascist, then every revolutionary movement (from that of the Americans in 1776 to that of the Israelis in 1947), every criminal organization (from the mafia to Mexican drug traffickers), every secret police (from the KGB to the CIA), and every assassin (from Brutus to Lee Harvey Oswald) is fascist—a claim that is almost as useless, and absurd, as the reduction of nationalism to "the national." Clearly, "looking like" somebody or something is no basis for claiming that things *are like* somebody or something.

To summarize: Nationalism's only precondition, both conceptually and empirically, is the non-existence of a state. Unlike fascists, nationalists build states *de novo*. Unsurprisingly, it is empirically the case that nationalism and nationalists are always found in stateless territories.

*

On Nationalism and Fascism, Part 3, *World Affairs Journal*, June 25, 2013

These reflections suggest that the most useful way of conceptualizing the interwar Organization of Ukrainian Nationalism (OUN) is as a nationalist movement with a na- tionalist ideology along the lines described above. In turn, this means that the OUN is most usefully compared to other nationalist movements that aspired to national liberation and the creation of nation-states (such as the American revolutionaries of 1776, the Palestine Liberation Organization, the Algerian National Liberation Front, the Irish Republican Army, the interwar Croatian Ustasha, the Vietnamese National Liberation Front, the Chinese Communist Party, and the Haganah in the British Mandate of Palestine, to name just a few) and not to fascist regimes or to fascist movements (such as Italian fascism, Nazism, the Polish Falanga, the Romanian Iron Guard, the Hungarian Arrow Cross, and the like). This is not to say that individual members of the OUN or individual planks of the OUN's constantly changing ideology were not, or could not have been, fascist, but it is to say that to focus on these fragmentary fascist elements is, first, to mistake the part for the whole and therefore to misunderstand the OUN; second and much worse, to misunderstand both fascism and nationalism; and, third and worst of all, to engage in conceptual nonsense.

The Ukrainian nationalist movement's relationship to political ideologies changed continually, proceeding from an apolitical militarism to authoritarianism to proto-fascism to democracy to social democracy. Thus, whereas nationalism as national liberation was a constant, the political ideology was a variable. The OUN's predecessor in the 1920s, the Ukrainian Military Organization, was a collection of patriotically inclined ex-soldiers with little sense of political ideology. The OUN began as a radical youth movement, then morphed into a quasi-authoritarian movement, adopted fascist elements by the late 1930s and early 1940s, abandoned them by 1943–1944, and began acquiring progressively more democratic and social-democratic characteristics in the mid- to late–1940s and 1950s. The picture looks even more complex if we consider that the OUN, throughout the 1930s, was divided into the émigré and homeland factions, with the former being more concerned with ideology and the latter more with action. As we would expect, post-World War II émigré Ukrainian nationalists were divided into liberal, moderate, and authoritarian wings.

If you really want to understand what made such Ukrainian nationalists as Stepan Bandera and Roman Shukhevych tick—both were made Heroes of Ukraine by President Viktor Yushchenko and both were subsequently unmade as Heroes by President Viktor Yanukovych—don't compare them to Adolf Hitler, Benito Mussolini, or Francisco Franco, but to George Washington, Jefferson Davis, Giuseppe Mazzini, Giuseppe Garibaldi, Menachem Begin, Vladimir Jabotinsky, Theodor Herzl, Ahmed Ben Bella, Ho Chi Minh, Mao Zedong, Josip Broz Tito, Simón Bolívar, and Emiliano Zapata. Personally, if I were doing comparative biographies, I'd do one on Bandera and Begin as political leaders and another on Shukhevych and Tito as military leaders. And then I'd compare the Ukrainian nationalist theorist Dmytro Dontsov with the Zionist theorist Jabotinsky.

If you want to understand what kind of arguments Ukrainian nationalists, like all nationalists, make and how they justify their claims for national self-determination, go no further than the American Declaration of Independence, Herzl's *The Jewish State*, or the PLO's National Charter. You won't find anything in any of those three documents that any nationalist in any country at any time wouldn't have agreed to. Consider the opening passage of the Declaration:

When in the Course of human events it becomes necessary for one people to dissolve the political bands which have connected them with another and to assume among the powers of the earth, the separate and equal station to which the Laws of Nature and of Nature's God entitle them, a decent respect to the opinions of mankind requires that they should declare the causes which impel them to the separation. We hold these truths to be self-evident, that all men are created equal, that they are endowed by their Creator with certain unalienable Rights, that among these are Life, Liberty and the pursuit of Happiness. —That to secure these rights, Governments are instituted among Men, deriving their just powers from the consent of the governed,—That whenever any Form of Government becomes destructive of these ends, it is the Right of the People to alter or to abolish it, and to institute new Government, laying its foundation on such principles and organizing its powers in such form, as to them shall seem most likely to effect their Safety and Happiness. ... But when a long train of abuses and usurpations, pursuing invariably the same Object evinces a design to reduce them under absolute Despotism, it is their right, it is their duty, to throw off such Government, and to provide new Guards for their future security.

Begin, Bandera, and Mao might have used different language, but they could easily have subscribed to the core logic of Thomas Jefferson's argument. Unsurprisingly, all four were equally nationalist, even though the first two tended toward authoritarianism, the third was a totalitarian Communist, and the fourth was a slave-owning democrat.

To summarize: Fascism is always anti-democratic and it always emerges within an already existing non-fascist state. Nationalism may or may not be anti-democratic and it always emerges within an already existing non-national state. Fascism aspires to change a state and make it fascist. Nationalism aspires to create a state. Like fascists and scores of other ideologically inspired individuals, nationalists can be violent. Like fascists and scores of other ideologically inspired individuals, nationalists can be chauvinists. But, like democrats, liberals, and other champions of human rights, nationalists can also be democratic and liberal champions of human rights. Unsurprisingly, Ukrainian nationalism, like Jewish nationalism (or Zionism), has contained all these elements at various times and in various places. The most striking thing about Ukrainian nationalism, therefore, is not that it is unique, but that it is so commonplace—no better and no worse than all other nationalisms: just as committed to liberation and just as likely to fall short of its ideals as to meet them.

It makes perfect sense for liberals and democrats always to oppose fascism. When it comes to nationalism, their attitude should be welcoming but cautious. Welcoming, because liberals and democrats should welcome every form of liberation: the political philosopher John Rawls even suggests in *The Law of Peoples* that liberalism demands recognizing the right of nations to self-determination and is, thus, intrinsically nationalist. Cautious, because nationalism, like all political projects, can be flawed. Like most things, come to think of it.

Searching for My Uncles' Soviet Killers, *World Affairs Journal*, July 1, 2013

Two of my uncles were killed by the Soviets and I'd like to know who the perpetrators were. The first, my aunt's husband, Bohdan, was killed exactly 72 years ago, on June 30, 1941, when the Soviet secret police shot somewhere between 9,000 and 20–25,000 (or possibly even more) mostly Ukrainian political prisoners in western Ukraine in the course of a week. The second, my father's kid brother, Teodozii, was arrested sometime in 1947, sent to a prison camp in Siberia, and never returned.

Bohdan was a member of the nationalist underground. In the 1930s, he spent five to six years in Polish prisons, where he was systematically beaten and tortured. When Hitler and Stalin destroyed Poland in September 1939, he was freed. He married my aunt in 1940 and then, on June 22, 1941, the day Hitler turned on his former collaborationist pal Stalin, Bohdan was arrested and placed in a provincial jail. Just before the Soviets withdrew, they massacred the inmates. Bohdan was mutilated and shot. He and the other prisoners were then dumped into a pit behind the jail, only to be discovered after the Soviets withdrew. My mother was there when the bodies were exhumed. Some 20 corpses had been found and he wasn't among them. Hoping that he might have survived, she took one last look into the pit and saw the outlines of another body. It was Bohdan. Evidently, he had been shot and dumped first.

Teodozii apparently had no political connections: he was an aspiring young actor who worked for a theater in Lviv. One weekend, he came home to his village at precisely the time that the nationalist underground had distributed some leaflets. Suspicion fell on him and he was arrested. In those days, it didn't take much for the Soviet secret police to imprison you. They placed Teodozii in a Lviv jail for a few months and then shipped him out to Siberia. He never came back. Did he fall ill? Did he starve to death? Was he shot? No one knows.

Neither my father nor my aunt ever spoke about their personal tragedies. I vaguely knew of their losses and learned of the details much later in life, when I began researching the history of Ukraine. I can't say that I have sleepless nights, but I am a tad angry. I'm angry at the Soviet Union, which killed two uncles. I'm angry at the Soviet secret policemen who tortured and shot Bohdan and maltreated Teodozii. And I'm angry at the reigning Western indifference to all Soviet deaths—and, by extension, to these two Ukrainian deaths.

I'd like to know who pulled the triggers and wielded the knives. I know there's virtually no chance of finding out—the documentation probably doesn't exist and, even if it does, it's certainly under lock and key—but finding out isn't the point, after all. Caring is, and the bottom line is that no one cares about the crimes committed by the KGB and its predecessor secret-police organizations. It was they who implemented the millions of deaths imposed by Stalin on the Soviet Union. It was they who incarcerated, tortured, and killed hundreds of thousands of their political opponents. It was they who deported entire peoples. Surely their crimes are at least roughly comparable to those of the SS and Gestapo. Or are victims of Soviet crimes less worthy of compassion than victims of Nazi crimes? And if we grant that all victims of violence deserve a smidgeon of our compassion, it surely follows that our outrage at the SS and Gestapo must extend to the KGB.

Except that it doesn't. A bar in New York is named after the KGB and it features readings by liberal-minded avant-garde writers and poets. Former KGB officers write memoirs and give lectures in the United States and Canada. Their affiliation with a criminal organization appears not to matter. They aren't even asked to say "oops" for their sins.

Consider the most egregious such example: Vladimir Putin, Russia's president. Putin resolved to join the secret police in the 1970s, a few years after Soviet tanks crushed the Prague Spring in Czechoslovakia, and during one of the largest KGB crackdowns on Soviet dissent. This kind of past should raise eyebrows. Instead, policymakers, scholars, and journalists accept Putin's choice as if it were merely a career move. They shake his hand at summits; they gladly let themselves be photographed in his presence; they attend elaborate meetings with him in Valdai. German Chancellor Gerhard Schröder went so far as to call Putin a "flawless democrat" at the height of Ukraine's Orange Revolution in late 2004. French President Jacques Chirac even bestowed his country's prestigious Grand-Croix de la Légion d'Honneur on Putin on September 23, 2006.

When I'm feeling bitter, I imagine how my uncles died. I see Bohdan getting a bullet in the back of his head. I see Teodozii starving in some barracks. And when I'm feeling cynical, I see Vladimir, Gerhard, and Jacques smoking cigars and drinking vodka in the KGB Bar.

*

Remembering the 1943 Volhynian Massacres, *World Affairs Journal*, July 12, 2013

This month marks the 70th anniversary of the brutal Polish-Ukrainian conflict that tore apart Volhynia in 1943 and produced tens of thousands of deaths.

There are several points of controversy. First, just how many people were killed? Second, who did the killing and why? Third, how should the killings be characterized? And fourth, who should condemn the killings and/or apologize for them?

Estimates of Polish victims of Ukrainian violence range from 30,000 to 100,000 (the spread is reminiscent of the estimates for the Ukrainian famine of 1932–1933: 3 to 10 million); estimates of Ukrainian victims of Polish violence range from 15,000 to 30,000. All the estimates are "guesstimates." After all, documentation is either non-existent or unreliable; it's difficult to determine who was killed and who fled (and many thousands obviously fled); and survivors always have a tendency to inflate the numbers of victims (earlier estimates of those who died in the Gulag reached as high as 40 million, many times the real number). In addition, some people count only one region and a narrow time period; others look at several regions and many years. Considering that Ukrainians were extremely poorly armed, a 100,000:15,000 "kill ratio" strikes me as implausible:

we'd expect that kind of imbalance from a conflict between a regular army and guerrillas. That said, it's pretty clear that Ukrainians did far more killing than Poles. The difference in the number of casualties may be due to the greater ruthlessness of the Ukrainians or, more likely, to the larger size of the Ukrainian population in the contested region. Other things being equal, majorities usually outfight minorities, and the Poles were a minority in Volhynia.

Who carried out the killings? Fingers usually get pointed at Ukrainian nationalists on the one hand and Polish nationalists on the other. According to the simplistic narratives, both sides were presumably driven by their extremist ideologies—the Ukrainians by a desire to cleanse the territory of Poles, the Poles by a desire to keep the Ukrainians oppressed. The reality was rather more complicated. Volhynia was part of the Reichskommissariat Ukraine, ruled by the brutal Erich Koch, who treated Slavs as *Untermenschen*. By 1942–1943, the Germans were playing Poles off against Ukrainians, while Soviet partisans were making forays into and destabilizing the region. After Stalingrad, Polish nationalists hoping to control Volhynia in anticipation of a Nazi withdrawal were cooperating with the Soviets. Ukrainian nationalists were fighting the Germans and the partisans and, fearful of a Soviet return, also aspired to control the area. Given the depth of preexisting Polish-Ukrainian animosity (in large part caused by the oppressive policies of the interwar Polish state), it was no surprise that the violence erupted as part peasant Jacquerie, part armed resistance, part political struggle, and part ethnic violence apparently initiated by one Ukrainian nationalist guerrilla commander.

How should the killings be characterized? There is no doubt that they were "mass killings." But were they also forms of ethnic cleansing, war crimes, and, perhaps, even genocide? Or were both sides simply conducting brutal "national liberation struggles" or a "war"?

The case for war is strong. Both Ukrainians and Poles had armed forces and political organizations attempting to establish, to quote Max Weber's definition of a state, "a monopoly of violence" in a given territory. When armies fight, we often call that a war. The case for national liberation struggle is also persuasive, as both Ukrainians and Poles were obviously hoping to free their nations from presumed oppression and build states. There is no doubt that both sides committed atrocities and war crimes, with Ukrainians probably committing more than Poles. The case for ethnic cleansing is weaker, inasmuch as the violence appears to have been only partly premeditated. The case for genocide is weakest. We usually restrict the term to the slaughter of hundreds of thousands, if not millions, and we usually insist that the perpetrators suffer few or no casualties. My own preference is for "ethnic violence," a category that immediately places the Polish-Ukrainian conflict in a comparative framework and enables us to make sense of it in social-science terms. Whatever your preferred term, it's clear that there was widespread savagery. For what it's worth, contemporary Poles and Ukrainians can take heart from the fact that the atrocities their countrymen and countrywomen committed pale in comparison to the Gulag and the Holocaust as well as to scores of World War II mass killings such as Hiroshima, Nagasaki, Nanking, Dresden, Lidice, and Katyn.

Who should condemn the violence and killings? The answer is obvious: everyone.

Whoever is concerned with violations of human rights in any part of the world has a moral obligation to condemn all violations of human rights in all parts of the world. But be careful. Human rights entail a huge responsibility: for your condemnation of violence by Ukrainians and Poles to be credible, you must be no less condemnatory of violence perpetrated by Americans, Russians, Germans, French, Chinese, Jews, Palestinians, Turks, Brazilians, Paraguayans, and everybody else. If only Ukrainian or Polish violence bothers you, than you are in fact being indifferent to human rights and pursuing a political agenda.

Who should apologize? It can't be "Poland" or "Ukraine," because neither state existed in 1943 (although there was a Polish government-in-exile in London) and neither existing state has the right to speak on behalf of individual Poles or Ukrainians in 1943. (And, besides, would it work for President Yanukovych to act as Ukraine's conscience given the harm his own party has done to the country?) It can't be "the Poles" or "the Ukrainians" either, because collective guilt does not exist.

Obviously, as in all cases of wrongdoing, the people who should apologize are the people who committed the wrongdoing. Truth and reconciliation committees along the lines of those in post-apartheid South Africa might be the way to go for both Poland and Ukraine: let the few surviving perpetrators confess and tell the truth and then go home.

Finally, the Ukrainian and Polish political organizations that claim lineage with their wartime undergrounds might want to issue apologies. They'll protest on the grounds that apologies would sully their sacrifices on behalf of the cause. But they'd be wrong. The best way to underscore that their principles are grounded in genuine liberation and genuine freedom is to condemn unsavory aspects of their pasts and thereby signal that their visions of national liberation rest on an unwavering commitment to human rights for all.

*

Misrepresenting History at the Kyiv Museum, *World Affairs Journal*, July 26, 2013

Does Kyiv have a history?

If you go to the Museum of the History of the City of Kyiv, you're likely to conclude that the answer is a resounding No. You're also likely to conclude that the people who set up the Museum at its present site a year ago have no idea of what the purpose of museums is.

The museum is currently lodged in a fancy new building on Khmelnytsky Street, just across the street from the Lesya Ukrainka Theater of Russian Drama. The building was constructed amid substantial controversy: its ornately neo-modernist, glass-and-steel-and marble, "Late Yanukovych" style doesn't quite jive with its surroundings, while its very placement in a formerly open space creates a sense of intrusiveness and crowding on an otherwise leisurely thoroughfare. (To be slightly fair, the recently constructed German

Embassy just up the road is just as much of an eyesore, and the Germans can't blame their bad taste on the woes of transitional societies.)

Whatever the merits or demerits of the museum as a building, you'd think that as important an institution as *the* city museum would tell an interesting story and aspire to look professional. Not so.

The exhibit consists of two floors. I get there just after opening at 10:05 a.m. I pay my 30 hryvnia (just under $4.00) and take the stairs to the second floor. The first thing that strikes me is that there are wet spots all around the landing. Evidently, the cleaners had just finished their mopping. A woman standing near the entrance to the right greets me in Russian. I walk in and notice more wet spots on the exhibit floor. Before me and to the right are some artifacts from the Kyivan Rus era of about a thousand years ago. They're enclosed in glass cases with crookedly placed pieces of paper identifying them. A stand holds a plastic-encased piece of paper with a typewritten narrative of a bit of Kyivan Rus history. Off to the right are several mosaics on the wall. They're unmarked. I ask the woman where they come from. She says they're copies. Of what? I ask. You should take the guided tour, she responds.

A few glass cases later, the Kyivan Rus period suddenly ends. Who were the grand dukes? Who were the princes? What happened in the several hundred years of its existence? The museum prefers not to say. And then, just as suddenly, I encounter a few glass cases from the Cossack period: some paintings, some articles of clothing, and the like. Who exactly were the Cossacks? What did they do? Who were their leaders? Once again, the museum, which is located on a street named after one of the most important Cossack leaders, is mum. And that may be just as well, because, inexplicably, the Cossack period suddenly morphs into a bunch of glass cases showing off everyday objects from the 19th and early 20th centuries.

Maybe the third floor will be better. There, too, the water on the landing and floor hasn't quite dried. There, too, a woman greets me in Russian. I enter, and right before me is a wall and glass-case exhibit about the Ukrainian revolution of 1917–1918. Highlighted are the anti-Soviet Ukrainian Central Rada and its president, the renowned historian Mykhailo Hrushevsky. The accompanying text, encased in plastic, typewritten on a single sheet, and placed on a wobbly stand, presents a non-Soviet interpretation of this period of Ukrainian history. Next come a few cases with artifacts from several Soviet Ukrainian writers of the interwar period. The accompanying text mentions repressions, but the exhibit fails to illustrate them.

And then, all of a sudden, it's World War II. One wall panel does mention the Nazi killing of Jews in Babyn Yar, but just about everything else is devoted to the uniforms, medals, and citations received by Soviet war heroes. If you'd like to know what life was like in Kyiv during the Nazi occupation, you'd be better off eading a book.

And then, with equal suddenness, the war is over and we're in some indefinite post-war period. You'd think there'd be something about the architectural reconstruction of post-war Kyiv, about the dissident movement, about Communist Party leaders Petro Shelest and Volodymyr Shcherbytsky, about the Chernobyl nuclear disaster, but, once again, you'd be dead wrong. Instead, the exhibit concludes with a roomful of hodgepodge from the 1960s until today.

The bottom line is that this is unlike any exhibit of any history I've ever seen. There are no narratives, no stories, no highlights, no themes—just a bunch of almost randomly collected stuff. Stuff may make for a great flea market, but it doesn't amount to a museum exhibit.

So who's to blame for this disaster? On the one hand, the answer is simple: the museum's director and curator (although the museum's Facebook site does not say who they are). On the other hand, the answer is even simpler: the Yanukovych regime. The ministries of culture and education are run by Regionnaires committed to emptying Ukrainian history, culture, and language of all content and reducing them to footnotes of some grand Soviet/Russian narrative. The last thing the Regionnaires want is a capital city with a genuine history: that might suggest that Ukraine has a history and that—heaven forbid—Ukrainians have an identity.

*

Opting for Deutsch in Ukraine, *World Affairs Journal*, September 4, 2013

Ukrainians are voting with their tongues, and they appear to be voting for Europe. In a little-noticed statistic just released by Ukraine's Ministry of Education and Science, 52 percent of the country's fifth-graders chose German as their second foreign language in the forthcoming school year. With another 14 percent of fifth-graders opting for French, 1.6 for Polish, and 1.2 for Spanish, non-Russian European languages accounted for 69 percent of their choices, while Russian accounted for 23—a ratio of three to one in favor of the former.

Since 92 percent of all grade-schoolers already study English as their first foreign language, it's clear that a linguistic sea change is taking place in Ukraine.

Twenty-five years ago, before independence, the only Ukrainians with a proficient knowledge of Western languages were those who studied them at university or attended elite schools (or worked for the KGB), while all Ukrainians had to be fluent in Russian. Unsurprisingly, their worldview was largely defined by their relationship, whether positive or negative, with Russian culture. Within a few years, it's quite possible that most of Ukraine's young people will be conversant, and possibly fluent, in English and German. Most of them will still speak Russian with varying degrees of facility, but their civilizational and cultural choices will now be a function of their encounter with and understanding of a different world.

Knowledge of English and German is no guarantee of liberalism and democracy, of course, but the ability to easily navigate among a multiplicity of cultures and countries can only enhance young people's disdain for hierarchy, authoritarianism, intolerance, and provincialism. The effects won't be felt immediately, but, within 10 to 15 years, expect this cohort of globally savvy Ukrainians to have very different values, norms, hopes, and expectations from their still-Sovietized elders.

Knowledge of Western languages is also likely to have a far-reaching impact on Ukrainian society. At present, about 70 percent of Ukrainian children study in schools with Ukrainian as the language of instruction. The statistic conceals important regional variations. In western Ukraine, the percentage is in the high 90s. In eastern and southern Ukraine, it's significantly smaller, with village schools being primarily in Ukrainian and urban schools primarily in Russian. In Donetsk, for instance, 28 percent study in Ukrainian-language schools. In Odessa, it's 52 percent. In Luhansk, it's only 13 percent.

Notwithstanding what the language of instruction is at school, the fact of the matter is that, with print media, television, pop music, and cinema so overwhelmingly Russian— Russia's cultural products have completely saturated the Ukrainian market, so much so that you'll be hard-pressed to find a Ukrainian-language publication at a newsstand anywhere in Ukraine—it's virtually impossible not to develop, by osmosis, a working knowledge of street Russian.

Ukrainian parents know that. They know that their fifth-grade kids will learn to speak some form of Russian anyway, even without trying. Acting as perfectly rational agents out to "maximize" their children's "utility," parents understand that knowledge of English and a second European language such as German, French, Polish, or Spanish will give their children a leg up over the kids who study Russian as a second foreign language. A middle-school graduate able to converse in Ukrainian, English, German, and street Russian will have far greater economic opportunities, whether at home or abroad, than a student with literary Russian, English, and Ukrainian. The former will be able to travel to and study in the West, work for Western multinationals in Ukraine, or get a job in a Russian company. The latter may be better qualified to teach Russian in Donetsk, Luhansk, and Odessa, but, other things being equal, will be a less attractive job candidate than the former in a rapidly globalizing world.

Expect the 23 percent of the parents who opted for Russian progressively to recognize their mistake. If so, the drift toward Western European languages should accelerate over time and street Russian will increasingly dominate literary Russian. Will parents in Donetsk, Luhansk, and Odessa follow suit and enroll their children in schools that give them greater linguistic flexibility or will they stick to literary Russian? The rational choice would be to opt for linguistic flexibility.

Consider, then, what the overall result might be in, say, a decade. As young Ukrainians become fluent in literary Ukrainian and street Russian as well as proficient in English and some other major European language, their country will finally be ready to join the world—while the tongue-tied Regionnaires currently running the country will be left behind.

PART FIVE: HISTORY, LANGUAGE, AND NATIONAL IDENTITY

Questioning War Monuments, *World Affairs Journal*, October 25, 2013

If you think the monument wars in Ukraine take the cake, think again. The Polish city of Gdansk is in the throes of a controversy over a statue of a Red Army soldier raping a woman. It was installed on October 12th, on the city's Victory Avenue, and uninstalled the next day for having been set up without a legal permit.

Here's how the *Moscow Times* reported the brouhaha:

> The offending work of art, entitled "Komm Frau," German for "Come Here Woman," had been installed on Gdansk's Avenue of Victory on Saturday. Polish authorities removed the statue on Sunday, saying that it had been put there illegally, while Szumczyk was brought in for questioning by the police before being released, Polish Radio reported.

> The sculptor, fifth-year art student Jerzy Szumczyk, said he "was unable to cope" with the accounts he read about rape by Soviet servicemen as they advanced toward Berlin in 1944 and 1945, and felt compelled to express his feelings.

> "I am deeply outraged by the stunt by a Gdansk Fine Arts Academy student, who has defiled by his pseudo-art the memory of 600,000 Soviet servicemen who gave their lives in the fight for the freedom and the independence of Poland," Russian ambassador Alexander Alexeyev said in a statement Tuesday.

> "We consider the installation of the statue as an expression of hooliganism, marked by an explicitly blasphemous nature," Alexeyev said. "The vulgar statue on the city's main street insults not only the feelings of Russians, but of all clear-headed people who remember to whom they owe their liberation from the Nazis."

What made Szumczyk's monument especially disturbing to his critics was its placement—right next to a Soviet T-34 tank intended to symbolize the city's liberation. The placement was, of course, an intentional provocation. As Szumczyk said: "It's a work from the heart. The idea came from the fact that the city's monuments are often in places where they shouldn't stand. Some monuments don't fit their surroundings, because great crimes took place there. We barely appreciate what the monuments represent."

The fact of the matter is that Red Army soldiers representing all the USSR's many nationalities did engage in systematic mass rape as they swept through the German-populated territories of Hitler's Reich. Danzig, as Gdansk was then called, was no exception. Here's how Yale University historian Timothy Snyder describes the violence in *Bloodlands*:

> The outburst of violence against German women was extraordinary. Men who tried to defend daughters or wives were beaten and sometimes killed. The women had few men to protect them. ... In some villages, every single female was raped, whatever her age. ... Gang rapes were very common. Many women died as a result of wounds sustained during successive rapes. German women often committed suicide, or tried to kill themselves, to prevent rape or to evade the shame of having been raped.

537

According to the *Moscow Times*, "Some historians estimate that up to 2 million German women, and large numbers of Polish women, were raped in the final months of World War II by soldiers of the advancing Red Army. However, Russian authorities maintain that the figures are flagrantly exaggerated."

Imagine that the real number of raped women was only one-fourth of the above estimate. That still comes out to an astoundingly large figure: 500,000. Even one-eighth amounts to 250,000 raped women.

Small wonder that Szumczyk felt impelled to counterbalance the tank with the soldier.

So whom do you believe—the outraged Russian ambassador or the outrageous Polish sculptor? Whose memories matter more? Or perhaps the better question is: whose memories matter?

In placing his statue next to the T-34 tank, Szumczyk was effectively claiming that memories of mass rape were as important as memories of liberation. The sculptor was arguing for parity: yes, there was liberation, he seems to be saying, but there was also enslavement, and both should be remembered. Not so Alexeyev. The Russian ambassador is arguing for priority and, indeed, for exclusivity: there was only liberation and any challenge to that claim is "blasphemous." Since one generally blasphemes only against God or holy writ, Alexeyev was effectively stating that the Soviet liberation of Poland was a religious matter, beyond memory, beyond history, beyond challenge.

Alexeyev's views are fully consistent with the Soviet mythmaking that transformed World War II into "The Great Patriotic War," glorified the Red Army, ignored Soviet crimes, and produced the thousands of war monuments and museums scattered throughout the former USSR. Those myths could stand only as long as Soviet ideological hegemony was unchallenged and the Soviet Union was whole. Once the empire collapsed and the ideology became a shambles, it was—and is—unsurprising that all the empire's subject peoples should seek to remember their own memories and construct their own histories. For them, the process is liberating and empowering. For many Russians, the process is insulting and diminishing. In succeeding the USSR, the Russian Federation inherited its diplomatic real estate, nuclear weapons, Security Council seat, and space program. But it also had to take possession of Lenin, Stalin, the Gulag, the Great Terror, the Holodomor, and the mass rapes.

It's no accident that other post-Soviet ambassadors failed to react with Alexeyev's invective. For them, the collapse of the Soviet Union spelled the emergence of their states. For Alexeyev, collapse probably was, as his boss Vladimir Putin once said, "the greatest geopolitical catastrophe of the 20th century."

Naturally, all memories *qua* memories are valid and deserve a hearing. But not all histories are equally valid: some are more complete, some are less complete; some are better, some are worse. And the moral of the story, for Ukraine and other post-Soviet states, is simple: acknowledge all memories and then try to set the historical record straight—or as straight as possible.

Remembering the Ukrainian Famine-Genocide, *World Affairs Journal*, December 13, 2013

Although the ongoing Euro Revolution in Ukraine is rightly the focus of much of the world's attention, we would do well to remember that on November 23rd Ukraine commemorated the 80th anniversary of the famine-genocide that took the lives of 3 to 4 million Ukrainian peasants in 1932–1933. As the United States contemplates whether or not it should threaten the Yanukovych regime with sanctions, we may want to remember that three Americans played key roles in reporting, denying, and remembering the events now known as the Holodomor.

Joseph Stalin's decision in 1928 to seize privately held agricultural land and transform it into collective farms caused massive hardship for all Soviet peasants. When authorities expropriated peasant grain stocks and farm animals, hunger broke out in much of the USSR. In Ukraine, where close to a million peasants actively rebelled against collectivization, such expropriations were especially severe, leading to widespread starvation that the state both refused to alleviate and purposely aggravated until millions had died and a massive crackdown on Ukrainian political, cultural, and religious elites had been completed. At the height of the Holodomor, 25,000 Ukrainians starved per day; cannibalism was rampant.

Harry Lang, a writer and labor editor of the New York–based, Yiddish-language *Jewish Daily Forward*, reported the following for the *New York Evening Journal*:

> A high official of the Ukrainian Soviet, with whom we established contact, confidentially advised me to take a trip to the villages. Only there, he said, would I see the full handiwork of the famine. And he added: "Six million people have perished from hunger in our country in 1932–33." In the office of a Soviet functionary I saw a poster on the wall which struck my attention. It showed the picture of a mother in distress, with a swollen child at her feet, and over the picture was the inscription: "EATING OF DEAD CHILDREN IS BARBARISM." I wondered. What was the purpose of such a poster? The Soviet official explained to me: "It is one of our methods of educating the people. We distributed such posters in hundreds of villages, especially in the Ukraine. We had to." "Is the situation that bad?" I asked in astonishment. "Are people really in such a condition as to eat their children's corpses?" The official was silent. It was a painful, disturbing silence. "Not all our people are enlightened," he remarked a little later. Again I shuddered. But I went down to the Ukraine and saw with my own eyes the destruction wrought there, the wreckage of a great country.

Unfortunately, Lang's honest reporting did not influence American public opinion as much as the mendacious stories written by Walter Duranty, Moscow bureau chief of the *New York Times* and winner of the Pulitzer Prize in 1932.

Here's what Duranty wrote in March 1933, at the height of the famine: "There is no actual starvation or deaths from starvation but there is widespread mortality from diseases due to malnutrition, especially in the Ukraine, North Caucasus, and Lower Volga." Later that year, Duranty wrote that any talk of famine is "a sheer absurdity."

Duranty knew he was lying. Privately, he told the British Embassy: "The Ukraine has been bled white. The population was exhausted and if the peasants were 'double-crossed' by the Government again no one could say what would happen." It was "quite possible that as many as 10 million people may have died directly or indirectly from lack of food in the Soviet Union during the past year."

Raphael Lemkin, the Polish-Jewish scholar who coined the term "genocide" and played a large role in the adoption of the United Nations Convention on the Prevention and Punishment of the Crime of Genocide, set the record straight in 1953. Lemkin, who lost scores of relatives in the Holocaust, immigrated to the United States in 1941 and taught at my university, Rutgers-Newark.

> Ukraine is highly susceptible to racial murder by select parts and so the Communist tactics there have not followed the pattern taken by the German attacks against the Jews. The nation is too populous to be exterminated completely with any efficiency. However, its leadership, religious, intellectual, political, its select and determining parts, are quite small and therefore easily eliminated, and so it is upon these groups particularly that the full force of the Soviet axe has fallen, with its familiar tools of mass murder, deportation and forced labor, exile and starvation. ... Between 1932 and 1933, 5,000,000 Ukrainians starved to death. ... This is not simply a case of mass murder. It is a case of genocide, of destruction, not of individuals only, but of a culture and a nation.

Unsurprisingly, Ukrainians refer to the famine of 1932–1933 as the "Holodomor"—or killing by famine. (An excellent documentary about the Holodomor is the Canadian film director Yurij Luhovy's award-winning *Genocide Revealed*.)

Bizarrely, some historians insist that remembering the Holodomor somehow diminishes the Holocaust. That's a bit like saying that remembering World War I diminishes World War II or that remembering slavery in Haiti diminishes slavery in America. Remembering or commemorating tragedies is not a zero-sum game; the human capacity for empathy is, after all, boundless. If I comprehend the horror of the Holodomor, I am better equipped to comprehend the horror of the Holocaust. And if I comprehend the horror of the Holocaust, I can better comprehend the horror of the Rwandan genocide. There are, alas, more than enough tragedies with which we can learn to empathize.

No less bizarrely, others suggest that Ukrainians concocted the word *Holodomor* to compete terminologically with the term *Holocaust*. That, too, is nonsense. The Ukrainian word for famine happens to be *holod*, which means the choice for a term is between *Holod* and *Holodomor*, the latter combining *holod* with part of the word *moryty* ("to kill"). By chance, both terms share their first four letters with *Holocaust*, yet neither of them have the same number of syllables.

Equally absurd are claims that Ukrainians have inflated estimates—to 6 or 10 million— to "beat" the Holocaust. As the above three citations illustrate, Lang reported 6 million dead, Duranty 10 million, and Lemkin 5 million. Where else were people to get numbers before more reliable demographic data became available recently and the 3 to 4 million figure became the most accurate current estimate (which isn't to say that it won't be revised upward or downward when still more detailed micro-data become available)?

Fortunately, despite Duranty's efforts to deny the Holodomor, honest men such as Lang and Lemkin saved it from the oblivion into which Stalin and his henchmen hoped it would disappear. Just as fortunately, despite some scholars' attempts to place the Holodomor in competition with the Holocaust, reasonable people can agree that such one-upmanship is obscene and that neither tragedy should ever be repeated.

Ukraine has a particular stake in remembering the Holodomor and the Holocaust, precisely because both genocides devastated its people. Since the Yanukovych regime is congenitally indifferent to human tragedy, the task of honoring the victims of both genocides will be up to a democratic post-Yanukovych government.

Now that the Lenin statue has been toppled in Kyiv, why not replace it with a simple statue honoring a great man who stood for everything the Bolshevik tyrant rejected—Raphael Lemkin?

*

Ukraine's Chief Rabbi Refutes Putin's Anti-Semitic Charges, *World Affairs Journal*, March 5, 2014

Russian President Vladimir Putin and his supporters in Russia and the West have accused the Ukrainian opposition that led the fight against the criminal Yanukovych regime and the democratic Ukrainian government that succeeded that regime of being fascist, neo-Nazi, and anti-Semitic.

The following quotations—by Putin and his most unremitting academic supporter in New York City on the one hand, and by three of Ukraine's leading Jewish officials on the other—should settle the issue. Putin is beyond redemption, of course, but Professor Cohen may want to take account of the evidence and, like a good revisionist historian, revise his views.

Vladimir Putin, president of the Russian Federation, March 4, 2014:

> Armed and masked militants are still roaming the streets of Kyiv. ... We see the rampage of reactionary forces, nationalist and anti-Semitic forces going on in certain parts of Ukraine, including Kyiv. ... [W]e understand what worries the citizens of Ukraine, both Russian and Ukrainian, and the Russian-speaking population in the eastern and southern regions of Ukraine. It is this uncontrolled crime that worries them.

Yaakov Dov Bleich, chief rabbi of Ukraine, March 3, 2014:

Rabbi Yaakov Dov Bleich, a chief rabbi of Ukraine, accused Russia of staging anti-Semitic "provocations" in Crimea in order to justify its invasion of the former Soviet republic. At a press conference in the Manhattan office of the United Jewish Communities of Eastern Europe, Bleich compared Russia's behavior to that of the Nazis prior to the Anschluss invasion of Austria in 1938.

"Things may be done by Russians dressing up as Ukrainian nationalists," he said, adding that it's "the same way the Nazis did when they wanted to go into Austria and created provocations."

Bleich, a vice president of the World Jewish Congress, also announced the creation of an aid effort, KyivRelief.org, to fund security for synagogues and mosques and to provide humanitarian relief for all Ukrainians. Bleich, who moved to Ukraine in 1989 from Brooklyn, was slated, along with other Ukrainian political and religious leaders, to meet with Secretary of State John Kerry on Tuesday. He said he will urge Kerry to be assertive with Russian President Vladimir Putin, to move the G8 Summit to Kyiv, as a show of solidarity with Ukrainians, and to consider sending military support to Ukraine. While acknowledging that Americans are "war-weary," he said Ukrainians need "boots on the ground to protect democracy" and to prevent "the cold war from getting hot." Asked about anti-Semitism among Ukrainian nationalists, particularly two far-right parties that have been included in the new government, Bleich acknowledged concerns but said the Jewish community has received assurances from top government leaders that their safety will be protected.

"The Russians are blowing this way, way out of proportion," he said, referring to the issue of anti-Semitism among some Ukrainian nationalist factions. He said that Ukrainians were united in response to the Russian intervention. "There were many differences of opinion throughout the revolution, but today all that is gone," he said. "We're faced by an outside threat called Russia. It's brought everyone together."

Rabbi Misha Kapustin, rabbi of the Simferopol Reform Synagogue Ner Tamid, Crimea, March 3, 2014:

Many here are against the Russians but are afraid to talk. I am a Ukrainian citizen and want to live in democratic Ukraine. The government has always provided protection for the Jews, and all the talk of anti-Semitism is exaggerated. The Russians have invaded illegally and that must be opposed. So far, people have encouraged me and I don't believe my petition will cause any harm to the Jews.

Stephen F. Cohen, professor of Russian studies and history at New York University, January 30, 2014:

... the street in Kyiv is now controlled by these right-wing extremists. And that extremism has spread to western Ukraine, where these people are occupying government buildings. So, in fact, you have a political civil war under way. What is the face of these people, this right wing? A, they hate Europe as much as they hate Russia. Their official statement is: Europe is homosexuals, Jews, and the decay of the Ukrainian state. They want nothing to do with Europe. They want nothing to do with Russia. I'm talking about this—it's not a fringe, but this very right-wing thing. What does their political activity include? It includes writing on buildings in western Ukraine, "Jews live here." That's exactly what the Nazis wrote on the homes of Jews when they occupied Ukraine. A priest who represents part of the political movement in western Ukraine—Putin quoted this, but it doesn't make it false. It doesn't make it false; it's been verified. A western Ukrainian priest said, "We, Ukraine, will not be governed by Negroes, Jews or Russians." So, these people have now come to the fore.

Josef Zissels, head of the Association of Jewish Communities of Ukraine and vice president of the World Jewish Congress, January 21, 2014:

On the websites of some parties close to the government, such as those of Viktor Medvedchuk [a Putin ally], Natalia Vitrenko [head of the pro-Stalin Progressive Socialist Party of Ukraine], and the Berkut [the riot police responsible for the mass killings in Kyiv], there have appeared in the last two-three weeks many anti-Semitic materials that state that the Jews organized the Maidan. That's completely absurd, but it's believed by those who with batons and shields face down the activists. They [the riot police] are being told: look, the Maidan is the work of Jews, so don't spare anyone, beat them all.

Josef Zissels, January 14, 2014:

The moving force of the Maidan is not the opposition parties, and certainly not the weakest of the opposition parties in the parliament, Svoboda. The moving force of the Maidan are the citizens of Ukraine. ... The Maidan has no leader. The Maidan is over 40 social organizations and various citizens' groups. They are Ukraine's civil society. ...

I view the coalition of three right parties in Ukraine (Svoboda does not appeal to me as a party) as a factor with which one must come to terms. Svoboda acquired 10.5 percent of the vote, entered parliament, and became a member of the opposition coalition. I view this situation as a phenomenon similar to the People's Front in France during World War II: against the common enemy there united communists, social democrats, monarchists, anarchists, and other very different forces.

Ukraine's key problem is not Svoboda, although Svoboda does indeed represent a certain kind of internal Ukrainian problem. The key problem is the government, its corruption, and its attempt to impose an authoritarian—and as its attack on the Maidan showed, even a totalitarian—form of rule on the country. The opposition united in that conflict with the government. Once the problem of the government is solved, once there will be the first unfalsified elections, then will be the time to deal with our "right-wingers" and "left-wingers." At the moment, we are all allies against a very powerful enemy.

P.S. On March 4th, Ukrainian Jews wrote an open letter to Putin in which they repeat many of the points made in the above quotations.

*

Kissinger Misunderstands Ukraine, *World Affairs Journal*, March 13, 2014

When a renowned American statesman such as Henry Kissinger exhibits alarming ignorance about Ukraine, you've got to worry. In a March 5th op-ed in the *Washington Post*, Kissinger got just about everything wrong, even though, remarkably, his prescriptions for resolving the Russo-Ukrainian standoff still managed to be worthy of consideration.

Consider this passage:

> The West must understand that, to Russia, Ukraine can never be just a foreign country. Russian history began in what was called Kyivan-Rus. The Russian religion spread from there. Ukraine has been part of Russia for centuries, and their histories were intertwined before then. Some of the most important battles for Russian freedom, starting with the Battle of Poltava in 1709, were fought on Ukrainian soil.

Russian history did not begin only in Kyivan (or Kyivan) Rus, as Kissinger says. It began in many places, including Russia. Similarly, America's history began in England as well as in many other places. Every country's history has multiple roots: Belarusian history also began in Kyivan Rus. Kissinger's mistake is to advance a tidy—and anti-historical—view of history that justifies imperial Russia's standing claims to Ukrainian territory. According to his logic, America would be justified in claiming Ontario. By the way, "what was called Kyivan-Rus" was in fact a state, one of Europe's largest at that time.

Pace Kissinger, the Russian religion did not spread from "what was called Kyivan-Rus." What spread was Orthodox Christianity and it spread from Constantinople, thanks in no small measure due to the proselyting efforts of Ss. Cyril and Methodius, both Greeks. True, Ukraine "has been part of Russia for centuries," but it's been no less a part of the Mongol empire, the Grand Duchy of Lithuania, the Polish Commonwealth, the Habsburg Empire, and the Ottoman Empire. The Battle of Poltava was a battle between two empires, the Swedish and Russian, and had nothing to do with "Russian freedom" or independence. Imperial struggles never do. And if anyone lost their freedom as a result of the battle, it was the Ukrainian Cossacks under Hetman Ivan Mazepa, who sided with King Charles XII against Tsar Peter I.

There's more:

Crimea, 60 percent of whose population is Russian, became part of Ukraine only in 1954, when Nikita Khrushchev, a Ukrainian by birth, awarded it as part of the 300th-year celebration of a Russian agreement with the Cossacks. The west is largely Catholic; the east largely Russian Orthodox. The west speaks Ukrainian; the east speaks mostly Russian.

Crimea's population was 58 percent Russian in 2001; with low birth rates and high death rates, the Russian probably comprise about 55 percent today. Crimea's population was mostly Crimean Tatar until 1944, when Stalin deported the entire Tatar population (numbering around 200,000) to Uzbekistan in a brazen act of ethnic cleansing and genocide (about half died en route). Moreover, Crimea possessed the status of an Autonomous Soviet Socialist Republic (with both Crimean Tatar and Russian as official languages) until 1945, when, cleansed of the Tatars, it was converted into a Russian province and rapidly populated with Russian settlers, mostly veterans.

Khrushchev was not a Ukrainian, but an ethnic Russian born in Ukraine. The Ukrainian west is as Orthodox as it is Catholic; the east is not "Russian Orthodox," but simply "Orthodox," with parishes being affiliated with the Moscow Patriarchate and the Kyiv Patriarchate. The west speaks more Ukrainian than Russian, the east speaks more Russian than Ukrainian, but most people, especially in the center, are at home with both languages.

One final passage:

> The politics of post-independence Ukraine clearly demonstrates that the root of the problem lies in efforts by Ukrainian politicians to impose their will on recalcitrant parts of the country, first by one faction, then by the other. That is the essence of the conflict between Viktor Yanukovych and his principal political rival, Yulia Tymoshenko. They represent the two wings of Ukraine and have not been willing to share power.

The ignorance on display here is especially alarming as it completely misrepresents the political reality in today's Ukraine: "the two wings of Ukraine" are not equally responsible for the mess Ukraine is in. Responsibility rests squarely with Yanukovych and his criminal Party of Regions, and for Kissinger to suggest otherwise is to engage in the greatest of ethical and political obfuscations and moral equivalences.

It is nonsense to suggest that Presidents Kravchuk, Kuchma, and even Yushchenko tried to "impose their will on recalcitrant parts of the country." Kravchuk and Kuchma always walked a fine middle line. Yushchenko adopted a more pro-western rhetoric, but never had the political will to impose on the east—or for that matter on anybody else. Yushchenko shared power with the Party of Regions, and Yanukovych himself served as Yushchenko's prime minister from August 4, 2006 to December 18, 2007. After losing the presidential elections of 2010, Tymoshenko "shared power" with the winner, Yanukovych, who, one and a half years later, threw her into jail. And the defining conflict in recent Ukrainian politics is not that between Tymoshenko and Yanukovych but between Tymoshenko and Yushchenko.

Fortunately, Kissinger does have some sensible things to say about resolving the ongoing war:

1. Ukraine should have the right to choose freely its economic and political associations, including with Europe.

2. Ukraine should not join NATO, a position I took seven years ago, when it last came up.

3. Ukraine should be free to create any government compatible with the expressed will of its people. Wise Ukrainian leaders would then opt for a policy of reconciliation between the various parts of their country. Internationally, they should pursue a posture comparable to that of Finland. That nation leaves no doubt about its fierce independence and cooperates with the West in most fields but carefully avoids institutional hostility toward Russia.

4. It is incompatible with the rules of the existing world order for Russia to annex Crimea. But it should be possible to put Crimea's relationship to Ukraine on a less fraught basis. To that end, Russia would recognize Ukraine's sovereignty over Crimea. Ukraine should reinforce Crimea's autonomy in elections held in the presence of international observers. The process would include removing any ambiguities about the status of the Black Sea Fleet at Sevastopol.

All four "principles" are reasonable starting points for a discussion. Of course, they all assume that President Putin is, as Kissinger writes, "a serious strategist—on the premises of Russian history." (That qualifier is worrisome: one could, by the same token, say that Adolf Hitler is "a serious strategist—on the premises of German history.") If Kissinger is right, then Putin just might be convinced to come around to considering these four points. If Kissinger is wrong—and Putin's warmongering rhetoric, continued military buildup in Crimea, and incursion into Kherson Province, north of Crimea, are not reassuring—then nothing short of a firm Western stand to contain Russia and protect Ukraine can end his imperialist assault on Ukraine and the international order.

*

Trading Barbs with Putin, *World Affairs Journal*, April 11, 2014

One of Ukraine's richest oligarchs, Igor Kolomoisky, has just taken another rude poke at Russian President Vladimir Putin. And this time the Jewish Ukrainian businessman hasn't just insulted Putin. By invoking Jewish support of Putin's Ukrainian nationalist bogeyman—Stepan Bandera (1909–1959)—Kolomoisky, who is president of the European Jewish Union and a leading Jewish philanthropist, has engaged in the ulti-mate provocation.

Kolomoisky, 51, was one of Ukraine's first oligarchs to side with the post-Yanukovych democratic government. Just after Putin's occupation of Crimea in early March, he agreed to serve as governor of his native Dnipropetrovsk Province and publicly **called** Putin "a schizophrenic of short stature." As if that weren't enough, Kolomoisky then went on to say: "He is completely inadequate. He has completely lost his mind. His messianic drive to recreate the Russian empire of 1913 or the USSR of 1991 could plunge the world into catastrophe."

A day later, Putin paid him back in kind:

> For example, Mr. Kolomoisky was appointed Governor of Dnepropetrovsk. This is a unique crook. He even managed to cheat our oligarch Roman Abramovich two or three years ago. Scammed him, as our intellectuals like to say. They signed some deal, Abramovich transferred several billion dollars, while this guy never delivered and pocketed the money. When I asked him [Abramovich]: "Why did you do it?" he said: "I never thought this was possible." I do not know, by the way, if he ever got his money back and if the deal was closed. But this really did happen a couple of years ago. And now this crook is appointed Governor of Dnepropetrovsk. No wonder the people are dissatisfied.

Kolomoisky's latest assault on Putin wasn't a statement, but a performance. He donned a T-shirt, which abounds with semiotic meanings that need some unpacking.

For starters, black and red are the colors of the Ukrainian nationalist movement that derives its ideological inspiration from the radical branch of the Organization of Ukrainian Nationalists affiliated with Bandera. The OUN was established in 1929 as a national liberation movement committed to attaining Ukrainian independence. Until its demise in the mid-1950s, it fought the Polish, German, and Soviet authorities by means of propaganda, terrorism, and guerrilla activities. Ideologically and behaviorally, the OUN closely resem-bled the Algerian National Liberation Front, the Palestine Liberation Organization, and the Jewish Irgun or "Stern Gang," while Bandera was the Ukrainian version of Ahmed Ben Bella, Yassir Arafat, Menachem Begin, or Avraham Stern.

Note as well that the image on the T-shirt represents a fusion of the Ukrainian national symbol, the trident, and a menorah.

The most semiotically charged part of the shirt is the term beneath the trident-menorah. If you read it in Russian, it's *zhidobandera*—or "kike-Bandera." If you read it in Ukrainian, it's *zhydobandera*—or "Jew-Bandera." Recall that, in the language of Soviet and Putin propaganda, "Bandera" is shorthand for "enemy of the Soviet Union," "enemy of Russia," "fascist," and "anti-Semite." According to this logic, enemies of the USSR/Russia must be fascists and anti-Semites. Hence, the T-shirt's Russian reading boils down to a fusion of "kike" and "anti-Semite." Its Ukrainian reading fuses "Jew" with "anti-Semite." Both readings fuse "Jew" with "enemy."

What, then, are the messages that the T-shirt, and Kolomoisky with it, are conveying?

First, and most obviously, Kolomoisky is claiming that ethnic Ukrainians and Jewish Ukrainians have a common cause in today's Ukraine and that that cause—building a democratic Ukrainian nation and state (or what most Ukrainian nationalists would call nationalism)—is deserving of Jewish support.

Second, Kolomoisky is implicitly accusing Putin of being both anti-Semitic and anti-Ukrainian. The term *zhidobandera* reverberates with the interwar anti-Semitic notion of *zhidokomuna*, which fused Jews with Communism. By identifying himself, a Jewish Ukrainian, with a benign version of *zhidobandera*, Kolomoisky is by the same token identifying Putin and his apologists with the malignant version, which views Jews as "kikes" and Ukrainians as "anti-Semites" and "fascists."

Third, in the manner of gays and African-Americans, who have appropriated such terms as "fag," "queer," and "nigger," in order to drain them of their offensive content and turn them against homophobes and racists, so, too, Kolomoisky is appropriating the offensive Russian *zhid* and the pejorative term, Bandera, and stating that, in Ukraine, his homeland, both terms will have the meaning that ethnic Ukrainians and Jewish Ukrainians choose to ascribe to them. In effect, Kolomoisky is taking control of both the Russian and Ukrainian languages and insisting that, not Putin, not Russia, and not Russian propaganda, but he, together with his Ukrainian/Jewish countrymen and women, will decide what words mean in Ukraine.

Finally, Kolomoisky's T-shirt is a plea for Jewish-Ukrainian understanding. Many of Ukraine's Jews, who are generally Russian speakers, find the Ukrainian word for Jew, *zhyd* (which is identical to the Polish, Czech, and Slovak words for Jew), to be too close to the Russian pejorative, *zhid*, to be acceptable and therefore prefer *yevrey*. Many Ukrainians defend their choice of *zhyd* on the grounds that *yevrey* came to Ukrainian from Russian. In effect, the pragmatic Kolomoisky is telling both communities to cool it, take a deep breath, transcend their complex past, and work out a solution that addresses current concerns.

*

Remembering the Red Army and Rape, *World Affairs Journal*, May 9, 2014

As May 9th, Victory Day, approaches and celebrations of the defeat of Nazi Germany take place throughout all the post-Soviet states, it may be worth remembering that many members of the Red Army traded in their heroism and self-sacrifice for criminality and rapine in the last days of the war.

Here's Cooper Union historian Atina Grossmann:

> It has been suggested that perhaps one out of every three of about one and a half million women in Berlin at the end of the war were raped—many but certainly

not all during the notorious week of "mass rapes," from April 24 to May 5, 1945, as the Soviets finally secured Berlin. The numbers cited for Berlin vary wildly; from 20,000 to 100,000, to almost one million, with the actual number of rapes higher because many women were attacked repeatedly. [Two German scholars] speak, perhaps conservatively, of about 110,000 women raped, many more than once, of whom up to 10,000 died in the aftermath. At the same time ... they announce on the basis of Hochrechnungen (projections or estimations) that 1.9 million German women altogether were raped at the end of the war by Red Army soldiers. This may be a horrifically accurate estimate ... ("A Question of Silence: The Rape of German Women by Occupation Soldiers," *October*, Spring 1995, pp. 42–63.)

According to Stanford University historian Norman Naimark:

It is highly unlikely that historians will ever know how many German women were raped by Soviet soldiers in the months before and years after the capitulation. ... R]ape became a part of the social history of the Soviet zone in ways unknown to the Western zones ... it is important to establish the fact that women in the Eastern zone—both refugees from further East and inhabitants of the towns, villages, and cities of the Soviet zone (including Berlin)—shared an experience for the most part unknown in the West, the ubiquitous threat as well as the reality of rape over a prolonged period of time. (Ibid.)

Here's Yale University historian Timothy Snyder:

[T]he outburst of violence against German women was extraordinary. ... In some villages, every single female was raped, whatever her age. ... Gang rapes were very common. ... German women often committed suicide, or tried to kill themselves, to prevent rape or to evade the shame of having been raped. As one recalled her flight, "With the darkness came an indescribable fright. Many women and girls were right there and raped by the Russians." Hearing their screams, she and her sister slit their wrists, but survived. ... They were spared during the night, probably because they had passed out and seemed to be dead. Indeed, death was one of the few defenses against rape. Martha Kurzmann and her sister were spared only because they were burying their mother. "Just as we had washed our dead mother and wished to dress her body, a Russian came and wanted to rape us." He spat and turned away. That was the exception. (*Bloodlands: Europe between Hitler and Europe*. New York: Basic Books, 2010.)

And, finally, historian James Mark about the Red Army and Hungary:

During the Soviet occupation of Budapest at the end of the Second World War, it is estimated that around fifty thousand women in Budapest were raped by soldiers from the Red Army. After Berlin, the women of Budapest suffered in greater numbers than those of any other Central or Eastern European capital. ("Remembering Rape: Divided Social Memory and the Red Army in Hungary 1944–1945," *Past & Present*, August 2005, pp. 133–61.)

All of the USSR's nations and nationalities—Russians, Ukrainians, Belarusians, Jews, Georgians, Armenians, Central Asians, and many others—were represented in the Soviet armed forces. Keep that in mind when you watch aged veterans taking part in Victory Day celebrations.

Now let's ask a few exceedingly uncomfortable questions.

Were Red Army soldiers who fought bravely but also committed rapes heroes or villains? Should they be celebrated or condemned?

On the one hand, there's no doubt that they made enormous sacrifices in World War II. Without them, Nazi Germany might not have been defeated. So, in that sense they are clearly heroes.

On the other hand, who could possibly condone mass rape? So, in that sense they are clearly villains.

Does it matter that their heroism lasted four years and their villainy two weeks? Do millions upon millions of war deaths negate thousands or hundreds of thousands or even 1 to 2 million rapes?

Should they be punished for their crimes? Should they be stripped of their medals? Or, at the least, reminded of their villainy?

Can any of these measures be undertaken without at the same time undermining the still-powerful Soviet-era myth of the "Great Fatherland War," which served to legitimize the Soviet Union and which still legitimizes authoritarian rule in a host of post-Soviet states, especially Russia? Are the peoples of the former Soviet Union ready to come to grips with one of the most shameful moments of their history? Are their Western fellow travelers?

And just who should judge the "hero-criminals"? Surely not the likes of Vladimir Putin and Viktor Yanukovych. Russia? No way. Ukraine? Too divided. Civil society? Too abstract. Europe? Too indecisive. The West? Too compromised. Intellectuals? Give me a break. You and me? Hardly.

Let's end with two questions with easy answers and one question with no easy answer.

Can heroes commit crimes? Of course. Can criminals be heroic? Why not?

Can we accommodate moral ambiguity, stop dividing the world into only two categories—saints and sinners, heroes and villains, victims and victimizers—and realize that there's far more gray around than black and white? I wouldn't bet on it.

*

Ukraine's Donbas Is Like America's Deep South, *Huffington Post*, January 15, 2015

Many journalistic accounts—as well as the Kremlin's propaganda machine—depict the Russian-speaking population in eastern Ukraine's separatist Donbas region and Crimea as an aggrieved ethnic minority clamoring for nothing more than greater autonomy and cultural and language rights. Seen in this light, Kyiv and ethnic Ukrainians are the victimizers. The Donbas and its Russians are the victims. To put the conflict in American terms, Kyiv is white America and the Russian-speaking regions are black America.

The analogy is false.

For starters, Crimea has enjoyed the status of an autonomous republic since 1991. The province ran itself, and Kyiv rarely meddled, so much so that it even neglected the physical needs and civil and cultural rights of the peninsula's Crimean Tatars and ethnic Ukrainians. The two Donbas provinces of Donetsk and Luhansk have also had de facto autonomy from Kyiv. Since the 1930s, they've been the bastions of Ukraine's Stalinist Communist Party, which remained highly influential until the revolution and war of 2013–2014. Since 2001, both provinces have been the stronghold of the Party of Regions, which largely drew its functionaries and electorate from the Communists and which served as the springboard for Ukraine's former president, Viktor Yanukovych. Ukraine's richest man, the oligarch Rinat Akhmetov, funded the Party of Regions, which, together with the Communists, ran the Donbas as its fiefdom.

Unsurprisingly, both Crimea and the Donbas witnessed the absolute hegemony of Russian language and culture. School instruction was largely in Russian; the media—whether books, magazines, newspapers, television or radio—were also overwhelmingly in Russian. Ethnic Ukrainians frequently complained that, if they tried to use Ukrainian in public, they'd be told to "speak human"—i.e. Russian. Most residents viewed Ukrainian as a "foreign" tongue and viewed the hegemony of Russian as a perfectly natural state of affairs. A supremacist minority detested all things Ukrainian.

I remember meeting one such supremacist at a conference in Kyiv in 1994. He insisted that the rights of Russians were persistently being violated in Crimea. Were there too many Ukrainian schools? I asked. No, he answered. Did Ukrainians dominate the media? No. Was he unable to speak Russian in public? No, again. What then was the problem? He finally fessed up: the very fact that Ukrainian existed in Crimea was an offense. Indeed, I can think of no instance of a Russian speaker being discriminated against in either the Donbas or Crimea since 1991.

A far more appropriate analogy for understanding Russo-Ukrainian relations is the Jim Crow South, with Russians as the whites and Ukrainians as the blacks. Not only have Russians and Russian speakers ruled Crimea and the Donbas and enjoyed complete language and cultural rights. They have also proven to be the most reactionary, intolerant and illiberal population within Ukraine.

During Viktor Yanukovych's four-year reign from 2010 to 2014, Ukraine's Jim Crow South captured Kyiv and began extending its norms to all of Ukraine. "Black" Ukrainians fought back, first with the Orange Revolution in 2004 and then with the Maidan Revolution of 2013–2014. The slogans of both revolutions centered on human and civil rights, dignity and personal autonomy—just as during the civil rights movement in the United States. The "white" Yanukovych regime fought back—in the same manner as racist whites in the Deep South—with violence, intimidation and the equivalent of its Ku Klux Klan, the armed fanatics that eventually formed the core of the separatist armies.

Unsurprisingly, "black" Ukrainians have divided into a variety of factions. The overwhelming majority supported, and continues to support, moderation, tolerance and inclusion, along the lines of Martin Luther King. Although there is, alas, no equivalent of Dr. King in contemporary Ukrainian politics, most Ukrainian democrats employ his rhetoric and promote his ideals. But there are also "black" Ukrainian radicals. The right-wing Svoboda party's leader, Oleh Tyahnybok, has sounded remarkably like Malcom X. The hyper-nationalist Azov Battalion resembles the Black Panthers, and its leader Andrii Biletskii could easily pass for Eldridge Cleaver.

The analogy with the Deep South breaks down because of Russia's annexation of Crimea and its invasion of eastern Ukraine. Russia's presence in these regions ensures that they will remain as reactionary, intolerant and illiberal as they have always been. If Kyiv were to reach some political accommodation with the pro-Russian separatists in the Donbas, Ukraine would face an impossible choice. If the Donbas retains the autonomy it has always had, it will remain a Jim Crow bastion that will prevent Ukraine from becoming a liberal democracy. If Ukraine attempts to spread liberal values to the Donbas Deep South, the region's "white" elites and Ku Klux Klan will, once again, rebel. Moscow will claim that their rights are being violated by the Ukrainian racists and fascists in Kyiv!

The United States could eventually overcome Jim Crow laws because Washington was stronger than the Deep South. As long as Russia supports the Donbas Deep South—and that is likely to be for a long time—Ukraine will be too weak to grant it autonomy or to absorb it. Faced with such an unenviable choice, Ukraine would be well advised to leave the Donbas to its own devices, borrow from Dr. King's rhetoric and "dream" of a sunny future.

*

Ukrainian Jewish Leader on Russian Aggression, *World Affairs Journal*, March 10, 2015

Josef Zissels is the chairman of the General Council of the Euro-Asian Jewish Congress. He is sitting in the middle of a long table in the Ukrainian Restaurant in downtown New York. Before him is a bowl of borscht. As he eats, he shares his views of the current crisis in Ukraine with nine specialists and activists.

Zissels does not mince words. "There is no civil war in Ukraine," he says. "There is a Russian aggression supported by local collaborators." The war with Russia will be "long," and Ukraine needs to construct a "militarist economy" like Israel's. The Maidan Revolution had nothing to do with ethnicity, language, or religion. It was a "civilizational conflict" between those Ukrainians who supported Europe and those who supported Russia.

Zissels is 69-year-old former dissident with prison sentences to prove it. Born in Tashkent, the capital of Uzbekistan, he's a staunch Ukrainian patriot who speaks perfect Ukrainian. In 1947, his family moved to Chernivtsi, in then-Soviet Ukraine, where he studied at the university. His dissident activity in both the Jewish and democratic movements began in the 1970s; in 1978, he joined the Ukrainian Helsinki Group. That same year, he received his first three-year prison sentence. In 1984, he got three more years. In 1989, as Mikhail Gorbachev's *perestroika* was taking off, he became co-chairman of the VAAD—the Confederation of Jewish Organizations and Communities. Two years later, in 1991, Zissels became chairman of the Association of Jewish Organizations and Communities of Ukraine and executive vice president of the Congress of National Communities of Ukraine and the Jewish Confederation of Ukraine.

As a Jewish Ukrainian democrat, Zissels took part in and supported both the 2004 Orange Revolution and the 2013–14 Maidan Revolution. On December 15, 2013, he delivered a stirring speech to the protesters on Kyiv's Independence Square:

> In 2004 I stood here, at this very Independence Square, this very Maidan, at the stage which had been built here, and thought of how happy my fate is. ... Today the situation in Ukraine is very similar to 2004, for once more the same propaganda is being used against Euromaidan, against the united opposition, against all of us. They are trying to sow the seeds of conflict, to pit us one against the other, and to create an artificial standoff—national minorities against Ukrainians. But Ukraine and its people have changed in these years, in this short time. ... When we go out to the Maidan desiring freedom, we have one joint goal: a united dignified future. ... We need a new government. ... Until we have such a government, we have only one peaceful weapon: these Maidans, which can grow into an all-national Maidan, into a perpetual campaign of civil dissent. Three thousand years ago my people took 40 years to walk from slavery to freedom. We, the people of Ukraine, have already gone halfway. There is not much longer to go!

Zissels ended his peroration with two explosive lines—the first from Ukraine's national poet, Taras Shevchenko: "If you fight, you shall win!"—and the second from the Ukrainian nationalist movement: "Glory to Ukraine!"

Zissels identifies himself completely with his homeland, Ukraine, which he sees as slowly overcoming centuries of Russian servitude and becoming a liberal, democratic country. His is the language of the 20th century's Ukrainian national liberation movements. Who, he asks, will "expel the Russian disease from our land?" Right-wing Ukrainians have, he says, mostly abandoned their Judeophobia and homophobia. They've still retained their Russophobia, but that's "largely justified."

Asked about the controversial Azov volunteer regiment, whose leader is a neo-Nazi,

Zissels brushes off the implication that the entire unit shares his extremist views. Perhaps 30 or 40 do, he says, but the important thing is that all the volunteers, including the Jews fighting in Azov, are on the front lines. Their ideological predilections don't matter, he emphasizes, as they're all united in defending their country against Russia.

In a July 6, 2014, interview in Toronto, Zissels openly associated himself with the controversial term *zhydobandera*, which the Ukrainian Jewish oligarch Igor Kolomoisky popularized by wearing on a T-shirt. (The term is a conjunction of *zhyd*, a word that can mean both "Jew" and "kike," and the surname of Stepan Bandera, a Ukrainian nationalist, that according to Soviet and Russian propaganda was a synonym for fascist. Hence, *zhydobandera* is the equivalent of both "Jew-Ukrainian nationalist" and "kike-fascist.") According to Zissels, "Back in 1978 when they were imprisoning me, the KGB couldn't understand me: 'as a Jew he should be a Zionist.' They had these stereotypes, but I became part of the Ukrainian Helsinki Group, a Ukrainian national group, and therefore back then I was already a *zhydobandera*."

Zissels is in the United States, meeting with Jewish, Ukrainian, and US government circles in order to lobby for his country. Putin, he notes, will stop at nothing, and will be willing to sacrifice untold numbers of his own people to crush Ukraine, which "opened a Pandora's box that will be hard to close." Ukraine, he stresses several times, needs weapons to defend itself against the Russian aggression. "This disease," he says, "must be stopped."

*

Soviet-Nazi Collaboration and World War II, *World Affairs Journal*, April 30, 2015

As May 9th, Victory Day in many post-Soviet states, approaches, decency demands that we celebrate the defeat of Adolf Hitler's Germany and honor the millions of soldiers and civilians who gave their lives to rid the world of the scourge of Nazism.

At the same time, if we truly want to honor the dead, we must take heed of the historical lies that the Kremlin, both in its Soviet and post-Soviet hypostases, promotes about the USSR's relationship with Nazi Germany.

For starters, the Moscow-controlled Communist International, and its sidekick, the Communist Party of Germany, made Hitler's rise to power possible, if not indeed inevitable, by tarring the German Social Democrats as "social fascists" who threatened to split the proletariat and were, thus, a greater evil than the Nazis. Had the German left remained united against the real threat—Nazism—Hitler might not have come to power. (Many leftists make a similar mistake today, preferring Vladimir Putin's fascism to American capitalism and thereby promoting war in Europe.)

And then there's the matter of the notorious Molotov-Ribbentrop Pact of 1939. The part that obligated Nazi Germany and the USSR to nonaggression vis-à-vis each other is arguably defensible in light of Moscow's desire to ward off a possible German attack.

Completely indefensible is the secret protocol that led to Poland's partition in September 1939 and the subsequent Soviet attack on and incorporation of Estonia, Latvia, and Lithuania. That was imperialism, pure and simple, though, naturally, the Soviets claimed that they were "liberating" the territories from "fascist" rule (sound familiar?).

More than indefensible—indeed, profoundly criminal—was Moscow's kowtowing to and enthusiastic support of the Hitler state and economy in 1939–1941, at precisely the time the Nazis were killing Poles, segregating Jews, and laying the groundwork for the Holocaust. Because the USSR *collaborated* with the Nazis, it bears a large part of the responsibility for World War II and the enormous destruction that Germany brought to Eastern Europe in general and Eastern European Jews, in particular.

By the way, during the two years the Soviets ruled Western Ukraine (the former eastern Poland), they destroyed civil society, dismantled all political and civil rights, deported hundreds of thousands of Poles, Jews, and Ukrainians to Siberia, and then, to top things off, massacred some 20,000–30,000 political prisoners in the week after the Nazis attacked in June of 1941. (About 70 percent were Ukrainian, 20 percent were Polish, and over 5 percent were Jewish.) A shot in the back of the head wasn't enough. The Soviet secret police also devised refined tortures for their helpless victims: noses, tongues, breasts, and genitalia were lopped off; skin was scalded with boiling water and peeled off; prisoners were buried alive. In one town, hundreds of prisoners were dumped, some dead, some still living, down a salt mine shaft.

The Soviet—as well as current Russian—designation for this monstrous enterprise is the "Great Patriotic War," a term that conveniently elides the two years of shameful collaboration and the USSR's direct contribution to World War II and the Holocaust.

Appropriately for the regnant Stalinist political culture in Putin's Russia, his neo-Nazi biker pals, the Night Wolves, want to celebrate Victory Day by retracing the Red Army's route from Russia to Berlin. Just as appropriately, Poland and Germany have refused them permission to cross their territory. (Unfazed by such legalities, the Wolves entered into Poland anyway on April 26th.) No less appropriately, Western states have declined to attend Victory Day celebrations in Moscow.

The West shouldn't boycott the anniversary events just because of Putin's invasion of Ukraine. They should do so because the Victory Day celebration covers up a raft of crimes that should be condemned along with Putin's regime.

*

Germany Must Lead in Europe, *World Affairs Journal*, May 21, 2015

Nothing could be more unlike the Russo-Ukrainian war in the Donbas than Munich's remarkably well-ordered condition. The desperate desire of Germans to look away from the death and destruction beyond their eastern border makes sense: War is too disruptive of their near-perfect orderliness to be thinkable, least of all real. Unfortunately for them, Germany has no choice but to play the role of Europe's "well-meaning hegemon." The European Union needs leadership, and, as distasteful as seizing the initiative may be to most Germans, who associate hegemony with the disaster of Nazism and World War II, only Germany has the geopolitical resources to be a consistent leader.

The lessons of Germany's catastrophic embrace of Nazism have been underscored in all the media these last few weeks, as Europe *sans* Russia and Russia *sans* Europe commemorated the 70th anniversary of the end of World War II. And rightly so, as long as Vladimir Putin's Russia continues to ignore the criminality of the Molotov-Ribbentrop Pact, the division of Poland, the incorporation of the Baltics, and the USSR's support of the Nazi killing machine. Unfortunately, all too many German policymakers and commentators still refer to the war as having been fought against *Russland* and insist that the *Russen* suffered immense casualties. The continued German blindness to the existence of the nations in between—Poland, Ukraine, and Belarus—and to their far greater population losses (not to mention the full-scale destruction of their cities, towns, and villages) is obscene. Poland at least exists in the German popular consciousness; Belarus and Ukraine are empty signifiers—terms that evoke no associations and, hence, little sympathy.

Paradoxically, part of the problem may lie in the fact that Germans are, appropriately, fixated on the Holocaust and their role in it. As a result, academic research, policy commentary, and media discussions of the German responsibility for Nazism and the Holocaust are extremely detailed and nuanced. In contrast, German attitudes toward the East are shaped by the categories of the Holocaust. The wartime experience of Poles, Belarusians, and Ukrainians matters only when Poles, Belarusians, and Ukrainians contributed to the persecution of Jews. Otherwise, they—and their narratives—take a back seat. Take a walk through Munich's newly opened Documentation Center for the History of National Socialism and you'll be hard-pressed to notice that the war actually affected the nations in between.

In fact, observing Adolf Hitler's rise to power cannot but evoke thoughts of Putin and Russia. A currently playing German docu-drama, *Elser*, focuses on the young Georg Elser's failed attempt to assassinate Hitler in late 1939. The film is especially good in depicting how the otherwise normal people of Elser's hometown acquiesce in or increasing-ly support the growing Nazi presence. Their faces glow at the mention of the Führer, their right arms rise in salute, their voices hail victory in the coming war. I doubt that most Germans will see the parallel, but I couldn't help but think of the millions of Russians who view Putin as their messiah and who, no less blindly and no less fanatically than the Germans, are welcoming their country's drive toward war. Swetlana Alexijewitsch, a Belarusian writer living in Moscow, writes in the May 13th edition of *Die Zeit* that "Russia has become a different country in the last one and a half years. ... We are people of war, because we know nothing else. ... A cult of war rules over us." A statue of Putin in St. Petersburg depicts him as a Roman emperor. A Russian scientist I met in Regensburg, Germany, says that he no longer recognizes his mother, still living in St. Petersburg. Meanwhile, former Chancellor Gerhard Schröder, who would never say that we should "understand" Hitler, continues to call on the West to understand Putin.

Munich's Literaturhaus, a cultural center, is currently showing an exhibit dedicated to the excellent Viennese Jewish writer Stefan Zweig, who left Salzburg for London in 1934 and, depressed by Hitler's aggression and persecution of Jews, committed suicide with his wife in Brazil in 1942. The poster highlights a citation from Zweig: "*Wir brauchen einen ganz anderen Mut!*" (We need a completely different courage!) The quote is profoundly misleading, suggesting that Zweig, who refrained from criticizing the Nazi regime pub-licly in the hope of having his books published in Germany again, was a heroic figure. He was not: He was tragic. The actual text also lacks the exclamation point, which suggests that Zweig's statement was meant as a call to arms. In fact, Zweig wrote the following to his friend Paul Zech on June 5, 1941: "My dear, it would be stupid and dishonest to want to say to you: be of good courage, we will win, all will be better. We need a com-pletely different courage, not that of an artificial optimism, but a courage of 'even so' and 'nevertheless.'"

In Munich, where Putin's immediate threat to world peace appears more abstract than the Nazi book-burning on Königsplatz in 1933, Zweig's words ring especially true.

*

Ukraine Is Still Caught between a Hammer and an Anvil, *Atlantic Council*, May 26, 2015

For most of the 20th century, Ukraine was the victim of two equally malevolent empires—Germany and Russia. Germany's contribution to Ukraine's devastation was the two World Wars; Russia's was the imposition of Soviet rule and the concomitant destruction of Ukraine's peasantry and elites. Unsurprisingly, one of the most constant images in 20th-century Ukrainian commentary is that of their country being caught between a hammer and an anvil.

The 21st century may be witnessing a fundamental break with Ukraine's tragic geopolitical position. While Russia is acting according to its historical script, post-Holocaust, post-unification Germany appears to be emerging as Europe's benevolent hegemon. As such, Germany has no choice but to exercise its clout and take a lead in Europe. But given its awful past and the continued importance of that past in shaping German foreign policy behavior, Germany also has no choice but to eschew the kind of crude realpolitik that produced two World Wars and took the lives of millions.

Ukraine's 20th-century encounter with Germany and Russia was devastating. According to a 2008 study by the Moscow-based Institute of Demography, Ukraine suffered close to fifteen million "excess deaths" between 1914 and 1948. About half of the deaths were attributable to Soviet Russian policies and half to the two World Wars with Germany. As a result of the destruction, approximately three million Ukrainians emigrated in this time period, and another six million failed to be born. Overall, Ukraine's population in 1948 (thirty million in 1900) was about twenty-three million less than it would have been if Germany and Russia had stayed out. And that's just population losses. The two World Wars also produced trillions of dollars of economic damage: cities, towns, and villages were destroyed, as were infrastructure and industrial and agricultural assets.

In sum, Germany and Russia set back Ukraine's political, social, and economic development by decades, if not centuries.

In 1945, the geopolitical Germany that had produced two world conflagrations was destroyed. In 1991, the Soviet empire collapsed. New democracies emerged on the ruins of both criminal dictatorships. In Germany, perhaps due to the extended US influence on the country's internal affairs, democracy took root and was consolidated. In Russia, democracy was blamed for the imperial collapse and subsequent economic hardships and, in 1999, effectively abandoned. By the late-2000s, Vladimir Putin had replaced Russia's democratic facade with a fascist regime.

Ironically, neither country has accepted its responsibility for the devastation it brought to Ukraine. Russia glorifies Stalinism, while Germany has still to fully appreciate that a people called Ukrainians in a country called Ukraine exist as more than an appendage of *Russland*. Heinrich Böll's 1949 novel, *The Train Was Punctual*, still captures the regnant mood among most Germans, if not among most German intellectuals. The novel's hero, a young soldier on furlough, is returning to his base in southern Ukraine. Remarkably, while repeatedly referring to Russians, Poles, and Jews—and peasants—he fails to mention the word Ukrainian or Ukrainians even once.

Now, as then, Ukrainians don't exist in most Germans' mental maps of Eastern Europe. Instead, most Germans insist that they fought a war against Russia and Russians, even though, as historian Timothy Snyder has shown in *Bloodlands*, Russian losses were less than those of Ukrainians, Belarusians, and Poles. And for a simple reason: most of World War II was fought in Ukraine, Belarus, and Poland, and not Russia.

On the other hand, Germany and Russia have adopted diametrically opposed foreign policies toward Ukraine. Despite the continued prominence of "*Russlandversteher*" insisting that the West provoked Putin to invade Ukraine, much of Germany's political and intellectual class has come to understand that Putin's unilateral revision of state borders is an unacceptable violation of the post-war security architecture that gave Europe more than seven decades of unprecedented peace and that Ukraine, as the victim of unprovoked Russian aggression, needs to be defended. Inasmuch as this stance is motivated largely by Russia's imperialism and not by any sense of moral responsibility toward Ukraine, it may be open to revision should German Chancellor Angela Merkel's government be replaced by the left, which is more prone to emphasize that Russia needs to be understood.

Putin's Russia, in contrast, has reverted to 20th-century Soviet Russian behavior, both insisting on its manifest destiny in the former Soviet space and refusing to countenance any degree of responsibility for its criminal acts vis-à-vis Ukraine and the other non-Russian states.

The ongoing war in Ukraine is thus a test for Germany and a test run for Russia. Germany must decide whether its role as a benevolent hegemon rests on both ethics and interests. Russia must decide whether its invasion of Crimea and the Donbas can serve as a model for its behavior with Estonia, Latvia, Belarus, and Kazakhstan. If Germany fails the test, Russia may well decide that its test run is positive.

*

What New Ukrainian Exceptionalism? *World Affairs Journal*, July 2, 2015

Having just lauded Kennan Institute Director Matthew Rojansky and two colleagues for a fine piece on Ukraine's relationship with the United States, I hate to change my tune and criticize him for a subsequent article co-written with a Ukrainian academic, but their views on the "new Ukrainian exceptionalism" are so divorced from reality as to be mystifying.

Rojansky and Mykhailo Minakov, associate professor in philosophy and religious studies at Kyiv's prestigious Mohyla Academy, begin their piece by paying due respect to Ukraine's "struggle not only for its sovereignty, but for its very survival as a nation-state." Rightly, they argue that "In this hour of need, every Ukrainian citizen and every self-described friend of Ukraine in the international community should not only speak but act in support of Ukraine."

Then they slip off he rails:

> But speaking out and taking action in support of Ukraine have become increasingly fraught in recent months. Russian-backed aggression, relentless propaganda and meddling in Ukraine's domestic politics have pushed many Ukrainians to adopt a deeply polarized worldview, in which constructive criticism, dissenting views, and even observable facts are rejected out of hand if they are seen as harmful to Ukraine. This phenomenon might be termed the new Ukrainian exceptionalism.

"This exceptionalist worldview," they write, "is nowhere more evident than in the discourse around Ukraine's President Petro Poroshenko," an oligarch supposedly committed to "de-oligarchization." According to Rojansky and Minakov, "when queried about whether, as an oligarch himself, Poroshenko can be effective in removing oligarchic influence from Ukraine's politics and economy, many Ukrainians feel compelled to defend their wartime leader by denying that he is, in fact, an oligarch in the first place. Or if he is one, they say, he's a different kind of oligarch, certainly the best of the bunch."

I don't know whom they've been talking to and what they've been reading, but it's obvious, at least to me, that their sources aren't at all reflective of majority views. I've been in Ukraine now for close to three weeks and have yet to meet a person who's spoken kindly of the president, prime minister, parliament, or any oligarch. And public opinion surveys back up my impression. Of the thousands of articles I've read about Ukraine in the last few months, I'd say at most 10 percent speak positively about the government. I can't think of a single one that's lauded the oligarchs. The fact is that Ukrainians are almost anarchically critical of every aspect of their political system. Indeed, from everyone I've talked to, from everything I've read, I'd say Ukrainians are almost destructively critical of *everything*. That may or may not be a good thing, but it's hardly reflective of the group think that Rojansky and Minakov supposedly encountered.

Rojansky and Minakov then focus their attention on

> the country's far right political forces. Cite the rise of Praviy Sektor, or Right Sector ... and many Ukrainians will point to the radical right movement's poor performance in last year's presidential and parliamentary elections. Point to the resurgence of symbols and slogans of the Second World War ultra-nationalist Union of Ukrainian Nationalists, OUN, or the newly passed laws banning 'Soviet symbols,' canonizing controversial Ukrainian nationalist figures Stepan Bandera and Roman Shukhevych, and they will say that Ukraine has every right to define its own history, even if it does so with blatant disregard and disrespect for that of millions of its citizens now living under Russian occupation or otherwise not fully represented in the government. ... [R]aise the problem of private armies in Ukraine, and one is told that the famous 'volunteer battalions' are actually completely legal and legitimate police, interior ministry or army units that have been integrated under a single, responsible national command. ... The same goes for so-called soldier deputies, commanders of the volunteer battalions elected to the parliament last October, many of whom still appear in uniform and demonstrate scant regard for the boundaries between civilian and military authority. Dashing but bellicose figures like Serhii Melnychuk, Semen Semenchenko and Dmytro Yarosh, we are told, are not really soldiers any more, their grandstanding is just a PR exercise.

Contrary to the authors' claims, the "observable" fact—to use Rojansky and Minakov's modifier—is that Ukraine's right really is insignificant, that the newly passed laws do not even come close to "canonizing controversial Ukrainian nationalist figures Stepan Bandera and Roman Shukhevych," that Ukraine has as much a right to "define its own history, even if it does so with blatant disregard and disrespect for that of millions of its [pro-Stalinist, pro-Putin] citizens" as does post-Jim Crow America and post-Nazi Germany, which blatantly disregarded and disrespected the history of millions of their racist and Nazi citizens, that Ukraine's problematic volunteer units represent a tiny fraction of the total volunteer movement, and that Melnychuk, Semenchenko, and Yarosh really are bit players.

But take note of what's just happened as a result of my disagreement with the authors' hyperventilation. I've effectively taken their bait and proven their point. For the observable fact is that Rojansky and Minakov frame their argument insidiously. They imply that disagreement with their (naturally correct!) views is reflective, not of genuine disagreement or, heaven forbid, the possibility of their being wrong, but of "exceptionalist" group think.

In other words, if I disagree with their claims, as I do, I am obviously incapable of the kind of critical thinking they claim to represent.

Just how is their stance supportive of the critical debate they supposedly endorse? It isn't. In effect, if not in intent, Rojansky and Minakov are insisting that their critics remain silent—that there be no debate, that group think reign. But, naturally, the group think that Rojansky and Minakov support.

Ironically, Rojansky and Minakov are the "new exceptionalists." Ukraine, in contrast, is becoming less exceptional, and more like everyone else in the West, with every day.

*

Here's Why More Ukrainians Admire Nationalists, and Why the West Shouldn't Freak Out, *Atlantic Council*, July 8, 2015

Here's a suggestion that will strike you as either painfully obvious or unnecessarily cumbersome. If you really want to understand contemporary Ukraine and Ukrainians, you need to know Ukrainian. If you accept that point, then discard all the writings by linguistically challenged analysts incapable of delving deeper into the Ukrainian psyche—and then go see two plays in Kyiv and visit two villages south of Kyiv.

The plays I have in mind are "Zacharovanyy" (The Enchanted Man) and "Divka (Maiden), a Ukrainian Love Story." The first, a modern adaptation of a nineteenth-century play by Ivan Karpenko-Karyy, tells the well-known story of two proud village lovers. They quar-rel, marry the wrong person out of spite, and then—unhappy in their new relationships—reignite their love illicitly. In the final scene, the young man, desperate and confused, accidentally kills his wife.

At first glance, there's nothing new here. Look a little closer, however, and you'll see that the play has the same structure and moral message as an ancient Greek tragedy. The Ukrainian lovers attempt to assert their autonomy, fail, and then succumb to their tragic fate: misery and death.

The second play is by a young Ukrainian playwright, Vira Makovii, from the Bukovyna region of western Ukraine. The plot line is similar to that of "The Enchanted Man"—but with one major difference. The heroine refuses to bow to her fate and, in the final scene, appears to escape its hold, avoiding the misery and death that befalls all the women in her village.

561

Makovii, obviously, is trying to move Ukrainian culture away from its traditional submissiveness to a dreadful fate and, in decidedly modern fashion, suggesting that Ukrainians can be masters—or mistresses—of their lives. That happened to be the message of the Maidan "Revolution of Dignity": that a humbled people can assert their humanity by rising up against tyranny.

The two villages, both about 170 kilometers south of Kyiv, are Moryntsi and Shevchenkove, where Ukraine's "national poet," Taras Shevchenko (1814–61), spent his youth as a serf—or, to use American terminology, a slave. Visit the huts he lived in and you can't help but compare them with the slave cabins found on American plantations. Shevchenko had the good fortune to be a "house serf," or page, in the employ of his master, Pavel Engelhardt, and accompany him to St. Petersburg in 1831. There, the young slave impressed local painters and writers with his artistic talents, and in 1838 they raised the money to buy his freedom. Arrested in 1847 for his revolutionary activity and writings, Shevchenko spent most of the rest of his life in exile.

There are many reasons for Shevchenko's canonical status as Ukraine's national poet. His poetry is outstanding, his art is impressive, and his commitment to freedom and justice is remarkable. But what may appeal most to many Ukrainians is that Shevchenko never gave up. He never buckled under, refusing to submit to his tragic fate like the slave he was. Instead, he had the courage to say no, loudly and repeatedly.

So much of Ukrainian culture—and perhaps of the Ukrainian "psyche"—is defined by these two dialectically related components. On the one hand, there is the fatalistic acceptance (still) of one's tragic fate. And for Ukrainians, who barely survived two monstrous totalitarian dictatorships, the Soviet and the Nazi, and lost some fifteen million people in the process, it's not hard to find evidence of the correctness of that view.

On the other hand, there is the rebellious rejection of fate, along with the deep-seated admiration of courageous individuals who have the strength of will to say no and to keep on saying no even in the face of overwhelming odds.

Small wonder that growing numbers of Ukrainians admire the nationalists—commonly known as Banderites, or followers of Stepan Bandera—who fought Polish rule in 1921–1939, Nazi rule in 1941–1944, and Soviet rule in 1939–1955. Western observers point to nationalist excesses and condemn them. But that's missing the point, somewhat like saying that Thomas Jefferson and George Washington don't deserve to be founding fathers because they had slaves. Ukrainians see strong-willed individuals who were willing to die for their ideals of independence and freedom. And, perhaps unsurprisingly, the contemporary Ukrainians who are most inclined to view the nationalists as symbols of resistance are the Russian-speaking easterners fighting Putin's troops in the Donbas and dying for the cause.

The similarity with Eastern European Jewish culture and Zionism is striking. Shtetl culture was generally resigned to the inevitability of tragedy, misery, and death. The Zionists were young men and women determined to reject that fatalistic worldview and create "new" Jews—strong, vigorous, and wilful. If necessary, the Zionists would also use violence. As Frantz Fanon, the author of the classic anti-colonial tract, *The Wretched of the Earth*, pointed out, colonial peoples in Asia and Africa have similar cultural mindsets and generate identical individuals committed to national liberation.

On July 2, I attended a book presentation at Kyiv's "YE" bookstore. Author Bohdan Zholdak had just published a novel about the ongoing war entitled *"UKRY"*—the derogatory name for Ukrainians that Russians use and that Ukrainians (like blacks with respect to "nigger" and gays with respect to "fag" have now appropriated. He dedicated the book to a young soldier, Zhora, who had been killed while returning to the front. Zhora's mother spoke at the gathering—in Russian. And she concluded her stirring words with the nationalist call, *"Slava Ukraini!"* [Glory to Ukraine!]. The audience responded with the nationalist response—*"Heroyam slava!"* [Glory to the heroes].

An outsider with no knowledge of Ukrainian language or culture might interpret the exchange as a right-wing nationalist ritual. It wasn't. It was an assertion of dignity, humanity, and the right to determine one's fate.

*

Two Mass Graves: Ukrainians and Jews, *World Affairs Journal*, July 15, 2015

I discovered two mass graves in the forest near my mother's home town in western Ukraine, Peremyshlyany, located 47 kilometers east-southeast of Lviv.

The former Przemyślany is also a former shtetl. Its prewar population was about 5,000; its current official population is 7,000–8,000, though, given the large number of residents working abroad, it's probably closer to the prewar level. The composition of the town has changed dramatically. The Jews and Poles, who comprised about 45 percent apiece of the prewar population, are gone: killed, expelled, or fled. About 90 percent of the prewar Ukrainian population had also been killed or expelled, or had fled. Most of the town's current Ukrainian inhabitants have no roots in Peremyshlyany, being the progeny of villagers who settled there after World War II.

In Peremyshlyany, as in most of western Ukraine's towns, there is little living historical memory—as opposed to a few monuments and plaques—because its bearers, whether Poles, Ukrainians, or Jews, are all dead. Ironically, I suspect that I, a native New Yorker, know more about the town's past than most of its inhabitants. I don't blame them. Peremyshlyany is dreadfully depressed and seems as far away from any possible socio-economic revival as one can imagine. (Visit some of the unremittingly gray former coal towns in eastern Pennsylvania for a sense of what it's like.) The past may look like a needless luxury when the sidewalks are cracked, the roads are crumbling, and most buildings haven't been plastered or painted in decades.

I had heard that there was a Jewish grave site somewhere in the forest behind the town hospital. It was another bit of the town's forgotten tragic past and an implicit connection to my mother's best friend, Fania Lacher, a Jewish girl who survived the Holocaust and became a Greek Catholic nun.

I climbed a steep slope and entered a shady wood populated by tall, straight pine trees. Several hundred yards into the forest, I came upon grassy flat terrain. An ideal killing field, I thought: close enough, but well out of earshot.

I was right. There, straight ahead, was the Jewish gravestone. The inscription, in English, read as follows:

THIS MONUMENT IS DEDICATED TO THE

SACRED MEMORY OF THE 385 JEWISH

MARTYRS WHO PERISHED HERE AT THE

HANDS OF THE NAZIS ON:

NOVEMBER 5TH, 1941

BLESSED BE THEIR MEMORY!

THE KIRSCHNER FAMILY, ISRAEL

THE ROHR FAMILY, U.S.A.

AND OTHERS.

Some 50 feet to the site's left, I came upon a surprising sight: another grave, this one adorned with a huge white cross. The faded (Ukrainian-language) inscription on the gravestone read as follows:

To the fi hters for Ukraine's freedom
who died at the hands of the
Muscovite-Bolshevik occupiers
1939–1950

The plaque attached to the cross behind the gravestone is only half legible:

On this place
[by?] Bolshevik [illegible]
executioners [illegible]
130[0?]
Ukrainians [illegible]
[their?] remains [illegible]

were reburied [illegible]

year in the local

ce[metery] [illegible]

May their memory be eternal!

So the clearing had been a mass grave for Ukrainian and Jewish victims of the 20th century's two totalitarian dictatorships—Soviet Union *and* Nazi Germany.

The Soviet secret police presumably started dumping the bodies of its Ukrainian opponents immediately after helping the Nazis dismember Poland in September 1939. The Nazis presumably decided that the Soviet mass grave was too conveniently located to ignore and used it to dump the bodies of Jews. After the Soviets returned to the region in 1944, they picked up where they had left off in 1939–1941 and used the area as a killing field until 1950, when the Ukrainian resistance movement was pretty much destroyed.

How fitting, I thought, for Ukrainians and Jews, who have needlessly hated, oppressed, exploited, and killed each other for centuries, to lie together, victims of two genocidal regimes.

*

De-Communization, Hannah Arendt, and Ukrainian Nationalism, *World Affairs Journal*, July 28, 2015

It's about 100 days since Ukraine passed its de-communization laws and guess what? The sky hasn't fallen. The fascists haven't taken over. Repression hasn't set in. Which is exactly what those of us who were arguing for the laws were saying all along.

The first bill provides a long list of "fighters for Ukraine's independence in the 20th cen-tury" with legal status. The second one gives people open access to secret police archives. The third reconceptualizes the Soviet-era Great Patriotic War as World War II. The fourth prohibits the propaganda of the Communist and Nazi totalitarian regimes and their symbols. Most of the controversy has centered on the first bill's list of "fighters," who include over 100 governments, organizations, movements, and parties, all excoriated by Soviet propaganda. They also include the controversial organized Ukrainian nationalist movement that flourished in western Ukraine in the interwar period and survived in the anti-Soviet underground until the mid-1950s. Opponents of the laws, in both Ukraine and especially the West, have argued that they amounted to *carte blanche* to persecute nationalist critics.

In fact, the brouhaha over the laws has exposed, yet again, one of the most depressing features of the Ukrainian intellectual landscape: the perennial war between absolutist supporters and absolutist critics of the interwar organized Ukrainian nationalist movement.

Supporters uncritically produce hagiographies. Critics uncritically produce jeremiads. Neither side tolerates nuance, complexity, or ambiguity: the nationalists must be either the whitest of heroes or the blackest of devils. People who hope to find a middle ground by arguing that the Ukrainian nationalists, like all nationalists, were black, white and gray, are lost in the noise. As you can imagine, the hagiographers have supported the laws (hey, even F students occasionally get an answer right), while the jeremiahs have damned 'em.

Both sets of absolutists would do well to read Hannah Arendt's *Eichmann in Jerusalem*, which unintentionally demonstrates that knowledge is not infallible even when its claims appear to be beyond dispute.

Israeli intelligence agents kidnapped Adolf Eichmann in Argentina on May 11, 1960, and brought him to Jerusalem, where he was tried as a Nazi war criminal and hanged on May 31, 1962. Arendt's account of the trial's philosophical and legal shortcomings, her criticism of the wartime Jewish Councils for effectively abetting Nazi policy, and her description of Eichmann as an ordinary man, and not a monster, whose behavior deserved to be characterized by the now-famous term, the "banality of evil," provoked a storm of protest. There were even attempts to revoke her teaching position at the New School for Social Research.

It was in the epilogue that Arendt addressed an issue of interest to contemporary Ukrainian debates. "Those who are convinced that justice, and nothing else, is the end of law will be inclined to condone the kidnaping act," she writes. "In this perspective, there existed but one real alternative to what Israel had done: instead of capturing Eichmann and flying him to Israel, the Israeli agents could have killed him right then and there." Arendt does not disagree. "The notion was not without merit," she says, "because the facts of the case were beyond dispute."

Arendt then discusses "two precedents" that involve taking the law into one's own hands: "There was the case of Shalom Schwartzbard, who in Paris on May 25, 1926, shot and killed Simon Petlyura, former hetman of the Ukrainian armies and responsible for the pogroms during the Russian civil war that claimed about a hundred thousand victims between 1917 and 1920. And there was the case of the Armenian Tehlirian, who, in 1921, in the middle of Berlin, shot to death Talaat Bey, the great killer in the Armenian pogroms of 1915." (Petliura is not on the "fighters" list, but the governments he headed are.)

Importantly for Arendt, "neither of these assassins was satisfied with killing 'his' criminal, but that both immediately gave themselves up to the police and insisted on being tried. Each used his trial to show the world through court procedure what crimes against his people had been committed and gone unpunished."

Although she never openly says it, it's clear that Arendt does not disapprove of both assassins' actions—because they gave themselves up and because the facts do appear to be beyond dispute.

Except that the facts turned out not to be beyond dispute, at least with respect to Petliura.

Arendt's brief description of Petliura is woefully inaccurate. He was never hetman—that was Pavlo Skoropadsky in 1918; he was not in charge of the "Ukrainian armies" in 1917–1920, but in 1919–1920; the Russian Civil War began in mid-1918 and not in 1917; and the pogroms that swept Ukraine in 1919 were the work of Ukrainians armies, Red Russian Bolshevik armies, White Russian armies, anarchists, and bandits.

But no matter. The key question is whether Petliura was "responsible for the pogroms." For years, Petliura's defenders argued that he was a philo-Semite, while his detractors argued the opposite. Recent academic research by Touro College historian Henry Abramson has shown that Petliura was indeed a philo-Semite who neither instigated, nor ordered the pogroms. Joshua Rubenstein neatly summarizes Abramson's complex conclusions:

> After a close review of the documentary record, Abramson rejects the accusation that Petliura was the architect of the pogroms or that he initiated the infamous attacks in Proskurov (where 1,500 Jews were slaughtered) by his subordinate Semesenko in 1919, an incident that rumor and accusation have long linked to Petliura. ... At the same time, Abramson accepts the view that Petliura's hands were tied, and that if he had "chastised his troops adequately," he would have lost the loyalty of his already disintegrating army at a time when the Red Army was able to field many more soldiers. Petliura was desperate to preserve Ukrainian independence. As Abramson implies, he could not hope to do this and protect Jews in far-flung towns and villages. In the end, though, Petliura's failure to act decisively against the pogroms did not save Ukraine.

Did Petliura do enough to prevent the pogroms? Some say yes, some say no. Some argue that Ukraine was a "failed state" and that no one could have stopped the killing. Meanwhile, don't forget that further research could revise Abramson's conclusions.

Many Ukrainians came to lionize Petliura after he was shot; many Jews demonized him because he "deserved" to be shot. Both sides are wrong. Petliura was a weak leader who was in the wrong place at the wrong time. Schwartzbard thought he was killing a bloodthirsty demon. In reality, he slaughtered a hapless man who was no match for the historical circumstances he faced. The putative hero, Schwartzbard, thus turns out to be a tragic half-devil, and the putative villain, Petliura, turns out to be a tragic half-angel. Both men appear rather more "banal"—and more like each other—than either imagined himself to be.

There is a lesson here for absolutist supporters and critics of Ukrainian nationalism.

Both sides should remember that, if as impressive a scholar as Arendt could have been dead wrong about Petliura, then significantly feebler minds than hers may be wrong about the targets of their venom or adulation. Only unfettered research, an open debate, and the abandonment of absolutist claims and hegemonic narratives can enable scholars to approximate the "facts of the case" about anything. Which is exactly what the de-communization laws will do.

It may be wise to remember that approximations of the truth are the best we can attain.

The number of facts comprising the truth about something is always infinite. Moreover, although facts, as by definition true statements about the world, may be "beyond dispute," their interpretation never is. The claim that the Ukrainian nationalists were angels or devils is at best a weak interpretation only partly supported by "the facts."

Just as most heroes and villains come and go, so, too, do seemingly infallible academic truths. Both hagiographers and demonizers of Ukrainian nationalism would do well to consider taking a pinch of intellectual and moral humility before they launch their next noise campaign.

*

Germany's Socialists, Russia's Fascism, and Ukrainian Deaths, *Atlantic Council*, June 20, 2016

On June 15, Ukraine's Minister of Defense Stepan Poltorak informed NATO that Ukraine had suffered 623 battle deaths in its war with Russia in 2016.

This astoundingly large figure—which amounts to three to four deaths per day—demonstrates conclusively that Russia and its proxies have no intention whatsoever of adhering to the Minsk accords.

The number also demonstrates the price Ukraine is willing to pay in order to defend itself—and Europe—from Russian President Vladimir Putin's aggression.

Meanwhile, Germany's Socialists appear increasingly committed to doing everything possible to appease Russian imperialism. The roots of their indifference to international norms and human rights may go back to the days of Ostpolitik. They certainly go back to 2005, when then Chancellor Gerhard Schröder—who called Putin a "flawless democrat" at the height of Ukraine's Orange Revolution in 2004—left his job in Berlin to become a highly-paid functionary of Russia's deeply corrupt, state-owned energy company, Gazprom. Since his move came immediately after his chancellorship ended, Schröder must have negotiated the terms of his new job while still in office. Unsurprisingly, Schröder has consistently turned a blind eye to Putin's fascism and imperialism while defending Russia's energy interests and supporting the continuation of Europe's energy dependence on Russian gas.

Sigmar Gabriel, the Socialist Democratic Party chairman, has been especially outspoken in his pro-Putin remarks. Think about what this means. Putin has dismantled democracy in Russia and replaced it with a dictatorial system centered on himself and his personality cult. Putin has also started wars in Georgia and Ukraine, violated international norms, and terrified all of his neighbors—from Kazakhstan to Belarus to Finland. It doesn't require much imagination to see the similarities with a certain German dictator who, back in the 1930s, dismantled democracy, replaced it with a dictatorial system centered on himself and his personality cult, started wars, violated international norms, and terrified his neighbors. And yet, despite the obvious similarities, Gabriel—who represents Germany's Socialists—remains committed to supporting Putin and his regime. That's not just appeasement. That's a complete betrayal of everything democratic socialists claim to stand for.

It's also a repudiation of the European Union's vaunted "European values." The EU, minus its values, is just a bunch of inward-focused countries who share a few buildings and procedures and a currency. It's the values—the commitment to democracy and human rights and the rejection of imperialism and colonialism—that make the EU special and worth preserving. In effect, German Socialist support of Putin is a rejection of Europe. That's far worse than Brexit, as the British are rejecting the EU's procedures, not its values. If the EU ever collapses, blame Germany's pious-sounding Socialists above all.

Pro-Putinite tendencies are also evident in Germany's authoritative, left-leaning newspaper, *Die Zeit*. In a recent article, its editor-at-large, Theo Sommer, discusses a variety of mass killings in the recent past—from Hiroshima, Nagasaki, and My Lai, to the Holocaust and Armenian genocide, the Battle of Verdun and the wars in Yugoslavia. Stalin's mass murders of Ukrainians, Russians, Crimean Tatars, and everybody else aren't on Sommer's list. He's too smart not to know, so the omission is obviously one of design. So much for *Die Zeit's* courageous stand for human rights. What's the moral of Sommer's blindness for Germany's young people? If a genocide is inconvenient to your agenda, ignore it.

But Gernot Erler, Berlin's Russia man and, of course, a Socialist, takes the cake. "Our highest priority is to maintain consensus within the EU," Erler recently said in reference to the possible easing of EU sanctions against Russia. "If a price has to be paid, then we should be ready" to pay it.

Now, just what price did Erler have in mind? He provides no answer, but Poltorak does: Ukrainian lives—623 in the first half of 2016, probably 1,250 in all of 2016, and many, many more to follow.

*

Should Ukraine Forget Its History? *Atlantic Council*, December 16, 2016

On November 25, 2010, while on a state visit to Kyiv, Israel's President Shimon Peres stated that, "If Ukrainians were to ask me for advice, I would say: forget history." Coming from the president of a country steeped in history, the comment was at first glance bizarre. Directed at a country embroiled in seemingly endless contentious debates over its history, the advice was at second glance intriguing. But *can* history be forgotten? And would forgetting be desirable, even if possible? And what would forgetting mean for a country such as Ukraine, which hopes to put its Soviet past behind it while discovering the neglected pages of its history?

Two Thought Experiments

Imagine what a society that forgets all history and its opposite—a society that remembers all history—would look like. The former would be even more nightmarish than George Orwell's *1984*. After all, Orwell's state needed history. It manipulated history by continually rewriting it to meet the political needs of Big Brother. A society that forgets history would have to destroy every single book, journal, article, blog, recording, film, and artwork no later than one day after it appeared. Such a society would live in the moment and be engaged in an unceasing attempt to obliterate everything that could serve as memory.

A society that remembers all history would, like Jorge Luis Borges's "Funes the Memorious," be equally dystopian. This society would not only preserve every single text—whether written, painted, filmed, or recorded—but it would have to record every conversation, every whisper, and every thought. It would have to incorporate every single recorded text into a continually evolving grand historical narrative.

Fortunately, neither of these societies is possible. An utterly remembering society is impossible, as a complete historical narrative could never assimilate an infinite number of facts. An utterly forgetful society is just as impossible, as it would entail a logical contradiction: forgetting how to remember.

National Narratives

There is another barrier to forgetfulness, one specific to Ukraine and other post-colonial nations. In order to forget history, one must first remember it. And in order to remember history, one must first have a history of the nation's development over time: a national narrative. Newly independent nations and states have a proclivity for these types of narratives, as independence creates a particular vantage point for history writing, demands that national narratives provide legitimacy for the new nations and states, and enables formerly oppressed peoples to find their voices and recover their memories.

There are three possible types of national narratives. First is a history of the national state. That entails tracing all the political formations that contributed to the emergence and consolidation of the administrative and coercive apparatus known as the state. Second is a history of the people, or nation. That entails tracing all the social, economic, political, and cultural developments that led to the emergence and consolidation of a self-conscious ethno-cultural community. Third is a history of the territory associated with the state or people. That entails tracing the relationships between all the peoples inhabiting that territory.

Which of these national narratives is best? Other things being equal, they are all equally good or bad as historical narratives. If the historians do their homework, write with integrity, and arrange genuine facts in logically coherent chronological narratives, each resulting narrative is valid. But is not the very notion of national narratives passé? Shouldn't truly serious historians develop non-national or post-national narratives that boldly venture into spaces outside the state and the nation? Isn't that kind of history intrinsically better? As we shall see, the answer is no.

Danto on History

The late philosopher Arthur Danto asked whether an "ideal chronicle" consisting of every single historical fact would amount to a genuine history. His answer was that an infinitely large collection of facts would not and could not be a usable historical narrative. Why not? For the simple, if somewhat counterintuitive, reason that complete comprehensiveness is antithetical to history. In reality, every history is and has to be partial and "slanted"; every history is and has to be a story. And stories are always stories, never of everything, but always of *something* with a beginning, middle, and end. As a result, all historians write intrinsically imperfect and incomplete narratives from particular vantage points reflective of their place in time. Every history is thus a never-ending work in progress, because the vantage point of the historian can never be frozen in time.

Although Danto's view of history may appear to coincide with postmodernist claims about indeterminacy, meaninglessness, subjectivism, and relativism, it is rooted in fairly traditional understandings of history. Facts exist in Danto's reading, and historians can determine what they are. Historians must therefore pay obeisance to chronological time, produce coherent narratives, and demonstrate that the facts they present are statements that, by virtue of their being supported by persuasive evidence, actually correspond to reality.

Histories can therefore give "objective" accounts of what happened, but they can never be full or final accounts produced from some transcendental vantage point. Multiple incomplete histories of anything are as inevitable and unavoidable as multiple lines intersecting a point. A feminist history can therefore be as good or as bad, as a historical narrative, as an anti- or non-feminist history. A nationalist or national history can, by the same logic, be as good or as bad as an anti-nationalist, non-national, post-national, or transnational history.

It follows that dominant, or hegemonic, historical narratives are not necessarily better as coherently organized chronological arrangements of facts. They only appear to be better because we—or, more precisely, historians and reading publics—deem them better. Certain histories strike us as better than others because they are more relevant to present-day concerns or more reflective of present-day views or norms. Thus, a feminist history may strike us as a better reading than a non-feminist history, but that is so, not because reality is demonstrably feminist, but because, inspired by feminism, we look for, and find, feminist facts in the story "as it really was."

The hegemony of dominant narratives transforms non-dominant narratives into unwelcome shifts that rock the boat. New, non-dominant narratives will always appear as upstarts that threaten to upend the only "correct" way of seeing things. Feminist and African-American histories were treated in just this manner until they became part of the mainstream. Similarly, the histories of all formerly colonized nations were in opposition to the hegemonic narratives generated by the former empire or by elites, groups, or professions with established historical narratives.

Ukrainian Narratives

Although Ukrainian historians have produced histories since at least the nineteenth century, they have never had the status of dominant narratives. As a result, Ukraine became independent in 1991 in a historical and historiographical setting of hegemonic non-Ukrainian narratives that had acquired institutionalized status over the course of decades or centuries. Emergent Ukrainian national narratives necessarily challenged the primacy of the historical status quo represented by existing dominant narratives.

Logically, emergent Ukrainian narratives had to correspond to the above three types of national narratives. Thus, a Ukrainian state narrative would necessarily begin Ukraine's history in Kyivan Rus. It would carry it through the Cossack rebellions of Bohdan Khmelnytsky and Ivan Mazepa, the failed attempt to build a state in 1917–1921, and the activity of the integral nationalists of the interwar period and World War II. And it would conclude with the development of the Ukrainian SSR, the collapse of the Soviet Union, and the role therein of Ukrainian national Communists and dissidents.

A Ukrainian people narrative would have the same historical sweep as the state narrative, while focusing on how state-building, together with developments in the society, culture, and economy, led to the emergence of nationally conscious Ukrainians and, eventually, a distinctly Ukrainian nation.

Finally, a Ukrainian territory narrative would tell the story of relations between and among peasants, landlords, merchants, workers, Ukrainians, Russians, Poles, Jews, Ruthenians, Catholics, Orthodox, and others in the territory of Ukraine.

Obviously, historians cannot ignore controversial individuals, organizations, or parties—be they nationalist, Stalinist, fascist, or liberal—in the writing of any kind of Ukrainian national narrative. Whatever their failings, these individuals, organizations, or parties played critically important, and arguably constructive, roles in the twin projects of Ukrainian state- and nation-building. To incorporate controversial figures into a Ukrainian national narrative is not to whitewash them. It is simply to tell the history of Ukraine as an ontologically legitimate story with a beginning, middle, and end embedded in a distinctly Ukrainian historical narrative—and not as a footnote in or disruption of non- or anti-Ukrainian historical narratives.

Such an approach entails a serious responsibility: to write Ukrainian national narratives honestly and with integrity—by eschewing hero-ization, demonization, casual myth-making, and obsessive myth-busting, by rejecting blank spots, and by addressing head-on all difficult, painful, complex, and embarrassing issues. The only way to counter popular depictions of Ukrainians as negations (as anti-Russians, anti-Soviets, anti-Semites, and thus as anti-human *Untermenschen*) is not to glorify them as *Übermenschen*, but to depict them as *Menschen*—as human beings capable of both good and evil, rationality and irrationality, and identical in these respects to all other human beings.

Taking Ukrainian History for Granted

For Ukraine to develop a "normal" relationship to history—one that might satisfy President Peres, historians, and Ukrainians—it must still go through two stages. Ukraine must first construct a national history or histories. Thanks to the Euromaidan and the 2015 <u>laws</u> on de-communization, the freedom to produce such narratives finally exists.

It is only after such national narratives are constructed and consolidated that Ukrainians will be able to move on—not forget per se, but stop obsessing about the past. Once Ukrainian national narratives become routinized and naturalized, they will lend themselves to commercialization, kitschification, satirizing, and the like. We will know that moment has arrived when a Ukrainian version of Mel Brooks' *The Producers* features "Springtime for Lenin" in Kharkiv and "Springtime for Bandera" in Lviv. Hollywood-ization will transform sacred historical narratives into mundane and secular artifacts and thereby enable the population to deal with history in the manner that it deserves—as the past and not the present, and as a taken-for-granted component of one's national identity.

Taken-for-grantedness will also take history out of the realm of society or the state and place it in the realm in which it is most suitably obsessed over—that of professional historians, who do not and cannot take history for granted. That, of course, is what President Peres really had in mind—that Ukrainians should let their historians worry about history. Peres was wrong to think that could happen at this point in Ukraine's historical and historiographical development. But once Ukraine catches up and has a history, Ukrainians will finally be able to forget it.

*

Facing the Past: In Defense of Ukraine's New Laws, *World Affairs Journal*, October 5, 2015

When Ukraine's Parliament, the Rada, approved four bills on April 9, 2015, stating that Communism and Nazism were equally evil, at least as far as Ukraine is concerned, some Western intellectuals reacted with pique to the de-Communization agenda the bills promoted. In particular, 70 Western and Ukrainian scholars wrote an open letter to Ukrainian President Petro Poroshenko and Rada Chairman Volodymyr Hroysman in which they claimed the "content and spirit" of the laws "contradicts one of the most fundamental political rights: the right to freedom of speech." According to the scholars, "Any legal or 'administrative' distortion of history is an assault on the most basic purpose of scholarly inquiry: pursuit of truth. Any official attack on historical memory is unjust.

Difficult and contentious issues must remain matters of debate."

The critics are right about the importance of the pursuit of truth. But they are wrong in claiming that these laws will impede that pursuit. Quite the contrary, they will finally make it possible.

Start with a truth that the Soviet regime, along with many Western scholars, assiduously denied: that Communism and Nazism were equally harmful to Ukraine. Americans and Europeans are uncomfortable with that equation, but it is hard to disagree with the Ukrainian view. The Moscow-based Institute of Demography estimated in 2008 that Ukraine suffered close to 15 million "excess deaths" between 1914 and 1948, and of that number about 6.5 million were due to the Nazis and 7.5 million to the Soviets. From the Ukrainian perspective, if de-Nazification was legitimate, then so, too, is de-Communization. And if de-Nazification was essential to Germany's reintegration into the civilized world, then so, too, de-Communization is essential to Ukraine's integration into the civilized world.

The bills are thus a coherent attempt to expunge both Communism and Nazism from the Ukrainian present and future. While the bills logically complement one another, critics make the mistake of treating them in isolation, thereby drawing alarming conclusions that are not warranted by the entire package.

The first bill, which has proven to be most controversial, makes an official list of those movements, governments, and organizations that qualify as "fighters" for an independent Ukraine. The second bill opens secret police archives to citizens. The third demystifies "the Great Patriotic War" of 1941–45, the truncated Soviet version of World War II, in which the USSR's two-year collaboration with Nazi Germany in 1939–41 disappeared into the memory hole. The fourth prohibits the "propaganda of the Communist and/or National Socialist totalitarian regimes" in Ukraine.

The stakes in the debate surrounding the bills are high. The de-Communization laws matter because Ukraine's move westward is impossible without a complete break with the Soviet past—and with the Soviet and neo-Soviet ideological constructs that reduced Ukraine and Ukrainians to passive objects of history. By pursuing both reform and de-Communization, Ukraine is acknowledging the demands of historical memory, taking control of its destiny, and breaking into the modern world.

Some episodes of what the West celebrates as its history have, as Malcolm X said of Plymouth Rock, landed especially heavily on Ukraine. France, for instance, celebrates Napoleon, who brought ruin and war to Ukrainian-populated territories. Virtually every German village has a monument to the "heroes" (*Helden*) who died in the two world wars that devastated Ukraine. Poland is replete with statues of and streets named after Jozef Pilsudski, who betrayed his Ukrainian allies while founding modern Poland. Even the Rutgers University–Newark campus, where I teach, celebrates Paul Robeson, the black singer and Communist civil rights activist who admired Stalin and justified his repressions, which hit Ukraine especially hard.

Look further and you'll find plenty of controversial expressions of memory. London is full of buildings, public artworks, and monuments celebrating the imperialism that immiserated people throughout the world. Turks deify Kemal Atatürk, who founded modern Turkey by imposing his will on a reluctant population, and in the process violating human rights and democratic procedures. In the American South, New Orleans, Charleston, and Richmond have (perhaps a tense change to "had" will soon be necessary) Confederate museums and grandiose monuments to Confederate heroes of the Civil War era. Russians venerate, through various public manifestations, Peter the Great, who was a tyrant, Joseph Stalin, who was a mass murderer, and Vladimir Putin, who is a warmonger and dictator. The Chinese still adore Mao Zedong, whose Great Leap Forward killed some 40 million of his compatriots. South Africa venerates Nelson Mandela, even though his African National Congress (and his own wife) committed terrorist atrocities against both whites and blacks.

When was the last time intellectuals expressed outrage over these controversial embodiments of the past? The question is rhetorical. Controversial monuments and controversial heroes are ubiquitous throughout the world. We ignore them because they already stand, and can therefore easily be regarded as inevitable and immovable. As the great Austrian writer Robert Musil once said: monuments are "invisible" and "impregnated with something that repels attention." Once erected, they become part of the background, and we notice them only when they are removed. In other words, it is not the historical memory itself that provokes controversy so much as changes in its public representations—a point reinforced by recent American debates over the Confederate flag.

Which brings us back to Ukraine and its de-Communization laws: they've been termed controversial and scandalous, when in fact they are neither. Because they hope to change a certain familiar attitude, one to which many Western observers are wedded, the laws have provoked an outraged response. The outrage stems from the fact that the laws challenge a taken-for-granted understanding of Ukraine that has its roots in Soviet propaganda and a variety of vicious stereotypes about Ukraine. Despite Ukraine's 25 years of independence, this view has remained "hegemonic," precisely because Ukraine never tried to challenge it. Now that it is doing just that, supporters of this profoundly illiberal mind-set are not unexpectedly outraged.

The hegemonic view these laws challenge reduces Ukrainian history to the status of a minor subplot in grander historical narratives, deprives Ukrainians of a voice, and depicts them as the quintessential "Other"—savage, violent, mindless, and destructive. The approach is strikingly reminiscent of the way in which black history and women's history were at one time considered illegitimate unless subsumed in white- or male-centered narratives that depicted African Americans as lust-filled and violent and women as irrational and hysterical. Colonial peoples have also been depicted in this manner, as Edward Said brilliantly argued in his classic study, *Orientalism*.

Ukraine's colonial status in the Polish Commonwealth, the Russian Empire, and the Soviet Union goes a long way to explaining why Ukrainians have been viewed by Soviet and Russian history as part of a brutish sideshow—lazy, violence-prone Little Russians with no language or culture of their own. (This is still the essence of Vladimir Putin's views of Ukraine.) Polish and Jewish narratives tend to view Ukrainians as savage peasants irrationally committed to killing Poles and Jews. Much contemporary Western Holocaust scholarship unconsciously adopts these Orientalist stereotypes by focusing only on Ukrainian anti-Semitism and thereby reducing Ukrainian history to a footnote in the history of pogroms.

Given these deep-seated ideological predilections, it logically follows that the "worst" form of Ukrainian is, like the "worst" form of African American, woman, or colonized person, the active, assertive individual who rejects the stereotype, claims to have a voice, and attempts to change the subordination that the hegemonic discourse supports. Such individuals must be condemned a priori, not because of what they did or failed to do, but because they exist, and because their very existence challenges accepted ways of perceiving the world.

When it comes to Ukraine, neo-colonial narratives assign the role of the evil "heavy" to the organized Ukrainian nationalist movement, in particular, to three 20th-century formations, the Ukrainian Military Organization (UVO), the Organization of Ukrainian Nationalists (OUN), and the Ukrainian Insurgent Army (UPA). The UVO, formed in 1920 in the Ukrainian-inhabited lands of eastern Poland by former participants in the national liberation struggle of 1918–1919, engaged throughout the 1920s in bombings, expropriations, and assassinations directed against Polish property and officials. The OUN was established in 1929 in Vienna and consisted of two segments—older émigrés resident in central and western Europe and young activists resident in eastern Poland. The former wrote the texts, developed the ideology, and sought alliances with Europe's revisionist powers, while the latter sought to topple Polish rule by means of the UVO's tactics. (In terms of their radicalism, the former were akin to Al Fatah and the Irish Republican Army, while the latter resembled the Popular Front for the Liberation of Palestine and the Provisional IRA.) Finally, the UPA was formed in late 1942 as a popular armed resistance movement that at various times and places fought the Germans, Poles, and Soviets. OUN members formed the core of the UPA, but the UPA itself drew on village youth for most of its membership, which numbered in the tens of thousands. Both the OUN and UPA continued their hopeless anti-Soviet struggle into the mid-1950s.

Unsurprisingly, many Poles, Russians, and Soviets have regarded, and still regard, the UVO, OUN, and UPA as terrorists, while many Ukrainians viewed, and still view, them as fighters who gave their lives for the cause of freedom and independence. Who's right?

There is no doubt that the UVO and OUN committed acts of terror, just as there is no doubt that units of the UPA engaged Polish settlers and armed units in Volhynia in a brutal war in 1943. There is also no doubt that some Ukrainian nationalists committed atrocities and collaborated with Germany in World War II. Where critics who stop with these facts fail is by not asking the obvious follow-up questions. Is this all the nationalists did? How, if at all, did the Ukrainians differ from other participants in the war? How does what the Ukrainians did compare with the acts of other national liberation struggles? And what was the proportion of good and bad in the activities of these movements?

The most controversial of the four de-Communization laws addresses these questions head-on by categorizing the UVO, OUN, and UPA as "fighters" (and decidedly not as "heroes"!) for Ukrainian independence. They are included in a long list containing scores of organizations, movements, and parties that for decades were ignored or demonized by Soviet and Russian propaganda. By recognizing all these movements as bona fide "fighters," the law is both stating an objective fact and challenging the extant historical narratives that demonize Ukrainians in general and their national liberation aspirations, in particular.

Did the UVO, OUN, and UPA fight for Ukrainian independence and, thus, qualify as "fighters"? Of course. Do their stories form an important part of the history of modern Ukraine? Obviously. Do they merit a place in Ukrainian history even if they have blemished records? How can they not?

The starting point of any level-headed, liberal approach to the Ukrainian nationalists is to view them as just that—nationalists, whose priority was the establishment of an independent Ukrainian state. As with all nationalists, political ideology played a secondary role for the Ukrainians. The kind of polity they wanted to create always took a backseat to something much simpler—attaining statehood and liberating the nation. Moreover, because the nationalists were an illegal underground movement, their political organization was necessarily conspiratorial and authoritarian. Critics who call the nationalists fascist entirely miss the point, which is that the Ukrainian nationalists were above all nationalists who regarded European ideas of nationalism with the utmost seriousness and whose views of politics were as fluid and contradictory as their commitment to a Ukrainian nation-state were constant and consistent. The UVO was indifferent to ideology; the OUN frankly embraced authoritarianism, while elements of the organization—primarily the émigrés—flirted with fascism in the late 1930s. But then in 1943, the OUN turned toward social democracy after discovering that authoritarianism did not travel well in Soviet Ukraine. The UPA almost from the start had an ethnically inclusive and pro-democratic bent, while also engaging in ethnic violence.

Ukrainian nationalist attitudes toward other countries were seen through a clear lens of national liberation and independent statehood. Poland and the Soviet Union were enemies because they occupied Ukrainian lands, although the OUN and UPA reached out to Polish nationalists after the Soviets overran Poland in 1944–1945. Jews were generally considered to be Communist supporters—a stereotype that led to bloodshed, although in the Ukrainian-inhabited territories of eastern Poland and Soviet Ukraine it had an empirical basis in reality. Germany and Italy were considered, not illogically, to be potential allies against Poland and the USSR. After the war, the Ukrainians sought alliances with the United Kingdom and the United States. Some nationalists were fascists and anti-Semites; some were democrats and socialists; most were self-styled revolutionaries determined to construct an independent state whatever the cost.

Read this brief history with a cool head and substitute IRA, PLO, Irgun, Viet Cong, or FLN for any of the corresponding Ukrainian acronyms, and you'll find that Ukrainian nationalist behavior differed in no fundamental way from the behavior of Irish, Palestinian, Jewish, Vietnamese, or Algerian nationalists. They were all illegal and conspiratorial; they all engaged in terrorism and violence; they all committed atrocities; they were all authoritarian in structure; they were all willing to sacrifice ideology to nationalism; they were all opportunistic in their choice of allies. And they were, and still are, all demonized by their opponents. But the Ukrainians, almost alone, remain the targets of disproportionately hysterical attacks—precisely because any level-headed interpretation of their activity directly challenges the hegemony of Orientalism.

No less important, whatever the Ukrainian nationalists did pales in comparison to what states did. Germany initiated the deadliest war in human history and killed 6 million Jews. The Soviet Union starved to death 4 million Ukrainian peasants in 1932–1933, set up the monstrous Gulag, collaborated with Nazi Germany by signing the 1939 Molotov-Ribbentrop Pact and feeding the German war machine through mid-1941, and later engaged in the mass rape of Germany, Austria, and Hungary in 1945. Inter-war Poland was openly anti-Semitic and anti-Ukrainian, while Polish armed forces cleansed eastern Poland of Ukrainians in 1947.

In contrast, the Ukrainian nationalists look like amateurs. They pursued an alliance of convenience with Germany in 1940–1941, which Berlin ended after the Ukrainians declared independence on June 30, 1941. There is evidence of individual nationalist involvement in anti-Jewish pogroms. And, in 1943 in Volhynia, units of the UPA killed 30,000–60,000 Poles while suffering 3,000–6,000 casualties of their own. Some Poles consider this "Volhynia Massacre" to be a genocide, but this inter-ethnic war and the resultant ethnic cleansing by Ukrainians of Volhynian Poles more accurately brings to mind the Israeli-Palestinian war of 1948 and the subsequent flight and expulsion of Palestinians from their territories of settlement.

The Ukrainian nationalists were no saints. And yet they were not just sinners, nor were their sins greater than those committed by other nationalist movements or states. In a word, the Ukrainian nationalists deserve to be neither demonized nor lionized. Yale historian Timothy Snyder puts it well: "A significant (and successful) effort has been made to document the role of Ukrainian nationalists in the Holocaust. But it is perfectly clear that this demonstration is chiefly of moral rather than practical importance. It means that Ukrainian nationalists do not have clean hands, which is not a great surprise; it does not at all mean that the Germans needed Ukrainian nationalists in order to perpetrate a Holocaust."

Is it possible that, as critics claim, one of the laws' controversial provisions—"Citizens of Ukraine, foreigners and persons without citizenship who publicly show contempt for persons referred to in Article 1 of this Law and prevent the exercise of rights by the fighters for independence of Ukraine in the twentieth century are responsible under the law."—could undermine the very freedom the laws hope to engender? Not at all, for at least five reasons.

First, the law in question also explicitly states that "The State encourages and supports the activities of non-governmental institutions and organizations engaged in research and education in the field of the study of the history of struggle and fighters for Ukraine's independence in the twentieth century." This sentence obviously cannot be interpreted as constraining scholarship. And, to the degree that there may be some confusion about what the law does or does not intend, President Poroshenko has promised to amend it accordingly.

Second, among the "fighters" the law lists are the People's Liberation Revolutionary Organization, a guerrilla army led by Taras Borovets, the Ukrainian Supreme Liberation Council, and its External Representation—all organizations that criticized, rejected, and, in the case of Borovets, even fought against the OUN in the 1940s. Clearly, the law itself recognizes criticism of the nationalists as perfectly legitimate.

Third, the laws form a package of mutually supportive and complementary pieces of legislation. Since one of the laws explicitly opens KGB archives to the public—thereby inviting controversy and contention—it makes little sense to suggest that the law on fighters is intended to quash debate.

Fourth, no one with any knowledge of contemporary Ukraine seriously believes that this legalistically challenged state committed to integration with the West will ever initiate a legal action against any critic of Ukrainian nationalism. (Unsurprisingly, no such action has been undertaken in the months since the laws' adoption.) That could change only if pro-Putin forces ever return to power in Kyiv.

Fifth, and most important, contrary to the Orientalist stereotype, Ukrainians are reasonable people who do not interpret legal ambiguities as a license to kill, repress, or oppress.

In fact, these new laws finally make a level-headed, liberal, and genuinely scholarly approach to the nationalists (and all the other "fighters") possible. Because the laws legitimize their inclusion in Ukrainian history, the nationalists are no longer savage Others who must be condemned or saintly heroes who must be worshipped. Liberal enquiry can replace hegemony. Liberal truth-seeking can replace Soviet and neo-Soviet truth-imposition. The fighters can, finally, be integrated into the Ukrainian historical narrative in a realistic way, neither as devils nor as angels, but as, quite simply, individuals and movements that played an important role in contemporary Ukrainian history. While deserving some praise and condemnation, they mostly deserve to have their stories told without the Orientalist assumptions of Soviet propaganda. Freed of these illiberal assumptions, Ukrainian debates about the painful pages of the country's past can now begin.

*

Stalin's Partisans in Ukraine, *World Affairs Journal,* February 9, 2016

Alexander Gogun's excellent study, *Stalin's Commandos: Ukrainian Partisan Forces on the Eastern Front,* sometimes reads like an analysis of Putin's commandos in the eastern Donbas. In both cases, the official Moscow line was and is that they're a popular movement generated by discontent from below. In fact, Stalin's commandos, like Putin's, were largely creatures of the Kremlin—a point Gogun, a Russian scholar currently based at the

Free University in Berlin, makes forcefully, repeatedly, and convincingly.

Gogun details how the partisans were structured and led (from abroad), what they did (terrorism) and whom they fought (the Germans and Ukrainians), how they interacted with the local population (with abandon), what their behavior looked like (robbery, drunkenness, and rape), and how they compared with the Ukrainian nationalist insurgents, the UPA, and the Polish nationalist guerrillas, the Home Army (AK). One table (p. 160) has a wealth of information: the 11 largest units of the Soviet Ukrainian partisan movement consisted of 45,478 fighters. Just over 11 percent were killed; 2 percent were executed or deserted; 7 percent were women; 57 percent were Ukrainians, 25 percent were Russians, and only 13 percent were members of the Communist Party. Their job was not to defend the people, but to fight the Germans, regardless of the exceedingly high toll the local population paid for their actions. Both the UPA and AK, in contrast, were careful to defend the people they claimed to represent.

Unsurprisingly, Stalin's commandos were most active in the forest and marsh regions of northern and northwestern Ukraine. That fact greatly contributed to one of the major secondary-theater wars during World War II: the bloody Ukrainian-Polish conflict in Volhynia. As Gogun's evidence demonstrates, the presence of Soviet partisans in this volatile region populated by large numbers of indigenous Ukrainian peasants and many Poles, both indigenous and recent settlers, may have sparked the large-scale violence that engulfed both communities in mid-1943.

Ethnic relations were anything but simple in Volhynia. The Germans terrorized the Poles and Ukrainians and fought the UPA, AK, and the Soviets. Many Poles, and above all the AK, viewed Ukrainians in general and Ukrainian nationalists in particular as their sworn enemies and sympathized with the Soviets, especially after the Polish government-in-exile allied with Moscow by means of the Sikorski-Maisky Pact of July 30, 1941. Many Ukrainians, and above all Ukrainian nationalists, viewed Poles, the AK, and the Soviets as their sworn enemies and the Germans as their situational allies (in early 1941 and 1944) or their situational enemies (1941–1943). The Soviets regarded the Germans and Ukrainian nationalists as their enemies, mistrusted the Ukrainians, and viewed the Poles and the AK as situational allies.

Soviet propagandists and neo-Soviet scholars generally ascribe the UPA's initiation of anti-Polish violence in mid-1943 to an innate proclivity to kill. The approach is racist and the evidence is unpersuasive, but more important, the story makes no sense as it excludes context. Thanks to Gogun, that context has been brought into focus. It's highly likely that Ukrainian nationalist suspicions of Poles reached a boiling point and translated into ethnic cleansing just as Soviet partisans began expanding their influence and threatening Ukrainian positions in Volhynia in early 1943, while many Poles looked on, or appeared to look on, approvingly.

One of Gogun's great virtues is to present this and other controversial issues objectively, without recourse to the *sub rosa* invective that frequently accompanies such narratives. His final chapter, a comparison of the UPA, AK, and the Soviet partisans, is especially useful, as it accomplishes what demonizers and hagiographers of these groups signally fail to do: provide a comparative analysis demonstrating that all three movements were guerrilla forces with pluses and minuses to their credit and detriment. All three could be brutal. All three resorted to extreme violence. And all three pursued wartime political agendas and none were simply crazed killers.

Gogun purposely shatters the Soviet mythology surrounding Stalin's commandos, but he also reminds us that myth-making is inimical to good history and that good history always rests on detailed demonstrations of complexity appropriately contextualized. The high standard he sets is welcome.

*

Ukraine Is Winning on the Linguistic Battle Front, *World Affairs Journal*, July 15, 2016

Many Ukrainians are persuaded that their language is dying out. Many Russians and Russian speakers believe Ukrainian is incapable of serving as a means of sophisticated communication among educated urban dwellers.

Both are wrong. In fact, the Ukrainian language may be doing far better than its supporters and detractors suspect.

Forget the statistics, which are useful but cannot capture what is really taking place on the ground. Instead, look at the remarkable growth of the YE chain of bookstores in Ukraine.

YE—written Є in Ukrainian—means "it is" or "there is," a boldly self-assertive claim that the Ukrainian language, despite the insistence of Russian chauvinists since tsarist times that "it never was, is not, or will be," in fact IS.

YE is unique in that it specializes in Ukrainian-language books. A few shelves might offer some Russian- and English-language products, but easily 95 percent of all the books YE sells are in Ukrainian. In most of Ukraine's bookstores, the proportion is likely to be tilted in favor of Russian-language books, sometimes overwhelmingly so.

For years, detractors of Ukrainian argued that bookstores were acting rationally, on the grounds that there was no demand for Ukrainian-language books. Indeed, how could there be demand for a peasant tongue and dialect of Russian? YE, the brainchild of Ukrainian journalist Yuri Makarov and Austria's ECEM Media GmBH, decisively proved them wrong. (ECEM also publishes the thriving Ukrainian- and English-language weekly, *Ukrainian Week*.)

YE's first bookstore opened on December 21, 2007 in Kyiv, behind the Opera House. Today, just 8 ½ years later, YE boasts 20 bookstores: seven in Kyiv, two apiece in Lviv, Kharkiv, and Dnipro (the former Dnipropetrovsk), and one apiece in Ivano-Frankivsk, Vinnytsia, Ternopil, Volodymyr-Volynsky, Rivne, Lutsk, and Khmelnytsky.

The geographic distribution is significant. Seven stores are located in western Ukraine (Lviv, Ivano-Frankivsk, Ternopil, Volodymyr-Volynsky, Rivne, Lutsk), where one expects demand for Ukrainian-language product to be highest. But nine are in central Ukraine (Kyiv city, Vinnytsia, Khmelnytsky). And—most impressive—four are in eastern Ukraine (Kharkiv, Dnipro), where, according to legend, no one cares to use Ukrainian. The seven in capital city Kyiv are also striking, as the language one hears on its streets is overwhelmingly Russian.

Clearly, Ukrainian-language books sell and can sell. Moreover, they sell even during times of extreme economic distress: YE opened several bookstores in the last two years, at just the time that Ukraine's GDP was contracting by about a fifth.

The message should be obvious: Ukrainians very much want to read books in their own language. Unsurprisingly, a large, and growing, number of publishers have emerged in recent years to meet that demand.

The implications of YE's success are clear. For starters, Ukrainians want the Ukrainian language and demand for Ukrainian-language products is high, perhaps even being what economists call "inelastic," remaining high despite rising costs and growing economic distress. Moreover, although demand is higher in the west, it's highest in Kyiv and quite respectable in the east.

But the most important implication is this: If Ukrainians want Ukrainian-language books, is it plausible to think that they do not want Ukrainian-language newspapers, magazines, radio, television, and film?

YE's success proves that Ukraine is, despite the indifference of its ruling elites, the hostility of Russian nationalists, and the opposition of Russia, experiencing a grassroots creeping Ukrainization. That's the most effective kind of linguistic change: from below. It takes time, and it annoys linguistic purists and radicals, but its major advantage is that it sticks.

And creeping Ukrainization heralds Vladimir Putin's worst nightmare: Ukraine's eventual separation from Russia, not just politically and economically, both also linguistically and culturally.

*

National Memory in Ukraine, *Foreign Affairs*, August 4, 2016

Are you a fascist?" I ask. "And are you an anti-Semite?"

Volodymyr Viatrovych, the 39-year-old director of the Ukrainian Institute of National Memory, in Kyiv, whose critics in the West demonize as an apologist of fascism and anti-Semitism, laughs. "Under no circumstances! I consider myself an anti-fascist. I value freedom, above all, and have the greatest respect for Jews. Indeed, I consider the Jewish struggle for liberation and equality to be a model for Ukrainians."

"Well," I continue, "are you a Banderite?" The reference is to the followers of Stepan Bandera, the controversial leader of the radical wing of the organized Ukrainian nationalist movement from the mid-1930s until his murder by a Soviet assassin in 1959.

"That depends on what you mean by 'Banderite,'" Viatrovych answers. "According to Russian propaganda, every nationally conscious Ukrainian is a Banderite. In that case, so am I. If by Banderite you mean a supporter of an interwar form of nationalism, then no."

We are sitting in Viatrovych's spacious office on the second floor of a building constructed in 1912 as a personal dwelling for Count Uvarov. The interior has seen better days. The floors squeak and haven't been varnished in decades. The corridors are dimly lit. The institute, founded as a governmental institution in 2007 by President Viktor Yushchenko, shares the building with a variety of nongovernmental organizations. Viatrovych has a staff of about 30, mostly young historians from various parts of Ukraine. Last year, there were about 40, but budgetary constraints and low salaries led ten to leave. All in all, the institute receives six million hryvnias (about $240,000) from the government for salaries and operating expenses and another five million (about $200,000) for its publications, conferences, and the like.

This shabby outfit is where, critics allege, Viatrovych is directing a full-fledged campaign to whitewash Ukraine's past, falsify documents, and impose censorship on scholarship and the media—all charges that he unconditionally rejects.

"I have never falsified a single document in all my work," he says. Viatrovych served as head of the Ukrainian secret police archive in 2008–2010 and is proud of having provided access to the formerly secret materials to researchers and of having begun to digitize the documents. "Various Polish scholars who are critical of my work have enjoyed open access to the archive and have never lodged a single complaint. When the [Viktor] Yanukovych regime fired me in 2010, they formed a commission to investigate my activity as director in the hope of finding compromising materials. Despite their best efforts, they found nothing, because there is nothing. The unconditional openness of the archives is a question of principle for me."

The charge of censorship derives from one of the four "decommunization" laws that Ukraine's parliament adopted in mid-2015. It states that insulting the organizations, groups, parties, and movements deemed "fighters for independence" is illegal, but it fails to specify what the legal mechanisms for dealing with such views might be. It's clear to me and most Ukrainians that the injunction, legally daft as it is, is exclusively exhortative. In any case, Viatrovych's institute didn't write that law; the son of one of the commanders of the Ukrainian nationalist underground did.

Likewise, "there hasn't been a single instance of censorship or repression," Viatrovych emphasizes. "Quite the contrary, scholars are actively studying Ukraine's communist past. After all, the point of the decommunization laws is not to stop discussion and research but to provide complete access to archives while removing the communist past from the everyday Ukrainian present—hence, the removal of monuments and the changing of street, city, town, and village names."

In truth, Viatrovych says, "what critics of the law find hardest to accept is its equation of communism with Nazism. As far as Ukraine is concerned, however, that equation is perfectly valid."

It's hard to disagree if one knows anything about twentieth-century Ukrainian history. In the 40 years between 1914, when World War I began, and 1953, when Stalin died, Ukraine experienced over 15 million "excess deaths" due to war, famine, and repression, a point emphasized by the historian George Liber in his recently published book, *Total Wars and the Making of Modern Ukraine, 1914–1954*. More than half were at the hands of the Communists. Mass deaths perpetrated against the Ukrainians, even genocide—the 1932–1933 Holodomor, in which four million Ukrainian peasants died as a result of Stalin's forced famine, is generally considered to be a genocide—does not absolve Ukrainians in general or Ukrainian nationalists or Communists in particular of unethical or criminal behavior. But nor can the fact that Ukraine is a central element in the region called "the bloodlands" by the historian Timothy Snyder be ignored, diminished, or relativized to the point of insignificance.

The controversy over how to interpret recent Ukrainian history underlies the controversy over Viatrovych. He is simply a stand-in for a form of Ukrainian history that some, mostly Western, historians reject. At first glance, the battle positions appear to be perfectly clear: good, enlightened, liberal Western historians versus bad, unenlightened, nationalist Ukrainian historians. That's also how Viatrovych's critics like to paint the confrontation. In fact, the conflict is far more complex and requires significant deconstruction in order to make sense of it.

One must start with the fact that as a people, the Ukrainians lacked the opportunity to develop their own narrative—their own self-understanding of their place in history, their own voice—for most of the twentieth century and the preceding centuries. And this was for a simple reason: they lacked statehood and full-fledged political, intellectual, and economic elites.

In fact, what all other states take for granted—a national history—is something that the Ukrainians have had the opportunity to develop only since attaining independence in 1991. Before 1918, what passed for Ukrainian history was subsumed under Russian, Austrian, or Polish history. From 1918 to the collapse of the Soviet Union in 1991, Ukrainian history was transformed into part of the Russian-led class struggle that the Communist Party decreed as the only valid form of history. There were of course genuine scholars, both Ukrainian and non-Ukrainian, who wrote intelligent, fair histories of Ukraine and the Ukrainians, but they were isolated, because an explicitly Ukrainian national project was banned in the Soviet Union.

Things began to change after the Soviet Union collapsed, but only slowly. Soviet-era institutions, elites, symbols, and language continued to dominate the Ukrainian intellectual landscape (and arguably still do). Complicating things was that after communism collapsed, other nations with a historical presence in Ukraine, such as the Russians, the Poles, and the Jews, had far more intellectual, political, and financial capital to structure post-communist narratives, ones that, once again, tended to marginalize the Ukrainians. At their worst, these histories, like the Soviet one, reduce Ukrainians to lazy, irresponsible, prejudiced country bumpkins with exaggerated penchants for vodka and violence.

These historical narratives depicted Ukrainian nationalists as cutthroats, killers, murderers, and rapists—unsurprisingly so, as the nationalists actively and violently rejected the stereotyping to which they and their nation had been subjected. Just as unsurprisingly, the nationalists countered these histories with their own—one that generally glorified the fighters and all their deeds. In effect, then, contemporary Ukraine has witnessed the ongoing clash of two competing narratives—the overwhelmingly powerful Soviet one (and its offshoots, such as contemporary Russian, Polish, and Jewish narratives) and the infinitely weaker nationalist story. They are binary opposites and are mutually exclusive. Just as the Soviet narrative charges all nationally conscious Ukrainians with being nationalist demons, so does the nationalist take glorify all Ukrainian nationalists and encourage all nationally conscious Ukrainians to become nationalists. There is little room for alternatives that avoid these two extremes.

Seen in this light, Viatrovych's Western critics are not quite the enlightened liberals they claim to be. Rather, they are exponents of a neo-Soviet narrative whose roots go back to the very earliest Russian Bolshevik excoriations of non-Russian opponents. Far from revisionist, such historians are in fact the continuators of a long tradition seeped in colonialist assumptions about non-Russians in general and Ukrainians, in particular.

Especially striking is the way in which these critics implicitly equate Ukrainian national identity, in even its most innocent forms, with a potentially virulent fascism. The historian Stephen Cohen provides a plethora of examples, having fully agreed with the Putin regime's characterization of the demonstrators during the 2013–14 Euromaidan protests and the post-Yanukovych government as fascist. To be sure, the organized nationalist movement of the interwar period was not democratic. Some Banderites flirted with fascism; others were true believers. But most were indifferent to questions of regime type and instead were willing to sacrifice their lives for the one tenet that all Ukrainian nationalists, and indeed all nationalists, have in common: the liberation of the nation and the construction of a national state.

Unsurprisingly, given their equation of Ukrainian identity with proto-fascism and fascism, Viatrovych's critics have spilled enormous amounts of ink warning of potential fascist threats in independent Ukraine, tending to magnify their importance far beyond what the reality justifies. There are several right-wing groups in Ukraine, but they have remained tiny and marginal. In contrast, the extremist left, as represented by the Communist Party and its successors, such as the Party of Regions, which catapulted Yanukovych to power in 2010, has remained less feared, even though its capacity to do harm, and the harm that it actually did, is immeasurably greater.

Within this field of neo-Soviets and nationalists, scholars such as Viatrovych are hoping to tread a middle way between the two extremes. Viatrovych's book *Druha polsko-ukray-inska viina, 1942–1947* (The Second Polish-Ukrainian War, 1942–1947, which I have reviewed positively) is a case in point. The neo-Soviets focus only on the ethnic cleansing of Poles by Ukrainian nationalists in 1943 in Volhynia. (Poland's parliament recently labeled Ukrainian nationalist actions in Volhynia a genocide.) The nationalists speak only of a national-liberation struggle. Viatrovych tries to place the violence of 1943 within the context of the interethnic Polish-Ukrainian violence of 1942–1947 and condemns the criminal activity of both Polish and Ukrainian nationalists at the time.

Another young Ukrainian historian, Oleksandr Zaytsev, vigorously disputes the fascist label for the Ukrainian nationalists while arguing that Bandera is undeservedly lionized and that the nationalists shared commonalities with the Ustasha, Croatia's World War II fascist movement—hardly a laudatory comparison. Still another historian, Ivan Patryliak, has written the equivalent of a social history of the nationalist movement without shirking from a discussion of the nationalists' moral lapses. Good history is perfectly possible in Ukraine, but only if the two extremes are avoided and historians are willing to be subjected to vicious criticism from both sides.

"Have you ever been attacked by the nationalist right?" I ask Viatrovych.

"Of course," he says, smiling. "The neo-Soviets call me a nationalist, while the nationalists accuse me of being a liberal. I know I must be doing something right."

Viatrovych openly acknowledges that Ukrainians and Ukrainian nationalists participated in anti-Jewish pogroms and in the ethnic cleansing of Poles. He insists only that that is not the whole story—and he is right. He also insists that the Ukrainian nationalists had no programmatic commitment to ethnic violence, a view that fully accords with my reading of the archival sources. His critics accuse him of whitewashing the crimes of the nationalists. Quite the contrary: by shifting the responsibility for ethnic violence from a small group of ideologically motivated individuals to the people at large, Viatrovych is effectively suggesting that Ukrainians—and Poles, Russians, and others—participated in violence. This seemingly small shift in focus has enormous consequences; it opens the door to an honest investigation of the social roots of violence and of the interethnic relations that spawned violence, both by Ukrainians and against Ukrainians. Naturally, this kind of complex argument, one of moral grays, cannot appeal to extremist neo-Soviets or to nationalists who prefer to see the world in terms of black and white.

By the same token, it is important to remember that Ukrainian nationalists are not just cutthroats and murderers; they are not just victimizers. They are also victims. And most important, although most banal, they are human beings who deserve to have a voice like any other people. Like all marginalized people, the Ukrainians should be able to participate in the writing of their own history. A fully open and frank discussion of all of Ukraine's history thus requires that the grand narratives that have stifled freedom of expression in the past be reduced to mere points of view that must compete in the marketplace of ideas.

Viatrovych's demonization by both the left and the right may be a testament to the fact that both extremes are losing influence and know it—and, as a result, are fighting rear-guard actions to hold on to their power. There is nothing inevitable about their ideas' demotion to mere points of view. Fortunately, Ukraine's remarkable post-Euromaidan ability to retain its democratic institutions, eschew right- and left-wing extremism, move toward the West, and regain its memory and voice bode well for the emergence of a contentious but honest middle ground. When that happens, Viatrovych is likely to be one of the heroes.

*

Trivializing Genocide: A Dangerous Distraction, *World Affairs Journal*, August 18, 2016

What do the Polish Sejm and the Donetsk People's Republic have in common? They've both contributed to the ongoing transformation of genocide into a term that has come to stand for little more than deplorable acts of violence.

On July 22, the Polish Sejm declared that the killing in 1943 by Ukrainian nationalists of "over 100,000" Polish citizens in Volhynia, in Ukraine's northwest, was a genocide. On June 2, Aleksandr Zakharchenko, the self-styled head of the separatist Donetsk People's Republic, stated that "The public of Donbas initiates an appeal to the international organisations to stop the genocide of the people of Donbas by the Ukrainian authorities. ..."

Did Ukrainians commit a Holocaust-like mass killing in Volhynia? Are they pursuing a Holocaust-like policy of extermination in eastern Ukraine? In my view, the answer to both questions must be no if we want genocide to designate an exceptional heinous crime. In contrast, the current legal definition embraces an array of wrongs that do not measure up to what many scholars and other experts consider to be genuine genocide.

Unfortunately, the Genocide Convention does not reasonably distinguish between geno-cide and lesser atrocities. Its definition of genocide is so broad as to include everything from a hate crime to the Holocaust. Inspired by the Convention's exceedingly loose defi-nitional criteria, the International Criminal Tribunal for the former Yugoslavia and the International Court of Justice ruled that the Srebrenica massacre of 1995, in which about 8,000 Muslim Bosniaks were killed by Serbian irregulars, was a genocide, while, in 1998, the International Criminal Tribunal for Rwanda ruled that systematic rape is also geno-cide, thereby decoupling genocide from killing altogether.

The Convention notwithstanding, a more reasonable definition of genocide should be based on two overriding criteria—magnitude and death. Genocides are mass kill-ings of defenseless and innocent civilians. The Holocaust involved 6 million European Jews; the Holodomor—4 million Ukrainians; the Armenian genocide—1.5 million; the Cambodian—2 million.

Several hundred thousand victims would reasonably qualify as genocidal if they represent a large portion of a relatively small population: hence the generally accepted view that Rwanda's Tutsis were genocide victims. A few thousand deaths, or even 100,000 deaths, should not qualify as genocidal, if the population concerned numbers about 25 million, as Poles did during the war. Zakharchenko's invocation of genocide is transparently absurd, as Kyiv is responsible for a few hundred or a few thousand, mostly military casualties in a region with a civilian population of about 2 million.

The 100,000 figure is also problematic. Most scholars, including those highly critical of Ukrainian nationalists, place the number of Polish dead in the 50,000 range. Some maintain it was closer to 35,000. In addition, the Ukrainian side also suffered casualties, about 10–20 percent as many as the Poles. That's not surprising, because Poles fought—or fought back, employing, as even the Sejm recognized, the same kind of brutal methods used by the Ukrainians and killing innocent men, women, and children.

Complicating the charge of genocide is the fact that the killings took place in the midst of armed conflict between Poles and Ukrainians in western Ukraine and between Poles, Ukrainians, Germans, and Soviets in World War II. The Ukrainians were organized in the Ukrainian Insurgent Army; the Poles were organized in the Home Army. Both sides also had armed individuals in the local police units that assisted the German authorities; Poles also enjoyed the support of Soviet partisans. Neither side had a state, and neither side was helpless.

In contrast, when genuine genocides occur, even if, like the Holocaust, in the midst of a war, the vast number of deaths are all on the side of innocent non-combatant victims, precisely because perpetrators of genocides are invariably states or state-affiliated militias that kill defenseless groups. As a result, states that perpetrate genocide suffer no, or almost no, casualties, while victims number in the millions.

Then there's the question of who started the fighting and when. Scholars legitimately disagree on this point. One could place the beginning of hostilities in 1918, when Poles and Ukrainians first fought over formerly Austrian Galicia. Or in the early 1920s, when Ukrainian nationalists first engaged in political violence against the Polish authorities. Or in 1930, when the Polish police and army brutally "pacified" Ukrainian inhabited-territories of eastern Poland. Or in 1934, when Ukrainian nationalists assassinated the Minister of Interior Bronislaw Pieracki. Or in the late 1930s, when Poland incarcerated thousands of Ukrainians in a concentration camp in Bereza Kartuska. Or in 1939, when Ukrainians rejoiced upon seeing Germany and the USSR partition Poland. Or in 1942, when Polish nationalists killed several thousand Ukrainians in the Chelm region just west of Volhynia. Or in 1648, when Ukrainian Cossacks rebelled against Polish authority. Or a century earlier, when Polish magnates viciously exploited their Ukrainian serfs …

Whatever the starting point, scholars agree that both sides fought and that the local Ukrainian population greatly outnumbered the local Polish population, with the result that their losses were smaller than those of the Poles. Did the Ukrainians commit atrocities? Yes. Crimes? Yes. Massacres? Yes. Ukrainians must ask themselves some tough questions about just what some of their compatriots did in Volhynia in 1943. By the same token, did Poles commit atrocities, crimes, and massacres? Alas, yes, and Poles, too, must ask themselves some tough questions about just what some of their compatriots did in Volhynia in 1943. Who committed more atrocities, crimes, and massacres? The answer depends entirely on where you place the starting point of the fighting. In any case, if thousands or hundreds of deaths constitute a genocide, then the history of Ukrainians and Poles, like the history of all nations everywhere, becomes transformed into an endless series of "genocides."

In an ideal world, Ukrainians and Poles would be asking themselves some tough moral questions, trying to come to some common understanding, and resolving to never let a mutual bloodletting happen again. Unfortunately, it is unrealistic to expect most Poles and Ukrainians to be reasonable and evenhanded about Volhynia, especially today, as Poland's right-wing government seems determined to rewrite Polish history and settle old scores, while Ukraine is embroiled in an existential war with Russia. Instead, charges and counter-charges will fly, more and more "genocides" are likely to be discovered, and the real questions—what actually happened in Volhynia in 1943 and how can some closure be achieved?—will be sacrificed to endless and self-destructive overreaching accusations of genocide. In the process, the concept of genocide will be trivialized and lost in demagoguery, and Poland and Ukraine, two countries that should be the closest of friends, could drift apart.

www.ingramcontent.com/pod-product-compliance
Lightning Source LLC
Chambersburg PA
CBHW080641270326
41928CB00017B/3156